T0297610

Data Science

Data Science

Concepts and Practice

Second Edition

Vijay Kotu

Bala Deshpande

MORGAN KAUFMANN PUBLISHERS

AN IMPRINT OF ELSEVIER

Morgan Kaufmann is an imprint of Elsevier
50 Hampshire Street, 5th Floor, Cambridge, MA 02139, United States

British Library Cataloguing-in-Publication Data
A catalogue record for this book is available from the British Library

Library of Congress Cataloging-in-Publication Data
A catalog record for this book is available from the Library of Congress

ISBN: 978-0-12-814761-0

For Information on all Morgan Kaufmann publications
visit our website at https://www.elsevier.com/books-and-journals

Working together
to grow libraries in
developing countries

www.elsevier.com • www.bookaid.org

Publisher: Jonathan Simpson
Acquisition Editor: Glyn Jones
Editorial Project Manager: Ana Claudia Abad Garcia
Production Project Manager: Sreejith Viswanathan
Cover Designer: Greg Harris

Typeset by MPS Limited, Chennai, India

Dedication

To all the mothers in our lives

Contents

Foreword

A lot has happened since the first edition of this book was published in 2014. There is hardly a day where there is no news on data science, machine learning, or artificial intelligence in the media. It is interesting that many of those news articles have a skeptical, if not an even negative tone. All this underlines two things: data science and machine learning are finally becoming mainstream. And people know shockingly little about it. Readers of this book will certainly do better in this regard. It continues to be a valuable resource to not only educate about how to use data science in practice, but also how the fundamental concepts work.

Data science and machine learning are fast-moving fields which is why this second edition reflects a lot of the changes in our field. While we used to talk a lot about "data mining" and "predictive analytics" only a couple of years ago, we have now settled on the term "data science" for the broader field. And even more importantly: it is now commonly understood that machine learning is at the core of many current technological breakthroughs. These are truly exciting times for all the people working in our field then!

I have seen situations where data science and machine learning had an incredible impact. But I have also seen situations where this was not the case. What was the difference? In most cases where organizations fail with data science and machine learning is, they had used those techniques in the wrong context. Data science models are not very helpful if you only have one big decision you need to make. Analytics can still help you in such cases by giving you easier access to the data you need to make this decision. Or by presenting the data in a consumable fashion. But at the end of the day, those single big decisions are often strategic. Building a machine learning model to help you make this decision is not worth doing. And often they also do not yield better results than just making the decision on your own.

Here is where data science and machine learning can truly help: these advanced models deliver the most value whenever you need to make lots of similar decisions quickly. Good examples for this are:

- Defining the price of a product in markets with rapidly changing demands.
- Making offers for cross-selling in an E-Commerce platform.
- Approving credit or not.
- Detecting customers with a high risk for churn.
- Stopping fraudulent transactions.
- And many others.

You can see that a human being who would have access to all relevant data could make those decisions in a matter of seconds or minutes. Only that they can't without data science, since they would need to make this type of decision millions of times, every day. Consider sifting through your customer base of 50 million clients every day to identify those with a high churn risk. Impossible for any human being. But no problem at all for a machine learning model.

So, the biggest value of artificial intelligence and machine learning is not to support us with those big strategic decisions. Machine learning delivers most value when we operationalize models and automate millions of decisions. One of the shortest descriptions of this phenomenon comes from Andrew Ng, who is a well-known researcher in the field of AI. Andrew describes what AI can do as follows: "If a typical person can do a mental task with less than one second of thought, we can probably automate it using AI either now or in the near future."

I agree with him on this characterization. And I like that Andrew puts the emphasis on automation and operationalization of those models—because this is where the biggest value is. The only thing I disagree with is the time unit he chose. It is safe to already go with a minute instead of a second.

However, the quick pace of changes as well as the ubiquity of data science also underlines the importance of laying the right foundations. Keep in mind that machine learning is not completely new. It has been an active field of research since the 1950s. Some of the algorithms used today have even been around for more than 200 years now. And the first deep learning models were developed in the 1960s with the term "deep learning" being coined in 1984. Those algorithms are well understood now. And understanding their basic concepts will help you to pick the right algorithm for the right task.

To support you with this, some additional chapters on deep learning and recommendation systems have been added to the book. Another focus area is using text analytics and natural language processing. It became clear in the past years that the most successful predictive models have been using unstructured input data in addition to the more traditional tabular formats. Finally, expansion of Time Series Forecasting should get you started on one of the most widely applied data science techniques in the business.

More algorithms could mean that there is a risk of increased complexity. But thanks to the simplicity of the RapidMiner platform and the many practical examples throughout the book this is not the case here. We continue our journey towards the democratization of data science and machine learning. This journey continues until data science and machine learning are as ubiquitous as data visualization or Excel. Of course, we cannot magically transform everybody into a data scientist overnight, but we can give people the tools to help them on their personal path of development. This book is the only tour guide you need on this journey.

Ingo Mierswa
Founder
RapidMiner Inc.
Massachusetts, USA

Preface

Our goal is to introduce you to *Data Science*.

We will provide you with a survey of the fundamental data science concepts as well as step-by-step guidance on practical implementations—enough to get you started on this exciting journey.

WHY DATA SCIENCE?

We have run out of adjectives and superlatives to describe the growth trends of data. The technology revolution has brought about the need to process, store, analyze, and comprehend large volumes of diverse data in meaningful ways. *However, the value of the stored data is zero unless it is acted upon*. The scale of data volume and variety places new demands on organizations to quickly uncover hidden relationships and patterns. This is where data science techniques have proven to be extremely useful. They are increasingly finding their way into the everyday activities of many business and government functions, whether in identifying which customers are likely to take their business elsewhere, or mapping flu pandemic using social media signals.

Data science is a compilation of techniques that extract value from data. Some of the techniques used in data science have a long history and trace their roots to applied statistics, machine learning, visualization, logic, and computer science. Some techniques have just reached the popularity it deserves. Most emerging technologies go through what is termed the "hype cycle." This is a way of contrasting the amount of hyperbole or hype versus the productivity that is engendered by the emerging technology. The hype cycle has three main phases: peak of inflated expectation, trough of disillusionment, and plateau of productivity. The third phase refers to the mature and value-generating phase of any technology. The hype cycle for data science indicates that it is in this mature phase. Does this imply that data science has stopped growing or has reached a saturation point? Not at all. On the contrary, this discipline has grown beyond the scope of its initial applications in marketing and has advanced to applications in technology, internet-based fields, health care, government, finance, and manufacturing.

WHY THIS BOOK?

The objective of this book is two-fold: to help clarify the basic *concepts* behind many data science techniques in an easy-to-follow manner; and to prepare anyone with a basic grasp of mathematics to *implement* these techniques in their organizations without the need to write any lines of programming code.

Beyond its practical value, we wanted to show you that the data science learning algorithms are elegant, beautiful, and incredibly effective. You will never look at data the same way once you learn the concepts of the learning algorithms.

To make the concepts stick, you will have to build data science models. While there are many data science tools available to execute algorithms and develop applications, the approaches to solving a data science problem are similar among these tools. We wanted to pick a fully functional, open source, free to use, graphical user interface-based data science tool so readers can follow the concepts and implement the data science algorithms. RapidMiner, a leading data science platform, fit the bill and, thus, we used it as a companion tool to implement the data science algorithms introduced in every chapter.

WHO CAN USE THIS BOOK?

The concepts and implementations described in this book are geared towards business, analytics, and technical professionals who use data everyday. You, the reader of the book will get a comprehensive understanding of the different data science techniques that can be used for prediction and for discovering patterns, be prepared to select the right technique for a given data problem, and you will be able to create a general-purpose analytics process.

We have tried to follow a process to describe this body of knowledge. Our focus has been on introducing about 30 key algorithms that are in widespread use today. We present these algorithms in the framework of:

1. A high-level practical use case for each algorithm.
2. An explanation of how the algorithm works in plain language. Many algorithms have a strong foundation in statistics and/or computer science. In our descriptions, we have tried to strike a balance between being accessible to a wider audience and being academically rigorous.

3. A detailed review of implementation using RapidMiner, by describing the commonly used setup and parameter options using a sample data set. You can download the processes from the companion website www.IntroDataScience.com and we recommend you follow-along by building an actual data science process.

Analysts, finance, engineering, marketing, and business professionals, or anyone who analyzes data, most likely will use data science techniques in their job either now or in the near future. For business managers who are one step removed from the actual data science process, it is important to know what is possible and not possible with these techniques so they can ask the right questions and set proper expectations. While basic spreadsheet analysis, slicing, and dicing of data through standard business intelligence tools will continue to form the foundations of data exploration in business, data science techniques are necessary to establish the full edifice of analytics in the organizations.

Vijay Kotu
California, USA
Bala Deshpande, PhD
Michigan, USA

Acknowledgments

Writing a book is one of the most interesting and challenging endeavors one can embark on. We grossly underestimated the effort it would take and the fulfillment it brings. This book would not have been possible without the support of our families, who granted us enough leeway in this time-consuming activity. We would like to thank the team at RapidMiner, who provided great help with everything, ranging from technical support to reviewing the chapters to answering questions on the features of the product. Our special thanks to Ingo Mierswa for setting the stage for the book through the foreword. We greatly appreciate the thoughtful and insightful comments from our technical reviewers: Doug Schrimager from Slalom Consulting, Steven Reagan from L&L Products, and Philipp Schlunder, Tobias Malbrecht and Ingo Mierswa from RapidMiner. Thanks to Mike Skinner of Intel and to Dr. Jacob Cybulski of Deakin University in Australia. We had great support and stewardship from the Elsevier and Morgan Kaufmann team: Glyn Jones, Ana Claudia Abad Garcia, and Sreejith Viswanathan. Thanks to our colleagues and friends for all the productive discussions and suggestions regarding this project.

CHAPTER 1

Introduction

Data science is a collection of techniques used to extract value from data. It has become an essential tool for any organization that collects, stores, and processes data as part of its operations. Data science techniques rely on finding useful patterns, connections, and relationships within data. Being a buzzword, there is a wide variety of definitions and criteria for what constitutes data science. Data science is also commonly referred to as knowledge discovery, machine learning, predictive analytics, and data mining. However, each term has a slightly different connotation depending on the context. In this chapter, we attempt to provide a general overview of data science and point out its important features, purpose, taxonomy, and methods.

In spite of the present growth and popularity, the underlying methods of data science are decades if not centuries old. Engineers and scientists have been using predictive models since the beginning of nineteenth century. Humans have always been forward-looking creatures and predictive sciences are manifestations of this curiosity. So, who uses data science today? Almost every organization and business. Sure, we didn't call the methods that are now under data science as *"Data Science."* The use of the term *science* in data science indicates that the methods are evidence based, and are built on empirical knowledge, more specifically historical observations.

As the ability to collect, store, and process data has increased, in line with Moore's Law - which implies that computing hardware capabilities double every two years, data science has found increasing applications in many diverse fields. Just decades ago, building a production quality regression model took about several dozen hours (Parr Rud, 2001). Technology has come a long way. Today, sophisticated machine learning models can be run, involving hundreds of predictors with millions of records in a matter of a few seconds on a laptop computer.

The process involved in data science, however, has not changed since those early days and is not likely to change much in the foreseeable future. To get meaningful results from any data, a major effort preparing, cleaning,

Data Science. DOI: https://doi.org/10.1016/B978-0-12-814761-0.00001-0

scrubbing, or standardizing the data is still required, before the learning algorithms can begin to crunch them. But what may change is the automation available to do this. While today this process is iterative and requires analysts' awareness of the best practices, soon smart automation may be deployed. This will allow the focus to be put on the most important aspect of data science: interpreting the results of the analysis in order to make decisions. This will also increase the reach of data science to a wider audience.

When it comes to the data science techniques, are there a core set of procedures and principles one must master? It turns out that a vast majority of data science practitioners today use a handful of very powerful techniques to accomplish their objectives: decision trees, regression models, deep learning, and clustering (Rexer, 2013). A majority of the data science activity can be accomplished using relatively few techniques. However, as with all 80/20 rules, the long tail, which is made up of a large number of specialized techniques, is where the value lies, and depending on what is needed, the best approach may be a relatively obscure technique or a combination of several not so commonly used procedures. Thus, it will pay off to learn data science and its methods in a systematic way, and that is what is covered in these chapters. But, first, how are the often-used terms artificial intelligence (AI), machine learning, and data science explained?

1.1   AI, MACHINE LEARNING, AND DATA SCIENCE

Artificial intelligence, Machine learning, and data science are all related to each other. Unsurprisingly, they are often used interchangeably and conflated with each other in popular media and business communication. However, all of these three fields are distinct depending on the context. Fig. 1.1 shows the relationship between artificial intelligence, machine learning, and data science.

Artificial intelligence is about giving machines the capability of mimicking human behavior, particularly cognitive functions. Examples would be: facial recognition, automated driving, sorting mail based on postal code. In some cases, machines have far exceeded human capabilities (sorting thousands of postal mails in seconds) and in other cases we have barely scratched the surface (search "artificial stupidity"). There are quite a range of techniques that fall under artificial intelligence: linguistics, natural language processing, decision science, bias, vision, robotics, planning, etc. Learning is an important part of human capability. In fact, many other living organisms can learn.

Machine learning can either be considered a sub-field or one of the tools of artificial intelligence, is providing machines with the capability of learning

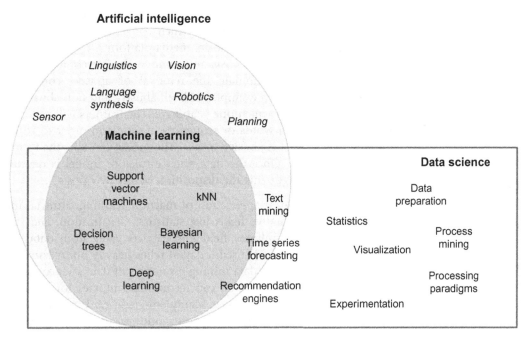

FIGURE 1.1
Artificial intelligence, machine learning, and data science.

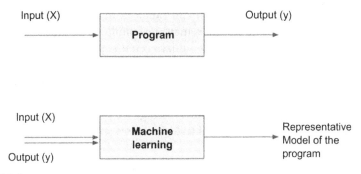

FIGURE 1.2
Traditional program and machine learning.

from experience. Experience for machines comes in the form of data. Data that is used to teach machines is called training data. Machine learning turns the traditional programing model upside down (Fig. 1.2). A program, a set of instructions to a computer, transforms input signals into output signals using predetermined rules and relationships. Machine learning algorithms, also called "learners", take both the known input and output (training data) to figure out a model for the program which converts input to output. For example, many organizations like social media platforms, review sites, or forums are required to moderate posts and remove abusive content. How can machines be taught to automate the removal of abusive content? The machines need to be shown examples of both abusive and non-abusive posts with a clear indication of which one is abusive. The learners will generalize a pattern based on certain words or sequences of words in order to conclude whether the overall post is abusive or not. The model can take the form of a set of "if--then" rules. Once the data science rules or model is developed, machines can start categorizing the disposition of any new posts.

Data science is the business application of machine learning, artificial intelligence, and other quantitative fields like statistics, visualization, and mathematics. It is an interdisciplinary field that extracts value from data. In the context of how data science is used today, it relies heavily on machine learning and is sometimes called data mining. Examples of data science user cases are: recommendation engines that can recommend movies for a particular user, a fraud alert model that detects fraudulent credit card transactions, find customers who will most likely churn next month, or predict revenue for the next quarter.

1.2 WHAT IS DATA SCIENCE?

Data science starts with *data*, which can range from a simple array of a few numeric observations to a complex matrix of millions of observations with thousands of variables. Data science utilizes certain specialized computational *methods* in order to discover meaningful and useful structures within a dataset. The discipline of data science coexists and is closely associated with a number of related areas such as database systems, data engineering, visualization, data analysis, experimentation, and business intelligence (BI). We can further define data science by investigating some of its key features and motivations.

1.2.1 Extracting Meaningful Patterns

Knowledge discovery in databases is the nontrivial process of identifying valid, novel, potentially useful, and ultimately understandable patterns or relationships within a dataset in order to make important decisions (Fayyad, Piatetsky-shapiro, & Smyth, 1996). Data science involves inference and iteration of many different hypotheses. One of the key aspects of data science is the process of *generalization* of patterns from a dataset. The generalization should be valid, not just for the dataset used to observe the pattern, but also for new unseen data. Data science is also a process with defined steps, each

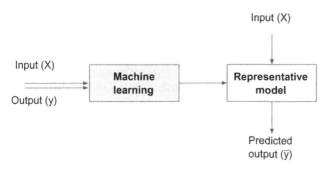

FIGURE 1.3
Data science models.

with a set of tasks. The term *novel* indicates that data science is usually involved in finding previously unknown patterns in data. The ultimate objective of data science is to find potentially useful conclusions that can be acted upon by the users of the analysis.

1.2.2 Building Representative Models

In statistics, a model is the representation of a relationship between variables in a dataset. It describes how one or more variables in the data are related to other variables. Modeling is a process in which a representative abstraction is built from the observed dataset. For example, based on credit score, income level, and requested loan amount, a model can be developed to determine the interest rate of a loan. For this task, previously known observational data including credit score, income level, loan amount, and interest rate are needed. Fig. 1.3 shows the process of generating a model. Once the representative model is created, it can be used to predict the value of the interest rate, based on all the input variables.

Data science is the process of building a representative model that fits the observational data. This model serves two purposes: on the one hand, it predicts the output (interest rate) based on the new and unseen set of input variables (credit score, income level, and loan amount), and on the other hand, the model can be used to understand the relationship between the output variable and all the input variables. For example, does income level really matter in determining the interest rate of a loan? Does income level matter more than credit score? What happens when income levels double or if credit score drops by 10 points? A Model can be used for both predictive and explanatory applications.

1.2.3   Combination of Statistics, Machine Learning, and Computing

In the pursuit of extracting useful and relevant information from large datasets, data science borrows computational techniques from the disciplines of statistics, machine learning, experimentation, and database theories. The algorithms used in data science originate from these disciplines but have since evolved to adopt more diverse techniques such as parallel computing, evolutionary computing, linguistics, and behavioral studies. One of the key ingredients of successful data science is substantial prior knowledge about the data and the business processes that generate the data, known as *subject matter expertise*. Like many quantitative frameworks, data science is an iterative process in which the practitioner gains more information about the patterns and relationships from data in each cycle. Data science also typically operates on large datasets that need to be stored, processed, and computed. This is where database techniques along with parallel and distributed computing techniques play an important role in data science.

1.2.4   Learning Algorithms

We can also define data science as a process of discovering previously unknown patterns in data using *automatic iterative methods*. The application of sophisticated learning algorithms for extracting useful patterns from data differentiates data science from traditional data analysis techniques. Many of these algorithms were developed in the past few decades and are a part of machine learning and artificial intelligence. Some algorithms are based on the foundations of Bayesian probabilistic theories and regression analysis, originating from hundreds of years ago. These iterative algorithms automate the process of searching for an optimal solution for a given data problem. Based on the problem, data science is classified into *tasks* such as classification, association analysis, clustering, and regression. Each data science task uses specific learning algorithms like decision trees, neural networks, k-nearest neighbors (k-NN), and k-means clustering, among others. With increased research on data science, such algorithms are increasing, but a few classic algorithms remain foundational to many data science applications.

1.2.5   Associated Fields

While data science covers a wide set of techniques, applications, and disciplines, there a few associated fields that data science heavily relies on. The techniques used in the steps of a data science process and in conjunction with the term "data science" are:

- *Descriptive statistics*: Computing mean, standard deviation, correlation, and other descriptive statistics, quantify the aggregate structure of a dataset. This is essential information for understanding any dataset in order to understand the structure of the data and the relationships within the dataset. They are used in the exploration stage of the data science process.

- *Exploratory visualization*: The process of expressing data in visual coordinates enables users to find patterns and relationships in the data and to comprehend large datasets. Similar to descriptive statistics, they are integral in the pre- and post-processing steps in data science.
- *Dimensional slicing*: Online analytical processing (OLAP) applications, which are prevalent in organizations, mainly provide information on the data through dimensional slicing, filtering, and pivoting. OLAP analysis is enabled by a unique database schema design where the data are organized as dimensions (e.g., products, regions, dates) and quantitative facts or measures (e.g., revenue, quantity). With a well-defined database structure, it is easy to slice the yearly revenue by products or combination of region and products. These techniques are extremely useful and may unveil patterns in data (e.g., candy sales decline after Halloween in the United States).
- *Hypothesis testing*: In confirmatory data analysis, experimental data are collected to evaluate whether a hypothesis has enough evidence to be supported or not. There are many types of statistical testing and they have a wide variety of business applications (e.g., A/B testing in marketing). In general, data science is a process where many hypotheses are generated and tested based on observational data. Since the data science algorithms are iterative, solutions can be refined in each step.
- *Data engineering*: Data engineering is the process of sourcing, organizing, assembling, storing, and distributing data for effective analysis and usage. Database engineering, distributed storage, and computing frameworks (e.g., Apache Hadoop, Spark, Kafka), parallel computing, extraction transformation and loading processing, and data warehousing constitute data engineering techniques. Data engineering helps source and prepare for data science learning algorithms.
- *Business intelligence*: Business intelligence helps organizations consume data effectively. It helps query the ad hoc data without the need to write the technical query command or use dashboards or visualizations to communicate the facts and trends. Business intelligence specializes in the secure delivery of information to right roles and the distribution of information at scale. Historical trends are usually reported, but in combination with data science, both the past and the predicted future data can be combined. BI can hold and distribute the results of data science.

1.3   CASE FOR DATA SCIENCE

In the past few decades, a massive accumulation of data has been seen with the advancement of information technology, connected networks, and the businesses it enables. This trend is also coupled with a steep decline in data storage and data processing costs. The applications built on these advancements like online businesses, social networking, and mobile technologies unleash a large amount of complex, heterogeneous data that are waiting to be analyzed. Traditional analysis techniques like dimensional slicing, hypothesis testing, and descriptive statistics can only go so far in information discovery. A paradigm is needed to manage the massive volume of data, explore the inter-relationships of thousands of variables, and deploy machine learning algorithms to deduce optimal insights from datasets. A set of frameworks, tools, and techniques are needed to intelligently assist humans to process all these data and extract valuable information (Piatetsky-Shapiro, Brachman, Khabaza, Kloesgen, & Simoudis, 1996). Data science is one such paradigm that can handle large volumes with multiple attributes and deploy complex algorithms to search for patterns from data. Each key motivation for using data science techniques are explored here.

1.3.1   Volume

The sheer volume of data captured by organizations is exponentially increasing. The rapid decline in storage costs and advancements in capturing every transaction and event, combined with the business need to extract as much leverage as possible using data, creates a strong motivation to store more data than ever. As data become more granular, the need to use large volume data to extract information increases. A rapid increase in the volume of data exposes the limitations of current analysis methodologies. In a few implementations, the time to create generalization models is critical and data volume plays a major part in determining the time frame of development and deployment.

1.3.2   Dimensions

The three characteristics of the Big Data phenomenon are high volume, high velocity, and high variety. The variety of data relates to the multiple types of values (numerical, categorical), formats of data (audio files, video files), and the application of the data (location coordinates, graph data). Every single record or data point contains multiple attributes or variables to provide context for the record. For example, every user record of an ecommerce site can contain attributes such as products viewed, products purchased, user demographics, frequency of purchase, clickstream, etc. Determining the most effective offer for an ecommerce user can involve computing information across these attributes. Each attribute can be thought of as a dimension in the data space. The user record has multiple attributes and can be visualized in multi-dimensional space. The addition of each dimension increases the complexity of analysis techniques.

A simple linear regression model that has one input dimension is relatively easy to build compared to multiple linear regression models with multiple dimensions. As the dimensional space of data increase, a scalable framework that can work well with multiple data types and multiple attributes is needed. In the case of text mining, a document or article becomes a data point with each unique word as a dimension. Text mining yields a dataset where the number of attributes can range from a few hundred to hundreds of thousands of attributes.

1.3.3 Complex Questions

As more complex data are available for analysis, the complexity of information that needs to get extracted from data is increasing as well. If the natural clusters in a dataset, with hundreds of dimensions, need to be found, then traditional analysis like hypothesis testing techniques cannot be used in a scalable fashion. The machine-learning algorithms need to be leveraged in order to automate searching in the vast search space.

Traditional statistical analysis approaches the data analysis problem by assuming a stochastic model, in order to predict a response variable based on a set of input variables. A linear regression is a classic example of this technique where the parameters of the model are estimated from the data. These hypothesis-driven techniques were highly successful in modeling simple relationships between response and input variables. However, there is a significant need to extract nuggets of information from large, complex datasets, where the use of traditional statistical data analysis techniques is limited (Breiman, 2001)

Machine learning approaches the problem of modeling by trying to find an algorithmic model that can better predict the output from input variables. The algorithms are usually recursive and, in each cycle, estimate the output and "learn" from the predictive errors of the previous steps. This route of modeling greatly assists in exploratory analysis since the approach here is not validating a hypothesis but generating a multitude of hypotheses for a given problem. In the context of the data problems faced today, both techniques need to be deployed. John Tuckey, in his article "We need both exploratory and confirmatory," stresses the importance of both exploratory and confirmatory analysis techniques (Tuckey, 1980). In this book, a range of data science techniques, from traditional statistical modeling techniques like regressions to the modern machine learning algorithms are discussed.

1.4 DATA SCIENCE CLASSIFICATION

Data science problems can be broadly categorized into *supervised* or *unsupervised* learning models. Supervised or directed data science tries to infer a function or relationship based on labeled training data and uses this function to map new unlabeled data. Supervised techniques predict the value of the output variables based on a set of input variables. To do this, a model is developed from a *training* dataset where the values of input and output are previously known. The model generalizes the relationship between the input and output variables and uses it to predict for a dataset where only input variables are known. The output variable that is being predicted is also called a class label or target variable. Supervised data science needs a sufficient number of labeled records to learn the model from the data. Unsupervised or undirected data science uncovers hidden patterns in unlabeled data. In unsupervised data science, there are no output variables to predict. The objective of this class of data science techniques, is to find patterns in data based on the relationship between data points themselves. An application can employ both supervised and unsupervised learners.

Data science problems can also be classified into tasks such as: classification, regression, association analysis, clustering, anomaly detection, recommendation engines, feature selection, time series forecasting, deep learning, and text mining (Fig. 1.4). This book is organized around these data science tasks. An overview is presented in this chapter and an in-depth discussion of the

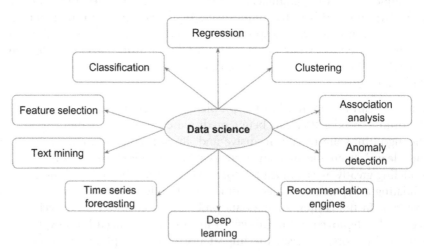

FIGURE 1.4
Data science tasks.

concepts and step-by-step implementations of many important techniques will be provided in the upcoming chapters.

Classification and *regression* techniques predict a target variable based on input variables. The prediction is based on a generalized model built from a previously known dataset. In regression tasks, the output variable is numeric (e.g., the mortgage interest rate on a loan). Classification tasks predict output variables, which are categorical or polynomial (e.g., the yes or no decision to approve a loan). *Deep learning* is a more sophisticated artificial neural network that is increasingly used for classification and regression problems. *Clustering* is the process of identifying the natural groupings in a dataset. For example, clustering is helpful in finding natural clusters in customer datasets, which can be used for market segmentation. Since this is unsupervised data science, it is up to the end user to investigate why these clusters are formed in the data and generalize the uniqueness of each cluster. In retail analytics, it is common to identify pairs of items that are purchased together, so that specific items can be bundled or placed next to each other. This task is called market basket analysis or *association analysis*, which is commonly used in cross selling. *Recommendation engines* are the systems that recommend items to the users based on individual user preference.

Anomaly or outlier detection identifies the data points that are significantly different from other data points in a dataset. Credit card transaction fraud detection is one of the most prolific applications of anomaly detection. *Time series forecasting* is the process of predicting the future value of a variable (e.g., temperature) based on past historical values that may exhibit a trend and seasonality. *Text mining* is a data science application where the input data is text, which can be in the form of documents, messages, emails, or web pages. To aid the data science on text data, the text files are first converted into document vectors where each unique word is an attribute. Once the text file is converted to document vectors, standard data science tasks such as classification, clustering, etc., can be applied. *Feature selection* is a process in which attributes in a dataset are reduced to a few attributes that really matter.

A complete data science application can contain elements of both supervised and unsupervised techniques (Tan et al., 2005). Unsupervised techniques provide an increased understanding of the dataset and hence, are sometimes called descriptive data science. As an example of how both unsupervised and supervised data science can be combined in an application, consider the following scenario. In marketing analytics, clustering can be used to find the natural clusters in customer records. Each customer is assigned a cluster label at the end of the clustering process. A labeled customer dataset can now be used to develop a model that assigns a cluster label for any new customer record with a supervised classification technique.

1.5 DATA SCIENCE ALGORITHMS

An algorithm is a logical step-by-step procedure for solving a problem. In data science, it is the blueprint for how a particular data problem is solved. Many of the learning algorithms are recursive, where a set of steps are repeated many times until a limiting condition is met. Some algorithms also contain a random variable as an input and are aptly called *randomized algorithms*. A classification task can be solved using many different learning algorithms such as decision trees, artificial neural networks, k-NN, and even some regression algorithms. The choice of which algorithm to use depends on the type of dataset, objective, structure of the data, presence of outliers, available computational power, number of records, number of attributes, and so on. It is up to the data science practitioner to decide which algorithm (s) to use by evaluating the performance of multiple algorithms. There have been hundreds of algorithms developed in the last few decades to solve data science problems.

Data science algorithms can be implemented by custom-developed computer programs in almost any computer language. This obviously is a time-consuming task. In order to focus the appropriate amount of time on data and algorithms, data science tools or statistical programing tools, like R, RapidMiner, Python, SAS Enterprise Miner, etc., which can implement these algorithms with ease, can be leveraged. These data science tools offer a library of algorithms as functions, which can be interfaced through programming code or configured through graphical user interfaces. Table 1.1 provides a summary of data science tasks with commonly used algorithmic techniques and example cases.

1.6 ROADMAP FOR THIS BOOK

It's time to explore data science techniques in more detail. The main body of this book presents: the concepts behind each data science algorithm and a practical implementation (or two) for each. The chapters do not have to be read in a sequence. For each algorithm, a general overview is first provided, and then the concepts and logic of the learning algorithm and how it works in plain language are presented. Later, how the algorithm can be implemented using RapidMiner is shown. RapidMiner is a widely known and used software tool for data science (Piatetsky, 2018) and it has been chosen particularly for ease of implementation using GUI, and because it is available to use free of charge, as an open source data science tool. Each chapter is

Table 1.1 Data Science Tasks and Examples

Tasks	Description	Algorithms	Examples
Classification	Predict if a data point belongs to one of the predefined classes. The prediction will be based on learning from a known dataset	Decision trees, neural networks, Bayesian models, induction rules, k-nearest neighbors	Assigning voters into known buckets by political parties, e.g., soccer moms Bucketing new customers into one of the known customer groups
Regression	Predict the numeric target label of a data point. The prediction will be based on learning from a known dataset	Linear regression, logistic regression	Predicting the unemployment rate for the next year Estimating insurance premium
Anomaly detection	Predict if a data point is an outlier compared to other data points in the dataset	Distance-based, density-based, LOF	Detecting fraudulent credit card transactions and network intrusion
Time series forecasting	Predict the value of the target variable for a future timeframe based on historical values	Exponential smoothing, ARIMA, regression	Sales forecasting, production forecasting, virtually any growth phenomenon that needs to be extrapolated
Clustering	Identify natural clusters within the dataset based on inherit properties within the dataset	k-Means, density-based clustering (e.g., DBSCAN)	Finding customer segments in a company based on transaction, web, and customer call data
Association analysis	Identify relationships within an item set based on transaction data	FP-growth algorithm, a priori algorithm	Finding cross-selling opportunities for a retailer based on transaction purchase history
Recommendation engines	Predict the preference of an item for a user	Collaborative filtering, content-based filtering, hybrid recommenders	Finding the top recommended movies for a user

LOF, *local outlier factor*; ARIMA, *autoregressive integrated moving average*; DBSCAN, *density-based spatial clustering of applications with noise*; FP, *frequent pattern.*

concluded with some closing thoughts and further reading materials and references are listed. Here is a roadmap of the book.

1.6.1 Getting Started With Data Science

Successfully uncovering patterns in a dataset is an iterative process. Chapter 2, Data Science Process, provides a framework to solve the data science problems. A five-step process outlined in this chapter provides guidelines on gathering subject matter expertise; exploring the data with statistics and visualization; building a model using data science algorithms; testing and deploying the model in the production environment; and finally reflecting on new knowledge gained in the cycle.

Simple data exploration either visually or with the help of basic statistical analysis can sometimes answer seemingly tough questions meant for data science. Chapter 3, Data Exploration, covers some of the basic tools used in knowledge discovery before deploying data science techniques. These practical tools increase one's understanding of data and are quite essential in understanding the results of the data science process.

1.6.2   Practice using RapidMiner

Before delving into the key data science techniques and algorithms, two specific things should be noted regarding how data science algorithms can be implemented while reading this book. It is believed that learning the concepts and implementing them enhances the learning experience. First, it is recommended that the free version of RapidMiner Studio software is downloaded from http://www.rapidminer.com and second, the first few sections of Chapter 15: Getting started with RapidMiner, should be reviewed in order to become familiar with the features of the tool, its basic operations, and the user interface functionality. Acclimating with RapidMiner will be helpful while using the algorithms that are discussed in this book. Chapter 15: Getting started with RapidMiner, is set at the end of the book because some of the later sections in the chapter build on the material presented in the chapters on tasks; however, the first few sections are a good starting point to become familiar with the tool.

Each chapter has a dataset used to describe the concept of a particular data science task and in most cases the same dataset is used for the implementation. The step-by-step instructions on practicing data science using the dataset are covered in every algorithm. All the implementations discussed are available at the companion website of the book at www.IntroDataScience.com. Though not required, it is advisable to access these files to as a learning aid. The dataset, complete RapidMiner processes (*.rmp files), and many more relevant electronic files can be downloaded from this website.

1.6.3   Core Algorithms

Classification is the most widely used data science task in business. The objective of a classification model is to predict a target variable that is binary (e.g., a loan decision) or categorical (e.g., a customer type) when a set of input variables are given. The model does this by learning the generalized relationship between the predicted target variable with all other input attributes from a known dataset. There are several ways to skin this cat. Each algorithm differs by how the relationship is extracted from the known training dataset. Chapter 4, Classification, on classification addresses several of these methods.

- *Decision trees* approach the classification problem by partitioning the data into purer subsets based on the values of the input attributes. The attributes that help achieve the cleanest levels of such separation are considered significant in their influence on the target variable and end up at the root and closer-to-root levels of the tree. The output model is a tree framework than can be used for the prediction of new unlabeled data.
- *Rule induction* is a data science process of deducing "if–then" rules from a dataset or from the decision trees. These symbolic decision rules explain an inherent relationship between the input attributes and the target labels in the dataset that can be easily understood by anyone.
- *Naïve Bayesian* algorithms provide a probabilistic way of building a model. This approach calculates the probability for each value of the class variable for given values of input variables. With the help of conditional probabilities, for a given unseen record, the model calculates the outcome of all values of target classes and comes up with a predicted winner.
- Why go through the trouble of extracting complex relationships from the data when the entire training dataset can be memorized and the relationship can appear to have been generalized? This is exactly what the *k-NN* algorithm does, and it is, therefore, called a "lazy" learner where the entire training dataset is memorized as the model.
- Neurons are the nerve cells that connect with each other to form a biological neural network in our brain. The working of these interconnected nerve cells inspired the approach of some complex data problems by the creation of *artificial neural networks*. The neural networks section provides a conceptual background of how a simple neural network works and how to implement one for any general prediction problem. Later on we extend this to deep neural networks which have revolutionized the field of artificial intelligence.
- *Support vector machines (SVMs)* were developed to address optical character recognition problems: how can an algorithm be trained to detect boundaries between different patterns, and thus, identify characters? SVMs can, therefore, identify if a given data sample belongs within a boundary (in a particular class) or outside it (not in the class).
- *Ensemble learners* are "meta" models where the model is a combination of several different individual models. If certain conditions are met, ensemble learners can gain from the wisdom of crowds and greatly reduce the generalization error in data science.

The simple mathematical equation $y = ax + b$ is a linear regression model. Chapter 5, Regression Methods, describes a class of data science techniques in which the target variable (e.g., interest rate or a target class) is functionally related to input variables.

- *Linear regression*: The simplest of all function fitting models is based on a linear equation, as previously mentioned. Polynomial regression uses higher-order equations. No matter what type of equation is used, the goal is to represent the variable to be predicted in terms of other variables or attributes. Further, the predicted variable and the independent variables all have to be numeric for this to work. The basics of building regression models will be explored and how predictions can be made using such models will be shown.
- *Logistic regression*: Addresses the issue of predicting a target variable that may be binary or binomial (such as 1 or 0, yes or no) using predictors or attributes, which may be numeric.

Supervised data science or directed data science predict the value of the target variables. Two important *unsupervised* data science tasks will be reviewed: Association Analysis in Chapter 6 and Clustering in Chapter 7. Ever heard of the beer and diaper association in supermarkets? Apparently, a supermarket discovered that customers who buy diapers also tend to buy beer. While this may have been an urban legend, the observation has become a poster child for association analysis. Associating an item in a transaction with another item in the transaction to determine the most frequently occurring patterns is termed *association analysis*. This technique is about, for example, finding relationships between products in a supermarket based on purchase data, or finding related web pages in a website based on clickstream data. It is widely used in retail, ecommerce, and media to creatively bundle products.

Clustering is the data science task of identifying natural groups in the data. As an unsupervised task, there is no target class variable to predict. After the clustering is performed, each record in the dataset is associated with one or more cluster. Widely used in marketing segmentations and text mining, clustering can be performed by a range of algorithms. In Chapter 7, Clustering, three common algorithms with diverse identification approaches will be discussed. The *k-means clustering* technique identifies a cluster based on a central prototype record. *DBSCAN* clustering partitions the data based on variation in the density of records in a dataset. *Self-organizing maps* create a two-dimensional grid where all the records related with each other are placed next to each other.

How to determine which algorithms work best for a given dataset? Or for that matter how to objectively quantify the performance of any algorithm on a dataset? These questions are addressed in Chapter 8, Model Evaluation, which covers performance evaluation. The most commonly used tools for evaluating classification models such as a confusion matrix, ROC curves, and lift charts are described.

Chapter 9, Text Mining, provides a detailed look into the area of text mining and text analytics. It starts with a background on the origins of text mining and provides the motivation for this fascinating topic using the example of IBM's Watson, the Jeopardy—winning computer program that was built using concepts from text and data mining. The chapter introduces some key concepts important in the area of text analytics such as term frequency—inverse document frequency scores. Finally, it describes two case studies in which it is shown how to implement text mining for document clustering and automatic classification based on text content.

Chapter 10, Deep Learning, describes a set of algorithms to model high level abstractions in data. They are increasingly applied to image processing, speech recognition, online advertisements, and bioinformatics. This chapter covers the basic concepts of deep learning, popular use cases, and a sample classification implementation.

The advent of digital economy exponentially increased the choices of available products to the customer which can be overwhelming. Personalized recommendation lists help by narrowing the choices to a few items relevant to a particular user and aid users in making final consumption decisions. Recommendation engines, covered in Chapter 11, are the most prolific utilities of machine learning in everyday experience. Recommendation engines are a class of machine learning techniques that predict a user preference for an item. There are a wide range of techniques available to build a recommendation engine. This chapter discusses the most common methods starting with *collaborative filtering* and *content-based filtering* concepts and implementations using a practical dataset.

Forecasting is a common application of time series analysis. Companies use sales forecasts, budget forecasts, or production forecasts in their planning cycles. Chapter 12 on Time Series Forecasting starts by pointing out the distinction between standard supervised predictive models and time series forecasting models. The chapter covers a few time series forecasting methods, starting with time series decomposition, moving averages, exponential smoothing, regression, ARIMA methods, and machine learning based methods using windowing techniques.

Chapter 13 on Anomaly Detection describes how outliers in data can be detected by combining multiple data science tasks like classification, regression, and clustering. The fraud alert received from credit card companies is the result of an anomaly detection algorithm. The target variable to be predicted is whether a transaction is an outlier or not. Since clustering tasks identify outliers as a cluster, distance-based and density-based clustering techniques can be used in anomaly detection tasks.

In data science, the objective is to develop a representative model to generalize the relationship between input attributes and target attributes, so that we can predict the value or class of the target variables. Chapter 14, Feature Selection, introduces a preprocessing step that is often critical for a successful predictive modeling exercise: *feature selection*. Feature selection is known by several alternative terms such as attribute weighting, dimension reduction, and so on. There are two main styles of feature selection: filtering the key attributes before modeling (filter style) or selecting the attributes during the process of modeling (wrapper style). A few filter-based methods such as principal component analysis (PCA), information gain, and chi-square, and a couple of wrapper-type methods like forward selection and backward elimination will be discussed.

The first few sections of Chapter 15, Getting Started with RapidMiner, should provide a good overview for getting familiar with RapidMiner, while the latter sections of this chapter discuss some of the commonly used productivity tools and techniques such as data transformation, missing value handling, and process optimizations using RapidMiner.

References

Breiman, L. (2001). Statistical modeling: Two cultures. *Statistical Science, 6*(3), 199−231.

Fayyad, U., Piatetsky-shapiro, G., & Smyth, P. (1996). From data science to knowledge discovery in databases. *AI Magazine, 17*(3), 37−54.

Parr Rud, O. (2001). *Data science Cookbook*. New York: John Wiley and Sons.

Piatetsky, G. (2018). Top Software for Analytics, Data Science, Machine Learning in 2018: Trends and Analysis. Retrieved July 7, 2018, from https://www.kdnuggets.com/2018/05/poll-tools-analytics-data-science-machine-learning-results.html.

Piatetsky-Shapiro, G., Brachman, R., Khabaza, T., Kloesgen, W., & Simoudis, E. (1996). An overview of issues in developing industrial data science and knowledge discovery applications. In: *KDD-96 conference proceedings. KDD-96 conference proceedings.*

Rexer, K. (2013). *2013 Data miner survey summary report*. Winchester, MA: Rexer Analytics. <www.rexeranalytics.com>.

Tan, P.-N., Michael, S., & Kumar, V. (2005). *Introduction to data science*. Boston, MA: Addison-Wesley.

Tuckey, J. (1980). We need exploratory and Confirmatory. *The American Statistician, 34*(1), 23−25.

CHAPTER 2

Data Science Process

The methodical discovery of useful relationships and patterns in data is enabled by a set of iterative activities collectively known as the data science process. The standard data science process involves (1) understanding the problem, (2) preparing the data samples, (3) developing the model, (4) applying the model on a dataset to see how the model may work in the real world, and (5) deploying and maintaining the models. Over the years of evolution of data science practices, different frameworks for the process have been put forward by various academic and commercial bodies. The framework put forward in this chapter is synthesized from a few data science frameworks and is explained using a simple example dataset. This chapter serves as a high-level roadmap to building deployable data science models, and discusses the challenges faced in each step and the pitfalls to avoid.

One of the most popular data science process frameworks is Cross Industry Standard Process for Data Mining (CRISP-DM), which is an acronym for Cross Industry Standard Process for Data Mining. This framework was developed by a consortium of companies involved in data mining (Chapman et al., 2000). The CRISP-DM process is the most widely adopted framework for developing data science solutions. Fig. 2.1 provides a visual overview of the CRISP-DM framework. Other data science frameworks are SEMMA, an acronym for Sample, Explore, Modify, Model, and Assess, developed by the SAS Institute (SAS Institute, 2013); DMAIC, is an acronym for Define, Measure, Analyze, Improve, and Control, used in Six Sigma practice (Kubiak & Benbow, 2005); and the Selection, Preprocessing, Transformation, Data Mining, Interpretation, and Evaluation framework used in the knowledge discovery in databases process (Fayyad, Piatetsky-Shapiro, & Smyth, 1996). All these frameworks exhibit common characteristics, and hence, a generic framework closely resembling the CRISP process will be used. As with any process framework, a data science process recommends the execution of a certain set of tasks to achieve optimal output. However, the process of extracting information and knowledge from the data is *iterative*. The steps within the data science process are not linear and have to undergo many

Data Science. DOI: https://doi.org/10.1016/B978-0-12-814761-0.00002-2

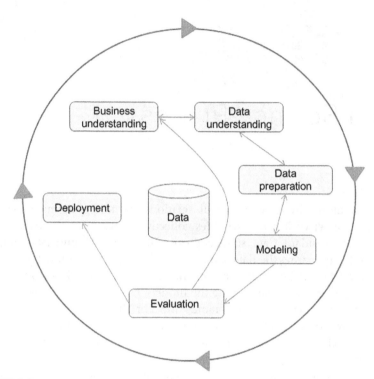

FIGURE 2.1
CRISP data mining framework.

loops, go back and forth between steps, and at times go back to the first step to redefine the data science problem statement.

The data science process presented in Fig. 2.2 is a generic set of steps that is problem, algorithm, and, data science tool agnostic. The fundamental objective of any process that involves data science is to address the analysis question. The problem at hand could be a segmentation of customers, a prediction of climate patterns, or a simple data exploration. The learning algorithm used to solve the business question could be a decision tree, an artificial neural network, or a scatterplot. The software tool to develop and implement the data science algorithm used could be custom coding, RapidMiner, R, Weka, SAS, Oracle Data Miner, Python, etc., (Piatetsky, 2018) to mention a few.

Data science, specifically in the context of big data, has gained importance in the last few years. Perhaps the most visible and discussed part of data science is the third step: *modeling*. It is the process of building representative models that can be inferred from the sample dataset which can be used for either predicting (*predictive modeling*) or describing the underlying pattern in the data (*descriptive or explanatory modeling*). Rightfully so, there is plenty of

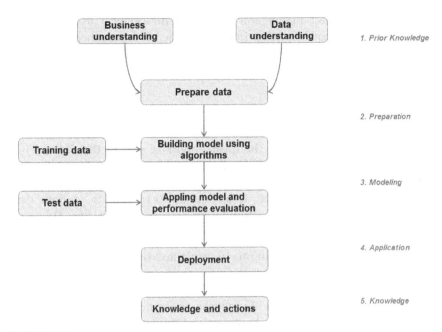

FIGURE 2.2
Data science process.

academic and business research in the modeling step. Most of this book has been dedicated to discussing various algorithms and the quantitative foundations that go with it. However, emphasis should be placed on considering data science as an end-to-end, multi-step, iterative process instead of just a model building step. Seasoned data science practitioners can attest to the fact that the most time-consuming part of the overall data science process is not the model building part, but the preparation of data, followed by data and business understanding. There are many data science tools, both open source and commercial, available on the market that can automate the model building. Asking the right business question, gaining in-depth business understanding, sourcing and preparing the data for the data science task, mitigating implementation considerations, integrating the model into the business process, and, most useful of all, gaining knowledge from the dataset, remain crucial to the success of the data science process. It's time to get started with Step 1: Framing the data science question and understanding the context.

2.1 PRIOR KNOWLEDGE

Prior knowledge refers to information that is already known about a subject. The data science problem doesn't emerge in isolation; it always develops on top of existing subject matter and contextual information that is already known. The prior knowledge step in the data science process helps to define what problem is being solved, how it fits in the business context, and what data is needed in order to solve the problem.

2.1.1 Objective

The data science process starts with a need for analysis, a question, or a business objective. This is possibly the most important step in the data science process (Shearer, 2000). Without a well-defined statement of the problem, it is impossible to come up with the right dataset and pick the right data science algorithm. As an iterative process, it is common to go back to previous data science process steps, revise the assumptions, approach, and tactics. However, it is imperative to get the first step—the objective of the whole process—right.

The data science process is going to be explained using a hypothetical use case. Take the consumer loan business for example, where a loan is provisioned for individuals against the collateral of assets like a home or car, that is, a mortgage or an auto loan. As many homeowners know, an important component of the loan, for the borrower and the lender, is the interest rate at which the borrower repays the loan on top of the principal. The interest rate on a loan depends on a gamut of variables like the current federal funds rate as determined by the central bank, borrower's credit score, income level, home value, initial down payment amount, current assets and liabilities of the borrower, etc. The key factor here is whether the lender sees enough reward (interest on the loan) against the risk of losing the principal (borrower's default on the loan). In an individual case, the status of default of a loan is Boolean; either one defaults or not, during the period of the loan. But, in a group of tens of thousands of borrowers, the default rate can be found—a continuous numeric variable that indicates the percentage of borrowers who default on their loans. All the variables related to the borrower like credit score, income, current liabilities, etc., are used to assess the default risk in a related group; based on this, the interest rate is determined for a loan. The business objective of this hypothetical case is: *If the interest rate of past borrowers with a range of credit scores is known, can the interest rate for a new borrower be predicted?*

2.1.2 Subject Area

The process of data science uncovers hidden patterns in the dataset by exposing relationships between attributes. But the problem is that it uncovers a lot of patterns. The false or spurious signals are a major problem in the data science process. It is up to the practitioner to sift through the exposed patterns and accept the ones that are valid and relevant to the answer of the objective question. Hence, it is essential to know the subject matter, the context, and the business process generating the data.

The lending business is one of the oldest, most prevalent, and complex of all the businesses. If the objective is to predict the lending interest rate, then it is important to know how the lending business works, why the prediction matters, what happens after the rate is predicted, what data points can be collected from borrowers, what data points cannot be collected because of the external regulations and the internal policies, what other external factors can affect the interest rate, how to verify the validity of the outcome, and so forth. Understanding current models and business practices lays the foundation and establishes known knowledge. Analysis and mining the data provides the new knowledge that can be built on top of the existing knowledge (Lidwell, Holden, & Butler, 2010).

2.1.3   Data

Similar to the prior knowledge in the subject area, prior knowledge in the data can also be gathered. Understanding how the data is collected, stored, transformed, reported, and used is essential to the data science process. This part of the step surveys all the data available to answer the business question and narrows down the new data that need to be sourced. There are quite a range of factors to consider: quality of the data, quantity of data, availability of data, gaps in data, does lack of data compel the practitioner to change the business question, etc. The objective of this step is to come up with a dataset to answer the business question through the data science process. It is critical to recognize that an inferred model is only as good as the data used to create it.

For the lending example, a sample dataset of ten data points with three attributes has been put together: identifier, credit score, and interest rate. First, some of the terminology used in the data science process are discussed.

- A *dataset* (*example set*) is a collection of data with a defined structure. Table 2.1 shows a dataset. It has a well-defined structure with 10 rows and 3 columns along with the column headers. This structure is also sometimes referred to as a "data frame".
- A *data point* (*record, object* or *example*) is a single instance in the dataset. Each row in Table 2.1 is a data point. Each instance contains the same structure as the dataset.
- An *attribute* (*feature, input, dimension, variable, or predictor*) is a single property of the dataset. Each column in Table 2.1 is an attribute. Attributes can be numeric, categorical, date-time, text, or Boolean *data types*. In this example, both the credit score and the interest rate are numeric attributes.

Table 2.1 Dataset

Borrower ID	Credit Score	Interest Rate (%)
01	500	7.31
02	600	6.70
03	700	5.95
04	700	6.40
05	800	5.40
06	800	5.70
07	750	5.90
08	550	7.00
09	650	6.50
10	825	5.70

Table 2.2 New Data With Unknown Interest Rate

Borrower ID	Credit Score	Interest Rate
11	625	?

- A *label* (*class label, output, prediction, target,* or *response*) is the special attribute to be predicted based on all the input attributes. In Table 2.1, the interest rate is the output variable.
- *Identifiers* are special attributes that are used for locating or providing context to individual records. For example, common attributes like names, account numbers, and employee ID numbers are identifier attributes. Identifiers are often used as lookup keys to join multiple datasets. They bear no information that is suitable for building data science models and should, thus, be excluded for the actual modeling step. In Table 2.1, the attribute ID is the identifier.

2.1.4   Causation Versus Correlation

Suppose the business question is inverted: *Based on the data in* Table 2.1, *can the credit score of the borrower be predicted based on interest rate?* The answer is yes— but it does not make business sense. From the existing domain expertise, it is known that credit score *influences* the loan interest rate. Predicting credit score based on interest rate inverses the direction of the causal relationship. This question also exposes one of the key aspects of model building. The correlation between the input and output attributes doesn't guarantee causation. Hence, it is important to frame the data science question correctly using the existing domain and data knowledge. In this data science example, the interest rate of the new borrower with an unknown interest rate will be predicted (Table 2.2) based on the pattern learned from known data in Table 2.1.

2.2 DATA PREPARATION

Preparing the dataset to suit a data science task is the most time-consuming part of the process. It is extremely rare that datasets are available in the form required by the data science algorithms. Most of the data science algorithms would require data to be structured in a tabular format with records in the rows and attributes in the columns. If the data is in any other format, the data would need to be transformed by applying pivot, type conversion, join, or transpose functions, etc., to condition the data into the required structure.

2.2.1 Data Exploration

Data preparation starts with an in-depth exploration of the data and gaining a better understanding of the dataset. Data exploration, also known as *exploratory data analysis*, provides a set of simple tools to achieve basic understanding of the data. Data exploration approaches involve computing descriptive statistics and visualization of data. They can expose the structure of the data, the distribution of the values, the presence of extreme values, and highlight the inter-relationships within the dataset. Descriptive statistics like mean, median, mode, standard deviation, and range for each attribute provide an easily readable summary of the key characteristics of the distribution of data. On the other hand, a visual plot of data points provides an instant grasp of all the data points condensed into one chart. Fig. 2.3 shows the scatterplot of credit score vs. loan interest rate and it can be observed that as credit score increases, interest rate decreases.

2.2.2 Data Quality

Data quality is an ongoing concern wherever data is collected, processed, and stored. In the interest rate dataset (Table 2.1), how does one know if the credit score and interest rate data are accurate? What if a credit score has a recorded value of 900 (beyond the theoretical limit) or if there was a data entry error? Errors in data will impact the representativeness of the model. Organizations use data alerts, cleansing, and transformation techniques to improve and manage the quality of the data and store them in companywide repositories called *data warehouses*. Data sourced from well-maintained data warehouses have higher quality, as there are proper controls in place to ensure a level of data accuracy for new and existing data. The data cleansing practices include elimination of duplicate records, quarantining outlier records that exceed the bounds, standardization of attribute values, substitution of missing values, etc. Regardless, it is critical to check the data using data exploration techniques in addition to using prior knowledge of the data and business before building models.

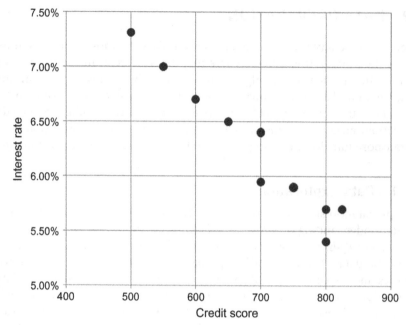

FIGURE 2.3
Scatterplot for interest rate dataset.

2.2.3   Missing Values

One of the most common data quality issues is that some records have missing attribute values. For example, a credit score may be missing in one of the records. There are several different mitigation methods to deal with this problem, but each method has pros and cons. The first step of managing missing values is to understand the reason behind why the values are missing. Tracking the data lineage (provenance) of the data source can lead to the identification of systemic issues during data capture or errors in data transformation. Knowing the source of a missing value will often guide which mitigation methodology to use. The missing value can be substituted with a range of artificial data so that the issue can be managed with marginal impact on the later steps in the data science process. Missing credit score values can be replaced with a credit score derived from the dataset (mean, minimum, or maximum value, depending on the characteristics of the attribute). This method is useful if the missing values occur randomly and the frequency of occurrence is quite rare. Alternatively, to build the representative model, all the data records with missing values or records with poor data quality can be ignored. This method reduces the size of the dataset. Some data science algorithms are good at handling records with missing values, while others expect the data preparation step to handle it before the model is inferred. For example, k-nearest neighbor (k-NN) algorithm for classification tasks are often robust with missing values. Neural network models for classification tasks do not perform well with missing attributes, and thus, the data preparation step is essential for developing neural network models.

2.2.4 Data Types and Conversion

The attributes in a dataset can be of different types, such as continuous numeric (interest rate), integer numeric (credit score), or categorical. For example, the credit score can be expressed as categorical values (poor, good, excellent) or numeric score. Different data science algorithms impose different restrictions on the attribute data types. In case of linear regression models, the input attributes have to be numeric. If the available data are categorical, they must be converted to continuous numeric attribute. A specific numeric score can be encoded for each category value, such as poor = 400, good = 600, excellent = 700, etc. Similarly, numeric values can be converted to categorical data types by a technique called *binning*, where a range of values are specified for each category, for example, a score between 400 and 500 can be encoded as "low" and so on.

2.2.5 Transformation

In some data science algorithms like k-NN, the input attributes are expected to be numeric and *normalized*, because the algorithm compares the values of different attributes and calculates distance between the data points. Normalization prevents one attribute dominating the distance results because of large values. For example, consider income (expressed in USD, in thousands) and credit score (in hundreds). The distance calculation will always be dominated by slight variations in income. One solution is to convert the range of income and credit score to a more uniform scale from 0 to 1 by normalization. This way, a consistent comparison can be made between the two different attributes with different units.

2.2.6 Outliers

Outliers are anomalies in a given dataset. Outliers may occur because of correct data capture (few people with income in tens of millions) or erroneous data capture (human height as 1.73 cm instead of 1.73 m). Regardless, the presence of outliers needs to be understood and will require special treatments. The purpose of creating a representative model is to generalize a pattern or a relationship within a dataset and the presence of outliers skews the representativeness of the inferred model. Detecting outliers may be the primary purpose of some data science applications, like fraud or intrusion detection.

2.2.7   Feature Selection

The example dataset shown in Table 2.1 has one *attribute* or *feature*—the credit score—and one *label*—the interest rate. In practice, many data science problems involve a dataset with hundreds to thousands of attributes. In text mining applications, every distinct word in a document forms a distinct attribute in the dataset. Not all the attributes are equally important or useful in predicting the target. The presence of some attributes might be counterproductive. Some of the attributes may be highly correlated with each other, like annual income and taxes paid. A large number of attributes in the dataset significantly increases the complexity of a model and may degrade the performance of the model due to the *curse of dimensionality*. In general, the presence of more detailed information is desired in data science because discovering nuggets of a pattern in the data is one of the attractions of using data science techniques. But, as the number of dimensions in the data increase, data becomes sparse in high-dimensional space. This condition degrades the reliability of the models, especially in the case of clustering and classification (Tan, Steinbach, & Kumar, 2005).

Reducing the number of attributes, without significant loss in the performance of the model, is called feature selection. It leads to a more simplified model and helps to synthesize a more effective explanation of the model.

2.2.8   Data Sampling

Sampling is a process of selecting a subset of records as a representation of the original dataset for use in data analysis or modeling. The sample data serve as a representative of the original dataset with similar properties, such as a similar mean. Sampling reduces the amount of data that need to be processed and speeds up the build process of the modeling. In most cases, to gain insights, extract the information, and to build representative predictive models it is sufficient to work with samples. Theoretically, the error introduced by sampling impacts the relevancy of the model, but their benefits far outweigh the risks.

In the build process for data science applications, it is necessary to segment the datasets into training and test samples. The training dataset is sampled from the original dataset using simple sampling or class label specific sampling. Consider the example cases for predicting anomalies in a dataset (e.g., predicting fraudulent credit card transactions). The objective of anomaly detection is to classify the outliers in the data. These are rare events and often the dataset does not have enough examples of the outlier class. *Stratified sampling* is a process of sampling where each class is equally represented in the sample; this allows the model to focus on the difference between the patterns of each class that is, normal and outlier records. In classification applications, sampling is used create multiple base models, each developed using a different set of sampled training datasets. These base models are used to build one meta model, called the *ensemble model*, where the error rate is improved when compared to that of the base models.

2.3 MODELING

A model is the abstract representation of the data and the relationships in a given dataset. A simple rule of thumb like *"mortgage interest rate reduces with increase in credit score"* is a model; although there is not enough quantitative information to use in a production scenario, it provides directional information by abstracting the relationship between credit score and interest rate.

There are a few hundred data science algorithms in use today, derived from statistics, machine learning, pattern recognition, and the body of knowledge related to computer science. Fortunately, there are many viable commercial and open source data science tools on the market to automate the execution of these learning algorithms. As a data science practitioner, it is sufficient to an overview of the learning algorithm, how it works, and determining what parameters need to be configured based on the understanding of the business and data. Classification and regression tasks are predictive techniques because they predict an outcome variable based on one or more input variables. Predictive algorithms require a prior known dataset to learn the model. Fig. 2.4 shows the steps in the modeling phase of predictive data science. Association analysis and clustering are descriptive data science techniques where there is no target variable to predict; hence, there is no test dataset. However, both predictive and descriptive models have an evaluation step.

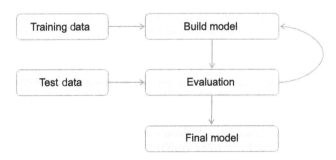

FIGURE 2.4
Modeling steps.

Table 2.3 Training Dataset

Borrower	Credit Score (X)	Interest Rate (Y) (%)
01	500	7.31
02	600	6.70
03	700	5.95
05	800	5.40
06	800	5.70
08	550	7.00
09	650	6.50

Table 2.4 Test Dataset

Borrower	Credit Score (X)	Interest Rate (Y)
04	700	6.40
07	750	5.90
10	825	5.70

2.3.1   Training and Testing Datasets

The modeling step creates a representative model inferred from the data. The dataset used to create the model, with known attributes and target, is called the *training dataset*. The validity of the created model will also need to be checked with another known dataset called the *test dataset* or *validation dataset*. To facilitate this process, the overall known dataset can be split into a training dataset and a test dataset. A standard rule of thumb is two-thirds of the data are to be used as training and one-third as a test dataset. Tables 2.3 and 2.4 show the random split of training and test data, based on the example dataset shown in Table 2.1. Fig. 2.5 shows the scatterplot of the entire example dataset with the training and test datasets marked.

2.3.2   Learning Algorithms

The business question and the availability of data will dictate what data science task (association, classification, regression, etc.,) can to be used. The practitioner determines the appropriate data science algorithm within the chosen category. For example, within a classification task many algorithms can be chosen from: decision trees, rule induction, neural networks, Bayesian models, k-NN, etc. Likewise, within decision tree techniques, there are quite a number of variations of learning algorithms like classification and regression tree (CART), CHi-squared Automatic Interaction Detector (CHAID) etc.

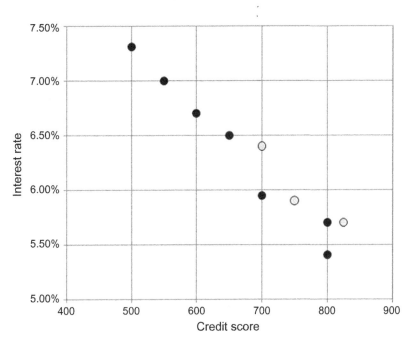

FIGURE 2.5
Scatterplot of training and test data.

These algorithms will be reviewed in detail in later chapters. It is not uncommon to use multiple data science tasks and algorithms to solve a business question.

Interest rate prediction is a regression problem. A simple linear regression technique will be used to model and generalize the relationship between credit score and interest rate. The training set of seven records is used to create the model and the test set of three records is used to evaluate the validity of the model.

The objective of simple linear regression can be visualized as fitting a straight line through the data points in a scatterplot (Fig. 2.6). The line has to be built in such a way that the sum of the squared distance from the data points to the line is minimal. The line can be expressed as:

$$y = a * x + b \tag{2.1}$$

where y is the output or dependent variable, x is the input or independent variable, b is the y-intercept, and a is the coefficient of x. The values of a and b can be found in such a way so as to minimize the sum of the squared residuals of the line.

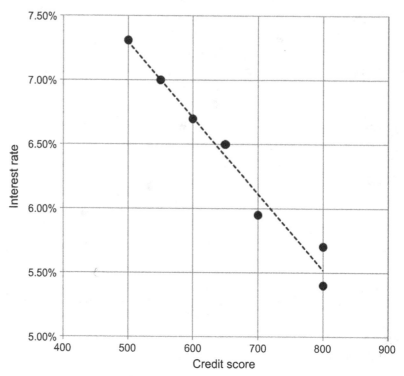

FIGURE 2.6
Regression model.

The line shown in Eq. (2.1) serves as a model to predict the outcome of new unlabeled datasets. For the interest rate dataset, the simple linear regression for the interest rate (y) has been calculated as (details in Chapter 5: Regression):

$$y = 0.1 + \frac{6}{100,000}x$$

$$\text{Interest rate} = 10 - \frac{6 \times \text{credit score}}{1000}$$

Using this model, the interest rate for a new borrower with a specific credit score can be calculated.

2.3.3 Evaluation of the Model

The model generated in the form of an equation is generalized and synthesized from seven training records. The credit score in the equation can be substituted to see if the model estimates the interest rate for each of the

Table 2.5 Evaluation of Test Dataset

Borrower	Credit Score (X)	Interest Rate (Y) (%)	Model Predicted (Y) (%)	Model Error (%)
04	700	6.40	6.11	− 0.29
07	750	5.90	5.81	− 0.09
10	825	5.70	5.37	− 0.33

seven training records. The estimation may not be exactly the same as the values in the training records. A model should not memorize and output the same values that are in the training records. The phenomenon of a model memorizing the training data is called *overfitting*. An overfitted model just memorizes the training records and will underperform on real unlabeled new data. The model should generalize or *learn* the relationship between credit score and interest rate. To evaluate this relationship, the validation or test dataset, which was not previously used in building the model, is used for evaluation, as shown in Table 2.5.

Table 2.5 provides the three testing records where the value of the interest rate is known; these records were not used to build the model. The actual value of the interest rate can be compared against the predicted value using the model, and thus, the *prediction error* can be calculated. As long as the error is acceptable, this model is ready for deployment. The error rate can be used to compare this model with other models developed using different algorithms like neural networks or Bayesian models, etc.

2.3.4 Ensemble Modeling

Ensemble modeling is a process where multiple diverse base models are used to predict an outcome. The motivation for using ensemble models is to reduce the generalization error of the prediction. As long as the base models are diverse and *independent*, the prediction error decreases when the ensemble approach is used. The approach seeks the wisdom of crowds in making a prediction. Even though the ensemble model has multiple base models within the model, it acts and performs as a single model. Most of the practical data science applications utilize ensemble modeling techniques.

At the end of the modeling stage of the data science process, one has (1) analyzed the business question; (2) sourced the data relevant to answer the question; (3) selected a data science technique to answer the question; (4) picked a data science algorithm and prepared the data to suit the algorithm; (5) split the data into training and test datasets; (6) built a generalized model from the training dataset; and (7) validated the model against the test dataset. This model can now be used to predict the interest rate of new borrowers by integrating it in the actual loan approval process.

2.4 APPLICATION

Deployment is the stage at which the model becomes production ready or *live*. In business applications, the results of the data science process have to be assimilated into the business process—usually in software applications. The model deployment stage has to deal with: assessing model readiness, technical integration, response time, model maintenance, and assimilation.

2.4.1 Production Readiness

The production readiness part of the deployment determines the critical qualities required for the deployment objective. Consider two business use cases: determining whether a consumer qualifies for a loan and determining the groupings of customers for an enterprise by marketing function.

The consumer credit approval process is a real-time endeavor. Either through a consumer-facing website or through a specialized application for frontline agents, the credit decisions and terms need to be provided in real-time as soon as prospective customers provide the relevant information. It is optimal to provide a quick decision while also proving accurate. The decision-making model has to collect data from the customer, integrate third-party data like credit history, and make a decision on the loan approval and terms in a matter of seconds. The critical quality of this model deployment is real-time prediction.

Segmenting customers based on their relationship with the company is a thoughtful process where signals from various customer interactions are collected. Based on the patterns, similar customers are put in cohorts and campaign strategies are devised to best engage the customer. For this application, batch processed, time lagged data would suffice. The critical quality in this application is the ability to find unique patterns amongst customers, not the response time of the model. The business application informs the choices that need to be made in the data preparation and modeling steps.

2.4.2 Technical Integration

Currently, it is quite common to use data science automation tools or coding using R or Python to develop models. Data science tools save time as they do not require the writing of custom codes to execute the algorithm. This allows the analyst to focus on the data, business logic, and exploring patterns from the data. The models created by data science tools can be ported to production applications by utilizing the Predictive Model Markup Language (PMML) (Guazzelli, Zeller, Lin, & Williams, 2009) or by invoking data science tools in the production application. PMML provides a portable and consistent format of model description which can be read by most data science tools. This allows the flexibility for practitioners to develop the model with one tool (e.g., RapidMiner) and deploy it in another tool or application. Some models such as simple regression, decision trees, and induction rules for predictive analytics can be incorporated directly into business applications and business intelligence systems easily. These models are represented by simple equations and the "if-then" rule, hence, they can be ported easily to most programming languages.

2.4.3 Response Time

Data science algorithms, like k-NN, are easy to build, but quite slow at predicting the unlabeled records. Algorithms such as the decision tree take time to build but are fast at prediction. There are trade-offs to be made between production responsiveness and modeling build time. The quality of prediction, accessibility of input data, and the response time of the prediction remain the critical quality factors in business application.

2.4.4 Model Refresh

The key criterion for the ongoing relevance of the model is the representativeness of the dataset it is processing. It is quite normal that the conditions in which the model is built change after the model is sent to deployment. For example, the relationship between the credit score and interest rate change frequently based on the prevailing macroeconomic conditions. Hence, the model will have to be refreshed frequently. The validity of the model can be routinely tested by using the new known test dataset and calculating the prediction error rate. If the error rate exceeds a particular threshold, then the model has to be refreshed and redeployed. Creating a maintenance schedule is a key part of a deployment plan that will sustain a relevant model.

2.4.5 Assimilation

In the descriptive data science applications, deploying a model to live systems may not be the end objective. The objective may be to assimilate the knowledge gained from the data science analysis to the organization. For example, the objective may be finding logical clusters in the customer database so that separate marketing approaches can be developed for each customer cluster. Then the next step may be a classification task for new customers to bucket them in one of known clusters. The association analysis provides a solution for the market basket problem, where the task is to find which two products are purchased together most often. The challenge for the data science practitioner is to articulate these findings, establish relevance to the original business question, quantify the risks in the model, and quantify the business impact. This is indeed a challenging task for data science practitioners. The business user community is an amalgamation of different points of view, different quantitative mindsets, and skill sets. Not everyone is aware about the process of data science and what it can and cannot do. Some aspects of this challenge can be addressed by focusing on the end result, the impact of knowing the discovered information, and the follow-up actions, instead of the technical process of extracting the information through data science.

2.5   KNOWLEDGE

The data science process provides a framework to extract nontrivial information from data. With the advent of massive storage, increased data collection, and advanced computing paradigms, the available datasets to be utilized are only increasing. To extract knowledge from these massive data assets, advanced approaches need to be employed, like data science algorithms, in addition to standard business intelligence reporting or statistical analysis. Though many of these algorithms can provide valuable knowledge, it is up to the practitioner to skillfully transform a business problem to a data problem and apply the right algorithm. Data science, like any other technology, provides various options in terms of algorithms and parameters within the algorithms. Using these options to extract the right information from data is a bit of an art and can be developed with practice.

The data science process starts with prior knowledge and ends with posterior knowledge, which is the incremental insight gained. As with any quantitative technique, the data science process can bring up spurious irrelevant patterns from the dataset. Not all discovered patterns lead to incremental knowledge. Again, it is up to the practitioner to invalidate the irrelevant patterns and identify the meaningful information. The impact of the information gained through data science can be measured in an application. It is the difference between gaining the information through the data science process and the insights from basic data analysis. Finally, the whole data science process is a framework to invoke the right questions (Chapman et al., 2000) and provide guidance, through the right approaches, to solve a problem. It is not meant to be used as a set of rigid rules, but as a set of iterative, distinct steps that aid in knowledge discovery.

In the upcoming chapters, the details of key data science concepts along with their implementation will be explored. Exploring data using basic statistical and visual techniques are an important first step in preparing the data for data science. The next chapter on data exploration provides a practical tool kit to explore and understand data. The techniques of data preparation are explained in the context of individual data science algorithms in the chapters on classification, association analysis, clustering, text mining, time series, and anomaly detection.

References

Chapman, P., Clinton, J., Kerber, R., Khabaza, T., Reinartz, T., Shearer, C., & Wirth, R. (2000). *CRISP-DM 1.0: Step-by-step data mining guide*. SPSS Inc. Retrieved from <ftp://ftp.software.ibm.com/software/analytics/spss/support/Modeler/Documentation/14/UserManual/CRISP-DM.pdf>.

Fayyad, U., Piatetsky-Shapiro, G., & Smyth, P. (1996). From data mining to knowledge discovery in databases. *AI Magazine, 17*(3), 37−54.

Guazzelli, A., Zeller, M., Lin, W., & Williams, G. (2009). PMML: An open standard for sharing models. *The R Journal, 1*(1), 60−65.

Kubiak, T., & Benbow, D. W. (2005). *The certified six sigma black belt handbook*. Milwaukee, WI: ASQQuality Press.

Lidwell, W., Holden, K., & Butler, J. (2010). *Universal principles of design, revised and updated: 125 ways to enhance usability, influence perception, increase appeal, make better design decisions, and teach through design*. Beverly, MA: Rockport Publishers.

Piatetsky, G. (2018). *Top software for analytics, data science, machine learning in 2018: Trends and analysis*. Retrieved from <https://www.kdnuggets.com/2018/05/poll-tools-analytics-data-science-machine-learning-results.html> Accessed 07.07.18.

SAS Institute. (2013). *Getting started with SAS enterprise miner 12.3*.

Shearer, C. (2000). The CRISP-DM model: The new blueprint for data mining. *Journal of Data Warehousing, 5*(4), 13−22.

Tan, P.-N., Steinbach, M., & Kumar, V. (2005). Introduction to data mining. *Journal of School Psychology, 19*, 51−56. Available from https://doi.org/10.1016/0022-4405(81)90007-8.

Weisstein, E. W. (2013). Retrieved from <http://mathworld.wolfram.com/LeastSquaresFitting.html> *Least squares fitting*. Champaign, Illinois: MathWorld—Wolfram Research, Inc.

CHAPTER 3

Data Exploration

The word "data" is derived from the Latin word *dare*, which means "something given"—an observation or a fact about a subject. (Interestingly, the Sanskrit word *dAta* also means "given"). Data science helps decipher the hidden useful relationships within data. Before venturing into any advanced analysis of data using statistical, machine learning, and algorithmic techniques, it is essential to perform basic data exploration to study the basic characteristics of a dataset. Data exploration helps with understanding data better, to prepare the data in a way that makes advanced analysis possible, and sometimes to get the necessary insights from the data faster than using advanced analytical techniques.

Simple pivot table functions, computing statistics like mean and deviation, and plotting data as a line, bar, and scatter charts are part of data exploration techniques that are used in everyday business settings. Data exploration, also known as exploratory data analysis, provides a set of tools to obtain fundamental understanding of a dataset. The results of data exploration can be extremely powerful in grasping the structure of the data, the distribution of the values, and the presence of extreme values and the interrelationships between the attributes in the dataset. Data exploration also provides guidance on applying the right kind of further statistical and data science treatment.

Data exploration can be broadly classified into two types—descriptive statistics and data visualization. Descriptive statistics is the process of condensing key characteristics of the dataset into simple numeric metrics. Some of the common quantitative metrics used are mean, standard deviation, and correlation. Visualization is the process of projecting the data, or parts of it, into multi-dimensional space or abstract images. All the useful (and adorable) charts fall under this category. Data exploration in the context of data science uses both descriptive statistics and visualization techniques.

Data Science. DOI: https://doi.org/10.1016/B978-0-12-814761-0.00003-4

3.1 OBJECTIVES OF DATA EXPLORATION

In the data science process, data exploration is leveraged in many different steps including preprocessing or data preparation, modeling, and interpretation of the modeling results.

1. *Data understanding*: Data exploration provides a high-level overview of each attribute (also called variable) in the dataset and the interaction between the attributes. Data exploration helps answers the questions like what is the typical value of an attribute or how much do the data points differ from the typical value, or presence of extreme values.
2. *Data preparation*: Before applying the data science algorithm, the dataset has to be prepared for handling any of the anomalies that may be present in the data. These anomalies include outliers, missing values, or highly correlated attributes. Some data science algorithms do not work well when input attributes are correlated with each other. Thus, correlated attributes need to be identified and removed.
3. *Data science tasks*: Basic data exploration can sometimes substitute the entire data science process. For example, scatterplots can identify clusters in low-dimensional data or can help develop regression or classification models with simple visual rules.
4. *Interpreting the results*: Finally, data exploration is used in understanding the prediction, classification, and clustering of the results of the data science process. Histograms help to comprehend the distribution of the attribute and can also be useful for visualizing numeric prediction, error rate estimation, etc.

3.2 DATASETS

Throughout the rest of this chapter (and the book) a few classic datasets, which are simple to understand, easy to explain, and can be used commonly across many different data science techniques, will be introduced. The most popular datasets used to learn data science is probably the *Iris dataset*, introduced by Ronald Fisher, in his seminal work on discriminant analysis, "The use of multiple measurements in taxonomic problems" (Fisher, 1936). Iris is a flowering plant that is found widely, across the world. The genus of Iris contains more than 300 different species. Each species exhibits different physical characteristics like shape and size of the flowers and leaves. The *Iris dataset* contains 150 observations of three different species, *Iris setosa*, *Iris virginica*, and *I. versicolor*, with 50 observations each. Each observation consists of four attributes: sepal length, sepal width, petal length, and petal width. The fifth attribute, the label, is the name of the species observed, which takes the values *I. setosa*, *I. virginica*, and *I. versicolor*. The petals are the brightly colored inner part of the flowers and the sepals form the outer part of the flower and are usually green in color. However, in an Iris flower, both sepals and petals are bright purple in color, but can be distinguished from each other by differences in the shape (Fig. 3.1).

All four attributes in the Iris dataset are numeric continuous values measured in centimeters. One of the species, *I. setosa*, can be easily distinguished from the other two using simple rules like the petal length is less than 2.5 cm. Separating the *virginica* and *versicolor* classes requires more complex rules that involve more attributes. The dataset is available in all standard data science tools, such as RapidMiner, or can be downloaded from public websites such as the University of California Irvine—Machine Learning repository[2] (Bache & Lichman, 2013). This dataset and other datasets used in this book can be accessed from the book companion website: www.IntroDataScience.com.

FIGURE 3.1

Iris versicolor. Source: *Photo by Danielle Langlois. July 2005 (Image modified from original by marking parts. "Iris versicolor 3." Licensed under Creative Commons Attribution-Share Alike 3.0 via Wikimedia Commons.[1])*

---

[1] http://commons.wikimedia.org/wiki/File:Iris_versicolor_3.jpg#mediaviewer/File:Iris_versicolor_3.jpg.
[2] https://archive.ics.uci.edu/ml/datasets.html.

The Iris dataset is used for learning data science mainly because it is simple to understand, explore, and can be used to illustrate how different data science algorithms approach the problem on the same standard dataset. The dataset extends beyond two dimensions, with three class labels, of which one class is easily separable (*I. setosa*) just by visual exploration, while classifying the other two classes is slightly more challenging. It helps to reaffirm the classification results that can be derived based on visual rules, and at the same time sets the stage for data science to build new rules beyond the limits of visual exploration.

3.2.1   Types of Data

Data come in different formats and types. Understanding the properties of each attribute or feature provides information about what kind of operations can be performed on that attribute. For example, the temperature in weather data can be expressed as any of the following formats:

- Numeric centigrade (31°C, 33.3°C) or Fahrenheit (100°F, 101.45°F) or on the Kelvin scale
- Ordered labels as in hot, mild, or cold
- Number of days within a year below 0°C (10 days in a year below freezing)

All of these attributes indicate temperature in a region, but each have different data types. A few of these data types can be converted from one to another.

Numeric or Continuous

Temperature expressed in Centigrade or Fahrenheit is numeric and continuous because it can be denoted by numbers and take an infinite number of values between digits. Values are ordered and calculating the difference between the values makes sense. Hence, additive and subtractive mathematical operations and logical comparison operators like greater than, less than, and equal to, operations can be applied.

An integer is a special form of the numeric data type which does not have decimals in the value or more precisely does not have infinite values between consecutive numbers. Usually, they denote a count of something, number of days with temperature less than 0°C, number of orders, number of children in a family, etc.

If a zero point is defined, numeric data become a *ratio* or *real* data type. Examples include temperature in Kelvin scale, bank account balance, and income. Along with additive and logical operations, ratio operations can be performed with this data type. Both integer and ratio data types are categorized as a *numeric* data type in most data science tools.

Categorical or Nominal

Categorical data types are attributes treated as distinct symbols or just names. The color of the iris of the human eye is a categorical data type because it takes a value like black, green, blue, gray, etc. There is no direct relationship among the data values, and hence, mathematical operators except the logical or "is equal" operator cannot be applied. They are also called a nominal or polynominal data type, derived from the Latin word for *name*.

An ordered nominal data type is a special case of a categorical data type where there is some kind of order among the values. An example of an ordered data type is temperature expressed as hot, mild, cold.

Not all data science tasks can be performed on all data types. For example, the neural network algorithm does not work with categorical data. However, one data type can be converted to another using a type conversion process, but this may be accompanied with possible loss of information. For example, credit scores expressed in poor, average, good, and excellent categories can be converted to either 1, 2, 3, and 4 or average underlying numerical scores like 400, 500, 600, and 700 (scores here are just an example). In this type conversion, there is no loss of information. However, conversion from numeric credit score to categories (poor, average, good, and excellent) does incur loss of information.

3.3 DESCRIPTIVE STATISTICS

Descriptive statistics refers to the study of the aggregate quantities of a dataset. These measures are some of the commonly used notations in everyday life. Some examples of descriptive statistics include average annual income, median home price in a neighborhood, range of credit scores of a population, etc. In general, descriptive analysis covers the following characteristics of the sample or population dataset (Kubiak & Benbow, 2006):

Characteristics of the Dataset	Measurement Technique
Center of the dataset	Mean, median, and mode
Spread of the dataset	Range, variance, and standard deviation
Shape of the distribution of the dataset	Symmetry, skewness, and kurtosis

The definition of these metrics will be explored shortly. Descriptive statistics can be broadly classified into univariate and multivariate exploration depending on the number of attributes under analysis.

3.3.1   Univariate Exploration

Univariate data exploration denotes analysis of one attribute at a time. The example Iris dataset for one species, *I. setosa*, has 50 observations and 4 attributes, as shown in Table 3.1. Here some of the descriptive statistics for sepal length attribute are explored.

Measure of Central Tendency

The objective of finding the central location of an attribute is to quantify the dataset with one central or most common number.

- *Mean*: The mean is the arithmetic average of all observations in the dataset. It is calculated by summing all the data points and dividing by the number of data points. The mean for sepal length in centimeters is 5.0060.
- *Median*: The median is the value of the central point in the distribution. The median is calculated by sorting all the observations from small to large and selecting the mid-point observation in the sorted list. If the number of data points is even, then the average of the middle two data points is used as the median. The median for sepal length is in centimeters is 5.0000.
- *Mode*: The mode is the most frequently occurring observation. In the dataset, data points may be repetitive, and the most repetitive data point is the mode of the dataset. In this example, the mode in centimeters is 5.1000.

Table 3.1 Iris Dataset and Descriptive Statistics (Fisher, 1936)

Observation	Sepal Length	Sepal Width	Petal Length	Petal Width
1	5.1	3.5	1.4	0.2
2	4.9	3.1	1.5	0.1
...	...	...	...	...
49	5	3.4	1.5	0.2
50	4.4	2.9	1.4	0.2
Statistics	**Sepal Length**	**Sepal Width**	**Petal Length**	**Petal Width**
Mean	5.006	3.418	1.464	0.244
Median	5.000	3.400	1.500	0.200
Mode	5.100	3.400	1.500	0.200
Range	1.500	2.100	0.900	0.500
Standard deviation	0.352	0.381	0.174	0.107
Variance	0.124	0.145	0.030	0.011

In an attribute, the mean, median, and mode may be different numbers, and this indicates the shape of the distribution. If the dataset has outliers, the mean will get affected while in most cases the median will not. The mode of the distribution can be different from the mean or median, if the underlying dataset has more than one natural normal distribution.

Measure of Spread

In desert regions, it is common for the temperature to cross above 110°F during the day and drop below 30°F during the night while the average temperature for a 24-hour period is around 70°F. Obviously, the experience of living in the desert is not the same as living in a tropical region with the same average daily temperature around 70°F, where the temperature within the day is between 60°F and 80°F. What matters here is not just the central location of the temperature, but the *spread* of the temperature. There are two common metrics to quantify spread.

- *Range:* The range is the difference between the maximum value and the minimum value of the attribute. The range is simple to calculate and articulate but has shortcomings as it is severely impacted by the presence of outliers and fails to consider the distribution of all other data points in the attributes. In the example, the range for the temperature in the desert is 80°F and the range for the tropics is 20°F. The desert region experiences larger temperature swings as indicated by the range.
- *Deviation:* The variance and standard deviation measures the spread, by considering all the values of the attribute. Deviation is simply measured as the difference between any given value (x_i) and the mean of the sample (μ). The variance is the sum of the squared deviations of all data points divided by the number of data points. For a dataset with N observations, the variance is given by the following equation:

$$\text{Variance} = s^2 = \frac{1}{N} \sum_{i=1}^{N} (x_i - \mu)^2 \tag{3.1}$$

Standard deviation is the square root of the variance. Since the standard deviation is measured in the same units as the attribute, it is easy to understand the magnitude of the metric. High standard deviation means the data points are spread widely around the central point. Low standard deviation means data points are closer to the central point. If the distribution of the data aligns with the *normal distribution*, then 68% of the data points lie within one standard deviation from the mean. Fig. 3.2 provides the univariate summary of the Iris dataset with all 150 observations, for each of the four numeric attributes.

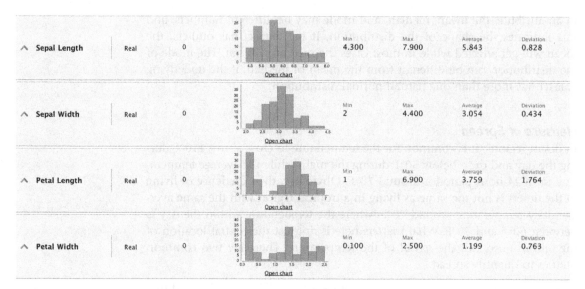

FIGURE 3.2
Descriptive statistics for the Iris dataset.

3.3.2 Multivariate Exploration

Multivariate exploration is the study of more than one attribute in the dataset simultaneously. This technique is critical to understanding the relationship between the attributes, which is central to data science methods. Similar to univariate explorations, the measure of central tendency and variance in the data will be discussed.

Central Data Point

In the Iris dataset, each data point as a set of all the four attributes can be expressed:

observation *i*: {sepal length, sepal width, petal length, petal width}

For example, observation one: {5.1, 3.5, 1.4, 0.2}. This observation point can also be expressed in four-dimensional Cartesian coordinates and can be plotted in a graph (although plotting more than three dimensions in a visual graph can be challenging). In this way, all 150 observations can be expressed in Cartesian coordinates. If the objective is to find the most "typical" observation point, it would be a data point made up of the mean of each attribute in the dataset independently. For the Iris dataset shown in Table 3.1, the central mean point is {5.006, 3.418, 1.464, 0.244}. This data point may not be an actual observation. It will be a hypothetical data point with the most typical attribute values.

Correlation

Correlation measures the statistical relationship between two attributes, particularly dependence of one attribute on another attribute. When two attributes are highly correlated with each other, they both vary at the same rate with each other either in the same or in opposite directions. For example, consider average temperature of the day and ice cream sales. Statistically, the two attributes that are correlated are dependent on each other and one may be used to predict the other. If there are sufficient data, future sales of ice cream can be predicted if the temperature forecast is known. However, correlation between two attributes does not imply causation, that is, one doesn't necessarily cause the other. The ice cream sales and the shark attacks are correlated, however there is no causation. Both ice cream sales and shark attacks are influenced by the third attribute—the summer season. Generally, ice cream sales spikes as temperatures rise. As more people go to beaches during summer, encounters with sharks become more probable.

Correlation between two attributes is commonly measured by the Pearson correlation coefficient (r), which measures the strength of *linear* dependence (Fig. 3.3). Correlation coefficients take a value from $-1 \leq r \leq 1$. A value closer to 1 or -1 indicates the two attributes are highly correlated, with perfect correlation at 1 or -1. Perfect correlation also exists when the attributes are governed by formulas and laws. For example, observations of the values of gravitational force and the mass of the object (Newton's second law) or the quantity of the products sold and total revenue (price* volume = revenue). A correlation value of 0 means there is no linear relationship between two attributes.

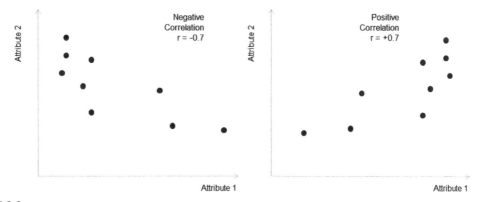

FIGURE 3.3
Correlation of attributes.

The Pearson correlation coefficient between two attributes x and y is calculated with the formula:

$$r_{xy} = \frac{\sum_{i=1}^{n} (x_i - \bar{x})(y_i - \bar{y})}{\sqrt{\sum_{i=1}^{n} (x_i - \bar{x})^2 \sum_{i=1}^{n} (y_i - \bar{y})^2}}$$
$$= \frac{\sum_{i=1}^{N} (x_i - \bar{x})(y_i - \bar{y})}{N \times s_x \times s_y} \tag{3.2}$$

where s_x and s_y are the standard deviations of random variables x and y, respectively. The Pearson correlation coefficient has some limitations in quantifying the strength of correlation. When datasets have more complex nonlinear relationships like quadratic functions, only the effects on linear relationships are considered and quantified using correlation coefficient. The presence of outliers can also skew the measure of correlation. Visually, correlation can be observed using scatterplots with the attributes in each Cartesian coordinate (Fig. 3.3). In fact, visualization should be the first step in understanding correlation because it can identify nonlinear relationships and show any outliers in the dataset. Anscombe's quartet (Anscombe, 1973) clearly illustrates the limitations of relying only on the correlation coefficient to understand the data (Fig. 3.4). The quartet consists of four different datasets, with two attributes (x, y). All four datasets have the same mean, the same variance for x and y, and the same correlation coefficient between x and y, but look drastically different when plotted on a chart. This evidence illustrates the necessity of visualizing the attributes instead of just calculating statistical metrics.

3.4   DATA VISUALIZATION

Visualizing data is one of the most important techniques of data discovery and exploration. Though visualization is not considered a data science technique, terms like visual mining or pattern discovery based on visuals are increasingly used in the context of data science, particularly in the business world. The discipline of data visualization encompasses the methods of expressing data in an abstract visual form. The visual representation of data provides easy comprehension of complex data with multiple attributes and their underlying relationships. The motivation for using data visualization includes:

- *Comprehension of dense information*: A simple visual chart can easily include thousands of data points. By using visuals, the user can see the big picture, as well as longer term trends that are extremely difficult to interpret purely by expressing data in numbers.

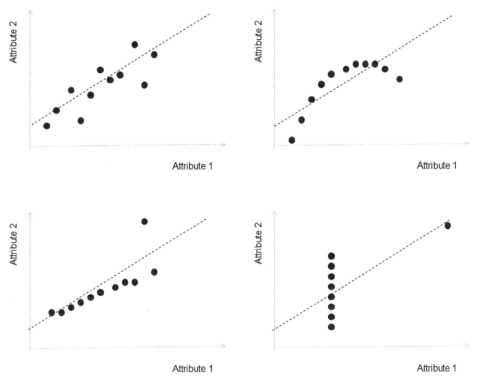

FIGURE 3.4

Anscombe's Quartet: descriptive statistics versus visualization. Source: *Adapted from: Anscombe, F. J., 1973. Graphs in statistical analysis, American Statistician, 27(1), pp. 19–20.*

- *Relationships*: Visualizing data in Cartesian coordinates enables exploration of the relationships between the attributes. Although representing more than three attributes on the *x*, *y*, and *z*-axes is not feasible in Cartesian coordinates, there are a few creative solutions available by changing properties like the size, color, and shape of data markers or using flow maps (Tufte, 2001), where more than two attributes are used in a two-dimensional medium.

Vision is one of the most powerful senses in the human body. As such, it is intimately connected with cognitive thinking (Few, 2006). Human vision is trained to discover patterns and anomalies even in the presence of a large volume of data. However, the effectiveness of the pattern detection depends on how effectively the information is visually presented. Hence, selecting suitable visuals to explore data is critically important in discovering and comprehending hidden patterns in the data (Ware, 2004). As with descriptive statistics, visualization techniques are also categorized into: univariate visualization, multivariate visualization and visualization of a large number of attributes using parallel dimensions.

Some of the common data visualization techniques used to analyze data will be reviewed. Most of these visualization techniques are available in commercial spreadsheet software like MS Excel. RapidMiner, like any other data science tool, offers a wide range of visualization tools. To maintain consistency with rest of the book, all further visualizations are output from RapidMiner using the Iris dataset. Please review Chapter 15, Getting Started With RapidMiner, to become familiar with RapidMiner.

3.4.1   Univariate Visualization

Visual exploration starts with investigating one attribute at a time using univariate charts. The techniques discussed in this section give an idea of how the attribute values are distributed and the shape of the distribution.

Histogram

A histogram is one of the most basic visualization techniques to understand the frequency of the occurrence of values. It shows the distribution of the data by plotting the frequency of occurrence in a range. In a histogram, the attribute under inquiry is shown on the horizontal axis and the frequency of occurrence is on the vertical axis. For a continuous numeric data type, the range or *binning* value to group a range of values need to be specified. For example, in the case of human height in centimeters, all the occurrences between 152.00 and 152.99 are grouped under 152. There is no optimal number of bins or bin width that works for all the distributions. If the bin width is too small, the distribution becomes more precise but reveals the noise due to sampling. A general rule of thumb is to have a number of bins equal to the square root or cube root of the number of data points.

Histograms are used to find the central location, range, and shape of distribution. In the case of the petal length attribute in the Iris dataset, the data is multimodal (Fig. 3.5), where the distribution does not follow the bell curve pattern. Instead, there are two peaks in the distribution. This is due to the fact that there are 150 observations of three *different* species (hence, distributions) in the dataset. A histogram can be *stratified* to include different classes in order to gain more insight. The enhanced histogram with class labels shows the dataset is made of three different distributions (Fig. 3.6). *I. setosa's* distribution stands out with a mean around 1.25 cm and ranges from 1−2 cm. *I. versicolor* and *I. virginica's* distributions overlap *I. setosa's* have separate means.

Quartile

A *box whisker* plot is a simple visual way of showing the distribution of a continuous variable with information such as quartiles, median, and outliers,

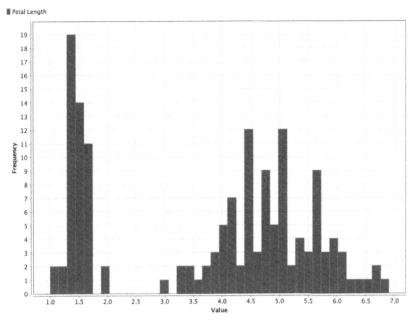

FIGURE 3.5
Histogram of petal length in Iris dataset.

overlaid by mean and standard deviation. The main attraction of box whisker or quartile charts is that distributions of multiple attributes can be compared side by side and the overlap between them can be deduced. The quartiles are denoted by Q1, Q2, and Q3 points, which indicate the data points with a 25% bin size. In a distribution, 25% of the data points will be below Q1, 50% will be below Q2, and 75% will be below Q3.

The Q1 and Q3 points in a box whisker plot are denoted by the edges of the box. The Q2 point, the median of the distribution, is indicated by a cross line within the box. The outliers are denoted by circles at the end of the whisker line. In some cases, the mean point is denoted by a solid dot overlay followed by standard deviation as a line overlay.

Fig. 3.7 shows that the quartile charts for all four attributes of the Iris dataset are plotted side by side. Petal length can be observed as having the broadest range and the sepal width has a narrow range, out of all of the four attributes.

One attribute can also be selected—petal length—and explored further using quartile charts by introducing a class label. In the plot in Fig. 3.8, we can see the distribution of three species for the petal length measurement. Similar to the previous comparison, the distribution of multiple species can be compared.

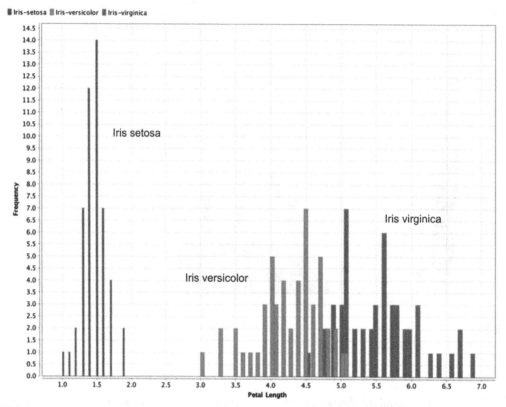

FIGURE 3.6

Class-stratified histogram of petal length in Iris dataset.

Distribution Chart

For continuous numeric attributes like petal length, instead of visualizing the actual data in the sample, its normal distribution function can be visualized instead. The normal distribution function of a continuous random variable is given by the formula:

$$f(x) = \frac{1}{\sqrt{2\pi}\sigma} e^{(x-\mu)^2/2\sigma^2} \tag{3.3}$$

where μ is the mean of the distribution and σ is the standard deviation of the distribution. Here an inherent assumption is being made that the measurements of petal length (or any continuous variable) follow the normal distribution, and hence, its distribution can be visualized instead of the actual values. The normal distribution is also called the *Gaussian distribution* or "bell curve" due to its bell shape. The normal distribution function

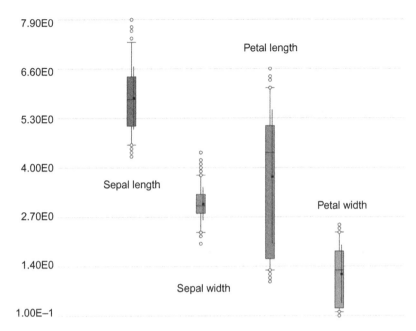

FIGURE 3.7
Quartile plot of Iris dataset.

shows the probability of occurrence of a data point within a range of values. If a dataset exhibits normal distribution, then 68.2% of data points will fall within one standard deviation from the mean; 95.4% of the points will fall within 2σ and 99.7% within 3σ of the mean. When the normal distribution curves are stratified by class type, more insight into the data can be gained. Fig. 3.9 shows the normal distribution curves for petal length measurement for each Iris species type. From the distribution chart, it can be inferred that the petal length for the *I. setosa* sample is more distinct and cohesive than *I. versicolor* and *I. virginica*. If there is an unlabeled measurement with a petal length of 1.5 cm, it can be predicted that the species is *I. setosa*. However, if the petal length measurement is 5.0 cm, there is no clear prediction, as the species could be either *Iris versicolor* and *I. virginica*.

3.4.2 Multivariate Visualization

The multivariate visual exploration considers more than one attribute in the same visual. The techniques discussed in this section focus on the relationship of one attribute with another attribute. These visualizations examine two to four attributes simultaneously.

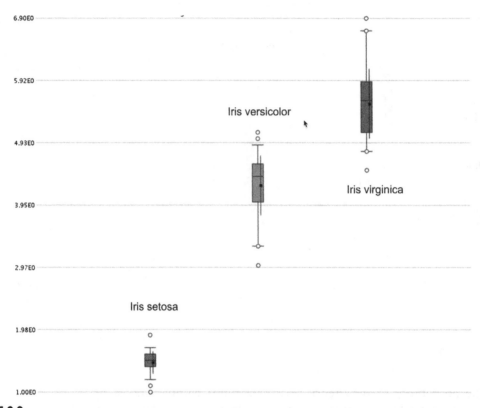

FIGURE 3.8
Class-stratified quartile plot of petal length in Iris dataset.

Scatterplot

A scatterplot is one of the most powerful yet simple visual plots available. In a scatterplot, the data points are marked in Cartesian space with attributes of the dataset aligned with the coordinates. The attributes are usually of continuous data type. One of the key observations that can be concluded from a scatterplot is the existence of a relationship between two attributes under inquiry. If the attributes are linearly correlated, then the data points align closer to an imaginary straight line; if they are not correlated, the data points are scattered. Apart from basic correlation, scatterplots can also indicate the existence of patterns or groups of clusters in the data and identify outliers in the data. This is particularly useful for low-dimensional datasets. Chapter 13: Anomaly detection, provides techniques for finding outliers in high-dimensional space.

Fig. 3.10 shows the scatterplot between petal length (x-axis) and petal width (y-axis). These two attributes are slightly correlated, because this is a measurement of the same part of the flower. When the data markers are colored to

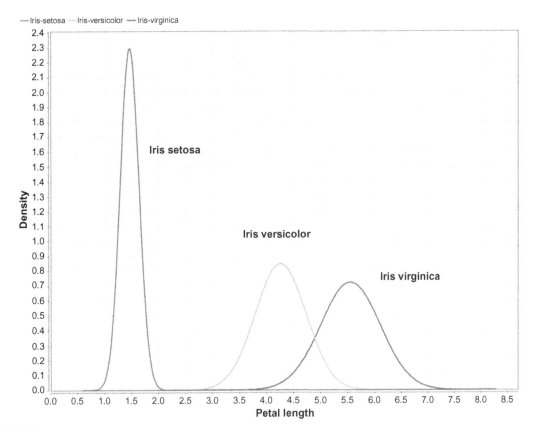

FIGURE 3.9
Distribution of petal length in Iris dataset.

indicate different species using class labels, more patterns can be observed. There is a cluster of data points, all belonging to species *I. setosa*, on the lower left side of the plot. *I. setosa* has much smaller petals. This feature can be used as a rule to predict the species of unlabeled observations. One of the limitations of scatterplots is that only two attributes can be used at a time, with an additional attribute possibly shown in the color of the data marker. However, the colors are usually reserved for class labels.

Scatter Multiple

A *scatter multiple* is an enhanced form of a simple scatterplot where more than two dimensions can be included in the chart and studied simultaneously. The primary attribute is used for the *x*-axis coordinate. The secondary axis is shared with more attributes or dimensions. In this example (Fig. 3.11), the values on the *y*-axis are shared between sepal length, sepal

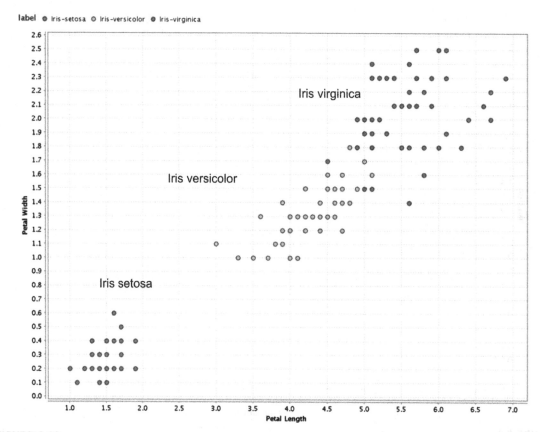

FIGURE 3.10
Scatterplot of Iris dataset.

width, and petal width. The name of the attribute is conveyed by colors used in data markers. Here, sepal length is represented by data points occupying the topmost part of the chart, sepal width occupies the middle portion, and petal width is in the bottom portion. Note that the data points are *duplicated for each attribute in the y-axis*. Data points are color-coded for each dimension in *y*-axis while the *x*-axis is anchored with one attribute—petal length. All the attributes sharing the y-axis should be of the same unit or normalized.

Scatter Matrix

If the dataset has more than two attributes, it is important to look at combinations of all the attributes through a scatterplot. A *scatter matrix* solves this need by comparing all combinations of attributes with individual scatterplots and arranging these plots in a matrix.

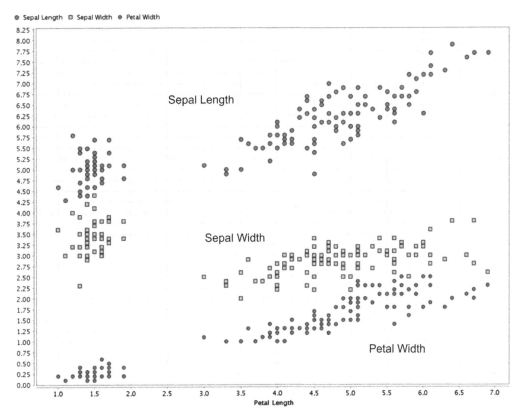

FIGURE 3.11
Scatter multiple plot of Iris dataset.

A scatter matrix for all four attributes in the Iris dataset is shown in Fig. 3.12. The color of the data point is used to indicate the species of the flower. Since there are four attributes, there are four rows and four columns, for a total of 16 scatter charts. Charts in the diagonal are a comparison of the attribute with itself; hence, they are eliminated. Also, the charts below the diagonal are mirror images of the charts above the diagonal. In effect, there are six distinct comparisons in scatter multiples of four attributes. Scatter matrices provide an effective visualization of comparative, multivariate, and high-density data displayed in small multiples of the similar scatterplots (Tufte, 2001).

Bubble Chart

A *bubble chart* is a variation of a simple scatterplot with the addition of one more attribute, which is used to determine the size of the data point. In the Iris dataset, petal length and petal width are used for *x* and *y*-axis, respectively

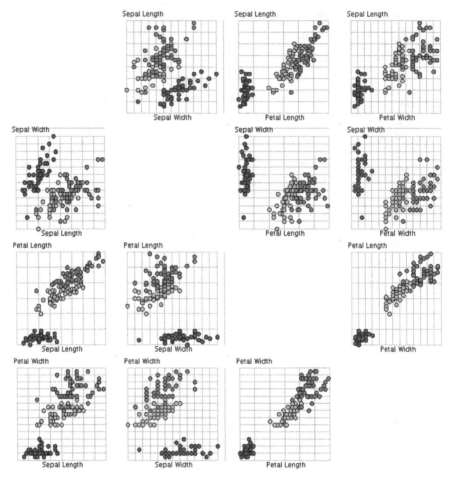

FIGURE 3.12
Scatter matrix plot of Iris dataset.

and sepal width is used for the size of the data point. The color of the data point represents a species class label (Fig. 3.13).

Density Chart

Density charts are similar to the scatterplots, with one more dimension included as a background color. The data point can also be colored to visualize one dimension, and hence, a total of four dimensions can be visualized in a density chart. In the example in Fig. 3.14, petal length is used for the *x*-axis, sepal length for the *y*-axis, sepal width for the background color, and class label for the data point color.

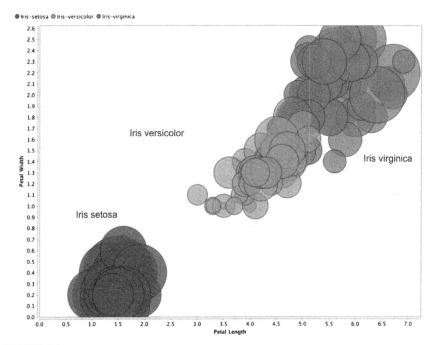

FIGURE 3.13
Bubble chart of Iris dataset.

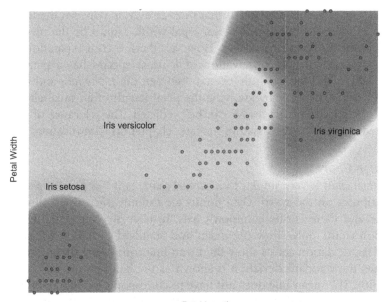

FIGURE 3.14
Density chart of a few attributes in the Iris dataset.

3.4.3 Visualizing High-Dimensional Data

Visualizing more than three attributes on a two-dimensional medium (like a paper or screen) is challenging. This limitation can be overcome by using transformation techniques to project the high-dimensional data points into parallel axis space. In this approach, a Cartesian axis is shared by more than one attribute.

Parallel Chart

A *parallel chart* visualizes a data point quite innovatively by transforming or projecting multi-dimensional data into a two-dimensional chart medium. In this chart, every attribute or dimension is linearly arranged in one coordinate (*x*-axis) and all the measures are arranged in the other coordinate (*y*-axis). Since the *x*-axis is multivariate, each data point is represented as a *line* in a parallel space.

In the case of the Iris dataset, all four attributes are arranged along the *x*-axis. The *y*-axis represents a generic distance and it is "shared" by all these attributes on the *x*-axis. Hence, parallel charts work only when attributes share a common unit of numerical measure or when the attributes are normalized. This visualization is called a *parallel axis* because all four attributes are represented in four parallel axes parallel to the *y*-axis.

In a parallel chart, a class label is used to color each data *line* so that one more dimension is introduced into the picture. By observing this parallel chart in Fig. 3.15, it can be noted that there is overlap between the three species on the sepal width attribute. So, sepal width cannot be the metric used to differentiate these three species. However, there is clear separation of species in petal length. No observation of *I. setosa* species has a petal length above 2.5 cm and there is little overlap between the *I. virginica* and *I. versicolor* species. Visually, just by knowing the petal length of an unlabeled observation, the species of Iris flower can be predicted. The relevance of this rule as a predictor will be discussed in the later chapter on Classification.

Deviation Chart

A *deviation chart* is very similar to a *parallel chart*, as it has parallel axes for all the attributes on the *x*-axis. Data points are extended across the dimensions as lines and there is one common *y*-axis. Instead of plotting all data lines, deviation charts only show the mean and standard deviation statistics. For each class, deviation charts show the mean line connecting the mean of each attribute; the standard deviation is shown as the band above and below the mean line. The mean line does not have to correspond to a data point (line). With this method, information is elegantly displayed, and the essence of a parallel chart is maintained.

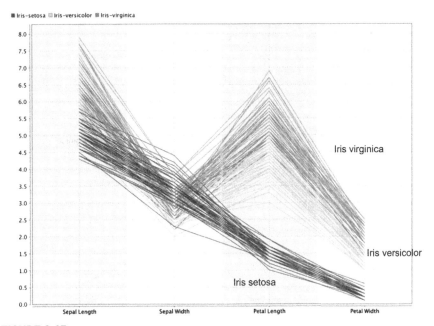

FIGURE 3.15
Parallel chart of Iris dataset.

In Fig. 3.16, a deviation chart for the Iris dataset stratified by species is shown. It can be observed that the petal length is a good predictor to classify the species because the mean line and the standard deviation bands for the species are well separated.

Andrews Curves

An *Andrews plot* belongs to a family of visualization techniques where the high-dimensional data are projected into a vector space so that each data point takes the form of a line or curve. In an Andrews plot, each data point X with d dimensions, $X = (x_1, x_2, x_3, \ldots, x_d)$, takes the form of a Fourier series:

$$f_x(t) = \frac{x_1}{\sqrt{2}} + x_2 \sin(t) + x_3 \cos(t) + x_4 \sin(2t) + x_5 \cos(2t) + \cdots \qquad (3.4)$$

This function is plotted for $-\pi < t < \pi$ for each data point. Andrews plots are useful to determine if there are any outliers in the data and to identify potential patterns within the data points (Fig. 3.17). If two data points are similar, then the curves for the data points are closer to each other. If curves are far apart and belong to different classes, then this information can be used classify the data (Garcia-Osorio & Fyfe, 2005).

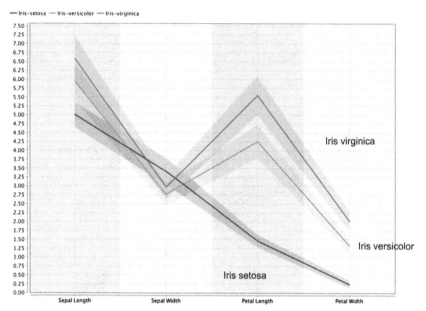

FIGURE 3.16
Deviation chart of Iris dataset.

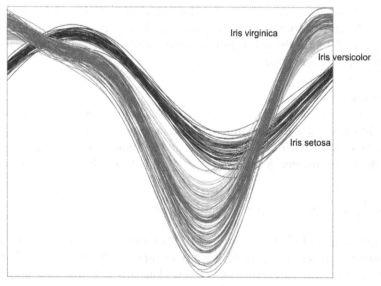

FIGURE 3.17
Andrews curves of Iris dataset.

Many of the charts and visuals discussed in this chapter explore the multivariate relationships within the dataset. They form the set of classic data visualizations used for data exploration, postprocessing, and understanding data science models. Some new developments in the area of visualization deals with networks and connections within the data objects (Lima, 2011). To better analyze data extracted from graph data, social networks, and integrated applications, connectivity charts are often used. Interactive exploration of data using visualization software provides an essential tool to observe multiple attributes at the same time but has limitations on the number of attributes used in visualizations. Hence, dimensional reduction using techniques discussed in Chapter 14, Feature Selection, can help in visualizing higher-dimensional data by reducing the dimensions to a critical few.

3.5 ROADMAP FOR DATA EXPLORATION

If there is a new dataset that has not been investigated before, having a structured way to explore and analyze the data will be helpful. Here is a roadmap to inquire a new dataset. Not all steps may be relevant for every dataset and the order may need to be adjusted for some sets, so this roadmap is intended as a guideline.

1. *Organize the dataset*: Structure the dataset with standard rows and columns. Organizing the dataset to have objects or instances in rows and dimensions or attributes in columns will be helpful for many data analysis tools. Identify the target or "class label" attribute, if applicable.
2. *Find the central point for each attribute*: Calculate *mean*, *median*, and *mode* for each attribute and the class label. If all three values are very different, it may indicate the presence of an outlier, or a multimodal or nonnormal distribution for an attribute.
3. *Understand the spread of each attribute*: Calculate the *standard deviation* and *range* for an attribute. Compare the standard deviation with the mean to understand the spread of the data, along with the max and min data points.
4. *Visualize the distribution of each attribute*: Develop the *histogram* and *distribution* plots for each attribute. Repeat the same for class-stratified histograms and distribution plots, where the plots are either repeated or color-coded for each class.
5. *Pivot the data*: Sometimes called dimensional slicing, a pivot is helpful to comprehend different values of the attributes. This technique can stratify by class and drill down to the details of any of the attributes. Microsoft Excel and Business Intelligence tools popularized this technique of data analysis for a wider audience.

6. *Watch out for outliers*: Use a scatterplot or quartiles to find outliers. The presence of outliers skews some measures like mean, variance, and range. Exclude outliers and rerun the analysis. Notice if the results change.

7. *Understand the relationship between attributes*: Measure the *correlation* between attributes and develop a correlation matrix. Notice what attributes are dependent on each other and investigate why they are dependent.

8. *Visualize the relationship between attributes*: Plot a quick scatter matrix to discover the relationship between multiple attributes at once. Zoom in on the attribute pairs with simple two-dimensional scatterplots stratified by class.

9. *Visualize high-dimensional datasets*: Create *parallel charts* and *Andrews curves* to observe the class differences exhibited by each attribute. *Deviation charts* provide a quick assessment of the spread of each class for each attribute.

References

Anscombe, F. J. (1973). Graphs in statistical analysis. *American Statistician, 27*(1), 17−21.

Bache, K., & Lichman, M. (2013) *University of California, School of Information and Computer Science*. Retrieved from UCI Machine Learning Repository <http://archive.ics.uci.edu/ml>.

Few, S. (2006). *Information dashboard design: The effective visual communication of data*. Sebastopol, CA: O'Reilly Media.

Fisher, R. A. (1936). The use of multiple measurements in taxonomic problems. *Annals of Human Genetics, 7*, 179−188, 10.1111/j.1469-1809.1936.tb02137.x.

Garcia-Osorio, C., & Fyfe, C. (2005). Visualization of high-dimensional data via orthogonal curves. *Journal of Universal Computer Science, 11*(11), 1806−1819.

Kubiak, T., & Benbow, D. W. (2006). *The certified six sigma black belt handbook*. Milwaukee, WI: ASQ Quality Press.

Lima, M. (2011). *Visual complexity: Mapping patterns of information*. New York: Princeton Architectural Press.

Tufte, E. R. (2001). *The visual display of quantitative information*. Cheshire, CT: Graphics Press.

Ware, C. (2004). *Information visualization: Perception for design*. Waltham, MA: Morgan Kaufmann.

CHAPTER 4

Classification

Enter the realm of data science—the process in which historical records are used to make a prediction about an uncertain future. At a fundamental level, most data science problems can be categorized into either class or numeric prediction problems. In classification or class prediction, one should try to use the information from the predictors or independent variables to sort the data samples into two or more distinct *classes* or *buckets*. In the case of numeric prediction, one would try to predict the numeric value of a dependent variable using the values assumed by the independent variables.

Here the classification process will be described with a simple example. Most golfers enjoy playing if the weather and outlook conditions meet certain requirements: too hot or too humid conditions, even if the outlook is sunny, are not preferred. On the other hand, overcast skies are no problem for playing even if the temperatures are somewhat cool. Based on the historic fictional records of these conditions and preferences, and information about a day's temperature, humidity level, and outlook, classification will allow one to predict if someone prefers to play golf or not. The outcome of classification is to categorize the weather conditions when golf is likely to be played or not, quite simply: *Play* or *Not Play* (two classes). The predictors can be continuous (temperature, humidity) or categorical (sunny, cloudy, windy, etc.). Those beginning to explore data science are confused by the dozens of techniques that are available to address these types of classification problems. In this chapter, several commonly used data science techniques will be described where the idea is to develop rules, relationships, and models based on predictor information that can be applied to classify outcomes from new and unseen data.

To begin with, fairly simple schemes will be used with a progression to more sophisticated techniques. Each section contains essential algorithmic details about the technique, describes how it is developed using simple examples, and finally closes with implementation details.

Data Science. DOI: https://doi.org/10.1016/B978-0-12-814761-0.00004-6

4.1   DECISION TREES

Decision trees (also known as classification trees) are probably one of the most intuitive and frequently used data science techniques. From an analyst's point of view, they are easy to set up and from a business user's point of view they are easy to interpret. Classification trees, as the name implies, are used to separate a dataset into classes belonging to the response variable. Usually the response variable has two classes: Yes or No (1 or 0). If the response variable has *more* than two categories, then variants of the decision tree algorithm have been developed that may be applied (Quinlan, 1986). In either case, classification trees are used when the response or target variable is categorical in nature.

Regression trees (Brieman, 1984) are similar in function to classification trees and are used for numeric prediction problems, when the response variable is numeric or continuous: for example, predicting the price of a consumer good based on several input factors. Keep in mind that in either case, the predictors or independent variables may be either categorical or numeric. It is the *target variable* that determines the type of decision tree needed.

4.1.1   How It Works

A decision tree model takes a form of decision flowchart (or an inverted tree) where an attribute is tested in each node. At end of the decision tree path is a leaf node where a prediction is made about the target variable based on conditions set forth by the decision path. The nodes split the dataset into subsets. In a decision tree, the idea is to *split* the dataset based on the homogeneity of data. Say for example, there are two variables, age and weight, that predict if a person is likely to sign up for a gym membership or not. In the training data if it was seen that 90% of the people who are older than 40 signed up, the data can be split into two parts: one part consisting of people older than 40 and the other part consisting of people under 40. The first part is now "90% pure" from the standpoint of which class they belong to. However, a rigorous measure of impurity is needed, which meets certain criteria, based on computing a proportion of the data that belong to a class. These criteria are simple:

1. The measure of impurity of a dataset must be at a maximum when all possible classes are equally represented. In the gym membership example, in the initial dataset, if 50% of samples belonged to "not signed up" and 50% of the samples belonged to "signed up," then this non-partitioned raw data would have maximum impurity.
2. The measure of impurity of a dataset must be zero when only one class is represented. For example, if a group is formed of only those people who signed up for the membership (only one class = members), then this subset has "100% purity" or "0% impurity."

Measures such as *entropy* or *Gini index* easily meet these criteria and are used to build decision trees as described in the following sections. Different criteria will build different trees through different biases, for example, *information gain* favors tree splits that contain many cases, while *information gain ratio* attempts to balance this.

HOW DATA SCIENCE CAN REDUCE UNCERTAINTY

Imagine a box that can contain one of three colored balls inside—red, yellow, and blue, see Fig. 4.1. Without opening the box, if one had to "predict" which colored ball is inside, then they are basically dealing with a lack of information or uncertainty. Now what is the *highest* number of "yes/no" questions that can be asked to reduce this uncertainty and, thus, increase our information?

1. Is it red? No.
2. Is it yellow? No.

Then it must be blue.

That is *two* questions. If there were a fourth color, green, then the highest number of yes/no questions is *three*. By extending this reasoning, it can be mathematically shown that the maximum number of *binary* questions needed to reduce uncertainty is essentially log(T), where the log is taken to base 2 and T is the number of possible outcomes (Meagher, 2005) [e.g., if there was only one color, that is,

one outcome, then log(1) = 0, which means there is no uncertainty!].

Many real-world business problems can be thought of as extensions to this "uncertainty reduction" example. For example, knowing only a handful of characteristics such as the length of a loan, borrower's occupation, annual income, and previous credit behavior, several available data science techniques can be used to rank the riskiness of a potential loan, and by extension, the interest rate of the loan. This is nothing but a more sophisticated uncertainty reduction exercise, similar in spirit to the ball-in-a-box problem. Decision trees embody this problem-solving technique by systematically examining the available attributes and their impact on the eventual class or category of a sample. Later in this section, how to predict the credit ratings of a bank's customers using their demographic and other behavioral data will be examined in detail using a decision tree, which is a practical implementation of the entropy principle for decision-making under uncertainty.

FIGURE 4.1
Playing 20 questions with entropy.

Continuing with the example in the box, if there are T events with equal probability of occurrence P, then $T = 1/P$. Claude Shannon, who developed the mathematical underpinnings for information theory (Shannon, 1948), defined entropy as $\log_2(1/p)$ or $-\log_2 p$ where p is the probability of an event occurring. If the probability for all events is not identical, a weighted expression is needed and, thus, entropy, H, is adjusted as follows:

$$H = -\sum_{k=1}^{m} p_k \log_2(p_k) \tag{4.1}$$

where $k = 1, 2, 3, \ldots, m$ represents the m classes of the target variable. p_k represents the proportion of samples that belong to class k. For the gym membership example from earlier, there are two classes: member or non-member. If the dataset had 100 samples with 50% of each, then the entropy of the dataset is given by $H = -[(0.5 \log_2 0.5) + (0.5 \log_2 0.5)] = -\log_2 0.5 = -(-1) = 1$. On the other hand, if the data can be partitioned into two sets of 50 samples each that exclusively contain all members and all nonmembers, the entropy of either of these two partitioned sets is given by $H = -1 \log_2 1 = 0$. Any other proportion of samples within a dataset will yield entropy values between 0 and 1 (which is the maximum). The Gini index (G) is similar to the entropy measure in its characteristics and is defined as

$$G = 1 - \sum_{k=1}^{m} p_k^2 \tag{4.2}$$

The value of G ranges between 0 and a maximum value of 0.5, but otherwise has properties identical to H, and either of these formulations can be used to create partitions in the data (Cover, 1991).

the golf example, introduced earlier, is used in this section to explain the application of entropy concepts for creating a decision tree. This was the same dataset used by J. Ross Quinlan to introduce one of the original decision tree algorithms, the *Iterative Dichotomizer* 3, or ID3 (Quinlan, 1986). The full data are shown in Table 4.1.

There are essentially two questions that need to be answered at each step of the tree building process: *where to split the data* and *when to stop splitting*.

Step 1: Where to Split Data?
There are 14 examples, with four attributes—Outlook, Temperature, Humidity, and Wind. The target attribute that needs to be predicted is Play with two classes: Yes and No. It's important to understand how to build a decision tree using this simple dataset.

Table 4.1 The Classic Golf Dataset

Outlook	Temperature	Humidity	Windy	Play
Sunny	85	85	false	no
Sunny	80	90	true	no
Overcast	83	78	false	yes
Rain	70	96	false	yes
Rain	68	80	false	yes
Rain	65	70	true	no
Overcast	64	65	true	yes
Sunny	72	95	false	no
Sunny	69	70	false	yes
Rain	75	80	false	yes
Sunny	75	70	true	yes
Overcast	72	90	true	yes
Overcast	81	75	false	yes
Rain	71	80	true	no

Start by partitioning the data on each of the four regular attributes. Let us start with Outlook. There are three categories for this variable: sunny, overcast, and rain. We see that when it is overcast, there are four examples where the outcome was Play = yes for all four cases (see Fig. 4.2) and so the proportion of examples in this case is 100% or 1.0. Thus, if we split the dataset here, the resulting four sample partition will be 100% pure for Play = yes. Mathematically for this partition, the entropy can be calculated using Eq. (4.1) as:

$$H_{outlook:overcast} = -(0/4)\log_2(0/4) - (4/4)\log_2(4/4) = 0.0$$

Similarly, the entropy in the other two situations for Outlook can be calculated:

$$H_{outlook:sunny} = -(2/5)\log_2(2/5) - (3/5)\log_2(3/5) = 0.971$$
$$H_{outlook:rain} = -(3/5)\log_2(3/5) - (2/5)\log_2(2/5) = 0.971$$

For the attribute on the whole, the total *information I* is calculated as the weighted sum of these component entropies. There are four instances of Outlook = overcast, thus, the proportion for overcast is given by $p_{outlook:overcast} = 4/14$. The other proportions (for Outlook = sunny and rain) are 5/14 each:

$$I_{outlook} = P_{outlook:overcast} \times H_{outlook:overcast} + P_{outlook:sunny} \times H_{outlook:sunny}$$
$$+ P_{outlook:rain} \times H_{outlook:rain}$$
$$I_{outlook} = (4/14) \times 0 + (5/14) \times 0.971 + (5/14) \times 0.971 = 0.693$$

Row No.	Play	Outlook
1	no	sunny
2	no	sunny
3	yes	overcast
4	yes	rain
5	yes	rain
6	no	rain
7	yes	overcast
8	no	sunny
9	yes	sunny
10	yes	rain
11	yes	sunny
12	yes	overcast
13	yes	overcast
14	no	rain

FIGURE 4.2
Splitting the data on the Outlook attribute.

Had the data *not* been partitioned along the three values for Outlook, the total information would have been simply the weighted average of the respective entropies for the two classes whose overall proportions were 5/14 (Play = no) and 9/14 (Play = yes):

$$I_{\text{outlook,no partition}} = -(5/14)\log_2(5/14) - (9/14)\log_2(9/14) = 0.940$$

By creating these splits or partitions, some entropy has been reduced (and, thus, some information has been gained). This is called, aptly enough, *information gain*. In the case of Outlook, this is given simply by:

$$I_{\text{outlook, no partition}} - I_{\text{outlook}} = 0.940 - 0.693 = 0.247$$

Similar information gain values for the other three attributes can now be computed, as shown in Table 4.2.

For numeric variables, possible split points to examine are essentially averages of available values. For example, the first potential split point for Humidity could be Average [65,70], which is 67.5, the next potential split point could be Average [70,75], which is 72.5, and so on. Similar logic can

Table 4.2 Computing the Information Gain for All Attributes

Attribute	Information Gain
Temperature	0.029
Humidity	0.102
Wind	0.048
Outlook	0.247

be used for the other numeric attribute, Temperature. The algorithm computes the information gain at each of these potential split points and chooses the one which maximizes it. Another way to approach this would be to discretize the numerical ranges, for example, Temperature $> = 80$ could be considered "Hot," between 70 and 79 "Mild," and less than 70 "Cool."

From Table 4.2, it is clear that if the dataset is partitioned into three sets along the three values of Outlook, the largest information gain would be experienced. This gives the first node of the decision tree as shown in Fig. 4.3. As noted earlier, the terminal node for the Outlook = overcast branch consists of four samples, all of which belong to the class Play = yes. The other two branches contain a mix of classes. The Outlook = rain branch has three yes results and the Outlook = sunny branch has three no results.

Thus, not all the final partitions are 100% homogenous. This means that the same process can be applied for each of these subsets till purer results are obtained. So, back to the first question once again—where to split the data? Fortunately, this was already answered for when the information gain for all attributes was computed. The other attributes, that yielded the highest gains, are used. Following that logic, the Outlook = sunny branch can be split along Humidity (which yielded the second highest information gain) and the Outlook = rain branch can be split along Wind (which yielded the third highest gain). The fully grown tree shown in Fig. 4.4 does precisely that.

Step 2: When to Stop Splitting Data?
In real-world datasets, it is very unlikely that to get terminal nodes that are 100% homogeneous as was just seen in the golf dataset. In this case, the algorithm would need to be instructed when to stop. There are several situations where the process can be terminated:

1. No attribute satisfies a minimum information gain threshold (such as the one computed in Table 4.2).
2. A maximal depth is reached: as the tree grows larger, not only does interpretation get harder, but a situation called "overfitting" is induced.
3. There are less than a certain number of examples in the current subtree: again, a mechanism to prevent *overfitting*.

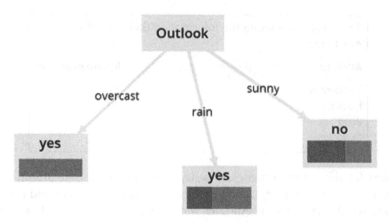

FIGURE 4.3
Splitting the Golf dataset on the Outlook attribute yields three subsets or branches. The middle and right branches may be split further.

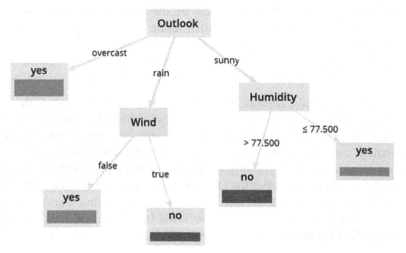

FIGURE 4.4
Decision Tree for the Golf data.

So, what exactly is overfitting? Overfitting occurs when a model tries to memorize the training data instead of generalizing the relationship between inputs and output variables. Overfitting often has the effect of performing well on the training dataset but performing poorly on any new data previously unseen by the model. As mentioned, overfitting by a decision tree results not only in difficulty interpreting the model, but also provides quite a useless model for unseen data. To prevent overfitting, tree growth may need to be restricted or reduced, using a process called *pruning*. All three stopping techniques mentioned constitute what is known of as *pre-pruning* the decision tree, because the pruning occurs before or during the growth of the tree. There are also methods that will not restrict the number of branches and allow the tree to grow as deep as the data will allow, and *then* trim or prune those branches that do not effectively change the classification error rates. This is called *post-pruning*. Post-pruning may sometimes be a better option because one will not miss any small but potentially significant relationships between attribute values and classes if the tree is allowed to reach its maximum depth. However, one drawback with post-pruning is that it requires additional computations, which may be wasted when the tree needs to be trimmed back.

Now the application of the decision tree algorithm can be summarized with this simple five-step process:

1. Using Shannon entropy, sort the dataset into homogenous (by class) and non-homogeneous variables. Homogeneous variables have low information entropy and non-homogeneous variables have high information entropy. This was done in the calculation of $I_{\text{outlook, no partition}}$.

2. Weight the influence of each independent variable on the target variable using the entropy weighted averages (sometimes called joint entropy). This was done during the calculation of I_{outlook} in the example.

3. Compute the information gain, which is essentially the reduction in the entropy of the target variable due to its relationship with each independent variable. This is simply the difference between the information entropy found in step 1 minus the joint entropy calculated in step 2. This was done during the calculation of $I_{\text{outlook, no partition}} - I_{\text{outlook}}$.

4. The independent variable with the highest information gain will become the root or the first node on which the dataset is divided. This was done using the calculation of the information gain table.

5. Repeat this process for each variable for which the Shannon entropy is nonzero. If the entropy of a variable is zero, then that variable becomes a "leaf" node.

4.1.2   How to Implement

Before jumping into a business use case of decision trees, a simple decision tree model will be implemented using the concepts discussed in the earlier section. The first implementation gives an idea about key building blocks in a data science implementation process. The second implementation provides a deep-dive into a business application. This is the first implementation of a data science technique, so some extra effort will be spent going into detail on many of the preliminary steps and also on introducing several additional tools and concepts that will be required throughout the rest of this chapter and other chapters that focus on supervised learning methods. These are the concepts of splitting data into testing and training samples and applying the trained model on testing. It may also be useful to first review Section 15.1 (Introduction to the GUI) and Section 15.2 (Data Import and Export) from Chapter 15, Getting started with RapidMiner before working through the rest of this implementation. As a final note, the ways and means to improve the performance of a classification model using RapidMiner will not be discussed in this section, but this very important part of data science will be revisited in several later chapters, particularly in the section on using optimization.

Implementation 1: To Play Golf or Not?

The complete RapidMiner process for implementing the decision tree model discussed in the earlier section is shown in Fig. 4.5. The key building blocks for this process are: training dataset, test dataset, model building, predicting using the model, predicted dataset, model representation, and performance vector.

The decision tree process has two input datasets. The *training dataset*, shown in Table 4.1, is used to build the decision tree with default parameter options. Fig. 4.6 shows the *test dataset*. The test dataset shares the same structure as the training dataset but with different records. These two operators constitute the inputs to the data science process.

The *modeling* block builds the decision tree using the training dataset. The *Apply model* block predicts the class label of the test dataset using the developed model and appends the predicted label to the dataset. The predicted dataset is one of the three outputs of the process and is shown in Fig. 4.7.

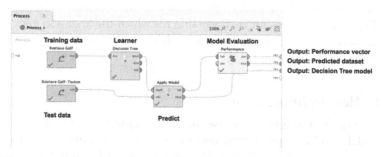

FIGURE 4.5

Building blocks of the Decision Tree process.

Row No.	Play	Outlook	Temperature	Humidity	Wind
1	yes	sunny	85	85	false
2	no	overcast	80	90	true
3	yes	overcast	83	78	false
4	yes	rain	70	96	false
5	yes	rain	68	80	true
6	no	rain	65	70	true
7	yes	overcast	64	65	true
8	no	sunny	72	95	false
9	yes	sunny	69	70	false
10	no	sunny	75	80	false
11	yes	sunny	68	70	true
12	yes	overcast	72	90	true
13	no	overcast	81	75	true
14	yes	rain	71	80	true

FIGURE 4.6

Test data.

Row ...	Play	prediction...	confidence(...	confidence(...	Outlook	Temperature	Humidity	Wind
1	yes	no	1	0	sunny	85	85	false
2	no	yes	0	1	overcast	80	90	true
3	yes	yes	0	1	overcast	83	78	false
4	yes	yes	0	1	rain	70	96	false
5	yes	no	1	0	rain	68	80	true
6	no	no	1	0	rain	65	70	true
7	yes	yes	0	1	overcast	64	65	true
8	no	no	1	0	sunny	72	95	false
9	yes	yes	0	1	sunny	69	70	false
10	no	no	1	0	sunny	75	80	false
11	yes	yes	0	1	sunny	68	70	true
12	yes	yes	0	1	overcast	72	90	true
13	no	yes	0	1	overcast	81	75	true
14	yes	no	1	0	rain	71	80	true

FIGURE 4.7

Results of applying the simple Decision Tree model.

Note the prediction test dataset has both the predicted and the original class label. The model has predicted correct class for nine of the records, but not for all. The five incorrect predictions are highlighted in Fig. 4.7.

The decision tree model developed using the training dataset is shown in Fig. 4.8. This is a simple decision tree with only three nodes. The leaf nodes are pure with a clean split of data. In practical applications, the tree will have dozens of nodes and the split will have mixed classes in the leaf nodes.

The *performance evaluation* block compares the predicted class label and the original class label in the test dataset to compute the performance metrics like accuracy, recall, etc. Fig. 4.9 shows the accuracy results of the model and the confusion matrix. It is evident that the model has been able to get 9 of the 14 class predictions correct and 5 of the 14 (in boxes) wrong, which translates to about 64% accuracy.

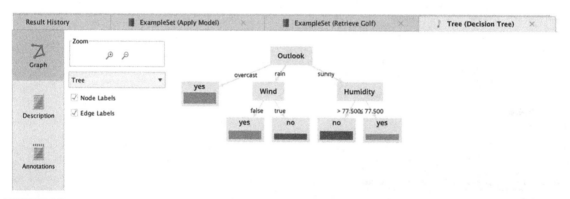

FIGURE 4.8
Decision Tree for Golf dataset.

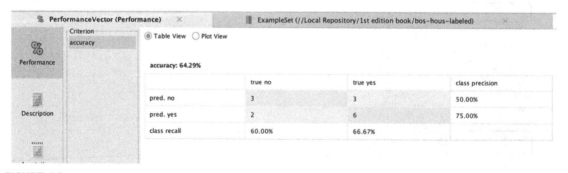

FIGURE 4.9
Performance vector.

Implementation 2: Prospect Filtering

A more involved business application will be examined to better understand how to apply decision trees for real-world problems. Credit scoring is a fairly common data science problem. Some types of situations where credit scoring could be applied are:

1. Prospect filtering: Identify which prospects to extend credit to and determine how much credit would be an acceptable risk.
2. Default risk detection: Decide if a particular customer is likely to default on a loan.
3. Bad debt collection: Sort out those debtors who will yield a good cost (of collection) to benefit (of receiving payment) performance.

The German Credit dataset from the University of California-Irvine Machine Learning (UCI-ML) data repository[1] will be used with RapidMiner to build a decision tree for addressing a *prospect filtering problem*. There are four main steps in setting up any supervised learning algorithm for a predictive modeling exercise:

1. Read in the cleaned and prepared data typically from a database or a spreadsheet, but the data can be from any source.
2. Split data into training and testing samples.
3. Train the decision tree using the training portion of the dataset.
4. Apply the model on the testing portion of the dataset to evaluate the performance of the model.

Step 1 may seem rather elementary but can confuse many beginners and, thus, sometime will be spent explaining this in somewhat more detail.

Step 1: Data Preparation

The raw data is in the format shown in Table 4.3. It consists of 1000 samples and a total of 20 attributes and 1 label or target attribute. There are seven numeric attributes and the rest are categorical or qualitative, including the label, which is a binominal variable. The label attribute is called Credit Rating and can take the value of 1 (good) or 2 (bad). In the data 70% of the samples fall into the good credit rating class. The descriptions for the data are shown in Table 4.3. Most of the attributes are self-explanatory, but the raw data has encodings for the values of the qualitative variables. For example, attribute 4 is the *purpose of the loan* and can assume any of 10 values (A40 for new car, A41 for used car, and so on). The full details of these encodings are provided under the dataset description on the UCI-ML website.

---

[1] http://archive.ics.uci.edu/ml/datasets/ All datasets used in this book are available at the companion website.

Table 4.3 A View of the Raw German Credit Data

Checking Account Status	Duration in Months	Credit History	Purpose	Credit Amount	Savings Account/ Bonds	Present Employment since	Credit Rating
A11	6	A34	A43	1169	A65	A75	1
A12	48	A32	A43	5951	A61	A73	2
A14	12	A34	A46	2096	A61	A74	1
A11	42	A32	A42	7882	A61	A74	1
A11	24	A33	A40	4870	A61	A73	2
A14	36	A32	A46	9055	A65	A73	1
A14	24	A32	A42	2835	A63	A75	1
A12	36	A32	A41	6948	A61	A73	1
A14	12	A32	A43	3059	A64	A74	1
A12	30	A34	A40	5234	A61	A71	2
A12	12	A32	A40	1295	A61	A72	2
A11	48	A32	A49	4308	A61	A72	2

RapidMiner's easy interface allows quick importing of spreadsheets. A useful feature of the interface is the panel on the left, called the *Operators*. Simply typing in text in the box provided automatically pulls up all available RapidMiner operators that match the text. In this case, an operator to needs to read an Excel spreadsheet, and so one would simply type excel in the box. Either double-click on the *Read Excel* operator or drag and drop it into the Main Process panel—the effect is the same. Once the *Read Excel* operator appears in the main process window as shown in Fig. 4.10, the data import process needs to be configured. What this means is telling RapidMiner which columns to import, what is contained in the columns, and if any of the columns need special treatment.

This is probably the most cumbersome part about this step. RapidMiner has a feature to automatically detect the type of values in each attribute (Guess Value types). But it is a good exercise for the analyst to make sure that the right columns are picked (or excluded) and the value types are correctly guessed. If not, as seen in Fig. 4.11, the value type can be changed to the correct setting by clicking on the button below the attribute name.

Once the data is imported, the target variable must be assigned for analysis, also known as a label. In this case, it is the Credit Rating. Finally, it is a good idea to run RapidMiner and generate results to ensure that all columns are read correctly.

An optional step is to convert the values from A121, A143, etc., to more meaningful qualitative descriptions. This is accomplished by the use of

FIGURE 4.10

Using the Read Excel operator.

✓	✓	✓	✓	✓	✓	✓	✓	✓	✓	✓	✓	✓
Checking A	Duration in	Credit Histo	Purpose	Credit Amo	Savings Acc	Present Em	Installment	Personal St	Other debtc	Present resi	Property	Age
polyn... ▼	integer ▼	polyn... ▼	polyn... ▼	integer ▼	polyn... ▼	polyn... ▼	integer ▼	polyn... ▼	polyn... ▼	integer ▼	polyn... ▼	integer ▼
attribute ▼	attribute ▼	attribute ▼	attribute ▼	attribute ▼	attribute ▼	attribute ▼	attribute ▼	attribute ▼	attribute ▼	attribute ▼	attribute ▼	attribute ▼
A11	6	A34	A43	1169	A65	A75	4	A93	A101	4	A121	67
A12	48	A32	A43	5951	A61	A73	2	A92	A101	2	A121	22
A14	12	A34	A46	2096	A61	A74	2	A93	A101	3	A121	49
A11	42	A32	A42	7882	A61	A74	2	A93	A103	4	A122	45
A11	24	A33	A40	4870	A61	A73	3	A93	A101	4	A124	53
A14	36	A32	A46	9055	A65	A73	2	A93	A101	4	A124	35
A14	24	A32	A42	2835	A63	A75	3	A93	A101	4	A122	53
...	..	...	..	....	...	...	.	...	....	.	....	..

FIGURE 4.11

Verifying data read-in and adjusting attribute value types if necessary.

another operator called *Replace (Dictionary)*, which will replace the values with bland encodings such as A121 and so on with more descriptive values. A dictionary will need to be created and supplied to RapidMiner as a comma-separated value (csv) file to enable this. Such a dictionary is easy to create and is shown in Fig. 4.12; Note that RapidMiner needs to be informed which column in the dictionary contains old values and which contain new values.

The last pre-processing step shown here is converting the numeric label into a binomial one by connecting the example output of *Replace (Dictionary)* to a *Numerical to Binominal* operator. To configure the *Numerical to Binominal* operator.

Finally, change the name of the label variable from Credit Rating to Credit Rating = Good so that it makes more sense when the integer values get converted to true or false after passing through the *Numerical to Binominal* operator. This can be done using the *Rename* operator. When this setup is run, the dataset shown in Fig. 4.13 will be generated. Comparing to Fig. 4.11, see

Row No.	OldValue	NewValue
1	A30	no credits taken all credits paid back duly
2	A31	all credits at this bank paid back duly
3	A32	existing credits paid back duly till now
4	A33	delay in paying off in the past
5	A34	critical account other credits existing (not at this bank)
6	A40	new car
7	A41	used car
8	A42	furniture equipment
9	A43	radio television
10	A44	domestic appliances
11	A45	repairs
12	A46	education

FIGURE 4.12
Attribute value replacement using a dictionary.

Row No.	Credit Rati...	Checking A...	Duration in...	Credit Hist...	Purpose	Credit Amo...	Savings Ac...	Present Em...	Installment...	Personal St...
1	false	Less than 0 ...	6	critical acco...	radio televis...	1169	unknown no...	Greater tha...	4	male single
2	true	0 to 200 DM	48	existing cre...	radio televis...	5951	Less than 1...	1 to 4 years	2	female divor...
3	false	no checking ...	12	critical acco...	education	2096	Less than 1...	4 to 7 years	2	male single
4	false	Less than 0 ...	42	existing cre...	furniture eq...	7882	Less than 1...	4 to 7 years	2	male single
5	true	Less than 0 ...	24	delay in pay...	new car	4870	Less than 1...	1 to 4 years	3	male single
6	false	no checking ...	36	existing cre...	education	9055	unknown no...	1 to 4 years	2	male single
7	false	no checking ...	24	existing cre...	furniture eq...	2835	500 to 100...	Greater tha...	3	male single
8	false	0 to 200 DM	36	existing cre...	used car	6948	Less than 1...	1 to 4 years	2	male single
9	false	no checking ...	12	existing cre...	radio televis...	3059	Greater tha...	4 to 7 years	2	male divorc...
10	true	0 to 200 DM	30	critical acco...	new car	5234	Less than 1...	unemployed	4	male marrie...

FIGURE 4.13
Data transformed for Decision Tree analysis.

that the label attribute is the first one shown and the values are *true* or *false*. The statistics tab of the results can be examined to get more information about the distributions of individual attributes and also to check for missing values and outliers. In other words, one must make sure that the data preparation step is properly executed before proceeding. In this implementation, there is no to worry about this because the dataset is relatively clean (for instance, there are no missing values), and one could proceed directly to the model development phase.

Step 2: Divide dataset Into Training and Testing Samples

As with all supervised model building, data must be separated into two sets: one for training or developing an acceptable model, and the other for testing or ensuring that the model would work equally well on a different dataset. The standard practice is to split the available data into a training set and a testing set. Typically, the training set contains 70%–90% of the original data. The remainder is set aside for testing. The *Split Validation* operator sets up splitting, modeling, *and* the validation check in one operator. Choose *stratified sampling* with a split ratio of 0.9 (90% training). Stratified sampling[2] will ensure that both training and testing samples have equal distributions of class values. The final sub step here is to connect the output from the *Numerical to Binominal* operator output to the *Split Validation* operator input (see Fig. 4.14).

Step 3: Modeling Operator and Parameters

A demonstration of how to build a decision tree model on this data will now be given. The *Validation* operator allows one to build a model and apply it on validation data in the same step. This means that two operations— model building and model evaluation—must be configured using the same operator. This is accomplished by double-clicking on the Validation operator, which is what is called a *nested* operator. When this operator is opened, note that there are two parts inside (see Fig. 4.15). The left box is where the *Decision Tree* operator has to be placed and the model will be built using the 90% of training data samples. The right box is for applying this trained model on the remaining 10% of the testing data samples using the *Apply Model* operator and evaluating the performance of the model using the *Performance* operator.

Step 4: Configuring the Decision Tree Model

The main parameters to pay attention to are the Criterion pull-down menu and the minimal gain box. This is essentially a partitioning criterion and offers information gain, Gini index, and gain ratio as choices. The first two criteria were covered earlier, and gain ratio will be briefly explained in the next section.

As discussed earlier in this chapter, decision trees are built up in a simple five-step process by increasing the information contained in the reduced

---

[2] Although not necessary, it is sometimes useful to check the *use local random seed* option, so that it is possible to compare models between different iterations. Fixing the random seed ensures that the same examples are chosen for training (and testing) subsets each time the process is run.

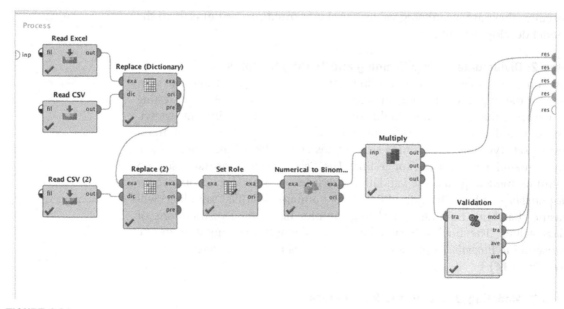

FIGURE 4.14
Decision Tree process.

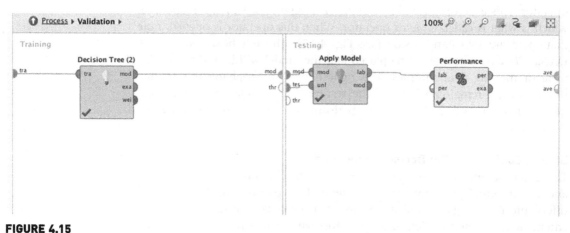

FIGURE 4.15
Setting up the split validation process.

dataset following each split. Data by its nature contains uncertainties. Uncertainties could possibly be systematically reduced, thus, increasing information by activities like sorting or classifying. When data have been sorted or classified to achieve the greatest reduction in uncertainty, basically, the greatest increase in information has been achieved. It has already been shown that entropy is a good measure of uncertainty and how keeping track of it allows information to be quantified. So, back to the options that are available within RapidMiner for splitting decision trees:

1. *Information gain:* This is computed as the information before the split minus the information after the split. It works fine for most cases, unless there are a few variables that have a large number of values (or classes). Information gain is *biased* toward choosing attributes with a large number of values as root nodes. This is not a problem, except in extreme cases. For example, each customer ID is unique and, thus, the variable has too many values (each ID is a unique value). A tree that is split along these lines has no predictive value.

2. *Gain ratio (default):* This is a modification of information gain that reduces its bias and is usually the best option. Gain ratio overcomes the problem with information gain by taking into account the number of branches that would result before making the split. It corrects information gain by taking the *intrinsic information* of a split into account. Intrinsic information can be explained using the golf example. Suppose each of the 14 examples had a unique ID attribute associated with them. Then the intrinsic information for the ID attribute is given by $14 \times (-1/14 \times \log(1/14)) = 3.807$. The gain ratio is obtained by dividing the information gain for an attribute by its intrinsic information. Clearly attributes that have high intrinsic information (high uncertainty) tend to offer low gains upon splitting and, hence, would not be preferred in the selection process.

3. *Gini index:* This is also used sometimes but does not have too many advantages over gain ratio.

4. *Accuracy:* This is also used to improve performance. The best way to select values for these parameters is by using many of the optimizing operators.

The other important parameter is the *minimal gain* value. Theoretically this can take any range from 0 upwards. The default is 0.1. It has been set as 0.01 for this example.

The other parameters *minimal size for a split, minimal leaf size, maximal depth* are determined by the size of the dataset. In this case, the values have been set as 4,5, and 5 respectively. The model is ready for training. Next, two more operators are added, *Apply Model* and *Performance (Binominal*

Classification), and the analysis is ready to be run. Configure the *Performance (Binominal Classification)* operator by selecting the *accuracy*, area under ROC (receiver operator characteristic) curve *(AUC)*, *precision*, and *recall* options.[3]

Remember to connect the ports correctly as this can be a source of confusion:

1. "mod"el port of the Testing window to "mod" on *Apply Model*
2. "tes"ting port of the Testing window to "unl"abeled on *Apply Model*
3. "lab"eled port of *Apply Model* to "lab"eled on *Performance*
4. "per"formance port on the *Performance* operator to "ave"rageable port on the output side of the testing box

The final step before running the model is to go back to the main process view (see Fig. 4.15) and connect the output ports model and "ave" of the *Validation* operator to the main process outputs.

Step 5: Process Execution and Interpretation

When the model is setup and run as explained, RapidMiner generates two tabs in the Results perspective. The *Performance Vector (Performance)* tab shows a confusion matrix that lists the model accuracy on the testing data, along with the other options selected above for the *Performance (Binominal Classification)* operator in step 3. The *Tree* (Decision Tree) tab shows a graphic of the tree that was built on the training data (see Fig. 4.16). Fig. 4.17 shows the tree model in the form of rules. Several important points must be highlighted before the performance of this model is discussed:

1. The root node—Checking Account Status—is the most important predictor in the dataset.
2. If the *Checking Account Status = No account*, a prediction can be made without the influence of other attributes.
3. For rest of the *Checking Account Status* values, other parameters come into effect and play an increasingly important role in deciding if someone is likely to have a *"good"* or *"bad"* credit rating.
4. Watch out for overfitting. Overfitting refers to the process of building a model specific to the training data that achieves close to full accuracy on the training data. However, when this model is applied to new data or if the training data changes somewhat, then there is a significant degradation in its performance. Overfitting is a potential issue with all supervised models, not just decision trees. One way this situation could be avoided is by changing the decision tree criterion *"Minimal leaf size"* to something like 10. But doing so, the classification influence of all the other parameters is also lost, except the root node.

---

[3] Performance criteria such as these are explained in more detail in Chapter 8, Model Evaluation.

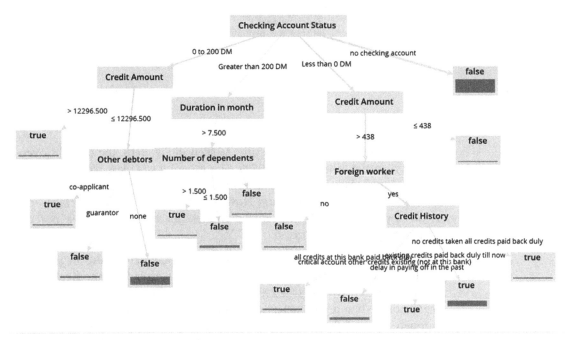

FIGURE 4.16
Decision Tree.

FIGURE 4.17
Decision Tree rules.

accuracy: 67.00%

	true false	true true	class precision
pred. false	65	28	69.89%
pred. true	5	2	28.57%
class recall	92.86%	6.67%	

FIGURE 4.18
Performance vector.

Now look at the Performance result. As seen in Fig. 4.18, the model's overall accuracy on the testing data is 67%. The model has a class recall of 92.86% for the "true" class implying that it is able to pick out customers with good credit rating with good accuracy. However, its class recall for the "false" class is an abysmal 6.67%! That is, the model can only pick out a potential defaulter in 1 out of 15 cases!

One way to improve this performance is by penalizing false negatives by applying a cost for every such instance. This is handled by another operator called *MetaCost*, which is described in detail in the next chapter on logistic regression. When a parameter search optimization is performed by iterating through three of the decision tree parameters, splitting criterion, minimum gain ratio, and maximal tree depth, significantly improved performance is gained. More details on how to set this type of optimization are provided in Chapter 15, Getting started with RapidMiner.

In addition to assessing the model's performance by aggregate measures such as accuracy, one can also use gain/lift charts, ROC charts, and AUC charts. An explanation of how these charts are constructed and interpreted is given in Chapter 8, Model Evaluation.

The RapidMiner process for a decision tree covered in the implementation section can be accessed from the companion site of the book at www.IntroDataScience.com. The RapidMiner process (*.rmp files) can be downloaded to one's computer and imported to RapidMiner through File > Import Process. Additionally, all the datasets used in this book can be downloaded from http://www. IntroDataScience.com.

4.1.3   Conclusion

Decision trees are one of the most commonly used predictive modeling algorithms in practice. The reasons for this are numerous. Some of the distinct advantages of using decision trees in many classification and prediction applications will be explained below along with some common pitfalls.

1. Easy to interpret and explain to non-technical users: As seen in the few examples discussed so far, decision trees are intuitive and easy to explain to non-technical people, who are typically the consumers of analytics.

2. Decision trees require relatively little effort from users for data preparation: If one has a dataset consisting of widely ranging attributes, for example, revenues recorded in millions and loan age recorded in years, many algorithms require scale normalization before model building and application. Such variable transformations are not required with decision trees because the tree structure will remain the same with or without the transformation. Another feature that saves data preparation time: missing values in training data will not impede partitioning the data for building trees. Decision trees are also not sensitive to outliers since the partitioning happens based on the proportion of samples within the split ranges and not on absolute values.

3. Nonlinear relationships between parameters do not affect tree performance. As described in Chapter 5, Regression Methods, highly nonlinear relationships between variables will result in failing checks for simple regression models, and thus, rendering such models invalid. However, decision trees do not require any assumptions of linearity in the data. Thus, one can use them in scenarios where one knows the parameters are nonlinearly related.

4. Decision trees implicitly perform variable screening or feature selection. When a decision tree is fitted to a training dataset, the top few nodes on which the tree is split are essentially the most important variables within the dataset and feature selection is completed automatically. In fact, RapidMiner has an operator for performing variable screening or feature selection using the information gain ratio. In Chapter 12, Time Series Forecasting, the importance of feature selection in data science will be discussed. A few common techniques for performing feature selection or variable screening will be introduced in that chapter.

However, all these advantages need to be tempered with the one key disadvantage of decision trees: without proper pruning or limiting tree growth, they tend to overfit the training data, making them somewhat poor predictors.

4.2 RULE INDUCTION

Rule induction is a data science process of deducing if-then rules from a dataset. These symbolic decision rules explain an inherent relationship between the attributes and class labels in a dataset. Many real-life experiences are based on intuitive rule induction. For example, one could come up with a rule that states that "if it is 8:00 a.m. on a weekday, then highway traffic will be heavy" and "if it is 8:00 p.m. on a Sunday, then the traffic will be light."

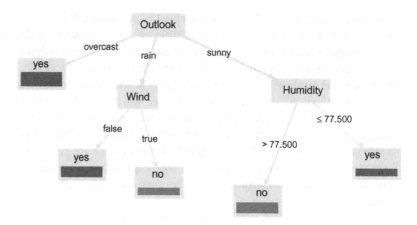

FIGURE 4.19
Decision tree model for Golf dataset

These rules are not necessarily right all the time. The 8:00 a.m. weekday traffic may be light during a holiday season. But, in general, these rules hold true and are deduced from real-life experience based on our everyday observations. The rule induction provides a powerful classification approach that can be easily understood by the general audience. Apart from its use in data science by classification of unknown data, rule induction is also used to describe the patterns in the data. The description is in the form of simple if-then rules that can be easily understood by general users.

The easiest way to extract rules from a dataset is from a decision tree that is developed on the same dataset. A decision tree splits data on every node and leads to the leaf where the class is identified. If one traces back from the leaf to the root node, they can combine all the split conditions to form a distinct rule. For example, in the Golf dataset (Table 4.1), based on four weather conditions, a rule set can be generalized to determine when a player prefers to play golf or not. Fig. 4.19 shows the decision tree developed from the Golf data with five leaf nodes and two levels. A rule can be extracted if one traces back the first leaf from the left: *If Outlook is overcast, then Play = yes*. Similarly, rules can be extracted from all the five leaves:

    Rule 1: if (Outlook = overcast) then Play = yes
    Rule 2: if (Outlook = rain) and (Wind = false) then Play = yes
    Rule 3: if (Outlook = rain) and (Wind = true) then Play = no
    Rule 4: if (Outlook = sunny) and (Humidity > 77.5) then Play = no
    Rule 5: if (Outlook = sunny) and (Humidity ≤ 77.5) then Play = yes

The set of all the five rules is called a *rule set*. Each individual rule r_i is called a *disjunct* or classification rule. The entire rule set can be represented as:

$$R = \{r_1 \cap r_2 \cap r_3 \cap \ldots r_k\}$$

where k is the number of disjuncts in a rule set. Individual disjuncts can be represented as:

r_i = (antecedent or condition) then (consequent)

For example, Rule 2 is r_2: if (Outlook = rain) and (Wind = false) then Play = yes.

In r_2, (Outlook = rain) and (Wind = false) is the *antecedent* or *condition* of the rule. The antecedent of the rule can have many attributes and values each separated by a logical *AND* operator. Each attribute and value test is called the *conjunct* of the rule. An example of a conjunct is (Outlook = rain). The antecedent is a group of conjuncts with the *AND* operator. Each conjunct is a node in the equivalent decision tree.

In the Golf dataset, one can observe a couple of properties of the rule set in relation with the dataset. First, the rule set R is mutually exclusive. This means that no example record will trigger more than one rule and hence the outcome of the prediction is definite. However, there can be rule sets that are not mutually exclusive. If a record activates more than one rule in a rule set and all the class predictions are the same, then there is no conflict in the prediction. If the class predictions differ, ambiguity exists on which class is the prediction of the induction rule model. There are a couple of techniques used to resolve conflicting class prediction by more than one rule. One technique is to develop an ordered list of rules where if a record activates many rules, the first rule in the order will take precedence. A second technique is where each active rule can "vote" for a prediction class. The predicted class with the highest vote is the prediction of the rule set R. The rule set discussed is also exhaustive. This means the rule set R is activated for all the combinations of the attribute values in the record set, not just limited to training records. If the rule set is not exhaustive, then a final catch all bucket rule "*else Class = Default Class Value*" can be introduced to make the rule set exhaustive.

Approaches to Developing a Rule Set
Rules can be directly extracted from the dataset or derived from previously built decision trees from the same dataset. Fig. 4.20 shows the approaches to generate rules from the dataset. The former approach is called the *direct* method, which is built on leveraging the relationship between the attribute and class label in the dataset. Deriving a rule set from a previously built classifier decision tree model is a passive or *indirect* approach. Since building a

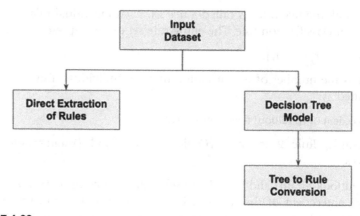

FIGURE 4.20
Approaches to rule generation

decision tree is covered in the previous section and the derivation of rules from the decision tree model is straightforward, the rest of the discussion will be focused on direct rule generation based on the relationships from the data. Specifically, the focus will be placed on the *sequential covering* technique used to build the rule set.

PREDICTING AND PREVENTING MACHINE BREAKDOWNS

A machine breakdown in the field almost always results in the disruption of a manufacturing process. In a large-scale process like an oil refinery, chemical plants, etc., it causes serious financial damage to the company and manufacturers of the machines. Rather than waiting for the machine to breakdown and react, it is much preferable to diagnose the problem and prevent the breakdown before a problem occurs. Industrial operations track thousands of real-time readings from multiple systems or sub-systems. (Such machines connected to networks that can gather readings and act based on smart logic or statistical learning constitute the Internet of Things.) One of the solutions is to leverage how these readings are trending and develop a rule base which says, for example, *if the cylinder temperature continues to report more than 852°C, then the machine will breakdown in the near future.* These types of the rules are simple to interpret, do not require

an expert to be around to take further action, and can be deployed by automated systems.

Developing learned rules requires historical analysis of all the readings that lead up to a machine failure (Langley & Simon, 1995). These learned rules are different, and in many cases, supersede the rule of thumb assumed by the machine operators. Based on the historic readings of failure and non-failure events, the learned rule set can predict the failure of the machine and, hence, alert the operator of imminent future breakdowns. Since these rules are simple to understand, these preventive measures can be easily deployed to line workers. This use case demonstrates the need of not only a predictive data model, but also a descriptive model where the inner working of the model can be easily understood by the users. A similar approach can be developed to prevent customer churn, or loan default, for example.

4.2.1 How It Works

Sequential covering is an iterative procedure of extracting rules from a dataset. The sequential covering approach attempts to find all the rules in the dataset class by class. One specific implementation of the sequential covering approach is called the RIPPER, which stands for Repeated Incremental Pruning to Produce Error Reduction (Cohen, 1995). Consider the dataset shown in Fig. 4.21, which has two attributes (dimensions) on the X and Y axis and two-class labels marked by " + " and " − ." The steps in sequential covering rules generation approach are provided here (Tan, Michael, & Kumar, 2005).

Step 1: Class Selection

The algorithm starts with the selection of class labels one by one. The rule set is class-ordered where all the rules for a class are developed before moving on to the next class. The first class is usually the least-frequent class label. From Fig. 4.21, the least-frequent class is " + " and the algorithm focuses on generating all the rules for " + " class.

Step 2: Rule Development

The first rule r_1 will need to be developed. The objective in this step is to cover all " + " data points using a rectilinear box with none or as few " − " as possible. For example, in Fig. 4.22, rule r_1 identifies the area of four " + " in

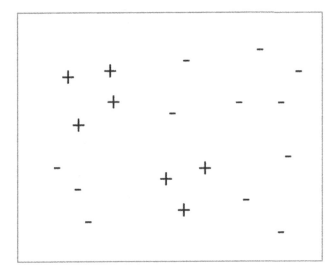

FIGURE 4.21
Dataset with two classes and two dimensions.

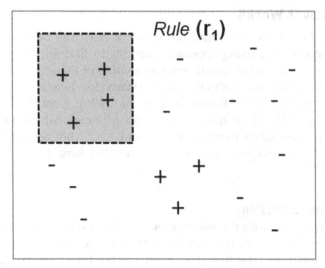

FIGURE 4.22
Generation of rule r_1.

the top left corner. Since this rule is based on simple logic operators in conjuncts, the boundary is rectilinear. Once rule r_1 is formed, the entire data points covered by r_1 are eliminated and the next best rule is found from the datasets. The algorithm grows in a greedy fashion using a technique called *Learn-One-Rule* which is described in the next section. One of the consequences of the greedy algorithms that start with initial configuration is that they yield *local optima* instead of a *global optimum*. A local optimum is a solution that is optimal in the neighborhood of potential solutions, but worse than the global optimum.

Step 3: Learn-One-Rule

Each disjunct rule r_i is grown by the learn-one-rule approach. Each rule starts with an empty rule set and conjuncts are added one by one to increase the rule accuracy. Rule accuracy is the ratio of the number of " + " covered by the rule to all records covered by the rule:

$$\text{Rule accuracy } A(r_i) = \frac{\text{Correct records covered by rule}}{\text{All records covered by the rule}}$$

Learn-one-rule starts with an empty rule set: if {} then class = " + ." Obviously, the accuracy of this rule is the same as the proportion of " + " data points in the dataset. Then the algorithm greedily adds conjuncts until the accuracy reaches 100%. If the addition of a conjunct decreases the accuracy, then the algorithm looks for other conjuncts or stops and starts the iteration of the next rule.

Step 4: Next Rule

After a rule is developed, then all the data points covered by the rule are eliminated from the dataset. All these steps are repeated for the next rule to cover the rest of the " + " data points. In Fig. 4.23, rule r_2 is developed after the data points covered by r_1 are eliminated.

Step 5: Development of Rule Set

After the rule set is developed to identify all " + " data points, the rule model is evaluated with a test dataset used for pruning to reduce generalization errors. The metric used to evaluate the need for pruning is $(p - n)/(p + n)$, where p is the number of positive records covered by the rule and n is the number of negative records covered by the rule. The conjunct is iteratively removed if it improves the metric. All rules that identify " + " data points are aggregated to form a rule group. In multi-class problems, the previous steps are repeated with for next class label. Since this is a two-class problem, any data points not covered by the rule set for identifying " + " are predicted to be " − ." The outcome of the sequential covering or RIPPER algorithm is a set of optimized rules that can describe the relationship between attributes and the class label (Saian & Ku-Mahamud, 2011).

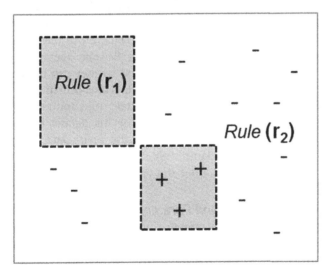

FIGURE 4.23
Elimination of r_1 data points and next rule.

4.2.2   How to Implement

Rules remain the most common expression to communicate the inherent relationship in the data. There are a few different ways to generate rules from the data using RapidMiner. The modeling operators for *rule induction* are available in the Modeling > Classification and Regression > Rule Induction folder. These modeling operators available:

1. *Rule Induction:* Commonly used generic rule induction modeler based on the RIPPER algorithm.
2. *Single Rule Induction (Attribute):* Uses only one attribute in antecedent, usually the attribute with the most predictive power.
3. *Single Rule Induction:* Generates only one rule with an if/else statement.
4. *Tree to Rule:* Indirect method of rule generation that is based on underlying decision tree.

Single rule induction is used for quick discovery of the most dominant rule. Because of its simplicity, single rule modeling operators are used to establish a baseline performance for other classification models. The implementation will be reviewed using the *Rule Induction* and *Tree to Rule* modeling operators in RapidMiner.

Step 1: Data Preparation

The dataset used in the implementation is the standard Iris dataset (See Table 3.1 and Fig. 3.1) with four attributes, sepal length, sepal width, petal length, and petal width, and a class label to identify the species of flower, viz., *Iris setosa*, *Iris versicolor*, and *Iris virginica*. The Iris dataset is available in the RapidMiner repository under Sample > Data. Since the original dataset refers to the four attributes as a1 to a4, the *Rename* operator was used to change the name of the attributes (not values) so they can be more descriptive. The *Rename* operator is available in Data Transformation > Name and Role modification. Similar to a decision tree, rule induction can accept both numeric and polynomial data types. The Iris dataset is split into two equal sets for training and testing, using the *Split Data* operator (Data Transformation > Filtering > Sampling). The split ratio used in this implementation is 50%−50% for training and test data.

Step 2: Modeling Operator and Parameters

The Rule Induction modeling operator accepts the training data and provides the rule set as the model output. The rule set is the text output of if-then rules, along with the accuracy and coverage statistics. These parameters are available in the model operator and can be configured for desired modeling behavior:

1. *Criterion:* Since the algorithm takes the greedy strategy, it needs an evaluation criterion to indicate whether adding a new conjunct helps in a rule. Information gain is commonly used for RIPPER and is similar to information gain for decision trees. Another easy-to-use criterion is accuracy, which was discussed in the sequential covering algorithm.
2. *Sample ratio:* This is the ratio of data used for training in the example set. The rest of the data is used for pruning. This sample ratio is different from the training/test split ratio that is used in the data preparation stage.
3. *Pureness:* This is the minimal ratio of accuracy desired in the classification rule.
4. *Minimal prune benefit:* This is the percentage increase in the prune metric required at the minimum.

The output of the model is connected to the *Apply Model* operator to apply the developed rule base against the test dataset. The test dataset from the *Split Data* operator is connected to the *Apply Model* operator. The *Performance* operator for classification is then used to create the performance vector from the labeled dataset generated from the *Apply Model* operator. The process can be saved and executed after the output ports are connected to the result ports. Fig. 4.24 shows the complete RapidMiner process for rule induction. The completed process and the dataset can be downloaded from the companion website of the book at: www. IntroDataScience.com.

Step 3: Results Interpretation

The results screen consists of the Rule Model window, the labeled test dataset, and the performance vector. The performance vector is similar to the decision tree performance vector. The Rule Model window, shown in Fig. 4.25, consists of a sequence of if-then rules with antecedents and consequents. The parentheses next to each classification rule indicate the class distribution of the rule covered from the training dataset. Note that these statistics are based on the training dataset, not the test dataset.

The Performance Vector window provides the accuracy statistics of the prediction based on the rules model applied to the test dataset. For the Iris dataset and the RapidMiner process shown in this example, the accuracy of

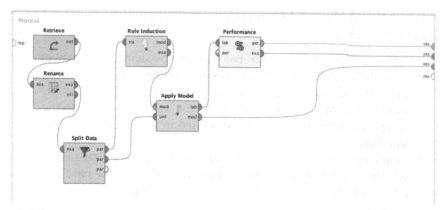

FIGURE 4.24
RapidMiner process for rule induction.

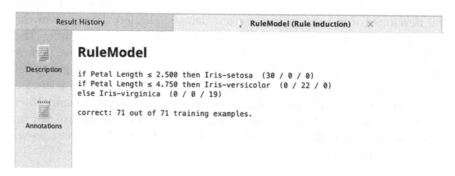

FIGURE 4.25
Rule output for rule induction.

prediction is 92%. 69 out of 75 test records are predicted accurately based on simple rules developed by the rule induction model. Not bad for a quick, easy-to-use and easy-to-understand model!

Alternative Approach: Tree-to-Rules
An indirect but easy way to generate a mutually exclusive and exhaustive rule set is to convert a decision tree to an induction rule set. Each classification

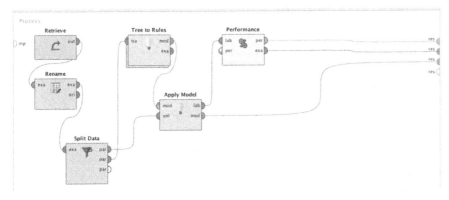

FIGURE 4.26
RapidMiner process for Tree to Rules operator.

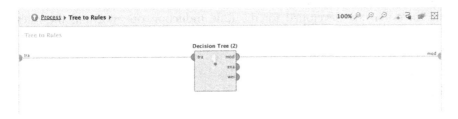

FIGURE 4.27
Decision Tree operator inside the sub-process for Tree to Rules.

rule can be traced from the leaf node to the root node, where each node becomes a conjunct and the class label of the leaf becomes the consequent. Even though tree-to-rules may be simple to implement, the resulting rule set may not be the most optimal to understand, as there are many repetitive nodes in the rule path.

In the rule induction process developed, the previous *Rule Induction* operator can simply be replaced with the *Tree to Rules* operator. This modeling operator does not have any parameters as it simply converts the tree to rules. However, the decision tree will have to be specified in the inner sub-process of the *Tree to Rules* operator. On double-clicking the *Tree to Rules* operator, the inner process can be seen, where a *Decision Tree* modeling operator has to be inserted as shown in Figs. 4.26 and 4.27.

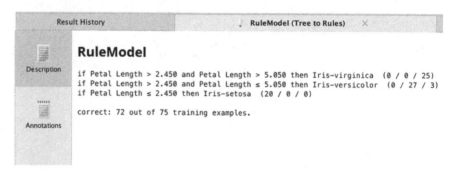

FIGURE 4.28
Rules based on Decision Tree.

The parameters for a decision tree are the same as reviewed in Section 4.1 of this chapter. The RapidMiner process can be saved and executed. The result set consists of a set of rule model, usually with repetitive conjuncts in antecedents, a fingerprint of rules derived from trees. Note the difference between the rules that are developed for the Rule Induction operator and the rules developed from *Tree to Rules* operator. The rules generated from Tree to Rules are shown in Fig. 4.28.

4.2.3 Conclusion

Classification using rules provides a simple framework to identify a relationship between attributes and the class label that is not only used as a predictive model, but also a descriptive model. Rules are closely associated to decision trees. They split the data space in a rectilinear fashion and generate a mutually exclusive and exhaustive rule set. When the rule set is not mutually exclusive, then the data space can be divided by complex and curved decision boundaries. Single rule learners are the simplest form of data science model and indicate the most powerful predictor in the given set of attributes. Since rule induction is a greedy algorithm, the result may not be the most globally optimal solution and like decision trees, rules can overlearn the example set. This scenario can be mitigated by pruning. Given the wide reach of rules, rule induction is commonly used as a tool to express the results of data science, even if other data science algorithms are used to create the model.

4.3 *k*-NEAREST NEIGHBORS

The predictive data science using decision trees and rule induction techniques were built by generalizing the relationship within a dataset and using it to predict the outcome of new unseen data. If one needs to predict the loan interest rate based on credit score, income level, and loan amount, one approach is to develop a mathematical relationship such as an equation $y = f(X)$ based on the known data and then using the equation to predict the interest rate for new unseen data points. These approaches are called *eager learners* because they attempt to find the best approximation of the actual relationship between the input and target variables. But there is also a simple alternative to this approach. One can "predict" the interest rate for a potential borrower with a known credit score, income level, and loan amount by *looking up* the interest rate of other customer loan records with a similar credit score, a closely matching income level and loan amount from the training dataset. This alternative class of learners adopts a blunt approach, where no "learning" is performed from the training dataset; rather the training dataset is used as a lookup table to match the input variables and find the outcome. These approaches that memorize the training set are called *lazy learners*.

The underlying idea here is somewhat similar to the old adage, "birds of a feather flock together." Similar records congregate in a neighborhood in *n*-dimensional space, with the same target class labels. This is the central logic behind the approach used by the *k*-nearest neighbor algorithm, or simply referred *k*-NN. The entire training dataset is "memorized" and when unlabeled example records need to be classified, the input attributes of the new unlabeled records are compared against the entire training set to find the closest match. The class label of the closest training record is the predicted class label for the unseen test record. This is a nonparametric method, where no generalization or attempt to find the distribution of the dataset is made (Altman, 1992). Once the training records are in memory, the classification of the test record is straightforward. The closest training record needs to be found for each test record. Even though no mathematical generalization or rule generation is involved, finding the closet training record for a new unlabeled record can be a tricky problem to solve, particularly when there is no exact match of training data available for a given test data record.

PREDICTING THE TYPE OF FOREST

Satellite imaging and digital image processing have provided a wealth of data about almost every part of the earth's landscape. There is a strong motivation for forestry departments, government agencies, universities, and research bodies to understand the makeup of forests, species of trees and their health, biodiversity, density, and forest condition. Field studies for developing forest databases and classification projects are quite tedious and expensive tasks. However, this process can be aided with the leveraging of satellite imagery, limited field data, elevation models, aerial photographs, and survey data (McInerney, 2005). The objective is to classify whether the particular

(Continued)

(Continued)

landscape is a forest or not and further predict the type of trees and species.

The approach to classifying a landscape involves dividing the area into land units (e.g., a pixel in a satellite image) and creating a vector of all the measurements for the land unit. Each unit's measurements are then compared against the measurements of known preclassified units. For every new unclassified pixel, one can find a pixel in the pre-classified catalog, which has measurements similar to the measurement of the pixel to be predicted. Say the pre-classified pixel with the closest measurement corresponds to birch trees. Thus, the pixel area can be predicted to be a birch forest. Each pixel's measurement is compared to measurements of the preclassified dataset to determine the like pixels and, hence, the same forest types. This is the core concept of the k-NN algorithm that is used to classify landscape areas (Haapanen, Lehtinen, Miettinen, Bauer, & Ek, 2001).

4.3.1   How It Works

Any record in a dataset can be visualized as a point in an n-dimensional space, where n is the number of attributes. While it is hard for us to visualize in more than three dimensions, mathematical functions are scalable to any dimension and, hence, all the operations that can be done in two-dimensional spaces and be performed in n-dimensional space. Consider the standard Iris dataset (150 examples, four attributes, one class label. See Fig. 3.1 and Table 3.1) and focus on two petal attributes, petal length and petal width. The scatterplot of these two dimensions is shown in Fig. 4.29. The colors indicate the species of Iris, the target class variable. For an unseen test record A, with (petal length, petal width) values (2.1, 0.5), one can visually deduce that the predicted species for the values of data point A would be *I. setosa*. This is based on the fact that test data point A is in the neighborhood of other data points that belong to the species *I. setosa*. Similarly, unseen test data point B has values (5.7, 1.9) and is in the neighborhood of *I. virginica*, hence, the test data point can be classified as *I. virginica*. However, if the data points are in between the boundaries of two species, for data points such as (5.0, 1.8), then the classification can be tricky because the neighborhood has more than one species in the vicinity. An efficient algorithm is needed in order to resolve these corner cases and measure the nearness of data points with more than two dimensions. One technique is to find the nearest training data point from an unseen test data point in multi-dimensional space. That is how the k-NN algorithm works.

The k in the k-NN algorithm indicates the number of close training record(s) that need to be considered when making the prediction for an unlabeled test record. When $k = 1$, the model tries to find the *first* nearest record and adopts

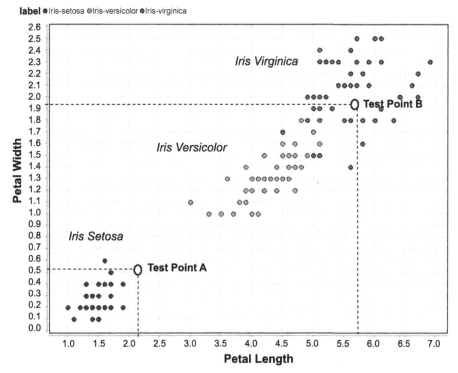

label ●Iris-setosa ●Iris-versicolor ●Iris-virginica

FIGURE 4.29
Two-dimensional plot of Iris dataset: petal length and petal width. Classes are stratified with colors.

the class label of the first nearest training record as the predicted target class value. Fig. 4.30 provides an example a training set with two dimensions and the target class values as circles and triangles. The unlabeled test record is the dark square in the center of the scatterplot. When $k = 1$, the predicted target class value of an unlabeled test record is *triangle* because the closest training record is a triangle. But, what if the closest training record is an outlier with the incorrect class in the training set? Then, all the unlabeled test records near the outlier will get wrongly classified. To prevent this misclassification, the value of k can be increased to, say, 3. When $k = 3$, the nearest *three* training records are considered instead of one. From Fig. 4.30, based on the majority class of the nearest three training records, the predicted class of the test record can be concluded as *circle*. Since the class of the target record is evaluated by voting, k is usually assigned an odd number for a two-class problem (Peterson, 2009).

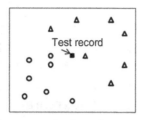 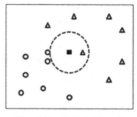 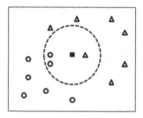

K = 1 Predicted Class is
triangle

K = 1 Predicted Class is
circle

FIGURE 4.30
(A) Dataset with a record of unknown class. (B) Decision boundary with $k = 1$ around unknown class record. (C) Decision boundary with $k = 3$ around unknown test record.

The key task in the k-NN algorithm is determination of the *nearest* training record from the unlabeled test record using a measure of proximity. Once the nearest training record(s) are determined, the subsequent class voting of the nearest training records is straightforward. The various techniques used to measure proximity are discussed here.

Measure of Proximity

The effectiveness of the k-NN algorithm hinges on the determination of how similar or dissimilar a test record is when compared with the memorized training record. A measure of proximity between two records is a measure of the proximity of its attributes. To quantify similarity between two records, there is a range of techniques available such as calculating distance, correlation, Jaccard similarity, and cosine similarity (Tan et al., 2005).

Distance

The distance between two points X (x_1, x_2) and Y (y_1, y_2) in two-dimensional space can be calculated by Eq. (4.3):

$$\text{Distance } d = \sqrt{(x_1 - y_1)^2 + (x_2 - y_2)^2} \tag{4.3}$$

One can generalize the two-dimensional distance formula shown in Eq. (4.3) for datasets with n attributes, where X is $(x_1, x_2, \ldots, x_n)$ and Y is $(y_1, y_2, \ldots, y_n)$, as:

$$\text{Distance } d = \sqrt{(x_1 - y_1)^2 + (x_2 - y_2)^2 + \cdots + (x_n - y_n)^2} \tag{4.4}$$

For example, the first two records of a four-dimensional Iris dataset is $X = (4.9, 3.0, 1.4, 0.2)$ and $Y = (4.6, 3.1, 1.5, 0.2)$. The distance between X and Y is: $d = \sqrt{(0.3)^2 + (0.1)^2 + (0.1)^2 + (0)^2} = 0.33$ centimeters.

All the attributes in the Iris dataset are homogenous in terms of measurements (size of the flower parts) and units (centimeters). However, in a typical practical dataset, it is common to see attributes in different measures (e.g., credit score, income) and varied units. One problem with the distance approach is that it depends on the scale and units of the attributes. For example, the difference in credit score between two records could be a few hundred points, which is minor in magnitude compared to the difference in income, which could be in the thousands. Consider two pairs of data points with credit score and annual income in USD. Pair A is (500, $40,000) and (600, $40,000). Pair B is (500, $40,000) and (500, $39,800). The first data point in both the pairs is same. The second data point is different from the first data point, with only one attribute changed. In Pair A, credit score is 600, which is significantly different to 500, while the income is the same. In Pair B, the income is down by $200 when compared to the first data point, which is only a 0.5% change. One can rightfully conclude that the data points in Pair B are more similar than the data points in Pair A. However, the distance [Eq. (4.4)] between data points in Pair A is 100 and the distance between Pair B is 200! The variation in income overpowers the variation in credit score. The same phenomenon can be observed when attributes are measured in different units, scales, etc. To mitigate the problem caused by different measures and units, all the inputs of *k*-NN are normalized, where the data values are rescaled to fit a particular range. Normalizing all the attributes provides a fair comparison between them. Normalization can be performed using a few different methods. Range transformation rescales all the values of the attributes to specified min and max values, usually 0 to 1. Z-transformation attempts to rescale all the values by subtracting the mean from each value and dividing the result by the standard deviation, resulting in a transformed set of values that have a mean of 0 and a standard deviation of 1. For example, when the Iris dataset is normalized using Z-transformation, sepal length, which takes values between 4.3 and 7.9 cm, and has a standard deviation of 0.828, is transformed to values between − 1.86 and 2.84, with a standard deviation of 1. The distance measurement discussed so far is also called *Euclidean distance*, which is the most common distance measure for numeric attributes. In addition to the Euclidean, *Manhattan*, and *Chebyshev* distance measures are sometimes used to calculate the distance between two numeric data points. Consider two data points X (1,2) and Y (3,1), as shown in Fig. 4.31. The Euclidean distance between X and Y is the straight-line distance between X and Y, which is 2.7. The Manhattan distance is the sum of the difference between individual attributes, rather than the root of squared difference. The Manhattan distance between X and Y is $(3-1) + (2-1) = 3$. The Manhattan distance is also called the taxicab distance, due to the similarities of the visual path traversed by a vehicle around city blocks (In Fig. 4.31, the total distance that is covered

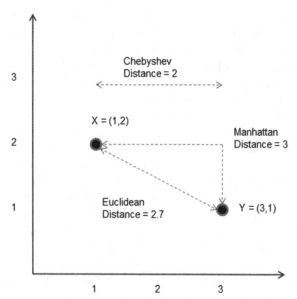

FIGURE 4.31
Distance measures.

by a cab that has to travel from X to Y in terms of number of city blocks is two blocks to the right and one block down). The Chebyshev distance is the maximum difference between all attributes in the dataset. In this example, the Chebyshev distance is the max of $[(3 - 1), (1 - 2)] = 2$. If Fig. 4.31 were a chess board, the Chebyshev distance would be the minimum number of moves required by the king to go from one position to another and the Manhattan distance is the minimum number of squares covered by the move of a rook from one position to another. All three aforementioned distance measures can be further generalized with one formula, the *Minkowski* distance measure. The distance between two points X $(x_1, x_2, \ldots, x_n)$ and Y $(y_1, y_2, \ldots, y_n)$ in n-dimensional space is given by Eq. (4.5):

$$d = \left(\sum_{i=1}^{n} |x_i - y_i|^p \right)^{\frac{1}{p}}$$

(4.5)

When $p = 1$, the distance measure is the Manhattan distance, when $p = 2$ the distance measure is the Euclidean distance, and when $p = \infty$ the distance measure is the Chebyshev distance. p is also called the *norm* and Eq. (4.5) is called the p-norm distance. The choice of distance measure depends on the data (Grabusts, 2011). The Euclidean measure is the most commonly used distance measure for numeric data. The Manhattan distance is used for binary attributes. For a new dataset with no prior knowledge, there is no rule-of-thumb for an ideal distance measure. Euclidean distance would be a good start and the model can be tested with a selection of other distance measures and the corresponding performance.

Once the nearest k neighbors are determined, the process of determining the predicted target class is straightforward. The predicted target class is the majority class of the nearest k neighbors. Eq. (4.6) provides the prediction of the k-NN algorithm:

$$y' = \text{majority class}(y_1, y_2, y_3, ... y_k) \tag{4.6}$$

where y' is the predicted target class of the test data point and y_i is the class of ith neighbor n_i.

Weights

The premise of the k-NN algorithm is that data points closer to each other are similar and, hence, have the same target class labels. When k is more than one, it can be argued that the closest neighbors should have more say in the outcome of the predicted target class than the farther neighbors (Hill & Lewicki, 2007). The farther away neighbors should have less influence in determining the final class outcome. This can be accomplished by assigned weights for all the neighbors, with the weights increasing as the neighbors get closer to the test data point. The weights are included in the final multi-voting step, where the predicted class is calculated. Weights (w_i) should satisfy two conditions: they should be proportional to the distance of the test data point from the neighbor and the sum of all weights should be equal to one. One of the calculations for weights shown in Eq. (4.7) follows an exponential decay based on distance:

$$w_i = \frac{e^{-d(x,n_i)}}{\sum_{i=1}^{k} e^{-d(x,n_i)}} \tag{4.7}$$

where w_i is the weight of ith neighbor n_i, k the is total number of neighbors, and x is the test data point. The weight is used in predicting target class y':

$$y' = \text{majority class}(w_1 * y_1, \ w_2 * y_2, \ w_3 * y_3, ..., \ w_k * y_k) \tag{4.8}$$

where y_i is the class outcome of neighbor n_i.

The distance measure works well for numeric attributes. However, if the attribute is categorical, the distance between two points is either 0 or 1. If the attribute values are the same, the distance is 0 and if the attribute values are different, the distance is 1. For example, distance between (overcast, sunny) = 1 and distance between (sunny, sunny) = 0. If the attribute is ordinal with more than two values, then the ordinal values can be converted to an integer data type with values 0, 1, 2, ..., $n - 1$ and the converted attribute can be treated as a numeric attribute for distance calculation. Obviously, converting ordinal into numeric retains more information than using it as a categorical data type, where the distance value is either 0 or 1.

Correlation similarity

The correlation between two data points X and Y is the measure of the linear relationship between the attributes X and Y. Pearson correlation takes a value from -1 (perfect negative correlation) to $+1$ (perfect positive correlation) with the value of zero being no correlation between X and Y. Since correlation is a measure of *linear* relationship, a zero value does not mean there is no relationship. It just means that there is no linear relationship, but there may be a quadratic or any other higher degree relationship between the data points. Also, the correlation between one data point and another will now be explored. *This is quite different from correlation between variables.* Pearson correlation between two data points X and Y is given by:

$$\text{Correlation } (X, Y) = \frac{s_{xy}}{s_x \times s_y} \tag{4.9}$$

where s_{xy} is the covariance of X and Y, which is calculated as:

$$s_{xy} = \frac{1}{n-1} \sum\nolimits_{i=1}^{n} (x_i - \overline{x})(y_i - \overline{y})$$

and s_x and s_y are the standard deviation of X and Y, respectively. For example, the Pearson correlation of two data points X $(1,2,3,4,5)$ and Y $(10,15,35,40,55)$ is 0.98.

Simple matching coefficient

The simple matching coefficient is used when datasets have binary attributes. For example, let X be $(1,1,0,0,1,1,0)$ and Y be $(1,0,0,1,1,0,0)$. One can measure the similarity between these two data points based on the simultaneous occurrence of 0 or 1 with respect to total occurrences. The simple matching coefficient for X and Y can be calculated as:

$$\text{Simple matching coefficient (SMC)} = \frac{\textit{Matching occurences}}{\textit{Total occurences}}$$

$$= \frac{m_{00} + m_{11}}{m_{10} + m_{01} + m_{11} + m_{00}} \tag{4.10}$$

In this example, $m_{11} = $ occurrences where $(X = 1$ and $Y = 1) = 2$; $m_{10} = $ occurrences where $(X = 1$ and $Y = 0) = 2$; $m_{01} = $ occurrences where $(X = 0$ and $Y = 1) = 1$; $m_{00} = $ occurrences where $(X = 0$ and $Y = 0) = 2$. Simple matching coefficient is, $(2 + 2) / (2 + 2 + 1 + 2) = 4/7$.

Jaccard similarity

If X and Y represent two text documents, each word will be an attribute in a dataset called a term document matrix or document vector. Each record in the document dataset corresponds to a separate document or a text blob. This is explained in greater detail in Chapter 9, Text Mining. In this application, the number of attributes would be very large, often in the thousands. However, most of the attribute values will be zero. This means that two documents do not contain the same rare words. In this instance, what is interesting is that the comparison of the *occurrence* of the same word and non-occurrence of the same word does not convey any information and can be ignored. The Jaccard similarity measure is similar to the simple matching similarity but the nonoccurrence frequency is ignored from the calculation. For the same example X (1,1,0,0,1,1,0) and Y (1,0,0,1,1,0,0),

$$\text{Jaccard coefficient} = \frac{\textit{Common occurences}}{\textit{Total occurences}}$$

$$= \frac{m_{11}}{m_{10} + m_{01} + m_{11}} = \frac{2}{5}$$

(4.11)

Cosine similarity

Continuing with the example of the document vectors, where attributes represent either the presence or absence of a word. It is possible to construct a more informational vector with the number of occurrences in the document, instead of just 1 and 0. Document datasets are usually long vectors with thousands of variables or attributes. For simplicity, consider the example of the vectors with X (1,2,0,0,3,4,0) and Y (5,0,0,6,7,0,0). The cosine similarity measure for two data points is given by:

$$\text{Cosine similarity}(|X, Y|) = \frac{x \cdot y}{||x|| \; ||y||}$$

(4.12)

where $x \cdot y$ is the dot product of the x and y vectors with, for this example,

$$x \cdot y = \sum_{i=1}^{n} x_i y_i \text{ and } ||x|| = \sqrt{x \cdot x}$$

$$x \cdot y = \sqrt{1 \times 5 + 2 \times 0 + 0 \times 0 + 0 \times 6 + 3 \times 7 + 4 \times 0 + 0 \times 0} = 5.1$$

$$||x|| = \sqrt{1 \times 1 + 2 \times 2 + 0 \times 0 + 0 \times 0 + 3 \times 3 + 4 \times 4 + 0 \times 0} = 5.5$$

$$||y|| = \sqrt{5 \times 5 + 0 \times 0 + 0 \times 0 + 6 \times 6 + 7 \times 7 + 0 \times 0 + 0 \times 0} = 10.5$$

$$\text{Cosine similarity}(|x \cdot y|) = \frac{x \cdot y}{||x|| \; ||y||} = \frac{5.1}{5.5 \times 10.5} = 0.08$$

The cosine similarity measure is one of the most used similarity measures, but the determination of the optimal measure comes down to the data structures. The choice of distance or similarity measure can also be parameterized, where multiple models are created with each different measure. The model with a distance measure that best fits the data with the smallest generalization error can be the appropriate proximity measure for the data.

4.3.2 How to Implement

Implementation of lazy learners is the most straightforward process amongst all the data science methods. Since the key functionality is referencing or looking up the training dataset, one could implement the entire algorithm in spreadsheet software like MS Excel, using lookup functions. Of course, if the complexity of the distance calculation or when the number of attributes rises, then one may need to rely on data science tools or programming languages. In RapidMiner, k-NN implementation is similar to other classification and regression process, with data preparation, modeling, and performance evaluation operators. The modeling step memorizes all the training records and accepts input in the form of real and nominal values. The output of this modeling step is just the dataset of all the training records.

Step 1: Data Preparation

The dataset used in this example is the standard Iris dataset with 150 examples and four numeric attributes. First, all attributes will need to be normalized using the *Normalize* operator, from the Data Transformation > Value Modification > Numerical Value Modification folder. The *Normalize* operator accepts numeric attributes and generates transformed numeric attributes. The user can specify one of four normalization methods in the parameter configurations: Z-transformation (most commonly used), range transformation, proportion transformation, and interquartile range. In this example, Z-transformation is used because all the attributes are being standardized.

The dataset is then split into two equal exclusive datasets using the *Split Data* operator. Split data (from Data Transformation > Filtering > Sampling) is used to partition the test and training datasets. The proportion of the partition and the sampling method can be specified in the parameter configuration of the split operator. For this example, the data is split equally between the training and test sets using shuffled sampling. One half of the dataset is used as training data for developing the k-NN model and the other half of the dataset is used to test the validity of the model.

Step 2: Modeling Operator and Parameters

The k-NN modeling operator is available in Modeling > Classification > Lazy Modeling. These parameters can be configured in the operator settings:

1. k: The value of k in k-NN can be configured. This defaults to one nearest neighbor. This example uses $k = 3$.

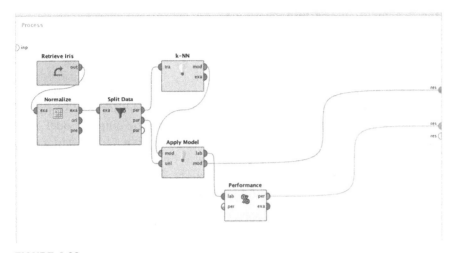

FIGURE 4.32
Data mining process for *k*-NN algorithm. *k*-NN, *k*-Nearest Neighbor.

2. *Weighted vote:* In the case of $k > 1$, this setting determines if the algorithm needs to take into consideration the distance value for the weights, while predicting the class value of the test record.
3. *Measure types:* There are more than two dozen distance measures available in RapidMiner. These measures are grouped in Measure Types. The selection of Measure Types drives the options for the next parameter (Measure).
4. *Measure:* This parameter selects the actual measure like Euclidean distance, Manhattan distance, and so on. The selection of the measure will put restrictions on the type of input the model receives. Depending on the weighting measure, the input data type choices will be limited and, hence, a data type conversion is required if the input data contains attributes that are not compatible with that measure.

Similar to other classification model implementations, the model will need to be applied to test the dataset, so the effectiveness of the model can be evaluated. Fig. 4.32 shows the RapidMiner process where the initial Iris dataset is split using a split operator. A random 75 of the initial 150 records are used to build the *k*-NN model and the rest of the data is the test dataset. The *Apply Model* operator accepts the test data and applies the *k*-NN model to predict the class type of the species. The *Performance* operator is then used to compare the predicted class with the labeled class for all of the test records.

Step 3: Execution and Interpretation

After the output from the *Performance* operator is connected to the result ports, as shown in Fig. 4.32, the model can be executed. The result output is observed as:

1. *k-NN model:* The model for *k*-NN is just the set of training records. Hence, no additional information is provided in this view, apart from the statistics of training records. Fig. 4.33 shows the output model.
2. *Performance vector:* The output of the *Performance* operator provides the confusion matrix with correct and incorrect predictions for all of the test dataset. The test set had 75 records. Fig. 4.34 shows the accurate prediction of 71 records (sum of diagonal cells in the matrix) and 4 incorrect predictions.
3. Labeled test dataset: The prediction can be examined at the record level.

KNNClassification

Description

3-Nearest Neighbour model for classification.
The model contains 75 examples with 4 dimensions of the following classes:
    Iris-setosa
    Iris-versicolor
    Iris-virginica

Annotations

FIGURE 4.33

k-NN model output. *k*-NN, *k*-Nearest Neighbor.

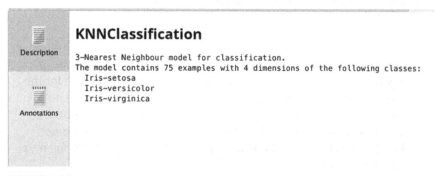

PerformanceVector (Performance)   ×   KNNClassification (k–NN)   ×

◉ Table View   ○ Plot View

accuracy: 96.00%

	true Iris-setosa	true Iris-versicolor	true Iris-virginica	class precision
pred. Iris-setosa	20	0	0	100.00%
pred. Iris-versicolor	0	26	2	92.86%
pred. Iris-virginica	0	1	26	96.30%
class recall	100.00%	96.30%	92.86%	

FIGURE 4.34

Performance vector for *k*-NN model. *k*-NN, *k*-Nearest Neighbor.

4.3.3 Conclusion

The k-NN model requires normalization to avoid bias by any attribute that has large or small units in the scale. The model is quite robust when there are any missing attribute values in the test record. If a value in the test record is missing, the entire attribute is ignored in the model, and the model can still function with reasonable accuracy. In this implementation example, if the sepal length of a test record is not known, then the sepal length is ignored in the model. k-NN becomes a three-dimensional model instead of the original four dimensions.

As a lazy learner, the relationship between input and output cannot be explained, as the model is just a memorized set of all training records. There is no generalization or abstraction of the relationship. Eager learners are better at explaining the relationship and providing a description of the model.

Model building in k-NN is just memorizing and does not require much time. But, when a new unlabeled record is to be classified, the algorithm needs to find the distance between the unseen record and *all* the training records. This process can get expensive, depending on the size of training set and the number of attributes. A few sophisticated k-NN implementations index the records so that it is easy to search and calculate the distance. One can also convert the actual numbers to ranges so as to make it easy to index and compare it against the test record. However, k-NN is difficult to be used in time-sensitive applications like serving an online advertisement or real-time fraud detection.

k-NN models can handle categorical inputs but the distance measure will be either 1 or 0. Ordinal values can be converted to integers so that one can better leverage the distance function. Although the k-NN model is not good at generalizing the input-output relationship, it is still quite an effective model and leverages the existing relationships between attributes and class label in the training records. For good quality outcome, it requires a significant number of training records with the maximum possible permutations values in input attributes.

4.4 NAÏVE BAYESIAN

The data science algorithms used for classification tasks are quite diverse. The objective of all these algorithms is the same—prediction of a target variable. The method of prediction is drawn from a range of multidisciplinary techniques. The naïve Bayes algorithm finds its roots in statistics and probability theory. In general, classification techniques try to predict class labels by best approximating the relationship between the attributes and the class label.

Every day, we mentally estimate a myriad of outcomes based on past evidence. Consider the process of guessing commuting time to work. First, commute time depends heavily on when one is leaving home or work. If one is traveling during peak hours, the commute is going to be longer. Weather conditions like rain, snow, or dense fog will slow down the commute. If the day is a school holiday, like summer break, then the commute will be lighter than on school days. If there is any road work, the commute usually takes longer. When more than one adverse factor is at play, then the commute will be even longer than if it is just one isolated factor is in the play. This *if-then* knowledge is based on previous experience of commuting when one or more factors come into play. Our experience creates a model in our brain and we mentally run the model before pulling out of the driveway!

Take the case of defaults in home mortgages and assume the average overall default rate is 2%. The likelihood of an average person defaulting on their mortgage loan is 2%. However, if a given individual's credit history is above average (or excellent), then the likelihood of their default would be less than average. Furthermore, if one knows that the person's annual income is above average with respect to loan value, then the likelihood of default falls further. As more evidence is obtained on the factors that impact the outcome, improved guesses can be made about the outcome using probability theory. The naïve Bayesian algorithm leverages the probabilistic relationship between the attributes and the class label. The algorithm makes a strong and sometimes *naïve* assumption of independence between the attributes, thus, its name. The independence assumption between attributes may not always hold true. It can be assumed that annual income and home value are independent of each other. However, homeowners with high income tend to buy more expensive houses. Although the independence assumption doesn't always hold true, the simplicity and robustness of the algorithm offsets the limitation introduced by the assumption.

PREDICTING AND FILTERING SPAM EMAIL

Spam is unsolicited bulk email sent to a wide number of email users. At best it is an annoyance to recipients but many of the spam emails hide a malicious intent by hosting false advertisements or redirecting clicks to phishing sites. Filtering spam email is one of the essential features provided by email service providers and administrators. The key challenge is balance between incorrectly flagging a legitimate email as spam (false positive) versus not catching all the spam messages. There is no perfect spam filtering solution and spam detection is a catch-up game. The spammers always try to deceive and outsmart

the spam filters and email administrators fortify the filters for various new spam scenarios. Automated spam filtering based on algorithms provides a promising solution in containing spam and in learning frameworks to update the changing filtering solutions (Process Software, 2013).

Some words occur in spam emails more often than in legitimate email messages. For example, the probability of the occurrence for words like free, mortgage, credit, sale, Viagra, etc., is higher in spam mails than in normal emails. The exact probabilities can be calculated if one

(Continued)

(Continued)

has a sample of previously known spam emails and regular emails. Based on the known word probabilities, the overall probability of an email being spam can be computed based on all the words in the email and the probability of each word being in spam versus regular emails. This is the foundation of Bayesian spam filtering systems (Zdziarski, 2005). Any misclassified spam messages that are subsequently reclassified by the user (by marking it as spam) are an opportunity to refine the model, making spam filtering adaptive to new spam techniques. Though current spam reduction methods use a combination of different algorithms, Bayesian-based spam filtering remains one of the foundational elements of spam prediction systems (Sahami, Dumais, Heckerman, & Horvitz, 1998).

4.4.1 How It Works

The naïve Bayesian algorithm is built on the Bayes' theorem, named after Reverend Thomas Bayes. Bayes' work is described in "Essay Towards Solving a Problem in the Doctrine of Chances" (1763), published posthumously in the *Philosophical Transactions of the Royal Society of London* by Richard Price. The Bayes' theorem is one of the most influential and important concepts in statistics and probability theory. It provides a mathematical expression for how a degree of subjective belief changes to account for new evidence. First, the terminology used in Bayes' theorem need to be discussed.

Assume $\mathbf{X}$ is the evidence (attribute set) and Y is the outcome (class label). Here $\mathbf{X}$ is a set, not individual attributes, hence, $\mathbf{X} = \{X_1, X_2, X_3, \ldots, X_n\}$, where X_i is an individual attribute, such as credit rating. The probability of outcome $P(Y)$ is called *prior probability*, which can be calculated from the training dataset. Prior probability shows the likelihood of an outcome in a given dataset. For example, in the mortgage case, $P(Y)$ is the default rate on a home mortgage, which is 2%. $P(Y|\mathbf{X})$ is called the *conditional probability*, which provides the probability of an outcome given the evidence, that is, when the value of $\mathbf{X}$ is known. Again, using the mortgage example, $P(Y|\mathbf{X})$ is the average rate of default given that an individual's credit history is known. If the credit history is excellent, then the probability of default is likely to be less than 2%. $P(Y|\mathbf{X})$ is also called *posterior probability*. Calculating posterior probability is the objective of data science using Bayes' theorem. This is the likelihood of an outcome as the conditions are learnt.

Bayes' theorem states that:

$$P(Y|\mathbf{X}) = \frac{P(Y) \times P(\mathbf{X}|Y)}{P(\mathbf{X})} \qquad (4.13)$$

$P(\mathbf{X}|Y)$ is another conditional probability, called the *class conditional probability*. $P(\mathbf{X}|Y)$ is the probability of the existence of conditions given an outcome. Like $P(Y)$, $P(\mathbf{X}|Y)$ can be calculated from the training dataset as well. If the training set of loan defaults is known, the probability of an "excellent" credit rating can be calculated given that the default is a "yes." As indicated in the Bayes' theorem, class conditional probability is crucial to calculating posterior probability. $P(\mathbf{X})$ is basically the probability of the evidence. In the mortgage example, this is simply the proportion of individuals with a given credit rating. To classify a new record, one can compute $P(Y|\mathbf{X})$ for *each class of Y* and see which probability "wins." Class label Y with the highest value of $P(Y|\mathbf{X})$ wins for given condition $\mathbf{X}$. Since $P(\mathbf{X})$ is the same for every class value of the outcome, one does not have to calculate this and it can be assumed as a constant. More generally, for an example set with n attributes $\mathbf{X} = \{X_1, X_2, X_3 \ldots X_n\}$,

$$P(Y|\mathbf{X}) = \frac{P(Y) \times \prod_{i=1}^{n} P(\mathbf{X}_i|Y)}{P(\mathbf{X})} \qquad (4.14)$$

If one knows how to calculate class conditional probability $P(\mathbf{X}|Y)$ or $\prod_{i=1}^{n} P(\mathbf{X}_i|Y)$, then it is easy to calculate posterior probability $P(Y|\mathbf{X})$. Since $P(\mathbf{X})$ is constant for every value of Y, it is enough to calculate the numerator of the equation $P(Y) \times \prod_{i=1}^{n} P(\mathbf{X}_i|Y)$ for every class value.

To further explain how the naïve Bayesian algorithm works, the modified Golf dataset shown in Table 4.4 will be used. The Golf table is an artificial dataset with four attributes and one class label. Note that the categorical data type is being used for ease of explanation (temperature and humidity have been converted from the numeric type). In Bayesian terms, weather condition is the *evidence* and decision to play or not play is the *belief*. Altogether there are 14 examples with 5 examples of Play = no and nine examples of Play = yes. The objective is to predict if the player will Play (yes or no), given the weather condition, based on learning from the dataset in Table 4.4. Here is the step-by-step explanation of how the Bayesian model works.

Table 4.4 Golf Dataset With Modified Temperature and Humidity Attributes

No.	Temperature X_1	Humidity X_2	Outlook X_3	Wind X_4	Play (Class Label) Y
1	High	Med	Sunny	false	no
2	High	High	Sunny	true	no
3	Low	Low	Rain	true	no
4	Med	High	Sunny	false	no
5	Low	Med	Rain	true	no
6	High	Med	Overcast	false	yes
7	Low	High	Rain	false	yes
8	Low	Med	Rain	false	yes
9	Low	Low	Overcast	true	yes
10	Low	Low	Sunny	false	yes
11	Med	Med	Rain	false	yes
12	Med	Low	Sunny	true	yes
13	Med	High	Overcast	true	yes
14	High	Low	Overcast	false	yes

Step 1: Calculating Prior Probability P(Y)

Prior probability $P(Y)$ is the probability of an outcome. In this example set there are two possible outcomes: Play = yes and Play = no. From Table 4.4, 5 out of 14 records with the "no" class and 9 records with the "Yes" class. The probability of outcome is

$P(Y = no) = 5/14$
$P(Y = yes) = 9/14$

Since the probability of an outcome is calculated from the dataset, it is important that the dataset used for data science is *representative* of the population, if sampling is used. The class-stratified sampling of data from the population will be ideal for naïve Bayesian modeling. The class-stratified sampling ensures the class distribution in the sample is the same as the population.

Step 2: Calculating Class Conditional Probability P(X$_i$|Y)

Class conditional probability is the probability of *each* attribute value for an attribute, for each outcome value. This calculation is repeated for all the attributes: Temperature (X_1), Humidity (X_2), Outlook (X_3), and Wind (X_4), and for every distinct outcome value. Here is a calculation of the class conditional probability of Temperature (X_1). For each value of the Temperature attribute, $P(X_1|Y = no)$ and $P(X_1|Y = yes)$ can be calculated by constructing a class conditional probability table as shown in Table 4.5. From the dataset there are five $Y = no$ records and nine $Y = yes$ records. Out of the five $Y = no$ records, the probability of occurrence can be calculated for when the temperature is high, medium, and low. The values will be 2/5, 1/5, and 2/5, respectively. The same process can be repeated when the outcome is $Y = yes$.

Similarly, the calculation can be repeated to find the class conditional probability for the other three attributes: Humidity (X_2), Outlook (X_3), and Wind (X_4). This class conditional probability table is shown in Table 4.6.

Step 3: Predicting the Outcome Using Bayes' Theorem

With the class conditional probability tables all prepared they can now be used in the prediction task. If a new, unlabeled test record (Table 4.7) has the conditions Temperature = high, Humidity = low, Outlook = sunny, and

Table 4.5 Class Conditional Probability of Temperature

Temperature (X_1)	$P(X_1|Y = no)$	$P(X_1|Y = yes)$
High	2/5	2/9
Med	1/5	3/9
Low	2/5	4/9

Table 4.6 Conditional Probability of Humidity, Outlook, and Wind

Humidity (X_2)	$P(X_2\|Y=no)$	$P(X_2\|Y=yes)$
High	2/5	2/9
Low	1/5	4/9
Med	2/5	3/9
Outlook (X_3)	**$P(X_3\|Y=no)$**	**$P(X_3\|Y=yes)$**
Overcast	0/5	4/9
Rain	2/5	3/9
Sunny	3/5	2/9
Wind (X_4)	**$P(X_4\|Y=no)$**	**$P(X_4\|Y=yes)$**
False	2/5	6/9
True	3/5	3/9

Table 4.7 Test Record

No.	Temperature X_1	Humidity X_2	Outlook X_3	Wind X_4	Play (Class Label) Y
Unlabeled test	high	Low	Sunny	False	?

Wind = false, what would the class label prediction be? Play = yes or no? The outcome class can be predicted based on Bayes' theorem by calculating the posterior probability $P(Y|X)$ for both values of Y. Once $P(Y=yes|X)$ and $P(Y=no|X)$ are calculated, one can determine which outcome has higher probability and the predicted outcome is the one that has the highest probability. While calculating both conditional probabilities using Eq. (4.14), it is sufficient to just calculate the numerator portion, as $P(X)$ is going to be the same for both the outcome classes (Table 4.7).

$$P(Y=yes|X) = \frac{P(Y) * \prod_{i=1}^{n} p(X_i|Y)}{P(X)}$$

$$= \frac{P(Y=yes) * \{P(Temp=high|Y=yes) * P(Humidity=low|Y=yes) * P(Outlook=sunny|Y=yes) * P(Wind=false|Y=yes)\}}{P(X)}$$

$$= \frac{9/14 * \{2/9 * 4/9 * 2/9 * 6/9\}}{P(X)}$$

$$= \frac{0.0094}{P(X)}$$

$$P(Y=no|X) = 5/14 * \{2/5 * 4/5 * 3/5 * 2/5\}$$
$$= \frac{0.0274}{P(X)}$$

Both the estimates can be normalized by dividing both conditional probability by (0.0094 + 0.027) to get:

$$\text{Likelihood of (Play} = \text{yes)} = \frac{0.0094}{0.0274 + 0.0094} = 26\%$$

$$\text{Likelihood of (Play} = \text{no)} = \frac{0.0094}{0.0274 + 0.0094} = 74\%$$

In this case $P(Y = \text{yes}|X) < P(Y = \text{no}|X)$, hence, the prediction for the unlabeled test record will be Play = no.

The Bayesian modeling is relatively simple to understand, once one gets past the probabilistic concepts, and is easy to implement in practically any programing language. The computation for model building is quite simple and involves the creation of a lookup table of probabilities. Bayesian modeling is quite robust in handling missing values. If the test example set does not contain a value, suppose temperature is not available, the Bayesian model simply omits the corresponding class conditional probability for all the outcomes. Having missing values in the test set would be difficult to handle in decision trees and regression algorithms, particularly when the missing attribute is used higher up in the node of the decision tree or has more weight in regression. Even though the naïve Bayes algorithm is quite robust to missing attributes, it does have a few limitations. Here are couple of the most significant limitations and methods of mitigation.

Issue 1: Incomplete Training Set
Problems arise when an attribute value in the testing record has no example in the training record. In the Golf dataset (Table 4.4), if an unseen test example consists of the attribute value Outlook = overcast, the probability of $P(\text{Outlook} = \text{overcast}|Y = \text{no})$ is zero. Even if one of the attribute's class conditional probabilities is zero, by nature of the Bayesian equation, the entire posterior probability will be zero.

$$P(Y = \text{no}|X) = P(Y = \text{No}) * \{P(\text{Team} = \text{high}|Y = \text{no}) * P(\text{Humidity} = \text{low}|$$
$$\frac{Y = \text{no}) * P(\text{Outlook} = \text{overcast}|Y = \text{no}) * P(\text{Wind} = \text{false}|Y = \text{no})\}}{P(X)}$$

$$= \frac{5/14 * \{2/5 * 1/5 * 0 * 2/5\}}{P(X)}$$

$$= 0$$

In this case $P(Y = \text{yes}|\mathbf{X}) > P(Y = \text{no}|\mathbf{X})$, and the test example will be classified as Play = yes. If there are no training records for any other attribute value, like Temperature = low for outcome *yes*, then probability of both outcomes, $P(Y = \text{no}|\mathbf{X})$ and $P(Y = \text{yes}|\mathbf{X})$, will also be zero and an arbitrary prediction shall be made because of the dilemma.

To mitigate this problem, one can assign small default probabilities for the missing records instead of zero. With this approach, the absence of an attribute value doesn't wipe out the value of $P(X|Y)$, albeit it will reduce the probability to a small number. This technique is called *Laplace correction*. Laplace correction adds a controlled error in all class conditional probabilities. If the training set contains Outlook = overcast, then $P(X|Y = no) = 0$. The class conditional probability for all the three values for Outlook is 0/5, 2/5, and 3/5, $Y = no$. Controlled error can be added by adding 1 to all numerators and 3 for all denominators, so the class conditional probabilities are 1/8, 3/8, and 4/8. The sum of all the class conditional probabilities is still 1. Generically, the Laplace correction is given by corrected probability:

$$P(X_i|Y) = \frac{0 + \mu p_3}{5 + \mu}, \frac{2 + \mu p_2}{5 + \mu}, \frac{3 + \mu p_2}{5 + \mu} \tag{4.15}$$

where $p_1 + p_2 + p_3 = 1$ and μ is the correction.

Issue 2: Continuous Attributes

If an attribute has continuous numeric values instead of nominal values, this solution will not work. The continuous values can always be converted to nominal values by discretization and the same approach as discussed can be used. But discretization requires exercising subjective judgment on the bucketing range, leading to loss of information. Instead, the continuous values can be preserved as such and the probability density function can used. One assumes the probability distribution for a numerical attribute follows a normal or Gaussian distribution. If the attribute value is known to follow some other distribution, such as Poisson, the equivalent probability density function can be used. The probability density function for a normal distribution is given by:

$$f(x) = \frac{1}{\sqrt{2\pi}\sigma} e^{\frac{(x-\mu)^2}{2\sigma^2}} \tag{4.16}$$

where μ is the mean and σ is the standard deviation of the sample.

In the Golf dataset shown in Table 4.8, temperature and humidity are continuous attributes. In such a situation, the mean and standard deviation can be computed for both class labels (Play = yes and Play = no) for temperature and humidity (Table 4.9).

If an unlabeled test record has a Humidity value of 78, the probability density can be computed using Eq. (4.16), for both outcomes. For outcome Play = yes, if the values $x = 78$, $\mu = 73$, and $\sigma = 6.16$ are plugged in to the probability density function, the equation renders the value 0.04. Similarly,

Table 4.8 Golf Dataset with Continuous Attributes

No.	Outlook X_1	Humidity X_2	Temperature X_3	Wind X_4	Play Y
1	Sunny	85	85	false	no
2	Sunny	80	90	true	no
6	Rain	65	70	true	no
8	Sunny	72	95	false	no
14	Rain	71	80	true	no
3	Overcast	83	78	false	yes
4	Rain	70	96	false	yes
5	Rain	68	80	false	yes
7	Overcast	64	65	true	yes
9	Sunny	69	70	false	yes
10	Rain	75	80	false	yes
11	Sunny	75	70	true	yes
12	Overcast	72	90	true	yes
13	Overcast	81	75	false	yes

Table 4.9 Mean and Deviation for Continuous Attributes

Play Value		Humidity X_2	Temperature X_3
$Y = no$	Mean	74.60	84.00
	Deviation	7.89	9.62
$Y = yes$	Mean	73.00	78.22
	Deviation	6.16	9.88

for outcome Play = no, $x = 78$, $\mu = 74.6$, $\sigma = 7.89$ can be plugged in and the probability density is computed to obtain 0.05:

$$P(\text{temperature} = 78|Y = yes) = 0.04$$
$$P(\text{temperature} = 78|Y = no) = 0.05$$

These values are probability densities and *not* probabilities. In a continuous scale, the probability of temperature being exactly at a particular value is zero. Instead, the probability is computed for a range, such as temperatures from 77.5 to 78.5 units. Since the same range is used for computing the probability density for both the outcomes, Play = yes and Play = no, it is not necessary to compute the actual probability. Hence, these temperature values can be substituted in the Bayesian Eq. 4.14 for calculating class conditional probability $P(\mathbf{X}|Y)$.

Issue 3: Attribute Independence

One of the fundamental assumptions in the naïve Bayesian model is *attribute independence*. Bayes' theorem is guaranteed only for independent attributes. In many real-life cases, this is quite a stringent condition to deal with. This is why the technique is called "naïve" Bayesian, because it assumes an attribute's independence. In practice the naïve Bayesian model works fine with slightly correlated features (Rish, 2001). This problem can be handled by pre-processing the data. Before applying the naïve Bayesian algorithm, it makes sense to remove strongly correlated attributes. In the case of all numeric attributes, this can be achieved by computing a weighted correlation matrix. An advanced application of Bayes' theorem, called a Bayesian belief network, is designed to handle datasets with attribute dependencies.

The independence of categorical attributes can be tested by the *chi-square* (χ^2) test for independence. The chi-square test is calculated by creating a contingency table of observed frequency like the one shown in Table 4.10A. A contingency table is a simple cross tab of two attributes under consideration.

A contingency table of expected frequency (Table 4.10B) is created based on the equation:

$$E_{r,c} = \frac{(\text{row total} \times \text{column total})}{(\text{table total})}$$ (4.17)

The chi-square statistic (χ^2) calculates the sum of the difference between these two tables. χ^2 is calculated by Eq. (4.18). In this equation, O is observed frequency and E is expected frequency:

$$x^2 = \sum \frac{(O-E)^2}{E}$$ (4.18)

If the chi-square statistic (χ^2) is less than the critical value calculated from the chi-square distribution for a given confidence level, then one can assume the two variables under consideration are independent, for practical purposes.

Table 4.10 Contingency Tables with *observed frequency* (A) and *expected frequency* (B)

Outlook	(A) Wind—Observed Frequency			Outlook	(B) Wind—Expected Frequency		
	False	True	Total		False	True	Total
Overcast	2	2	4	Overcast	2.29	1.71	4
Rain	3	2	5	Rain	2.86	2.14	5
Sunny	3	2	5	Sunny	2.86	2.14	5
Total	**8**	**6**	**14**	**Total**	**8**	**6**	**14**

4.4.2   How to Implement

The naïve Bayesian model is one of the few data science techniques that can be easily implemented in any programing language. Since the conditional probability tables can be prepared in the model building phase, the execution of the model in runtime is quick. Data science tools have dedicated naïve Bayes classifier functions. In RapidMiner, the *Naïve Bayes* operator is available under Modeling > Classification. The process of building a model and applying it to new data is similar to with decision trees and other classifiers. The *naïve Bayesian* models can accept both numeric and nominal attributes.

Step 1: Data Preparation

The Golf dataset shown in Table 4.8 is available in RapidMiner under Sample > Data in the repository section. The Golf dataset can just be dragged and dropped in the process area to source all 14 records of the dataset. Within the same repository folder, there is also a Golf-Test dataset with a set of 14 records used for testing. Both datasets need to be added in the main process area. Since the Bayes operator accepts numeric and nominal data types, no other data transformation process is necessary. Sampling is a common method to extract the training dataset from a large dataset. It is especially important for naïve Bayesian modeling for the training dataset to be representative and proportional to the underlying dataset.

Step 2: Modeling Operator and Parameters

The *Naïve Bayes* operator can now be connected to the Golf training dataset. The *Naïve Bayesian* operator has only one parameter option to set: whether or not to include Laplace correction. For smaller datasets, Laplace correction is strongly encouraged, as a dataset may not have all combinations of attribute values for every class value. In fact, by default, Laplace correction is checked. Outputs of the *Naïve Bayes* operator are the model and original training dataset. The model output should be connected to *Apply Model* (Model Application folder) to execute the model on the test dataset. The output of the *Apply Model* operator is the labeled test dataset and the model.

Step 3: Evaluation

The labeled test dataset that one gets after using the *Apply Model* operator is then connected to the *Performance—Classification* operator to evaluate the performance of the classification model. The *Performance—Classification* operator can be found under Evaluation>Performance Measurement> Performance. Fig. 4.35 shows the complete naïve Bayesian predictive classification process. The output ports should be connected to the result ports and the process can be saved and executed.

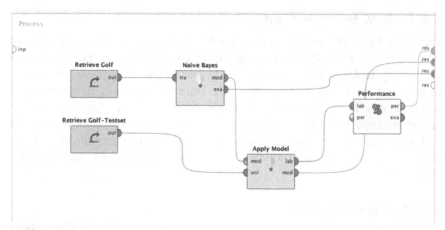

FIGURE 4.35
Data mining process for naïve Bayes algorithm.

Step 4: Execution and Interpretation

The process shown in Fig. 4.35 has three result outputs: a model description, performance vector, and labeled dataset. The labeled dataset contains the test dataset with the predicted class as an added column. The labeled dataset also contains the confidence for each label class, which indicates the prediction strength.

The model description result contains more information on class conditional probabilities of all the input attributes, derived from the training dataset. The Charts tab in model description contains probability density functions for the attributes, as shown in Fig. 4.36. In the case of continuous attributes, the decision boundaries can be discerned across the different class labels for the Humidity attribute. It has been observed that when Humidity exceeds 82, the likelihood of Play = no increases. The Distribution Table shown in Fig. 4.37 contains the familiar class conditional probability table similar to Tables 4.5 and 4.6.

The performance vector output is similar to previously discussed classification algorithms. The performance vector provides the confusion matrix describing accuracy, precision, and recall metrics for the predicted test dataset.

4.4.3   Conclusion

The Bayesian algorithm provides a probabilistic framework for a classification problem. It has a simple and sound foundation for modeling data and

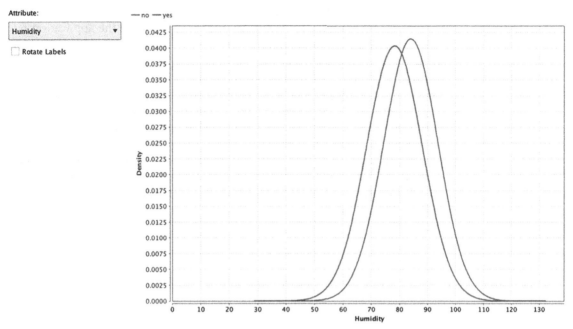

FIGURE 4.36
Naïve Bayes model output: probability density function for humidity attribute.

Attribute	Parameter	no	yes
Outlook	value = rain	0.392	0.331
Outlook	value = overcast	0.014	0.438
Outlook	value = sunny	0.581	0.223
Outlook	value = unknown	0.014	0.008
Temperature	mean	74.600	73
Temperature	standard deviation	7.893	6.164
Humidity	mean	84	78.222
Humidity	standard deviation	9.618	9.884
Wind	value = true	0.589	0.333
Wind	value = false	0.397	0.659
Wind	value = unknown	0.014	0.008

Result History   ExampleSet (Retrieve Golf)   SimpleDistribution (Naïve Bayes)   PerformanceVector (Performance)

Description   Charts   Distribution Table   Annotations

FIGURE 4.37
Naïve Bayes distribution table output.

is quite robust to outliers and missing values. This algorithm is deployed widely in text mining and document classification where the application has a large set of attributes and attributes values to compute. The naïve Bayesian classifier is often a great place to start for a data science project as it serves as a good benchmark for comparison to other models. Implementation of the Bayesian model in production systems is quite straightforward and the use of data science tools is optional. One major limitation of the model is the assumption of independent attributes, which can be mitigated by advanced modeling or decreasing the dependence across the attributes through pre-processing. The uniqueness of the technique is that it leverages new information as it arrives and tries to make a best prediction considering new evidence. In this way, it is quite similar to how our minds work. Talking about the mind, the next algorithm mimics the biological process of human neurons!

4.5   ARTIFICIAL NEURAL NETWORKS

The objective of a supervised learner is to model the relationship between input and output variables. The neural network technique approaches this problem by developing a functional relationship between input and output variables by mimicking the architecture of the biological process of a *neuron*. Although the developers of this technique have used many biological terms to explain the inner workings of neural network modeling process, it has a simple mathematical foundation. Consider the linear model:

$$Y = 1 + 2X_1 + 3X_2 + 4X_3$$

where Y is the calculated output and X_1, X_2, and X_3 are input attributes. 1 is the intercept and 2, 3, and 4 are the scaling factors or coefficients for the input attributes X_1, X_2, and X_3, respectively. This simple linear model can be represented in a topological form as shown in Fig. 4.38.

In this topology, X_1 is the input value and passes through a node, denoted by a circle. Then the value of X_1 is multiplied by its weight, which is 2, as noted in the connector. Similarly, all other attributes (X_2 and X_3) go through a node and scaling transformation. The last node is a special case with no input variable; it just has the intercept. Finally, the values from all the connectors are summarized in an output node that yields the predicted output Y. The topology shown in Fig. 4.38 represents the simple linear model $Y = 1 + 2X_1 + 3X_2 + 4X_3$. The topology also represents a simple *artificial neural network* (ANN). The neural networks model more complex nonlinear

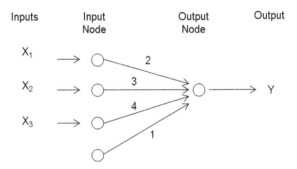

FIGURE 4.38
Model topology.

relationships of data and *learn* though adaptive adjustments of weights between the nodes. The ANN is a computational and mathematical model inspired by the biological nervous system. Hence, some of the terms used in an ANN are borrowed from biological counterparts.

In neural network terminology, nodes are called *units*. The first layer of nodes closest to the input is called the input layer or input nodes. The last layer of nodes is called the output layer or output nodes. The output layer performs an *aggregation function* and can also have a *transfer function*. The transfer function scales the output into the desired range. Together with the aggregation and transfer function, the output layer performs an *activation function*. This simple two-layer topology, as shown in Fig. 4.38, with one input and one output layer is called a *perceptron*. It is the most simplistic form of an ANN. A perceptron is a feed-forward neural network where the input moves in one direction and there are no loops in the topology.

An ANN is typically used for modeling *nonlinear*, complicated relationships between input and output variables. This is made possible by the existence of more than one layer in the topology, apart from the input and output layers,

BIOLOGICAL NEURONS

The functional unit of cells in the nervous system is the neuron. An ANN of nodes and connectors has a close resemblance to a biological network of neurons and connections, with each node acting as a single neuron. There are close to 100 billion neurons in the human brain and they are all interconnected to form this extremely important organ of the human body (see Fig. 4.39). Neuron cells are found in most animals; they transmit information through electrical and chemical signals. The interconnection between one neuron with another neuron happens through a *synapse*. A neuron consists of a cell body, a thin structure that forms from the cell body called a dendrite, and a long linear cellular extension called an axon. Neurons are composed of a number of dendrites and one axon. The axon of one neuron is connected to the dendrite of another neuron through a synapse, and electro-chemical signals are sent from one neuron to another. There are about 100 trillion synapses in the human brain.

(Continued)

(Continued)

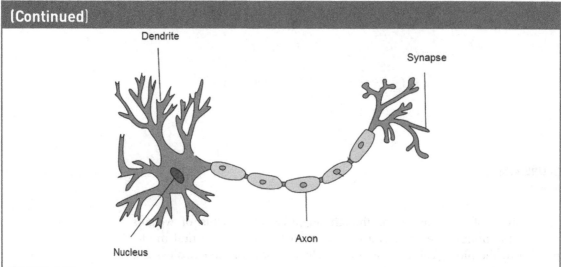

FIGURE 4.39

Anatomy of a neuron. *Modified from original "Neuron Hand-tuned." Original uploader: Quasar Jarosz at en.wikipedia.org. Transferred from en.wikipedia.org to Commons by user Faigl.ladislav using CommonsHelper. Licensed under Creative Commons Attribution-Share Alike 3.0 via Wikimedia Commons.*[4]

called *hidden layers*. A hidden layer contains a layer of nodes that connects input from previous layers and applies an activation function. The output is now calculated by a more complex combination of input values, as shown in Fig. 4.40.

Consider the example of the Iris dataset. It has four input variables, sepal length, sepal width, petal length, and petal width, with three classes (*I. setosa, I. versicolor, I. virginica*). An ANN based on the Iris dataset yields a three-layer structure (the number of layers can be specified by the user) with three output nodes, one for each class variable. For a categorical label problem, as in predicting the species for Iris, the ANN provides output for each class type. A winning class type is picked based on the maximum value of the output class label. The topology in Fig. 4.40 is a feed-forward ANN with one hidden layer. Of course, depending on the problem to be solved, one can use a topology with multiple hidden layers and even with looping where the output of one layer is used as input for preceding layers. Chapter 10 on Deep Learning introduces more complex topologies to solve sophisticated use cases. Specifying what topology to use is a challenge in neural network modeling.

The *activation function* used in the output node consists of a combination of an aggregation function, usually summarization, and a *transfer function*.

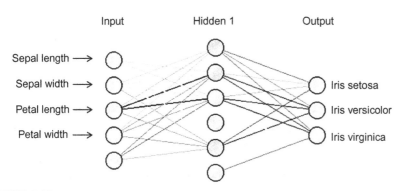

FIGURE 4.40

Topology of a Neural Network model.

Transfer functions commonly used are: sigmoid, normal bell curve, logistic, hyperbolic, or linear functions. The purpose of sigmoid and bell curves is to provide a linear transformation for a particular range of values and a nonlinear transformation for the rest of the values. Because of the transfer function and the presence of multiple hidden layers, one can model or closely approximate almost any mathematical continuous relationship between input variables and output variables. Hence, a multilayer ANN is called a *universal approximator*. However, the presence of multiple user options such as topology, transfer function, and a number of hidden layers makes the search for an optimal solution quite time consuming.

OPTICAL CHARACTER RECOGNITION

Character recognition is the process of interpreting handwritten text and converting it into digitized characters. It has a multitude of practical applications in everyday life, including converting handwritten notes to standardized text, automated sorting of postal mail by looking at the zip codes (postal area codes), automated data entry from forms and applications, digitizing classic books, license plate recognition, etc. How does it work?

In its most basic form, character recognition has two steps: digitization and a predictive model. In the digitization step, every individual character is converted to a digital matrix, say 12×12 pixel, where each cell takes a value of either 0 or 1 based on the handwritten character overlay. The input vector now has 144 binary attributes (12×12) indicating the information of the handwritten characters. Assume the objective is to decipher a numeric handwritten zip code (Matan et al., 1990).

An ANN model can be developed which accepts 144 inputs and has 10 outputs, each indicating a digit from 0 to 9. The model has to be learnt in such a way that when the input matrix is fed, one of the outputs shows the highest signal indicating the prediction for the character. Since a neural network is adaptable and relatively easy to deploy, it is getting used increasingly in character recognition, image processing, and related applications (Li, 1994). This specific use case is also an example where the explanatory aspect of the model is less important—maybe because no one knows exactly how the human brain does it. So, there is less expectation that the model should be understandable as long as it works with acceptable performance. ANN models are not easy to explain, and, in many situations, this alone will remove them from consideration of the data science techniques to use. One can only wish this wasn't the case!

4.5.1 How It Works

An ANN learns the relationship between input attributes and the output class label through a technique called *back propagation*. For a given network topology and activation function, the key training task is to find the weights of the links. The process is rather intuitive and closely resembles the signal transmission in biological neurons. The model uses every training record to estimate the error between the predicted and the actual output. Then the model uses the error to adjust the weights to minimize the error for the next training record and this step is repeated until the error falls within the acceptable range (Laine, 2003). The rate of correction from one step to another should be managed properly, so that the model does not overcorrect. The steps in developing an ANN from a training dataset include:

Step 1: Determine the Topology and Activation Function

For this example, imagine a dataset with three numeric input attributes (X_1, X_2, X_3) and one numeric output (Y). To model the relationship, a topology with two layers and a simple aggregation activation function is being used, as shown in Fig. 4.41. There is no transfer function used in this example.

Step 2: Initiation

Assume the initial weights for the four links are 1, 2, 3, and 4. Take an example model and a training record with all the inputs as 1 and the known output as 15. So, X_1, X_2, $X_3 = 1$ and output $Y = 15$. Fig. 4.42 shows initiation of the first training record.

Step 3: Calculating Error

The predicted output of the record from Fig. 4.42 can be calculated. This is a simple feed-forward process when the input data passes through the nodes

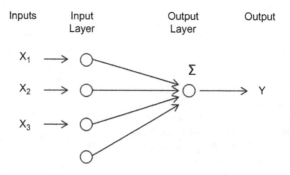

FIGURE 4.41
Two-layer topology with summary aggregation.

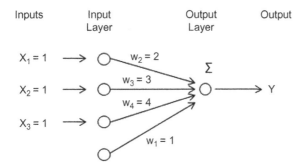

FIGURE 4.42
Initiation and first training record.

and the output is calculated. The predicted output $\overline{Y}$ according to the current model is $1 + 1 \times 2 + 1 \times 3 + 1 \times 4 = 10$. The difference between the actual output from the training record and the predicted output is the model error:

$$e = Y - \overline{Y}$$

The error for this example training record is $15 - 10 = 5$.

Step 4: Weight Adjustment
Weight adjustment is the most important part of *learning* in an ANN. The error calculated in the previous step is passed back from the output node to all other nodes in the reverse direction. The weights of the links are adjusted from their old value by a *fraction* of the error. The fraction λ applied to the error is called the learning rate. λ takes values from 0 to 1. A value close to 1 results in a drastic change to the model for each training record and a value close to 0 results in smaller changes and, hence, less correction. The new weight of the link (w) is the sum of the old weight (w') and the product of the learning rate and proportion of the error $(\lambda \times e)$.

$$w = w' + \lambda \times e$$

The choice of λ can be tricky in the implementation of an ANN. Some model processes start with λ close to 1 and reduce the value of λ while training each cycle. By this approach any outlier records later in the training cycle will not degrade the relevance of the model. Fig. 4.43 shows the error propagation in the topology.

The current weight of the first link is $w_2 = 2$. Assume the learning rate is 0.5. The new weight will be $w_2 = 2 + 0.5 \times 5/3 = 2.83$. The error is divided by 3 because the error is back propagated to three links from the output node. Similarly, the weight will be adjusted for all the links. In the next

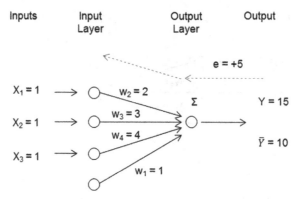

FIGURE 4.43
Neural Network error back propagation.

cycle, a new error will be computed for the next training record. This cycle goes on until all the training records are processed by iterative runs. The same training example can be repeated until the error rate is less than a threshold. It was an extremely simple case of an ANN that was reviewed. In reality, there will be multiple hidden layers and multiple output links—one for each nominal class value. Because of the numeric calculations, an ANN model works well with numeric inputs and outputs. If the input contains a nominal attribute, a pre-processing step should be included to convert the nominal attribute into multiple numeric attributes—one for each attribute value. This process is similar to dummy variable introduction, which will be further explored in Chapter 12, Time Series Forecasting. This specific pre-processing increases the number of input links for a neural network in the case of nominal attributes and, thus, increases the necessary computing resources. Hence, an ANN is more suitable for attributes with a numeric data type.

4.5.2 How to Implement

An ANN is one of the most popular algorithms available for data science tools. In RapidMiner, the ANN model operators are available in the Classification folder. There are three types of models available: A simple perceptron with one input and one output layer, a flexible ANN model called *Neural Net* with all the parameters for complete model building, and an advanced *AutoMLP* algorithm. AutoMLP (for Automatic Multilayer Perceptron) combines concepts from genetic and stochastic algorithms.

It leverages an ensemble group of ANNs with different parameters like hidden layers and learning rates. It also optimizes by replacing the worst performing models with better ones and maintains an optimal solution. For the rest of the discussion, the *Neural Net* model operator will be focused on.

Step 1: Data Preparation

The Iris dataset is used to demonstrate the implementation of an ANN. All four attributes for the Iris dataset are numeric and the output has three classes. Hence the ANN model will have four input nodes and three output nodes. The ANN model will not work with categorical or nominal data types. If the input has nominal attributes, it should be converted to numeric using data transformation, see Chapter 15, Getting started with RapidMiner. In this example, the *Rename* operator is used to name the four attributes of the Iris dataset and the *Split Data* operator to split 150 Iris records equally into the training and test data.

Step 2: Modeling Operator and Parameters

The training dataset is connected to the *Neural Net* operator. The *Neural Net* operator accepts real data type and normalizes the values. These parameters are available in ANN for users to change and customize in the model:

1. *Hidden layer:* Determines the number of layers, size of each hidden layer, and names of each layer for easy identification in the output screen. The default size of the node is -1, which is calculated by (*number of attributes + number of classes*)/2 + 1. The default node size can be overwritten by specifying a number, not including a no-input threshold node per layer.
2. *Training cycles:* This is the number of times a training cycle is repeated; it defaults to 500. In a neural network, every time a training record is considered, the previous weights are quite different, and hence, it is necessary to repeat the cycle many times.
3. *Learning rate:* The value of λ determines the sensitivity of the change while back propagating the error. It takes a value from 0 to 1. A value closer to 0 means the new weight would be more based on the previous weight and less on error correction. A value closer to 1 would be mainly based on error correction.
4. *Momentum:* This value is used to prevent local maxima and seeks to obtain globally optimized results by adding a fraction of the previous weight to the current weight.
5. *Decay:* During the neural network training, ideally the error would be minimal in the later portion of the training record sequence. One

wouldn't want a large error due to any outlier records in the last few records, as it would thereby impact the performance of the model. Decay reduces the value of the learning rate and brings it closer to zero for the last training record.

6. *Shuffle:* If the training record is sorted, one can randomize the sequence by shuffling it. The sequence has an impact in the model, particularly if the group of records exhibiting nonlinear characteristics are all clustered together in the last segment of the training set.

7. *Normalize:* Nodes using a sigmoid transfer function expect input in the range of −1 to 1. Any real value of the input should be normalized in an ANN model.

8. *Error epsilon:* The objective of the ANN model should be to minimize the error but not make it zero, at which the model memorizes the training set and degrades the performance. The model building process can be stopped when the error is less than a threshold called the error epsilon.

The output of the *Neural Net* operator can be connected to the *Apply Model* operator, which is standard in every data science workflow. The *Apply Model* operator also gets an input dataset from the *Split data* operator for the test dataset. The output of the *Apply Model* operator is the labeled test dataset and the ANN model.

Step 3: Evaluation
The labeled dataset output after using the *Apply Model* operator is then connected to the *Performance—Classification* operator, to evaluate the performance of the classification model. Fig. 4.44 shows the complete ANN predictive classification process. The output connections should be connected to the result ports and the process can be saved and executed.

Step 4: Execution and Interpretation
The output results window for the model provides a visual on the topology of the ANN model. Fig. 4.45 shows the model output topology. With a click on a node, one can get the weights of the incoming links to the node. The color of the link indicates relative weights. The description tab of the model window provides the actual values of the link weights.

The output performance vector can be examined to see the accuracy of the ANN model built for the Iris dataset. Fig. 4.46 shows the performance vector for the model. A two-layer ANN model with the default parameter options and equal splitting of input data and training set yields 93% accuracy. Out of 75 examples, only 5 were misclassified.

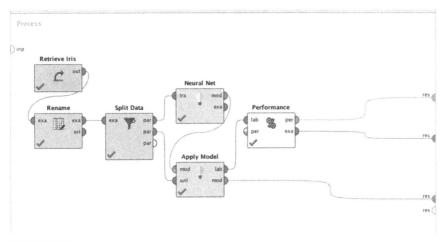

FIGURE 4.44
Data mining process for Neural Network.

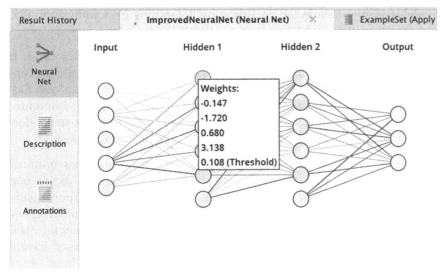

FIGURE 4.45
Neural Network model output with three hidden layers and four attributes.

4.5.3   Conclusion

Neural network models require stringent input constraints and pre-processing. If the test example has missing attribute values, the model cannot function, similar to a regression or decision tree model. The missing values

accuracy: 93.33%

	true Iris–setosa	true Iris–versicolor	true Iris–virginica	class precision
pred. Iris–setosa	20	0	0	100.00%
pred. Iris–versicolor	0	25	3	89.29%
pred. Iris–virginica	0	2	25	92.59%
class recall	100.00%	92.59%	89.29%	

FIGURE 4.46
Performance vector for Artificial Neural Network.

can be replaced with average values or any default values to mitigate the constraint. The relationship between input and output cannot be explained clearly by an ANN. Since there are hidden layers, it is quite complex to understand the model. In many data science applications explanation of the model is as important as the prediction itself. Decision trees, induction rules, and regression do a far better job at explaining the model.

Building a good ANN model with optimized parameters takes time. It depends on the number of training records and iterations. There are no consistent guidelines on the number of hidden layers and nodes within each hidden layer. Hence, one would need to try out many parameters to optimize the selection of parameters. However, once a model is built, it is straightforward to implement, and a new unseen record gets classified quite fast.

An ANN does not handle categorical input data. If the data has nominal values, it needs to be converted to binary or real values. This means one input attribute explodes into multiple input attributes and exponentially increases nodes, links, and complexity. Also, converting non-ordinal categorical data, like zip code, to a numeric value provides an opportunity for ANN to make numeric calculations, which doesn't make sense. However, having redundant correlated attributes is not going to be a problem in an ANN model. If the example set is large, having outliers will not degrade the performance of the model. However, outliers will impact the normalization of the signal, which most ANN models require for input attributes. Because model building is by incremental error correction, ANN can yield local optima as the final model. This risk can be mitigated by managing a momentum parameter to weigh the update.

Although model explanation is quite difficult with an ANN, the rapid classification of test examples makes an ANN quite useful for anomaly detection and classification problems. An ANN is commonly used in fraud detection, a scoring situation where the relationship between inputs and output is non-linear. If there is a need for something that handles a highly nonlinear land-scape along with fast real-time performance, then the ANN fits the bill.

4.6 SUPPORT VECTOR MACHINES

Support vector algorithms are a relatively new concept, like so many other machine learning techniques. Cortes (1995) provided one of the first formal introductions to the concept while investigating algorithms for optical character recognition at the AT&T Bell Labs.

The term "support vector machine" (SVM) is a confusing name for a data science *algorithm*. The fact is this term is very much a misnomer: there is really no specialized hardware. But it is a powerful algorithm that has been quite successful in applications ranging from pattern recognition to text mining. SVM emphasizes the interdisciplinary nature of data science by drawing equally from three major areas: computer science, statistics, and mathematical optimization theory.

Firstly, the essential terminology and definitions that are unique to SVMs will be introduced. Then the functioning of the algorithm will be explained for a simple linear dataset and then for a slightly more complex nonlinear dataset. A brief mathematical explanation of the workings of the algorithm will be provided before a case study based demonstration of how to implement SVMs in practice. Finally, the way SVMs perform better in some situations compared to other classification techniques will be highlighted and a list of the advantages and disadvantages of SVMs in general will be described.

Concept and Terminology

At a basic level, a SVM is a classification method. It works on the principle of fitting a boundary to a region of points that are all alike (that is, belong to one class). Once a boundary is fitted on the training sample, for any new points (test sample) that need to be classified, one must simply check whether they lie inside the boundary or not. The advantage of a SVM is that once a boundary is established, most of the training data is redundant. All it needs is a *core set of points* that can help identify and fix the boundary. These data points are called *support vectors* because they "support" the boundary. Why are they called vectors? Because each data point (or observation) is a vector: that is, it is a row of data that contains values for a number of different attributes.

This boundary is traditionally called a *hyperplane*. In a simple example of two dimensions, this boundary can be a straight line or a curve (as shown in

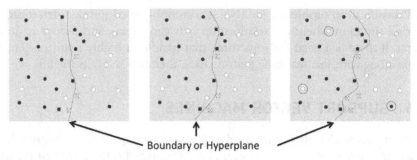

Boundary or Hyperplane

FIGURE 4.47
Three different hyperplanes for the same set of training data. There are two classes in this dataset, which are shown as filled and open circles.

Fig. 4.47). In three dimensions it can be a plane or an irregular complex surface. Higher dimensions are difficult to visualize, and a hyperplane is, thus, a generic name for a boundary in more than three dimensions.

As seen in Fig. 4.47, a number of such hyperplanes can be found for the same dataset. Which one is the "correct" one? Clearly a boundary that separates the classes with minimal misclassification is the best one. In the sequence of images shown, the algorithm applied to the third image appears to have zero misclassifications and may be the best one. Additionally, a boundary line that ensures that the average geometric distance between the two regions (or classes) is maximized is even better. This *n*-dimensional distance is called a *margin*. An SVM algorithm, therefore, essentially runs an optimization scheme to maximize this margin. The points with the "X" through them are the support vectors.

But it is not always possible to ensure that data can be cleanly separated. It may be rare to find that the data are *linearly separable*. When this happens, there may be many points within the margin. In this case, the best hyperplane is the one that has a *minimum* number of such points within the margin. To ensure this, a *penalty* is charged for every "contaminant" inside the margin and the hyperplane that has a minimum aggregate penalty cost is chosen. In Fig. 4.48, ξ represents the penalty that is applied for each error and the sum of all such errors is minimized to get the best separation.

What would happen if the data are not linearly separable (even without such contaminating errors)? For example, in Fig. 4.49A, the data points belong to two main classes: an inner ring and an outer ring. Clearly these two classes are not "linearly separable." In other words, a straight line can be drawn to split the two classes. However, it is intuitively clear that an elliptical or circular "hyperplane" can easily separate the two classes. In fact, if a simple linear

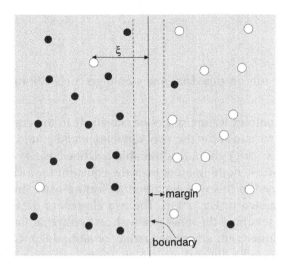

FIGURE 4.48
Key concepts in SVM construction: boundary, margin, and penalty, ξ. *SVM*, Support Vector Machine.

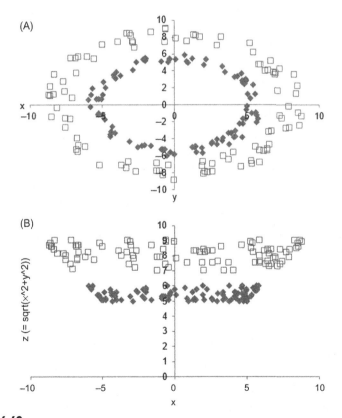

FIGURE 4.49
(A) Linearly non-separable classes. (B) Transformation to linearly separable.

SVM were to be run on this data, one would get a classification accuracy of around 46%.

How can such complex feature spaces be classified? In the example, a simple trick would be to transform the two variables x and y into a new feature space involving x (or y) and a new variable z defined as $z = \sqrt{(x^2 + y^2)}$. The representation of z is nothing more than the equation for a circle. When the data is transformed in this way, the resulting feature space involving x and z will appear as shown in Fig. 4.49B. The two clusters of data correspond to the two radii of the rings: the inner one with an average radius of around 5.5 and the outer cluster with an average radius of around 8.0. Clearly this new problem in the x and z dimensions is now linearly separable and a standard SVM can be applied to do the classification. When a linear SVM is run on this transformed data, one would get a classification accuracy of 100%. After classifying the transformed feature space, the transformation can be inverted to get back the original feature space.

Kernel functions offer the user the option of transforming nonlinear spaces into linear ones. Most packages that include SVM will have several nonlinear kernels ranging from simple polynomial basis functions to sigmoid functions. The user does not have to do the transformation beforehand, but simply has to select the appropriate kernel function; the software will take care of transforming the data, classifying it, and retransforming the results back into the original space.

Unfortunately, with a large number of attributes in a dataset it is difficult to know which kernel would work best. The most commonly used ones are polynomial and radial basis functions. From a practical standpoint, it is a good idea to start with a quadratic polynomial and work ones way up into some of the more exotic kernel functions until the desired accuracy level is reached. This flexibility of SVMs does come at the cost of computation. Now that an intuitive understanding of how SVMs work is reached, the working of the algorithm can be examined with a more formal mathematical explanation.

4.6.1 How It Works

Given a training dataset, how does one go about determining the boundary and the hyperplane? The case of a simple linearly separable dataset will be used consisting of two attributes, x_1 and x_2. Ultimately by using proper kernels any complex feature space can be mapped into a linear space, so this formulation will apply to any general dataset. Furthermore, extending the algorithm to more than two attributes is conceptually straightforward.

There are three essential tasks involved here: the first step is to find the boundary of each class. Then the best hyperplane, H, is the one that maximizes the margin or the distance to each of the class boundaries (see Fig. 4.48). Both of these steps use the training data. The final step is to determine on which side of this hyperplane a given test example lies in order to classify it.

Step 1: Finding the class boundary. When one connects every point in one class of a dataset to every other in that class, the outline that emerges defines the boundary of this class. This boundary is also known as the *convex hull*, as shown in Fig. 4.50.

Each class will have its own convex hull and because the classes are (assumed to be) linearly separable, these hulls do not intersect each other.

Step 2: Finding the hyperplane. There are infinitely many available hyperplanes, two of which are shown in Fig. 4.51. How does one know which hyperplane maximizes the margin? Intuitively one knows that H_0 has a larger margin than H_1, but how can this be determined mathematically?

First of all, any hyperplane can be expressed in terms of the two attributes, x_1 and x_2, as:

$$H = b + \mathbf{w} \cdot \mathbf{x} = 0 \tag{4.19}$$

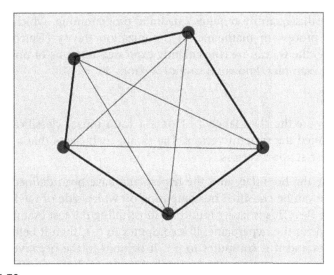

FIGURE 4.50
A convex hull for one class of data.

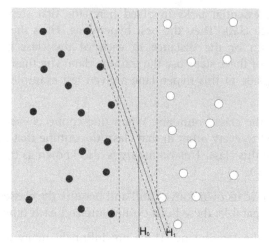

FIGURE 4.51
Both hyperplanes shown can separate data. It is intuitively clear that H_0 is better.

where $\mathbf{x}$ is (x_1, x_2), the weight $\mathbf{w}$ is (w_1, w_2), and b_0 is an intercept-like term usually called the *bias*. Note that this is similar to the standard form of the equation of a line. An optimal hyperplane, H_0, is uniquely defined by $(b_0 + \mathbf{w_0} \cdot \mathbf{x} = 0)$. Once the hyperplane is defined in this fashion, it can be shown that the margin is given by $2/\sqrt{(w_0 . w_0)}$ Cortes (1995).

Maximizing this quantity requires quadratic programming, which is a well-established process in mathematical optimization theory (Fletcher, 1987). Furthermore, the w_0 can be conveniently expressed in terms of only a few of the training examples, known as support vectors, as:

$$\mathbf{w_0} = \sum |\gamma_i \mathbf{x}_i| \tag{4.20}$$

where the γ_i are the class labels ($+1$ or -1 for a binary classification), and the $\mathbf{x}_i$ are called the support vectors. The i's are coefficients that are nonzero only for these support vectors.

Step 3: Once the boundary and the hyperplane have been defined, any new test example can be classified by computing on which side of the hyperplane the example lies. This is easily found by substituting the test example, $\mathbf{x}$, into the equation for the hyperplane. If it computes to $+1$, then it belongs to the positive class and if it computes to -1 it belongs to the negative class. For more in depth information refer to Smola (2004) or Cortes (1995) for a full mathematical description of the formulation. Hsu (2003) provides a more practical demonstration of programming an SVM.

4.6.2   How to Implement

How to use RapidMiner to perform classification with SVMs will now be described using two simple cases.[4]

Implementation 1: Linearly Separable Dataset

The default SVM implementation in RapidMiner is based on the so-called "dot product" formulation shown in the equations above. In this first example an SVM will be built using a two-dimensional dataset that consists of two classes: A and B (Fig. 4.52). A RapidMiner process reads in the training dataset, applies the default SVM model, and then classifies new points based on the model trained.

The dataset consists of 17 rows of data for three attributes: x_1, x_2, and **class**. The attributes x_1 and x_2 are numeric and **class** is a binomial variable consisting of the two classes A and B. Table 4.11 shows the full dataset and Fig. 4.52 shows the plot of the dataset. The model will be used to classify the three test examples: (1.50, 1.00), (1.50, 4.00), and (2.00, 7.00).

Step 1: Data Preparation

1. Read simpleSVMdemo.csv into RapidMiner by either using the *Read csv* operator or import the data into the repository using Import csv file. The dataset can be downloaded from the companion website of the book: www.IntroDataScience.com.
2. Add a *Set Role* operator to indicate that *class* is a label attribute and connect it to the data retriever. See Fig. 4.53A.

Step 2: Modeling Operator and Parameters

1. In the Operators tab, type in SVM, drag and drop the operator into the main window, and connect it to Set Role. Leave the parameters of this operator in their default settings.
2. Connect the "mod" output port of SVM to an *Apply Model* operator.
3. Insert a *Generate Data by User Specification* operator and click on the Edit List button of the attribute values parameter. When the dialog box opens up, click on Add Entry twice to create two test attribute names: x_1 and x_2. Set $x_1 = 2$ and $x_2 = 7$ under "attribute value." Note that the attribute values will need to be changed for each new test point that one wants to classify.
4. When this simple process is run, RapidMiner builds an SVM on the training data and applies the model to classify the test example, which was manually input using the *Generate Data by User Specification* operator.

---

[4] A pair of simplistic datasets were deliberately chosen to illustrate how SVMs can be implemented. A more sophisticated case study will be used to demonstrate how to use SVMs for text mining in Chapter 9, Text Mining.

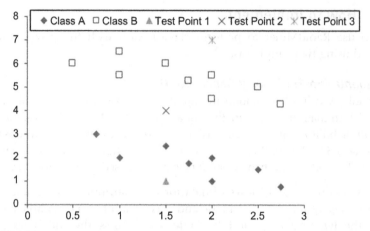

FIGURE 4.52

Two-class training data: class A (diamond) and class B (square). Points 1 to 3 are used to test the capability of the SVM. *SVM*, Support Vector Machine.

x_1	x_2	Class
1.50	2.50	A
2.00	2.00	A
1.00	2.00	A
0.75	3.00	A
2.00	1.00	A
1.75	1.75	A
2.75	0.75	A
2.50	1.50	A
0.50	6.00	B
1.50	6.00	B
2.00	5.50	B
1.00	5.50	B
1.00	6.50	B
2.00	4.50	B
1.75	5.25	B
2.75	4.25	B
2.50	5.00	B
1.50	1.00	Test point 1
1.50	4.00	Test point 2
2.00	7.00	Test point 3

Table 4.11 A Simple Dataset to Demonstrate SVM

SVM, *Support vector machine.*

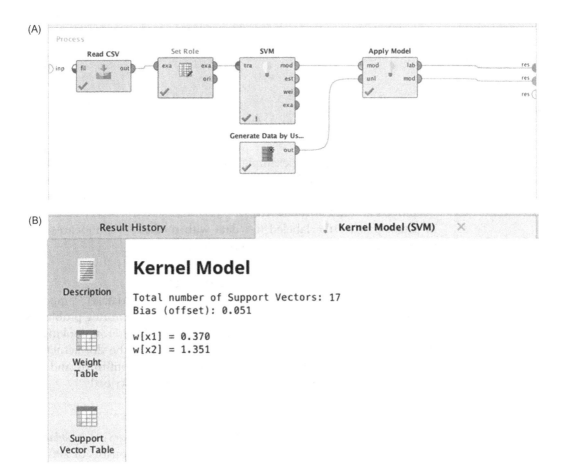

FIGURE 4.53
(A) A simple SVM setup for training and testing. (B) The accompanying SVM model. *SVM*, Support Vector Machine.

Step 3: Process Execution and Interpretation

For more practical applications, the Kernel Model output may not be very interesting, it is shown here (Fig. 4.53B) to observe what the hyperplane for this simplistic example looks like. Note that this is essentially the same form as Eq. (4.19) with bias $b_0 = 0.051$, $w_1 = 0.370$, and $w_2 = 1.351$. The more interesting result in this case is the output from the "lab" port of the Apply Model, which is the result of applying the SVM model on the test point (2, 7).

As can be seen in Fig. 4.54, the model has correctly classified this test point as belonging to class B [see the "prediction(class)" column]. Furthermore, it says that the confidence that this point belongs in class B is 92.6%. Looking at the chart, one can see that indeed there is little ambiguity about the classification of test point (2, 7).

ExampleSet (1 example, 3 special attributes, 2 regular attributes)

	Row No.	prediction(...	confidence(...	confidence(...	x1	x2
Data	1	B	0.074	0.926	2	7

FIGURE 4.54

Applying the simple SVM to classify test point 1 from Fig. 4.52. *SVM*, Support Vector Machine.

If one changes the test example input to the point (1.5, 1), it can be seen that this point would be classified under class A, with 88% confidence. However, the same cannot be said of test point (1.5, 4); one can run the process and test for themselves!

In actual practice the labeled test data with prediction confidences are the most useful results from an SVM application.

Example 2: Linearly Non-Separable Dataset

The first example showed a linearly separable training dataset. Suppose one wants to now apply the same SVM (dot) kernel to the two-ring problem seen earlier in this chapter: what would the results look like? From looking at the dataset it's clear that this is a nonlinear problem and the dot kernel would not work well. This intuitive understanding will be confirmed and how it can be easily fixed will be demonstrated in the steps described:

Step 1: Data Preparation

1. Start a new process and read in the dataset *nonlinearSVMdemodata.csv* using the same procedure as before. This dataset consists of 200 examples in four attributes: x_1, x_2, y, and ring. The ring is a binomial attribute with two values: inner and outer.
2. Connect a *Set Role* operator to the data and select the "ring" variable to be the label.
3. Connect a *Select Attributes* operator to this and select a subset of the attributes: x_1, x_2, and ring. Make sure that the *Include Special Attributes* checkbox is on.
4. Connect a *Split Validation* operator. Set the "split" to relative, "split ratio" to 0.7, and "sampling type" to stratified.

Step 2: Modeling Operator and Parameters

1. Double-click the *Split Validation* box and when the nested layer is entered, add an SVM operator in the training panel and *Apply Model* and *Performance (Classification)* operators in the testing panel.
2. Once again, do not change the parameters for the SVM operator from its default values.

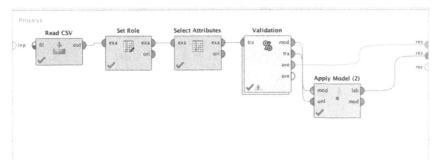

FIGURE 4.55
Setup for the nonlinear SVM demo model. *SVM*, Support Vector Machine.

3. Go back to the main level and add another *Apply Model* operator. Connect the "mod" output from the *Validation* box to the "mod" input port of *Apply Model (2)* and the "exa" output from the Validation box to the "unl" input port of *Apply Model (2)*. Also connect the "ave" output from the *Validation* box to the "res" port of the Main Process. Finally, connect the "lab" output from *Apply Model (2)* to the "res" port of the Main Process. The final process should look like Fig. 4.55.

Step 3: Execution and Interpretation

1. When this model is run, RapidMiner will generate two result tabs: *ExampleSet (Select Attributes)* and *Performance Vector (Performance)*. Check the *performance* of the SVM classifier. Recall that 30% of the initial input examples are now going to be tested for classification accuracy (which is a total of 60 test samples).
2. As seen in Fig. 4.56, the linear SVM can barely get 50% of the classes correct, which is to be expected considering linearly non-separable data is being used with a linear (dot) kernel SVM.
3. A better way to visualize this result is by means of the Scatter 3D Color plot. Click on the *ExampleSet (Select Attributes)* results tab and select Plot View and set up the Scatter 3D Color plot as shown in Fig. 4.57.

The red-colored examples in the upper (outer) ring are correctly classified as belonging to the class outer while the cyan-colored examples have been incorrectly classified as belonging to class inner. Similarly, the blue-colored examples in the lower (inner) ring have been correctly classified as belonging to class inner, whereas, the yellow-colored ones are not. As can be seen, the classifier roughly gets about half the total number of test examples right.

To fix this situation, all one needs to do is to go back to the SVM operator in the process and change the *kernel type* to *polynomial* (default degree 2.0) and

accuracy: 46.67%

	true inner	true outer	class precision
pred. inner	16	18	47.06%
pred. outer	14	12	46.15%
class recall	53.33%	40.00%	

FIGURE 4.56
Prediction accuracy of a linear (dot) kernel SVM on nonlinear data. *SVM*, Support Vector Machine.

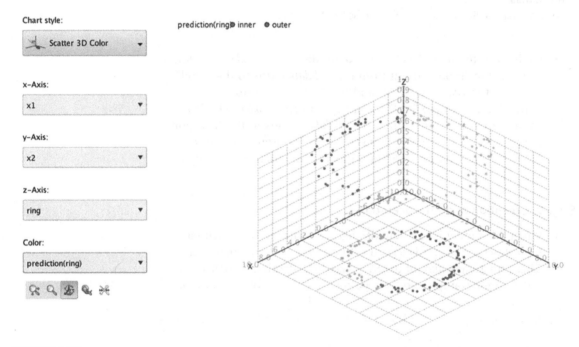

FIGURE 4.57
Visualizing the prediction from linear SVM. *SVM*, Support Vector Machine.

rerun the analysis. This time the points will be able to be classified with 100% accuracy as seen in Fig. 4.58. The same result will be obtained if a radial kernel is tried as well.

The point of this exercise was to demonstrate the flexibility of SVMs and the ease of performing such trials using RapidMiner. Unfortunately, with more realistic datasets, there is no way of knowing beforehand which kernel type would work best. The solution is to nest the SVM within an Optimization operator and explore a host of different kernel types and kernel parameters until one is

◉ Table View ○ Plot View

accuracy: 100.00%

	true inner	true outer	class precision
pred. inner	30	0	100.00%
pred. outer	0	30	100.00%
class recall	100.00%	100.00%	

FIGURE 4.58
Classifying the two-ring nonlinear problem using a polynomial SVM kernel. *SVM*, Support Vector Machine.

found that performs reasonably well. (Optimization using RapidMiner is described in Chapter 15: Getting started with RapidMiner.)

Parameter Settings

There are many different parameters that can be adjusted depending on the type of kernel function that is chosen. There is, however, one parameter that is critical in optimizing SVM performance: this is the SVM complexity constant, C, which sets the penalties for misclassification, as was described in an earlier section. Most real-world datasets are not cleanly separable and, therefore, will require the use of this factor. For initial trials, however, it is best to go with the default settings.

4.6.3 Conclusion

A disadvantage with higher order SVMs is the computational cost. In general, since SVMs have to compute the dot product for every classification (and during training), extremely high dimensions or a large number of attributes can result in slow computation times. However, this disadvantage is offset by the fact that once an SVM model is built, small changes to the training data will not result in significant changes to the model coefficients as long as the support vectors do not change. This overfitting resistance is one of the reasons why SVMs have emerged as one of the most versatile among machine learning algorithms.

In summary, the key advantages of SVM are:

1. *Flexibility in application:* SVMs have been applied for activities from image processing to fraud detection to text mining.
2. *Robustness:* Small changes in data do not require expensive remodeling.
3. *Overfitting resistance:* The boundary of classes within datasets can be adequately described usually by only a few support vectors.

These advantages have to be balanced with the somewhat high computational costs.

4.7   ENSEMBLE LEARNERS

In supervised machine learning, the objective is to build a model that can explain the relationship between inputs and output. The model can be considered as a hypothesis that can map new input data to predicted output. For a given training set, multiple hypotheses can explain the relationship with varying degrees of accuracy. While it is difficult to find the exact hypothesis from an infinite hypothesis space, one would like the modeling process to find the hypothesis that can *best* explain the relationship with least error.

Ensemble methods or learners optimize the hypothesis-finding problem by employing an array of individual prediction models and then combining them to form an aggregate hypothesis or model. These methods provide a technique for generating a better hypothesis by combining multiple hypotheses into one. Since a single hypothesis can be locally optimal or overfit a particular training set, combining multiple models can improve the accuracy by forcing a meta-hypothesis solution. It can be shown that in certain conditions, the combined predictive power of the ensemble model is better than the predictive power of individual models. Since different methods often capture different features of the solution space as part of any one model, the model ensembles have emerged as the most important technique for many practical classification problems.

Wisdom of the Crowd

Ensemble models have a set of base models that accept the same inputs and predict the outcome independently. Then the outputs from all of these base models are combined, usually by voting, to form an ensemble output. This approach is similar to decision-making by a committee or a board. The method of improving accuracy by drawing together the prediction of multiple models is called *meta learning*. A similar decision-making methodology is seen in higher courts of justice, corporate boards, and various committees. The logic here is: while individual members of the committee have biases and opinions, collective decision-making is better than one individual's assessment. Ensemble methods are used to improve the error rate and overcome the modeling bias of individual models. They can produce one strong learner by combining many weak learners. Fig. 4.59 provides the framework of ensemble models.

The predicted class with more votes from the base learners is the output of the combined ensemble model. Base models predict the outcome with varied degrees of accuracy. Hence, one can weigh the vote by the accuracy rate of individual models, which causes base models with higher accuracy to have higher representation in the final aggregation than models with a lower accuracy rate (Dietterich, 2007).

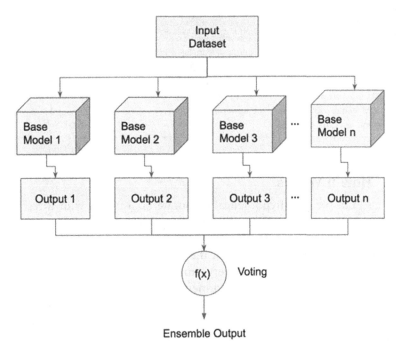

FIGURE 4.59
Ensemble model.

PREDICTING DROUGHT

Drought is a period of time where a region experiences far less than average water supply. With the onset of climate change, there has been an increase in frequency and duration of drought conditions in many parts of the world. Immediate drought is caused by the development of high-pressure regions, thereby inhibiting the formation of clouds, which results in low precipitation and lower humidity. Predicting drought conditions in a region is an extremely challenging task. There is no clear start and end point for drought duration. There are too many variables that impact the climate patterns that lead to drought conditions. Hence, there is no strong model to predict drought well ahead of time (Predicting Drought, 2013). Predicting drought seasons in advance would provide time for regional administrations to mitigate the consequences of the drought.

Droughts involve myriad factors including groundwater level, air stream flow, soil moisture, topology, and large-scale global weather patterns like El Nino and La Nina (Patel, 2012). With thousands of attributes and many unknown variables that influence the conditions for drought, there is no "silver bullet" massive model for predicting when drought is going to hit a region with a high

(Continued)

(Continued)

degree of accuracy. What there is, is many different "weak" models that use some of the thousands of attributes available, which make predictions marginally better than pure chance. These weak models may provide different drought predictions for the same region and time, based on the diverse input variables for each model. The prediction can be summarized by combining the predictions of individual models. Ensemble models provide a systematic method to combine many weak models into one better model. Most of the data science models deployed in production applications are ensemble models.

4.7.1   How It Works

Here's an example of a hypothetical corporate boardroom with three board members. Assume that individually each board member makes wrong decisions about 20% of time. The board needs to make a yes/no decision for a major project proposal by looking at the merits. If all board members make consistent unanimous decisions every time, then the error rate of the board as a whole is 20%. But, if each board member's decisions are *independent* and if their outcomes are not correlated, the board makes an error only when more than *two board members make an error* at the same time. The board makes an error only when the majority of its members make an error. The error rate of the board can be calculated using the binomial distribution.

In binomial distribution, the probability of k successes in n independent trials each with a success rate of p is given by a probability mass function:

$$p(k) = \binom{n}{k} p^k (1-p)^{n-k}$$

$$
\begin{aligned}
P(\text{Board wrong}) &= \binom{n}{3} p^k (1-p)^{n-k} + \binom{n}{2} p^k (1-p)^{n-k} \\
&= \binom{3}{3} 0.2^3 (1-0.2)^0 + \binom{3}{2} 0.2^2 (1-0.2)^1 \\
&= 0.008 + 0.96 \\
&= 0.104 \\
&= 10.4\%
\end{aligned}
$$

(4.21)

In this example, the error rate of the board (10.4%) is *less* than the error rate of the individuals (20%)! One can, therefore, see the impact of collective decision-making. A generic formula for calculating error rate for the ensemble is given by:

$$P(\text{ensemble wrong}) = P(k \geq \text{round } (n/2)) = \sum_{k=n/2}^{n} \binom{n}{k} P^k (1-P)n - k$$

where n is the number of the base models. Some important criteria to note are:

1. Each member of the ensemble should be independent.
2. The individual model error rate should be less than 50% for binary classifiers.

If the error rate of the base classifier is more than 50%, its prediction power is worse than pure chance and hence, it is not a good model to begin with. Achieving the first criterion of independence amongst the base classifier is difficult. However, there are a few techniques available to make base models as diverse as possible. In the board analogy, having a board with diverse and independent members makes statistical sense. Of course, they all have to make the right decision more than half the time.

Achieving the Conditions for Ensemble Modeling

One will be able to take advantage of the combined decision-making power of the ensemble model only if the base models are good to begin with. While meta learners can form a strong learner from several weak learners, those weak learners should be better than random guessing. Because all the models are developed based on the same training set, the diversity and independence condition of the model is difficult to accomplish. While complete independence of the base models cannot be achieved, one can take steps to promote independence by changing the training sets for each base model, varying the input attributes, building different classes of modeling techniques and algorithms, and changing the modeling parameters to build the base models. To achieve diversity in the base models, one can alter the conditions in which the base model is built. The most commonly used conditions are:

1. *Different model algorithms*: The same training set can be used to build different classifiers, such as decision trees using multiple algorithms, naïve Bayesian, *k*-NNs, ANNs, etc. The inherent characteristics of these models are different, which yield different error rates and a diverse base model set.
2. *Parameters within the models:* Changing the parameters like depth of the tree, gain ratio, and maximum split for the decision tree model can produce multiple decision trees. The same training set can be used to build all the base models.
3. *Changing the training record set:* Since the training data is the key contributor to the error in a model, changing the training set to build the base model is one effective method for building multiple independent base models. A training set can be divided into multiple sets and each set can be used to build one base model. However, this technique requires a sufficiently large training set and is seldom used.

Instead, one can sample training data with replacements from a dataset and repeat the same process for each base model.

4. *Changing the attribute set:* Similar to changing the training data where a sample of records is used for the building of each base model, one can sample the attributes for each base model. This technique works if the training data have a large number of attributes.

In the next few sections, specific approaches to building ensemble models will be reviewed based on the mentioned techniques for promoting independence among base models. There are some limitations to using ensemble models. If different algorithms are used for the base models, they impose different restrictions on the type of input data that can be used. Hence, it could create a superset of restrictions to inputs for an ensemble model.

4.7.2   How to Implement

In data science tools, ensemble modeling operators can be found in meta learning or ensemble learning groupings. In RapidMiner, since ensemble modeling is used in the context of predicting, all the operators are located in Modeling > Classification and Regression > Meta Modeling. The process of building ensemble models is similar to that of building any classification models like decision trees or neural networks. Please refer to previous classification algorithms for steps to develop individual classification processes and models in RapidMiner. In the next few pages the implementation of ensemble modeling will be reviewed with simple voting and a couple of other techniques to make the base models independent by altering examples for the training set.

Ensemble by Voting

Implementing an ensemble classifier starts with building a simple base classification process. For this example, a decision tree process can be built with the Iris dataset as shown in Section 4.1 Decision Trees. The standard decision tree process involves data retrieval and a decision tree model, followed by applying the model to an unseen test dataset sourced from the Iris dataset and using a performance evaluation operator. To make it an ensemble model, the *Decision Tree* operator has to be replaced with the *Vote* operator from the meta learning folder. All other operators will remain the same. The ensemble process will look similar to the process shown in Fig. 4.60.

The *Vote* operator is an ensemble learner that houses multiple base models in the *inner sub-process*. The model output from the vote process behaves like

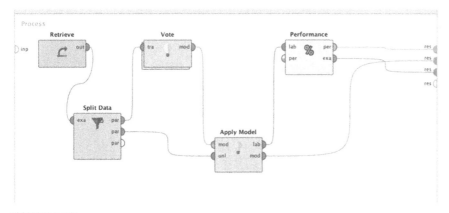

FIGURE 4.60
Data mining process using ensemble model.

any other classification model and it can be applied in any scenario where a decision tree can be used. In the apply model phase, the predicted classes are tallied up amongst all the base classifiers and the class with the highest number of votes is the predicted class for the ensemble model.

On double-clicking the nested *Vote* meta modeling operator, multiple base classification models can be added inside the nested operator. All these models accept the same training set and provide an individual base model as output. In this example three models have been added: decision tree, *k*-NN, and naïve Bayes. Fig. 4.61 shows the inner sub-process of the *Vote* meta modeling operator. The act of tallying all the predictions of these base learners and providing the majority prediction is the job of the meta model—the *Vote* modeling operator. This is the aggregation step in ensemble modeling and in RapidMiner it is called a stacking model. A stacking model is built into the *Vote* operator and is not visible on the screen.

The ensemble process with the *Vote* meta model can be saved and executed. Once the process is executed, the output panel of the performance vector is no different than a normal performance vector. Since this process has a meta model, the model panel in the results window shows new information (Fig. 4.62). The model sub-process shows all the individual base models and one stacking model. The *Vote* meta model is simple to use wherever an individual base model could have been used independently. The limitation of the model is that all the base learners use the same training dataset and different base models impose restrictions on what data types they can accept.

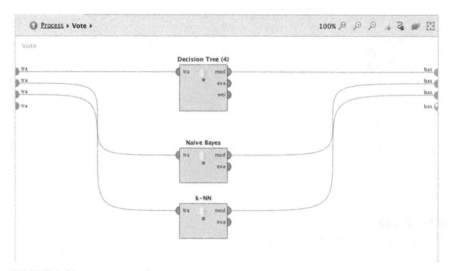

FIGURE 4.61
Sub-process inside the Vote operator.

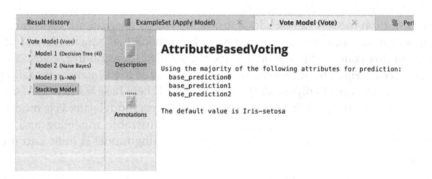

FIGURE 4.62
Output of ensemble model based on voting.

Bootstrap Aggregating or Bagging

Bagging is a technique where base models are developed by changing the training set for every base model. In a given training set T of n records, m training sets are developed each with n records, by sampling with replacement. Each training set T_1, T_2, T_3, ..., T_m will have the same record count of n as the original training set T. Because they are sampled with replacement, they can contain duplicate records. This is called *bootstrapping*. Each sampled training set is then used for a base model preparation. Through bootstrapping, one has a set of m base models and the prediction of each model is aggregated for an ensemble model. This combination of bootstrapping and aggregating is called *bagging*.

On average, each base training set T_i contains about 63% unique training records as compared to the original training set T. Sampling with replacement of n records contains $1 - (1 - 1/n)^n$ unique records. When n is sufficiently large one gets $1 - 1/e = 63.2\%$ unique records on average. The rest of the data contains duplicates from already sampled data. The process of bagging improves the stability of unstable models. Unstable models like decision trees and neural network are highly susceptible even to slight changes in the training data. Because a bagging ensemble combines multiple hypotheses of the same data, the new aggregate hypothesis helps neutralize these training data variations.

Implementation

The *Bagging* operator is available in the meta learning folder: Modeling > Classification and Regression > Meta modeling > Bagging. Like the *Vote* meta operator, *Bagging* is a nested operator with an inner sub-process. Unlike the vote process, bagging has only one model in the inner sub-process. Multiple base models are generated by changing the training dataset internally. The *Bagging* operator has two parameters.

1. *Sample ratio:* Indicates the fraction of records used for training.
2. *Iterations (m):* Number of base modes that need to be generated.

Fig. 4.63 shows the RapidMiner process for the *Bagging* operator. Fig. 4.64 shows the inner sub-process for the *Bagging* operator with one model specification. Internally, multiple base models are generated based on iterations (*m*) configured in the Bagging parameter. The RapidMiner process for bagging can be saved and executed. Similar to the *Vote* meta model, the *Bagging* meta model acts as one model with multiple base models inside. The results window shows the labeled example set, performance vector, and bagging model description. In the results window, all *m* (in this case 10) models can be examined that are developed based on *m* iterations of the training set. The base model results are aggregated using simple voting. Bagging is particularly useful when there is an anomaly in the training dataset that impacts the individual model significantly. Bagging provides a useful framework where the same data science algorithm is used for all base learners. However, each base model differs because the training data used by the base learners are different. Fig. 4.65 shows the model output of the *Bagging* meta model with constituent decision trees.

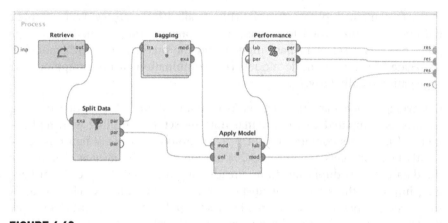

FIGURE 4.63
Ensemble process using bagging.

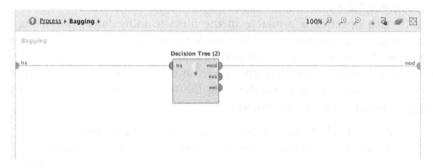

FIGURE 4.64
Bagging sub-process.

Boosting

Boosting offers another approach to building an ensemble model by manipulating training data similar to bagging. As with bagging, it provides a solution to combine many weak learners into one strong learner, by minimizing bias or variance due to training records. Unlike bagging, boosting trains the base models in sequence one by one and assigns weights for all training records. The boosting process concentrates on the training records that are hard to classify and over-represents them in the training set for the next iteration.

The boosting model is built with an iterative and sequential process where a base model is built and tested with all of the training data. Based on the outcome, the next base model is developed. To start with, all training records

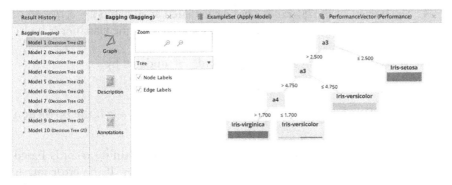

FIGURE 4.65
Output of bagging models.

have equal weight. The weight of the record is used for the sampling selection with replacement. A training sample is selected based on the weight and then used for model building. Then the model is used for testing with the whole training set. Incorrectly classified records are assigned a higher weight so hard-to-classify records have a higher propensity of selection for the next round. The training sample for the next round will be over-represented with incorrectly classified records from the previous iteration. Hence, the next model will focus on the hard-to-classify data space.

Boosting assigns the weight for each training record and has to adaptively change the weight based on the difficulty of classification. This results in an ensemble of base learners specialized in classifying both easy-to-classify and hard-to-classify records. When applying the model, all base learners are combined through a simple voting aggregation.

AdaBoost
AdaBoost is one of the most popular implementations of the boosting ensemble approach. It is adaptive because it assigns weights for base models (α) based on the accuracy of the model and changes the weights of the training records (w) based on the accuracy of the prediction. Here is the framework of the AdaBoost ensemble model with m base classifiers and n training records $((x_1, y_1), (x_2, y_2), \ldots, (x_n, y_n))$. The steps involved in AdaBoost are:

1. Each training record is assigned a uniform weight $w_i = 1/n$.
2. Training records are sampled and the first base classifier $b_k(x)$ is built.
3. The error rate for the base classifier can be calculated by Eq. (4.22):

$$e_k = \sum_{k=1}^{n} w_i \times I\,(b_k(x_i) \neq y_i) \tag{4.22}$$

where $I(x) = 1$ when the prediction is right and 0 when the prediction is incorrect.

4. The weight of the classifier can be calculated as $\alpha_k = \ln\ (1 - e_k)/e_k$. If the model has a low error rate, then the weight of the classifier is high and vice versa.

5. Next, the weights of all training records are updated by:

$$w_{k+1}(i+1) = w_k(i) \times e^{(\alpha_k F(bk(xi) \neq yi)}$$

where $F(x) = -1$ if the prediction is right and $F(x) = 1$ if the prediction is wrong.

Hence, the AdaBoost model updates the weights the training records based on the prediction and the error rate of the base classifier. If the error rate is more than 50%, the record weight is not updated and reverted back to the next round.

Implementation

The *AdaBoost* operator is available in the meta learning folder: Modeling > Classification and Regression > Meta modeling > AdaBoost. The operator functions similar to Bagging and has an inner sub-process. The number of iterations or base models is a configurable parameter for the *AdaBoost* operator. Fig. 4.66 shows the AdaBoost data science process. This example uses the Iris dataset with the *Split Data* operator for generating training and test datasets. The output of the AdaBoost model is applied to the test set and the performance is evaluated by the *Performance* operator.

The number of iterations used in the AdaBoost is ten, which is specified in the parameter. In the inner process, the model type can be specified. In this example the decision tree model is used. The completed RapidMiner process is saved and executed. The result window has the output ensemble model, base models, predicted records, and the performance vector. The model

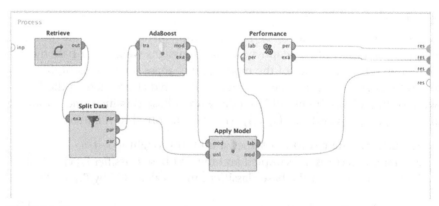

FIGURE 4.66
Data mining process using AdaBoost.

FIGURE 4.67
Output of AdaBoost model.

window shows the decision trees for the base classifiers. Fig. 4.67 shows the result output for the AdaBoost model.

Random Forest

Recall that in the bagging technique, for every iteration, a sample of training records is considered for building the model. The random forest technique uses a concept similar to the one used in bagging. When deciding on splitting each node in a decision tree, the random forest only considers a random subset of the *attributes* in the training set. To reduce the generalization error, the algorithm is randomized in two levels, training record selection and attribute selection, in the inner working of each base classifier. The random forests concept was first put forward by Leo Breiman and Adele Cutler (Breiman, 2001).

In general, the model works using the following steps. If there are n training records with m attributes, and k number of trees in the forest; then for each tree:

1. An *n-size* random sample is selected with replacement. This step is similar to bagging.
2. A number D is selected, where $D \ll m$. D determines the number of attributes to be considered for node splitting.
3. A decision tree is started. For each node, instead of considering all m attributes for the best split, a random number of D attributes are considered. This step is repeated for every node.
4. As in any ensemble, the greater the diversity of the base trees, the lower the error of the ensemble.

Once all the trees in the forest are built, for every new record, all the trees predict a class and vote for the class with equal weights. The most predicted class by the base trees is the prediction of the forest (Gashler, Giraud-Carrier, & Martinez, 2008).

Implementation

The *Random Forest* operator is available in Modeling > Classification and Regression > Tree Induction > Random Forest. It works similarly to the other ensemble models where the user can specify the number of base trees. Since the inner base model is always a decision tree, there is no explicit inner subprocess specification. Bagging or boosting ensemble models require explicit inner sub-process specification. All the tree-specific parameters like leaf size, depth, and split criterion can be specified in the *Random Forest* operator. The key parameter that specifies the number of base trees is *Number of Trees* parameter. Fig. 4.68 shows the RapidMiner process with the Iris dataset, the *Random Forest* modeling operator, and the *Apply Model* operator. For this example, the number of base trees is specified as 10. The process looks and functions similarly to a simple decision tree classifier.

Once the process is executed, the results window shows the model, predicted output, and performance vector. Similar to other meta model outputs, the Random Forest model shows the trees for all base classifiers. Fig. 4.69 shows the model output for the *Random Forest* operator. Notice that the nodes are different in each tree. Since the attribute selection for each node is randomized, each base tree is different. Thus, the Random Forest models strive to reduce the generalization error of the decision tree model. The Random Forest models are extremely useful as a baseline ensemble model for comparative purposes.

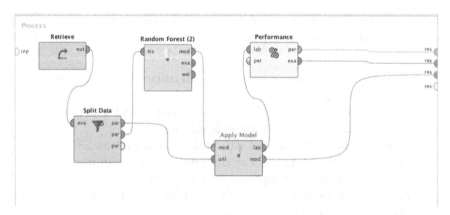

FIGURE 4.68
Data mining process using the Random Forest operator.

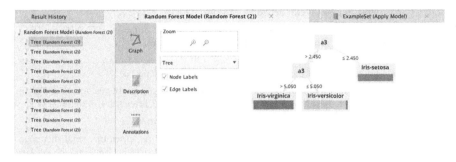

FIGURE 4.69
Output of Random Forest models.

4.7.3 Conclusion

Most of the data science models developed for production applications are built on ensemble models. They are used in a wide range of applications, including political forecasting (Montgomery, Hollenbach, & Ward, 2012), weather pattern modeling, media recommendation, web page ranking (Baradaran Hashemi, Yazdani, Shakery, & Pakdaman Naeini, 2010), etc. Since many algorithms approach the problem of modeling the relationship between input and output differently, it makes sense to aggregate the predictions of a diverse set of approaches. Ensemble modeling reduces the generalization error that arises due to overfitting the training dataset. The four ensemble techniques discussed provide fundamental methods of developing a cohort of base models by choosing different algorithms, changing parameters, changing training records, sampling, and changing attributes. All these techniques can be combined into one ensemble model. There is no one approach for ensemble modeling; all the techniques discussed in this chapter were proven to perform better than base models as long as they are diverse (Polikar, 2006). The wisdom of crowds makes sense in data science as long as "group thinking" is controlled by promoting independence amongst base models.

References

Altman, N. S. (1992). An introduction to kernel and nearest-neighbor nonparametric regression. *The American Statistician, 46*(3), 175−185.

Baradaran Hashemi, H., Yazdani, N., Shakery, A., & Pakdaman Naeini, M. (2010). Application of ensemble models in web ranking. In: *2010 5th International symposium on telecommunications* (pp. 726−731). doi:10.1109/ISTEL.2010.5734118.

Breiman, L. (2001). Random forests. *Machine Learning, 45*, 5−32.

Brieman, L. F. (1984). *Classification and regression trees.* Chapman and Hall.

Cohen W.W. (1995). Fast effective rule induction. Machine learning. In: *Proceedings of the twelfth international conference.*

Cortes, C. A. (1995). Support vector networks. *Machine Learning*, 273–297.

Cover, T. A. (1991). Entropy, relative information, and mutual information. In T. A. Cover (Ed.), *Elements of information theory* (pp. 12–49). John Wiley and Sons.

Dietterich, T.G. *Ensemble methods in machine learning.* (2007). Retrieved from <http://www.eecs.wsu.edu/~holder/courses/CptS570/fall07/papers/Dietterich00.pdf>.

Fisher, R. A. (1936). The use of multiple measurements in taxonomic problems. *Annals of Human Genetics*, 7, 179–188. Available from https://doi.org/10.1111/j.1469-1809.1936.tb02137.x.

Fletcher, R. (1987). *Practical methods of optimization.* New York: John Wiley.

Gashler, M., Giraud-Carrier, C., & Martinez T. (2008) Decision tree ensemble: small heterogeneous is better than large homogeneous. In: *2008 Seventh international conference on machine learning and applications* (pp. 900–905). doi:10.1109/ICMLA.2008.154.

Grabusts, P. (2011). The choice of metrics for clustering algorithms. In: *Proceedings of the 8th international scientific and practical conference II* (1) (pp. 70–76).

Haapanen, R., Lehtinen, K., Miettinen, J., Bauer, M.E., & Ek, A.R. (2001). Progress in adapting *k*-NN methods for forest mapping and estimation using the new annual forest inventory and analysis data. In: *Third annual forest inventory and analysis symposium* (p. 87).

Hill, T., & Lewicki, P. (2007). Statistics methods and applications methods. StatSoft, Inc. Tulsa, OK.

Hsu, C.-W., Chang, C.-C., & Lin, C.-J. (2003). *A practical guide to support vector classification* (4th ed.). Taipei: Department of Computer Science, National Taiwan University.

Laine, A. (2003). *Neural networks. Encyclopedia of computer science* (4th ed., pp. 1233–1239). John Wiley and Sons Ltd.

Langley, P., & Simon, H. A. (1995). Applications of machine learning and rule induction. *Communications of the ACM*, *38*(11), 54–64. doi:10.1145/219717.219768.

Li, E. Y. (1994). Artificial neural networks and their business applications. *Information & Management*, *27*(5), 303–313. Available from https://doi.org/10.1016/0378-7206(94)90024-8.

Matan, O., et al. (1990). Handwritten character recognition using neural network architectures. In: *4th USPS advanced technology conference* (pp. 1003–1011).

McInerney, D. (2005). Remote sensing applications *k*-NN classification. In: *Remote sensing workshop.*   <http://www.forestry.gov.uk/pdf/DanielMcInerneyworkshop.pdf/$FILE/DanielMcInerneyworkshop.pdf> Retrieved on April 27, 2014.

Meagher, P. *Calculating entropy for data mining. PHP Dev Center.* (2005). <http://www.onlamp.com/pub/a/php/2005/01/06/entropy.html?page = 1> Retrieved from O'Reilly OnLamp.com.

Mierswa, I., Wurst, M., Klinkenberg, R., Scholz, M., & Euler, T. (2006). YALE: Rapid prototyping for complex data mining tasks. In: *Proceedings of the ACM SIGKDD international conference on knowledge discovery and data mining* (Vol. 2006, pp. 935–940). doi:10.1145/1150402.1150531.

Montgomery, J. M., Hollenbach, F. M., & Ward, M. D. (2012). Improving predictions using ensemble Bayesian model averaging. *Political Analysis*, *20*(3), 271–291.

Patel, P. *Predicting the future of drought prediction. IEEE Spectrum.* (2012). <http://spectrum.ieee.org/energy/environment/predicting-the-future-of-drought-prediction> Retrieved April 26, 2014.

Peterson, L. *k-Nearest neighbors. Scholarpedia.* (2009). Retrieved from <http://www.scholarpedia.org/article/K-nearest_neighbor>.

Polikar, R. (2006). Ensemble based systems in decision making. *IEEE Circuits and Systems Magazine*, 21–45.

National Drought Mitigation Center. *Predicting drought.* (2013). <http://drought.unl.edu/DroughtBasics/PredictingDrought.aspx> Retrieved April 26, 2014.

Process Software, (2013). Introduction to Bayseian filtering. In: PreciseMail whitepapers (pp. 1−8). Retrieved from <www.process.com>.

Quinlan, J. R. (1986). Induction of decision trees. *Machine Learning, 1*(1), 81−106.

Rish, I. (2001). An empirical study of the naïve Bayes classifier. In: *IBM research report.*

Sahami, M., Dumais, S., Heckerman, D., & Horvitz, E. (1998). A Bayesian approach to filtering junk e-mail. Learning for text categorization. In: *Papers from the 1998 workshop.* vol. 62, pp. 98−105.

Saian, R., & Ku-Mahamud, K. R. (2011) Hybrid ant colony optimization and simulated annealing for rule induction. In: *2011 UKSim 5th European symposium on computer modeling and simulation* (pp. 70−75). doi:10.1109/EMS.2011.17.

Shannon, C. (1948). A mathematical theory of communication. *Bell Systems Technical Journal,* 379−423.

Smola, A. J., & Schölkopf, B. (2004). A tutorial on support vector regression. *Statistics and Computing, 14*(3), 199−222.

Tan, P.-N., Michael, S., & Kumar, V. (2005). Classfication and classification: Alternative techniques. In P.-N. Tan, S. Michael, & V. Kumar (Eds.), *Introduction to data mining* (pp. 145−315). Boston, MA: Addison-Wesley.

Zdziarski, J. A. (2005). *Ending spam: Bayesian content filtering and the art of statistical language classification.* No Starch Press.

CHAPTER 5

Regression Methods

In this chapter, one of the most commonly used data science techniques—fitting data with functions or *function fitting* will be explored. The basic idea behind function fitting is to predict the value (or class) of a dependent attribute y, by combining the predictor attributes **X** into a function, $y = f(\mathbf{X})$. Function fitting involves many different techniques and the most common ones are *linear regression* for numeric prediction and *logistic regression* for classification. These two, form the majority of the material in this chapter. Regression models continue to be one of the most common analytics tools used by practitioners today.[1]

Regression is a relatively old technique dating back to the Victorian era (1830s to the early 1900s). Much of the pioneering work was done by Sir Francis Galton, a distant relative of Charles Darwin, who came up with the concept of *regressing toward the mean* while systematically comparing children's heights against their parents' heights. He observed there was a strong tendency for tall parents to have children slightly shorter than themselves, and for short parents to have children slightly taller than themselves. Even if the parents' heights were at the tail ends of a bell curve or normal distribution, their children's heights tended toward the mean of the distribution. Thus, in the end, all the samples regressed toward a population mean. Therefore, this trend was called *regression* by Galton (Galton, 1888) and, thus, the foundations for linear regression were laid.

In the first section of this chapter, the theoretical framework for the simplest of function-fitting methods: the *linear regression model*, will be provided. The main focus will be on a case study that demonstrates how to build regression models. Due to the nature of the function-fitting approach, one limitation

---

[1] Rexer Analytics survey available from http://www.rexeranalytics.com.

Data Science. DOI: https://doi.org/10.1016/B978-0-12-814761-0.00005-8

that modelers have to deal with is what is called the *curse of dimensionality*. As the number of predictors **X**, increases, not only will our ability to obtain a good model reduce, it also adds computational and interpretational complexity. *Feature selection* methods will be introduced that can reduce the number of predictors or factors required to a minimum and still obtain a good model. The mechanics of implementation, will be explored, to do the data preparation, model building, and validation. Finally, in closing some checkpoints to ensure that linear regression is used correctly will be described.

In the second section of this chapter *logistic regression* will be discussed. Strictly speaking, it is a classification technique, closer in its application to decision trees or Bayesian methods. But it shares an important characteristic with linear regression in its function-fitting methodology and, thus, merits inclusion in this chapter, rather than the previous one on classification.

5.1   LINEAR REGRESSION

Linear regression is not only one of the oldest data science methodologies, but it also the most easily explained method for demonstrating function

PREDICTING HOME PRICES

What features would play a role in deciding the value of a home? For example, locality, the number of rooms, its age, the quality of schools in the vicinity, its location with respect to major sources of employment, and its accessibility to major highways, are some of the important considerations most potential home buyers would like to factor in. But which of these are the most significant influencers of the price? Is there a way to determine these? Once these factors are known, can they be incorporated into a model that can be used for predictions? The case study that will be discussed later in this chapter addresses this problem, using multiple linear regressions to predict the median home prices in an urban region given the characteristics of a home.

A common goal that all businesses have to address in order to be successful is growth, in revenues and profits. Customers are what will enable this to happen. Understanding and increasing the likelihood that someone will buy again from the company is, therefore, critical. Another question that would help strategically, for example in customer segmentation, is being able to predict how much money a customer is likely to spend, based on data about their previous purchase habits. Two very important distinctions need to be made here: understanding why someone purchased from the company will fall into the realm of *explanatory modeling*, whereas, predicting how much someone is likely to spend will fall into the realm of predictive modeling. Both these types of models fall under a broader category of *surrogate* or empirical models which relies on historical data to develop rules of behavior as opposed to *system* models which use fundamental principles (such as laws of physics or chemistry) to develop rules. See Fig. 1.2 for a taxonomy of data science. In this chapter, the predictive capability of models will be focused on as opposed to the explanatory capabilities. Historically much of applied linear regression in statistics has been used for explanatory needs. Later on in this chapter with the case of logistic regression, it will be demonstrated, how *both* needs can be met with good analytical interpretation of models.

(Continued)

(Continued)

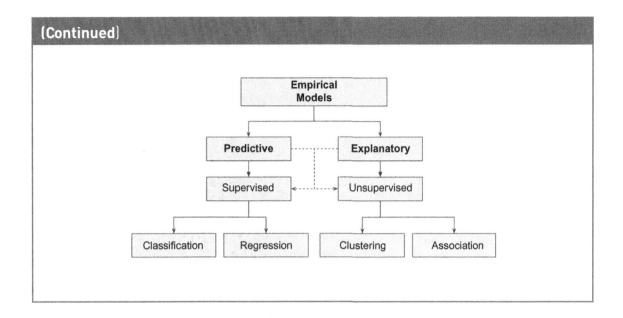

fitting. The basic idea is to come up with a function that explains and pre-dicts the value of the target variable when given the values of the predictor variables.

5.1.1   How it Works

A simple example is shown in Fig. 5.1: if one would like to know the effect of the number of rooms in a house (predictor) on its median sale price (tar-get). Each data point on the chart corresponds to a house (Harrison, 1978). It is evident that on average, increasing the number of rooms tends to also increase median price. This general statement can be captured by drawing a straight line through the data. The problem in linear regression is, therefore, finding a line (or a curve) that best explains this tendency. If there are two predictors, then the problem is to find a surface (in a three-dimensional space). With more than two predictors, visualization becomes difficult and one has to revert to a general statement where the dependent variables are expressed as a linear combination of independent variables:

$$y = b_0 + b_1 x_1 + b_2 x_2 + \cdots + b_n x_n \qquad (5.1)$$

Consider the problem with one predictor. Clearly, one can fit an infinite number of straight lines through a given set of points such as the ones shown in Fig. 5.1. How does one know which one is the best? A metric is

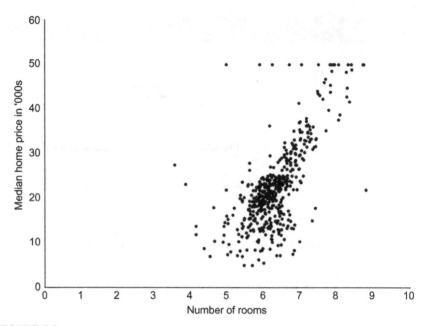

FIGURE 5.1
A simple regression model.

needed, one that helps quantify the different straight line fits through the data. Once this metric is found, then selecting the best line becomes a matter of finding the optimum value for this quantity.

A commonly used metric is the concept of an error function. Suppose one fits a straight line through the data. In a single predictor case, the *predicted* value, $\hat{y}$, for a value of x that exists in the dataset is then given by:

$$\hat{y} = b_0 + b_1 x \qquad (5.2)$$

Then, error is simply the difference between the actual target value and predicted target value:

$$e = y - \hat{y} = y - (b_0 + b_1 x) \qquad (5.3)$$

This equation defines the error at a single location (x, y) in the dataset. One could easily compute the error for all existing points to come up with an aggregate error. Some errors will be positive, and others will be negative. The difference can be squared to eliminate the sign bias and an average error for a given fit can be calculated as:

$$\frac{J}{n} = \frac{\sum e^2}{n} = \frac{\sum (y_i - \hat{y}_i)^2}{n} = \frac{\sum (y_i - b_0 - b_i x_i)^2}{n} \qquad (5.4)$$

where n represents the number of points in the dataset. J is the total squared error. For a given dataset, the best combination of (b_0, b_1) can then be found, which minimizes the total error, e. This is a classical minimization problem, which is handled with methods of calculus. Stigler provides some interesting historical details on the origins of the method of least squares, as it is known (Stigler, 1999). Using the methods of calculus, the values of b can be found, which minimize the total error J. Specifically, one can take partial derivatives of J with respect to b_1 and b_0 and set them equal to zero. Chain rule of differential calculus gives us:

$$\partial J/\partial b_1 = \partial J/\partial \hat{y} \ \ \partial \hat{y}/\partial b_1$$
$$\Rightarrow \partial J/\partial b_1 = 2(\Sigma(y_i - b_0 - b_1 x_i))\partial \hat{y}/\partial b_1 = 0$$
$$\Rightarrow \Sigma(y_i - b_0 - b_1 x_i)(-x_i) = 0$$
$$\Rightarrow -\Sigma(y_i x_i) + \Sigma(b_0 x_i) + \Sigma(b_1 x^2{}_i) = 0$$
$$\Rightarrow \Sigma(y_i x_i) = b_0 \Sigma(x_i) + b_1 \Sigma(x^2{}_i) \tag{5.5}$$

Similarly, one can use:

$$\partial J/\partial b_0 = 2(\Sigma(y_i - b_0 - b_1 x))\partial \hat{y}/\partial b_0 = 0$$
$$\Rightarrow \Sigma(y_i - b_0 - b_1 x_i)(-1) = 0$$
$$\Rightarrow -\Sigma(y_i) + \Sigma(b_0.1) + \Sigma(b_1 x_i)1 = 0$$
$$\Rightarrow -\Sigma(y_i) + b_0 \Sigma(1) + b_1 \Sigma(x_i) = 0$$
$$\Rightarrow \Sigma(y_i) = b_0 N + b_1 \Sigma(x_i) \tag{5.6}$$

Eqs. (5.5) and (5.6) are two equations in two unknowns, b_0 and b_1, which can be further simplified and solved to yield the expressions:

$$b_1 = (\Sigma x_i y_i - \bar{y}\Sigma x_i)/(\Sigma x^2{}_i - \bar{x} - \Sigma x_i) \tag{5.7}$$

$$b_0 = (\bar{y}\Sigma x^2{}_i - \bar{x}\Sigma x_i y_i)/(\Sigma x^2{}_i - \bar{x}\Sigma x_i) \tag{5.8}$$

b_1 can also be written as (5.9a):

$$b_1 = \text{Correlation } (y, x) \times \frac{s_y}{s_x} \tag{5.9a}$$

$$b_0 = y_{\text{mean}} - b_1 \times x_{\text{mean}} \tag{5.9b}$$

where Correlation(x, y) is the correlation between x and y and s_y, s_x are the standard deviations of y and x. Finally, x_{mean} and y_{mean} are the respective mean values.

Practical linear regression algorithms use an optimization technique known as *gradient descent* (Fletcher, 1963; Marquardt, 1963) to identify the combination of b_0 and b_1 which will minimize the error function given in Eq. (5.4). The advantage of using such methods is that even with several predictors, the optimization works fairly robustly. When such a process is applied to the simple example shown, one gets an equation of the form:

Median price $= 9.1 \times$ (*number of rooms*) $- 34.7$ (5.10)

where b_1 is 9.1 and b_0 is -34.7. From this equation, it can be calculated that for a house with six rooms, the value of the median price is about 20 (the prices are expressed in thousands of US dollars, c. 1970). In Fig. 5.1 it's evident that for a house with six rooms, the actual price can range between 10.5 and 25. An infinite number of lines could have been fit in this band, which would have all predicted a median price within this range—but the algorithm chooses the line that minimizes the average error over the full range of the independent variable and is, therefore, the best fit for the given dataset.

For some of the points (houses) shown in Fig. 5.1 (at the top of the chart, where median price = 50) the median price appears to be independent of the number of rooms. This could be because there may be other factors that also influence the price. Thus, more than one predictor will need to be modeled and *multiple linear regression (MLR)*, which is an extension of simple linear regression, will need to be used. The algorithm to find the coefficients of the regression Eq. (5.1) can be easily extended to more than one dimension.

The single variable expression for error function in (5.4) can be generalized to multiple variables quite easily, $\hat{y}_i = b_0 + b_1 x_1 + \dots + b_D x_D$. If we let $x = [x_0, x_1, \dots, x_D]$ and recognize that the intercept term can be written as $b_0 x_0$ where $x_0 = 1$, then we can write (5.4) as $E = \sum_{i=1}^{N}(y_i - B^T x_i)^2$ where B is a vector of weights $[b_0, b_1, \dots, b_D]$ for a dataset with D columns or features and N samples. Similar to how we computed (5.7) and (5.8), we can take a derivative of E with respect to each weight B and will end up with D equations to be solved for D weights (one corresponding to each feature). The partial derivative for each weight is

$$\partial E / \partial b_j = \partial E / \partial \hat{y} * \partial \hat{y}_i / \partial b_j$$
$$\Rightarrow \partial E / \partial b_j = 2\Sigma(y_i - B^T x_i)\partial \hat{y}_i / \partial b_j$$
$$\Rightarrow \partial E / \partial b_j = 2\Sigma(y_i - B^T x_i)(-x_i)$$
$$\Rightarrow \Sigma y_i(-x_i) - B^T \Sigma(x_i)(-x_i)$$

When we consider all D weights at the same time, this can be very simply written in matrix form as follows:

$$\partial E / \partial B = -(Y^T X) + B(X^T X) \tag{5.11}$$

Here B is a $1 \times D$ matrix or vector. As in the case of simple linear regression, we can set this derivative to zero, to solve for the weights, B and get the following expression: $-(Y^T X) + B(X^T X) = 0$. In this case, solving for B now becomes a matrix inversion problem and results in $B = (X^T X)^{-1} Y^T X$. The reader can verify as an exercise that this matrix is dimensionally consistent (Hint: Use the fact that the matrix shape of X is $N \times D$, Y is $N \times 1$ and B is $1 \times D$). MLR can be applied in any situation where a numeric prediction, for example "how much will something sell for," is required. This is in contrast to making categorical predictions such as "will someone buy/not buy" or "will/will not fail," where classification tools such as decision trees or logistic regression models are used. In order to ensure regression models are not arbitrarily deployed, several checks must be performed on the model to ensure that the regression is accurate which will be the focus of a later section in this chapter.

Table 5.1 Sample View of the Classic Boston Housing Dataset

CRIM	ZN	INDUS	CHAS	NOX	RM	AGE	DIS	RAD	TAX	PTRATIO	B	LSTAT	Target = MEDV
0.00632	18	2.31	0	0.538	6.575	65.2	4.09	1	296	15.3	396.9	4.98	24
0.02731	0	7.07	0	0.469	6.421	78.9	4.9671	2	242	17.8	396.9	9.14	21.6
0.02729	0	7.07	0	0.469	7.185	61.1	4.9671	2	242	17.8	392.83	4.03	34.7
0.03237	0	2.18	0	0.458	6.998	45.8	6.0622	3	222	18.7	394.63	2.94	33.4
0.06905	0	2.18	0	0.458	7.147	54.2	6.0622	3	222	18.7	396.9	5.33	36.2
0.02985	0	2.18	0	0.458	6.43	58.7	6.0622	3	222	18.7	394.12	5.21	28.7
0.08829	12.5	7.87	0	0.524	6.012	66.6	5.5605	5	311	15.2	395.6	12.43	22.9
0.14455	12.5	7.87	0	0.524	6.172	96.1	5.9505	5	311	15.2	396.9	19.15	27.1

Table 5.2 Attributes of Boston Housing Dataset

1. CRIM per capita crime rate by town
2. ZN proportion of residential land zoned for lots over 25,000 sq.ft.
3. INDUS proportion of non-retail business acres per town
4. CHAS Charles River dummy variable (=1 if tract bounds river; 0 otherwise)
5. NOX nitric oxide concentrations (parts per 10 million)
6. RM average number of rooms per dwelling
7. AGE proportion of owner-occupied units built prior to 1940
8. DIS weighted distances to five Boston employment centers
9. RAD index of accessibility to radial highways
10. TAX full-value property-tax rate per $10,000
11. PTRATIO pupil-teacher ratio by town
12. B 1000(Bk − 0.63)^2 where Bk is the proportion of blacks by town
13. LSTAT percent lower status of the population
14. MEDV Median value of owner-occupied homes in $1000's

The housing example can be extended in order to include additional variables. This comes from a study of urban environments conducted in the late 1970s[2] (Harrison, 1978). The objectives of this are:

1. Identify which of the several attributes are required to accurately predict the median price of a house.
2. Build a multiple linear regression model to predict the median price using the most important attributes.

The original data consist of thirteen predictors and one response variable, which is the variable that needs to be predicted. The predictors include physical characteristics of the house (such as number of rooms, age, tax, and location) and neighborhood features (schools, industries, zoning) among others. The response variable is of course the median value (MEDV) of the house in thousands of dollars. Table 5.1 shows a snapshot of the dataset, which has altogether 506 examples. Table 5.2 describes the features or attributes of the dataset.

---

[2] http://archive.ics.uci.edu/ml/datasets/Housing.

5.1.2   How to Implement

In this section, how to set up a RapidMiner process to build a multiple linear regression model for the Boston Housing dataset will be demonstrated. The following will be described:

1. Building a linear regression model
2. Measuring the performance of the model
3. Understanding the commonly used options for the *Linear Regression* operator
4. Applying the model to predict MEDV prices for unseen data

Step 1: Data Preparation

As a first step, the data is separated into a training set and an unseen test set. The idea is to build the model with the training data and test its performance on the unseen data. With the help of the *Retrieve* operator, import the raw data (available in the companion website www.IntroDataScience.com) into the RapidMiner process. Apply the *Shuffle* operator to randomize the order of the data so that when the two partitions are seperated, they are statistically similar. Next, using the *Filter Examples Range* operator, divide the data into two sets as shown in Fig. 5.2. The raw data has 506 examples, which will be linearly split into a training set (from row 1 to 450) and a test set (row 451−506) using the two operators.

Insert the *Set Role* operator, change the role of MEDV to label and connect the output to a *Split Validation* operator's input training port as shown in Fig. 5.3. The training data is now going to be further split into a training set and a validation set (keep the default Split Validation options as

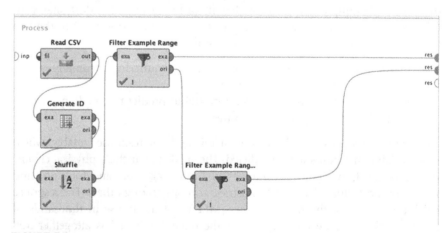

FIGURE 5.2
Separating the data into training and testing samples.

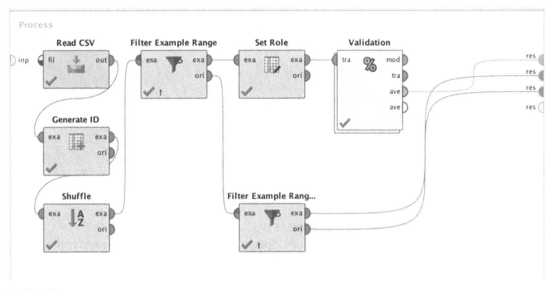

FIGURE 5.3
Using the split validation operator.

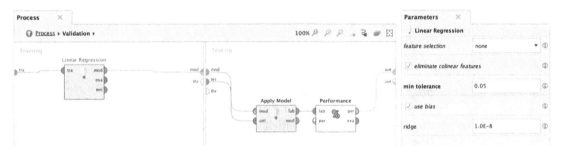

FIGURE 5.4
Applying the linear regression operator and measuring performance.

is, i.e., *relative*, *0.7*, and *shuffled*). This will be needed in order to measure the performance of the linear regression model. It is also a good idea to set the local random seed (to default the value of 1992), which ensures that RapidMiner selects the same samples if this process is run at a later time.

After this step, double-click the *Validation* operator to enter the nested process. Inside this process insert the *Linear Regression* operator on the left window and *Apply Model* and *Performance (Regression)* in the right window as shown in Fig. 5.4. Click on the *Performance* operator and check squared error, correlation, and squared correlation inside the Parameters options selector on the right (Fig. 5.5).

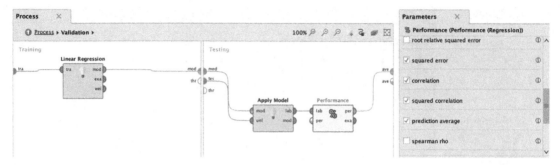

FIGURE 5.5
Selecting performance criteria for the MLR.

Step 2: Model Building

Select the *Linear Regression* operator and change the *feature selection* option to none. Keep the default eliminate collinear features checked, which will remove factors that are linearly correlated from the modeling process. When two or more attributes are correlated to one another, the resulting model will tend to have coefficients that cannot be intuitively interpreted and, furthermore, the statistical significance of the coefficients also tends to be quite low. Also keep the use bias checked to build a model with an intercept [the b_0 in Eq. (5.2)]. Keep the other default options intact (Fig. 5.4).

When this process is run the results shown in Fig. 5.6 will be generated.

Step 3: Execution and Interpretation

There are two views that one can examine in the *Linear Regression* output tab: the Description view, which actually shows the function that is fitted (Fig. 5.6A) and the more useful Data view, which not only shows the coefficients of the linear regression function, but also gives information about the significance of these coefficients (Fig. 5.6B). The best way to read this table is to sort it by double-clicking on the column named Code, which will sort the different factors according to their decreasing level of significance. RapidMiner assigns four stars (****) to any factor that is highly significant.

In this model, no *feature selection* method was used and as a result all 13 factors are in the model, including AGE and INDUS, which have very low significance. However, if the same model were to be run by selecting any of the options that are available in the drop-down menu of the *feature selection* parameter, RapidMiner would have removed the least significant factors from the model. In the next iteration, the *greedy* feature selection is used, and this will have removed the least significant factors, INDUS and AGE, from the function (Fig. 5.7A & B).

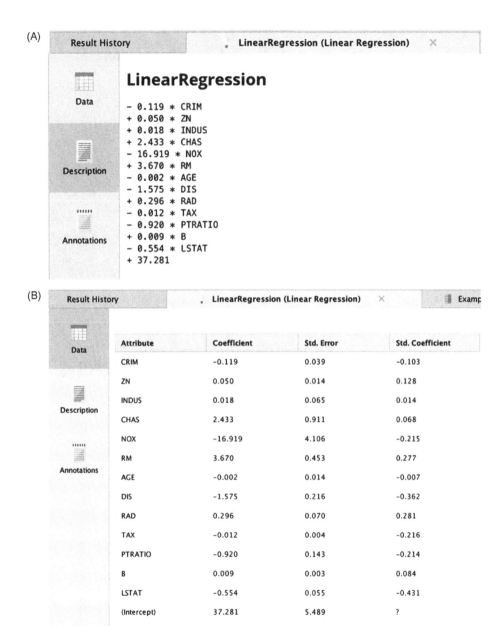

(A)

LinearRegression

```
- 0.119 * CRIM
+ 0.050 * ZN
+ 0.018 * INDUS
+ 2.433 * CHAS
- 16.919 * NOX
+ 3.670 * RM
- 0.002 * AGE
- 1.575 * DIS
+ 0.296 * RAD
- 0.012 * TAX
- 0.920 * PTRATIO
+ 0.009 * B
- 0.554 * LSTAT
+ 37.281
```

(B)

Attribute	Coefficient	Std. Error	Std. Coefficient
CRIM	−0.119	0.039	−0.103
ZN	0.050	0.014	0.128
INDUS	0.018	0.065	0.014
CHAS	2.433	0.911	0.068
NOX	−16.919	4.106	−0.215
RM	3.670	0.453	0.277
AGE	−0.002	0.014	−0.007
DIS	−1.575	0.216	−0.362
RAD	0.296	0.070	0.281
TAX	−0.012	0.004	−0.216
PTRATIO	−0.920	0.143	−0.214
B	0.009	0.003	0.084
LSTAT	−0.554	0.055	−0.431
(Intercept)	37.281	5.489	?

FIGURE 5.6

(A) Description of the linear regression model. (B) Tabular view of the model. Sort the table according to significance by double-clicking on the Code column.

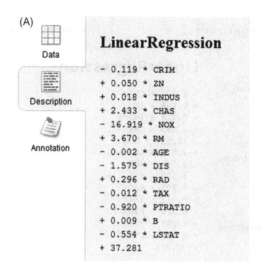

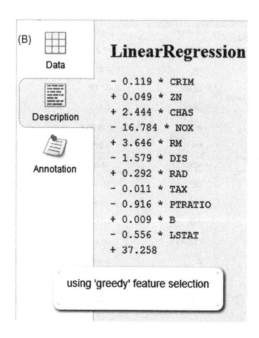

FIGURE 5.7

(A) Model without any feature selection. (B) Model with greedy feature selection.

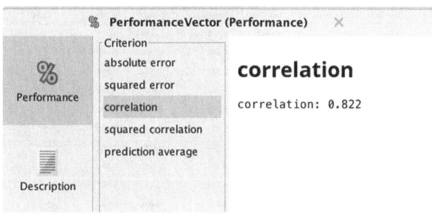

FIGURE 5.8
Generating the r^2 for the model.

Feature selection in RapidMiner can be done automatically within the *Linear Regression* operator as described or by using external wrapper functions such as forward selection and backward elimination. These will be discussed separately in Chapter 14, Feature Selection.

The second output to pay attention to is the Performance: a handy check to test the goodness of fit in a regression model is the *squared correlation*. Conventionally this is the same as the adjusted r^2 for a model, which can take values between 0.0 and 1.0, with values closer to 1 indicating a better model. For either of the models shown above, a value around 0.822 can be obtained (Fig. 5.8). The squared error output was also requested: the raw value in itself may not reveal much, but this is useful in comparing two different models. In this case it was around 25.

One additional insight that can be extracted from the modeling process is ranking of the factors. The easiest way to check this is to rank by *p*-value. As seen in Fig. 5.9, RM, LSTAT, and DIS seem to be the most significant factors. This is also reflected in their absolute *t*-stat values. The *t*-stat and *P*-values are the result of the hypothesis tests conducted on the regression coefficients. For the purposes of predictive analysis, the key takeaway is that a higher *t*-stat signals that the null hypothesis—which assumes that the coefficient is zero—can be safely rejected. The corresponding *p*-value indicates the probability of wrongly rejecting the null hypothesis. Its already been noted how the number of rooms (RM) was a good predictor of the home prices, but it was unable to explain all of the variations in median price. The r^2 and squared

Attribute	Coefficient	Std. Error	Std. Coeff...	Tolerance	t–Stat	p–Value ↑	Code
LSTAT	-0.556	0.052	-0.432	0.490	-10.661	0	****
RM	3.646	0.443	0.275	0.581	8.236	0.000	****
DIS	-1.579	0.199	-0.363	0.823	-7.928	0.000	****
(Intercept)	37.258	5.440	?	?	6.849	0.000	****
PTRATIO	-0.916	0.140	-0.213	0.793	-6.547	0.000	****
NOX	-16.784	3.794	-0.213	0.812	-4.424	0.000	****
RAD	0.292	0.068	0.276	0.769	4.318	0.000	****
ZN	0.049	0.014	0.128	0.877	3.465	0.001	****
TAX	-0.011	0.004	-0.208	0.749	-3.219	0.001	***
CRIM	-0.119	0.039	-0.103	0.843	-3.088	0.002	***
B	0.009	0.003	0.083	0.905	2.953	0.003	***
CHAS	2.444	0.905	0.068	0.991	2.701	0.007	***

FIGURE 5.9
Ranking variables by their *P*-values.

error for that one-variable model were 0.405 and 45, respectively. This can be verified by rerunning the model built so far using only one independent variable, the number of rooms, RM. This is done by using the *Select Attributes* operator, which has to be inserted in the process before the *Set Role* operator. When this model is run, the equation shown earlier, Eq. (5.10), will be obtained in the model *Description*. By comparing the corresponding values from the MLR model (0.676 and 25) to the simple linear regression model, it's evident that both of these quantities have improved, thus, affirming the decision to use multiple factors.

One now has a more comprehensive model that can account for much of the variability in the response variable, MEDV. Finally, a word about the sign of the coefficients: LSTAT refers to the percentage of low-income households in the neighborhood. A lower LSTAT is correlated with higher median home price, and this is the reason for the negative coefficient on LSTAT.

Step 4: Application to Unseen Test Data

This model is now ready to be deployed against the unseen data that was created at the beginning of this section using the second *Filter Examples* operator (Fig. 5.2). A new *Set Role* operator will need to be added, select MEDV under parameters and set it to target role prediction from the pull-down menu. Add another *Apply Model* operator and connect the output of *Set Role* to its unlabeled port; additionally, connect the output model from the Validation

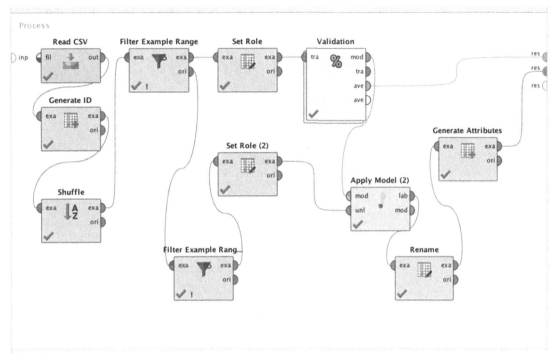

FIGURE 5.10
Setting up a process to do the comparison between the unseen data and the model predicted values.

process to the input model port of the new *Apply Model*. What has been done is, the attribute MEDV has been changed from the unseen set of 56 examples to a prediction. When the model is applied to this example set, one will be able to compare the prediction (MEDV) values to the original MEDV values (which exist in the set) to test how well the model would behave on new data. The difference between prediction (MEDV) and MEDV is termed residual. Fig. 5.10 shows one way to quickly check the residuals for the models application. A *Rename* operator would be needed to change the name of "prediction (MEDV)" to predictedMEDV to avoid confusing RapidMiner when the next operator, *Generate Attributes*, is used to calculate residuals (try without using the *Rename* operator to understand this issue as it can pop up in other instances where *Generate Attributes* is used). Fig. 5.11 shows the statistics for the new attribute residuals which indicate that the mean is close to 0 (-0.27) but the standard deviation (and hence, variance) at 4.350 is not quite small. The histogram also seems to indicate that the residuals are not quite normally distributed, which would be another motivation to continue to improve the model.

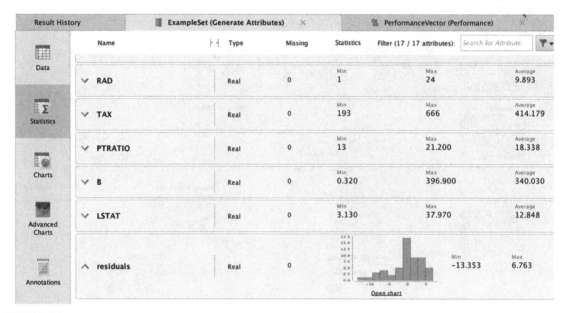

FIGURE 5.11
Statistics of the residuals for the unseen data show that some model optimization may be necessary.

5.1.3   Checkpoints

This section on linear regression can be wrapped up with a brief discussion of several checkpoints to ensure that any models are valid. This is a critical step in the analytics process because all modeling follows the garbage in, garbage out (GIGO) dictum. It is incumbent upon the data scientist to ensure these checks are completed.

Checkpoint 1: One of the first checkpoints to consider before accepting any regression model is to quantify the r^2, which is also known as the coefficient of determination which effectively explains how much variability in the dependent variable is explained by the independent variables (Black, 2008). In most cases of linear regression, the r^2 value lies between 0 and 1. The ideal range for r^2 varies across applications; for example, in social and behavioral science models typically low values are acceptable. Generally, extremely low values ($\sim$ <0.2) indicate that the variables in the model do not explain the outcome satisfactorily. A word of caution about overemphasizing the value of r^2: when the intercept is set to zero (in RapidMiner, when one unchecks *use bias*, Fig. 5.5), r^2 values tend to be inflated because of the manner in which they are calculated. In such situations where a zero intercept are required, it makes sense to use other checks such as the mean and variance of the residuals.

The most common metric used for measuring how well a regression model fits the data is by using the coefficient of determination, r^2. This is defined as:

$$r^2 = 1 - \text{SSE}/\text{SSYY} \tag{5.12}$$

SSE is simply the sum of squared errors which is given by $\sum e^2$ in Eq. (5.4). SSYY is the aggregate mean deviation defined by:

$$\text{SSYY} = \sum (y - \bar{y})^2 \tag{5.13}$$

Intuitively, it is easy to see that if SSE is close to zero, then r^2 is close to 1—a perfect fit. If SSE is close to SSYY then r^2 is close to zero—the model is simply predicting the average value of y for all values of x. The nice thing about r^2 is that because it only depends on y and not the weights or independent variables, it can be used for any form of regression model: simple or multiple.

Checkpoint 2: This leads to the next check, which is to ensure that all error terms in the model are normally distributed. To do this check in RapidMiner, a new attribute called error can be generated, which is the difference between the predicted MEDV and the actual MEDV in the test dataset. This can be done using the *Generate Attributes* operator. This is what was done in step 5 in the last section. Passing checks 1 and 2 will ensure that the independent and dependent variables are related. However, this does not imply that the independent variable is the cause and the dependent is the effect. Remember that *correlation is not causation*!

Checkpoint 3: Highly nonlinear relationships, result in simple regression models failing these checks. However, this does not mean that the two variables are not related. In such cases it may become necessary to resort to somewhat more advanced analytical methods to test the relationship. This is best described and motivated by Anscombe's quartet, presented in Chapter 3, Data Exploration.

Checkpoint 4: In addition to testing the goodness of a model fit using r^2, it is also important to ensure that there is no *overfitting* of data. Overfitting refers to the process of developing a model that is so well tuned to represent the training data that its least squares error is as low as possible, but this error becomes high when the model is used on unseen or new data. That is, the model fails to generalize. The following example illustrates this and also develops intuition for avoiding such behavior by using what is called Regularization.

Consider some sample data which represent an underlying simple function $y = 3x + 1$. If the data were to be plotted it would look like Fig. 5.12.

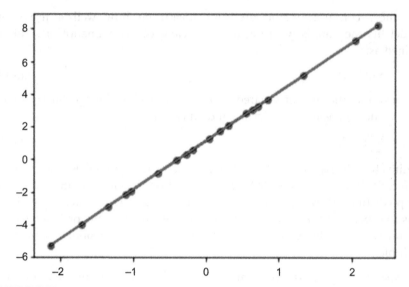

FIGURE 5.12
Linear regression line.

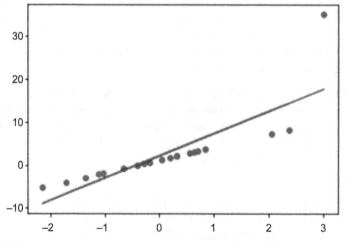

FIGURE 5.13
Linear regression line with an outlier.

A regression model could be fit to this data and a nice linear fit obtained, as shown by the line, as well as obtaining the following coefficients: $b_0 = 1.13$ and $b_1 = 3.01$, which is close to the underlying function. Now suppose that there is a new data point [3, 30] which is somewhat of an outlier and now the model has to be refit, the results would be similar to those shown in Fig. 5.13.

Compared to the previous fit, the outlier tends to pull the fitted line up toward the outlying point. In other words, as the model tries to minimize the squared distance between it and every point, a few outlying points tend to exert a disproportionate influence on the model's characteristics.

Another way to look at this is that the model tries to fit all the training data points to the best of its ability or causes *overfitting*. A consequence of overfitting is that the overall error on the training data will be minimized, but if the same model is tried on new data points (which were not used for training), the error tends to increase till it's out of proportion. One symptom of overfitting is the generation of large coefficients. In the example above, these coefficients are now $b_0 = 2.14$ and $b_1 = 6.93$, that is, they have increased by a factor of nearly 2 or more in each case

In order to avoid overfitting by ensuring that none of the weights or coefficients become large, one can add a penalty factor to the cost function that penalizes large weights. This process is known as *Ridge regression or L2-norm regularization*. The penalty includes the sum of the squared magnitude of all weights, $||b||^2 = b^2{}_1 + b^2{}_2 + \ldots$, that is, *L2-Norm* of b_m, where m is the number of attributes.

The cost function is modified as shown:

$$J_{RIDGE} = \Sigma N_i = (y_i - B^T x_i)^2 + \lambda |b|^2 \tag{5.14}$$

By following the usual steps and switching to a matrix form shown earlier, one arrives at the new solution for the weights as:

$$B = (\lambda I + X^T X)^{-1} X^T Y \tag{5.15}$$

where I is the identity matrix and λ is a penalty factor > 0.

Compare this to the standard solution that can be derived from Eq. (5.11):

$$B = (X^T X)^{-1} Y^T X. \tag{5.16}$$

When L2-norm is implemented, the fit looks much improved and the coefficients are $b_0 = 1.5$ and $b_1 = 4.02$ which are closer to the underlying function (shown in Fig. 5.14).

Ridge regression tends to push all the weights toward zero in order to minimize the cost function.

There is another scenario of overfitting, that involves selecting more than the optimal number of independent variables (and, thus, weights). Not all features exert the same influence on the predicted outcome, some features have more influence than others. However, as more features are included in a model, the training error continues to reduce. But the test error may spiral out of control and result in another form of overfitting.

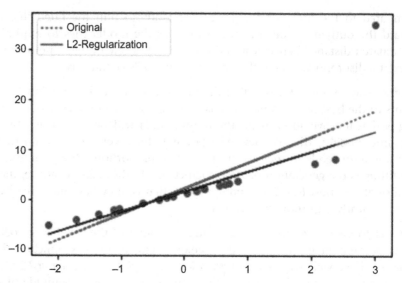

FIGURE 5.14
L2-regularization.

Lasso regression or *L1-norm regularization* addresses this concern where the goal is to select the optimal number of features. The formulation is similar to Ridge, but using the L1-norm: $||b|| = |b_1| + |b_2| + \cdots$

$$J_{LASSO} = \Sigma N_i = (y_i - B^T x_i)^2 + \lambda |b| \tag{5.17}$$

Sometimes the features are correlated with each other—when this happens the $X^T X$ matrix becomes singular and the closed form solution cannot be used. However, this should not be any concern if gradient descent is used to approximate the solution. Gradient descent is a technique that allows us to incrementally evaluate the coefficients, **b** for which the error **J** is minimized, when obtaining a closed form derivative for **dJ/db** is not possible. The idea is to take small computational steps toward the direction of minimum J by choosing the fastest path. In this case we can however get the derivative of the error function in closed form, which turns out to be:

$$\partial J/\partial b = -2X^T Y + 2X^T X b + \lambda \text{sign}(b) = 0 \tag{5.18}$$

here $\text{sign}(b) = 1$ if $b > 0$, -1 if $b < 0$, 0 if $b = 0$.

Typically for practical situations, such closed form derivatives are seldom available and the gradient descent formulation is the alternative. The final gradient descent setup for both types of regularization are:

LASSO or L1:

$$b_{i+1} = b_i - \eta X^T(Y - \hat{Y}) + \lambda \times \text{sign}(b_i) \tag{5.19}$$

RIDGE or L2:

$$b_{i+1} = b_i - \eta X^T(Y - \hat{Y}) + \lambda \times b_i \tag{5.20}$$

where η is the same *learning rate* parameter that crops up in neural networks (Chapter 4: Classification) and deep learning (Chapter 10). The number of steps, i is determined by the rate of convergence of the solution or by other stopping criteria. In RapidMiner, Rigde regression is implemented by providing a non-zero penalty factor in the box for 'ridge' under parameters—see Fig. 5.4.

5.2 LOGISTIC REGRESSION

From a historical perspective, there are two main classes of data science techniques: those that evolved (Cramer, 2002) from statistics (such as regression) and those that emerged from a blend of statistics, computer science, and mathematics (such as classification trees). Logistic regression arose in the mid-twentieth century as a result of the simultaneous development of the concept of the *logit* in the field of biometrics and the advent of the digital computer, which made computations of such terms easy. So, to understand logistic regression, the logit concept first needs to be explored. The chart in Fig. 5.15, adapted from data shown in Cramer (2002) shows the evolving trend from initial acceptance of the logit concept in the mid-1950s to the surge in references to this concept toward the latter half of the twentieth century. The chart is an indicator of how important logistic regression has become over the last few decades in a variety of scientific and business applications.

To introduce the logit, a simple example will be used. Recall that linear regression is the process of finding a function to fit the x's that vary linearly with y with the objective of being able to use the function as a model for prediction. The key assumption here are that both the predictor and target variables are continuous, as seen in the chart in Fig. 5.16. Intuitively, one can state that when x increases, y increases along the slope of the line. For example, advertisement spend and sales.

What happens if the target variable is not continuous? Suppose the target variable is the response to advertisement campaigns—if more than a threshold number of customers buy for example, then the response is considered

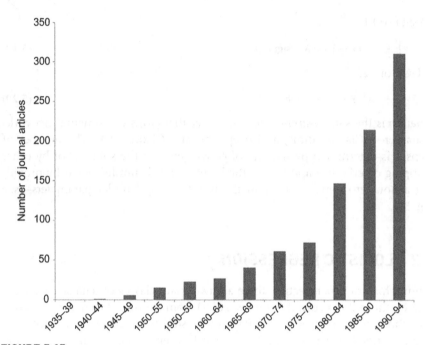

FIGURE 5.15

Growth of logistic regression applications in statistical research.

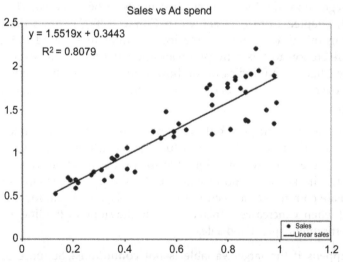

Linear Regression Model. We can make an intuitive assessment that increase in *Ad spend* also increases *Sales*. Using the straight line, we may also be able to predict.

FIGURE 5.16

Goal of linear regression.

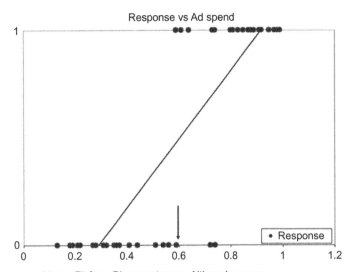

Linear Fit for a Binary outcome: Although we can make an intuitive assessment that increase in *Ad spend* increases *Response*, the switch is abrupt - around 0.6. Using the straight line, we cannot really predict outcome.

FIGURE 5.17
Fitting a linear model to discrete data.

to be 1; if not the response is 0. In this case, the target (y) variable is discrete (as in Fig. 5.17); the straight line is no longer a fit as seen in the chart. Although one can still estimate—approximately—that when x (advertising spend) increases, y (response or no response to a mailing campaign) also increases, there is no gradual transition; the y value abruptly jumps from one binary outcome to the other. Thus, the straight line is a poor fit for this data.

On the other hand, take a look at the S-shaped curve in Fig. 5.18. This is certainly a better fit for the data shown. If the equation to this "sigmoid" curve is known, then it can be used as effectively as the straight line was used in the case of linear regression.

Logistic regression is, thus, the process of obtaining an appropriate nonlinear curve to fit the data when the target variable is discrete. How is the sigmoid curve obtained? How does it relate to the predictors?

5.2.1 How It Works

The dependent variable, y, will be re-examined. If it is binomial, that is, it can take on only two values (yes/no, pass/fail, respond/does not respond, and so on), then y can be coded to assume only two values: 1 or 0.

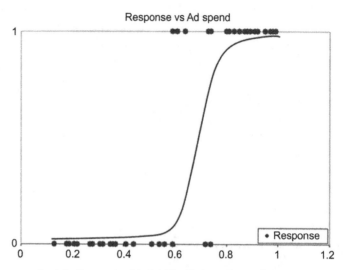

Logistic Regression Model. The S-shaped curve is clearly a better fit for *most* of the data. we can state *Ad spend* increases *Sales*, **and**. we may also be able to predict using this model.

FIGURE 5.18

Fitting a nonlinear curve to discrete data.

The challenge is to find an equation that functionally connects the predictors, *x*, to the outcome y where y can only take on two values: 0 or 1. However, the predictors themselves may have no restrictions: they could be continuous or categorical. Therefore, the functional range of these unrestricted predictors is likely to also be unrestricted (between $-\infty$ to $+\infty$). To overcome this problem, one must map the continuous function to a discrete function. This is what the logit helps to achieve.

How Does Logistic Regression Find the Sigmoid Curve?

As observed in Eq. (5.1), a straight line can be depicted by only two parameters: the slope (b_1) and the intercept (b_0). The way in which *x*'s and *y* are related to each other can be easily specified by b_0 and b_1. However, an S-shaped curve is a much more complex shape and representing it parametrically is not as straightforward. So how does one find the mathematical parameters to relate the *x*'s to the *y*?

It turns out that if the target variable *y* is transformed to the *logarithm of the odds of y*, then the *transformed* target variable is *linearly* related to the predictors, *x*. In most cases where the use of logistic regression is needed; the y is usually a yes/no type of response. This is usually interpreted as the probability of an event happening ($y = 1$) or not happening ($y = 0$). This can be deconstructed as:

- If y is an event (response, pass/fail, etc.),
- and p is the probability of the event happening ($y = 1$),
- then $(1 - p)$ is the probability of the event *not* happening ($y = 0$),
- and $p/(1 - p)$ are the *odds* of the event happening.

The logarithm of the odds, log $(p/(1 - p))$ is linear in the predictors, X, and log $(p/(1 - p))$ or the log of the odds is called the *logit function*.

The logit can be expressed as a linear function of the predictors X, similar to the linear regression model shown in Eq. (5.1) as:

$$\text{logit} = \log p/(1 - p) = b_0 x + b_1 \tag{5.21}$$

For a more general case, involving multiple independent variables, x, there is:

$$\text{logit} = b_0 + b_1 x_1 + b_2 x_2 + \cdots + b_n x_n \tag{5.22}$$

The logit can take any value from $-\infty$ to $+\infty$. For each row of predictors in a dataset, the logit an now be computed. From the logit, it is easy to then compute the probability of the response y (occurring or not occurring) as seen below:

$$p = e^{\text{logit}}/(1 + e^{\text{logit}}) \tag{5.23}$$

The logistic regression model from Eq. (5.22) ultimately delivers the probability of y occurring (i.e., $y = 1$), given specific value(s) of x via Eq. (5.23). In that context, a good definition of logistic regression is that it is a mathematical modeling approach in which a best-fitting, yet least-restrictive model is selected to describe the relationship between several independent explanatory variables and a dependent binomial response variable. It is least-restrictive because the right side of Eq. (5.22) can assume any value from $-\infty$ to $+\infty$. Cramer (2002) provides more background on the history of the logit function.

From the data given the x's are known and using Eqs. (5.22) and (5.23) one can compute the p for any given x. But to do that, the coefficients first need to be determined, b, in Eq. (5.22). How is this done? Assume that one starts out with a trial of values for b. Given a training data sample, one can compute the quantity:

$$p^y \times (1-p)^{(1-y)}$$

where y is the original outcome variable (which can take on 0 or 1) and p is the probability estimated by the logit equation [Eq. (5.23)]. For a specific training sample, if the actual outcome was $y = 0$ and the model estimate of p was high (say 0.9), that is, the model was wrong, then this quantity reduces to 0.1. If the model estimate of probability was low (say 0.1), that is, the model was good, then this quantity increases to 0.9. Therefore, this quantity, which is a simplified form of a *likelihood* function, is *maximized for good estimates* and *minimized for poor estimates*. If one computes a summation of the simplified likelihood function across *all* the training data samples, then a high value indicates a good model (or good fit) and vice versa.

In reality, gradient descent or other nonlinear optimization techniques are used to search for the coefficients, b, with the objective of maximizing the likelihood of correct estimation (or $p^y \times (1 - p)^{(1 - y)}$, summed over all training samples). More sophisticated formulations of likelihood estimators are used in practice (Eliason, 1993).

A Simple but Tragic Example

In the 1912 shipwreck of the HMS Titanic, hundreds of people perished as the ship struck an iceberg in the North Atlantic (Hinde, 1998). When the data is dispassionately analyzed, a couple of basic patterns emerge. 75% of the women and 63% of the first-class passengers survived. If a passenger was a woman and if she traveled first class, her probability of survival was 97%! The scatterplot in Fig. 5.19 depicts this in an easy to understand way (see the bottom left cluster).

A data science competition used the information from this event and challenged analysts to develop an algorithm that could classify the passenger list into survivors and non-survivors.[3] The training dataset provided will be used as an example to demonstrate how logistic regression could be employed to make this prediction and also to interpret the coefficients from the model.

Table 5.3 shows part of a reduced dataset consisting only of three variables: travel class of the passenger (pclass = 1st, 2nd, or 3rd), sex of the passenger (0 for male and 1 for female), and the label variable "survived" (true or false). When a logistic regression model is fit to this data consisting of 891 samples, the following equation is obtained for predicting the class *survived* = *false* (the details of a generic setup process will be described in the next section):

$$\text{logit} = -0.6503 - 2.6417 \times \text{sex} + 0.9595 \times \text{pclass} \tag{5.24}$$

Comparing this to Eq. (5.22), $b_0 = -0.6503$, $b_1 = -2.6417$, and $b_2 = 0.9595$. How are these coefficients interpreted? In order to do this, Eq. (5.23) will need to be recalled,

---

[3] http://www.kaggle.com/c/titanic-gettingStarted.

Survived ● Yes ● No

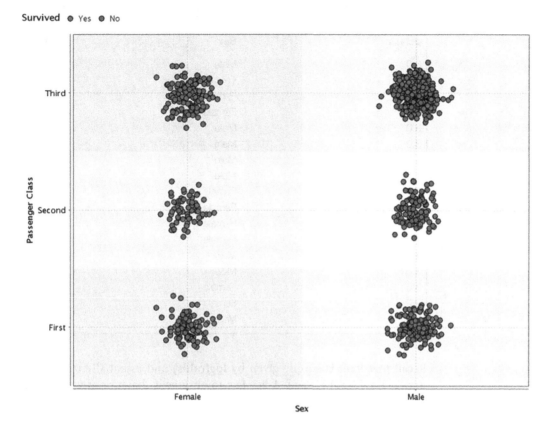

FIGURE 5.19
Probability of survival in the Titanic wreck based on gender and travel class.

$p = e^{\text{logit}}/[1 + e^{\text{logit}}]$

which indicates that as logit increases to a large positive quantity, the probability that the passenger did not survive (survived = false) approaches 1. More specifically, when logit approaches $-\infty$, p approaches 0 and when logit approaches $+\infty$, p approaches 1. The negative coefficient on variable *sex* indicates that this probability reduces for females (*sex* = 1) and the positive coefficient on variable p indicates that the probability of not surviving (*survived* = false) increases the higher the *number* of the travel class. This verifies the intuitive understanding that was provided by the scatterplot shown in Fig. 5.19.

The odds form of the logistic regression model can also be examined, which is given as:

$$\text{odds (survived = false)} = e^{-0.6503} \times 2.6103^{\text{pclass}} \times 0.0712^{\text{sex}} \qquad (5.25)$$

Table 5.3 Portion of the Dataset From the Titanic Example

pclass	Sex	Survived?
3.0	Male	0.0
1.0	Female	1.0
3.0	Female	1.0
1.0	Female	1.0
3.0	Male	0.0
3.0	Male	0.0
1.0	Male	0.0
3.0	Male	0.0
3.0	Female	1.0
2.0	Female	1.0
3.0	Female	1.0
1.0	Female	1.0
3.0	Male	0.0
3.0	Male	0.0
3.0	Female	0.0
2.0	Female	1.0
3.0	Male	0.0

Recall that logit is simply given by log(odds) and essentially the same equation as Eq. (5.24) is used. A key fact to observe is that a positive coefficient in the logit model translates into a coefficient higher than 1 in the odds model (the number 2.6103 in the above equation is $e^{0.9595}$ and 0.0712 is $e^{-2.6417}$) and a negative coefficient in the logit model translates into coefficients smaller than 1 in the odds model. Again, it is clear that the odds of not surviving increases with travel class and reduces with gender being female.

An *odds ratio analysis* will reveal the value of computing the results in this format. Consider a female passenger (*sex* = 1). The survivability for this passenger could be calculated if she was in 1st class (*pclass* = 1) versus if she was in 2nd class as an odds ratio:

$$\text{odds (survived = false 2nd class)}/\text{odds(survived = false 1st class)}$$
$$= 2.6103^2/2.6103^1 = 2.6103 \tag{5.26}$$

Based on the Titanic dataset, the odds that a female passenger would not survive if she was in 2nd class increases by a factor of 2.6 compared to her odds if she was in 1st class. Similarly, the odds that a female passenger would not survive increases by nearly seven times if she was in 3rd class! In the next section, the mechanics of logistic regression are discussed as well as the process of implementing a simple analysis using RapidMiner.

Table 5.4 A Sample From the Loan Default Dataset

[Busage]	[Daysdelq]	[Default]
87.0	2.0	N
89.0	2.0	N
90.0	2.0	N
90.0	2.0	N
101.0	2.0	N
110.0	2.0	N
115.0	2.0	N
115.0	2.0	N
115.0	2.0	N
117.0	2.0	N

5.2.2 How to Implement

The data used come from an example for a credit scoring exercise. The objective is to predict DEFAULT (Y or N) based on two predictors: loan age (business age) and number of days of delinquency. There are 100 samples Table 5.4.

Step 1: Data Preparation
Load the spreadsheet into RapidMiner. Remember to set the DEFAULT column as Label. Split the data into training and test samples using the *Split Validation* operator.

Step 2: Modeling Operator and Parameters
Add the *Logistic Regression* operator in the training subprocess of the *Split Validation* operator. Add the *Apply Model* operator in the testing subprocess of the *Split Validation* operator. Just use default parameter values. Add the *Performance (Binominal)* evaluation operator in the testing subprocess of *Split Validation* operator. Check the Accuracy, AUC, Precision, and Recall boxes in the parameter settings. Connect all ports as shown in Fig. 5.20.

Step 3: Execution and Interpretation
Run the model and view the results. In particular, check for the kernel model, which shows the coefficients for the two predictors and the intercept. The bias (offset) is -1.820 and the coefficients are given by: w[BUSAGE] = 0.592 and w[DAYSDELQ] = 2.045. Also check the confusion matrix for Accuracy, Precision, and Recall and finally view the ROC curves and check the area under the curve or AUC. Chapter 8, Model Evaluation, provides further details on these important performance measures.

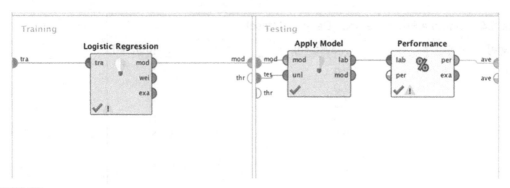

FIGURE 5.20
Setting up the RapidMiner process for a logistic regression model.

accuracy: 83.33%

	true N	true Y	class precision
pred. N	21	3	87.50%
pred. Y	2	4	66.67%
class recall	91.30%	57.14%	

FIGURE 5.21
Confusion matrix for the testing sample.

The accuracy of the model based on the 30% testing sample is 83%. (The ROC curves have an AUC of 0.863). The next step would be to review the kernel model and prepare for deploying this model. Are these numbers acceptable? In particular, pay attention to the class recall (bottom row of the confusion matrix in Fig. 5.21). The model is quite accurate in predicting if someone is NOT a defaulter (91.3%), however, its performance when it comes to identifying if someone IS a defaulter is questionable. For most predictive applications, the cost of wrong class predictions is not uniform. That is, a false positive (in the case of identifying someone as a defaulter, when they are not) may be less expensive than a false negative (in the case of identifying someone as a non-defaulter, when they actually are). There are ways to weight the cost of misclassification, and RapidMiner allows this through the use of the *MetaCost* operator.

Step 4: Using MetaCost
Nest the *Logistic Regression* operator inside a *MetaCost* operator to improve class recall. The *MetaCost* operator is now placed inside *Split Validation* operator. Configure the *MetaCost* operator as shown in Fig. 5.22. Notice that false

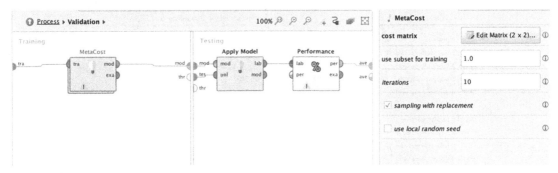

FIGURE 5.22
Configuring the MetaCost operator to improve class recall performance.

accuracy: 83.33%

	true N	true Y	class precision
pred. N	20	2	90.91%
pred. Y	3	5	62.50%
class recall	86.96%	71.43%	

FIGURE 5.23
Improved classification performance with the usage of MetaCost operator.

negatives have twice the cost of false positives. The actual values of these costs can be further optimized using an optimization loop—optimization is discussed for general cases in Chapter 15, Getting Started with RapidMiner.

When this process is run, the new confusion matrix that results is shown in Fig. 5.23. The overall accuracy has not changed much. Note that while the class recall for the Default = Yes class has increased from 57% to 71%, this has come at the price of reducing the class recall for Default = No from 91% to 87%. Is this acceptable? Again, the answer to this comes from examining the actual business costs. More details about interpreting the confusion matrix and evaluating the performance of classification models is provided in Chapter 8, Model Evaluation.

Step 5: Applying the Model to an Unseen Dataset
In RapidMiner, logistic regression is calculated by creating a support vector machine (SVM) with a modified loss function (Fig. 5.24). SVMs were introduced in Chapter 4 on Classification. That's the reason why support vectors are seen at all.

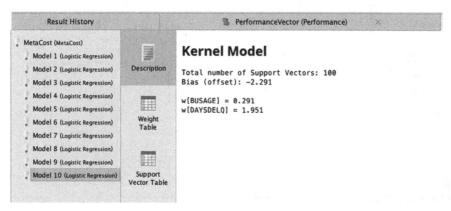

FIGURE 5.24
Default logistic regression model in RapidMiner is based on SVM. *SVM*, Support vector machine.

5.2.3 Summary Points

- Logistic regression can be considered equivalent to using linear regression for situations where, when the target (or dependent) variable is discrete, that is, not continuous. In principle, the response variable or label is binomial. A binomial response variable has two categories: Yes/No, Accept/Not Accept, Default/Not Default, and so on. Logistic regression is ideally suited for business analytics applications where the target variable is a binary decision (fail/pass, response/no response, etc.).

- Logistic regression comes from the concept of the logit. The logit is the logarithm of the odds of the response, y, expressed as a function of independent or predictor variables, x, and a constant term. That is, for example, log (odds of y = Yes) = $b_1 x + b_0$.

- This logit gives the odds of the Yes event, however if one wants probabilities, the transformed equation will need to be used:
$$p(y = \text{"Yes"}) = 1/(1 + e^{(-b_1 x - b_0)})$$

- The predictors can be either numerical or categorical for standard logistic regression. However, in RapidMiner, the predictors can only be numerical, because it is based on the SVM formulation.

5.3 CONCLUSION

This chapter explored two of the most common function-fitting methods. Function-fitting methods are one of the earliest data science techniques based on the concept of supervised learning. The multiple linear regression model works with numeric predictors and a numeric label and is, thus, one of the go-to methods for numeric prediction tasks. The logistic regression model works with numeric or categorical predictors and a categorical (typically, binomial) label. How a simple linear regression model is developed was explained using the methods of calculus and how feature selection impacts the coefficients of a model was discussed. It was explained, how the significance of the coefficients can be interpreted using the t-stat and p-values and finally several checkpoints that one must follow to build good quality models were laid down. Logistic regression was then introduced, by comparing the similar structural nature of the two function-fitting methods. How a sigmoid curve can better fit predictors to a binomial label was discussed and the concept of logit was introduced, which enables the transformation of a complex function into a more recognizable linear form. How the coefficients of logistic regression can be interpreted was discussed as well as how to measure and improve the classification performance of the model.

References

Black, K. (2008). Multiple regression analysis. In K. Black (Ed.), *Business statistics* (pp. 601–610). Hoboken, NJ: John Wiley and Sons.

Cramer, J. (2002). *The origins of logistic regression* (pp. 1–15). Tinbergen Institute Discussion Paper.

Eliason, S. (1993). *Maximum likelihood estimation: Logic and practice*. Newbury Park, CA: Sage Publishers.

Fletcher, R. A. (1963). A rapidly convergent descent method for minimization. *The Computer Journal, 6*(2), 163–168.

Galton, F. (1888). Co-relations and their measurement, chiefly from anthropometric data. *Proceedings of the Royal Society of London, 45*(273-279), 135–145.

Harrison, D. A. (1978). Hedonic prices and the demand for clean air. *Journal of Environmental Economics and Management, 5*(1), 81–102.

Hinde, P. (1998). Encyclopedia titanica. Retrieved from <http://www.encyclopedia-titanica.org/>.

Marquardt, D. (1963). An algorithm for least-squares estimation of nonlinear parameters. *Journal of the Society for Industrial and Applied Mathematics, 11*(2), 431–441.

Stigler, S. (1999). *Statistics on the table: The history of statistical concepts and methods*. Cambridge: Harvard University Press.

CHAPTER 6

Association Analysis

The beer and diaper association story in the analytics circle is (urban) legendary (Power, 2002). There are many variations of this story, but the basic plot is that a supermarket company discovered that customers who buy diapers also tend to buy beer. The beer and diaper relationship heralded unusual, unknown, and quirky nuggets that could be learned from the transaction data of a supermarket. How did the supermarket determine that such a relationship between products existed? The answer: Data Science (It was called data mining back in the 2000s). Specifically, association analysis.

Association analysis measures the strength of co-occurrence between one item and another. The objective of this class of data science algorithms is not to predict an occurrence of an item, like classification or regression algorithms do, but to find usable patterns in the co-occurrences of the items. Association rules learning is a branch of unsupervised learning processes that discover hidden patterns in data, in the form of easily recognizable *rules*.

Association algorithms are widely used in retail analysis of transactions, recommendation engines, and online clickstream analysis across web pages, etc. One of the popular applications of this technique is called *market basket analysis*, which finds co-occurrences of one retail item with another item within the same retail purchase transaction (Agrawal, Imieliński, & Swami, 1993). If patterns within transaction data tell us that baby formula and diapers are usually purchased together in the same transaction, a retailer can take advantage of this association for bundle pricing, product placement, and even shelf space optimization within the store layout. Similarly, in an online business setting, this information can be leveraged for real-time cross selling, recommendations, cart offers, and post-purchase marketing strategies. The results of association analysis are commonly known, for example a burger with fries or baby formula with diapers; however, uncommon relationships are the

Data Science. DOI: https://doi.org/10.1016/B978-0-12-814761-0.00006-X

prized discoveries, the ones businesses can take advantage of. The downside is that association analysis may also yield spurious relationships between items. When dealing with data containing billions of transactions, transactions with all kinds of possibilities with strange combinations of itemsets (e.g., nicotine patch and cigarettes) can be found. It takes analytical skill and business knowledge to successfully apply the outcomes of an association analysis. The model outcome of an association analysis can be represented as a set of rules, like the one below:

{Item A} → {Item B}

This rule indicates that based on the history of all the transactions, when Item A is found in a transaction or a basket, there is a strong propensity of the occurrence of Item B within the *same* transaction. Item A is the *antecedent* or *premise* of the rule and Item B is the *consequent* or *conclusion* of the rule. The antecedent and consequent of the rule can contain more than one item, like Item A and Item C. To mine these kinds of rules from the data, previous customer purchase transactions would need to be analyzed. In a retail business, there would be millions of transactions made in a day with thousands of stock keeping units, which are unique for an item. Hence, two of the key

CROSS SELLING: CUSTOMERS WHO BOUGHT THIS ALSO BOUGHT...

Consider an e-commerce website that sells a large selection of products online. One of the objectives of managing an e-commerce business is to increase the average order value of a visit. Optimizing order size is even more critical when the businesses pay for acquisition traffic through search engine marketing, online advertisements, and affiliate marketing. Businesses attempt to increase average order value by cross-selling and up-selling relevant products to the customer, based on what they have purchased or are currently purchasing in the current transaction (a common fast-food equivalent: "Do you want fries with the burger?"). Businesses need to be careful by weighing the benefit of suggesting an extremely relevant product against the risk of irritating a customer who is already making a transaction. In a business where there are limited products (e.g., fast-food industry), cross-selling a product with another product is straightforward and is quite embedded in the business. But, when the number of unique products runs into the thousands or millions, determining a set of *affinity* products when customers are looking at a product is quite challenging.

To better learn about product affinity, understanding purchase history data is helpful. The information on how one product creates affinity to another product relies on the fact that both the products appear in the same transaction. If two products are bought together, then it can be hypothesized, that the necessity of those products arise simultaneously for the customer. If the two products are bought together many times, by a large number of customers, then there is a strong possibility of an affinity pattern within these products. In a new later transaction, if a customer picks one of those affinity products, then there is an increased likelihood that the other product will be picked by the customer, in the same transaction.

The key input for affinity analysis is a list of past transactions with product information. Based on the analysis of these transactions, the most frequent product pairs can

(Continued)

> **(Continued)**
>
> be determined. A threshold will need to be defined for "frequent" because a few appearances of a product pair doesn't qualify as a pattern. The result of an affinity analysis is a rule set that says, "If product A is purchased, there is an increased likelihood that product B will be purchased in the same transaction." This rule set can be leveraged to provide cross sell recommendations on the product page of product A. Affinity analysis is the concept behind the web widgets which state, "Customers who bought this also bought…"

considerations of association analysis are computational time and resources. However, over the last two decades newer and more efficient algorithms have been developed to mitigate this problem.

6.1 MINING ASSOCIATION RULES

Basic association analysis just deals with the *occurrence* of one item with another. More advanced analysis can take into consideration the quantity of occurrence, price, and sequence of occurrence, etc. The method for finding association rules through data science involves sequential steps:

> *Step 1*: Prepare the data in transaction format. An association algorithm needs input data to be formatted in transaction format $t_x = \{i_1, i_2, i_3\}$.
> *Step 2*: Short-list frequently occurring *itemsets*. Itemsets are combinations of items. An association algorithm limits the analysis to the most frequently occurring items, so that the final rule set extracted in the next step is more meaningful.
> *Step 3*: Generate *relevant* association rules from itemsets. Finally, the algorithm generates and filters the rules based on the interest measure.

To start with, consider a media website, like BBC or Yahoo News, with categories such as news, politics, finance, entertainment, sports, and arts. A session or transaction in this example is one visit for the website, where the same user accesses content from different categories, within a certain session period. A new session usually starts after 30 minutes of inactivity. Sessions are quite similar to transactions in a traditional brick and mortar model and the pages accessed can be related to items purchased. In online news sites, items are *visits* to the categories such as News, Finance, Entertainment, Sports, and Arts. The data can be collected as shown in Table 6.1, with a list of sessions and media categories accessed during a given session. The objective in this data science task is to find associations between media categories.

For association analysis of these media categories, a dataset in a particular transaction format would be needed. To get started with association analysis, it would be helpful to pivot the data in the format shown in Table 6.2.

Table 6.1 Clickstream

Session ID	List of Media Categories Accessed
1	{News, Finance}
2	{News, Finance}
3	{Sports, Finance, News}
4	{Arts}
5	{Sports, News, Finance}
6	{News, Arts, Entertainment}

Table 6.2 Clickstream Dataset

Session ID	News	Finance	Entertainment	Sports	Arts
1	1	1	0	0	0
2	1	1	0	0	0
3	1	1	0	1	0
4	0	0	0	0	1
5	1	1	0	1	0
6	1	0	1	0	1

This binary format indicates the presence or absence of article categories and ignores qualities such as minutes spent viewing or the sequence of access, which can be important in certain sequence analysis. For now, the focus is on basic association analysis and the terminologies used in association rules will be reviewed.

6.1.1   Itemsets

In the examples of association rules discussed so far, the antecedent and consequent of the rules had only one item. But, as mentioned before, they can involve multiple items. For example, a rule can be of the following sort:

{News, Finance} → {Sports}

This rule implies that, if users have accessed news and finance in the same session, there is a high likelihood that they would also access sports articles, based on historical transactions. The combination of news and finance items is called an *itemset*. An itemset can occur either in the antecedent or in the consequent portion of the rule; however, both sets should be disjointed, which means there should not be any common item on both sides of the rule. Obviously, there is no practical relevance for rules like "News and Finance users are most likely to visit the News and Sports pages." Instead, rules like "If users visited the Finance page they are more likely to visit the News and Sports pages" make more sense. The introduction of the itemset with more than one item greatly increases the permutations of the rules to be considered and tested for the strength of relationships.

The strength of an association rule is commonly quantified by the *support* and *confidence* measures of a rule. There are a few more quantifications like *lift* and *conviction* measures that can be used in special cases. All these measures are based on the relative frequency of occurrences of a particular itemset in the transactions dataset used for training. Hence, it is important that the training set used for rule generation is unbiased and truly represents a universe of transactions. Each of these frequency metrics will be elaborated on in the coming sections.

Support

The *support of an item* is simply the relative frequency of occurrence of an itemset in the transaction set. In the dataset shown in Table 6.2, support of {News} is five out of six transactions, $5/6 = 0.83$. Similarly, support of an itemset {News, Finance} is the co-occurrence of both news and finance in a transaction with respect to all the transactions:

$$\text{Support}(\{\text{News}\}) = 5/6 = 0.83$$
$$\text{Support}(\{\text{News, Finance}\}) = 4/6 = 0.67$$
$$\text{Support}(\{\text{Sports}\}) = 2/6 = 0.33$$

The *support of a rule* is a measure of how all the items in a rule are represented in the overall transactions. For example, in the rule {News} → {Sports}, News and Sports occur in two of six transactions and hence, support for the rule {News} → {Sports} is 0.33. The support measure for a rule indicates whether a rule is worth considering. Since the support measure favors the items where there is high occurrence, it uncovers the patterns that are worth taking advantage of and investigating. This is particularly interesting for businesses because leveraging patterns in high volume items leads to incremental revenue. Rules with low support have either infrequently occurring items or an item relationship occurs just by chance, which may yield spurious rules. In association analysis, a threshold of support is specified to filter out infrequent rules. Any rule that exceeds the support threshold is then considered for further analysis.

Confidence

The *confidence of a rule* measures the likelihood of the occurrence of the consequent of the rule out of all the transactions that contain the antecedent of the rule. Confidence provides the reliability measure of the rule. Confidence of the rule $(X \rightarrow Y)$ is calculated by

$$\text{Confidence } (X \to Y) = \frac{\text{Support } (X \cup Y)}{\text{Support } (X)} \qquad (6.1)$$

In the case of the rule {News, Finance} → {Sports}, the question that the confidence measure answers is, if a transaction has both News and Finance, what is the likelihood of seeing Sports in it?

$$\begin{aligned}\text{Confidence } (\{\text{News, Finance}\} \to \{\text{Sports}\}) &= \frac{\text{Support } (\{\text{News, Finance, Sports}\})}{\text{Support } (\{\text{News, Finance}\})} \\ &= \frac{2/6}{4/6} \\ &= 0.5\end{aligned}$$

Half of the transactions that contain News and Finance also contain Sports. This means that 50% of the users who visit the news and finance pages also visit the sports pages.

Lift

Though confidence of the rule is widely used, the frequency of occurrence of a rule consequent (conclusion) is largely ignored. In some transaction item-sets, this can provide spurious scrupulous rule sets because of the presence of infrequent items in the rule consequent. To solve this, the support of a consequent can be put in the denominator of a confidence calculation. This measure is called the *lift of the rule*. The lift of the rule can be calculated by

$$\text{Life } (X \to Y) = \frac{\text{Support } (X \cup Y)}{\text{Support } (X) \times \text{Support } (Y)}$$

In the case of our example:

$$\begin{aligned}\text{Life } (\{\text{News, Finance}\} \to \{\text{Sports}\}) &= \frac{\text{Support } (X \cup Y)}{\text{Support } (X) \times \text{Support } (Y)} \qquad (6.2) \\ &= \frac{0.333}{0.667 \times 0.33} = 1.5\end{aligned}$$

Lift is the ratio of the observed support of {News and Finance} and {Sports} with what is expected if {News and Finance} and {Sports} usage were completely independent. Lift values closer to 1 mean the antecedent and consequent of the rules are independent and the rule is not interesting. The higher the value of lift, the more interesting the rules are.

Conviction

The *conviction of the rule* $X \to Y$ is the ratio of the expected frequency of X occurring in spite of Y and the observed frequency of incorrect predictions. Conviction takes into account the direction of the rule. The conviction of $(X \to Y)$ is not the same as the conviction of $(Y \to X)$. The conviction of a rule $(X \to Y)$ can be calculated by

$$\text{Conviction } (X \to Y) = \frac{1 - \text{Support } (Y)}{1 - \text{Confidence } (X \to Y)}$$

For our example, $\hspace{7cm}$ (6.3)

$$\text{Conviction}(\{\text{News, Finance}\} \to \{\text{Sports}\}) = \frac{1 - 0.33}{1 - 0.5} = 1.32$$

A conviction of 1.32 means that the rule ($\{\text{News, Finance}\} \to \{\text{Sports}\}$) would be incorrect 32% more often if the relationship between $\{\text{News, Finance}\}$ and $\{\text{Sports}\}$ is purely random.

6.1.2 Rule Generation

The process of generating meaningful association rules from the dataset can be broken down into two basic tasks.

1. *Finding all frequent itemsets.* For an association analysis of n items it is possible to find $2^n - 1$ itemsets excluding the null itemset. As the number of items increase, there is an exponential increase in the number of itemsets. Hence it is critical to set a minimal support threshold to discard less frequently occurring itemsets in the transaction universe. All possible itemsets can be expressed in a visual lattice form like the diagram shown in Fig. 6.1. In this figure one item {Arts} is excluded from the itemset generation. It is not uncommon to exclude items so that the association analysis can be focused on subsets of important relevant items. In the supermarket example, some filler items like grocery bags can be excluded from the analysis. An itemset tree (or lattice) helps demonstrate the methods to easily find frequent itemsets.
2. *Extracting rules from frequent itemsets.* For the dataset with n items it is possible to find $3^n - 2^{n+1} + 1$ rules (Tan, Steinbach, & Kumar, 2005). This step extracts all the rules with a confidence higher than a minimum confidence threshold.

This two-step process generates hundreds of rules even for a small dataset with dozens of items. Hence, it is important to set a reasonable support and confidence threshold to filter out less frequent and less relevant rules in the search space. The generated rules can also be evaluated with support, confidence, lift, and conviction measures. In terms of computational requirements, finding all the frequent itemsets above a support threshold is more expensive than extracting the rules. Fortunately, there are some algorithmic approaches to efficiently find the frequent itemsets. The Apriori and Frequent Pattern (FP)-Growth algorithms are two of the most popular association analysis algorithms.

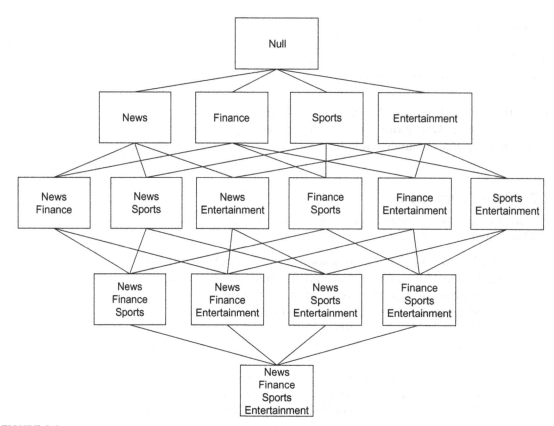

FIGURE 6.1
Itemset tree.

6.2 APRIORI ALGORITHM

All association rule algorithms should efficiently find the frequent itemsets from the universe of all the possible itemsets. The Apriori algorithm leverages some simple logical principles on the lattice itemsets to reduce the number of itemsets to be tested for the support measure (Agrawal & Srikant, 1994). The Apriori principles states that "If an itemset is frequent, then all its subset items will be frequent." (Tan et al, 2005). The itemset is "frequent" if the support for the itemset is more than that of the support threshold.

For example, if the itemset {News, Finance, Sports} from the dataset shown in Table 6.2 is a frequent itemset, that is, its support measure (0.33) is higher than the threshold support measure k (say, 0.25), then all of its subset items or itemsets will be frequent itemsets. Subset itemsets will have a support measure higher than or equal to the parent itemset. Fig. 6.2 shows the

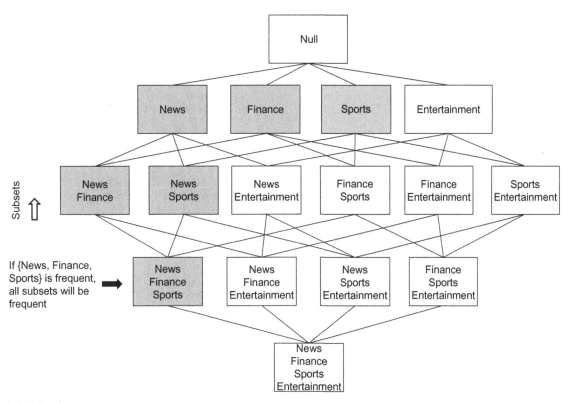

FIGURE 6.2

Frequent itemsets using Apriori principle.

application of the Apriori principle in a lattice. The support measures of the subset itemsets for {News, Finance, Sports} are

Support {News, Finance, Sports} = 0.33 (above threshold support)
Support {News, Finance} = 0.66
Support {News, Sports} = 0.33
Support {News} = 0.83
Support {Sports} = 0.33
Support {Finance} = 0.66

Conversely, if the itemset is infrequent, then all its *supersets* will be infrequent. In this example, support of Entertainment is 0.16, and the support of all the supersets that contain Entertainment as an item will be less than or equal to 0.16, which is infrequent when considering the support threshold of 0.25. Superset exclusion of an infrequent item is shown in Fig. 6.3.

The Apriori principle is helpful because not all itemsets have to be considered for a support calculation and tested for the support threshold; hence,

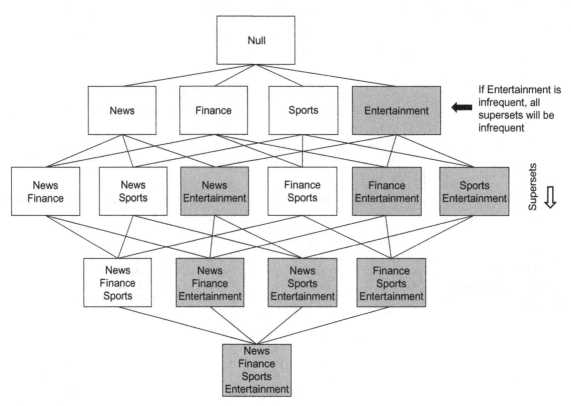

FIGURE 6.3

Frequent itemsets using Apriori principle: exclusion.

generation of the frequent itemsets can be handled efficiently by eliminating a bunch of itemsets that have an infrequent item or itemsets (Bodon, 2005).

6.2.1   How it Works

Consider the dataset shown in Table 6.3, which is the condensed version of the prior example set discussed. In this dataset there are six transactions. If the support threshold is assumed to be 0.25, then all items are expected to appear in at least two out of six transactions.

Frequent Itemset Generation

The support count and support for all itemset(s) can now be calculated. *Support count* is the absolute count of the transactions and support is the ratio of support count to total transaction count. Any one itemset below the threshold support count (which is 2 in this example) can be eliminated from further processing. Table 6.4 shows the support count and support calculation for each

Table 6.3 Clickstream Dataset: Condensed Version

Session	News	Finance	Entertainment	Sports
1	1	1	0	0
2	1	1	0	0
3	1	1	0	1
4	0	0	0	0
5	1	1	0	1
6	1	0	1	0

Table 6.4 Frequent Itemset Support Calculation

Item	Support Count	Support
{News}	5	0.83
{Finance}	4	0.67
{Entertainment}	1	0.17
{Sports}	2	0.33
Two-Itemsets	**Support Count**	**Support**
{News, Finance}	4	0.67
{News, Sports}	2	0.33
{Finance, Sports}	2	0.33
Three-Itemsets	**Support Count**	**Support**
{News, Finance, Sports}	2	0.33

item. Since {Entertainment} has a support count less than the threshold, it can be eliminated for the next iteration of itemset generation. The next step is generating possible two-itemset generations for {News}, {Finance}, and {Sports}, which yield three two-itemsets. If the {Entertainment} itemset is not eliminated, six two-itemsets would be obtained. Fig. 6.4 shows the visual representation of the itemsets with elimination of the {Entertainment} item.

This process is continued until all n-itemsets are considered from previous sets. At the end, there are seven frequent itemsets passing the support threshold. The total possible number of itemsets is 15 ($=2^4 - 1$). By eliminating {Entertainment} in the first step, seven additional itemsets do not have to be generated that would not pass the support threshold anyway (Witten & Frank, 2005).

Rule Generation

Once the frequent itemsets are generated, the next step in association analysis is generating useful rules which have a clear antecedent (premise) and consequent (conclusion), in the format of the rule:

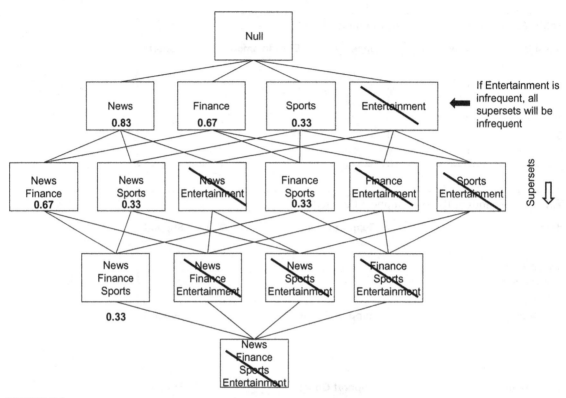

FIGURE 6.4
Frequent itemset with support.

{Item A} → {Item B}

The usefulness of the rule can be approximated by an objective measure of interest such as confidence, conviction, or lift. Confidence for the rule is calculated by the support scores of the individual items as given in Eq. (6.1). Each frequent itemset of n items can generate $2^n - 2$ rules. For example {News, Sports, Finance} can generate rules with confidence scores as follows:

Rules and confidence scores

$$\{News, Sports\} \rightarrow \{Finance\} - 0.33/0.33 = 1.0$$
$$\{News, Finance\} \rightarrow \{Sports\} - 0.33/0.67 = 0.5$$
$$\{Sports, Finance\} \rightarrow \{News\} - 0.33/0.33 = 1.0$$
$$\{News\} \rightarrow \{Sports, Finance\} - 0.33/0.83 = 0.4$$
$$\{Sports\} \rightarrow \{News, Finance\} - 0.33/0.33 = 1.0$$
$$\{Finance\} \rightarrow \{News, Sports\} - 0.33/0.67 = 0.5$$

Since all the support scores have already been calculated in the itemset generation step, there is no need for another set of computations for calculating confidence. However, it is possible to prune potentially low confidence rules using the same Apriori method. For a given frequent itemset {News, Finance, Sports}, if the rule {News, Finance} → {Sports} is a low confidence rule, then it can be concluded that any rules within the subset of the antecedent will be a low confidence rule. Hence, all the rules like {News} → {Sports, Finance} and {Finance} → {News, Sports} can be discarded, which are in the subsets of the antecedent of the rule. The reason is that all three rules have the same numerator in the confidence score calculation [Eq. (6.1)], which is 0.33. The denominator calculation depends on the support of the antecedent. Since the support of a subset is always greater or equal to the set, it can be concluded that all further rules within a subset of an itemset in the premises will be a low confidence rule, and hence, can be ignored.

All the rules passing a particular confidence threshold are considered for output along with both support and confidence measures. These rules should be further evaluated for rational validity to determine if a useful relationship was uncovered, if there was an occurrence by chance, or if the rule confirms a known intuitive relationship.

6.3 FREQUENT PATTERN-GROWTH ALGORITHM

The FP-Growth algorithm provides an alternative way of calculating a frequent itemset by compressing the transaction records using a special graph data structure called *FP-Tree*. FP-Tree can be thought of as a transformation of the dataset into graph format. Rather than the generate and test approach used in the Apriori algorithm, FP-Growth first generates the FP-Tree and uses this compressed tree to generate the frequent itemsets. The efficiency of the FP-Growth algorithm depends on how much compression can be achieved in generating the FP-Tree (Han, Pei, & Yin, 2000).

6.3.1 How it Works

Consider the dataset shown in Table 6.5 containing six transactions of four items—news, finance, sports, and entertainment. To visually represent this dataset in a tree diagram (Fig. 6.6), the list of transactions need to be transformed into a tree map, preserving all the information and representing the *frequent paths*. Here is a break-down of the FP-Tree for this dataset step by step.

1. The first step is to sort all the items in each transaction in descending order of frequency (or support count). For example, News is the most frequent item and Sports is the least frequent item in the transaction, based on the data in Table 6.5. The third transaction of {Sports, News, Finance} has to be rearranged to {News, Finance, Sports}. This will help to simplify mapping frequent paths in later steps.

Table 6.5 Transactions List: Session and Items	
Session	**Items**
1	{News, Finance}
2	{News, Finance}
3	{News, Finance, Sports}
4	{Sports}
5	{News, Finance, Sports}
6	{News, Entertainment}

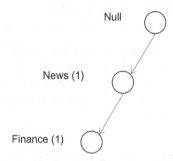

FIGURE 6.5

FP-Tree: Transaction 1.

2. Once the items within a transaction are rearranged, the transaction can now be mapped to the FP-Tree. Starting with a null node, the first transaction {News, Finance} can be represented by Fig. 6.5. The number within the parenthesis next to the item name is the number of transactions following the path.

3. Since the second transaction {News, Finance} is the same as the first one, it follows the same path as the first one. In this case, the numbers can simply be incremented.

4. The third transaction contains {News, Finance, Sports}. The tree is now extended to include Sports and the item path count is incremented (Fig. 6.6).

5. The fourth transaction only contains the {Sports} item. Since Sports is not preceded by News and Finance, a new path should be created from the null item and the item count should be noted. This node for Sports is different from the Sports node next to Finance (the latter co-occurs with News and Finance). However, since both nodes indicate the same item, they should be linked by a dotted line.

6. This process is continued until all the transactions are scanned. All of the transaction records can be now represented by a compact FP-Tree (Fig. 6.7).

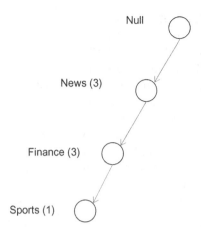

FIGURE 6.6
FP-Tree: Transactions 1—3.

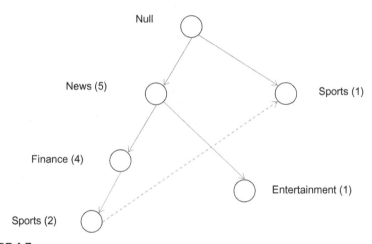

FIGURE 6.7
FP-Tree: Transactions 1—6.

The compression of the FP-Tree depends on how frequently a path occurs within a given transaction set. Since the key objective of association analysis is to identify these common paths, the datasets used from this analysis contain many frequent paths. In the worst case, all transactions contain unique itemset paths and there wouldn't be any compression. In that case the rule generation itself would be less meaningful for association analysis.

Frequent Itemset Generation

Once the transaction set is expressed by a compact FP-Tree, the most frequent itemset can be generated from the FP-Tree effectively. To generate the frequent itemset, the FP-Growth algorithm adopts a bottom-up approach of generating all the itemsets starting with the least frequent items. Since the structure of the tree is ordered by the support count, the least frequent items can be found in the leaves of the tree. In Fig. 6.8, the least frequent items are {Entertainment} and {Sports}, because the support count is just one transaction. If {Entertainment} is indeed a frequent item, because the support exceeds the threshold, the algorithm will find all the itemsets ending with entertainment, like {Entertainment} and {News, Entertainment}, by following the path from the bottom-up. Since the support counts are mapped to the nodes, calculating the support for {News, Entertainment} will be instant. If {Entertainment} is not frequent, the algorithm skips the item and goes with the next item, {Sports}, and finds all possible itemsets ending with sports: {Sports}, {Finance, Sports}, {News, Finance, Sports}.

Finding the entire itemset ending with a particular item number is actually made possible by generating a prefix path and conditional FP-Tree for an item, as shown in Fig. 6.9. The prefix path of an item is a subtree with only paths that contain the item of interest. A conditional FP-Tree for an item, say {Sports}, is similar to the FP-Tree, but with the {Sports} item removed. Based on the conditional FP-Tree, the algorithm repeats the process of finding leaf nodes. Since leaf nodes of the sports conditional tree co-exist with {Sports}, the algorithm finds the association with finance and generates {Finance, Sports}.

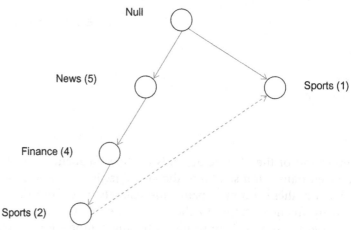

FIGURE 6.8
Trimmed FP-Tree.

Rule generation in the FP-Growth algorithm is very similar to the Apriori algorithm. Since the intent is to find frequently occurring items, by definition, many of the transactions should have essentially the same path. Hence, in many practical applications the compaction ratio is very high. In those scenarios, the FP-Growth algorithm provides efficient results. Since the FP-Growth algorithm uses graphs to map the relationship between frequent items, it has found applications beyond association analysis. It is now applied in research as a preprocessing phase for document clustering, text mining, and sentiment analysis (Akbar & Angryk, 2008). However, in spite of the execution differences, both the FP-Growth and Apriori algorithms yield similar results. Rule generation from the frequent itemsets is similar to the Apriori algorithm. Even though the concepts and explanations include analyzing graphs and subgraphs, FP-Growth algorithms can be easily ported to programming languages, particularly to SQL and PL/SQL programs on top of relational databases, where the transactions are usually stored (Shang, Sattler, & Geist, 2004).

6.3.2 How to Implement

The retrieval of association rules from a dataset is implemented through the FP-Growth algorithm in RapidMiner. Since the modeling parameters and the results for most of the association algorithms are the same, the FP-Growth algorithm will be used to observe the inputs, process, and the result of an association analysis implementation.

Step 1: Data Preparation
The Association analysis process expects transactions to be in a particular format. The input grid should have binominal (true or false) data with items in the columns and each transaction as a row. If the dataset contains transaction IDs or session IDs, they can either be ignored or tagged as a special attribute in RapidMiner. Datasets in any other format have to be converted to this

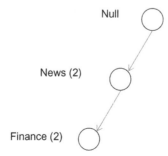

FIGURE 6.9
Conditional FP-Tree.

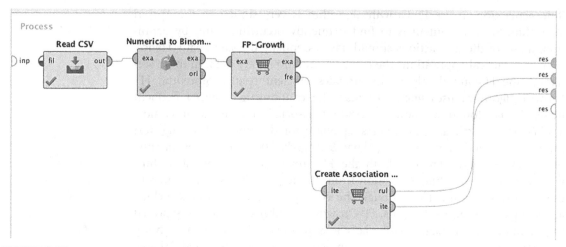

FIGURE 6.10
Data science process for FP-Growth algorithm.

transactional format using data transformation operators. In this example, the data shown in Table 6.3 has been used, with a session ID on each row and content accessed in the columns, indicated by 1 and 0. This integer format has to be converted to a binomial format by a *numerical to binominal* operator. The output of *numerical to binominal* is then connected to the *FP-Growth* operator to generate frequent itemsets. The dataset and RapidMiner process for association analysis can be accessed from the companion site of the book at www.IntroDataScience.com. Fig. 6.10 shows the RapidMiner process of association analysis with the FP-Growth algorithm.

Step 2: Modeling Operator and Parameters

The *FP-Growth* operator in RapidMiner generates all the frequent itemsets from the input dataset meeting a certain parameter criterion. The modeling operator is available at Modeling > Association and itemset Mining folder. This operator can work in two modes, one with a specified number of high support itemsets (default) and the other with minimum support criteria. These parameters can be set in this operator, thereby, affecting the behavior of the model:

- *Min Support:* Threshold for support measure. All the frequent itemsets passing this threshold will be provided in the output.
- *Max Items:* Maximum number of items in an itemset. Specifying this parameter limits too many items in an itemset.
- *Must Contain:* Regular expression to filter itemsets to contain specified items. Use this option to filter out items.

| Result History | FrequentItemSets (FP-Growth) × | AssociationRules (Create Association Rules) × | ExampleSet (Numerical to Binominal) × |

	No. of Sets: 7	Size	Support	Item 1	Item 2	Item 3
Data	Total Max. Size: 3	1	0.833	News		
	Min. Size: 1	1	0.667	Finance		
Annotations	Max. Size: 3	1	0.333	Sports		
	Contains Item:	2	0.667	News	Finance	
		2	0.333	News	Sports	
	Update View	2	0.333	Finance	Sports	
		3	0.333	News	Finance	Sports

FIGURE 6.11
Frequent itemset output.

- *Find Minimum Number of Itemsets:* This option allows the *FP-Growth* operator to lower the support threshold, if fewer itemsets are generated with the given threshold. The support threshold is decreased by 20% in each retry.
  - *Min Number of Itemsets:* Value of minimum number of itemsets to be generated.
  - *Max Number of Retries:* Number of retries allowed in achieving minimum itemsets

In this example, *Min Support* is set to 0.25. The result of the *FP-Growth* operator is the set of itemsets generated, which can be viewed in the results page. The reporting options include filtering based on the number of items and sorting based on the support threshold. Fig. 6.11 shows the output of frequent itemsets operator where all possible itemsets with support higher than the threshold can be seen.

Step 3: Create Association Rules
The next step in association analysis is generation of the most interesting rules from the frequent itemsets created from the *FP-Growth* operator. The *Create Association Rules* operator generates relevant rules from frequent itemsets. The interest measure of the rule can be specified by providing the correct interest criterion based on the dataset under investigation. The input of the *Create Association Rules* operator are frequent itemsets from the *FP-Growth* operator and the output generates all the association rules meeting the interest criterion. These parameters govern the functionality of this operator:

- *Criterion:* Used to select the interest measure to filter the association rules. All other parameters change based on the criterion selection. Confidence, lift, and conviction are commonly used interest criterion.

- *Min Criterion Value:* Specifies the threshold. Rules not meeting the thresholds are discarded.
- The *Gain theta* and *Laplace* parameters are the values specified when using Gain and Laplace parameters for the interest measure.

In this example process, we are using confidence as the criterion and a confidence value of 0.5. Fig. 6.10 shows the completed RapidMiner process for association analysis. The process can be saved and executed.

Step 4: Interpreting the Results

The filtered association analysis rules extracted from the input transactions can be viewed in the results window (Fig. 6.12). The listed association rules are in a table with columns including the premise and conclusion of the rule, as well as the support, confidence, gain, lift, and conviction of the rule. The interactive control window on the left-hand side of the screen allows the users to filter the processed rules to contain the selected item and there is a slide bar to increase the confidence or criterion threshold, thereby, showing fewer rules.

The main purpose of association analysis is to understand the relationship between items. Since the items take the role of both premise and conclusion, a visual representation of relationships between all the items, through a rule,

	AssociationRules (Create Association Rules) ✕								
No.	Premises	Conclusion	Support	Confidence	LaPlace	Gain	p-s	Lift	Convic...
1	Finance	Sports	0.333	0.500	0.800	−1	0.111	1.500	1.333
2	Finance	News, Sports	0.333	0.500	0.800	−1	0.111	1.500	1.333
3	News, Finance	Sports	0.333	0.500	0.800	−1	0.111	1.500	1.333
4	News	Finance	0.667	0.800	0.909	−1	0.111	1.200	1.667
5	Finance	News	0.667	1	1	−0.667	0.111	1.200	∞
6	Sports	News	0.333	1	1	−0.333	0.056	1.200	∞
7	Sports	Finance	0.333	1	1	−0.333	0.111	1.500	∞
8	Sports	News, Finance	0.333	1	1	−0.333	0.111	1.500	∞
9	News, Sports	Finance	0.333	1	1	−0.333	0.111	1.500	∞
10	Finance, Sports	News	0.333	1	1	−0.333	0.056	1.200	∞

FIGURE 6.12

Association rules output.

can help comprehend the analysis. Fig. 6.13 shows the rules in text format and by interconnected graph format through the results window, for selected items. Fig. 6.13B shows the items selected, connected with the rules through arrows. The incoming item to a rule is the premise of the rule and the outgoing item is the conclusion of the association rule.

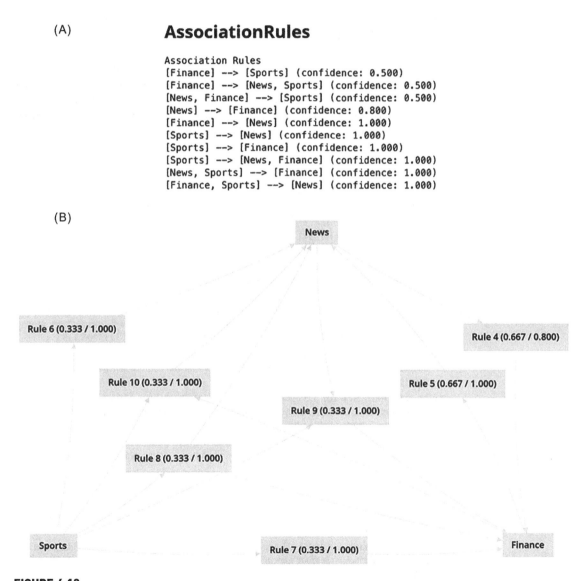

(A)

AssociationRules

Association Rules
[Finance] --> [Sports] (confidence: 0.500)
[Finance] --> [News, Sports] (confidence: 0.500)
[News, Finance] --> [Sports] (confidence: 0.500)
[News] --> [Finance] (confidence: 0.800)
[Finance] --> [News] (confidence: 1.000)
[Sports] --> [News] (confidence: 1.000)
[Sports] --> [Finance] (confidence: 1.000)
[Sports] --> [News, Finance] (confidence: 1.000)
[News, Sports] --> [Finance] (confidence: 1.000)
[Finance, Sports] --> [News] (confidence: 1.000)

(B)

News

Rule 6 (0.333 / 1.000)

Rule 4 (0.667 / 0.800)

Rule 10 (0.333 / 1.000)

Rule 5 (0.667 / 1.000)

Rule 9 (0.333 / 1.000)

Rule 8 (0.333 / 1.000)

Sports

Rule 7 (0.333 / 1.000)

Finance

FIGURE 6.13
Association rules output (A) text view and (B) graph view.

6.4 CONCLUSION

Association rules analysis has gained popularity in the last two decades particularly in retail, online cross selling, recommendation engines, text analysis, document analysis, and web analysis. Typically, a commercial data science tool offers association analysis in its tool package. Though there may be a variation in how the algorithm is implemented in each commercial package, the framework of generating a frequent itemset using a support threshold and generating rules from the itemsets using an interest criterion is the same. Applications that involve large amount of items and real-time decision making, demand new approaches with efficient and scalable association analysis (Zaki, 2000). Association analysis is also one of the prevalent algorithms that is applied to information stored using big data technologies, data streams, and large databases (Tanbeer, Ahmed, Jeong, & Lee, 2008).

References

Agrawal, R., Imieliński, T., & Swami, A. (1993). Mining association rules between sets of items in large databases. In *SIGMOD '93 proceedings of the 1993 ACM SIGMOD international conference on management of data* (pp. 207–216).

Agrawal, R., & Srikant, R. (1994). Fast algorithms for mining association rules. *The international conference on very large databases*, 487–499.

Akbar, M., & Angryk, R. (2008). Frequent pattern-growth approach for document organization. In *Proceeding of the 2nd international workshop on Ontologies and information systems for the semantic web*, ACM (pp. 77–82). Available from http://dl.acm.org/citation.cfm?id = 1458496.

Bodon, F. (2005). A trie-based APRIORI implementation for mining frequent item sequences. In *Proceedings of the 1st international workshop on open source data science frequent pattern mining implementations – OSDM '05* (pp. 56–65). http://dx.doi.org/10.1145/1133905.1133913.

Han, J., Pei, J., & Yin, Y. (2000). Mining frequent patterns without candidate generation. In *SIGMOD '00 proceedings of the 2000 ACM SIGMOD international conference on management of data* (pp. 1–12).

Power, D.J. (2002, Nov 10). *DSS News*. Retrieved Jan 21, 2014, from Desicion Support Systems (DSS). Retrieved Jan 21, 2014, from Desicion Support Systems (DSS), http://www.dssresources.com/newsletters/66.php.

Shang, X., Sattler, K.U., Geist, I. (2004). SQL based frequent pattern mining without candidate generation. In *2004 ACM symposium on applied computing – Poster Abstract* (pp. 618–619).

Tan, P.-N., Steinbach, M., & Kumar, V. (2005). *Association analysis: Basic concepts and algorithms. Introduction to data mining* (pp. 327–404). Boston, MA: Addison Wesley.

Tanbeer, S.K., Ahmed, C.F., Jeong, B.-S., Lee, Y.-K. (2008). Efficient frequent pattern mining over data streams. In *Proceeding of the 17th ACM conference on information and knowledge mining – CIKM '08* (Vol. 1, pp. 1447–1448). http://dx.doi.org/10.1145/1458082.1458326.

Witten, I. H., & Frank, E. (2005). *Algorithms: The basic methods: Mining association rules. Data science: Practical machine learning tools and techniques* (pp. 112–118). San Francisco, CA: Morgan Kaufmann.

Zaki, M. Jk (2000). Scalable algorithms for association mining. *IEEE Transactions on Knowledge and Data Engineering*, 12(3), 372–390. Available from https://doi.org/10.1109/69.846291.

CHAPTER 7

Clustering

Clustering is the process of finding meaningful groups in data. In clustering, the objective is not to predict a target class variable, but to simply capture the possible natural groupings in the data. For example, the customers of a company can be grouped based on purchase behavior. In the past few years, clustering has even found a use in political elections (Pearson & Cooper, 2012). The prospective electoral voters can be clustered into different groups so that candidates can tailor the messages to resonate within each group. the difference between classification and clustering can be illustrated with an example. Categorizing a *given* voter as a "soccer mom" (a known user group) or not, based on previously available labeled data, is supervised learning—Classification. Segregating a population of electorates into different groups, based on similar demographics is unsupervised learning—Clustering. The process of identifying whether a data point belongs to a particular known group is classification. The process of dividing the dataset into meaningful groups is clustering. In mostcases, one would not know ahead what groups to look for and, thus, the inferred groups might be difficult to explain. The task of clustering can be used in two different classes of applications: to *describe* a given dataset and as a *preprocessing* step for other data science algorithms.

CLUSTERING TO DESCRIBE THE DATA

The most common application of clustering is to explore the data and find all the possible meaningful groups in the data. Clustering a company's customer records can yield a few groups in such a way that customers within a group are more like each other than customers belonging to a different group. Depending on the clustering technique used, the number of groups or clusters is either user-defined or automatically determined by the algorithm from the dataset. Since clustering is not about predicting the membership of a customer in a well-defined meaningful group (e.g., frequent high-volume purchaser), the similarities of customers within a group need

221

to be carefully investigated to make sense of the group as a whole. Some of the common applications of clustering to describe the underlying natural structure of data are:

1. *Marketing:* Finding the common groups of customers based on all past customer behaviors, and/or purchase patterns. This task is helpful to segment the customers, identify prototype customers (description of a typical customer of a group), and to tailor a marketing message to the customers in a group.
2. *Document clustering:* One common text mining task is to automatically group documents (or text blobs) into groups of similar topics. Document clustering provides a way of identifying key topics, comprehending and summarizing these clustered groups rather than having to read through whole documents. Document clustering is used for routing customer support incidents, online content sites, forensic investigations, etc.
3. *Session grouping:* In web analytics, clustering is helpful to understand common groups of clickstream patterns and to discover different kinds of clickstream profiles. One clickstream profile may be that of a customer who knows what they want and proceeds straight to checkout. Another profile may be that of a customer who has researched the products, read through customer reviews, and then makes a purchase during a later session. Clustering the web sessions by profile helps the e-commerce company provide features fitting each customer profile.

CLUSTERING FOR PREPROCESSING

Since a clustering process considers all the attributes of the dataset and *reduces* the information to a cluster, which is really another attribute (i.e., the ID of the cluster to which a record would belong to), clustering can be used as a data compression technique. The output of clustering is the cluster ID for each record and it can be used as an input variable for other data science tasks. Hence, clustering can be employed as a preprocessing technique for other data science processes. In general, clustering can be used for two types of preprocessing:

1. *Clustering to reduce dimensionality:* In an n-dimensional dataset (n number of attributes), the computational complexity is proportional to the number of dimensions or "n." With clustering, n-dimensional attributes can be converted or reduced to one categorical attribute— "Cluster ID." This reduces the complexity, although there will be some loss of information because of the dimensionality reduction to one

single attribute. Chapter 14, Feature Selection provides an in-depth look at feature selection techniques.

2. *Clustering for object reduction:* Assume that the number of customers for an organization is in the millions and the number of cluster groups is 100. For each of these 100 cluster groups, one "poster child" customer can be identified that represents the typical characteristics of all the customers in that cluster group. The poster child customer can be an actual customer or a fictional customer. The prototype of a cluster is the most common representation of all the customers in a group. Reducing millions of customer records to 100 prototype records provides an obvious benefit. In some applications, instead of processing millions of records, just the prototypes can be processed for further classification or regression tasks. This greatly reduces the record count and the dataset can be made appropriate for classification by algorithms like k-nearest neighbor (k-NN) where computation complexity depends on the number of records.

TYPES OF CLUSTERING TECHNIQUES

Regardless of the types of clustering applications, the clustering process seeks to find groupings in data, in such a way that data points within a cluster are more *similar* to each other than to data points in the other clusters (Witten & Frank, 2005). One common way of measuring similarity is the Euclidean distance measurement in n-dimensional space. In Fig. 7.1 all data points in Cluster 2 are closer to other data points in Cluster 2 than to other data points in Cluster 1. Before explaining the different ways to implement clustering, the different types of clusters have to be defined. Based on a data point's membership to an identified group, a cluster can be:

- *Exclusive or strict partitioning clusters*: Each data object belongs to one exclusive cluster, like the example shown in Fig. 7.1. This is the most common type of cluster.
- *Overlapping clusters*: The cluster groups are not exclusive, and each data object may belong to more than one cluster. These are also known as multi-view clusters. For example, a customer of a company can be grouped in a high-profit customer cluster and a high-volume customer cluster at the same time.
- *Hierarchical clusters*: Each child cluster can be merged to form a parent cluster. For example, the most profitable customer cluster can be further divided into a long-term customer cluster and a cluster with new customers with high-value purchases.

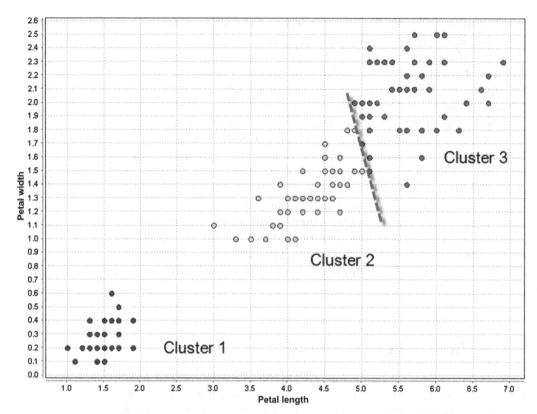

FIGURE 7.1
Example of a clustering of the Iris dataset without class labels.

- *Fuzzy or probabilistic clusters*: Each data point belongs to all cluster groups with varying degrees of membership from 0 to 1. For example, in a dataset with clusters A, B, C, and D, a data point can be associated with all the clusters with degree A = 0.5, B = 0.1, C = 0.4, and D = 0. Instead of a definite association of a data point with one cluster, fuzzy clustering associates a probability of membership to all the clusters.

Clustering techniques can also be classified based on the algorithmic approach used to find clusters in the dataset. Each of these classes of clustering algorithms differ based on what relationship they leverage between the data objects.

- *Prototype-based clustering*: In the prototype-based clustering, each cluster is represented by a central data object, also called a prototype. The prototype of each cluster is usually the center of the cluster, hence, this clustering is also called centroid clustering or center-based clustering. For example, in clustering customer segments, each customer cluster will have a central prototype customer and customers with similar properties are associated with the prototype customer of a cluster.

- **Density clustering**: In Fig. 7.1, it can be observed that clusters occupy the area where there are more data points per unit space and are separated by sparse space. A cluster can also be defined as a dense region where data objects are concentrated surrounded by a low-density area where data objects are sparse. Each dense area can be assigned a cluster and the low-density area can be discarded as noise. In this form of clustering not all data objects are clustered since noise objects are unassigned to any cluster.
- **Hierarchical clustering**: Hierarchical clustering is a process where a cluster hierarchy is created based on the distance between data points. The output of a hierarchical clustering is a *dendrogram*: a tree diagram that shows different clusters at any point of precision which is specified by the user. There are two approaches to create a hierarchy of clusters. A bottom-up approach is where each data point is considered a cluster, and the clusters are merged to finally form one massive cluster. The top-down approach is where the dataset is considered one cluster and they are recursively divided into different sub-clusters until individual data objects are defined as separate clusters. Hierarchical clustering is useful when the data size is limited. A level of interactive feedback is required to cut the dendrogram tree to a given level of precision.
- **Model-based clustering**: Model-based clustering gets its foundation from statistics and probability distribution models; this technique is also called distribution-based clustering. A cluster can be thought of as a grouping that has the data points belonging to the same probability distribution. Hence, each cluster can be represented by a distribution model (like Gaussian or Poisson), where the parameter of the distribution can be iteratively optimized between the cluster data and the model. With this approach, the entire dataset can be represented by a mixture of distribution models. *Mixture of Gaussians* is one of the model-based clustering techniques used where a fixed number of distributions are initialized, and parameters are optimized to fit the cluster data.

In the rest of the chapter, the common implementations of clustering will be discussed. First, *k*-means clustering will be covered, which is a kind of prototype-clustering technique. This is followed by the Density-Based Spatial Clustering of Applications with Noise (DBSCAN), which provides a view into density clustering, and the chapter is concluded with an explanation of a novel approach called self-organizing maps (SOMs).

SEGMENTING CUSTOMER RECORDS

All business entities record most of their interactions with customers, including but not limited to monetary transactions, customer service, customer location and details, online interactions, product usage, and warranty and service information. Take the telecommunications industry as an example. Telecommunications companies have now evolved to provide multiple services to different types of customers by packaging products like phones, wireless, internet, data communications, corporate backbones, entertainment content, home security, etc. To better understand customers, whose numbers often range in the millions, it is necessary to combine multiple datasets about the customers and their interactions with each product. The vastness of the number and variety of attributes in the dataset provides both an opportunity and challenge to better know their customers (Berry & Linoff, 2000a,b). One logical way to understand the customer beyond straightforward classifications like customer type (residential, corporate, government, etc.) or revenue volume (high-, medium-, and low-revenue customers), is to segment the customer based on usage patterns, demographics, geography, and behavior patterns for product usage.

For a customer segmentation task, the data need to be prepared in such a way that each record (row) is associated with each customer and the columns contain all the attributes about the customer, including demographics, address, products used, revenue details, usage details of the product, call volume, type of calls, call duration, time of calls, etc. Table 7.1 shows an example structure of a denormalized customer dataset. Preparing this dataset is going to be a time-consuming task. One of the obvious methods of segmentation is stratifying based on any of the existing attributes. For example, one can segment the data based on a customer's geographical location.

A clustering algorithm consumes this data and groups the customers with similar patterns into clusters based on all the attributes. Based on the data, clustering could be based on a combination of call usage, data patterns, and monthly bills. The resulting clusters could be a group of customers who have low data usage but with high bills at a location where there is weak cellular coverage, which may indicate dissatisfied customers.

The clustering algorithm doesn't explicitly provide the reason for clustering and doesn't intuitively label the cluster groups. While clustering can be performed using a large number of attributes, it is up to the practitioner to carefully select the attributes that will be relevant for clustering. Automated feature selection methods can reduce the dimensions for a clustering exercise. Clustering could be iteratively developed further by selecting or ignoring other attributes in the customer dataset.

Table 7.1 Dataset for Customer Segmentation

Customer ID	Location	Demographics	Call Usage	Data Usage (MB)	Monthly Bill ($)
01	San Jose, CA	Male	1400	200	75.23
02	Miami, FL	Female	2103	5000	125.78
03	Los Angeles, CA	Male	292	2000	89.90
04	San Jose, CA	Female	50	40	59.34

7.1 *K*-MEANS CLUSTERING

k-Means clustering is a prototype-based clustering method where the dataset is divided into *k*-clusters. *k*-Means clustering is one of the simplest and most commonly used clustering algorithms. In this technique, the user specifies the number of clusters (*k*) that need to be grouped in the dataset.

The objective of *k*-means clustering is to find a *prototype* data point for each cluster; all the data points are then assigned to the nearest prototype, which then forms a cluster. The prototype is called as the *centroid*, the center of the cluster. The center of the cluster can be the mean of all data objects in the cluster, as in *k*-means, or the most represented data object, as in *k*-medoid clustering. The cluster centroid or mean data object does not have to be a real data point in the dataset and can be an imaginary data point that represents the characteristics of all the data points within the cluster.

The *k*-means clustering algorithm is based on the works of Stuart Lloyd and E.W. Forgy (Lloyd, 1982) and is sometimes referred to as the Lloyd—Forgy algorithm or Lloyd's algorithm. Visually, the *k*-means algorithm divides the data space into *k* partitions or boundaries, where the centroid in each partition is the prototype of the clusters. The data objects inside a partition belong to the cluster. These partitions are also called *Voronoi partitions*, and each prototype is a seed in a Voronoi partition. A Voronoi partition is a process of segmenting a space into regions, around a set of points called seeds. All other points are then associated to the nearest seed and the points associated with the seed from a unique partition. Fig. 7.2 shows a sample Voronoi partition around seeds marked as black dots.

k-Means clustering creates *k* partitions in *n*-dimensional space, where *n* is the number of attributes in a given dataset. To partition the dataset, a proximity measure has to be defined. The most commonly used measure for a numeric attribute is the Euclidean distance. Fig. 7.3 illustrates the clustering of the Iris dataset with only the petal length and petal width attributes. This Iris dataset is two-dimensional (selected for easy visual explanation), with numeric attributes and *k* specified as 3. The outcome of *k*-means clustering provides a clear partition space for Cluster 1 and a narrow space for the other two clusters, Cluster 2 and Cluster 3.

7.1.1 How It Works

The logic of finding *k*-clusters within a given dataset is rather simple and always converges to a solution. However, the final result in most cases will be locally optimal where the solution will not converge to the best global solution. The process of *k*-means clustering is similar to Voronoi iteration, where the objective is to divide a space into cells around points. The difference is Voronoi iteration partitions the space, whereas, *k*-means clustering partitions the points in data space. Take the example of a two-dimensional dataset (Fig. 7.4). The step-by-step process of finding three clusters is provided below (Tan, Michael, & Kumar, 2005).

FIGURE 7.2

Voronoi partition "Euclidean Voronoi Diagram" by Raincomplex—personal work. Licensed under Creative Commons Zero, Public Domain Dedication via Wikimedia Commons. http://commons.wikimedia.org/wiki/File:Euclidean_Voronoi_Diagram.png#mediaviewer/File:Euclidean_Voronoi_Diagram.png.[1])

Step 1: Initiate Centroids

The first step in k-means algorithm is to initiate k random centroids. The number of clusters k should be specified by the user. In this case, three centroids are initiated in a given data space. In Fig. 7.5, each initial centroid is given a shape (with a circle to differentiate centroids from other data points) so that data points assigned to a centroid can be indicated by the same shape.

Step 2: Assign Data Points

Once centroids have been initiated, all the data points are now assigned to the nearest centroid to form a cluster. In this context the "nearest" is calculated by a proximity measure. Euclidean distance measurement is the most common proximity measure, though other measures like the Manhattan measure and Jaccard coefficient can be used. The Euclidean distance between two data points X $(x_1, x_2,..., x_n)$ and C $(c_1, c_2,..., c_n)$ with n attributes is given by (7.1)

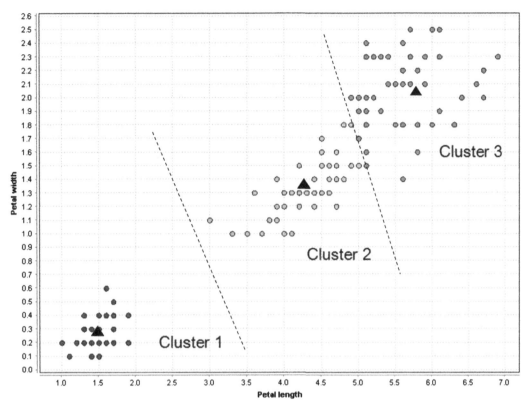

FIGURE 7.3
Prototype-based clustering and boundaries.

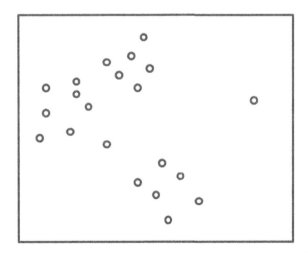

FIGURE 7.4
Dataset with two dimensions.

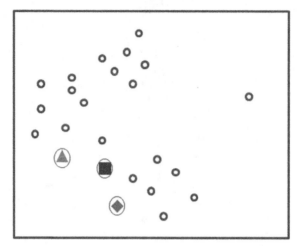

FIGURE 7.5
Initial random centroids.

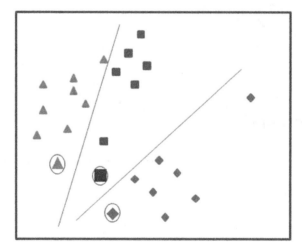

FIGURE 7.6
Assignment of data points to nearest centroids.

$$\text{Distance } d = \sqrt{(x_1 - c_1)^2 + (x_2 - c_2)^2 + \ldots + (x_n - c_n)^2} \qquad (7.1)$$

All the data points associated to a centroid now have the same shape as their corresponding centroid as shown in Fig. 7.6. This step also leads to partitioning of data space into Voronoi partitions, with lines shown as boundaries.

Step 3: Calculate New Centroids

For each cluster, a new centroid can now be calculated, which is also the prototype of each cluster group. This new centroid is the most representative data point of all data points in the cluster. Mathematically, this step can be expressed as minimizing the sum of squared errors (SSEs) of all data points in a cluster to the centroid of the cluster. The overall objective of the step is to minimize the SSEs of individual clusters. The SSE of a cluster can be calculated using Eq. (7.2).

$$SSE = \sum_{i=1}^{k} \sum_{x_j \in C_i} \|x_j - \mu_i\|^2 \tag{7.2}$$

where C_i is the ith cluster, j are the data points in a given cluster, μ_i is the centroid for i^{th} cluster, and x_j is a specific data object. The centroid with minimal SSE for the given cluster i is the new mean of the cluster. The mean of the cluster can be calculated using (7.3)

$$\mu_i = \frac{1}{j_i} \sum_{x \in C_i} X \tag{7.3}$$

where X is the data object vector $(x_1, x_2, \ldots, x_n)$. In the case of k-means clustering, the new centroid will be the mean of all the data points. k-Medoid clustering is a variation of k-means clustering, where the median is calculated instead of the mean. Fig. 7.7 shows the location of the new centroids.

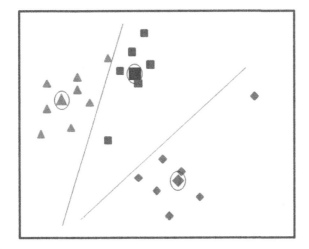

FIGURE 7.7
New centroids.

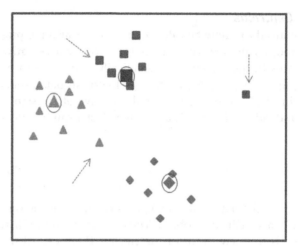

FIGURE 7.8
Assignment of data points to new centroids.

Step 4: Repeat Assignment and Calculate New Centroids

Once the new centroids have been identified, assigning data points to the nearest centroid is repeated until all the data points are reassigned to new centroids. In Fig. 7.8, note the change in assignment of three data points that belonged to different clusters in the previous step.

Step 5: Termination

Step 3—calculating new centroids, and step 4—assigning data points to new centroids, are repeated until no further change in assignment of data points happens. In other words, no significant change in centroids are noted. The final centroids are declared the prototypes of the clusters and they are used to describe the whole clustering model. Each data point in the dataset is now tied with a new clustering ID attribute that identifies the cluster.

Special Cases

Even though k-means clustering is simple and easy to implement, one of the key drawbacks of k-means clustering is that the algorithm seeks to find a *local optimum*, which may not yield globally optimal clustering. In this approach, the algorithm starts with an initial configuration (centroids) and continuously improves to find the best solution possible for that initial configuration. Since the solution is optimal to the initial configuration (locally optimal), there might be a better optimal solution if the initial configuration changes. The locally optimal solution may not be the most optimal solution for the given clustering problem. Hence, the success of a k-means algorithm much depends on the initiation of centroids. This limitation can be addressed by having multiple random initiations; in each run one could measure the cohesiveness of the clusters by a *performance criterion*. The clustering run with the best performance metric can be chosen as the final run. Evaluation of clustering is discussed in the next section. Some key issues to be considered in *k*-means clustering are:

- *Initiation:* The final clustering grouping depends on the random initiator and the nature of the dataset. When random initiation is used, one can run the entire clustering process (also called "runs") with a different set of random initiators and find the clustering process that has minimal total SSE. Another technique is hierarchical clustering, where each cluster is in turn split into multiple clusters and, thereby, minimal SSE is achieved. Hierarchical clustering is further divided into agglomerative or bottom-up clustering and divisive or top-down clustering, depending on how the clustering is initiated. Agglomerative clustering starts with each data point as an individual cluster and proceeds to combine data points into clusters. Divisive clustering starts with the whole dataset as one big cluster and proceeds to split that into multiple clusters.

- *Empty clusters:* One possibility in *k*-means clustering is the formation of empty clusters in which no data objects are associated. If empty clusters are formed, a new centroid can be introduced in the cluster that has the highest SSE, thereby, splitting the cluster that contributes to the highest SSE or selecting a new centroid that is at the farthest point away from any other centroid.

- *Outliers:* Since SSE is used as an objective function, *k*-means clustering is susceptible to outliers; they drift the centroid away from the representative data points in a cluster. Hence, the prototype is no longer the best representative of the clusters it represents. While outliers can be eliminated with preprocessing techniques, in some applications finding outliers or a group of outliers is the objective of clustering, similar to identifying fraudulent transactions.

- *Post-processing:* Since *k*-means clustering seeks to be locally optimal, a few post-processing techniques can be introduced to force a new solution that has less SSE. One could always increase the number of clusters, *k*, and reduce SSE. But, this technique can start overfitting the dataset and yield less useful information. There are a few approaches that can be deployed, such as bisecting the cluster that has the highest SSE and merging two clusters into one even if SSE increases slightly.

Evaluation of Clusters

Evaluation of *k*-means clustering is different from regression and classification algorithms because in clustering there are no known external labels for comparison. The evaluation parameter will have to be developed from the very dataset that is being evaluated. This is called unsupervised or internal evaluation. Evaluation of clustering can be as simple as computing total SSE. Good models will have low SSE within the cluster and low overall SSE among all clusters. SSE can also be referred to as the average within-cluster distance and can be calculated for each cluster and then averaged for all the clusters.

Another commonly used evaluation measure is the Davies–Bouldin index (Davies & Bouldin, 1979). The Davies–Bouldin index is a measure of uniqueness of the clusters and takes into consideration both cohesiveness of the cluster (distance between the data points and center of the cluster) and separation between the clusters. It is the function of the ratio of within-cluster separation to the separation between the clusters. The lower the value of the Davies–Bouldin index, the better the clustering. However, both SSE and the Davies–Bouldin index have the limitation of not guaranteeing better clustering when they have lower scores.

7.1.2   How to Implement

k-Means clustering implementation in RapidMiner is simple and straightforward with one operator for modeling and one for unsupervised evaluation. In the modeling step, the parameter for the number of clusters, k, is specified as desired. The output model is a list of centroids for each cluster and a new attribute is attached to the original input dataset with the cluster ID. The cluster label is appended to the original dataset for each data point and can be visually evaluated after the clustering. A model evaluation step is required to calculate the average cluster distance and Davies–Bouldin index.

For this implementation, the Iris dataset will be used with four attributes and 150 data objects (Fisher, 1936). Even though a class label is not needed for clustering, it was kept for later explanation to see if identified clusters from an unlabeled dataset are similar to natural clusters of species in the dataset.

Step 1: Data Preparation

k-Means clustering accepts both numeric and polynominal data types; however, the distance measures are more effective with numeric data types. The number of attributes increases the dimension space for clustering. In this example the number of attributes has been limited to two by selecting petal width (a3) and petal length (a4) using the *Select attribute* operator as shown in Fig. 7.9. It is easy to visualize the mechanics of k-means algorithm by looking at two-dimensional plots for clustering. In practical implementations, clustering datasets will have more attributes.

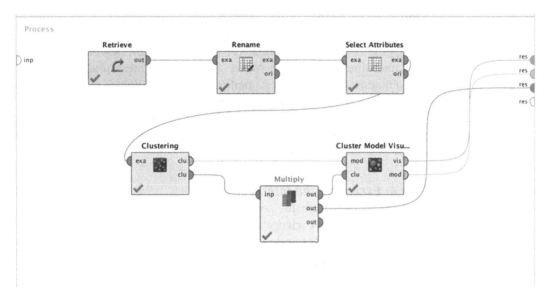

FIGURE 7.9
Data science process for *k*-means clustering.

Step 2: Clustering Operator and Parameters

The *k*-means modeling operator is available in the Modeling > Clustering and Segmentation folder of RapidMiner. These parameters can be configured in the model operator:

- *k*: *k* is the desired number of clusters.
- *Add cluster as attribute*: Append cluster labels (IDs) into the original dataset. Turning on this option is recommended for later analysis.
- *Max runs*: Since the effectiveness of *k*-means clustering is dependent on random initial centroids, multiple runs are required to select the clustering with the lowest SSE. The number of such runs can be specified here.
- *Measure type*: The proximity measure can be specified in this parameter. The default and most common measurement is Euclidean distance (L2). Other options here are Manhattan distance (L1), Jaccard coefficient, and cosine similarity for document data. Please refer to Chapter 4, Classification section *k*-NN for description on distance measures.
- *Max optimization steps*: This parameter specifies the number of iterations of assigning data objects to centroids and calculating new centroids.

The output of the modeling step includes the cluster model with *k* centroid data objects and the initial dataset appended with cluster labels. Cluster labels are named generically such as cluster_0, cluster_1,..., cluster_*k*−1.

Step 3: Evaluation

Since the attributes used in the dataset are numeric, the effectiveness of clustering groups need to be evaluated using SSE and the Davies—Bouldin index. In RapidMiner, the *Cluster Model Visualizer* operator under Modeling > Segmentation is available for a performance evaluation of cluster groups and visualization. *Cluster Model Visualizer* operator needs both inputs from the modeling step: cluster centroid vector (model) and the labeled dataset. The two measurement outputs of the evaluation are average cluster distance and the Davies—Bouldin index.

Step 4: Execution and Interpretation

After the outputs from the *performance* operator have been connected to the result ports, the data science process can be executed. These outputs can be observed from results window:

- *Cluster Model (Clustering):* The model output contains the centroid for each of the k-clusters, along with their attribute values. As shown in Fig. 7.10, in the text view and folder view sections, all the data objects associated with the each cluster can be seen. The centroid plot view provides the parallel chart view (Chapter 3: Data Exploration) of the centroids. A large separation between centroids is desirable, because well-separated clusters divide the dataset cleanly.
- *Labeled example set:* The appended dataset has some of the most important information on clustering. The generic Iris dataset of 150 observations is clustered in three groups. The cluster value is appended as a new special polynominal attribute and takes a generic label format. In the scatterplot view of this output dataset, the x- and y-axes can be configured to be attributes of the original dataset, petal length and petal width. In the plot in Fig. 7.11, it can be noted how the algorithm identified clusters. This output can be compared against the original label (Iris species). and only five data points in the border of I. *versicolor* and I. *virginica* are mis-clustered! The k-means clustering process identified the different species in the dataset almost exactly.
- *Visualizer and Performance vector:* The output of the Cluster Model Visualizer shows the centroid charts, table, scatter plots, heatmaps, and performance evaluation metrics like average distance measured and the Davies—Bouldin index (Fig. 7.12). This step can be used to compare multiple clustering processes with different parameters. In advanced implementations, it is possible to determine the value of "k" using *Optimize Parameters* operator, based on the number of looped clustering runs with various values of k. Amongst multiple clustering runs each with a distinct value for k, the k value with the lowest average-within-centroid distance or Davies—Bouldin index is selected as the most optimal.

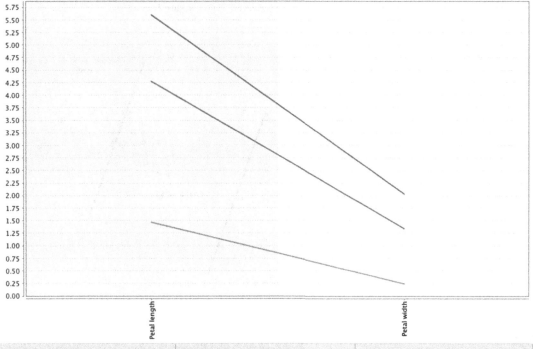

Cluster	Petal length	Petal width
Cluster 0	4.269	1.342
Cluster 1	1.464	0.244
Cluster 2	5.596	2.037

FIGURE 7.10
k-Means clustering centroids output.

The *k*-means clustering algorithm is simple, easy to implement, and easy to interpret. Although the algorithm can effectively handle an *n*-dimensional dataset, the operation will be expensive with a higher number of iterations and runs. One of the key limitations of *k*-means is that it relies on the user to assign the value of *k* (Berry & Linoff, 2000a,2000b). The number of clusters in the dataset will be unknown to begin with and an arbitrary number can limit the ability to find the right number of natural clusters in the dataset. There are a variety of methods to estimate the right number for *k*, ranging from the Bayesian Information Criterion to hierarchical methods that increase the value of *k* until the data points assigned to the cluster are Gaussian (Hamerly & Elkan, 2003). For a start, it is recommended to use a

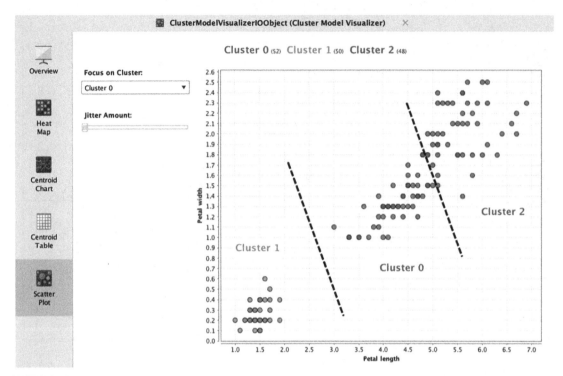

FIGURE 7.11
k-Means clustering visual output.

value of *k* in the low single digits and increasing it until it fits. Clustering using density methods will help provide an idea into the number of clusters and could be used as a value of *k* in *k*-means clustering.

Since the centroid prototype approach is used, *k*-means tends to find globular clusters in the dataset. However, natural clusters can be of all shapes and sizes. The presence of outliers possesses a challenge in the modeling of *k*-means clustering. The simplicity of the *k*-means clustering technique makes it a great choice for quick evaluation of globular clusters and as a preprocessing technique for data science modeling and for dimensionality reduction.

7.2   DBSCAN CLUSTERING

A cluster can also be defined as an area of high concentration (or density) of data objects surrounded by areas of low concentration (or density) of data objects. A density-clustering algorithm identifies clusters in the data based on the measurement of the density distribution in *n*-dimensional space. Unlike

FIGURE 7.12
Performance measures of *k*-means clustering.

centroid methods, specifying the number of the cluster parameters (*k*) is not necessary for density-based algorithms. Thus, density-based clustering can serve as an important data exploration technique. DBSCAN is one of the most commonly used density-clustering algorithms (Ester, Kriegel, Sander, & Xu,1996). To understand how the algorithm works, the concept of density in a data space first needs to be defined.

Density can be defined as the number of data points in a unit *n*-dimensional space. The number of dimensions *n* is the number of attributes in a dataset. To simplify the visualization and to further understand how the model works, consider a two-dimensional space or a dataset with two numeric attributes. From looking at the dataset represented in Fig. 7.13, it can be visually concluded that the density in the top-left section is higher than the density in top-right, bottom-left, and bottom-right sections. Technically, density relates to the number of points in unit space, in this case a quadrant. Wherever there is high-density space amongst relatively low-density spaces, there is a cluster.

One can also measure density within a circular space around a point as in Fig. 7.14. The number of points within a circular space with radius ε

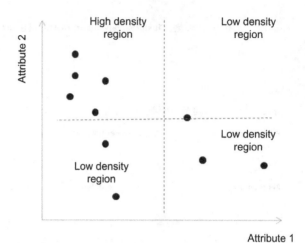

FIGURE 7.13
Dataset with two attributes.

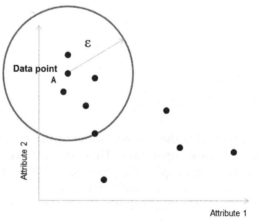

FIGURE 7.14
Density of a data point within radius ε.

(epsilon) around a data point A is six. This measure is called center-based density since the space considered is globular with the center being the point that is considered.

7.2.1   How It Works

The DBSCAN algorithm creates clusters by identifying high-density and low-density space within the dataset. Similar to k-means clustering, it is preferred that the attributes are numeric because distance calculation is still used. The algorithm can be reduced to three steps: defining threshold density, classification of data points, and clustering (Tan et al., 2005).

Step 1: Defining Epsilon and MinPoints

The DBSCAN algorithm starts with calculation of a density for all data points in a dataset, with a given fixed radius ε (epsilon). To determine whether a neighborhood is high-density or low-density, a threshold of data points (MinPoints) will have to be defined, above which the neighborhood is considered high-density. In Fig. 7.14, the number of data points inside the space is defined by radius ε. If MinPoints is defined as 5, the space ε surrounding data point A is considered a high-density region. Both ε and MinPoints are user-defined parameters and can be altered for a dataset.

Step 2: Classification of Data Points

In a dataset, with a given ε and MinPoints, all data points can be defined into three buckets (Fig. 7.15):

- *Core points*: All the data points inside the high-density region of at least one data point are considered a core point. A high-density region is a space where there are at least *MinPoints* data points within a radius of ε for any data point.
- *Border points*: Border points sit on the circumference of radius ε from a data point. A border point is the boundary between high-density and

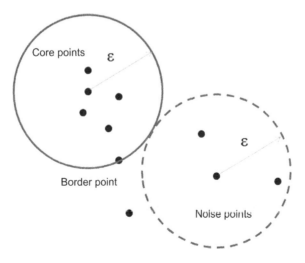

FIGURE 7.15
Core, border, and density points.

low-density space. Border points are counted within the high-density space calculation.

- *Noise points*: Any point that is neither a core point nor border point is called a noise point. They form a low-density region around the high-density region.

Step 3: Clustering

Once all data points in the dataset are classified into density points, clustering is a straightforward task. Groups of core points form distinct clusters. If two core points are within ε of each other, then both core points are within the same cluster. All these clustered core points form a cluster, which is surrounded by low-density noise points. All noise points form low-density regions around the high-density cluster, and noise points are not classified in any cluster. Since DBSCAN is a partial clustering algorithm, a few data points are left unlabeled or associated to a default noise cluster.

Optimizing Parameters

One of the key advantages of using a density algorithm is that there is no need for specifying the number of clusters (k). Clusters are automatically found in the dataset. However, there is an issue with selecting the distance parameter ε and a minimum threshold (MinPoints) to identify the dense region. One technique used to estimate optimal parameters for the DBSCAN clustering algorithm relates to the k-NN algorithm. The initial values of the parameter can be estimated by building a k-distribution graph. For a user-specified value of k (say, four data points), the distance of the k-th NN can be calculated for a data point. If the data point is a core point in a high-density region, then the distance of the k-th NN will be smaller. For a noise point, the distance will be larger. Similarly, the k-distance can be calculated for all data points in a dataset. A k-distance distribution graph can be built by arranging all the k-distance values of individual data points in descending order, as shown in Fig. 7.16. This arrangement is similar to Pareto charts. Points on the right-hand side of the chart will belong to data points inside a cluster, because the distance is smaller. In most datasets, the value of k-distance sharply rises after a particular value. The distance at which the chart rises will be the optimal value ε (epsilon) and the value of k can be used for MinPoints.

Special Cases: Varying Densities

The DBSCAN algorithm partitions data based on a certain threshold density. This approach creates an issue when a dataset contains areas of varying data density. The dataset in Fig. 7.17 has four distinct regions numbered from 1–4. Region 1 is the high-density area A, regions 2 and 4 are of medium-density B, and between them is region 3, which is extremely low-density C. If

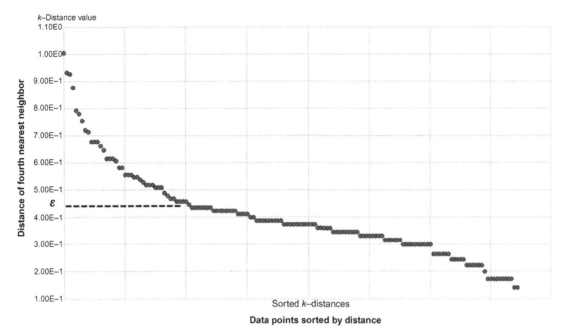

FIGURE 7.16
k-Distribution chart for the Iris dataset with $k = 4$.

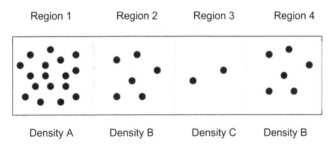

FIGURE 7.17
Dataset with varying densities.

the density threshold parameters are tuned in such a way as to partition and identify region 1, then regions 2 and 4 (with density B) will be considered noise, along with region 3. Even though region 4 with density B is next to an extremely low-density area and clearly identifiable visually, the DBSCAN algorithm will classify regions 2 through 4 as noise. The k-means clustering algorithm is better at partitioning datasets with varying densities.

7.2.2   How to Implement

The implementation of the DBSCAN algorithm is supported in RapidMiner through the DBSCAN modeling operator. The DBSCAN operator accepts numeric and polynominal datasets with provisions for user-specified ε (epsilon) and MinPoints parameters. Here are the implementation steps.

Step 1: Data Preparation

As with the k-means section, the number of attributes in the dataset will be limited to a3 and a4 (petal length and petal width) using the *Select Attribute* operator, so that the cluster can be visualized and the clustering process better understood.

Step 2: Clustering Operator and Parameters

The modeling operator is available in the Modeling > Clustering and Segmentation folder and is labeled DBSCAN. These parameters can be configured in the model operator:

- *Epsilon (ε)*: Size of the high-density neighborhood. The default value is 1.
- *MinPoints*: Minimum number of data objects within the epsilon neighborhood to qualify as a cluster.
- *Distance measure*: The proximity measure can be specified in this parameter. The default and most common measurement is Euclidean distance. Other options here are Manhattan distance, Jaccard coefficient, and cosine similarity for document data. Please refer to Chapter 4, Classification for a summary of different distance measures.
- *Add cluster as attributes*: To append cluster labels into the original dataset. This option is recommended for later analysis.

Step 3: Evaluation

Similar to k-means clustering implementation, the effectiveness of clustering groups can be evaluated using average within-cluster distance. In RapidMiner, the *Cluster Density Performance* operator under Evaluation > Clustering is available for performance evaluation of cluster groups generated by Density algorithms. The clustering model and labeled dataset are connected to *performance* operator for cluster evaluation. Additionally, to aid the calculation, *performance* operator expects Similarity Measure objects. A similarity measure vector is a distance measure of every example data object with the other data object. The similarity measure can be calculated by using *Data to Similarity* Operator on the example dataset.

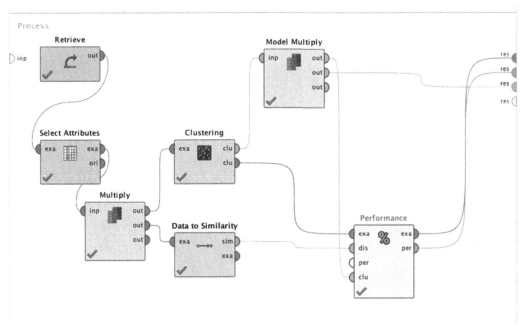

FIGURE 7.18
Data science process with density clustering.

Step 4: Execution and Interpretation

After the outputs from the *performance* operator have been connected to the result ports, as shown in Fig. 7.18, the model can be executed. The result output can be observed as:

1. *Model*: The cluster model output contains information on the number of clusters found in the dataset (Cluster 1, Cluster 2, etc.) and data objects identified as noise points (Cluster 0). If no noise points are found, then Cluster 0 is an empty cluster. As shown in Fig. 7.19, the Folder view and Graph view from the output window provide the visualization of data points classified under different clusters.

2. *Clustered example set*: The example set now has a clustering label that can be used for further analysis and visualization. In the scatterplot view of this dataset (Fig. 7.20), x- and y-axes can be configured to be attributes of the original dataset, petal length and petal width. The Color Column can be configured to be the new cluster label. In the plot, it can be noted how the algorithm found two clusters within the example set. The I. *setosa* species data objects have clear high-density areas but there is a density bridge between the I. *versicolor* and I. *virginica* species data points. There is no clear low-density area to

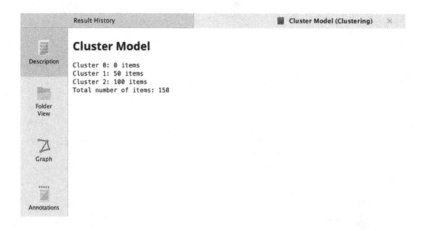

FIGURE 7.19
Density-clustering model output.

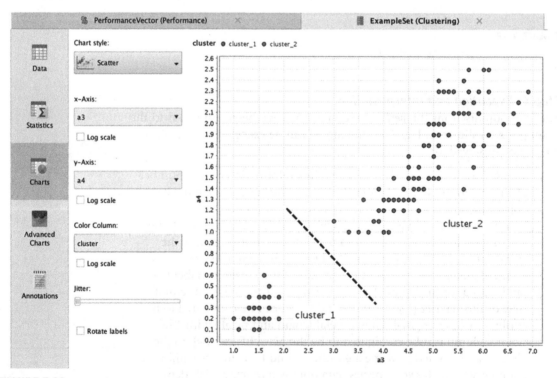

FIGURE 7.20
Density-clustering visual output.

partition these two species of data points. Hence, I. *versicolor* and I. *virginica* natural clusters are combined to one artificial predicted cluster. The epsilon and MinPoints parameters can be adjusted to find different results for the clustering.

3. *Performance vector*: The performance vector window shows the average distance within each cluster and the average of all clusters. The average distance is the distance between all the data points within the cluster divided by number of data points. These measures can be used to compare the performance of multiple model runs.

The main attraction of using DBSCAN clustering is that one does not have to specify the value of k, the number of clusters to be identified. In many practical applications, the number of clusters to be discovered will be unknown, like finding unique customers or electoral segments. DBSCAN uses variations in the density of the data distribution to find the concentration of structures in the data. These clusters can be of any shape and they are not confined to globular structures as in the k-means approach. But the density algorithms run into the risk of finding bridges between two natural clusters and merging them into one cluster.

Since the density-clustering technique yields partial clustering, DBSCAN ignores noise and outlier data points and they are not clustered in the final results. The inability to identify varying densities within a dataset is one of the major limitations of the DBSCAN clustering technique. Centroid methods are more successful at finding varying density patterns in a dataset. A dataset with a high number of attributes will have processing challenges with density-clustering methods. Given the complementary pros and cons of the k-means and DBSCAN methods, it is advisable to cluster the dataset by both methods and understand the patterns of both result sets.

7.3 SELF-ORGANIZING MAPS

A self-organizing map (SOM) is a powerful visual clustering technique that evolved from a combination of neural networks and prototype-based clustering. A SOM is a form of neural network where the output is an organized visual matrix, usually a two-dimensional grid with rows and columns. The objective of this neural network is to transfer all input data objects with n attributes (n dimensions) to the output lattice in such a way that objects next to each other are closely related to each other. Two examples of SOM layouts are provided in Fig. 7.21. This two-dimensional matrix becomes an exploration tool in identifying the clusters of objects related to each other by visual examination. A key distinction in this neural network is the absence of an output target function to optimize or predict, hence, it is an unsupervised learning algorithm. SOMs effectively arrange the data points in a lower

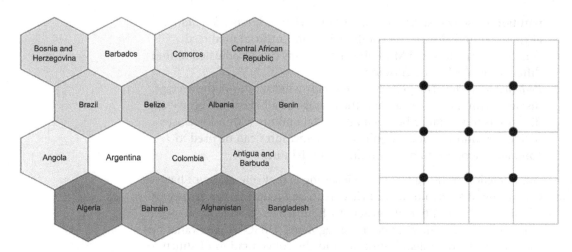

FIGURE 7.21

Self-organizing maps of countries by GDP data using a (A) hexagonal grid and (B) rectangular lattice. *GDP*, Gross domestic product.

dimensional space, thereby, aiding in the visualization of high-dimensional data through a low-dimensional space.

SOMs are relevant to clustering because the most common SOM output is a two-dimensional grid with data objects placed next to each other based on their similarity to one another. Objects related to each other are placed in close proximity. SOMs differ from other clustering techniques because there is no explicit clustering labels assigned to data objects. Data objects are arranged based on their attribute proximity and the task of clustering is left to visual analysis by the user. Hence, SOM is used as a *visual* clustering and data exploration technique (Germano, 1999).

SOMs were first proposed by Kohonen (1982) and, hence, this technique is also known as Kohonen networks; it is sometimes also referred to by a more specific name, self-organizing feature maps. SOM methodology is used to project data objects from *data space*, mostly in *n* dimensions, to *grid space*, usually resulting in two dimensions. Though other output formats are possible, the most common output formats for SOMs are: (1) a hexagonal lattice or a (2) rectangular grid as shown in Fig. 7.21. Each data point from the dataset occupies a cell or a node in the output lattice, with arrangement constraints depending on the similarity of data points. Each cell in the SOM grid, called a *neuron*, corresponds to one or a group of data points. In a hexagonal grid, each neuron has six neighbors while a rectangular lattice has four neighbors.

SOMs are commonly used in comparing data points with a large number of numeric attributes. The objective of this kind of analysis is to compare the relative features of data objects in a simple two-dimensional setting where the placement of objects is related to each other. In Fig. 7.21A, the SOM compares relative gross domestic product (GDP) data from different countries where countries with similar GDP profiles are placed either in the same cells or next to each other. All similar countries around a particular cell can be considered a grouping. Although the individual data objects (countries) do not have a cluster membership, the placement of objects together aides in visual data analysis. This application is also called competitive SOMs.

7.3.1 How It Works

The algorithm for a SOM is similar to centroid-based clustering but with a neural network foundation. Since a SOM is essentially a neural network, the model accepts only numerical attributes. However, there is no target variable in SOM because it is an unsupervised learning model. The objective of the algorithm is to find a set of centroids (neurons) to represent the cluster but with topological constraints. The topology refers to an arrangement of centroids in the output grid. All the data objects from the dataset are assigned to each centroid. Centroids closer to each other in the grid are more closely "related" to each other than to centroids further away in the grid. A SOM converts numbers from the data space to a grid space with additional inter-topology relationships.

Step 1: Topology Specification

The first step for a SOM is specifying the topology of the output. Even though multi-dimensional output is possible, two-dimensional rows and columns with either a rectangular lattice or a hexagonal lattice are commonly used in SOMs to aid in the visual discovery of clustering. One advantage in using a hexagonal lattice is that each node or centroid can have six neighbors, two more than in a rectangular lattice. Hence, in a hexagonal lattice, the association of a data point with another data point can be more precise than for a rectangular grid. The number of centroids can be specified by providing the number of rows and columns in the grid. The number of centroids is the product of the number of rows and columns in the grid. Fig. 7.22 shows a hexagonal lattice SOM.

Step 2: Initialize Centroids

A SOM starts the process by initializing the centroids. The initial centroids are values of random data objects from the dataset. This is similar to initializing centroids in k-means clustering.

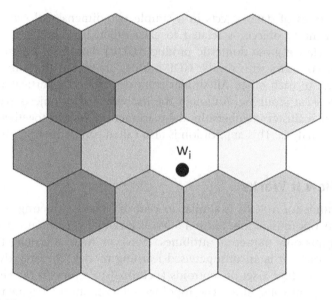

FIGURE 7.22
Weight of the centroid is updated.

Step 3: Assignment of Data Objects

After centroids are selected and placed on the grid in the intersection of rows and columns, data objects are selected one by one and assigned to the nearest centroid. The nearest centroid can be calculated using a distance function like Euclidean distance for numeric data or a cosine measure for document or binary data.

Step 4: Centroid Update

The centroid update is the most significant and distinct step in the SOM algorithm and is repeated for every data object. The centroid update has two related sub-steps.

The first sub-step is to update the closest centroid. The objective of the method is to update the data values of the nearest centroid of the data object, proportional to the difference between the centroid and the data object. This is similar to updating weights in the back-propagation algorithm of neural networks. In the neural network section of Chapter 4, Classification, how the weights of neurons are updated based on the error difference between the predicted and actual values was discussed. Similarly, in the context of a SOM, the values of centroids are updated. In fact, centroids are considered neurons in a SOM. Through this update, the closest centroid moves closer to the data object in the data space.

The centroid update step is repeated for a number of iterations, usually in the thousands. Denote t as the tth iteration of the update where the data point $d(t)$ is picked up. Let w_1, w_2, w_3, ..., w_k represent all the centroids in the grid space. Fig. 7.22 shows the lattice with centroid weight. Let r and c be the number of rows and columns in the grid. Then k will be equal to $r * c$. Let w_i be the nearest centroid for a data object $d(t)$. During iteration t, the nearest centroid w_i is updated using Eq. (7.4).

$$w_i(t + 1) = w_i(t) + f_i(t) \times [d(t) - w_i(t)] \qquad (7.4)$$

The effect of the update is determined by the difference between the centroid and the data point in the data space and the neighborhood function $f_i(t)$. The neighborhood function decreases for every iteration so that there are no drastic changes made in the final iteration. In addition to updating the nearest primary centroid, all other centroids in the grid space neighborhood of the primary centroid are updated as well. This will be reviewed in more detail in the next sub-step.

The second sub-step is to update all centroids in the grid space neighborhood as shown in Fig. 7.23. The neighborhood update step has to be proportional to the distance from the closest centroid to the centroid that is being updated. The update function has to be stronger when the distance is closer. Taking into account time decay and distance between neighborhood centroids, a Gaussian function is commonly used for:

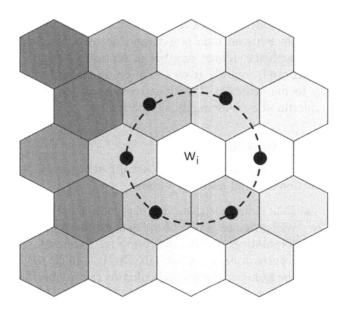

FIGURE 7.23
The weight of the neighborhood centroids are updated.

$$f_i(t) = \lambda_i(t)e^{\left(-\frac{(g_i - g_j)^2}{2\sigma^2}\right)}$$

(7.5)

where $\lambda_i(t)$ is the learning rate function that takes a value between 0 and 1 and decays for every iteration. Usually it is either a linear rate function or an inverse of the time function. The variable in the exponential parameter $g_i - g_j$ is the distance between the centroid being updated and the nearest centroid of the data point in the grid space. The variable σ determines the radius of the centroid update or the neighborhood effect. By updating the entire neighborhood of centroids in the grid, the SOM self-organizes the centroid lattice. Effectively, the SOM converts data from the data space to a location-constrained grid space.

Step 5: Termination

The entire algorithm is continued until no significant centroid updates take place in each run or until the specified number of run count is reached. The selection of the data object can be repeated if the dataset size is small. Like with many data science algorithms, a SOM tends to converge to a solution in most cases but doesn't guarantee an optimal solution. To tackle this problem, it is necessary to have multiple runs with various initiation measures and to compare the results.

Step 6: Mapping a New Data Object

A SOM model itself is a valuable visualization tool that can describe the relationship between data objects and be used for visual clustering. After the grids with the desired number of centroids have been built, any new data object can be quickly given a location on the grid space, based on its proximity to the centroids. The characteristics of new data objects can be further understood by studying the neighbors.

7.3.2   How to Implement

SOM can be implemented in a few different ways in RapidMiner, with varied functionality and resulting output.

- *Data exploration chart*: In Chapter 3, Data Exploration, the SOM chart was reviewed as one of the data exploration techniques. In RapidMiner, any dataset connected to a result port has a SOM chart feature under the Chart tab. This is a quick and easy method where the number of rows and columns can be specified, and a SOM chart can be rendered.
- *Data Transformation > Attribute set reduction > SOM Operator*: The SOM operator available under the Data Transformation folder is used to reduce the number of dimensions in the dataset. It is similar to the

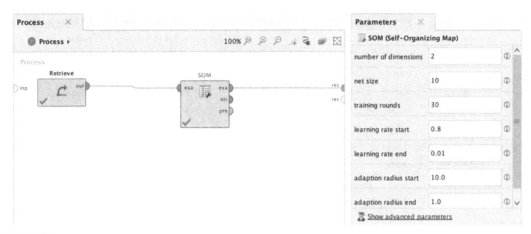

FIGURE 7.24
SOM in data transformation. *SOM*, Self-organizing map.

application of principal component analysis where the dataset is
reduced to a lower dimensionality. In theory, a SOM can help reduce
the data to any number of dimensions below the dimension count of
the dataset. In this operator, the number of desired output dimensions
can be specified in the parameters, as shown in Fig. 7.24. The net size
parameter indicates the unique values in each of the SOM dimensions.
There is no visual output for this operator and in two dimensions, only
a square topography can be achieved through the SOM *data
transformation* operator.

- *RapidMiner Extension > SOM Modeling Operator*: The *SOM modeling*
operator is available in the SOM extension (Motl, 2012) and offers rich
SOM visuals. SOM extensions will be used for the rest of this
implementation section, so installing the SOM extension is
recommended before proceeding further.

RapidMiner provides a marketplace platform called
Extensions for specialized data science tasks which has
operators, data science algorithms, data transformation
operators, and visual exploration tools. The extensions can
be installed and uninstalled easily from Help > Updates
and Extensions. SOM is one of the extensions, along with
text mining, the R extension, Recommenders, Weka extension, etc. Extensions will be used in the upcoming chapters.

The dataset used in this section is the relative GDP information by country
(IMF, 2012) from the *World Economic Outlook Database October 2012* by the
International Monetary Fund. The dataset has 186 records, one for each
country, and four attributes in percentage of GDP: relative GDP invested, relative GDP saved, government revenue, and current account balance. Fig. 7.25
shows the actual raw data for a few rows and Fig. 7.26 shows the quartile
plot for all the attributes.

Row No.	Country	Current account balance	General government revenue	Gross national savings	Total investment
1	Afghanistan	3.877	21.977	30.398	26.521
2	Albania	−11.372	25.835	14.509	25.886
3	Algeria	7.489	36.458	48.947	41.428
4	Angola	9.024	43.479	21.692	12.668
5	Antigua and...	−13.109	22.430	16.194	29.303
6	Argentina	0.658	37.199	22.595	24.451
7	Armenia	−14.653	20.970	16.660	31.313
8	Australia	−2.870	31.846	23.925	26.794
9	Austria	3.009	48.105	24.611	21.602
10	Azerbaijan	28.423	45.652	46.955	18.532

FIGURE 7.25

GDP by country dataset. *GDP*, Gross domestic product.

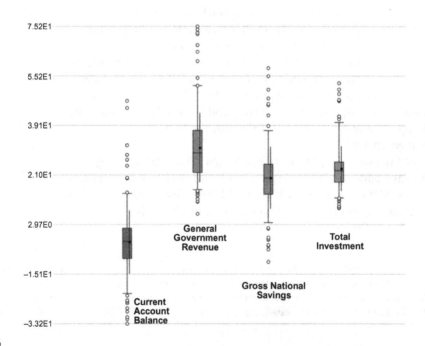

FIGURE 7.26

GDP by country: box-whisker (quartile) plot for all four attributes. *GDP*, Gross domestic product.

The objective of the clustering is to compare and contrast countries based on their percentage of GDP invested and saved, government revenue, and current account balance. Note that they are not compared using the size of the economy through absolute GDP but by the size of investment, national savings, current account, and the size of government relative to the country's GDP. The goal of this modeling exercise is to arrange countries in a grid so that countries with similar characteristics of investing, savings, size of government, and current accounts are placed next to each other. The four-dimensional information is being compressed into a two-dimensional map or grid. The dataset and RapidMiner process can be accessed from the companion site of the book at www.IntroDataScience.com.

Step 1: Data Preparation

As a neural network, a SOM cannot accept polynominal or categorical attributes because centroid updates and distance calculations work only with numeric values. Polynominal data can be either ignored with information loss or converted to a numeric attribute using the *Nominal to Numerical* type conversion operator available in RapidMiner. The country attribute is set as a label using Set role operator. In this dataset, there are records (each record is a country) where there is no data in few attributes. Neural networks cannot handle missing values and, hence, they need to be replaced by either zero or the minimum or average value for the attribute using the *Replace Missing Value* operator. In this example the average was chosen as the default missing value.

Step 2: SOM Modeling Operator and Parameters

The *SOM modeling extension* operator is available in the Self-Organizing Map folder, labeled with the same name. Please note that the SOM folder is visible only when the SOM extension has been installed. The coming parameters can be configured in the model operator. The modeling operator accepts the example set with numeric data and a label attribute if applicable. In this example set, the country name is a label attribute. Fig. 7.27 shows the RapidMiner process for developing a SOM model.

- *Training Rounds*: Defaults to 1000. This value indicates the number of training rounds for the data object selection process.
- *Net Size*: Indicates whether the grid size should be specified by the user or automatically approximated by the system. In this exercise select user input for *X* and *Y*.
- *Net Size X*: Specifies the number of columns in the grid (horizontal direction). This is the same as the possible values for the SOM_0 attribute in the output. In this example this value will be set to 10.

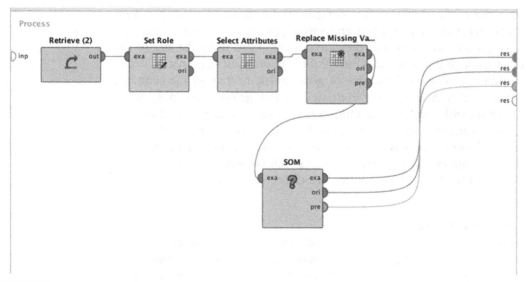

FIGURE 7.27

Clustering with SOM. *SOM*, Self-organizing map.

- *Net Size Y*: Specifies the number of rows in the grid (vertical direction). This also indicates the values for the SOM_1 attribute in the output grid. In this example this value will be set to 10.
- *Learning Rate*: The neural network learning parameter (λ), which takes a value from 0 to 1. The value of λ determines how sensitive the change in weight is to the previous weights. A value closer to 0 means the new weight would be mostly based on previous weight and an λ closer to 1 means that the weight would be mainly based on error correction. The initial λ will be assigned as 0.9 (see Section 4.5 on Neural Networks).
- *Learning Rate function*: The learning rate function in a neural network is a time decay function of the learning process. The default and most commonly used time decay function is the inverse of time.

Step 3: Execution and Interpretation

The RapidMiner process can be saved and executed. The output of the *SOM modeling* operator consists of a visual model and a grid dataset. The visual model is a lattice with centroids and mapped data points. The grid dataset output is the example set labeled with location coordinates for each record in the grid lattice.

Visual Model

The visual model of the SOM displays the most recognizable form of SOM in a hexagonal grid format. The size of the grid is configured by the input parameters that set the net size of X and Y. There are several advanced visualization styles available in the Visualization results window. The SOM visual output can be customized using these parameters:

- *Visualization Style*: This selection controls the visual layout and background color of the SOM hexagons. The value of the selected measure is represented as a background gradient color. The default, U-Matrix, presents a background gradient color proportional to the distance of the central data points in adjacent hexagons. The P-Matrix option shows the number of example data points through the background gradient color. The selection of an individual attribute name for the visualization style renders the background gradient proportional to the value of the selected attribute. The visualization style selection does not rearrange the data points assigned to hexagons.
- *Label*: Selection shows the attribute value selected in the hexagons.
- *Color Schema*: Selection of monochrome or color scheme.

Fig. 7.28 shows a SOM with the default selection of the label as Country and the visualization style as U-Matrix. It can be observed how countries are

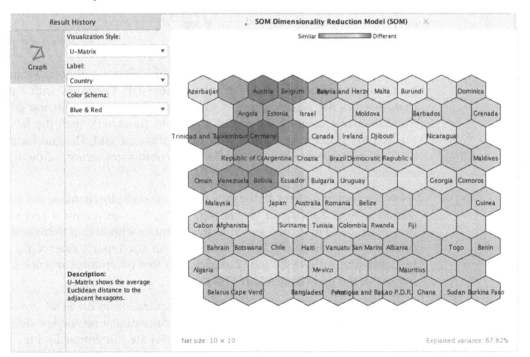

FIGURE 7.28

SOM output in the hexagonal grid. *SOM*, Self-organizing map.

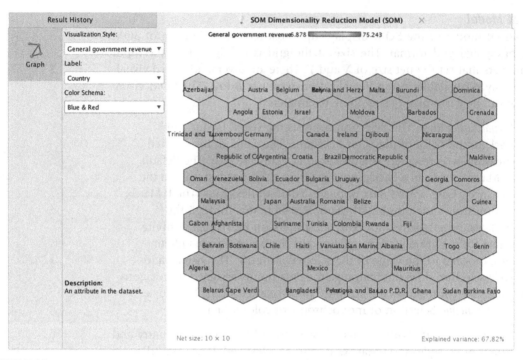

FIGURE 7.29

SOM output with color overlay related to government revenue. *SOM*, Self-organizing map.

placed on the grid based on their relationship with each other, as evaluated by the four economic metrics in relation to GDP. Countries with similar characteristics are placed closer to each other than to others in the grid. If more than one country belongs to a centroid (hexagon), then the label of one country closer to the centroid is displayed on the grid. The grid locations of all the counties are listed in the location coordinates section of the results window.

A few interesting patterns in the data can be observed by changing the visualization style as a metric in the dataset. In Fig. 7.29, government revenue as percentage of GDP is used and visually, countries with high government revenue as a percentage of GDP is displayed on the top-left side of the grid (e.g., Belgium with 48%) and countries with low government revenue are at bottom of the grid (Bangladesh 11%).

Fig. 7.30 shows the national savings rate visualization in the SOM; countries with a high savings rate (Algeria 49%) are concentrated on the left side and countries with a low savings rate (Maldives 2%) are concentrated on the right side of the SOM.

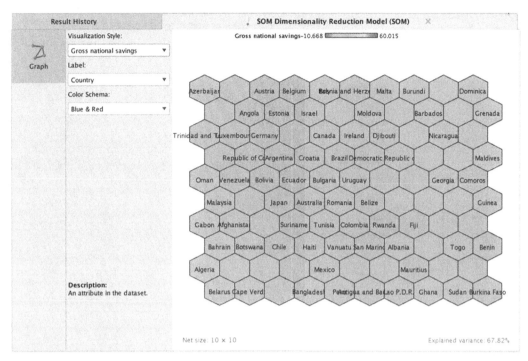

FIGURE 7.30

SOM output with color overlay related to national savings rate. *SOM*, Self-organizing map.

Location Coordinates

The second output of the *SOM* operator contains the location coordinates of the *x*- and *y*-axes of grid with labels SOM_0 and SOM_1. The coordinate values of location range from 0 to net size—1, as specified in the model parameters, since all data objects, in this case countries, are assigned to a specific location in the grid. This output, as shown in Fig. 7.31, can be further used for post-processing such as distance calculation of locations between countries in the grid space.

Conclusion

The methodology of SOMs is derived from the foundations of both neural network and prototype-clustering approaches. SOMs are an effective visual clustering tool to understand high-dimensional numeric data. They reduce the features of the dataset to two or three features, which is used to specify the topology of the layout. Hence, SOMs are predominantly used as a visual discovery and data exploration technique. Some of the applications of SOMs include the methods that are used in conjunction with other data science techniques such as graph mining (Resta, 2012), text mining (Liu, Liu, & Wang, 2012), speech recognition (Kohonen, 1988), etc.

	ExampleSet (Replace Missing Values)	✕		ExampleSet (SOM)

ExampleSet (186 examples, 1 special attribute, 2 regular attributes)   Filter (186 / 186 examples):

Row No.	Country	SOM_0	SOM_1
1	Afghanistan	1	6
2	Albania	6	7
3	Algeria	0	8
4	Angola	1	1
5	Antigua and...	5	9
6	Argentina	2	3
7	Armenia	5	9
8	Australia	3	5
9	Austria	2	0
10	Azerbaijan	0	0
11	Bahrain	0	7
12	Bangladesh	3	9
13	Barbados	7	1
14	Belarus	0	9

Left sidebar icons: Data, Statistics, Charts, Advanced Charts, Annotations

FIGURE 7.31

SOM output with location coordinates. *SOM*, Self-organizing map.

References

Bache, K., & Lichman, M. (2013). *UCI machine learning repository*. University of California, School of Information and Computer Science. Retrieved from <http://archive.ics.uci.edu/ml>.

Berry, M. J., & Linoff, G. (2000a). Converging on the customer: Understanding the customer behavior in the telecommunications industry. In M. J. Berry, & G. Linoff (Eds.), *Mastering data science: The art and science of customer relationship management* (pp. 357–394). John Wiley & Sons, Inc.

Berry, M. J., & Linoff, G. (2000b). Data science techniques and algorithms. In M. J. Berry, & G. Linoff (Eds.), *Mastering data science: The art and science of customer relationship management* (pp. 103–107). John Wiley & Sons, Inc.

Davies, D. L., & Bouldin, D. W. (1979). A cluster separation measure. *IEEE Transactions on Pattern Analysis and Machine Intelligence, 1*(2), 224–227.

Ester, M., Kriegel, H. -P., Sander, J., & Xu X. (1996). A density-based algorithm for discovering clusters in large spatial databases with noise. In *AAAI Press proceedings of 2nd international conference on knowledge discovery and data science KDD-96* (Vol. 96, pp. 226–231). AAAI Press.

Fisher, R. A. (1936). The use of multiple measurements in taxonomic problems. *Annals of Human Genetics, 7*, 179–188. Retrieved from <https://doi.org/10.1111/j.1469-1809.1936.tb02137.x>.

Germano, T. (March 23, 1999) Self-organizing maps. Retrieved from <http://davis.wpi.edu/~matt/courses/soms/> Accessed 10.12.13.

Hamerly, G., & Elkan, C. (2003). Learning the *k* in *k*-means. *Advances in Neural Information Processing Systems, 17,* 1−8. Available from http://dx.doi.org/10.1.1.9.3574.

IMF, (2012, October). *World economic outlook database.* International Monetary Fund. Retrieved from <http://www.imf.org/external/pubs/ft/weo/2012/02/weodata/index.aspx> Accessed 15.03.13.

Kohonen, T. (1982). Self-organized formation of topologically correct feature maps. *Biological Cybernetics, 43,* 59−69.

Kohonen, T. (1988). The "neural" phonetic typewriter. *Computer, IEEE, 21*(3), 11−22. Available from https://doi.org/10.1109/2.28.

Liu, Y., Liu, M., & Wang, X. (2012). Application of self-organizing maps in text clustering: A review. In M. Johnsson (Ed.), *Applications of self-organizing maps* (pp. 205−220). InTech.

Lloyd, S. (1982). Least squares quantization in PCM. *IEEE Transactions on Information Theory, 28,* 129−137.

Motl, J. (2012). *SOM extension for rapid miner.* Prague: Czech Technical University.

Pearson, P., & Cooper, C. (2012). Using self organizing maps to analyze demographics and swing state voting in the 2008 U.S. presidential election. In N. Mana, F. Schwenker, & E. Trentin (Eds.), *Artificial neural networks in pattern recognition ANNPR'12 Proceedings of the 5th INNS IAPR TC 3 GIRPR conference* (pp. 201−212). Heidelberg: Springer Berlin Heidelberg, Berlin10.1007/978-3-642-33212-8.

Resta, M. (2012). Graph mining based SOM: A tool to analyze economic stability. In M. Johnsson (Ed.), *Applications of self-organizing maps* (pp. 1−26). InTech. Retrieved from <http://www.intechopen.com/books/applications-of-self-organizing-maps>.

Tan, P.-N., Michael, S., & Kumar, V. (2005). Clustering analysis: Basic concepts and algorithms. In P.-N. Tan, S. Michael, & V. Kumar (Eds.), *Introduction to data science* (pp. 487−555). Boston, MA: Addison-Wesley.

Witten, I. H., & Frank, E. (2005). *Algorithms: The basic methods. Data science: Practical machine learning tools and techniques* (pp. 136−139). San Francisco, CA: Morgan Kaufmann.

CHAPTER 8

Model Evaluation

In this chapter, the most commonly used methods for testing the quality of a data science model will be formally introduced. Throughout this book, various *validation* techniques have been used to split the available data into a training set and a testing set. In the implementation sections, different types of performance operators in conjunction with validation have been used without an in detail explanation of how these operators really function. Several ways in which predictive data science models are evaluated for their performance will now be discussed.

There are a few main tools that are available to test a classification model's quality: *confusion matrices (or truth tables), lift charts, ROC (receiver operator characteristic) curves, area under the curve (AUC)*. How these tools are constructed will be defined in detail and how to implement performance evaluations will be described. To evaluate a numeric prediction from a regression model, there are many conventional statistical tests that may be applied (Black, 2008) a few of which were discussed in Chapter 5, Regression Methods.

DIRECT MARKETING

Direct marketing (DM) companies, which send out postal mail (or in the days before do-not-call lists, they called prospects) were one of the early pioneers in applying data science techniques (Berry, 1999). A key performance indicator for their marketing activities is of course the improvement in their bottom line as a result of their utilization of predictive models.

Assume that a typical average response rate for a direct mail campaign is 10%. Further assume that: cost per mail sent = $1 and potential revenue per response = $20.

If they have 10,000 people to send out their mailers to, then they can expect to receive potential revenues of 10,000 × 10% × $20 = $20,000, which would yield a net return of $10,000. Typically, the mailers are sent out in batches to spread costs over a period of time. Further assume that these are sent out in batches of 1000. The first question someone would ask is how to divide the list of names into these batches. If the average expectation of return is 10%, then would it not make a lot of sense to just send one batch of mails to those prospects that make up this 10% and be done with the campaign?

(Continued)

Data Science. DOI: https://doi.org/10.1016/B978-0-12-814761-0.00008-3

(Continued)

Clearly this would save a lot of time and money and the net return would jump to $19,000!

Can all of these 10 percenters be identified? While this is clearly unrealistic, classification techniques can be used to rank or score prospects by the likelihood that they would respond to the mailers. Predictive analytics is after all about converting future uncertainties into usable probabilities (Taylor, 2011). Then a predictive method can be used to order these probabilities and send out the mailers

to only those who score above a particular threshold (say 85% chance of response).

Finally, some techniques may be better suited to this problem than others. How can the different available methods be compared based on their performance? Will logistic regression capture these top 10 percenters better than support vector machines? What are the different metrics that can be used to select the best performing methods? These are some of the things that will be discussed in this chapter in more detail.

8.1 CONFUSION MATRIX

Classification performance is best described by an aptly named tool called the *confusion matrix* or truth table. Understanding the confusion matrix requires becoming familiar with several definitions. But before introducing the definitions, a basic confusion matrix for a binary or binomial classification must first be looked at where there can be two classes (say, Y or N). The accuracy of classification of a specific example can be viewed in one of four possible ways:

- The predicted class is Y, and the actual class is also Y → this is a True Positive or TP
- The predicted class is Y, and the actual class is N → this is a False Positive or FP
- The predicted class is N, and the actual class is Y → this is a False Negative or FN
- The predicted class is N, and the actual class is also N → this is a True Negative or TN

A basic confusion matrix is traditionally arranged as a 2×2 matrix as shown in Table 8.1. The predicted classes are arranged horizontally in rows and the

Table 8.1 Confusion Matrix

		Actual Class (Observation)	
		Y	N
Predicted class (expectation)	Y	*TP* correct result	*FP* unexpected result
	N	*FN* missing result	*TN* correct absence of result
TP, *true positive*; FP, *false positive*; FN, *false negative*; TN, *true negative*.			

actual classes are arranged vertically in columns, although sometimes this order is reversed (Kohavi & Provost, 1998). A quick way to examine this matrix or a truth table as it is also called is to scan the diagonal from top left to bottom right. An ideal classification performance would only have entries along this main diagonal and the off-diagonal elements would be zero.

These four cases will now be used to introduce several commonly used terms for understanding and explaining classification performance. As mentioned earlier, a perfect classifier will have no entries for FP and FN (i.e., the number of FP = number of FN = 0).

1. *Sensitivity* is the ability of a classifier to select all the cases that *need* to be selected. A perfect classifier will select all the actual Y's and will not miss any actual Y's. In other words it will have no FNs. In reality, any classifier will miss some true Y's, and thus, have some FNs. Sensitivity is expressed as a ratio (or percentage) calculated as follows: TP/(TP + FN). However, sensitivity alone is not sufficient to evaluate a classifier. In situations such as credit card fraud, where rates are typically around 0.1%, an ordinary classifier may be able to show sensitivity of 99.9% by picking nearly all the cases as legitimate transactions or TP. The ability to detect illegitimate or fraudulent transactions, the TNs, is also needed. This is where the next measure, specificity, which ignores TPs, comes in.

2. *Specificity* is the ability of a classifier to reject all the cases that *need* to be rejected. A perfect classifier will reject all the actual N's and will not deliver any unexpected results. In other words, it will have no FPs. In reality, any classifier will select some cases that need to be rejected, and thus, have some FPs. Specificity is expressed as a ratio (or percentage) calculated as: TN/(TN + FP).

3. *Relevance* is a term that is easy to understand in a document search and retrieval scenario. Suppose a search is run for a specific term and that search returns 100 documents. Of these, let us say only 70 were useful because they were *relevant* to the search. Furthermore, the search actually missed out on an additional 40 documents that could actually have been useful. With this context, additional terms can be defined.

4. *Precision* is defined as the proportion of cases found that were actually relevant. From the example, this number was 70, and thus, the precision is 70/100 or 70%. The 70 documents were TP, whereas the remaining 30 were FP. Therefore, precision is TP/(TP + FP).

5. *Recall* is defined as the proportion of the relevant cases that were actually found among all the relevant cases. Again, with the example, only 70 of the total 110 (70 found + 40 missed) relevant cases were

Table 8.2 Evaluation Measures

Term	Definition	Calculation
Sensitivity	Ability to select what needs to be selected	TP/(TP + FN)
Specificity	Ability to reject what needs to be rejected	TN/(TN + FP)
Precision	Proportion of cases found that were relevant	TP/(TP + FP)
Recall	Proportion of all relevant cases that were found	TP/(TP + FN)
Accuracy	Aggregate measure of classifier performance	(TP + TN)/ (TP + TN + FP + FN)

TP, *true positive*; FP, *false positive*; FN, *false negative*; TN, *true negative*.

actually found, thus, giving a recall of 70/110 = 63.63%. It is evident that recall is the same as sensitivity, because recall is also given by TP/(TP + FN).

6. *Accuracy* is defined as the ability of the classifier to select all cases that need to be selected and reject all cases that need to be rejected. For a classifier with 100% accuracy, this would imply that FN = FP = 0. Note that in the document search example, the TN has not been indicated, as this could be really large. Accuracy is given by (TP + TN)/ (TP + FP + TN + FN). Finally, *error* is simply the complement of accuracy, measured by (1 − accuracy).

Table 8.2 summarizes all the major definitions. Fortunately, the analyst does not need to memorize these equations because their calculations are always automated in any tool of choice. However, it is important to have a good fundamental understanding of these terms.

8.2   ROC AND AUC

Measures like accuracy or precision are essentially aggregates by nature, in the sense that they provide the average performance of the classifier on the dataset. A classifier can have a high accuracy on a dataset but have poor class recall and precision. Clearly, a model to detect fraud is no good if its ability to detect TP for the fraud = yes class (and thereby its class recall) is low. It is, therefore, quite useful to look at measures that compare different metrics to see if there is a situation for a trade-off: for example, can a little overall accuracy be sacrificed to gain a lot more improvement in class recall? One can examine a model's rate of detecting TPs and contrast it with its ability to detect FPs. The receiver operator characteristic (ROC) curves meet this need and were originally developed in the field of signal detection (Green, 1966). A ROC curve is created by plotting the fraction of TPs (TP rate) versus the fraction of FPs (FP rate). When a table of such values is generated, the FP rate can be plotted on the horizontal axis and the TP rate (same as sensitivity or recall) on the vertical axis. The FP can also be expressed as (1 − specificity) or TN rate.

Consider a classifier that could predict if a website visitor is likely to click on a banner ad: the model would be most likely built using historic click-through rates based on pages visited, time spent on certain pages, and other characteristics of site visitors. In order to evaluate the performance of this model on test data, a table such as the one shown in Table 8.3 can be generated.

The first column "Actual Class" consists of the actual class for a particular example (in this case a website visitor, who has clicked on the banner ad). The next column, "Predicted Class" is the model prediction and the third column, "Confidence of response" is the confidence of this prediction. In order to create a ROC chart, the predicted data will need to be sorted in decreasing order of confidence level, which has been done in this case. By comparing columns Actual class and Predicted class, the type of prediction can be identified: for instance, spreadsheet rows 2 through 5 are all TPs and row 6 is the first instance of a FP. As observed in columns "Number of TP" and "Number of FP," one can keep a running count of the TPs and FPs and also calculate the fraction of TPs and FPs, which are shown in columns "Fraction of TP" and "Fraction of FP."

Observing the "Number of TP" and "Number of FP" columns, it is evident that the model has discovered a total of 6 TPs and 4 FPs (the remaining 10 examples are all TNs). It can also be seen that the model has identified nearly 67% of all the TPs before it fails and hits its first FP (row 6 above). Finally, all TPs have been identified (when Fraction of TP = 1) before the next FP was run into. If Fraction of FP (FP rate) versus Fraction of TP (TP rate) were now to be plotted, then a ROC chart similar to the one shown in Fig. 8.1 would be seen. Clearly an ideal classifier would have an accuracy of 100% (and thus, would have identified 100% of all TPs). Thus, the ROC for an ideal classifier would look like the dashed line shown in Fig. 8.1. Finally, an ordinary or random classifier (which has only a 50% accuracy) would possibly be able to find one FP for every TP, and thus, look like the 45-degree line shown.

As the number of test examples becomes larger, the ROC curve will become smoother: the random classifier will simply look like a straight line drawn between the points (0,0) and (1,1)—the stair steps become extremely small. The area under this random classifier's ROC curve is basically the area of a

Table 8.3 Classifier Performance Data Needed for Building a ROC Curve

Actual Class	Predicted Class	Confidence of "Response"	Type?	Number of TP	Number of FP	Fraction of FP	Fraction of TP
Response	Response	0.902	TP	1	0	0	0.167
Response	Response	0.896	TP	2	0	0	0.333
Response	Response	0.834	TP	3	0	0	0.500
Response	Response	0.741	TP	4	0	0	0.667
No response	Response	0.686	FP	4	1	0.25	0.667
Response	Response	0.616	TP	5	1	0.25	0.833
Response	Response	0.609	TP	6	1	0.25	1
No response	Response	0.576	FP	6	2	0.5	1
No response	Response	0.542	FP	6	3	0.75	1
No response	Response	0.530	FP	6	4	1	1
No response	No response	0.440	TN	6	4	1	1
No response	No response	0.428	TN	6	4	1	1
No response	No response	0.393	TN	6	4	1	1
No response	No response	0.313	TN	6	4	1	1
No response	No response	0.298	TN	6	4	1	1
No response	No response	0.260	TN	6	4	1	1
No response	No response	0.248	TN	6	4	1	1
No response	No response	0.247	TN	6	4	1	1
No response	No response	0.241	TN	6	4	1	1
No response	No response	0.116	TN	6	4	1	1

ROC, *receiver operator characteristic*; TP, *true positive*; FP, *false positive*; TN, *true negative*.

right triangle (with side 1 and height 1), which is 0.5. This quantity is termed Area Under the Curve or AUC. AUC for the ideal classifier is 1.0. Thus, the performance of a classifier can also be quantified by its AUC: obviously any AUC higher than 0.5 is better than random and the closer it is to 1.0, the better the performance. A common rule of thumb is to select those classifiers that not only have a ROC curve that is closest to ideal, but also an AUC higher than 0.8. Typical uses for AUC and ROC curves are to compare the performance of different classification algorithms for the same dataset.

8.3 LIFT CURVES

Lift curves or lift charts were first deployed in direct marketing where the problem was to identify if a particular prospect was worth calling or sending an advertisement by mail. It was mentioned in the use case at the beginning

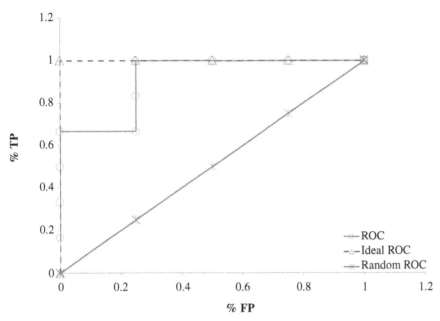

FIGURE 8.1

Comparing ROC curve for the example shown in Table 8.3 to random and ideal classifiers. *ROC*, receiver operator characteristic.

of this chapter that with a predictive model, one can *score* a list of prospects by their propensity to respond to an ad campaign. When the prospects are sorted by this score (by the decreasing order of their propensity to respond), one now ends up with a mechanism to systematically select the most valuable prospects right at the beginning, and thus, maximize their return. Thus, rather than mailing out the ads to a random group of prospects, the ads can now be sent to the first batch of "most likely responders," followed by the next batch and so on.

Without classification, the "most likely responders" are distributed randomly throughout the dataset. Suppose there is a dataset of 200 prospects and it contains a total of 40 responders or TPs. If the dataset is broken up into, say, 10 equal sized batches (called deciles), the likelihood of finding TPs in each batch is also 20%, that is, four samples in each decile will be TPs. However, when a predictive model is used to classify the prospects, a good model will tend to pull these "most likely responders" into the top few deciles. Thus, in this simple example, it might be found that the first two deciles will have all 40 TPs and the remaining eight deciles have none.

Lift charts were developed to demonstrate this in a graphical way (Rud, 2000). The focus is again on the TPs and, thus, it can be argued that they indicate the sensitivity of the model unlike ROC curves, which can show the relation between sensitivity and specificity.

The motivation for building lift charts was to depict how much better the classifier performs compared to *randomly selecting x% of the data (for prospects to call) which would yield x% targets (to call or not)*. Lift is the improvement over this random selection that a predictive model can potentially yield because of its scoring or ranking ability. For example, in the data from Table 8.3, there are a total of 6 TPs out of 20 test cases. If one were to take the unscored data and randomly select 25% of the examples, it would be expected that 25% of them were TPs (or 25% of 6 = 1.5). However, scoring and reordering the dataset by confidence will improve this. As can be seen in Table 8.4, the first 25% or quartile of scored (reordered) data now contains four TPs. This translates to a lift of 4/1.5 = 2.67. Similarly, the second quartile of the unscored data can be expected to contain 50% (or three) of the TPs. As seen in Table 8.4, the scored 50% data contains all six TPs, giving a lift of 6/3 = 2.00.

The steps to build lift charts are:

1. Generate scores for all the data points (prospects) in the test set using the trained model.
2. Rank the prospects by decreasing score or confidence of response.
3. Count the TPs in the first 25% (quartile) of the dataset, and then the first 50% (add the next quartile) and so on; see columns Cumulative TP and Quartile in Table 8.4.
4. *Gain* at a given quartile level is the ratio of the cumulative number of TPs in that quartile to the total number of TPs in the entire dataset (six in the example). The 1st quartile gain is, therefore, 4/6 or 67%, the 2nd quartile gain is 6/6 or 100%, and so on.
5. *Lift* is the ratio of gain to the random expectation at a given quartile level. Remember that random expectation at the xth quartile is x%. In the example, the random expectation is to find 25% of 6 = 1.5 TPs in the 1st quartile, 50% or 3 TPs in the 2nd quartile, and so on. The corresponding 1st quartile lift is, therefore, 4/1.5 = 2.667, the 2nd quartile lift is 6/3 = 2.00, and so on.

The corresponding curves for the simple example are shown in Fig. 8.2. Typically lift charts are created on deciles not quartiles. Quartiles were chosen here because they helped to illustrate the concept using the small 20-sample test dataset. However, the logic remains the same for deciles or any other groupings as well.

Table 8.4 Scoring Predictions and Sorting by Confidences Is the Basis for Generating Lift Curves

Actual Class	Predicted Class	Confidence of "Response"	Type?	Cumulative TP	Cumulative FP	Quartile	Gain	Lift
Response	Response	0.902	TP	1	0	1st	67%	2.666667
Response	Response	0.896	TP	2	0	1st		
Response	Response	0.834	TP	3	0	1st		
Response	Response	0.741	TP	4	0	1st		
No response	Response	0.686	FP	4	1	1st		
Response	Response	0.616	TP	5	1	2nd	100%	2
Response	Response	0.609	TP	6	1	2nd		
No response	Response	0.576	FP	6	2	2nd		
No response	Response	0.542	FP	6	3	2nd		
No response	Response	0.530	FP	6	4	2nd		
No response	No response	0.440	TN	6	4	3rd	100%	1.333333
No response	No response	0.428	TN	6	4	3rd		
No response	No response	0.393	TN	6	4	3rd		
No response	No response	0.313	TN	6	4	3rd		
No response	No response	0.298	TN	6	4	3rd		
No response	No response	0.260	TN	6	4	4th	100%	1
No response	No response	0.248	TN	6	4	4th		
No response	No response	0.247	TN	6	4	4th		
No response	No response	0.241	TN	6	4	4th		
No response	No response	0.116	TN	6	4	4th		

TP, *true positive*; FP, *false positive*; TN, *true negative*.

8.4 HOW TO IMPLEMENT

A built-in dataset in RapidMiner will be used to demonstrate how all the three classification performances (confusion matrix, ROC/AUC, and lift/gain charts) are evaluated. The process shown in Fig. 8.3 uses the *Generate Direct Mailing Data* operator to create a 10,000 record dataset. The objective of the modeling (Naïve Bayes used here) is to predict whether a person is likely to respond to a direct mailing campaign or not based on demographic attributes (age, lifestyle, earnings, type of car, family status, and sports affinity).

Step 1: Data Preparation
Create a dataset with 10,000 examples using the *Generate Direct Mailing Data* operator by setting a local random seed (default = 1992) to ensure

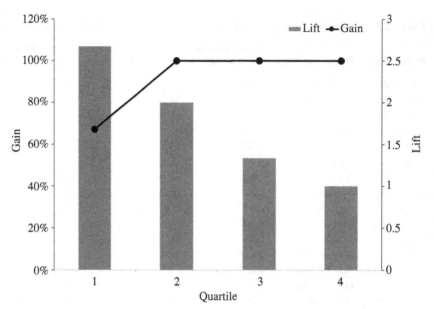

FIGURE 8.2
Lift and gain curves.

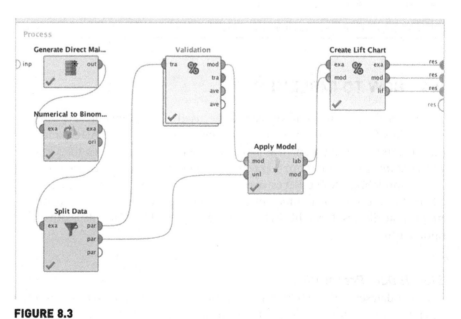

FIGURE 8.3
Process setup to demonstrate typical classification performance metrics.

repeatability. Convert the label attribute from polynomial (nominal) to binominal using the appropriate operator as shown. This enables one to select specific binominal classification performance measures.

Split data into two partitions: an 80% partition (8000 examples) for model building and validation and a 20% partition for testing. An important point to note is that data partitioning is not an exact science and this ratio can change depending on the data.

Connect the 80% output (upper output port) from the *Split Data* operator to the *Split Validation* operator. Select a relative split with a ratio of 0.7 (70% for training) and shuffled sampling.

Step 2: Modeling Operator and Parameters

Insert the *naïve Bayes* operator in the Training panel of the *Split Validation* operator and the usual *Apply Model* operator in the Testing panel. Add a *Performance (Binomial Classification)* operator. Select the following options in the performance operator: accuracy, FP, FN, TP, TN, sensitivity, specificity, and AUC.

Step 3: Evaluation

Add another *Apply Model* operator outside the *Split Validation* operator and deliver the model to its mod input port while connecting the 2000 example data partition from Step 3 to the unl port. Add a *Create Lift Chart* operator with these options selected: target class = response, binning type = frequency, and number of bins = 10. Note the port connections as shown in Fig. 8.3.

Step 4: Execution and Interpretation

When the above process is run, the confusion matrix and ROC curve for the validation sample should be generated (30% of the original 80% = 2400 examples), whereas a lift curve should be generated for the test sample (2000 examples). There is no reason why one cannot add another *Performance (Binomial Classification)* operator for the test sample or create a lift chart for the validation examples. (The reader should try this as an exercise—how will the output from the *Create Lift Chart* operator be delivered when it is inserted inside the *Split Validation* operator?)

The confusion matrix shown in Fig. 8.4 is used to calculate several common metrics using the definitions from Table 8.1. Compare them with the RapidMiner outputs to verify understanding.

	true no response	true response	class precision
pred. no response	1231	146	89.40%
pred. response	394	629	61.49%
class recall	75.75%	81.16%	

FIGURE 8.4

Confusion matrix for validation set of direct marketing dataset.

$$TP = 629, \quad TN = 1231, \quad FP = 394, \quad FN = 146$$

Term	Definition	Calculation
Sensitivity	TP/(TP + FN)	629/(629 + 146) = 81.16%
Specificity	TN/(TN + FP)	1231/(1231 + 394) = 75.75%
Precision	TP/(TP + FP)	629/(629 + 394) = 61.5%
Recall	TP/(TP + FN)	629/(629 + 146) = 81.16%
Accuracy	(TP + TN)/ (TP + TN + FP + FN)	(629 + 1231)/(629 + 1231 + 394 + 146) = 77.5%

Note that RapidMiner makes a distinction between the two classes while calculating precision and recall. For example, in order to calculate a class recall for "no response," the *positive* class becomes "no response" and the corresponding TP is 1231 and the corresponding FN is 394. Therefore, a class recall for "no response" is 1231/(1231 + 394) = 75.75%, whereas the calculation above assumed that "response" was the positive class. Class recall is an important metric to keep in mind when dealing with highly unbalanced data. Data are considered unbalanced if the proportion of the two classes is skewed. When models are trained on unbalanced data, the resulting class recalls also tend to be skewed. For example, in a dataset where there are only 2% responses, the resulting model can have a high recall for "no responses" but a very low class recall for "responses." This skew is not seen in the overall model accuracy and using this model on unseen data may result in severe misclassifications.

The solution to this problem is to either balance the training data so that one ends up with a more or less equal proportion of classes or to insert penalties or costs on misclassifications using the *Metacost* operator as discussed in Chapter 5, Regression Methods. Data balancing is explained in more detail in Chapter 13, Anomaly Detection.

The AUC is shown along with the ROC curve in Fig. 8.5. As mentioned earlier, AUC values close to 1 are indicative of a good model. The ROC captures the sorted confidences of a prediction. As long as the prediction is correct for the examples the curve takes one step up (increased TP). If the prediction is wrong the curve takes one step to the right (increased FP). RapidMiner can

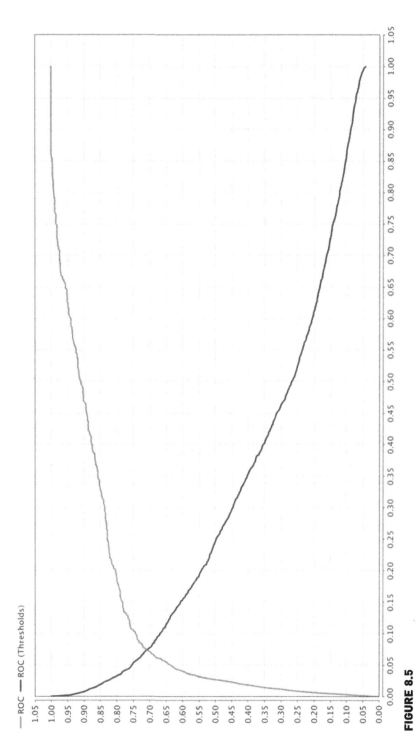

FIGURE 8.5

ROC curve and AUC. *ROC*, receiver operator characteristic; *AUC*, area under the curve.

show two additional AUCs called optimistic and pessimistic. The differences between the optimistic and pessimistic curves occur when there are examples with the same confidence, but the predictions are sometimes false and sometimes true. The optimistic curve shows the possibility that the correct predictions are chosen first so the curve goes steeper upwards. The pessimistic curve shows the possibility that the wrong predictions are chosen first so the curve increases more gradually.

Finally, the lift chart outputs do not directly indicate the lift values as has been demonstrated with the simple example earlier. In Step 5 of the process, 10 bins were selected for the chart and, thus, each bin will have 200 examples (a decile). Recall that to create a lift chart all the predictions will need to be sorted by the confidence of the positive class (response), which is shown in Fig. 8.6.

The first bar in the lift chart shown in Fig. 8.7 corresponds to the first bin of 200 examples after the sorting. The bar reveals that there are 181 TPs in this bin (as can be seen from the table in Fig. 8.6 that the very second example, Row No. 1973, is an FP). From the confusion matrix earlier, 629 TPs can be seen in this example set. A random classifier would have identified 10% of these or 62.9 TPs in the first 200 examples. Therefore, the lift for the first decile is $181/62.9 = 2.87$. Similarly the lift for the first two deciles is $(181 + 167)/(2 \times 62.9) = 2.76$ and so on. Also, the first decile contains $181/629 = 28.8\%$ of the TPs, the first two deciles contain $(181 + 167)/629 = 55.3\%$ of the TPs, and so on. This is shown in the cumulative (percent) gains curve on the right hand y-axis of the lift chart output.

As described earlier, a good classifier will accumulate all the TPs in the first few deciles and will have extremely few FPs at the top of the heap. This will result in a gain curve that quickly rises to the 100% level within the first few deciles.

8.5 CONCLUSION

This chapter covered the basic performance evaluation tools that are typically used in classification methods. Firstly the basic elements of a confusion matrix were described and then the concepts that are important to understanding it, such as sensitivity, specificity, and accuracy were explored in detail. The ROC curve was then described, which has its origins in signal detection theory and has now been adopted for data science, along with the equally useful aggregate metric of AUC. Finally, two useful tools were described that have their origins in direct marketing applications: lift and gain charts. How to build these curves in general and how they can be

Row No.	label	prediction(l...	confidence(no response)	confidence(response)	name	age	lifestyle	zip code
1	no response	no response	0.881	0.119	iHHbMWkc	27	cozily	70096
2	response	response	0.090	0.910	ZWkb86b8	69	active	96274
3	no response	response	0.389	0.611	C1JDpJQO	49	active	37767
4	no response	no response	0.681	0.319	FjYd8PWL	42	healthy	59235
5	no response	no response	0.911	0.089	y7rkBg7t	22	active	57999
6	response	response	0.125	0.875	sPJLeRoj	68	cozily	66375
7	response	response	0.066	0.934	etE6NiMS	67	cozily	95286
8	no response	no response	0.515	0.485	goA2OOUe	45	healthy	60108
9	no response	no response	0.861	0.139	WQkOyMLF	32	healthy	78263
10	response	response	0.248	0.752	A1KrhHiP	51	healthy	98457

FIGURE 8.6

Table of scored responses used to build the lift chart.

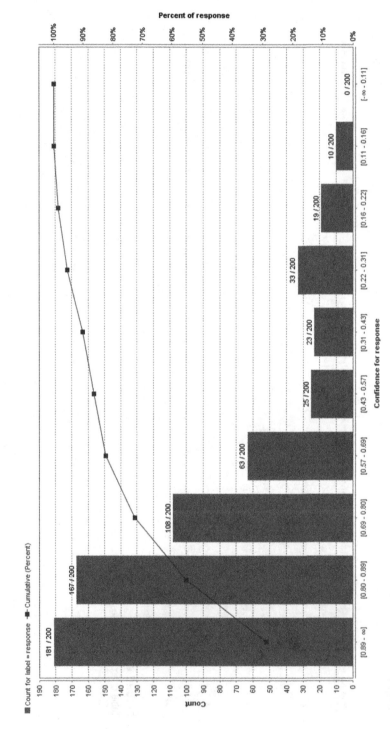

FIGURE 8.7

Lift chart generated.

constructed using RapidMiner was discussed. In summary, these tools are some of the most commonly used metrics for evaluating predictive models and developing skill and confidence in using these is a prerequisite to developing data science expertise.

One key to developing good predictive models is to know when to use which measures. As discussed earlier, relying on a single measure like accuracy can be misleading. For highly unbalanced datasets, rely on several measures such as class recall and precision in addition to accuracy. ROC curves are frequently used to compare several algorithms side by side. Additionally, just as there are an infinite number of triangular shapes that have the same area, AUC should not be used alone to judge a model—AUC and ROCs should be used in conjunction to rate a model's performance. Finally, lift and gain charts are most commonly used for scoring applications where the examples in a dataset need to be rank-ordered according to their propensity to belong to a particular category.

References

Berry, M. A. (1999). *Mastering data mining: The art and science of customer relationship management.* New York: John Wiley and Sons.

Black, K. (2008). *Business statistics for contemporary decision making.* New York: John Wiley and Sons.

Green, D. S. (1966). *Signal detection theory and psychophysics.* New York: John Wiley and Sons.

Kohavi, R., & Provost, F. (1998). Glossary of terms. *Machine Learning, 30,* 271–274.

Rud, O. (2000). *Data mining cookbook: Modeling data for marketing, risk and customer relationship management.* New York: John Wiley and Sons.

Taylor, J. (2011). *Decision management systems: A practical guide to using business rules and predictive analytics.* Boston, Massachusetts: IBM Press.

CHAPTER 9

Text Mining

This chapter explores and formalizes how to extract patterns and discover new knowledge by applying many of the techniques learned so far, not on ordered data, but on unstructured natural language. This constitutes the vast area of text and web mining. For all the techniques described up to this point, a cleaned and organized table consisting of rows and columns of data was fed as input to an algorithm. The output from the algorithm was a model that could then be used to predict outcomes from a new data set or to find patterns in data. But are the same techniques applicable to extract patterns and predict outcomes when the input data looks like normal written communication? This might seem baffling at first, but as shall be seen in this chapter, there are ways of presenting text data to the same algorithms that process normal data.

To start out a brief historical introduction to the field of text mining is given to establish some context. In the following section, techniques that can convert common text into a semi-structured format will be described that we, and the algorithms introduced so far, can recognize. Finally, the text mining concepts will be implemented using two case studies: one involving an unsupervised (clustering) model and another involving a supervised support vector machine (SVM) model. The chapter will be closed with some key considerations to keep in mind while implementing text mining.

Unstructured data (including text, audio, images, videos, etc.) is the new frontier of data science. Eric Siegel in his book *Predictive Analytics* (Siegel, 2013) provides an interesting analogy: if all the data in the world was equivalent to the water on earth, then textual data is like the ocean, making up a majority of the volume. Text analytics is driven by the need to process natural human language, but unlike numeric or categorical data, natural language does not exist in a structured format consisting of rows (of examples) and columns (of attributes). Text mining is, therefore, the domain of unstructured data science.

Data Science. DOI: https://doi.org/10.1016/B978-0-12-814761-0.00009-5

Some of the first applications of text mining came about when people were trying to organize documents (Cutting, 1992). Hearst (1999) recognized that text analysis does not require artificial intelligence but "... a mixture of computationally-driven and user-guided analysis," which is at the heart of the supervised models used in predictive analytics that have been discussed so far.

IT IS NLP, MY DEAR WATSON!

Perhaps the most famous application of text mining is IBM's Watson program, which performed spectacularly when competing against humans on the nightly game show Jeopardy! How does Watson use text mining? Watson has instant access to hundreds of millions of structured and unstructured documents, including the full content of Wikipedia entries.

When a Jeopardy! question is transcribed to Watson, it searches for and identifies candidate documents that score a close match to the words of the question. The search and comparison methods it uses are similar to those used by search engines, and include many of the techniques, such as *n*-grams and stemming, which will be discussed in this chapter. Once it identifies candidate documents, it again uses other text mining (also known as natural language processing or NLP) methods to rank them. For example, if the answer is, *regarding this device, Archimedes said, "give me a place to stand on, and I will move the earth,"* a Watson search for this sentence in its

databases might reveal among its candidate documents several with the term "lever." Watson might insert the word "lever" inside the answer text and rerun a new search to see if there are other documents with the new combination of terms. If the search result has many matches to the terms in the sentence—as it most likely would in this case—a high score is assigned to the inserted term.

If a broad and non-domain-focused program like Watson, which relies heavily on text mining and NLP, can answer open-ended quiz show questions with nearly 100% accuracy, one can imagine how successful specialized NLP tools would be. In fact IBM has successfully deployed a Watson-type program to help in decision making at health care centers (Upbin, 2013).

Text mining also finds applications in numerous business activities such as email spam filtering, consumer sentiment analysis, and patent mining to name a few. A couple of these will be explored in this chapter.

People in the data management domains can appreciate text mining in a slightly different context. Here, the objective is not so much discovering new trends or patterns, but cleaning data stored in business databases. For example, when people make manual entries into a customer relationship management software, there is a lot of scope for typographic errors: a salesperson's name may be spelled "Osterman" in several instances (which is perhaps the correct spelling) and "Ostrerman" in a few instances, which is a misspelling. Text mining could be used in such situations to identify the right spelling and suggest it to the entry operator to ensure that data consistency is maintained. Similar application logic could be used in identifying and streamlining call center service data (McKnight, 2005).

Text mining, more than any other technique within data mining, fits the *mining* metaphor. Traditionally, mining refers to the process of separating dirt from valuable metal and in the case of text mining, it is an attempt to separate valuable keywords from a mass of other words (or relevant documents from a sea of documents) and use them to identify meaningful patterns or make predictions.

9.1 HOW IT WORKS

The fundamental step in text mining involves converting text into semi-structured data. Once the unstructured text is converted into semi-structured data, there is nothing to stop one from applying any of the analytics techniques to classify, cluster, and predict. The unstructured text needs to be converted into a semi-structured data set so that patterns can be found and even better, models could be trained to detect patterns in new and unseen text. The chart in Fig. 9.1 identifies the main steps in this process at a high level.

Each of the main processes will now be examined in detail and some necessary terminology and concepts will be introduced. But before these processes are described, a few core ideas essential to text analytics will need to be defined.

9.1.1 Term Frequency–Inverse Document Frequency

Consider a web search problem where the user types in some keywords and the search engine extracts all the documents (essentially, web pages) that contain these keywords. How does the search engine know which web pages to serve up? In addition to using network rank or page rank, the search engine also runs some form of text mining to identify the most relevant web pages. Suppose for example, that the user types in the following keywords: "RapidMiner books that describe text mining." In this case, the search engines run on the following basic logic:

1. Give a high weightage to those keywords that are relatively rare.
2. Give a high weightage to those web pages that contain a large number of instances of the rare keywords.

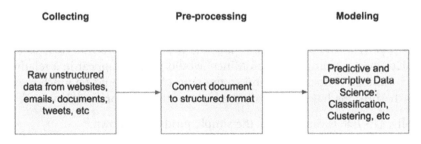

FIGURE 9.1
A high-level process for text mining.

In this context, what is a rare keyword? Clearly, English words like "that," "books," "describe," and "text" possibly appear in a large number of web pages, whereas "RapidMiner" and "mining" may appear in a relatively smaller number of web pages. (A quick web search returned 7.7 billion results for the word "books," whereas only 584,000 results were returned for "RapidMiner" at the time of this writing.) Therefore, these rarer keywords would receive a higher rating to begin with according to logic 1. Next, among all those pages that contain the rare keywords, only those pages that contain the largest number of instances of the rare keywords are likely to be the most relevant for the user and will receive high weightage according to logic 2. Thus, the highest-weighted web pages are the ones for which the *product* of these two weights is the highest. Therefore, only those pages that not only contain the rare keywords, but also have a high number of instances of the rare keywords should appear at the top of the search results.

The technique of calculating this weighting is called term *TF–IDF*, which stands for term frequency–inverse document frequency.

Calculating TF is extremely easy: it is simply the ratio of the number of times a keyword appears in a given document, n_k (where k is the keyword), to the total number of terms in the document, n:

$$\text{TF} = \frac{n_k}{n} \tag{9.1}$$

Considering the mentioned example, a common English word such as "that" will have a fairly high TF score and a word such as "RapidMiner" will have a much lower TF score.

IDF is defined as follows:

$$\text{IDF} = \log_2\left(\frac{N}{N_k}\right) \tag{9.2}$$

where N is the number of documents under consideration (in a search engine context, N is the number of all the indexed web pages). For most text mining problems, N is the number of documents that one is trying to mine, and N_k is the number of documents that contain the keyword, k. Again, a word such as "that" would arguably appear in every document and, thus, the ratio (N/N_k) would be close to 1, and the IDF score would be close to zero for. However, a word like "RapidMiner" would possibly appear in a relatively fewer number of documents and so the ratio (N/N_k) would be much greater than 1. Thus, the IDF score would be high for this less common keyword.

Finally, TF–IDF is expressed as the simple product as shown:

$$\text{TF} - \text{IDF} = \frac{n_k}{n} \times \log_2\left(\frac{N}{N_k}\right) \tag{9.3}$$

Going back to the mentioned example, when the high TF for "that" is multiplied by its corresponding low IDF, a low (or zero) TF−IDF will be reached, whereas when the low TF for "RapidMiner" is multiplied by its corresponding fairly high IDF, a relatively higher TF−IDF would be obtained.

Typically, TF−IDF scores for every word in the set of documents is calculated in the preprocessing step of the three-step process described earlier. Performing this calculation will help in applying any of the standard data science techniques that have been discussed so far in this book. In the following sections additional concepts that are commonly employed in text mining will be described.

9.1.2 Terminology

Consider the following two sentences: "This is a book on data mining" and "This book describes data mining and text mining using RapidMiner." Suppose the objective is to perform a comparison between them, or a similarity mapping. For this purpose, each sentence is one unit of text that needs to be analyzed.

These two sentences could be embedded in an email message, in two separate web pages, in two different text files, or else they could be two sentences in the same text file. In the text mining context, each sentence is considered a distinct *document*. Furthermore, in the simplest case, words are separated by a special character: a blank space. Each word is called a *token*, and the process of discretizing words within a document is called *tokenization*. For the purpose here, each sentence can be considered a separate document, although what is considered an individual document may depend upon the context. For now, a document here is simply a sequential collection of tokens.

| Document 1 | This is a book on data mining |
| Document 2 | This book describes data mining and text mining using RapidMiner |

Some form of structure can be imposed on this raw data by creating a matrix where the columns consist of all the tokens found in the two documents and the cells of the matrix are the counts of the number of times a token appears, as shown in Table 9.1.

Each token is now an attribute in standard data science parlance and each document is an example. One, therefore, has a structured *example set*, to use standard terminology. Basically, unstructured raw data is now transformed into a format that is recognized, not only by the human users as a data table, but more importantly by all the machine learning algorithms which require

Table 9.1 Building a Matrix of Terms From Unstructured Raw Text

	This	is	a	book	on	data	mining	describes	text	rapidminer	and	using
Document 1	1	1	1	1	1	1	1	0	0	0	0	0
Document 2	1	0	0	1	0	1	2	1	1	1	1	1

such tables for training. This table is called a *document vector* or *term document matrix (TDM)* and is the cornerstone of the preprocessing required for text mining. Suppose a third statement is added, "RapidMiner is offered as an open source software program." This new document will increase the number of rows of the matrix by one (Document 3); however, it increases the number of columns by seven (seven new words or tokens were introduced). This results in zeroes being recorded in nine other columns for row 3. As more new statements are added that have little in common, one would end up with a very sparse matrix.

Note that one could have also chosen to use the term frequencies for each token instead of simply counting the number of occurrences and it would still be a sparse matrix. TF can be obtained by dividing each row of Table 9.1 by number of words in the row (document). This is shown in Table 9.2.[1]

Similarly, one could have also chosen to use the TF−IDF scores for each term to create the document vector. This is also shown in Fig. 9.2.

One thing to note in the two sample text documents was the occurrence of common words such as "a," "this," "and," and other similar terms. Clearly in larger documents a higher number of such terms would be expected that do not really convey specific meaning. Most grammatical necessities such as articles, conjunctions, prepositions, and pronouns may need to be filtered before additional analysis is performed. Such terms are called *stop words* and usually include most articles, conjunctions, pronouns, and prepositions. *Stop word filtering* is usually the second step that follows immediately after *tokenization*. Notice that the document vector has a significantly reduced size after applying standard English stop word filtering (see Fig. 9.3).

In addition to filtering standard stop words, some specific terms might also need to be filtered out. For example, in analyzing text documents that pertain to the automotive industry, one may want to filter away terms that are common to this industry such as "car," "automobile," "vehicle," and so on. This

---

[1] RapidMiner does a double normalization while calculating TF scores. For example, in case of Document 1, the TF score for the term "data" would be $(0.1498)/\sqrt{(0.1498^2 + 0.1498^2 + ... + 0.1498^2)} = 0.1498/\sqrt{7*(0.1498^2)} = 0.3779$. Similarly for all other terms, double normalization makes it easier to apply algorithms such as SVM. This change in TF calculation is reflected in the TF-IDF scores.

Table 9.2 Using Term Frequencies Instead of Term Counts in a TDM

	This	is	a	book	on	data	mining	describes	text	rapidminer	and	using
Document 1	1/7 = 0.1428	0.1428	0.1428	0.1428	0.1428	0.1428	0.1428	0	0	0	0	0
Document 2	1/10 = 0.1	0	0	0.1	0	0.1	0.2	0.1	0.1	0.1	0.1	0.1

TDM, *Term document matrix.*

ExampleSet (2 examples, 0 special attributes, 12 regular attributes)											
Row No.	RapidMiner	This	a	and	book	data	describes	is	mining	on	text	using
1	0	0	0.577	0	0	0	0	0.577	0	0.577	0	0
2	0.447	0	0	0.447	0	0	0.447	0	0	0	0.447	0.447

FIGURE 9.2

Calculating TF−IDF scores for the sample TDM. *TF−IDF*, Term Frequency−Inverse Document Frequency; *TDM*, term document matrix.

Row No.	RapidMiner	book	data	describes	mining	text	using
1	0	1	1	0	1	0	0
2	1	1	1	1	2	1	1

FIGURE 9.3

Stop word filtering reduces the size of the TDM significantly.

is generally achieved by creating a separate dictionary where these context-specific terms can be defined and then *term filtering* can be applied to remove them from the data. (*Lexical substitution* is the process of finding an alternative for a word in the context of a clause and is used to align all the terms to the same term based on the field or subject which is being analyzed—this is especially important in areas with specific jargon, e.g., in clinical settings.)

Words such as "recognized," "recognizable," or "recognition" may be encountered in different usages, but contextually they may all imply the same meaning. For example, "Einstein is a *well-recognized* name in physics" or "The physicist went by the easily *recognizable* name of Einstein" or "Few other physicists have the kind of name *recognition* that Einstein has." The so-called root of all these highlighted words is "recognize." By reducing terms in a document to their basic stems, the conversion of unstructured text to structured data can be simplified because now only the occurrence of the root terms has to be taken into account. This process is called *stemming*. The most common stemming technique for text mining in English is the Porter method (Porter, 1980). Porter stemming works on a bunch of rules where the basic idea is to remove and/or replace the suffix of words. For example, one rule would be: *Replace all terms which end in 'ies' by 'y,'* such as replacing the term "anomalies" with "anomaly." Similarly, another rule would be to stem all terms ending in "s" by removing the "s," as in "algorithms" to "algorithm." While the Porter stemmer is extremely efficient, it can make mistakes that could prove costly. For example, "arms" and "army" would both be stemmed to "arm," which would result in somewhat different contextual meanings. There are other stemmers available; which one is chosen is usually guided by ones experience in various domains. Stemming is usually the next process step following term filtering. (A word of caution: stemming is

Row	label	RapidMiner	book	book_data	book_descr..	data	data_mining	describes	describes_data	mining	mining_text	mining_usi..	text_0	text_mining	using	using_RapidMiner
1	text1	0	0.447	0.447	0	0.447	0.447	0	0	0.447	0	0	0	0	0	0
2	text2	0.243	0.243	0	0.243	0.243	0.243	0.243	0.243	0.485	0.243	0.243	0.243	0.243	0.243	0.243

FIGURE 9.4

Meaningful *n*-grams show higher TF–IDF scores. *TF–IDF*, Term Frequency–Inverse Document Frequency.

Table 9.3 A Typical Sequence of PreProcessing Steps to Use in Text Mining

Step	Action	Result
1	Tokenize	Convert each word or term in a document into a distinct attribute
2	Stop word removal	Remove highly common grammatical tokens/words
3	Filtering	Remove other very common tokens
4	Stemming	Trim each token to its most essential minimum
5	*n*-grams	Combine commonly occurring token pairs or tuples (more than 2)

completely dependent on the human language being processed as well as the period of the language being processed. Historical usage varies so widely that comparing text across generations—Shakespeare to present-day literature for instance—can raise concerns.)

There are families of words in the spoken and written language that typically go together. For example, the word "Good" is usually followed by either "Morning," "Afternoon," "Evening," "Night," or in Australia, "Day." Grouping such terms, called *n-grams*, and analyzing them statistically can present new insights. Search engines use word *n*-gram models for a variety of applications, such as automatic translation, identifying speech patterns, checking misspelling, entity detection, information extraction, among many other different uses. Google has processed more than a trillion words (1,024,908,267,229 words back as far back as 2006) of running text and has published the counts for all 1,176,470,663 five-word sequences that appear at least 40 times (Franz, 2006). While most text mining applications do not require 5-grams, bigrams and trigrams are quite useful. The final preprocessing step typically involves forming these *n*-grams and storing them in the document vector. Also, most algorithms providing *n*-grams become computationally expensive and the results become huge so in practice the amount of "*n*" will vary based on the size of the documents and the corpus.

Fig. 9.4 shows a TF-based document vector for bigrams ($n = 2$) from the examples and as can be seen, terms like "data mining" and "text mining" and "using RapidMiner" can be quite meaningful in this context. Table 9.3

summarizes a typical sequence of preprocessing steps that will convert unstructured data into a semi-structured format.

Usually there is a preprocessing step before tokenization such as removing special characters, changing the case (up-casing and down-casing), or sometimes even performing a simple spell check beforehand. Data quality in text mining is just as important as in other areas.

9.2   HOW TO IMPLEMENT

A few essential concepts have been introduced that would be needed for a basic text mining project. In the following sections, two case studies will be examined that apply text mining. In the first example, several documents (web pages) will be taken and keywords found in them will be grouped into similar *clusters*. In the second example, a *blog gender classification* will be attempted. To start with several blogs (documents) written by men and women authors, will be used as training data. Using the article keywords as features, several classification models will be trained, including a couple of SVMs, to recognize stylistic characteristics of authors and to classify new unseen blogs as belonging to one of the two author classes (male or female).

9.2.1   Implementation 1: Keyword Clustering

In this first example, some of the web mining features of RapidMiner will be introduced and then a clustering model will be created with keywords data mined from a website. The objective of this case study is to scan several pages from a given website and identify the most frequent words within these pages that also serve to characterize each page, and then to identify the most frequent words using a clustering model. This simple example can be easily extended to a more comprehensive document-clustering problem where the most common words occurring in a document would be used as flags to group multiple documents. The predictive objective of this exercise is to then use the process to identify any random webpage and determine if the page pertains to one of the two categories which the model has been trained to identify.

The site (http://www.detroitperforms.org) that is being looked into is hosted by a public television station and is meant to be used as a platform for reaching out to members of the local community who are interested in arts and culture. The site serves as a medium for the station to not only engage with community members, but also to eventually aid in targeted marketing campaigns meant to attract donors to public broadcasting. The site has pages for several related categories: Music, Dance, Theater, Film, and so on. Each of these pages contains articles and events related to that category. The goal here is to characterize each page on the site and identify the top keywords that appear on each page. To that end, each category page will be crawled, the content extracted, and the information converted into a structured document vector consisting of keywords. Finally, a *k*-medoids clustering process will be run to sort the keywords and rank them. Medoid clustering is similar to the *k*-means clustering described in Chapter 7, Clustering. A medoid is the most centrally located object in a cluster (Park & Jun, 2009). *k*-Medoids are less susceptible to noise and outliers when compared to *k*-means. This is because *k*-medoids tries to minimize dis-similarities rather than Euclidean distances, which is what *k*-means does.

Before beginning with web page clustering in RapidMiner, make sure that the web mining and text mining extensions are installed. *(This is easily done by going to Help → Updates and Extensions on the main menu bar.)* RapidMiner provides three different ways to crawl and get content from websites. The *Crawl Web* operator will allow setting up of simple crawling rules and based on these rules will store the crawled pages in a directory for further processing. The *Get Page* operator retrieves a single page and stores the content as an example set. The *Get Pages* operator works similarly but can access multiple pages identified by their URLs contained in an input file. The *Get Pages* operator will be used in this example. Both of the *Get Page(s)* operators allow the choosing of either the GET or POST HTTP request methods for retrieving content.[2]

Step 1: Gather Unstructured Data
The first step in this process is to create an input text file containing a list of URLs to be scanned by the *Get Pages* operator. This is specified in the *Read CSV* (renamed in the process shown in Fig. 9.6 to *Read URL List*) operator, which initiates the whole process. The text file consists of three lines: a header line that is needed for the link attribute parameter for Get Pages and two lines containing the two URLs that are going to be crawled, as shown in Fig. 9.5.[3]

```
        pages.txt
1   links_to_scan
2   http://www.detroitperforms.org/category/dance/
3   https://www.detroitperforms.org/category/film/
4
```

FIGURE 9.5
Creating a URL read list.

---

[2] For more information on the differences between the two methods, and when to use which type of request, refer to the tutorials on www.w3schools.com.

[3] Be aware that websites may frequently change their structure or content or be taken down altogether. The results shown here for this example were obtained when the website listed was crawled at the time of writing. Your results may differ depending upon when the process is executed.

The first URL is the Dance category page and the second one is the Film category page on the website. Save the text file as pages.txt as shown in the figure.

The output from the *Get Pages* operator consists of an example set that will contain two main attributes: the URL and extracted HTML content. Additionally, it also adds some metadata attributes that are not needed in this example, such as content length (characters), date, and so on. These extra attributes can be filtered out using the *Select Attributes* operator.

Step 2: Data Preparation

Next, connect the output from this to a *Process Documents from Data* operator. This is a nested operator, which means this operator contains an inner sub-process where all the preprocessing takes place. The first step in this preprocessing is removing all the HTML tags and only preserving the actual content. This is enabled by the *Extract Content* operator. Put this operator inside the *Process Documents from Data* operator and connect the different operators as shown in Figs. 9.6 and 9.7. Refer to Table 9.3 from earlier to see which operators to use. The inset shows the operators inside the nested *Process Documents from Data* operator. In this case, the word occurrences will need to be used for the clustering. So, select Term Occurrences for the vector creation parameter option when configuring the *Process Documents from Data* operator.

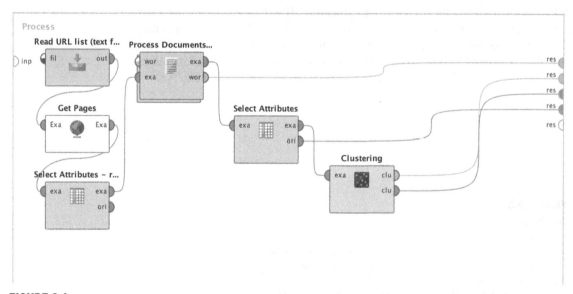

FIGURE 9.6

Overall process of creating keyword clustering from websites.

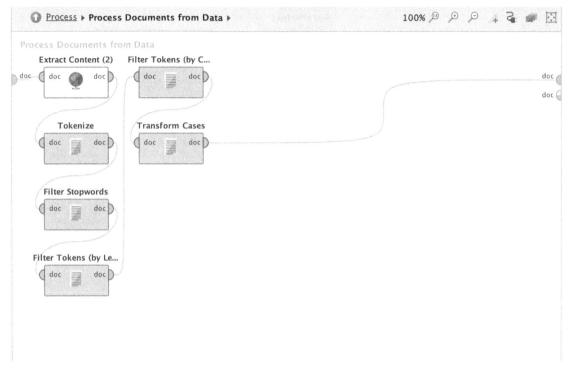

FIGURE 9.7
Configuring the nested preprocessing operator: process documents from data.

Step 3: Apply Clustering

The output from the *Process Documents from Data* operator consists of (1) a word list and (2) a document vector or TDM. The word list is not needed for clustering; however, the document vector is. Recall that the difference between the two is that in the document vector, each word is considered an attribute and each row or example is a separate document (in this case the web pages crawled). The values in the cells of the document vector can of course be word occurrences, word frequencies, or TF—IDF scores, but as noted in step 2, in this case the cells will have word occurrences. The output from the *Process Documents from Data* operator is filtered further to remove attributes that are less than 5 (that is all words that occur less than five times in *both* documents). Notice that RapidMiner will only remove those attributes (words) which occur less than five times in *both* documents—for example, the word "dance" appears only two times in the Film category but is the most common word in the Dance category; it is not and should not be removed! Finally, this cleaned output is fed into a *k*-medoids clustering operator, which is configured as shown in Fig. 9.8.

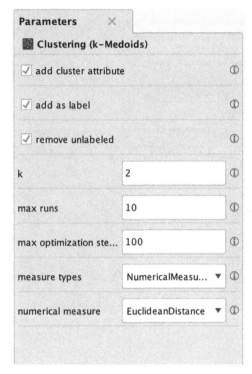

FIGURE 9.8

Configuring the *k*-medoids operator.

Upon running the process, RapidMiner will crawl the two URLs listed and execute the different operations to finally generate two clusters. To view these clustering outputs, select either the Centroid Table or Centroid Plot views in the Cluster Model (Clustering) results tab, which will clearly show the top keywords from each of the two pages crawled. In Fig. 9.9, see the top few keywords that characterize each cluster. One can then use this model to identify if the content of any random page would belong to either one of the categories.

9.2.2 Implementation 2: Predicting the Gender of Blog Authors

The objective of this case study is to attempt to predict the gender of blog authors based[4] on the content of the blog (should it be predicted? why? can it be predicted?).

---

[4] A compressed version of this data can be downloaded from the Opinion Mining, Sentiment Analysis, and Opinion Spam Detection website (http://www.cs.uic.edu/~liub/FBS/sentiment-analysis.html). The data set is called Blog Author Gender Classification dataset associated with the paper (Mukherjee, 2010). This site contains a lot of relevant information related to text mining and sentiment analysis, in addition to several other useful data sets.

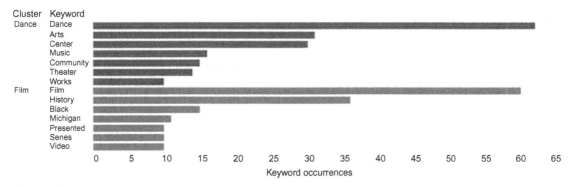

FIGURE 9.9
Results of the website keyword clustering process.

Step 1: Gather Unstructured Data

The data set for this case study consists of more than 3000 individual blog entries (articles) by men and women from around the world (Mukherjee, 2010). The data[4] is organized into a single spreadsheet consisting of 3227 rows and two columns as shown in the sample in Table 9.4. The first column is the actual blog content and the second column is the author's gender, which has been labeled.

For the purpose of this case study, the raw data will be split into two halves: the first 50% of the data is treated as training data with known labels and the remaining 50% is set aside to verify the performance of the training algorithm.

While developing models involving large amounts of data, which is common with unstructured text analysis, it is a good practice to divide the process into several distinct processes and store the intermediate data, models, and results from each process for recall at a later stage. RapidMiner facilitates this by providing special operators called *Store* and *Retrieve*. The *Store* operator stores an input-ouput (IO) Object in the data repository and *Retrieve* reads an object from the data repository. The use of these operators is introduced in the coming sections.

Step 2: Data Preparation

Once the data is downloaded and uncompressed, it yields a single MS Excel file, which can then be imported into the RapidMiner database using the *Read Excel* operator. The raw data consists of 290 examples that do not have a label and one example that has no blog content but has a label! This needs to be cleaned up. It is easier to delete this entry in the raw data—simply delete the row (#1523) in the spreadsheet that contains this missing entry and save the file before reading it into RapidMiner. Also

Table 9.4 Raw Data for the Blog Classification Study

Blog	Gender
This game was a blast. You (as Drake) start the game waking up in a train that is dangling over the side of a cliff. You have to climb up the train car, which is slowly teetering off the edge of the cliff, ready to plummet miles down into a snowy abyss. From the snowy beginning there are flashbacks to what led Drake to this predicament. The story unfolds in a very cinematic manner, and the scenes in between levels, while a bit clichéd by Hollywood standards, are still just as good if not better than your average brainless Mel Gibson or Bruce Willis action movie. In fact, the cheese is part of the fun and I would venture to say it's intentional	M
My mother was a contrarian, she was. For instance, she always wore orange on St. Patrick's Day, something that I of course did not understand at the time, nor, come to think of it do I understand today. Protestants wear orange in Ireland, not here, but I'm pretty sure my mother had nothing against the Catholics, so why did she do it? Maybe it had to do with the myth about Patrick driving the snakes, a.k.a. pagans, out of Ireland. Or maybe it was something political. I have no idea and since my mother is long gone from this earth, I guess I'll never know	F
LaLicious Sugar Soufflé body scrub has a devoted following and I now understand why. I received a sample of this body scrub in Tahitian Flower and after one shower with this tub of sugary goodness, I was hooked. The lush scent is deliciously intoxicating and it ended up inspiring compliments and extended sniffing from both loved ones and strangers alike. Furthermore, this scrub packs one heck of a punch when it comes to pampering dry skin. In fact, LaLicious promises that this body scrub is so rich that it will eliminate the need for applying your post-shower lotion. This claim is true—if you follow the directions	F
Stopped by the post office this morning to pick up a package on my way to the lab. I thought it would be as good a time as any to clean up my desk and at the very least make it appear that I am more organized than I really am (seriously, it's a mess). It's pretty nice here on the weekends, it's quiet, there's less worry of disturbing undergrad classes if I do any experiments in the daytime	M
Anyway, it turns out the T-shirt I ordered from Concrete Rocket arrived! Here's how the design looks	
See here's the thing: Men have their neat little boxes through which they compartmentalize their lives. Relationship over? Oh, I'll just close that box. It's not that easy for women. Our relationships are not just a section of our lives—they run through the entire fabric, a hot pink thread which adds to the mosaic composing who we are. Take out a relationship and you grab that thread and pull. Have you ever pulled a thread on a knit sweater? That's what it's like. The whole garment gets scrunched and disfigured just because that one piece was removed. And then you have to pull it back apart, smooth it out, fill in the gaps. See here's the thing: men have their neat little boxes through which they compartmentalize their lives. Relationship over? Oh, I'll just close that box. It's not that easy for women	F

make sure that the *Read Excel* operator is configured to recognize the data type in the first column as text and not polynominal (default) as shown in Fig. 9.10. Connect the output from *Read Excel* to a *Filter Examples* operator, where the entries with missing labels will then be removed. (If inclined, store these entries with missing labels for use as testing samples—this can be accomplished with another *Filter Examples*, but by checking *Invert Filter* box and then storing the output. In this case, however, examples with missing labels will simply be discarded.) The cleaned data can now be separated with a 50/50 split using a *Split Data* operator. Save the latter 50%

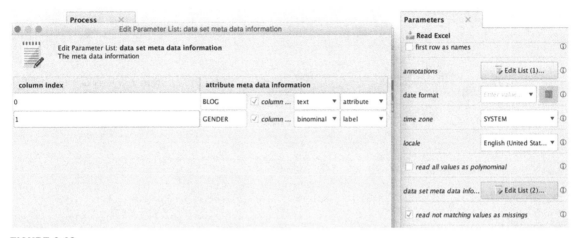

FIGURE 9.10
Properly configuring the Read Excel operator to accept text (not polynomial).

testing data (1468 samples) to a new file with a *Write Excel* operator and pass the remaining 50% training portion to a *Process Documents from Data* operator.

This is a nested operator where all the preprocessing happens. Recall that this is where the conversion of unstructured data into a structured format will take place. Connect the different operators within as shown in Fig. 9.13. The only point to note here is that a *Filter Stop word (Dictionary)* operator will be needed to remove any "nbsp" (" " is used to represent a nonbreaking space) terms that may have slipped into the content. Create a simple text file with this keyword inside it and let RapidMiner know that this dictionary exists by properly configuring the operator. To configure the *Process Documents from Data* operator, use the options as shown in Fig. 9.11.

The output from the process for step 2 consists of the document vector and a word list. While the word list may not be of immediate use in the subsequent steps, it is a good idea to store this along with the very important document vector. The final process is shown in Fig. 9.12.

Step 3.1: Identify Key Features
The document vector that is the result of the process in step 2 is a structured table consisting of 2055 rows—one for every blog entry in the training set—and 2815 attributes or columns—each token within an article that meets the filtering and stemming criteria defined by operators inside *Process Documents* is converted into an attribute. Training learning algorithms using 2815 features or variables is clearly an onerous task. The right approach is to further filter these attributes by using feature selection methods.

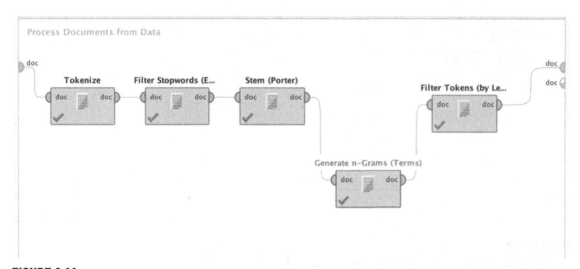

FIGURE 9.11
Configuring the preprocessing operator.

Two feature selection methods will be employed using the *Weight by Information Gain* and *Weight by SVM* operators that are available. *Weight by Information Gain* (more details in Chapter 14: Feature Selection, on this operator) will rank a feature or attribute by its relevance to the label attribute (in this case, gender) based on the information gain ratio and assign weights to them accordingly. *Weight by SVM* will set the coefficients of the SVM hyperplane as attribute weights. Once they are ranked using these techniques, only a handful of attributes can be selected (e.g., the top 20) to build the models. Doing so will result in a reasonable reduction in modeling costs.

The results of this intermediate process will generate two weight tables, one corresponding to each feature selection method. The process is started by retrieving the document vector saved in step 2 and then the process is ended by storing the weight tables for use in step 3.2 (see Fig. 9.14).

In the paper by Mukherjee and Liu (Mukherjee, 2010) from which this data set comes, they demonstrate the use of several other feature selection methods, including a novel one developed by the authors that is shown to yield a much higher prediction accuracy than the stock algorithms (such as the ones demonstrated here).

Step 3.2: Build Models
With the document vector and attribute weights now ready, one can experiment using several different machine learning algorithms to understand

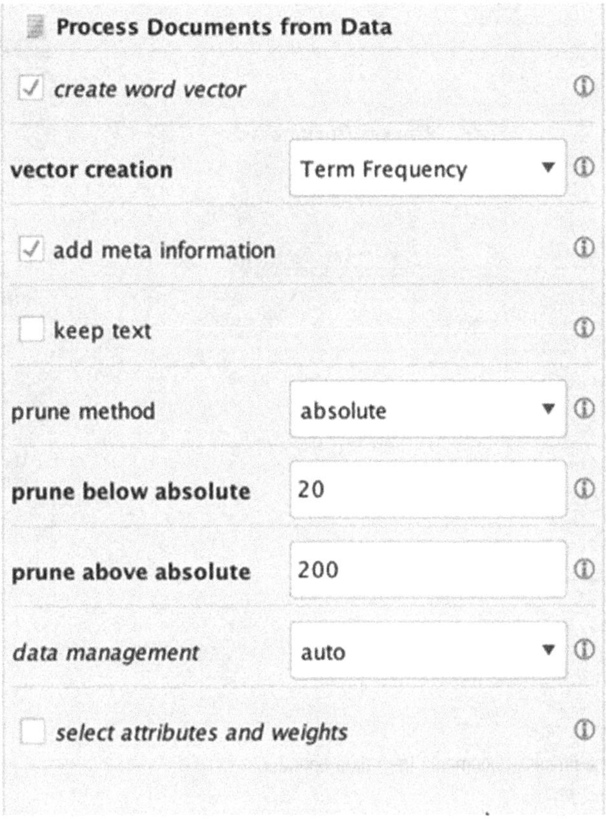

FIGURE 9.12
Overall process for blog gender classification.

which gives the best accuracy. The process illustrated in Figs. 9.15 and 9.16 will generate the models and store them (along with the corresponding performance results) for later application. This is a key strength of RapidMiner: once one has built up the necessary data for predictive modeling, switching back and forth between various algorithms requires nothing more than dragging and dropping the needed operators and making the connections. As seen in Fig. 9.16, there are four different algorithms nested inside the *X-Validation* operator and can conveniently be switched back and forth as needed. Table 9.5 shows that the *LibSVM (linear)* and *W-Logistic* operators (Available through Weka extension for RapidMiner) seem to give the best performance. Keep in mind that these accuracies are still not the highest and are in line with the performances reported by Mukherjee and Liu in their paper for generic algorithms.

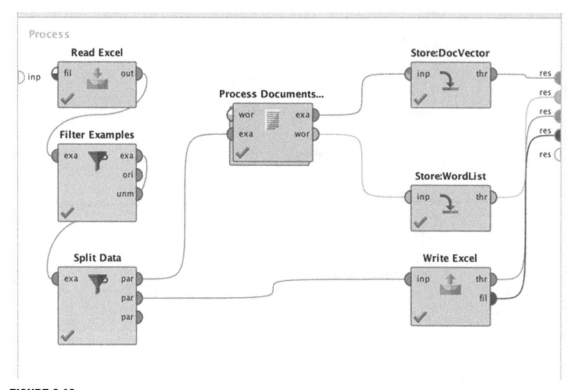

FIGURE 9.13
Preprocessing text data using the process documents from data operator.

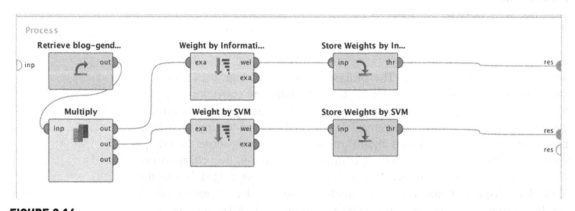

FIGURE 9.14
Using feature selection methods to filter attributes from the TDM. *TDM*, Term Document Matrix.

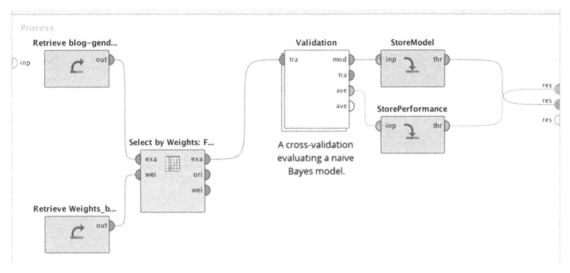

FIGURE 9.15
Training and testing predictive models for blog gender classification.

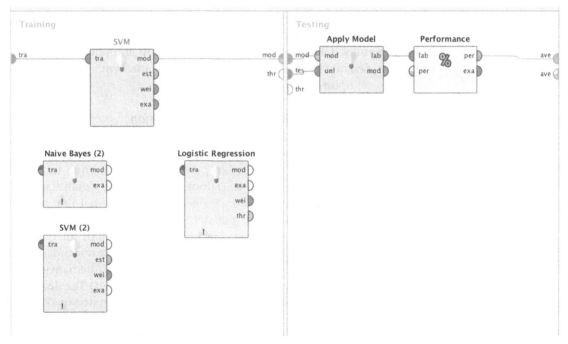

FIGURE 9.16
Switching between several algorithms.

Table 9.5 Comparing the Performance of Different Training Algorithms for Blog Gender Classification

Algorithm	Class Recall (M)	Class Recall (F)	Accuracy
LibSVM (linear)	87	53	72
W-Logistic	85	58	73
Naïve Bayes	86	55	72
SVM (polynomial)	82	42	63

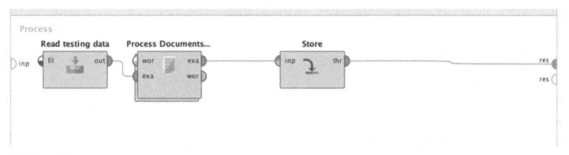

FIGURE 9.17
Preparing the unseen data for model deployment.

To improve upon these, we may need to further optimize the best performers so far by nesting the entire validation process within an optimization operator. This is described in the Chapter 15: Getting started with RapidMiner, in the section on optimization.

Step 4.1: Prepare Test Data for Model Application

Going back to the original 50% of the unseen data that was saved for testing purposes, the real-world performance of the best algorithm can actually be evaluated in classifying blogs by author gender. However, keep in mind that the raw data that was set aside as is, cannot be used (what would happen if one did?). This raw test data would also need to be converted into a document vector first. In other words, the step 2 process needs to be repeated (without the filtering and split data operators) on the 50% of the data that were set aside for testing. The *Process Documents from Data* operator can be simply copied and pasted from the process in step 2. (Alternatively, the entire data set could have been preprocessed before splitting!) The document vector is stored for use in the next step. This process is illustrated in Fig. 9.17.

Step 4.2: Applying the Trained Models to Testing Data

This is where the rubber hits the road! The last step will take any of the saved models created in step 3.2 and the newly created document vector from step

4.1 and apply the model on this test data. The process is shown in Figs. 9.18 and 9.19. One useful operator to add is the *Set Role* operator, which will be used to indicate to RapidMiner the label variable. Doing so will allow the results to be sorted from the Apply Model by Correct Predictions and Wrong Predictions using the View Filter in the Results perspective as shown here.

When this process is run, it can be observed that the LibSVM (linear) model can correctly predict only 828 of the 1468 examples, which translates to a poor 56% accuracy! The other models fare worse. Clearly the model and the process are in need of optimization and further refinement. Using RapidMiner's optimization operators, one can easily improve on this baseline accuracy. A discussion about how to use the optimization operators in general is provided in Chapter 15, Getting started with RapidMiner. The truly adventurous can implement the Mukherjee and Liu algorithm for feature selection in RapidMiner based on the instructions given in their paper! Although this implementation did not return a stellar predictive performance (and the motivation of this classification is digital advertisement, as specified in the paper), a word of caution is in order: algorithms have become increasingly more powerful and reckless application of machine learning may lead to undesirable consequences of discrimination (via gender, in this instance). Data scientists are responsible for ensuring that their products are used in an ethical and non-discriminatory manner.

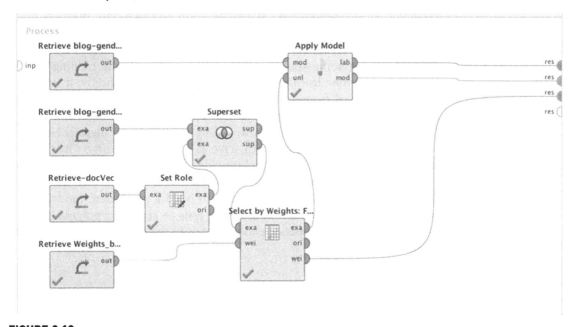

FIGURE 9.18
Applying the models built in step 3 on the unseen data.

Row No.	GENDER	predict...	confide...	confide...	abil	activ	adapt	admir	ador	adult	advanc	ahead	amount
1	M	M	1	0	0	0	0	0	0	0	0	0	0
2	M	M	1	0	0	0	0	0	0	0	0	0	0
3	M	M	0.500	0.500	0	0	0	0	0	0	0	0	0
4	M	M	1	0	0	0	0	0	0	0	0	0	0
5	M	M	0.500	0.500	0	0	0	0	0	0.186	0	0	0
6	M	M	1	0	0	0	0	0	0	0	0	0	0
7	M	M	0.500	0.500	0	0	0	0	0	0	0	0	0
8	M	M	0.500	0.500	0	0	0	0	0	0	0	0	0
9	M	M	1	0	0	0	0	0	0	0	0	0	0
10	M	M	0.500	0.500	0	0	0	0	0	0	0	0	0
11	M	M	0.500	0.500	0	0	0	0	0	0	0	0	0
12	M	M	1	0	0	0	0	0	0	0	0	0	0

FIGURE 9.19
The results view.

Bias in Machine Learning

Data Science is a powerful tool to extract value from data. Just like any other tool, it can be put to good use, inappropriate use, malicious use or use it in such a way that yield unintended consequences. Recently, a data science model that was developed to filter and sort the resumes of job applicants started to discriminate against women (Gershgorn, 2018). The data science modeling process would have started as a solution to a right business problem, which is to manage the influx of resumes and sorting the most relevant ones to the top. In doing so, the text mining model favoured one applicant class, leveraging some spurious pattern in the data. If the training data is biased, the machine learning model will be biased. Specifically, if the training data is derived from a biased process, the machine learning automation just amplifies the phenomenon. A loan approval model might not ask for the race of the applicant (which would be unethical and illegal). However, the location of an applicant might serve as a proxy for the race. It is important to test and audit if the model provides fair prediction for all the classes of users. These machine learning models have real world consequences. The responsibility lies with the data scientist to build a transparent model adhering to ethical principles. Creating robust tests to check for potential unfairness in the models is imperative to gain trust in the discipline of data science (Loukides et al., 2018).

9.3 CONCLUSION

Unstructured data, of which text data is a major portion, appears to be doubling in volume every three years (Mayer-Schonberger, 2013). The ability to automatically process and mine information from such digital data will become an important skill in the future. These techniques can be used to classify and predict just as the other techniques throughout the book, except one is now working on text documents and even voice recordings that have been transcribed to text.

This chapter described how unstructured data can be mined using any of the available algorithms presented in this book. The key to being able to apply these techniques is to convert the unstructured data into a semi-structured format. A high-level three-step process that will enable this was introduced. Some key tools for transforming unstructured data, such as tokenization, stemming, *n*-gramming, and stop word removal were discussed. How concepts such as TF–IDF allow us to make the final transformation of a corpus of text to a matrix of numbers, that can be worked on by the standard machine learning algorithms was explained. Finally, a couple of implementation examples were presented, which will allow one to explore the exciting world of text mining.

References

Cutting, D. K. (1992). Scatter/gather: A cluster-based approach to browsing large document collections. In: *Copenhagen proceedings of the 15th annual international ACM SIGIR conference on research and development in information retrieval* (pp. 318–329). Copenhagen.

Franz, A. A. (2006, August 3). *All our N-gram are belong to you.* Research blog. Retrieved from <http://googleresearch.blogspot.com/2006/08/all-our-n-gram-are-belong-to-you.html> Accessed 01.11.13.

Gershgorn, D. (2018). Companies are on the hook if their hiring algorithms are biased – Quartz. Retrieved October 24, 2018, from <https://qz.com/1427621/companies-are-on-the-hook-if-their-hiring-algorithms-are-biased/>.

Hearst, M. (1999, June 20–26). Untangling text data mining. In: *Proceedings of Association for Computational Linguistics, 37th annual meeting 1999.* University of Maryland.

Loukides, M., Mason, H., & Patil, D. J. (2018). *Ethics and Data Science.* Sebastopol. CA: O'Reilly Media.

Mayer-Schonberger, V. A. (2013). *Big data: A revolution that will transform how we live, work and think.* London: John Murray and Co.

McKnight, W. (2005, January 1). *Text data mining in business intelligence.* Information Management. Retrieved from <http://www.information-management.com/issues/20050101/1016487-1.html#Login> Accessed 01.11.13.

Mukherjee, A. L. (2010). Improving gender classification of blog authors. In: *Proceedings of conference on Empirical Methods in Natural Language Processing (EMNLP-10).* Cambridge, MA.

Park, H. S., & Jun, C. H. (2009). A simple and fast algorithm for K-medoids clustering. *Expert Systems with Applications, 36*(2), 3336–3341.

Porter, M. F. (1980). An algorithm for suffix stripping. *Program, 14*(3), 130–137.

Siegel, E. (2013). *Predictive analytics: The power to predict who will click, buy, lie or die.* Hoboken, NJ: John Wiley and Sons.

Upbin, B. (2013, February 8). IBM's Watson gets its first piece of business in healthcare. *Forbes.* Retrieved from <https://www.forbes.com/sites/bruceupbin/2013/02/08/ibms-watson-gets-its-first-piece-of-business-in-healthcare/#7010113b5402/>.

CHAPTER 10

Deep Learning

To get a deep-learning system to recognize a hot dog, you might have to feed it 40 million pictures of hot dogs. To get [a two year old] to recognize a hot dog, you show her a hot dog.[1]

The newest and shiniest member of the data science algorithm toolbox is deep learning. Today deep learning has captured the imagination of scientists, business leaders, and lay people. A local bank teller may not understand what deep learning is but talk to her about artificial intelligence (AI)—which is the ubiquitous avatar of deep learning and it would be surprising to learn how much she may have heard about it. The mentioned quote humorously captures the essence of what makes today's AI methods. Deep learning is a vast and rapidly emerging field of knowledge and requires a book on its own merit considering the wide-ranging architectures and implementation details it encompasses.

This chapter aims to provide an intuitive understanding of this complex topic. The hope is that this would establish a solid framework for a much more sophisticated understanding of the subject. Firstly, what constitutes the core of deep learning will be discussed and in order to do that a little computing history will be covered. The similarities between deep learning and familiar algorithms like regression will then be discussed and how deep learning is an extension of regression and artificial neural networks encountered in Chapter 4, Classification will be demonstrated. The essential differences between "traditional" algorithms like multiple linear regression, artificial neural networks and deep learning will, be pointed out by introducing the core concepts of deep learning that set it apart. One type of deep learning technique will then be explored in sufficient detail and implementation information will be provided to make this knowledge applicable to real life problems. Finally, a quick overview of some of the other newly emerging

---

[1] https://www.technologyreview.com/s/608911/is-ai-riding-a-one-trick-pony/.

Data Science. DOI: https://doi.org/10.1016/B978-0-12-814761-0.00010-1

BRINGING ARTIFICIAL INTELLIGENCE TO ENGINEERING

Computer-aided engineering (CAE) is a mainstay of analytical methods used by engineers (Fig. 10.1). CAE works by solving higher order partial differential equations to predict how engineered products respond to service loads that are put on them. This helps engineers design shapes and select materials for different components. For example, how does an F-15 wing behave at supersonic speeds? How much energy does the front bumper of a car absorb in a crash event?.

So how can AI help in such sophisticated activities? To understand this, one needs to dissect CAE its constituent steps. CAE is not a monolithic endeavor, but involves interaction between designers, engineers, and oftentimes computer systems people. The core activities include: creating geometric models of products, subdividing the geometries into discrete "finite elements" on which the laws of physics are applied, converting these physical laws into mathematical equations or formulations, solving these formulations, visualizing the solutions on the original geometric models (using intuitive heat maps, such as the one shown in Fig. 10.1.[2]). This entire process is not only time consuming, but also requires deep domain knowledge in graphics, mechanics, math, and high-performance computing.

All this would suggest that today's state-of-the-art AI could probably not help a whole lot. After all, from what is heard on the popular press AI is mostly chat-bots and identifying cats on the internet! However, that would be a superficial assessment. There are many smaller steps in each of the mentioned processes which are prime candidates for some of the techniques that will be learnt in this chapter.

As an illustration, we can expand on one of these tasks: subdivide the geometries in CAE. This is a crucial step and poor handling of this step will compromise all of the downstream activities. Unfortunately, it is also highly dependent on the skill of the designer who actually works on the discretization. Luckily CAE process engineers have developed many "expert" rules which even an entry level designer can use to make sure that the end product of their activities will meet rigorous standards. One expert rule is something like this: "if a part looks like a rubber gasket, use method A to discretize the geometry; if it looks like an aluminum fastener, then use method B." One can imagine in a modern-day car, for example, that there are hundreds of such similar looking parts. It is a time-consuming task—to go through an entire vehicle to correctly identify components and apply the right discretization method. It would be real value added if an AI could take over the determination of what "a part looks like" before letting an automated process apply the proper method to discretize. In a way this is essentially an application of the "cat identification" AI in a new—and more

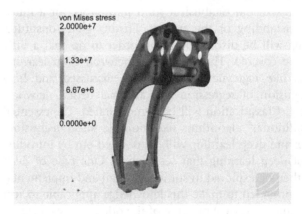

FIGURE 10.1
Computer-aided engineering.

(Continued)

(Continued)

serious domain. But that is not the only task which AI can turbocharge. As will be covered in this chapter, neural networks are at the core of deep learning. But what does a neural network really do? ANN's establish a mapping between the behavior of a complicated system and the environment it functions in. For instance, they help create a mapping between the behavior of a customer (churn vs stay) and the customer's shopping and purchasing habits. Or they create a mapping between the nature of a transaction (fraud vs legitimate) and the characteristics of the transactional environment (location, amount, frequency, and so on).

Another challenging task in CAE is to determine the performance of a system given highly variable environmental conditions. Will the fuselage require maintenance after 10,000 hours of flying or 1000 hours? Will an airbag deploy as intended by design, in tropical climates? Will the reduction in gage thickness still meet the crash safety requirements? Today CAE helps to answer these questions by utilizing physics based computational models to make predictions—this is the mathematical formulation and solution phase identified earlier. Such computations can be costly (in CPU time) and cumbersome (model development time) so that minor changes in design cannot be quickly studied. Deep learning can help speed these up by creating mappings between the product's design elements and its final on-field performance provided sufficient data is

generated (a one-time process) to train a model initially. This idea is not new—classical CAE can be used to develop what are called response surfaces to help with this. The objective of a response surface is to effectively map the design space and then attempt to find an optimum. But a crucial problem with response surfaces was that highly nonlinear or discontinuous behavior that physical systems often exhibit would make it impossible to find optima using conventional mathematical techniques and, thus, would reduce response surfaces to mere toys. In an engineering setting, the independent variable could represent a geometric design feature such as the gage thickness of a metal part whereas the dependent variable could represent a performance metric such as energy absorption.[3] If the data is linearly separable it can be handled by many of the traditional classification algorithm we encountered earlier.

However, complex physical systems rarely exhibit such behavior. Classifying (or mapping) such responses is not possible without ANNs and more specifically without "deep" neural networks. As will be seen in this chapter, a key strength of deep learning networks is in generating nonlinear mappings.

---

[2]https://commons.wikimedia.org/wiki/File:
Static_Structural_Analysis_of_a_Gripper_Arm.jpg.
[3]For an actual example, see Fig. 3 here: https://pdfs.semanticscholar.
org/2f26/c851cab16ee20925c4e556eff5198d92ef3c.pdf.

techniques will be provided, which are now considered as part of the deep learning repertoire of techniques.

10.1 THE AI WINTER

The first ANN were the Perceptrons developed in the 1950s which were a class of pattern recognition elements that weighed evidence and tested if it exceeded a certain threshold in order to make a decision, that is, to classify patterns. Fig. 10.2 shows the architecture of a single perceptron (later on called neuron) which has retained its basic structure through the years.

Each input, x_i has a weight w_i associated with it and a dot product $\Sigma w_i x_i$ is computed at the perceptron and passed to the activation function g. If g $(\Sigma w_i x_i)$ evaluates above a threshold then the output is set to 1 (true) or

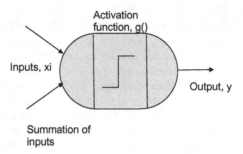

FIGURE 10.2
Conceptual architecture of a perceptron.

otherwise to 0 (false). The process of obtaining the weights, w_i, is called "learning" or "training" the perceptron. The *perceptron learning rule* was originally developed by Frank Rosenblatt (1957). Training data are presented to the network's inputs and the output is computed. The weights w_i are modified by an amount that is proportional to the product of the difference between the actual output, y, and the desired output, d, and the inputs, x_i.

The perceptron learning rule is basically:

1　Initialize the weights and threshold to small random numbers.
2　Feed the inputs x_i to the perceptron and calculate the output.
3　Update the weights according to: $w_i(t + 1) = w_i(t) + \eta(d - y)x$
　Where:
　　d is the desired output,
　　t is the time step, and
　　η is the learning rate, where $0.0 < \eta < 1.0$
4　Repeat steps 2 and 3 until:
　　a.　the iteration error is less than a user-specified error threshold or
　　b.　a predetermined number of iterations have been completed.

Note that learning only happens when the error is above a preset threshold, otherwise the weights are not updated. Also, every time the weights need an update, reading the input data (i.e., step 2) is required.

AI Winter: 1970's

Perceptrons were able to solve a range of decision problems, in particular they were able to represent logic gates such as "AND", "OR," and "NOT." The *perceptron learning rule* tended to converge to an optimal set of weights for several classes of input patterns. However, this was not always guaranteed. Another limitation arose when the data were not linearly separable— for example, the classic "XOR." A XOR gate resolves to "true" if the two

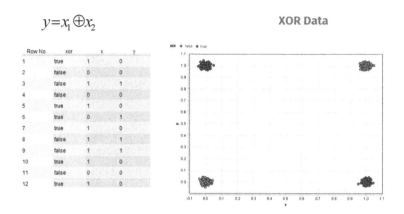

$$y = x_1 \oplus x_2$$

Perceptron will not find a hyper-plane that partitions the classes perfectly

FIGURE 10.3
RapidMiner XOR example.

inputs are different and resolves to "false" if both inputs are the same (Fig. 10.3). Minsky and Papert published these and other core limitations of perceptrons in a 1969 book called *Perceptrons*, which arguably reduced further interest in these types of ANN and the so-called AI Winter had set in.

Mid-Winter Thaw of the 1980s

ANN, however, had a brief resurgence in the 1980s with the development of the multi-layer perceptron (MLP) which was heralded as the solution for nonlinearly separable functions: for example, changing the activation function in an MLP from a linear step function to a nonlinear type (such as sigmoid) could overcome the decision boundary problem seen in the XOR case.

Fig. 10.4 shows that with a linear activation function a two-layer MLP still fails to achieve more than 50% accuracy on the XOR problem using TensorFlow [4] playground. However, a simple switch of the activation function to the nonlinear "sigmoid" helps achieve more than 80% accuracy with the same architecture (Fig. 10.5).

Another important innovation in the 1980s that was able to overcome some of the limitations of the perceptron training rule was the use of "backpropagation" to calculate or update the weights (rather than reverting back to the

---

[4] playground.tensorflow.org.

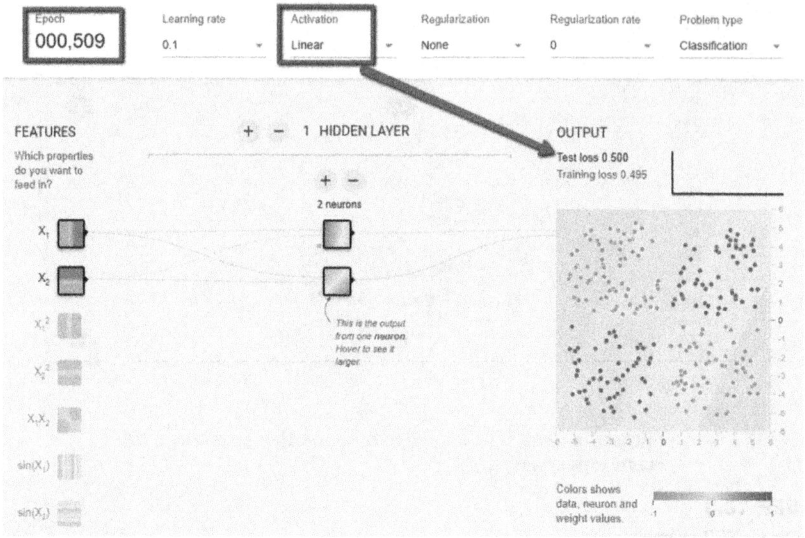

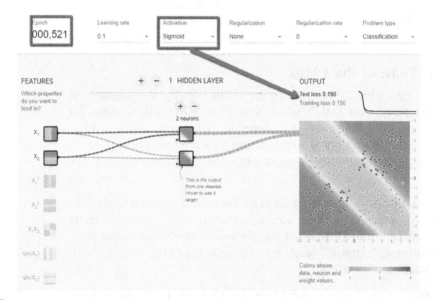

FIGURE 10.4
Exploring network architectures using TensorFlow playground.

FIGURE 10.5
Modifying network architecture to solve the XOR problem using Tensorflow playground.

inputs every time there was an error—step 2 of the perceptron learning rule). The perceptron learning rule updated the weights by an amount that was proportional to the error times of the inputs (the quantity $\eta(d - y)x$ in step 2). These weights w_i are the heart of the network and training an multi-layer perceptron (MLP) or ANN is really all about finding these weights. Finding a robust and repeatable process for updating the weights becomes critical. To do this an extra layer of neurons were added in between the input and the output nodes. Now the error quantity $(d - y)$ becomes a summation and to avoid sign bias, the error may be squared, that is, $\Sigma(d_j - y_j)^2$. The challenge now was determining which direction to change the weights, w_i so that this error quantity is minimized. The algorithm now involved these steps:

1. Computing the output vector given the inputs and a random selection of weights in a "forward" computational flow.
2. Computing the error quantity.
3. Updating the weights to reduce this error at the output layer.
4. Repeat two and three for the hidden layer going backward.

This backpropagation method was introduced by Rumelhart, Hinton, and Williams (1986).[5] Their network was trainable to detect mirror symmetry; to predict one word in a triplet when two of the words were given and other such basic applications. More sophisticated ANNs were built using backpropagation, that could be trained to read handwriting (LeCun, 1989).[6] However, successful business applications of ANN were still limited and it failed to capture the public imagination the way it has currently.

Part of the reason was the state of computing hardware at the time when these algorithms were introduced. But one can argue that a bigger hurdle preventing a wider adoption back in the 1980s and 1990s was a lack of data. Many of the machine learning algorithms were developed and successfully demonstrated during this time: Hidden Markov Models and Convolutional Neural Nets were described in 1984 and 1989 respectively. However, a successful deployment of these algorithms on a practical business scale did not occur until nearly a decade later. Data (or lack thereof) was the primary reason for this. Data became more readily available and accessible only after the introduction of the internet in 1993. Wissner-Gross (2016) cites several interesting examples of breakthroughs in AI algorithms, effectively concluding that the average time period for an AI innovation to become practical was 18 years (after the introduction of the algorithm) but only 3 years after the first large scale datasets (that could be used to train that algorithm) became available.[7]

---

[5] https://www.iro.umontreal.ca/~vincentp/ift3395/lectures/backprop_old.pdf.
[6] http://yann.lecun.com/exdb/publis/pdf/lecun-89.pdf.
[7] http://www.spacemachine.net/views/2016/3/datasets-over-algorithms.

This brings us to the defining moment in the short but rapidly evolving history of deep learning. In 2006, Hinton (the same Hinton who was part of the team that introduced backpropagation) and Salakhutdinov, demonstrated that by adding more layers of computation to make neural networks "deep," larger datasets could be better utilized to solve problems such as handwriting recognition (Hinton and Salakhutdinov, 2006). These 3-hidden layer deep learning networks had significantly lower errors than the traditional single hidden layer ANNs that were discussed in Chapter 5, Regression Methods. With this innovation, the field of AI emerged from its long winter. This emergence is best summarized in the authors' own words[8]:

> It has been obvious since the 1980s that backpropagation through deep autoencoders would be very effective...provided that computers were fast enough, data sets were big enough, and the initial weights were close enough to a good solution. All three conditions are now satisfied.

Using massive datasets, deep network architectures with new and powerful graphics processing units (GPUs) originally developed for video games, real-world AI applications such as facial recognition, speech processing and generation, machines defeating humans at their own board games have become possible. ANNs had moved decisively from the research lab to mainstream media hype.

The Spring and Summer of Artificial Intelligence: 2006—Today

In spite of all these exciting developments, today's AI is still far from being what is considered artificial general intelligence (AGI). The quote at the beginning of the chapter summarizes the main aspect of today's AI: the need for massive amounts of data to train a machine to recognize concepts which seem simple even to a 2-year-old human brain. There are two main questions one would have at this point: How far away from AGI is AI today? What are the hurdles that stand in the way?

Defense Advanced Research Projects Agency (DARPA) has developed a nice classification[9] of the evolution of AI into three "waves" based on the main dimensions which reflect the capabilities of the systems: ability to learn, ability to abstract, and ability to reason.[10]

---

[8] https://www.cs.toronto.edu/~hinton/science.pdf.
[9] https://www.darpa.mil/attachments/AIFull.pdf.
[10] DARPA also lists a 4th dimension: ability to perceive. However this dimension is very close to "ability to learn". According to Webster, the difference between 'learn' and 'perceive' is tied to the senses. Learning is defined as understanding by study or experience, perception is defined as understanding or awareness through senses. For our purposes, we ignored these subtle differences."

The first wave of AI evolution includes "handcrafted knowledge" systems. These are the expert systems and chess playing programs of the 1980s and 1990s. Humans encode into the machines an ability to make decisions based on input data from a specific domain. In other words, these systems have a limited ability to reason but no ability to learn let alone abstract.

Second wave systems include today's machine learning and deep learning systems and are generally terms systems capable of "statistical learning." The uniqueness of these systems is the ability to separate data into different sets or patterns based on learning by relying on large volumes of data. While a rule engine can be added to these statistical learners, these systems still lack the ability to abstract knowledge. To clarify this: consider that while a facial recognition system is successful at identifying faces, it cannot explicitly explain why a particular face was categorized as such. On the other hand, a human can explain that a particular face was classified as a man because of the facial hair and body dimensions, for example.

In the yet-to-be developed third wave systems, AI cannot only apply encoded rules and learn from data, but can also explain why a particular data point was classified in a particular way. This is termed a "contextually adaptive" system. DARPA also calls these systems "Explainable AI" or XAI[11] that *"produce more explainable models, while maintaining a high level of learning performance (prediction accuracy)."* A first step toward developing XAI is the integration of the now conventional deep machine learning with reinforcement learning (RL), which is introduced later in this chapter.

To conclude this section, before the technical brass-tacks of deep learning are explained, it is helpful to acknowledge/recognize these facts:

- Majority of AI today is machine learning and deep learning.
- Majority of that learning is supervised.
- Majority of that supervised learning is classification.

10.2 HOW IT WORKS

In this section, the connection between conventional machine learning and deep learning will be further discussed. Firstly, linear regression and how it can be represented using an ANN will be examined more closely and then logistic regression will be discussed to reinforce the similarities between conventional machine learning techniques and deep learning. This will serve as an entry point to introduce some of the fundamental concepts in ANN and by extension deep learning. This in-depth understanding is essential to

---

[11] https://www.darpa.mil/program/explainable-artificial-intelligence.

confidently navigate some of the more sophisticated and specialized deep learning techniques that will come later.

To begin with, ANNs (and deep learning) should be regarded as a mathematical process. An ANN basically creates a mapping of data between outputs and inputs that is established using calculus-based optimization techniques. In a simplified mathematical format, an ANN can be essentially represented as:

$$Y = f(X)$$
$$Y = f(g(b)) \quad \text{where } X = g(b) \tag{10.1}$$

where b, X and Y are vectors or more generally, tensors. In this context, vectors are one dimensional array of numbers, matricies are two dimensional arrays and tensors are more general n-dimensional arrays. The process of training ANN is mostly about finding values for the coefficients, b, to complete the mapping. The coefficients are calculated by performing a constrained optimization of an error function (error is the difference between a predicted output y' and the known output, y). A technique to iteratively perform this optimization is called backpropagation which will be discussed in this section. A basic difference between deep learning and "shallow" machine learning is in the count of the coefficients, b. Deep learning deals with weight or coefficient counts in the hundreds of thousands to millions whereas conventional machine learning may deal with a few hundred at best. This enhancement of the numerosity in the computation gives deep learning their significant power to detect patterns within data.

10.2.1 Regression Models As Neural Networks

Eq. (10.1) is a vectorized form of Eq. (5.1) which was the general statement of a multiple linear regression problem. Section 5.1.1 discussed how a linear regression problem would be solved using methods of calculus, in particular, gradient descent. The gradient descent technique is the cornerstone of all deep learning algorithms and it is advisable to revisit Section 5.1.1 at this time to become comfortable with it. The linear regression model of Section 5.1.1 can be rewritten as an ANN: Fig. 10.6 is the simple linear regression model shown as a network. Note that when $x_0 = 1$, this captures Eq. (5.2). This network is only two layers deep: it has an input layer and an output layer. Multiple regression models simply require additional nodes (one node for each variable/feature) in the input layer and no additional/intermediate layers.

Similarly, a logistic regression model can also be represented by a simple two-layer network model with one key difference. As was discussed in Section 5.2.2 on Logistic Regression, the output of logistic regression is the probability of an event, p rather than a real number value as in linear

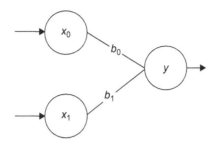

FIGURE 10.6
Regression depicted as a network.

regression. So, what needed to be done was transform the output variable in such a way that its domain now ranges from 0 to 1 instead of $-\infty-$ to $+\infty$. It was observed that by replacing the right-hand side expression of 5.6 with the log of the odds-ratio or the *logit*, this transformation was achieved.[12]

$$\log\left(\frac{p}{1-p}\right) = b_0 + b_1 x_1 \qquad (10.2)$$

$$\Rightarrow p = \left(\frac{1}{1+e^{-z}}\right) \quad \text{where } z = b_0 + b_1 x_1 \text{ after rearranging the terms} \qquad (10.3a)$$

more generally, the output is summarized as:

$$p(y) = \sigma(z) \qquad (10.3b)$$

So, the output node in the above network could be rewritten as shown in Fig. 10.7.

Eqs. (10.3a) and (10.3b) represent the *sigmoid* function. The sigmoid's domain is $[0,1]$ for $z \in [-\infty,\infty]$ so that any arbitrary values for b and x will always result in $p(y_n) = [0,1]$. Note that $p(y_n)$ is the prediction from the logistic regression model for sample n, which needs to be compared with the actual class value, p_n for that sample, in order to evaluate the model. How would one quantitatively compare these two across all data samples? Recall that in linear regression squared error $\Sigma(y_n - y_n')^2$ was used. The binary nature of p_n requires that the error be maximum when the predicted $p(y_n)$ and actual p_n are opposite and vice versa.

10.2.2 Gradient Descent

In Section 5.2.2 on Logistic Regression, an error function or a cost function was introduced, which can now be generalized by taking a log on the terms so that a summation is obtained instead of a product when one needs to

---

[12] Note that we are shortening probability of y, that is $p(y)$ to p for ease of notation in this line.

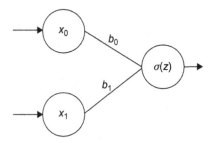

FIGURE 10.7
Adding an activation function to the regression "network."

compute across all samples. Note that y_n is the calculated value of probability based on the model and can range between $[0-1]$ and p_n is the target which is either 0 or 1. N is the number of samples.

$$J = -\sum_{n=1}^{N}\left[p_n log(y_n) + (1 - p_n)log(1 - y_n)\right] \qquad (10.4)$$

J is called the *cross-entropy cost function*. In the spirit of considering this as a cost function, a negative sign is added in front and with the aim of minimizing the value. Thus, b's need to be found which minimizes this function.[13] This has been done before using calculus in the case of linear regression (Section 5.1.1). It is easy to use the chain rule of differentiation to compute the derivative. But as will be seen this will turn out to be a constant and, thus, b cannot be solved for by setting it equal to 0. Instead, once an initial slope is obtained, gradient descent will be used to iteratively find the location where it is minimum.

Note that the cross-entropy cost function is easily expressed in terms of weights b, by substituting:

$$y = \sigma(z) = \frac{1}{(1 + e^{-z})} \quad \text{where} \ z = b_0 x_0 + b_1 x_1$$

The weights, b, can now be found by minimizing J, expressed in terms of b by using the chain rule of differentiation and setting this derivative to 0:

$$\frac{dJ}{db} = 0$$

$$\Rightarrow \frac{dJ}{dy} \times \frac{dy}{dz} \times \frac{dz}{db} = 0 \qquad (10.5)$$

---

[13] Why can the same cost function not be used that was used for linear regression? That is, $\frac{1}{2} \times (p_n - y_n)^2$? It turns out that this function is not a "convex" function—in other words does not necessarily have a single global optimum.

Calculate each derivative listed in 10.5 with these three steps:

Step I. $\frac{dJ}{dy} = \left(\frac{p_n}{y_n}\right) - \left(\frac{1-p_n}{1-y_n}\right)$ using Eq. (10.3a) and (10.3b)

Step II. $y = 1/1 + e^{-z}$

$$\Rightarrow \frac{dy}{dz} = \frac{-e^{-z}}{(1+e^{-z})}$$

with proper substitution and rearrangement of terms, the right side of the derivative can be reduced to:

$$\Rightarrow \frac{dy}{dz} = \frac{y_n}{(1-y_n)}$$

Finally, Step III. $z = b_0 x_0 + b_1 x_1 = b_0 + b_1 x_1$, noting that x_0 is usually set to 1 for the bias term, b_0

Using subscript notation:

$$\Rightarrow \frac{dz}{db} = x_i \quad \text{where } i = 1, 2, \ldots, n.$$

Putting them all together now, the derivative can be written as:

$$\frac{dJ}{db} = -\sum_{n=1}^{N}\left[\left(\frac{p_n}{y_n}\right) - \left(\frac{1-p_n}{1-y_n}\right)\right] \times [y_n(1-y_n)] \times [x_1]$$

which simplifies to:

$$\frac{dJ}{db} = -\sum_{n=1}^{N}(p_n - y_n)x_1$$

Expanding it to a general matrix form, where B, P, X, and Y are vectors:

$$\frac{dJ}{dB} = (P_n - Y_n)^T \cdot X \tag{10.6}$$

Note that B is a $(d \times 1)$ vector, where d is the number of independent variables and the other three vectors are $(n \times 1)$ where n is the number of samples. J and its derivative are scalars. The dot product between the two vectors in 10.6, will account for the summation.

As mentioned before, rather than setting the above equation to 0, an iterative approach is adopted to solve for the vector B using gradient descent. Start with an initial value for weight vector, B_j, where j is the iteration step and a step size (called the learning rate) and use this slope Eq. (10.6), to iteratively reach the point where J is minimized.

$$B_{j+1} = B_j - \text{Learning Rate} \times [P_n - Y_n]^T \cdot X \tag{10.7}$$

In practice one would stop after a set number of iterations or when the incremental difference between B_j and B_{j+1} is very small. In general, one can calculate the weights for any error function using a formula similar to 10.6. The key is to compute the gradient of the cost function, dJ/dB, and plug it into this form:

$$B_{j+1} = B_j + Learning\ Rate \times \frac{dJ}{dB} \cdot X \tag{10.8}$$

Notice that the iterative update component of gradient computation for logistic regression in (10.6) is remarkably similar to the one derived for linear regression, $X^T(\hat{Y} - Y_i)$—see Section 5.1.1. They both have the same form:

(Predicted Vector − Target Vector)·(Matrix of Input Data)

if the slight inconsistency in the nomenclature of Y is disregarded. The key difference is the way the Y's and the P are computed. In logistic regression these are evaluated using the *sigmoid transformation* $(y = \sigma(b_0 + b_1 x))$, whereas in linear regression a *unit transformation* $(y = b_0 + b_1 x)$ is used that is, no scaling or transformation is applied to the computed output.

This is essentially the concept of an *activation function* in ANN and deep learning. Think of activation functions like a rule based weighted averaging scheme. If the weighted average $(b_0 + b_1 x)$ crosses a preset threshold, the output evaluates to 1, if not it evaluates to 0—which is what happens if the activation function is the *sigmoid*. Clearly there are many candidate functions which can be used (sigmoid is simply one of them). Shown below are examples of the most commonly used activation functions used in deep learning: (1) *sigmoid*, (2) *tanh,* and (3) *rectified linear unit (RELU)* (Fig. 10.8).

Observe the similarity in shape between *sigmoid* and *tanh*—the only difference between the two is the scaling: *tanh* scales the output between $[-1, 1]$. The *RELU* is also an interesting function—the output linearly increases if the

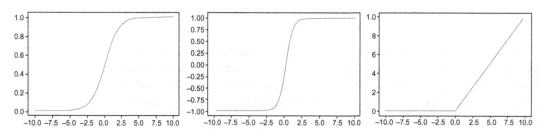

FIGURE 10.8
Commonly used activation functions: sigmoid (left), tanh (center), and RELU (right). *RELU,* Rectified linear unit.

weighted average exceeds a set threshold, otherwise it is set to 0. Note that all three are *nonlinear* functions which is an important characteristic that enables ANN and deep learning networks to classify linearly *nonseparable* data discussed in Section 10.2.

The table below summarizes the formulation of some common quantities that arise in the application of gradient descent for linear and logistic regression. For the cost functions that arise in a general ANN, calculation of the gradient in a closed form, like in Section 5.1.1, is not feasible, and it has to be computed using numerical approximation. In practice, this is what packages such as TensorFlow (TF) help implement. Such implementations rely heavily on TF for the purposes of gradient calculation and associated tensor or matrix method bookkeeping that is required.

Method	Cost Function	Derivative of Cost Function	Closed Form Solution	Gradient Form Solution
Linear egression	$J = 1/N \sum_{i=1}^{N}(y_i - b^T x_i)^2$	$dJ/db = 2/N \sum_{i=1}^{N}$ $(y_i - b^T x_i)(-x_i)$	$B = (X^T X)^{-1} Y^T X$	$b_{i+1} = b_i - \eta \, dJ/dB$, where η is the learning rate and $dJ/dB =$ $X^T \bullet (\hat{Y} - Y_i)$
Logistic regression	$J = -\sum(p_n \log y_n$ $+ (1 - p_n)\log(1 - y_n))$	$\dfrac{dJ}{db} = \dfrac{dJ}{dy}\dfrac{dy}{dz}\dfrac{dz}{db}$ where $y = \sigma(z)$ and $z = \Sigma b_i x_i$	None	$b_{i+1} = b_i - \eta dJ/dB$; where $dJ/dB = (P_n - Y_n)^T \cdot X$

10.2.3 Need for Backpropagation

Weighted averaging is one intuition that would allow a full ANN to be conceptualized starting from the simple two-layer models of logistic and linear regression. As discussed, in Section 10.2.2, gradient descent is about incrementally updating the weights based on the output generated from a previous iteration. The first iteration is kicked off by randomly choosing the weights. Can the process be made a bit more efficient and "well-rounded" by choosing a series of starting weights in parallel? That is, can one start by building, say 3 logistic (or linear) regression units or models in parallel so that instead of (b_1, b_2) as the starting weights, there are 3 sets: (b_{11}, b_{21}), (b_{12}, b_{22}), and (b_{13}, b_{23})? Here the first subscript refers to the input node or feature and the second subscript refers to the node in the intermediate or so-called "hidden" layer. This is illustrated in the Fig. 10.9. It turns out that by doing this, a small computational price might be paid at each iteration, but the output may be arrived at quicker by reducing the number of iterations. Finally, the output from the hidden layer is once again weight-averaged by 3 more weights (c_1, c_2, and c_3) before the final output

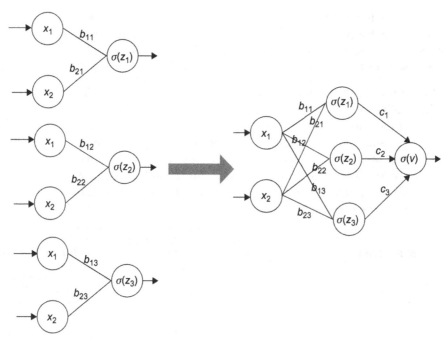

FIGURE 10.9
Combining multiple logistic regression models into a neural network.

is computed. Also observe that the right-hand side figure is exactly equivalent to the left-hand side, but representationally simpler. With the hidden layer in place, the output is first computed starting from left to right: that is, $\sigma(z_1)$, $\sigma(z_2)$, and $\sigma(z_3)$ are computed as usual and weights for c_1:c_3 are assumed in order to compute the final sigmoid $\sigma(v)$. This would be the first iteration. The output can now be compared to the correct response and the model performance evaluated using the cross-entropy cost function. The goal is now to reduce this error function for which one would first need to incrementally update the weights c_1:c_3 and then work *backwards* to then update the weights b_{11}:b_{23}. This process is termed "backpropagation" for obvious reasons. Backpropagation remains relevant no matter how many hidden layers or output nodes are in question and is fundamental to understanding of how all ANNs work. The actual mechanics of this computation was described with a simple example in Section 4.6 and will not be repeated here. The main difference between the example used in that case and this present one is the computation of the error function.

10.2.4   Classifying More Than 2 Classes: Softmax

Recall that by using logistic regression one is able to address a binary classification problem. However, most real-world classifications require categorization into one of more than two classes. For example, identifying faces,
numerals, or objects, and so on. One needs a handy tool to identify which of
the several classes a given sample belongs to. Also recall that in the network
models discussed so far in this chapter, there was only one output node and
the probability that a given sample belonged to a class was obtained. By
extension, one could add an output node for every class that needs to be categorized into and the probability that a sample belonged to that particular
class (see Fig. 10.10) could simply be computed. This is intuitively how the
"softmax" function works.

Softmax does two calculations: it exponentiates the value received at each
node of the output layer and then normalizes this value by the sum of the
exponentiated values received at all the output nodes. For instance, when the
output layer has two nodes (one each for class one and class two), the probability of each class can be expressed as:

$$p(Y = \text{class 1}): \frac{e^{z_1}}{(e^{z_1} + e^{z_2})}$$

$$p(Y = \text{class 2}): \frac{e^{z_2}}{(e^{z_1} + e^{z_2})}$$

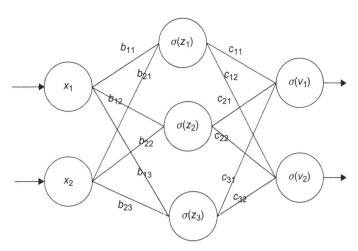

FIGURE 10.10
Softmax output layer in a network.

If one divides the numerator and the denominator of the first class by e^{z_1}, one would get:

$$p(Y = \text{class } 1): \frac{1}{(1 + e^{z_2 - z_1})}$$

which is the same expression as the sigmoid, Eq. (10.3a), if one had only one output node for a binary classification problem (i.e. $z_2 = 0$). In general, for a k-class problem, softmax is computed as:

$$p(Y = k) = \frac{e^{z_k}}{\sum_{i=1}^{k} [e^{z_i}]} \tag{10.9}$$

Note that what the z_i are has not been stated. In practice they have the same form as in Eq. (10.3a), that is, $z_i = \Sigma b_i x_i$. Another thing to keep in mind is that in logistic regression based on the sigmoid, the thresholding is used or the cut-off value of the output probability to assign the final class—if the value is >0.5 then a "hard maximum" is applied to assign it to one class over the other.

The triple concepts of activation functions, backpropagation, and (calculus based) gradient descent form what may be loosely termed as the "ABCs" of deep learning and remain at the mathematical core of these algorithms. Hopefully this section provided an intuitive understanding of these important concepts using simple networks such as linear and logistic regression models. In combination with the material presented on ANN in Chapter 4, on Classification one should now be in a strong enough position to grasp the extension of these techniques to larger scale networks such as convolutional neural networks.

There is no strict definition of what constitutes a "deep" learning network. A common understanding is that any network with three or more hidden layers between the input and output layers is considered "deep." Based on the math described in the preceding section it should be easy to understand how adding more hidden layers increases the number of weight parameters, b_{ij}. In practice it is not uncommon to have networks where the number of weight parameters (termed *trainable parameters*) run into millions. In the next few sections some typical use cases or applications of deep learning methods will be explored and the practical implementations discussed.

10.2.5 Convolutional Neural Networks

A convolution is a simple mathematical operation between two matrices. Consider a 6×6 matrix A, and a 3×3 matrix B.

$$A = \begin{bmatrix} 10 & 9 & 9 & 8 & 7 & 7 \\ 9 & 8 & 8 & 7 & 6 & 6 \\ 9 & 8 & 8 & 7 & 6 & 6 \\ 1 & 1 & 1 & 0 & 0 & 0 \\ 1 & 1 & 1 & 0 & 0 & 0 \\ 0 & 0 & 0 & 1 & 0 & 0 \end{bmatrix}$$

$$B = \begin{bmatrix} 1 & 1 & 1 \\ 0 & 0 & 0 \\ -1 & -1 & -1 \end{bmatrix}$$

Convolution between A and B, mathematically denoted as A (*) B, results in a new matrix, C whose elements are obtained by a sum-product between the individual elements of A and B. For the given example,

$c_{11} = 10 \times 1 + 9 \times 1 + 9 \times 1 + 9 \times 0 + 8 \times 0 + 8 \times 0 + 9 \times -1 + 8 \times -1 + 8 \times -1 = 3$
$c_{12} = 9 \times 1 + 8 \times 1 + 8 \times 1 + 8 \times 0 + 8 \times 0 + 7 \times 0 + 8 \times -1 + 8 \times -1 + 7 \times -1 = 3$

and so on.

It is easier to understand this operation by visualizing as shown in Fig. 10.11. Matrix B is the lighter shaded one which essentially slides over the larger matrix A (darker shade) from left (and top) to right (and bottom). At each overlapping position, the corresponding elements of A and B are multiplied and all the products are added as indicated in the figure to obtain the corresponding element for C. The resulting output matrix C will be smaller in dimension than A but larger than B. So, what is the utility of this

c_{ij} = sum.product of overlapping cells

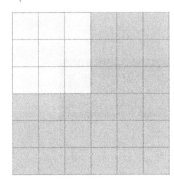 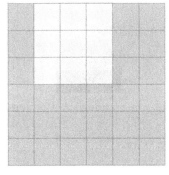 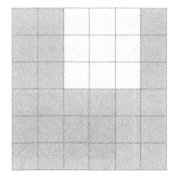

$c_{11} = a_{11}b_{11} + a_{12}b_{12} + a_{13}b_{13} + \ldots + a_{33}b_{33}$ $c_{12} = a_{12}b_{11} + a_{13}b_{12} + a_{14}b_{13} + \ldots + a_{34}b_{33}$ $c_{13} = a_{13}b_{11} + a_{14}b_{12} + a_{15}b_{13} + \ldots + a_{35}b_{33}$

FIGURE 10.11
Computing a convolution.

convolution operation? Matrix *A* is typically a raw image where each cell in the matrix is a pixel value and matrix *B* is called a filter (or kernel) which when convolved with the raw image results in a new image that highlights only certain features of the raw image.

As shown in the Fig. 10.12, *A* and *B* are basically pixel maps which when convolved together yield another pixel map, *C*. One can see that *C* accentuates or highlights the horizontal edge in *A* where the pixels jump from a high value to a low value. In this case, the accent appears to be thick—but in the case of a real image where the matrix sizes are in the order of 1000s (e.g., a 1-megapixel image is approximately a 1000×1000 matrix of pixels)—the accent line will be finer and clearly demarcate or detect any horizontal edge in the picture. Another thing to note about the filter is that when it is flipped by 90 degrees or transposed, that is, use B^T instead of *B*, a convolution performed on a raw image would be able to detect *vertical* edges. By judiciously choosing *B*, it will be possible to identify edges in any orientation.

Thus, convolutions are useful in order to identify and detect basic features in images such as edges. The challenge is of course to determine the right filter for a given image. In the example this was done intuitively—however, machine learning can be used to optimally determine the filter values. Observe that determining the filter was a matter of finding the $3 \times 3 = 9$ values for the matrix *B* in the example. A couple of things to note: the matrix *A* is $n_{width} \times n_{height}$ in terms of pixels for a grayscale image. Standard color images have three channels: red, green, and blue. Color images are easily handled by considering a 3-dimensional matrix $n_{width} \times n_{height} \times n_{channels}$ which are convolved with as many different filters are there are color channels.

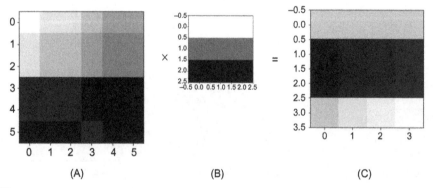

FIGURE 10.12
Effect of performing a convolution on a raw image.

In Fig. 10.12, one can observe that C is smaller than the raw image A. If the dimensions of A and B are known, the dimensions of C can be determined. For simplicity, assume that $n_{width} = n_{height} = n$ which is quite common in real applications. If the filter is also a square matrix of size f, then the output C is square of dimension $n - f + 1$. In this case $n = 6$, $f = 3$ and, therefore, C was 4×4.

As the process of convolution reduces the raw image size, it is sometimes useful to enlarge the raw image with dummy pixels so that the original size is retained. This process is called "*padding*" as illustrated in Fig. 10.13. If p is the number of padded pixels, then the output dimension is given by $n + 2p - f + 1$. Thus, in the example, the output of C will be 6×6 if one unit of padding is added.

Another important consideration in computing convolutions is the "*stride*." This is the number of pixels the filter is advanced each time to compute the next element of the output. In the examples discussed so far, a stride of 1 has been assumed. Fig. 10.14 illustrates this point. With stride, s, the output dimension can be computed as $(n + 2p - f)/s + 1$.

So far, it has been taken on intuition that a convolution helps to identify basic image features such as edges. Thus, a filter strides over an image and at each location of the output a sum-product of the corresponding elements can be computed between the image and filter. However, instead of performing a sum-product if one simply used the highest pixel value in the overlapping cells at each compute location (Fig. 10.15), a process called *max pooling* would be obtained. Max pooling can be thought of as an operation that highlights the most dominant feature in an image (e.g., an eye within a face). Max pooling is another feature detection tactic that is widely used for

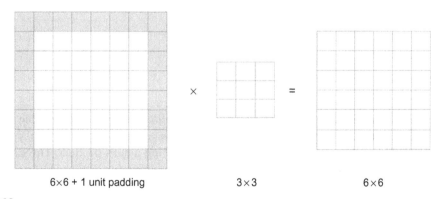

6×6 + 1 unit padding   3×3   6×6

FIGURE 10.13

Padding a convolution.

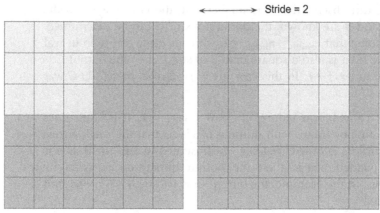

FIGURE 10.14
Visualizing the stride during a convolution.

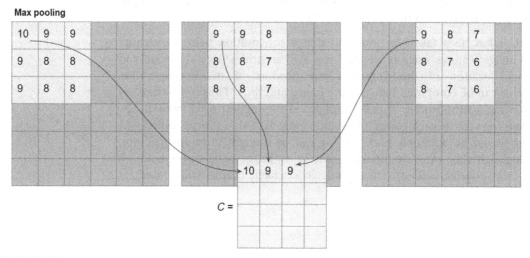

FIGURE 10.15
Max pooling visualized.

image processing. Similar to max pooling, an *average pooling* can also be done to somewhat "airbrush" the raw image, where the values are averaged in the overlapping cells instead of doing a sum-product. The calculation for output dimension after pooling still remains $(n + 2p-f)/s + 1$.

A convolution is a linear function similar to Eq. **10.1** which is a general form of any neural networkwhere the weights, B are now the pixels of the filter matrix and the inputs, A are the image pixel values. The sum-product output C is analogous to z in 10.3a . Similar to applying a nonlinear opera-tor to z in 10.3b, the elements of C are typically passed through a RELU non-linearity. This entire process, as will be summarized, forms one convolutional layer. The output of this convolutional layer is sent to the next layer which can be another convolutional layer (with a different filter) or "flattened" and sent to a regular layer of nodes, called a "Fully Connected" layer which will be described later on.

In the Fig. 10.16, $A[0]$ is the raw image and C is the result of its convolution with the filter B. $A[1]$ is the result of adding a bias term to each element of C and passing them through a RELU activation function. B is analogous to a weight matrix b of **10.1**, while C is analogous to $\sigma(z)$ in **10.2b**. The point of making these comparisons is to highlight how convolutions can be used as a part of a deep learning network. In a neural network, backpropagation can be used to compute the elements of the weight matrix, b, and a similar pro-cess can be applied to determine the elements of the filter matrix B.

One additional note: TF and such tools allow one to apply multiple filters in the same layer. So for example, one can let B_1 be a horizontal edge detector, B_2 be a vertical edge detector, and apply both filters on $A[0]$. The output C can be tensorially represented as a volume, in this example, C will have the dimension of $4 \times 4 \times 2$, which is essentially a stack of two 4×4 matrices, each one is the result of convolution between A and B_i $(i = 1,2)$. Fig. 10.17 shows how adding multiple filters at a layer will result in a volumetric network.

In order to determine the filter elements, remember that backpropagation will be used. So, a cost-function will need to be computed, such as the one in **10.3**, and minimize/maximize it using gradient descent. The cost function is now dependent on $3 \times 3 \times 2 = 18$ parameters in this example. In order to

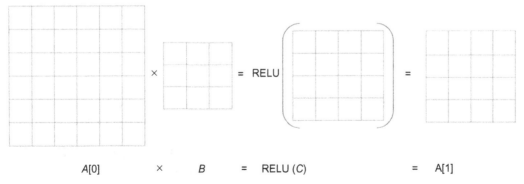

$A[0]$ $\times$ B $=$ RELU (C) $=$ $A[1]$

FIGURE 10.16

Combining a convolution with an activation function.

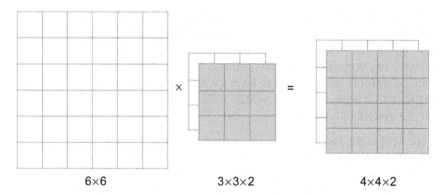

6×6   3×3×2   4×4×2

FIGURE 10.17
Multiple filters of convolution.

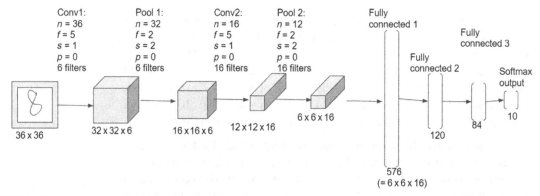

FIGURE 10.18
Architecture of a typical CNN model.

completely define the cost-function one can "flatten" the output $4 \times 4 \times 2$ matrix into $32(=4 \times 4 \times 2)$ nodes and connect each node to a logistic regression output node or softmax output nodes.

Fig. 10.18 shows a classic CNN architecture introduced by LeCun (1989). It consists of several convolutional layers interspersed with max pool layers and finally followed by what are known as fully connected layers where the last convolution output matrix is flattened into its constituent elements and passed through a few hidden layers before terminating at a softmax output layer. This was one of the first CNNs and was used to recognize handwritten digits.

CNNs are highly capable deep learning networks which function highly efficiently because of a couple of reasons. The feature detection layers (such as

Conv1, Conv2, etc.,) are computationally quite quick because there are few parameters to train (e.g., each Conv1 filter is 5×5 which yields $25 + 1$ for bias $= 26$ times 6 filters $= 156$ parameters) and not every parameter in the output matrix is connected to every other parameter of the next layer as in a typical neural network (as happens in the fully connected layers down the network). Thus the fully connected layers FC1 and FC2 have 576 times $120 = 69,120$ parameters to train. Because of their flexibility and computational efficiency, CNNs are now one of the most common deep learning techniques in practical applications.

Layers are the high-level building blocks in deep learning. As observed in Fig. 10.18, there are several convolutional layers and several fully connected layers (also called "*Dense*" layers) Each layer receives the inputs from the previous layer, applies the weights and aggregates with an activation function. A couple of other key concepts that are in usage in deep learning are summarized here.

10.2.6 Dense Layer

A dense or fully connected layer is one where all the nodes in the prior layer are connected to all the nodes in the next layer. Several layers of dense layers form different levels of representation in the data. (Fig. 10.19).

10.2.7 Dropout Layer

A dropout layer helps to prevent model overfitting by dropping the nodes randomly in the layer. The probability of dropping a node is controlled by a factor which ranges from 0 to 1. A dropout factor closer to one drops more nodes from the layer. This is a form of regularization that reduces the complexity of the model. This concept is depicted in Fig. 10.20

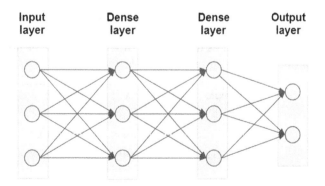

FIGURE 10.19
Illustrating a dense or fully connected layer.

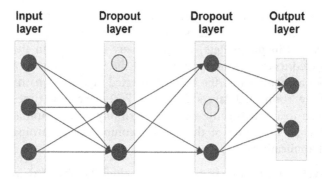

FIGURE 10.20
Illustrating a dense or fully connected layer.

10.2.8 Recurrent Neural Networks

The field of deep learning has exploded in the last decade due to a variety of reasons outlined in the earlier sections. This chapter provided an intuition into one of the most common deep learning methodologies: CNN. These are but one representation of a deep neural network architecture. The other prominent deep learning method in widespread use is called recurrent neural network (RNN). RNNs find application in any situation where the data have a temporal component. Prominent examples are time series coming from financial data or sensor data, language related data such as analyzing the sentiment from a series of words which make up a sentence, entity recognition within a sentence, translating a series of words from one language to another and so on. In each of these instances, the core of the network still consists of a processing node coupled with an activation function as depicted in Fig. 10.1.

Suppose the time series problem is a text entity recognition. So, here is a set of training examples consisting of sentences from which one can identify certain named entities in each sentence such as proper nouns, places, dates, and so on. The training set, thus, looks like:

Sample	$x^{<1>}$	$x^{<2>}$	$x^{<3>}$	$x^{<4>}$
1	This	is	an	egg
2	I	love	scrambled	eggs
3	Do	you	like	omelettes?
4	Green	eggs	and	Ham
5	My	name	is	Sam
...	...	...	...	...

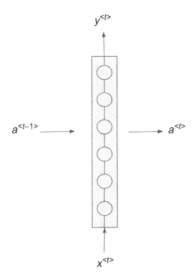

FIGURE 10.21
A basic representation of RNN. *RNN,* Recurrent neural network.

The objective here is to predict that $y^{<j>}$ is a named entity such as a proper noun. So, $y^{<4>}$ would be 1, whereas $y^{<1,2,3>}$ are 0's. The idea behind an RNN is to train a network by passing the training data through it in a sequence (where each example is an ordered sequence). In the schematic in Fig. 10.21, $x^{<t>}$ are the inputs where $<t>$ indicates the position in the sequence. Note that there are as many sequences as there are samples. $y^{<t>}$ are the predictions which are made for each position based on the training data. What does the training accomplish? It will determine the set of weights of this (vertically depicted) network, b_x which in a linear combination with $x_i^{<t>}$ and passed through a nonlinear activation (typically tanh), produces an activation matrix $a^{<t>}$. So:

$$a^{<t>} = g(b_x x^{<t>})$$

However, RNNs also use the value of the activation from the previous time step (or previous word in the sequence) because typically in most sequences—such as sentences—the prediction of a next word is usually dependent on the previous word or set of words. For example, the previous words "My", "name", and "is" would almost certainly make the next word a proper noun (so $y = 1$). This information is helpful in strengthening the prediction. Therefore, the value of the activation matrix can be modified by adding the previous steps' activation multiplied by another coefficient, b_a:

$$a^{<t>} = g(b_a a^{<t-1>} + b_x x^{<t>})$$

Finally, the prediction itself for the position $<t>$ is given by:

$$y^{<t>} = g\left(b_y a^{<t>}\right)$$

where b_y is another set of coefficients. All the coefficients are obtained during the learning process by using the standard process of backpropagation. Because of the temporal nature of data, RNNs typically do not have structures that are as deep as in CNNs. It is not common to see more than 4–5 layers which are all temporally connected.

10.2.9   Autoencoders

So far, deep learning has been discussed in the context of supervised learning where an explicit labeled output dataset was used to train a model. Deep learning can also be used in an unsupervised context and this is where Autoencoders are useful.

An autoencoder is deep learnings answer to dimensionality reduction (which is introduced in chapter 14 on Feature Selection). The idea is pretty simple: transform the input through a series of hidden layers but ensure that the final output layer is the same dimension as the input layer. However, the intervening hidden layers have progressively smaller number of nodes (and hence, reduce the dimension of the input matrix). If the output matches or encodes the input closely, then the nodes of the smallest hidden layer can be taken as a valid dimension reduced dataset.

This concept is illustrated in Fig. 10.22.

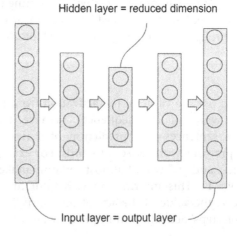

FIGURE 10.22
Concept of dropout.

10.2.10 Related AI Models

Two other algorithms will briefly be mentioned which fall more into the domain of AI rather than the straightforward function approximation objective used so far. However, many researchers and experts tend to consider these as newer applications of deep learning because deep networks may be used as part of the algorithms.

Reinforcement Learning (RL) is an agent-based goal seeking technique where an (AI) agent tries to determine the best action to take in a given environment depending on a reward. The agent has access to data which correspond to the various states in an environment and a label for each action. A deep learning network may be used to take in an observation or state-array and output probabilities for each action (or label). The most popular implementation of RL is Google's alpha-go AI which defeated a top-ranked human Go player. Practical applications of RL include route optimization strategies for a self-driving vehicle, for example. Most such applications are experimental as of this publication.

Generative adversarial network (GAN) are at the cutting edge of deep learning implementations—they were first introduced in 2014 and are yet to find mainstream applications. GANs are proposed to be used to generate new samples similar to the data they were originally trained on. For example, creating new "photographs of faces" after being trained on a large set of facial recognition data. GANs consist of two parts: A Generator and a Discriminator. Both of these are deep neural networks, the generator "mashes" up new samples while the discriminator evaluates if the new samples are "valid" or not. One can think of the analogy of counterfeiting currency. A counterfeiter tries to pass off poorly forged notes at first to be rejected by say, a vendor. The counterfeiter learns from this experience and gets increasingly sophisticated in his forgery until such time that the vendor can no longer discriminate between a forged note and a real one and, thereby, accepts the new note as a valid sample of the known distribution.

10.3 HOW TO IMPLEMENT

Deep-learning architecture in RapidMiner can be implemented by a couple of different paths. The simple artificial neural networks with multiple hidden layers can be implemented by the *Neural Net* operator introduced in Chapter 4, Classification, Artificial Neural Network. The operator parameter can be configured to include multiple hidden layers and nodes within each layer. By default, the layer configuration is *dense*. This operator lacks the variety of different layer designs that distinguishes deep-learning architecture from simple Neural Networks.

The *Keras* extension for RapidMiner offers a set of operators specific for deep learning. It utilizes the Keras neural network library for Python. Keras is designed to run on top of popular deep learning frameworks like TensorFlow and Microsoft Cognitive Toolkit. The *Keras* extension in RapidMiner enables a top-level, visual, deep-learning process along with data science preprocessing and postprocessing. The Keras extension requires Python and related libraries to be installed.[14] The modeling and execution of the deep-learning process in production application requires machines running GPUs as computation using normal machines can be time consuming. The following implementation uses Keras extension operators and can be run on general-purpose machines[15].

Handwritten Image Recognition

Optical character recognition is an image recognition technique where handwritten or machine-written characters are recognized by computers. A deep learning-based (convolutional neural network) numeric character recognition model is developed in this section. As with any deep-learning model, the learner needs plenty of training data. In this case, a large number of labeled handwritten images are needed to develop a deep learning model. The MNIST database[16] (Modified National Institute of Standards and Technology database) is a large database of labeled handwritten digits used commonly for training image processing systems. The dataset consists of 70,000 images of handwritten digits (0,1,2,...,9). Fig 10.23 shows sample training images for the digits 2, 8, and 4.

The complete RapidMiner process for implementing handwritten image recognition on the MNIST dataset is shown in Fig. 10.24.[17] The process has a Execute Python operator to convert the 28 x 28 image pixels to a data frame. The Keras Model contains a deep-learning model with several convolutional and dense layers. The model was applied to the test dataset and performance was evaluated. The dataset and the process are available at www. IntroDataScience.com

---

[14] https://community.rapidminer.com/t5/RapidMiner-Studio-Knowledge-Base/Keras-Deep-Learning-extension/ta-p/40839.

[15] Note that on CPU the runtime is likely to be 100x to 1000x slower than on GPU. For this example, the run time was 37 hours on a 2.5 GHz core i7.

[16] MNIST Database - http://yann.lecun.com/exdb/mnist/.

[17] This implementation example was generously provided by Dr. Jacob Cybulski of Deakin University, Australia.

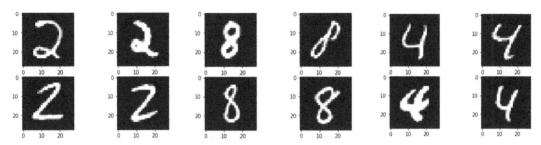

FIGURE 10.23
Three different handwritten samples of the digits 2,8, and 4 from the MNIST dataset.

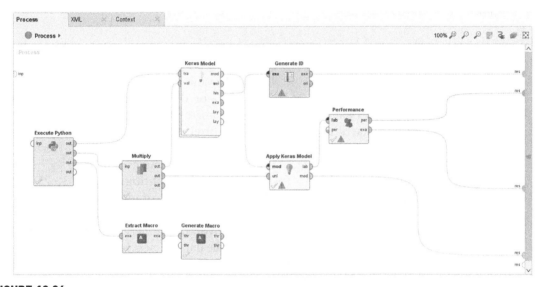

FIGURE 10.24
RapidMiner process for Deep learning

Step 1: Dataset Preparation

The key challenge in implementing this well-known model using RapidMiner is in preparing the dataset. RapidMiner expects the data in the form of a standard data frame (a table of rows as samples and columns as attributes) organized into rows and columns and in its current version (as of this publication) cannot use the raw image data. The raw data consist of 70,000 images which are 28 x 28 pixels. This needs to be transformed into a Pandas data frame which is 70,000 rows (or samples) by 784 columns (pixel values) and then split up into 60,000 sample training and 10,000 sample test sets. The 28 x 28 (pixels) yields 784 pixel values. The first

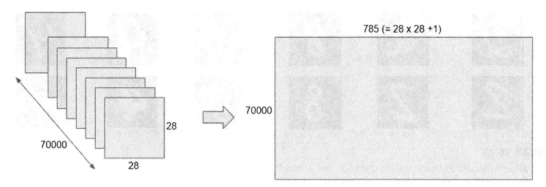

FIGURE 10.25
Reshaping the MNIST image tensor into a data frame.

operator in this process is a Python script executor which takes the raw data and transforms it. In the Execute Python operator (Note: this is very similar to the Execute R operator discussed in Chapter 15: Getting started with RapidMiner, and works analogously), the data is read from the MNIST dataset, its shape saved, the pixel data transformed into floats from integers, and finally both training and test "x" and "y" vectors are "unfolded" and merged into Pandas data frames with the "y" column defined as a "label" (using rm_metadata attribute). Fig. 10.25 shows graphically what the Execute Python block accomplishes. The shape information is alsoreturned as a data frame, so that it can later be used to set image sizes and shapes in the convolutional nets. The results from the Execute Python block consists of three data frames: (i) a training data frame 60,000 rows x 785 columns; (ii) test data frame 10,000 x 785; and (iii) and a shape information data frame which stores information about the data (each image is 28 x 28 x 1 tensor, the 1 refers to the channel). After flattening the 28 x 28 image we have 784 columns and we add one more column to contain the "label" information (i.e., which digit is encoded by the 784 columns).

Step 2: Modeling using the Keras Model

The rest of process is very straightforward after the image data is transformed. It passes the training data through the Keras Model and applies the model on the test dataset (Apply Keras Model) and then checks the model performance. The Extract Macro and Generate Macro operators pull the shape information into variables called img_shape, img_row, img_cols, and img_channels which are the used to reshape the data frame into a tensor that the Keras Model operator can then use. The main modeling operator for

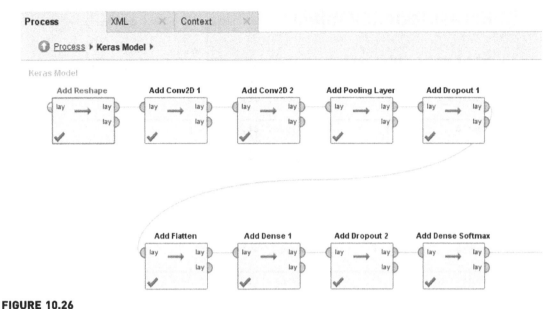

FIGURE 10.26
Deep learning subprocess for keras operators.

deep learning is the Keras Model operator under Keras > Modelling folder. The Keras operator is a meta operator which has a subprocess of deep-learning layers within it. The main parameters for the Keras modeling operator chosen are: Input shape: [img_size (=img_rows*img_cols*img_channels)], Loss: categorical_crossentropy, Optimizer: Adadelta, Learning rate, Epochs, batch_size are initially set at 1.0, 12 and 128 respectively. These can be adjusted later for optimal performance.

The architecture of the Keras deep learning network is shown in Fig. 10.26. The main thing to note is that we need to include an extra initial step (Add reshape) to fold the data back into its original form (28 x 28 x 1) based on the size and shape information passed into RapidMiner. There are two Conv2D layers: the first uses 32 filters (n = 32) and the second uses 64 filters. All filters are 3 x 3 (i.e., f = 3) and stride (s = 1). MaxPooling (with f = 2 and s = 2) and a Dropout layer which randomly eliminates 25% of the nodes (see Fig. 10.20), complete the CNN portion of the network before a flattened layer converts the 2D images into a column of 9216 nodes. This is connected to a 128-node layer, and another Dropout layer (50%) is applied before terminating in a 10-unit softmax output layer. As an exercise, the reader is encouraged to write this process as a schematic similar to Fig. 10.18 to make sure the internal workings of the network are clearer. As you move from one layer to the next, Keras

KerasModelIOObject

Layer (type)	Output Shape	Param #
reshape_1 (Reshape)	(None, 28, 28, 1)	0
conv2d_1 (Conv2D)	(None, 26, 26, 32)	320
conv2d_2 (Conv2D)	(None, 24, 24, 64)	18496
max_pooling2d_1 (MaxPooling2	(None, 12, 12, 64)	0
dropout_1 (Dropout)	(None, 12, 12, 64)	0
flatten_1 (Flatten)	(None, 9216)	0
dense_1 (Dense)	(None, 128)	1179776
dropout_2 (Dropout)	(None, 128)	0
dense_2 (Dense)	(None, 10)	1290

Total params: 1,199,882
Trainable params: 1,199,882
Non-trainable params: 0

FIGURE 10.27
A summary of the deep-learning model and its constituent layers.

automatically calculates the output size (i.e., number of output nodes for that layer). The user must make sure that the output of the previous layer is compatible with the input of the next layer by specifying the correct input_size. The reader should also try to calculate the number of weights or parameters that need to be learned at each layer. Fig. 10.27 shows the model summary. As seen, this model has more than one million weights (called "Trainable params") that need to be trained or learned making it a truly deep-learning model. Observe that the largest number of weights occur in the first dense layer.

Step 3: Applying the Keras Model
The model developed by the Keras modeling operator can be applied on the test dataset using Apply Keras model under Keras > Scoring folder. This

accuracy: 99.04%

	true 7	true 2	true 1	true 0	true 4	true 9	true 5	true 6	true 3	true 8	class precision
pred. 7	1015	4	0	1	0	0	0	0	0	1	99.41%
pred. 2	5	1023	1	0	0	0	0	0	2	2	99.03%
pred. 1	2	1	1130	0	0	1	0	2	0	0	99.47%
pred. 0	1	1	0	975	0	1	3	4	0	3	98.68%
pred. 4	0	1	0	0	969	3	0	1	0	0	99.49%
pred. 9	2	0	0	0	5	994	0	0	0	4	98.81%
pred. 5	0	0	0	1	0	5	881	1	1	1	98.99%
pred. 6	0	0	2	2	5	0	3	949	0	0	98.75%
pred. 3	2	1	2	0	0	3	5	0	1006	1	98.63%
pred. 8	1	1	0	1	2	2	0	1	1	962	99.07%
class recall	98.74%	99.13%	99.56%	99.49%	98.60%	98.51%	98.77%	99.06%	99.60%	98.77%	

FIGURE 10.28
Comparing the deep learning predicted values to actual values.

operator is similar to other Apply Model operators. The input for the operator is the test dataset with 10,000 labeled image data frame and the model. The output is the scored dataset. The scored output is then connected to the Performance (Classification) operator to compare the deep learning-based digits recognition with the actual value of the label.

Step 4: Results
Fig. 10.28 shows the results of the prediction performed by the CNN-based deep-learning model. As seen from the confusion matrix, the performance measured via recall, precision, or overall accuracy is around 99% across all the digits, indicating that the model performs exceptionally well. This implementation shows both the power and the complexity of the deep learning process.

10.4 CONCLUSION

Deep learning is a fast-growing field of research and its applications run the gamut of structured and unstructured data (text, voice, images, video, and others). Each day brings new variants of the deep architectures and with it, new applications. It is difficult to do justice to this field within the scope of a broad data science focused book. This chapter provided a brief high-level overview of the collection of techniques known as deep learning. An overview on how the majority of today's AI applications are supported solely by deep learning was provided. The fundamental similarity between deep learning and function fitting methods such as multiple linear regression and logistic regression were demonstrated. The essential differences between deep learning and traditional machine learning was also discussed. Some time was then spent detailing one of the most common deep learning techniques—convolutional neural networks and how it can be implemented using

Rapidminer was discussed. Finally, some of the other deep learning techniques were highlighted which are rapidly gaining ground in research and industry.

References

Explainable Artificial Intelligence. (2016). *Broad agency announcement.* Defense Advanced Research Projects Agency. <https://www.darpa.mil/program/explainable-artificial-intelligence>.

Hinton, G. E., & Salakhutdinov, R. R. (2006). Reducing the dimensionality of data with neural networks. *Science, 313,* 504–507.

Le Cun, Y. (1989). Generalization and network design Strategies. *University of Toronto technical report CRG-TR-89-4.*

Marczyk, J., Hoffman, R., Krishnaswamy, P. (1999). *Uncertainty management in automotive crash: From analysis to simulation.* <https://pdfs.semanticscholar.org/2f26/c851cab16ee20925-c4e556eff5198d92ef3c.pdf>.

Minsky, M., and Papert, S (1969). *Perceptrons: an introduction to computational geometry.* Cambridge, Massachusetts: MIT Press.

Rosenblatt, F. (1957) The perceptron: A Probabilistic model for Visual Perception, Procs. of the 15th International Congress of Psychology, North Holland, 290-297.

Rumelhart, D. E., Hinton, G. E., & Williams, R. J. (1986). Learning representations by back-propagating errors. *Nature, 323*(9), 533–536.

Somers, J. (2017). Is AI riding a one-trick pony? MIT Technology Review, September 29, 2017. <https://www.technologyreview.com/s/608911/is-ai-riding-a-one-trick-pony/>.

Wissner-Gross, A. (2016). Datasets over algorithms. Edge <https://www.edge.org/response-detail/26587>.

CHAPTER 11

Recommendation Engines

Now a days, everyone experiences the increasing impact of products and applications that utilize machine learning. Out of all the applications of machine learning, recommendation engine techniques underwrite some of the most prolific utilities in everyday experience. Recommendation engines are a class of machine learning techniques that predict *a user* preference for an *item*. A user is a customer or a prospective customer of an item or a product. In essence, the purpose of an enterprise is to connect a customer to a product that the customer wants. Recommendation engines influence this important connection between the customer and the product. Hence, recommendation engines play a cardinal role in how a relevant product is introduced to a customer. Whether it is a snippet of news feed on a social media homepage, what to watch next in a streaming service, suggested article in an online news portal, a new friend recommendation, or a suggested product to buy from an e-commerce site, the influence of automated recommendation engines are inescapable in today's digital economy.

WHY DO WE NEED RECOMMENDATION ENGINES?

A brick and mortar store has a limitation of space which dictates the number of unique products it can hold. An enterprise with a few dozen products, by design, has a limited number of choices for its customers. In either case, it is relatively easy to predict what available products the customers want. It is common to see retailers recommending their top selling products to their customers. To capitalize on what readers might commonly buy, bookstores often display the top selling books, new releases, or store recommendations at the front of the store. Newspapers run top stories in politics, business, sports, and entertainment on the front page, anticipating they would be the most likely read articles. These tactics became the recommendations or product predictions for customer consumption as a whole. In this approach, there is one common recommendation list for *all* the customers. It served well for the customers because most of them purchased top selling products (and,

Data Science. DOI: https://doi.org/10.1016/B978-0-12-814761-0.00011-3

hence, they are in best sellers!) and served the enterprise well because they made it easy for customers to purchase the top sellers.

The legacy recommendation tactics that served the brick and mortar settings do not take into account an *individual* customer preference. After all, not all the customers are the same. Some may prefer business books, but not mystery novels, some may like to read sports news and may not really care about current affairs or politics. At a deeper level, none of the users are the same and everyone has their own unique interests and preferences of the products they want to consume. It would be ideal to have a unique recommendation list for every user, taking into consideration their unique interests and wants. The customers and the enterprises alike want a personalized storefront to maximize the positive experience of customer-product interactions. Both the editor-curated and best-selling lists are good global approximations of what customers would purchase. However, both the approaches do not fit the preferences of an individual user, unless the user is the prototypical average user.

The advent of online businesses greatly expanded the access of the product selection an enterprise can offer. In the span of a few years, customers could have instant access to half a million movies on a streaming service, millions of products on an e-commerce platform, millions of news articles and user generated content. Shelf space is not a constraint anymore and there is an abundance of unique products at the customer's disposal. However, not all products are consumed at the same rate. There are blockbuster movies and there is a long tail of obscure movies that are consumed less frequently. The long tail of products tend to serve customers with unique interests. A customer who is interested in thrillers might have watched the movie *The Girl with the Dragon Tattoo*, a Swedish-American psychological thriller from 2011. Given that the customer watched *The Girl with the Dragon Tattoo*, the customer might be extremely interested in an obscure subgenre of *Scandinavian Crime Fiction* and discovers titles like *Headhunters*, *The Killing*, *The Bridge*, etc. This pattern of consumption is made possible when there is an abundant selection of products that can be consumed instantly. It is also a scenario where the one size fits all approach of the best seller lists and common editorial staff picks are insufficient. The more customer-product connections an enterprise makes, the more it can keep the customer engaged. Moreover, the long tail products tend to be less expensive than licensing the best seller products. In those cases, it will be more profitable for the business to keep the customer engaged in the long tail products.

Search engines offer a good solution to discover items in the long tail only if the user knows what to look for. The information retrieval system works if the customer types in a specific movie title, like "Headhunters" or in some cases, if the information retrieval system is capable, users can search for "Scandinavian crime fiction" and get a list of movies. But, what if there is no such thing as a Scandinavian crime fiction subgenre or if the user is unaware of such a genre? There is nothing recommended when the credits roll.

Most customers are best served by their personalized storefronts where they can discover the most relevant products for them, out of the millions of available products. If an enterprise can predict what the user is going to consume next, it will be serving both the customers and itself. Recommendation engines make the personalized experience happen.

APPLICATIONS OF RECOMMENDATION ENGINES

Recommendation engines have become an indispensable part of online, and in some cases offline, experiences. It is difficult to escape the reach of the applications that utilize recommendation engines every day. These models are behind some of the familiar phrases in digital life: friends you may know, who to follow, recommended connections, news feeds, tweet feeds, customers who bought this item also bought, featured products, suggested dates, you may also like, related stories, recommended movies, what to watch next, etc. Recommendation engines power these online experiences (Underwood, 2017). Some of the applications of the recommenders are:

Product recommendations: An e-commerce website or any organization that has thousands of products, use product recommendation engines. It is one of the earliest applications of recommenders in the digital realm (Schafer, Konstan, & Riedl, 2001). The recommended listings, which are predicted by the company as the most relevant products for a specific customer, are shown in the homepage, product pages, shopping cart, checkout, and even in the order confirmation page. The recommendation list is based on past purchases or past clickstream data of the customer. E-commerce companies often complement the list with the best seller lists, new products, and curated featured products. Once the customer is in a product page, assuming the customer is interested in the product, a new modified recommendation list is shown as "related products" or as "other customer also bought this," lists. Similar features can be extended to offline enterprises, to an extent. Customizable marketing offers, customer relevant coupon codes, and dynamic call center scripts are some of the ways recommendation engines are used in offline experiences.

Content recommendation: A personalized news feed is one way to increase the stickiness of content sites. Whether it is a desktop, mobile, or any other device, users have limited time to consume the content. Content companies are motivated to keep users on the site by feeding them the most relevant news stories, a friend's social update, or a tweet. All these recommendations are based on the past behavior of the user and the behavior of other users on the site (Thorson, 2008).

Entertainment recommendation: Binge watching as a phenomenon was unknown just a few years ago. Digital consumption of entertainment products has become the predominant way the media is consumed in many segments. Music streaming providers have a vast collection of tracks and cater to a user's unique taste in music. They can recommend a new artist's track to a listener because it shares the same traits as the track *For What it is Worth* by Buffalo Springfield that has already been *liked* by the listener.

In 2006, when Netflix Inc. announced Netflix Prize, a public competition to award the best recommendation engine model that could beat the company's own recommender—CineMatch, research into recommendation engines came into the spotlight. For its part Netflix released about half a million anonymized user ratings of 17,000 movies. Movies are rated with a 1−5-star scale by the users, presumably after watching the movie. Even though, recommendation engines existed before this, new research began into this problem of predicting user-product interactions (Koren, Bell, & Volinsky, 2009).

11.1 RECOMMENDATION ENGINE CONCEPTS

Whatever the application may be, a recommendation engine should predict a customer's interest in a particular product and provide highly personalized recommendations to the customer. To do this, the recommendation engine needs some information about the customer, the product and the customer-product preference. The input information for the recommendation engine takes the form of the past inclinations of the customer's preference of the product, for example, the movie ratings by a customer of the content streaming service. The customer discloses this rating information with an implicit understanding that the company will keep offering them highly relevant titles and with the satisfaction of their voice being heard. The company uses this data point and the data points collected from other users to feed into the recommendation engine. They invest in recommendation engines in an effort to keep offering customers highly personalized content, keep customers engaged, and maintain the trust of the customers for giving them information about the products they like.

The general model of a recommendation engine is shown in Fig. 11.1. Throughout this chapter, the customer will be referred to as the *user* and the

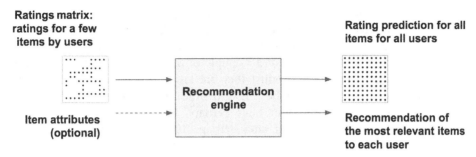

FIGURE 11.1
The general model of a recommendation engine.

Table 11.1 Known Ratings Matrix

	The Godfather	2001: A Space Odyssey	The Hunt for Red October	Fargo	The Imitation Game	...
Josephine	5	4	1		1	
Olivia			2	2	4	
Amelia	5	1	4	4	1	
Zoe	2	2	5	1	1	
Alanna	5	5		1	1	
Kim		4	1	2	5	
...						

product as an *item*. An item can be a product, movie, track, album, artist, topic, news article, etc. The user-item preference is quantified in the form of *ratings*. The ratings can be of any ordinal scale: 1–5-star ratings, scores, like or dislike flags, etc.

The most common input format for a recommendation engine is the *Utility matrix* or *Ratings matrix*. It is a simple two-dimensional crosstab with items in the columns, users in the rows and ratings in the cells. A few cells in the ratings matrix have rating values which indicate the user's preference for an item. Table 11.1 shows the ratings matrix with the user Josephine rating the movie *The Godfather* as 5 stars, on a 1–5-star scale. Alternatively, the cells in the ratings matrix may indicate a Boolean flag, whether or not a user has purchased, viewed, or searched for an item. In the ratings matrix with rating data, the blank cells may represent a few possibilities. Most likely the reason is that the user has not used or experienced the item yet. Other reasons can be that the user has not bothered to give a rating after using the item. In either case, the lack of rating cannot be assumed to indicate that the user disliked the item.

It is lucky to see so many ratings for the items by the users in the ratings matrix shown in Table 11.1. In reality, however, most of the cells would be empty in a ratings matrix. Say there is an "Etsy" style e-commerce company with 500,000 items and a couple of million users. Each user can give a 1−5-star rating for a product they are familiar with. If all the users rate all the items, that would be 10^{12} possible ratings! How many distinct products would a typical user buy? Perhaps 100. Out of which, how many items would a typical user rate? Perhaps 10. The remaining of 499,990 items for the user will have a blank cell in the ratings matrix. A sparse matrix provides both a challenge and an opportunity for recommendation engines. The model would have to sift through the user's potential preference in the other 499,990 items and provide a list of a dozen or so items the user would be most interested in. *The objective of the recommendation engine is to fill the blank cells of the ratings matrix with predicted ratings for each user and the item, which the user presumably hasn't used or experienced yet.*

The association analysis technique discussed in Chapter 6, Association Analysis is similar in approach to a recommendation engine. After all, both the techniques recommend items to a user and both employ machine learning algorithms. However, the results of the association analysis technique are not personalized to a specific user. If the association analysis model recommends beer the moment diapers are placed in the user's shopping basket, this same recommendation would be served to *all* users, whether or not a user liked beer or ever even bought beer in the past. It is a global rule-based recommendation for all users. Moreover, in the association analysis model, the session window of consideration is restricted to the current visit to the supermarket. The purchase history of the individual user in previous visits is not taken into account. In the case of recommendation engines, past ratings or purchase history of a specific user is central to building future user-item recommendations. The past history data is not readily accessible when a user enters a supermarket or is visiting a website as an anonymous user. In these cases, the global recommendation by association analysis provides a good approximation of user-item preferences.

Building up the Ratings Matrix

The ratings matrix shown in Table 11.1 can be represented with a ratings function f.

Ratings function $f: U \times I \rightarrow R$ ⁣   (11.1)

where U is the set of users, I is the item set and R is the ratings matrix. The initial *known* ratings in matrix R is sparse because the user-item interaction is miniscule compared to all the possible item-user combinations. The objective of the recommender is to fill the blank cells with predicted *unknown* ratings. The process of building a completed ratings matrix consists of three steps.

1. Assemble known ratings
2. Predict unknown ratings
3. Prediction evaluation

Step 1: Assemble Known Ratings

Collecting and assembling known ratings in the form of a ratings matrix is the most time-consuming step, riddled with data capture challenges. The ratings can be explicit, where the user directly provides ratings about an item. The user can be offered a list of previously consumed items or be provided with choices to select their favorite items out of a pre-selected list. The choice list is helpful to seed some ratings when a user is new to the service. The ratings could also be derived from the wish-lists where the user has expressed interest in an item. The challenge in the explicit rating is that it is not scalable. A typical user is not good at voluntarily providing a rating. How often does one leave a rating for a product that has been purchased or seen? The typical response rate is very low, in the range of 1%−10% (Weise, 2017). This limits the amount of data that can be used to build a reliable recommendation engine.

The implicit collection of ratings provides an alternative to, or complements, explicit data collection. Implicit data collection is inferred preference of an item from the past user actions, for example, searching for an item, previous purchases (not ratings), watching a movie, product views, etc. While one can get an abundance of data about user-item interactions using implicit collection, the challenge is that it is very difficult to interpret low or high ratings from implicit action. The user might have seen the movie and completely detested the movie. It is incorrect to assume that a user liked the movie just because the user watched it. A hybrid combination of both explicit and implicit rating is used in large scale production deployments to overcome the limitations of individual methods (Hu, Koren, & Volinsky, 2008).

Regardless of either explicit or implicit data collection, there is no available known rating for a new user or a new item. Hence, providing relevant recommendations is difficult when a new user or new item is introduced into the system. This is called the *cold start* problem. The recommenders cannot conclude any inferences from users or items when the system has not obtained sufficient data about them. Cold start is a major issue to recommenders because new items and users are continuously added to the system. Some of the algorithms used to build a recommendation engine discussed in this chapter are highly susceptible to dealing with the cold start problem, while others are robust.

Step 2: Rating Prediction

Predicting ratings for prospective user-item interaction is the key objective for a recommendation engine. In some cases, the objective is to show 1–5-star ratings for all the movies in the catalog indicating how much a user will prefer a movie. In most cases, however, it is not essential to predict ratings for *all* the user-item interactions. The objective is just to show only the *top* recommended items from the massive catalog of movies. Hence, it might be adequate to show items with top predicted ratings instead of all the items with the predicted ratings.

Step 3: Evaluation

Any machine learning-based prediction model needs to go through an evaluation step to check if the prediction is generalized and the model is not overfitting the training dataset. Some of the known rating data can be reserved as a test dataset to evaluate the training prediction. The performance of the recommendation engine is often measured as RMSE (root mean square error) or MAE (mean absolute error) of ratings, which measures the delta between the actual ratings and the predicted ratings. RMSE metric is penalized for larger errors, while MAE has the advantage of easy interpretation. The accuracy of the deployed recommendation engine has to be continuously measured whenever a new known rating is captured in the system. The new actual rating is compared against the previous prediction of the recommender.

The Balance

A good recommendation engine has reasonable accuracy of predicted ratings, balanced with a few other secondary objectives. Sometimes a user might not have discovered a particular genre and could benefit from serendipitous discovery of an item appearing on the recommendation list. A new popular movie might not have a user's favorite cast or director but might be worth recommending because the movie is popular. The recommendation engine accentuates a phenomenon called the *Filter bubble*, where users are cocooned with a singular viewpoint (Bozdag, 2013). It is not uncommon to find recommended articles leaning towards one political affiliation or all the recommended movies from one genre, because the user happened to sample a particular news article or watched a movie from a specific genre. The same user might like a different genre, say classic drama, had the user been provided with an opportunity to watch it. Providing a mix of diverse selection and enabling serendipitous discovery might complement the recommendation engine's predictions on user-item preferences. Companies deal with the

filter bubble problem by creating hybrid lists like new, noteworthy, or popular items along with the listing from recommendation engines.

11.1.1   Types of Recommendation Engines

The machine learning methods for building a recommendation engine can
be classified into a taxonomy shown in Fig. 11.2. There is a wide selection of
algorithms for building a recommendation engine, each with its own
strengths and limitations (Bobadilla, Ortega, Hernando, & Gutiérrez, 2013).
Association analysis is included as a type of recommendation engine method
in this taxonomy, but it is distinct because of the absence of user personalization and the window of data it considers for a recommendation (Cakir &
Aras, 2012). Recommendation engine methods are broadly classified into
Collaborative Filtering and *Content-based Filtering*.

Collaborative filtering: Collaborative filtering is a class of recommenders that
leverage only the past user-item interactions in the form of a ratings matrix.
It operates under the assumption that similar users will have similar likes. It
uses rating information from all *other* users to provide predictions for a user-
item interaction and, thereby, whittles down the item choices for the users,
from the complete item set. Hence, the name collaborative filtering. The collaborative filtering techniques can be further classified into:

1. *Neighborhood methods*: Neighborhood methods predict the user-item
   preferences by first finding a cohort of users or items which are similar
   to the user or the item whose ratings are to be predicted. In the case of

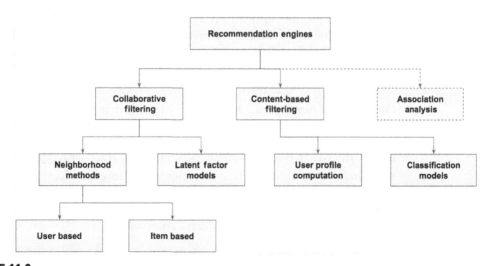

FIGURE 11.2

Taxonomy of recommendation engines.

the *user-based* neighborhood method, the algorithm is designed to find a cohort of users who have a similar rating pattern to the user in question and who have rated the item in question. The predicted rating is deduced from those cohort of similar users. The case is the same with the *item-based* neighborhood method where a cohort of similar items is found which have been given similar ratings when rated by the same user. The rating of similar items approximates the rating of the item in question for a user. Both these techniques leverage the similarity scores discussed in the k-Nearest Neighbor section in Chapter 4, Classification.

2. *Latent factor models*: Actively managed mutual fund managers look for suitable companies to invest in their pursuit to outperform the market averages. Out of hundreds of thousands of publicly traded companies, the fund managers select dozens of companies using certain criteria or factors. The factors can be management stability, market positioning, strength of the balance sheet, cash flow metrics, or market share of the products. They even explain the preference of the dozens of companies where they have taken positions using the factors. Factors are the same generalized dimensions that the company is ranked against (Company *Acme Inc.* has products with high market share) and the fund manager's preference for the factor (The fund *Cash cow* looks for companies with high market share). The latent factor models tend to explain the ratings by representing both the users and the items on a set of common factors. This set of factors is inferred from the known user-item ratings matrix. The factors can take the form of interpretable dimensions like "science-fiction movies with aliens" or uninterpretable dimensions. It maps both the users and items against the same set of factors. For example, if a science-fiction movie has a plot involving aliens and if a user has a preference for movies with aliens, a recommendation is made. Both the movie and the user are mapped with a degree of association with the factor—aliens.

Content-based filtering: In addition to the ratings matrix used by collaborative filtering methods, content-based filtering leverages *attribute* data about items. For example, it may use all the available information about the contents of a movie (item): the cast, the producer, the director, released year, genre, description, etc., in addition to the user-item ratings matrix. Content-based filtering uses the information about an item in the format of an *item profile*. After the item profile is sourced, the content-based recommenders predict the user-item preference with two different approaches:

1. *User profile method*: Once an item profile is developed, a user profile can be developed to show the affinity of a user to the attribute used in the item profile. For example, if a user has given high ratings for the

movies *Fargo*, *The Big Lebowski*, and *No Country for Old Men*, the user profile can be built to show the preference for the *Coen brothers'* (filmmakers, Joel Coen and Ethan Coen) work, who directed all the aforementioned movies. This technique is leveraged by user profile methods. The predicted rating for a user-item is computed by the similarity of the user and the item profiles. Since the movie *True Grit* is associated with the *Coen brothers* in the item profile and the user has shown an association with the *Coen brothers* in the user profile, a user-item recommendation can be made.

2. *Supervised learning (Classification or Regression) models:* Consider the case of a user who has shown explicit preference for a few movies by providing ratings. The item profile of the movies has a set of attributes, for example, the cast, the director, genre, key words in the plot description, etc., for all the items. If these two datasets were joined viz., the ratings matrix for *one user* and the item profile using the common link—*the item*, then movie ratings (response or label) and item attributes (input or predictor) are obtained for the user. The joined dataset is similar to the training data used to create classification or regression models. With the item profile and ratings matrix, it is possible to develop a classification or a regression model, say a decision tree, for *each* user and predict the rating for an unseen item using its attributes. By the supervised learning method, a personalized classification or regression model is built for every single user in the system. The model scores the items based on the user's affinity towards specific item attributes.

11.2 COLLABORATIVE FILTERING

Collaborative Filtering is based on a simple idea—a user will prefer an item if it is recommended by their like-minded friends. Suppose there is a new restaurant in town. If a friend, who happens to have the same interests as the user, raves about it—the user might like it as well. The idea makes intuitive sense. Collaborative filtering leverages this insight into an algorithm that predicts a user's preference of an item by finding a cohort of users who happen to have the same preference as the user. The preference or predicted rating for an item can be deduced by the rating given by a cohort of similar users.

The distinguishing feature of the collaborative filtering method is that the algorithm considers only the ratings matrix that is, the past user-item interactions. Hence, the collaborative filtering method is item domain independent. The same algorithm can be applied to predicting ratings for movies, music, books, and gardening tools. In fact, the algorithm does not have any knowledge about the items except the ratings given by the users.

Some of the real-world applications of collaborative filtering include Google News recommendations (Das, Datar, Garg, & Rajaram, 2007), music recommendations by Last.fm, and recommended Twitter follows (Gupta et al., 2013). The general framework for collaborative filtering is shown in Fig. 11.3. There are two distinct approaches in processing the ratings matrix and extracting the rating prediction. The neighborhood method finds a cohort of similar users or items. The latent factor method explains the ratings matrix through a set of dimensions called latent factors. *Matrix factorization* is the common realization of the latent factor method, where both users and items are mapped to a common set of self-extracted factors.

11.2.1 Neighborhood-Based Methods

Neighborhood methods calculate how similar the users (or the items) are in the known ratings matrix. The similarity scores or the measure of proximity, discussed in the k-Nearest Neighbor section in Chapter 4, Classification techniques, are used in neighborhood-based methods to identify similar users and items. Commonly used similarity measures are: Jaccard similarity, Cosine similarity, and Pearson correlation coefficient.

The general approach for neighborhood-based methods consists of two steps to find the predicted rating for a user-item:

1. Find the cohort of other similar users (or the items) who have rated the item (or the user) in question.
2. Deduce the rating from the ratings of similar users (or the items).

The two methods for the neighborhood-based systems, that is, user-based and item-based, are extremely similar. The former starts to identify similar users and the latter starts by identifying similarly rated items by the same

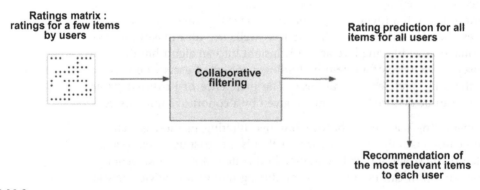

FIGURE 11.3

Collaborative filtering recommender.

users. For the ratings matrix shown in Table 11.1, both the methods share the same technique, where one starts with finding similar rows and the other finds similar columns.

User-Based Collaborative Filtering
The user-based collaborative filtering method operates on the assumption that similar users have similar likes. The two-step process of identifying new unseen user-item preferences consists of filtering similar users and deducing the ratings from similar users. The approach for user-based collaborative filtering is quite similar to the k-NN classification algorithm.

1. For every user x, find a set of N other users who are similar to the user x and who have rated the item i.
2. Approximate the rating of the user x for the item i, by aggregating (averaging) the rating of N similar users.

Consider the known ratings matrix shown in Table 11.2. Say the task is to find whether the user Olivia will like the movie *2001: A Space Odyssey*. The first step will be to find N users similar to the user Olivia who have already rated the movie *2001: A Space Odyssey*. The second step will be to deduce a rating for the user Olivia from the cohort of similar users.

Step 1: Identifying Similar Users
The users are similar if their rating *vectors* are close according to a distance measure. Consider the rating matrix shown in Table 11.2 as a set of rating vectors. The rating for the user Amelia is represented as $r_{amelia} = \{5,1,4,4,1\}$. The similarity between the two users is the similarity between the rating vectors. A quantifying metric is needed in order to measure the similarity between the user's vectors. Jaccard similarity, Cosine similarity, and Pearson correlation coefficient are some of the commonly used distance and

Table 11.2 Known Ratings Matrix and a User-item Rating Prediction

	The Godfather	2001: A Space Odyssey	The Hunt for Red October	Fargo	The Imitation Game
Josephine	5	4	1		1
Olivia		?	2	2	4
Amelia	5	1	4	4	1
Zoe	2	2	5	1	1
Alanna	5	5		1	1
Kim		4	1	2	5

similarity metrics. The cosine similarity measure between two nonzero user vectors for the user Olivia and the user Amelia is given by the Eq. (11.2)

$$\text{Cosine similarity } (|x \cdot y|) = \frac{x\,y}{||x||\ ||y||}$$

$$\text{Cosine similarity } (r_{\text{olivia}}, r_{\text{amelia}}) = \frac{0 \times 5 + 0 \times 1 + 2 \times 4 + 2 \times 4 + 4 \times 1}{\sqrt{2^2 + 2^2 + 4^2} \times \sqrt{5^2 + 1^2 + 4^2 + 4^2 + 1^2}} = 0.53$$

$$(11.2)$$

Note that the cosine similarity measure equates the lack of ratings as zero value ratings, which can also be considered as a low rating. This assumption works fine for the applications for where the user has purchased the item or not. In the movie recommendation case, this assumption can yield the wrong results because the lack of rating does not mean that the user dislikes the movie. Hence, the similarity measure needs to be enhanced to take into consideration the lack of rating being different from a low rating for an item. Moreover, biases in the ratings should also be dealt with. Some users are more generous in giving ratings than others who are more critical. The user's bias in giving ratings skews the similarity score between users.

Centered cosine similarity measure addresses the problem by normalizing the ratings across all the users. To achieve this, all the ratings for a user is subtracted from the average rating of the user. Thus, a negative number means below average rating and a positive number means above average ratings given by the same user. The normalized version of the ratings matrix is shown in Table 11.3. Each value of the ratings matrix is normalized with the average rating of the user.

Centered cosine similarity or *Pearson correlation* between the ratings for the users Olivia and Amelia is calculated by:

$$\text{Centered cosine similarity } (r_{\text{olivia}}, r_{\text{amelia}})$$
$$= \frac{0 \times 2.0 + 0 \times -2.0 + -0.7 \times 1.0 + 0.7 \times 1.0 + 1.3 \times -2.0}{\sqrt{(-0.7)^2 + (0.7)^2 + (1.3)^2} * \sqrt{(2.0)^2 + (-2.0)^2 + (1.0)^2 + (1.0)^2 + (-2.0)^2}} = -0.65$$

Table 11.3 Normalized Ratings Matrix

	The Godfather	2001: A Space Odyssey	The Hunt for Red October	Fargo	The Imitation Game
Josephine	2.3	1.3	−1.8		−1.8
Olivia			−0.7	−0.7	1.3
Amelia	2.0	−2.0	1.0	1.0	−2.0
Zoe	−0.2	−0.2	2.8	−1.2	−1.2
Alanna	2.0	2.0		−2.0	−2.0
Kim		1.0	−2.0	−1.0	2.0

Table 11.4 User-to-User Similarity Matrix

	Josephine	Olivia	Amelia	Zoe	Alanna	Kim
Josephine	1.00	− 0.20	0.28	− 0.30	0.74	0.11
Olivia		1.00	− 0.65	− 0.50	− 0.20	0.90
Amelia			1.00	0.33	0.13	− 0.74
Zoe				1.00	0.30	− 0.67
Alanna					1.00	0.00
Kim						1.00

The similarity score can be pre-computed between all the possible pairs of users and the results can be kept ready in a user-to-user matrix shown in sample Table 11.4 for ease of calculation in the further steps. At this point the neighborhood or cohort size, k, has to be declared, similar to k in the k-NN algorithm. Assume k is 3 for this example. The goal of this step is to find three users similar to the user Olivia who have also rated the movie *2001: A Space Odyssey*. From the table, the top three users can be found similar to the user Olivia, who are Kim (0.90), Alanna (− 0.20), and Josephine (− 0.20).

Step 2: Deducing Rating From Neighborhood Users

$$\text{Rating } R = \sum_{\text{neighborhood}} (\text{similarity score} \times \text{rating}) \qquad (11.3)$$

Once the cohort of users are found, deducing the predicted rating is straight forward. The predicted rating for Olivia for the movie *2001: A Space Odyssey* is the average of the ratings given by Kim, Alanna, and Josephine, for the same movie. One can use weighted average based on the similarity score for more accuracy and the general formula for the predicted ratings is given by Eq. (11.4).

$$r_{xi} = \frac{\sum_{u \in N} s_{xu} r_{ui}}{\sum_{u \in N} s_{xu}} \qquad (11.4)$$

where N is a set of k users similar to user x and have rated the item i, r is the predicted rating for user x and item i. s_{xu} is the similarity score of user x and user u. Using Eq. (11.4) and the similarity matrix, the predicted rating for Movie 2: *2001: A Space Odyssey* can be computed for Olivia as:

$$r_{xi} = \frac{(0.9 \times 1) + (-0.2 \times 2) + (-0.2 \times 1.25)}{(0.9 - 0.2 - 0.2)} = 0.05$$

The predicted rating is 0.05 above the average score for Olivia, which is 2.7. The *final* predicted rating for the movie is therefore 2.75 stars. If k is 1, the rating would have been 3.7 stars.

The user-based neighborhood technique provides an intuitive way to fill the ratings matrix. The steps for finding similar users and rating deductions is repeated for every blank ratings cell in the ratings matrix. However, the collaborative filtering process can be time consuming. One way to speed-up the process is to pre-compute the user-to-user similarity matrix shown in Table 11.4 once for all the users and reuse the results for the first step in identifying similar users. The user-to-user similarity matrix should be updated for any new user. However, a new user similarity with other users can be computed only when their preference information is known—*cold start problem*!

The cold start problem is the most significant limitation of the collaborative filtering technique (Isinkaye, Folajimi, & Ojokoh, 2015). A new user to the system would not have item preference ratings. The system could ask the new user to declare the preferences by providing information on their most preferred items. Regardless, the user will have a minimal number of item ratings to start with. For the new users, the cohort neighborhoods will be small and, thus, matching the user with other cohort users will be limited, which in turn leads to less recommendations. Similarly, a new item will not be part of any previous user-item interactions and will lead to less recommendations for the new item to the users. In some cases, because of the fewer recommendations, the new items stay less popular. For existing users or items, the neighborhood method needs more data for the algorithm to be more effective, which can be a limiting factor for the applications that rely exclusively on the explicit data collection method.

The cold start problem can be mitigated by a couple of strategies. First, the system can ask all the new users to select or enter their preferred items once they have signed up. This can be selecting a few movies from a curated list of movies or tagging them from the movie catalog. The new user onboarding process incorporates this step, so the recommendation engines have some seed information about the new users. Second, the system can rely heavily on implicit data collection through search or clickstream activity until a solid item preference profile can be build.

Popular items are preferred by a large number of users. Collaborative filtering tends to recommend popular items to users because the cohort selection might be skewed towards higher ratings for popular items. Recommending the popular items is not necessarily a bad decision. However, one of the objectives of recommendation engine is to discover the personalized idiosyncratic and unique items of the user. Moreover, the nonpersonalized popular items are usually shown by *best seller* or *trending now* lists, which have the same content for all the users.

Item-Based Collaborative Filtering

The item-based neighborhood method operates on the assumption that users prefer items that are similar to previously preferred items. In this context, items that are similar tend to be rated similarly by the same users. If a user liked the dark comedy crime movie *Fargo*, then the user might like the crime thriller movie *No Country for Old Men*, provided that both movies are rated similarly by the same users. Both the movies are created by the same writers-directors and it is presumed that if a user has given high ratings for *Fargo*, the same user might have given high ratings for *No Country for Old Men* as well. If the rating patterns of two items are similar, then the items are in the neighborhood and their item vectors are close to each other. Hence, the item's neighbor is a set of other items that tend to get similar ratings when rated by the same user. The two-step process of identifying new user-item preference using item-based collaborative filtering include identifying similar items and deducing a rating from similar items.

1. For every item *i*, find a set of *N* other items which have similar ratings when rated by the same user.
2. Approximate the rating for the item *i* by aggregating (averaging) the rating of *N* similar items rated by the user.

The ratings matrix shown in Table 11.2 can be used to compute the predicted rating for the same unseen cell—for the user Olivia for the movie *2001: A Space Odyssey-using the item-based method*. To realize the item-based neighborhood method, the rating matrix shown in Table 11.2 has to be transposed (swapping rows and columns) and continued with the same steps as the user-based (or row based) neighborhood method. Table 11.5 shows the transposed version of the original ratings matrix.

The centered cosine or Pearson correlation coefficient metric is used to calculate the similarity between movies based on the ratings pattern. Since the objective is to find the rating for *2001: A Space Odyssey*, the similarity score would need to be found for all the movies with *2001: A Space Odyssey*.

Table 11.5 Transposed Ratings Matrix

	Josephine	Olivia	Amelia	Zoe	Alanna	Kim
The Godfather	5		5	2	5	
2001: A Space Odyssey	4	?	1	2	5	4
The Hunt for Red October	1	2	4	5		1
Fargo		2	4	1	1	2
The Imitation Game	1	4	1	1	1	5

Table 11.6 Normalized Ratings and Similarity With a Movie

	Josephine	Olivia	Amelia	Zoe	Alanna	Kim	Similarity with the Movie 2001: A Space Odyssey
The Godfather	2.3		2.0	− 0.2	2.0		− 0.10
2001: A Space Odyssey	1.3		− 2.0	− 0.2	2.0	1.0	1.00
The Hunt for Red October	− 1.8	− 0.7	1.0	2.8		− 2.0	− 0.36
Fargo		− 0.7	1.0	− 1.2	− 2.0	− 1.0	0.24
The Imitation Game	− 1.8	1.3	− 2.0	− 1.2	− 2.0	2.0	− 0.43

Table 11.6 shows the centered rating values along with the similarity score of all the movies with *2001: A Space Odyssey*. The similarity score is calculated using Eq. (11.2) on the centered rating values. Since the centered ratings can be negative, the similarity score can be positive or negative. Depending on the number of neighbors specified, the top k neighbors to the movie *2001: A Space Odyssey* can now be narrowed down using the magnitude of the similarity score. Assume k is 2.

From Table 11.6 the nearest two movies to *2001: A space Odyssey* can be concluded, rated by Olivia, are *Fargo* and *The Hunt for Red October*. The predicted centered rating for the *2001: A space Odyssey* for Olivia, using Eq. (11.4) is:

$$r_{xi} = \frac{(0.24 \times -0.7) + (-0.36 \times -0.7)}{(0.24 - 0.36)} = -0.67$$

The normalized rating for Olivia and *2001: A space Odyssey* is − 0.67 and the real ratings for *2001: A space Odyssey* by Olivia is 2. Note that the predicted ratings for the same user-item pair is different when user-based collaborative filtering is used.

User-Based or Item-Based Collaborative Filtering?

The neighborhood technique for predicting a rating for a user-item combination, either with user-based or item-based, is very similar. After all, if the ratings matrix is transposed at the beginning, the item-based approach is exactly the same as the user-based approach. However, the predicted rating is *different* when these two approaches are used on the *same* ratings matrix.

Conceptually, finding similar items is relatively easier than finding similar users. Items tend to get aligned with specific genres or types of the items. A movie can belong to either Classics or Science fiction genres or, less likely, in both the genres. However, a user may like both Classics and Science fiction genres. It is common for the users to have interests in multiple genres and develop unique taste profiles. It is easier to find similar courtroom drama movies. It is difficult to find similar users when a user has preference to courtroom drama, science fiction, movies directed by Francis Ford Coppola and Pixar movies. If all the users prefer one genre, it is easy to isolate the preferences and, thereby, have no confounding of ratings. In practice, that doesn't work, and it is difficult to extract the user preference from the ratings matrix when users have multiple overlapping preference profiles. Hence, finding similar items is more effective than finding similar users and yields better performance in most applications.

In some business applications, the objective of the recommendation engine is to provide a list of top recommended items for each user. To accomplish this in the user-based approach, for every user, one can pre-compute the step of finding similar users and then aggregate the ratings for items. This vastly narrows the search space. However, in the item-based approach, all the item-to-item similarity combinations need to be pre-computed before getting into user level recommendation. The user-based approach has a leg up when it comes to computational time because most applications are concerned with providing recommendations at the user level.

Neighborhood based Collaborative Filtering - How to Implement
The neighbor-based method involves relatively simple calculations, albeit time consuming. The entire step-by-step process of finding similar users (or similarly rated items) and deducing a rating can be implemented in a programming tool or by using RapidMiner. If using the latter, ratings data should be prepared in the form of a ratings matrix to find similar users or items. Similar users can be found using the operator *Data to Similarity Data* operator with Cosine Similarity as the parameter. Alternatively, the prebuilt operators for Recommendation Engines using the Recommenders extension (Mihelčić, Antulov-Fantulin, Bošnjak, & Šmuc, 2012) can be leveraged. The operators that come with the extension expand the available library and abstract the low level tasks to high-level tasks geared toward Recommendation Engine application.

Dataset
The dataset used in this chapter is sourced from MovieLens database. It is a sample of real-world anonymized data from GroupLens Inc. The ratings data can be downloaded from the GroupLens website[1] which provides multiple data size options. The following implementation uses 100,000 ratings given

[1] http://grouplens.org/datasets/movielens

Table 11.7 MovieLens Datasets—Ratings and Movie Attributes

User ID	Movie ID	Rating	Timestamp
1	31	2.5	1260759144
1	1029	3	1260759179
1	1061	3	1260759182
1	1129	2	1260759185
1	1172	4	1260759205
1	1263	2	1260759151
1	1287	2	1260759187
1	1293	2	1260759148
1	1339	3.5	1260759125
1	1343	2	1260759131

Movie ID	Title	Genres
1	Toy Story (1995)	Adventure|Animation|Children|Comedy|Fantasy
2	Jumanji (1995)	Adventure|Children|Fantasy
3	Grumpier Old Men (1995)	Comedy|Romance
4	Waiting to Exhale (1995)	Comedy|Drama|Romance
5	Father of the Bride Part II (1995)	Comedy
6	Heat (1995)	Action|Crime|Thriller
7	Sabrina (1995)	Comedy|Romance
8	Tom and Huck (1995)	Adventure|Children
9	Sudden Death (1995)	Action
10	GoldenEye (1995)	Action|Adventure|Thriller

by 1000 users for 1700 titles. There are two datasets in each of the down-loaded packages. The first dataset (ratings dataset) contains ratings, user IDs, and movie ID attributes. The second dataset (items dataset) contains limited metadata about each movie—movie ID, movie title, and concatenated genre attributes. The attributes of the movies can be further expanded from other third-party databases like IMDB[2] using the movie name. Table 11.7 shows the MovieLens input data.

Implementation Steps
The outline of the full RapidMiner process is shown in Fig. 11.4. The high-level process for a recommendation engine is no different from the other pre-dictive analytics process. It contains data preparation, modeling, applying the model to a test set, and performance evaluation steps to predict the user-item ratings.

---

[2] http://imdb.com

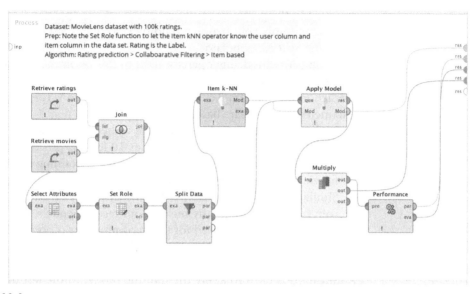

FIGURE 11.4
Item *k*-NN recommender process.

1. **Data Preparation:** The central operator in the neighborhood-based recommender process is the modeling operator called *User—KNN* or *Item—KNN*. The former implements a user-based and the latter implements an item-based neighborhood recommender. As a collaborative filtering method, the only input needed for the modeling operator is the ratings matrix. The ratings matrix is in the form of User identification, Item identification, and the label (rating). Any other attribute from the dataset is not used in the core modeling operator. Whatever the format of the input data, it needs to be transformed to a dataset with user identification, item identification, and numerical rating label.

   All the information needed for the modeling is available in the MovieLens rating dataset. However, more context can be added to the movies by joining the ratings dataset with the item dataset. Attributes not needed for the process are discarded using the *Select attribute* operator. The *Set role* operator is used to declare which attribute is "user identification," "item identification," and the label. The "user identification" and "item identification" are custom roles used by Recommender operators. Mapping the attribute user ID to "user identification" role and item ID to "item identification" role is specified in the parameter settings for the *Set role* operator. The ratings data is randomly split between training (95%) and test dataset (5%) using the *Split data* operator

2. **Modeling:** The modeling operator used in this recommender process *item K-NN* can be found under Recommenders > Item rating prediction > Collaborative Filtering Rating Prediction. There are a few parameters to configure based on the application.

   a. k: Nearest neighbor cohort size. This is the same "k" as in k-NN classification. The cohort size is set as 10 for this process.
   b. Min and Max ratings: The ratings range in the training dataset. The movie ratings dataset has ratings from 0 to 5.
   c. Similarity measure: Pearson or Cosine similarity measure is the commonly used similarity measure for recommenders. Cosine similarity measure is used for this recommender process.

3. **Apply Model to test set:** The *Apply Model (Rating Prediction)* operator under Recommenders > Recommender Performance > Model Application is used to apply the training model to the test dataset. A portion of the original dataset that is reserved for testing is used as an input for the Apply Model operator which calculates the predicted ratings for each user-item combination in the test dataset. The Apply Model is also used in the final deployment where one can supply user-item combinations for which the rating is to be predicted.

4. **Performance evaluation:** The output of the predicted test dataset from the *Apply Model* operator is connected to the *Performance (Rating Prediction)* operator under the Recommender extension folder to evaluate if the predicted rating is close to the actual rating provided by the users. As in the *Apply Model* operator, the ratings range is declared in the parameters for *Performance (Rating Prediction)* operator.

The whole process shown in Fig. 11.4 can be saved and executed. The Results window shows the predicted values for the test dataset. In addition to the attributes in the original test dataset, a new prediction column is appended to the dataset. A sample of the first ten records are shown in Fig. 11.5, where recommender model prediction and the actual rating given by the users can be observed.

The performance vector tab in the Results window shows the output of the Performance evaluation operator. RMSE of the rating prediction is 0.873 stars for the neighborhood-based recommender using the MovieLens dataset. The MAE is 0.665 stars. On an average, the predicted star rating will be off from the actual prediction by 0.665 stars. Not bad for using a simple recommender model!

Row No.	rating	userId	movieId	title	genres	prediction
1	2.500	1	2455	Fly, The (1986)	Drama|Horror|Sci–Fi|Thriller	2.292
2	3	2	339	While You Were Sleeping (1995)	Comedy|Romance	3.382
3	3	2	410	Addams Family Values (1993)	Children|Comedy|Fantasy	3.447
4	3	2	539	Sleepless in Seattle (1993)	Comedy|Drama|Romance	3.232
5	3	2	550	Threesome (1994)	Comedy|Romance	3.399
6	3	2	588	Aladdin (1992)	Adventure|Animation|Childr...	3.954
7	4	2	661	James and the Giant Peach (1996)	Adventure|Animation|Childr...	3.418
8	4	2	720	Wallace & Gromit: The Best of Aardman ...	Adventure|Animation|Comedy	3.777
9	3	4	431	Carlito's Way (1993)	Crime|Drama	4.608
10	5	4	1194	Cheech and Chong's Up in Smoke (1978)	Comedy	4.297

FIGURE 11.5
Predicted ratings for Item k-NN recommender.

Conclusion

Neighborhood-based recommendation systems use just the ratings matrix as in input for training the model. It is content agnostic or domain independent and does not have to learn about the details of the items a priori. Moreover, the same model can be used to recommend different types of items. An ecommerce platform can recommend books, movies, and other products with the same recommendation engine. *The model using the neighborhood method does not care about what the items mean, it just focuses on the user-item interactions using past ratings.* As with all the collaborative filtering techniques, the neighborhood method suffers from the cold start problem and popular item bias.

One limitation of neighborhood techniques is the processing complexity and scalability. It is computationally intensive to find similar users or similar items for every user or an item, when there are millions of users and items. Since it is practically impossible to carry out these calculations at runtime, the neighborhood calculation for finding neighborhoods for each user or item can be pre-computed. If R is the ratings matrix, the processing complexity of the neighborhood-based approach is given by $O(|R|)$. The pre-computation processing complexity increases to $O(n.|R|)$ where, n is the number of items (Lee, Sun, & Lebanon, 2012). As the number of items or users increase in the system, so to do the computations required for collaborative filtering approaches. In the current form, collaborative filtering approaches do not scale well with the increase in users and items in a system.

The items like a pack of Oatmeal and a pack of Instant Oatmeal may look quite similar, but they are different items. Synonymy is the tendency of particularly similar items with different distinctions. Collaborative filtering techniques will have a hard time equating these two items because they do not have any information on the content of the items. Ideally, two users having preferences on two similar items should be treated the same. Collaborative filtering techniques have difficulty managing the synonymy of the items.

GLOBAL BASELINE

The recommendation engine methods discussed in this chapter so far have underpinnings in machine learning. Alternatively, there is a simple straightforward (naive) method to calculate the predicted rating for a user-item interaction - Global baseline, as shown in Eq. (11.5).

$$r_{ui} = \mu + b_u + b_i \qquad (11.5)$$

where μ is the global average of all ratings, b_u is the user bias. On average, the rating given by a user u is $\mu + b_u$, b_i is the item bias. On average, the rating for the item i by all the users is $\mu + b_i$. b_u and b_i is the delta from the global average of all the ratings, given by the user u and for the item i. For example, consider the average star rating for all the movies is 2.5. The user Amelia tends to be generous in her rating and on average she has given 3.5 stars for all the movies rated by her. The user bias is +1.0 stars. On an average the movie *Interstellar* received 2.0 stars from all the users. The item bias is −0.5. The predicted star rating, using Global baseline, by the user Amelia for the movie *Interstellar* is 3.0

$$r_{ui} = 2.5 + 1.0 - 0.5 = 3.0$$

The global average serves as a baseline to measure the performance of more complex machine learning-based recommenders discussed in this chapter.

11.2.2   Matrix Factorization

The ratings matrix discussed so far in this chapter has information on the user, item, and the strength of user-item interaction. For every user, the ratings information is at the level of individual item, that is, every individual movie, track, product. The number of items usually ranges from thousands to millions of unique values. If one were to ask someone what movies or books they would prefer to watch or read, the answer is usually in the form of some generalized dimension. For example, expressing the preference for science fiction movies, movies directed by Christopher Nolan, movies with strong female leads, crime novels or 1920s literature. The subsequent follow-up might be providing specific item examples which belong to those groupings, for example titles like, *Interstellar, Iron Lady, The Great Gatsby*, etc. The generalized categories can be a predefined genre, works by a creator, or sometimes it might be a yet-to-be named or vague categorization. Perhaps the user just likes a set of items with no specific generalized category.

The *Latent Factor* model, like the neighborhood methods, uses just the ratings matrix as the only input. It tries to generalize and explain the ratings matrix with a set of *latent factors* or generalized dimensions. The factors, which usually range from a dozen to a few hundred, are automatically inferred from the ratings matrix, as long as the number of factors is specified. There is no separate input to the model that provides pre-classified genres or factors. In fact, there are no interpretable names for the latent factors. The inferred factors might resemble genre like classification (science fiction or family movies) and in some cases they are just uninterpretable groupings of items. It will be interesting to research and generalize why a group of items are rated highly against a factor. Once the factors are discovered, the model associates an item's membership towards a factor and a user's inclination towards the *same* factor. If the user and item are near to each other when plotted against a factor or a set of factors, then there is a strong user-item preference.

Fig. 11.6 shows the users (circles) and items (squares) mapped against two illustrative factors: production scale and comedic content. The items or movies are plotted on the chart based on how movies express themselves against the latent factors. The users are plotted based on their preferences against the same latent factors. From the chart, it can be concluded that the user Amelia prefers the movie *No country for Old men* because both the user and the movie are close to one another when expressed against the latent factors. Similarly, Alanna prefers the movie *Headhunters* instead of *Titanic*. The user-item preference is calculated by the dot product of the user vector and the item vector expressed latent factors. The similarity between the user and the item vectors dictates the preference of the user to the item (Koren et al., 2009).

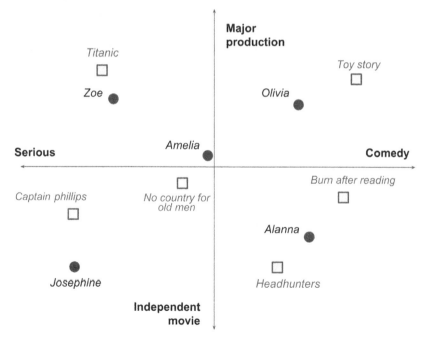

FIGURE 11.6
Items and users in latent factor space.

Matrix Factorization is a technique to discover the latent factors from the ratings matrix and to map the items and the users against those factors. Consider a ratings matrix R with ratings by n users for m items. The ratings matrix R will have $n \times m$ rows and columns. The matrix R can be decomposed into two thin matrices P and Q. P will have $n \times f$ dimensions and Q will have $m \times f$ dimensions where f is the number of latent factors. In the example used in Fig. 11.6, there are two latent factors. The matrix R can be decomposed in such a way that the dot product of the matrix P and transposed Q will yield a matrix with $n \times m$ dimensions that closely approximates the original ratings matrix R (Fig. 11.7).

$$R \approx P \cdot Q^T \qquad (11.6)$$

The decomposition of the ratings matrix into the user matrix and the item matrix makes intuitive sense. The rating of a user-item combination, say Olivia to *Toy Story*, can be explained by Olivia's preference to comedy movies and whether the movie *Toy Story* is acclaimed highly in a comedic content scale or not. This generalization approach greatly reduces the size of the matrices. The massive $m \times n$ dimensional ratings matrix with 2 million users and a half a million items can be decomposed to two thin matrices: P with 2 million users against 100 factors and Q with half a million items against 100 factors. The dot product of P and Q will closely yield the original ratings matrix, with 2 million users and a half a million items, but with more information! *All* the cells in the rating matrix will be filled with the predicted ratings from the dot product, including the sparse known ratings and the vast unknown ratings, using the matrix dot product of P and Q.

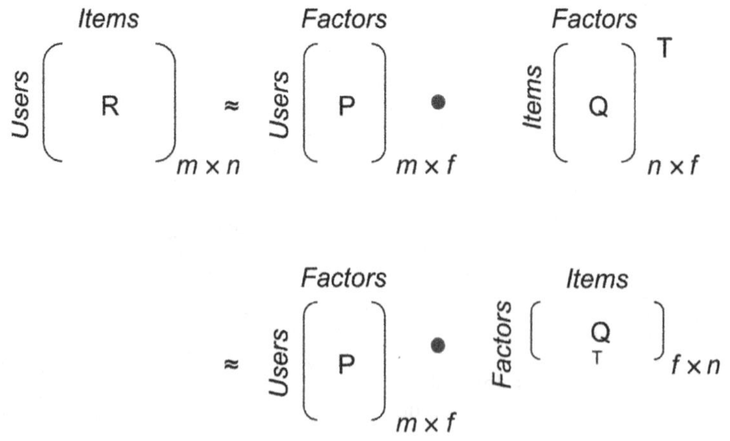

FIGURE 11.7
Decomposition of ratings matrix into latent factor matrices.

The approach is similar to expressing a number, 61, as a product of two numbers. As a prime number, it is not possible to decompose 61 as a product of two numbers, but the original number can be closely approximated with 6×10. The error in this decomposition is 1. Similarly, each rating r can be expressed by the user u for the item i as:

$$\widehat{r_{ui}} = p_u . q_i^T \tag{11.7}$$

where p_u is the user vector with f dimensions and q_i is the item vector with f dimensions. For each item i, the vector q_i measures the extent to which the item i possesses the latent factors. For each user u, the vector p_u measures the preference of the user for the items that have a high possession of those factors. The dot product of the vectors p_u and $q^T{}_i$ gives the approximation of the user's preference for the item.

The objective of the matrix factorization method is to learn the vectors P and Q from the ratings matrix R, where P expresses an item's rating in terms of the factors f and Q expresses the interest of users to the factors. P and Q should be learned in such a way that one can minimize the delta between known ratings and predicted ratings. Assume K is the set of known, non-blank cells in the ratings matrix R. The objective is to minimize the prediction error or the loss function, in Eq. (11.8)

$$\min \sum_{(u,i) \in K} (r_{ui} - \widehat{r_{ui}})^2$$
$$\min \sum_{(u,i) \in K} (r_{ui} - p_u q_i^T)^2 \tag{11.8}$$

where K is the set of (u,i) pairs of known ratings.

Similar to all machine learning algorithms for predictive tasks, overfitting is a problem for recommenders using the matrix factorization method. The key objective is to predict the ratings of items which are not rated, more than accurately predicting the ratings of the known items. To reduce the impact of overfitting, one can introduce *regularization* models (as introduced in Chapter 5: Regression Methods). Regularization is a technique that penalizes learning more complex and flexible models to avoid the risk of overfitting. Regularization avoids overfitting by minimizing the regularized square error shown in Eq. (11.9). It regularizes or forces the coefficient estimates toward zero. Hence, the magnitude of the learned parameters (coefficients) is penalized through regularization. The extent of regularization is controlled through the tuning parameter λ, which ranges from 0 (no effect) to ∞ (maximum effect)

$$\min \sum_{(u,i) \in K} (r_{ui} - p_u q_i^T)^2 + \lambda(||p_u||^2 + ||q_i||^2) \tag{11.9}$$

Much of the observed variance in the rating matrix can be explained by the user-item interactions. However, in real-world applications, there are significant biases that affect the user-item preference. After all, some users are more critical in providing ratings than others. Some blockbuster movies gather generous ratings because they are... blockbusters. To factor in the effects of bias to overall ratings the Global Baseline model can be used given by Eq. (11.5), as a proxy for overall bias in the system.

$$b_{ui} = \mu + b_u + b_i \tag{11.10}$$

The effects of the bias can be used in the predicted ratings, in addition to the user-item interactions as calculated by the matrix factorization method. Eq. (11.11) shows the predicted rating with bias taken into consideration.

$$\widehat{r_{ui}} = \mu + b_u + b_i + p_u.q_i^T \tag{11.11}$$

The overall objective function for the matrix factorization methods is shown in Eq. (11.12). The parameters for the learning algorithm are: regularization λ, user bias b_u, item bias b_i, and the global average rating μ

$$\min \sum_{(u,i) \in K} (r_{ui} - (\mu + b_u + b_i + p_u.q_i^T))^2 + \lambda(||p_u||^2 + ||q_i||^2 + b_u^2 + b_i^2) \tag{11.12}$$

The algorithm commonly used to learn the factor vectors p_u and q_i by minimizing the loss function is *Stochastic Gradient Descent* (SGD). SGD is an iterative optimization method based on gradient descent touched upon in chapter 5 and also in chapter 10, to minimize the objective function like the one in Eq. (11.9). For the given factor dimension f, the SGD algorithm initializes the vectors P and Q and calculates the error rate, which is the delta between the real and predicted ratings. The algorithm slowly changes the value of P and Q to minimize the error and halts when there is no meaningful change in the error rate (Gemulla, Nijkamp, Haas, & Sismanis, 2011).

Matrix Factorization - How to Implement

Implementing a matrix factorization-based recommender from scratch is an effort intensive process. The Recommenders extension (Mihelčić et al., 2012) offers prebuilt operators to implement Biased Matrix Factorization recommendation engines. As with the neighborhood-based recommender implementation, the MovieLens dataset from GroupLens[3] with 100,000 ratings given by 1000 users for 1700 titles is used for building the recommender using matrix factorization.

---

[3] http://grouplens.org/datasets/movielens

Implementation Steps

The outline of the RapidMiner process for the matrix factorization-based recommender is shown in Fig. 11.8. The process is similar to the process used in neighborhood-based methods, with the only change to the modeling operator—Biased Matrix Factorization (BMF)

1. **Data Preparation:** The central operator in this is process is the modeling operator called BMF. As a collaborative filtering method, the only input needed for the modeling operator is ratings matrix. The *Set role* operator is used to declare the attributes for "user identification", "item identification," and the label. The data is randomly split between training (95%) and test dataset (5%).

2. **Modeling:** The modeling operator is BMF—found under Recommenders > Item rating prediction > Collaborative Filtering Rating Prediction. These parameters can be configured in the modeling operator to suit the application:

   a. **Min and Max ratings:** The ratings range in the training dataset. The movie ratings dataset has ratings from 0 to 5.

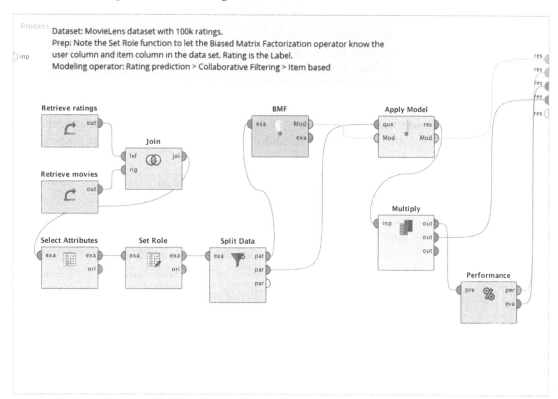

FIGURE 11.8

Matrix factorization recommender process.

b. **Num Factors (_f_):** The number of latent factors inferred from the ratings dataset. Specifying the number of latent factors is critical in matrix factorization modeling. However, similar to _k_-NN and clustering techniques, specifying an optimal number of factors is tricky. Hence, the parameter optimization technique discussed in Chapter 15 Getting started with RapidMiner may need to be employed to find the best number of latent factors for the dataset to obtain optimal performance. In this process, the number of latent factors is set as 12.

c. **Bias:** Bias regularization parameter. The default value is set as 0.0001.

d. **Learn Rate (α):** Learning rate in the Stochastic Gradient Descent algorithm. SGD is used to optimize the parameters to minimize the function in Eq. (11.12). The value is set as 0.005 for this process.

e. **Regularization (λ):** Regularization tuning parameter. The default value is set as 0.015.

3. **Apply Model to test set:** The _Apply Model (Rating Prediction)_ operator is used to apply the training model to the test dataset. The model and the test dataset serve as input to the apply model operator and the output is the predicted rating for all the test records.

4. **Performance evaluation:** The output of the predicted test dataset from the _Apply Model_ operator is connected to the _Performance (Rating Prediction)_ operator to evaluate if the predicted rating is close to the actual rating provided by the users.

The RapidMiner process shown in Fig. 11.8 can be saved and executed. The result window shows the predicted dataset, the recommender model and the performance vector. In addition to the attributes in the test dataset, a new

Row No.	rating	userId	movieId	title	genres	prediction
1	2.500	1	2455	Fly, The (1986)	Drama|Horror|Sci-Fi|Thriller	2.854
2	3	2	339	While You Were Sleeping (1995)	Comedy|Romance	3.078
3	3	2	410	Addams Family Values (1993)	Children|Comedy|Fantasy	2.813
4	3	2	539	Sleepless in Seattle (1993)	Comedy|Drama|Romance	3.059
5	3	2	550	Threesome (1994)	Comedy|Romance	2.838
6	3	2	588	Aladdin (1992)	Adventure|Animation|Childre...	3.505
7	4	2	661	James and the Giant Peach (19...	Adventure|Animation|Childre...	3.158
8	4	2	720	Wallace & Gromit: The Best of A...	Adventure|Animation|Comedy	3.733
9	3	4	431	Carlito's Way (1993)	Crime|Drama	4.411
10	5	4	1194	Cheech and Chong's Up in Smok...	Comedy	4.444

FIGURE 11.9
Predicted ratings using matrix factorization recommender.

rating prediction column is appended to the dataset. A sample of ten test records are shown in Fig. 11.9 with the original unseen ratings and the predicted ratings.

The results window also contains the performance vector which shows the RMSE and MAE for the ratings prediction for the test dataset. The RMSE for the BMF model is 0.953 stars and MAE is 0.730 stars.

11.3 CONTENT-BASED FILTERING

The collaborative filtering method uses the past user-item interaction data as the only input for building the recommenders. Content or attribute-based recommenders use the explicit properties of an item (attributes) in addition to the past user-item interaction data as inputs for the recommenders. They operate under the assumption that the items with similar properties have similar ratings at the user level. This assumption makes intuitive sense. If a user liked the movies *Frago, No Country for Old Men*, and *Burn After Reading*, then the user would most likely prefer *The Big Lebowski*, which are all directed by the same people—the Coen brothers. Content-based recommendation engines keep suggesting an item to a user similar to the items rated highly by the same user. The user will most likely get recommendations about movies with the same cast or director as the user preferred in the past.

The distinguishing feature of the content-based recommendation engine is that it sources attributes of an item, also known as building the item profile. The attribute data about the movies are readily available in public databases like IMDB,[4] where the cast, directors, genre, description, and the year of the title can be sourced. The item attributes can be derived from structured catalogs, tags, or unstructured data from the item description and images.

The general framework of a content-based recommendation engine is shown in Fig. 11.10. The model consumes ratings matrix and item profiles. The output of the model either fills the entire ratings matrix or provides just the top item recommendation for each user.

Predicting ratings using a content-based recommendation method involves two steps. The first step is to build a good item profile. Each item in the catalog can be represented as a vector of its profile attributes. The second step is to extract the recommendations from the item profile and ratings matrix. There are two distinct methods used for extracting recommendations: a user profile-based approach and a supervised learning-based approach.

---

[4] https://www.imdb.com/

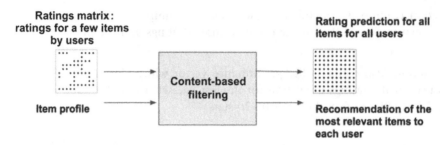

FIGURE 11.10
Model for content-based recommendation engine.

The user profile approach computes the preference of users to the item attributes from the ratings matrix. The proximity of the users and the items against the item attribute space indicates the preference of the user to the items. Whereas, the supervised learning approach treats the user preference of attributes as a *user level* classification or regression problem with the ratings matrix serving as the label (target) and item attributes as the predictors (feature). If one uses a decision tree as the supervised learning technique, then *each* user will have a personalized decision tree. The nodes in the decision tree will be checking an item attribute to predict whether the user will prefer the item or not.

Building an Item Profile

An item profile is a set features or discrete characteristics about an item in the form of a matrix. Features, also called attributes, provide a description of an item. Each item can be considered as a vector against the set of attributes. In case of the books, the attributes may be the publisher, author, genre, subgenre, etc. In the case of movies, the attributes may be individual cast members, year, genre, director, producer, etc. A matrix can be built with columns as the universe of attributes for *all the items* where each row is a distinct item. The cells can be Boolean flags indicating if the item is associated with the attribute or not. Similar to the document vectors discussed in Chapter 9, Text Mining, the number of columns or attributes will be large and the matrix will be sparse. Table 11.8 shows a sample item profile or item feature matrix for the movies with the attributes as cast, directors, genre, etc.

The item profile can be sourced from the providers of the item (e.g., product sellers in an e-commerce platform) or from third-party metadata providers (IMDB has metadata on a vast selection of movies). The item description provides a wealth of features about the products. Chapter 9, Text Mining discusses relevant tools like term frequency-inverse document frequency (TF-IDF) to

Table 11.8 Item Profile

Movie	Tom Hanks	Helen Miren	...	Joel Coen	Kathryn Bigelow	...	Romantic	Action
Fargo				1				
Forrest Gump	1							
Queen		1						
Sleepless in Seattle	1						1	
Eye in the Sky		1						1

extract features from documents such as item description. If the items are news articles in an online news portal, text mining is used to extract features from news articles. In this case, the item profile contains important words in the columns and the cells of the matrix indicate whether the words appear in the document of the individual items. At the end item profile creation process, there will be a set of attributes that best describe the characteristics of each item. The matrix contains information on whether each item possess those attributes or not. Once the item profile is assembled, the recommendations can be extracted using either a user profile computation approach or a supervised learning approach.

11.3.1 User Profile Computation

The user profile approach computes the user-item preference by building a user feature matrix in addition to the item feature matrix. The user feature matrix or the user profile maps the user preference to the *same features* used in the item feature matrix, thereby, measuring the strength of preference of the user to the features. Just like item profile vector, a user profile can be represented in a vector form in the feature space. The proximity of the user and the item vector indicates the strength of preference of the items to the users. Proximity measures like centered cosine metric discussed in the neighborhood based methods is used to measure the preference between a user and an item. The proximity measure between user and item is used to provide recommendations of the item to the user. This approach is similar to matrix factorization as both the methods express the ratings in terms of a user's preference to a set of features and items associated to the same features. Content-based recommenders using user profile computation differs from matrix factorization with regards to how the features are derived. Content-based recommenders start with a known feature set for the items and matrix factorization infers a set of specified features from the ratings matrix.

The user profile is built from the combination of the item profile and the known ratings matrix. Suppose R is the ratings matrix with m users and n items. I is the item profile matrix with n items and f features or attributes. The extracted user profile will be the matrix U with m users and exactly the same f features from the item profile. Fig. 11.11 shows the visual representation of the matrix operation.

Consider the two matrices shown in Tables 11.9 and 11.10. The matrix R is the ratings matrix with six users and five movies. This is a Boolean matrix with 1 indicating that the user likes the movie and the blank indicating no explicit preference for the movie. The matrix I is the item profile with f columns, starting with the cast, ..., director, movie genre. In practice, f will span thousands of columns, which is a superset of all the cast members, directors, and genres of all the movies in the catalog.

The user profile U can be derived in such a way than the value-shown user profile is percent of the time that the feature appears in the movies liked by the user. For example, Olivia likes the movies *Fargo*, *Queen*, and *Eye in the Sky*. Two-thirds of all the movies liked by Olivia have Helen Mirren in the cast (*Queen* and *Eye in the Sky*). All the movies (*Forrest Gump* and *Sleepless in Seattle*) liked by Josephine have Tom Hanks in the cast. The generic formula for the cells in the user profile U is the number of times the feature appears

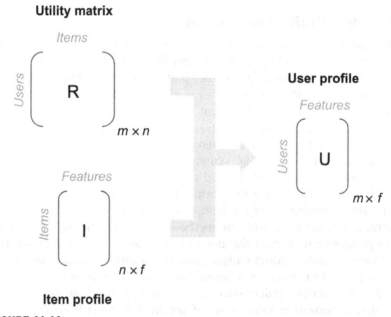

FIGURE 11.11
User profile from utility matrix and item profile.

Table 11.9 Ratings Matrix R

	Fargo	Forrest Gump	Queen	Sleepless in Seattle	Eye in the Sky
Josephine		1		1	
Olivia	1		1		1
Amelia		1			
Zoe	1				
Alanna					
Kim		1			

Table 11.10 Item Profile I

Movie	Tom Hanks	Helen Mirren	...	Joel Coen	Kathryn Bigelow	...	Romantic	Action
Fargo				1				
Forrest Gump	1							
Queen		1						
Sleepless in Seattle	1						1	
Eye in the Sky		1						1

in the movies liked by the user divided by the number of movies liked by the user. Table 11.11 shows the user profile U.

The user feature vector for Amelia is $U = \{1,0,\ldots,0,0,\ldots,0,0\}$ and the item feature vector for *Fargo* is $I = \{0,0,\ldots,1,0,\ldots,0,0\}$ and *Forrest Gump* is $I = \{1,0,\ldots,0,0,\ldots,0,0\}$. Out of these two item vectors, *Forrest Gump* is closer (in fact, perfect match in this example) to Amelia's user vector and, hence, it gets recommended.

As more becomes known about the user's preferences (when the user "likes" a title), the user profile is updated. Consequently, the weights of the user-feature matrix are updated and the latest user profile is used to compare against all the items in the item profile. Note that in this method, unlike the collaborative filtering approach, no information from *other users* is needed to make recommendations. This feature makes the content-based recommendation system a good fit to address the cold start problem, especially when a new item is added to the system. When a new movie title is added to the system, the item attributes are already known a priori. Therefore, the new items can be instantly recommended to the relevant users. However, the content-based method needs more consistent information about each item to make

Table 11.11 User Profile U

	Tom Hanks	Helen Mirren	...	Joel Coen	Kathryn Bigelow	...	Romantic	Action
Josephine	1						1/2	
Olivia		2/3						1/3
Amelia	1							
Zoe				1				
Alanna								
Kim	1							

meaningful recommendations to the users. The content-based recommenders do not entirely address the cold start problem for new users. Some information is still needed on the new user's item preferences to make a recommendation for new users.

Content-Based Filtering - How to Implement

In addition to the standard ratings matrix, a content-based recommender needs the item profile. Sourcing item attribute dataset is one more additional data pre-processing step to be built in the data science tool for creating a content-based recommendation engine. In RapidMiner, implementing the content-based recommenders can be accomplished using the Recommender extension operators.

Dataset

The same MovieLens[5] ratings matrix dataset used earlier in collaborative filtering is used to implement content-based recommenders. There are two datasets provided by MovieLens. The first datafile contains a ratings matrix, with user ID, movie ID, and ratings. The ratings matrix has 100,000 ratings given by 1000 users for 1700 titles. The movie datafile contains limited metadata about the movie ID: title and concatenated genres. This second dataset will serve as the item profile to build the content-based filtering.

Implementation steps

The outline of the RapidMiner process for the recommender is shown in Fig. 11.12. The high-level process for building a content-based recommendation engine consists of preparing the ratings matrix, preparing the item profile, recommender model building, applying the model to known test ratings, and the performance evaluation.

1. **Data preparation:** The modeling operator for the content-based recommender process is item attribute k-NN which can be found under

---

[5] GroupLens.org

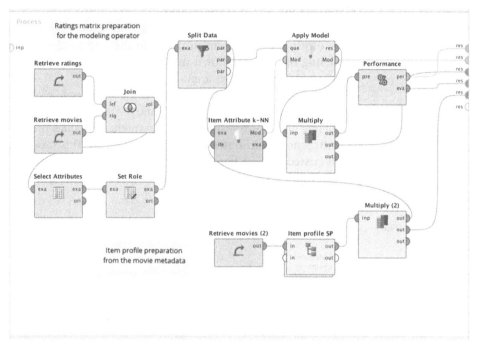

FIGURE 11.12
Recommender process using content-based filtering.

Recommenders > Item rating prediction > Attribute-based Rating Prediction. The inputs for the modeling operator are (1) the ratings matrix and (2) the item profile. The ratings matrix is in the form of User identification (user ID), Item identification (movie ID), and the label (Rating), similar to the process used in collaborative filtering. *Set role* operator is used to declare which attribute is the "user identification", "item identification," or the label.

2. **Item profile preparation:** Content-based recommenders will need the item profile for building the recommender model. The second dataset from MovieLens is in the form of Movie ID, Title, and Genres, as shown in Fig. 11.14A. The column Genres is a concatenated list of genres that a title will belong to with each genre separated by | character. For example, the movie *Toy Story* belongs to Adventure, Animation, Children, Comedy, and Fantasy genres. However, the format of the item profile that is needed by the *Item attribute k-NN* modeling operator is shown in Fig. 11.14C where each record has one distinct movie-genre combination. The movie *Toy Story* (Movie ID = 1) is pivoted into five rows, one for each genre (Genre = 4,5,6,7,11). The item profile dataset represented in Fig. 11.14A would need to be transformed into the item profile shown in Fig. 11.15C. The following section

highlights the fact that the most time-consuming part of a data science process is gathering and processing data. The subprocess of transforming the raw item profile into the one needed for the modeling operator is shown in Fig. 11.13A. The key steps in this data transformation task are:

a. *Text mining*: The Genre attributes contain values like Adventure| Animation|Children|Comedy|Fantasy. The *text to attributes using text mining* operator transforms the concatenated values into independent attributes shown in Fig. 11.14B. This process is discussed in the Chapter 9, Text Mining. The key operator in the text mining subprocess is *Tokenize*—to convert the genre words to

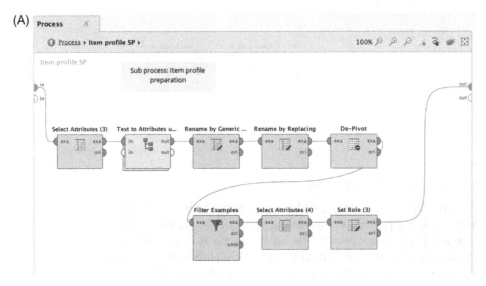

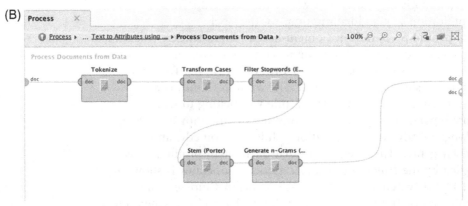

FIGURE 11.13

(A) Subprocess to create an Item profile. (B) Text mining subprocess to convert text to attributes.

(A)

Row No.	movieId	title	genres
1	1	Toy Story (1995)	Adventure|Animation|Children|Comedy|Fantasy
2	2	Jumanji (1995)	Adventure|Children|Fantasy
3	3	Grumpier Old Men (1995)	Comedy|Romance
4	4	Waiting to Exhale (1995)	Comedy|Drama|Romance
5	5	Father of the Bride Part II (19…	Comedy
6	6	Heat (1995)	Action|Crime|Thriller
7	7	Sabrina (1995)	Comedy|Romance
8	8	Tom and Huck (1995)	Adventure|Children
9	9	Sudden Death (1995)	Action
10	10	GoldenEye (1995)	Action|Adventure|Thriller

(B)

movieId	(no genres …	?	action	adventur	anim	children	comedi	crime	documentari
1	0	0	0	1	1	1	1	0	0
2	0	0	0	1	0	1	0	0	0
3	0	0	0	0	0	0	1	0	0
4	0	0	0	0	0	0	1	0	0
5	0	0	0	0	0	0	1	0	0
6	0	0	1	0	0	0	0	1	0
7	0	0	0	0	0	0	1	0	0
8	0	0	0	1	0	1	0	0	0
9	0	0	1	0	0	0	0	0	0
10	0	0	1	1	0	0	0	0	0

(C)

Row No.	movieId	Genre
1	1	4
2	1	5
3	1	6
4	1	7
5	1	11
6	2	4
7	2	6
8	2	11
9	3	7
10	3	17

FIGURE 11.14

(A) Item profile with concatenated genre. (B) Item profile with attributes. (C) Item profile with attribute information in rows.

attributes. The parameter to split the words is the character (|) which is specified in the *tokenize* operator.

b. ***Attribute naming for De-Pivot:*** Before the columns can be de-pivoted to rows, the columns should be renamed so the *de-Pivot* operator can work this dataset. The columns are renamed to generic attr1, attr2, ..., etc.

c. ***De-Pivot:*** The *de-pivot* operator converts the columns information to rows. The Genre in the column for each movie is now a distinct row. This operator expands the row count of the table from count (movie ID) to count [movie ID × distinct (genre)].

d. ***Filtering and set role:*** The output of de-pivot has both the negative and positive examples. Only the positive examples are needed, and the negative examples can be filtered out. The *Set role* operator is used to declare Movie ID as "item identification" and Genre as "attribute identification". The dataset is now suitable to be used for the modeling operator. The attribute columns for the items are folded into one column (Genre) which indicates all the attributes the item possesses.

3. **Recommender Modeling**: The modeling operator *item attribute K-NN* receives both the ratings matrix and the item profile as the inputs. There are a few parameters to configure based on the application and the input data

   a. **k:** Nearest neighbor cohort size. The predicted rating is based on the distance between the user vector and the item vector. k is set as 10 in this process.

   b. **Min and Max ratings:** Ratings range in the dataset. It is set as 0 and 5 for minimum and maximum ratings.

4. **Apply Model to test set:** The *Apply Model (Rating Prediction)* operator is used to apply the training model to the test dataset. A portion of the original dataset that was reserved for testing is used as an input for the Apply Model operator which calculates the predicted ratings for each user-item combination in the test dataset.

5. **Performance evaluation:** The output of the predicted test dataset from the *Apply Model* operator is connected to the *Performance (Rating Prediction)* operator to evaluate if the predicted rating is close to the actual rating provided by the users.

The RapidMiner process shown in Fig. 11.12 can be saved and executed. The result window shows the original dataset with a new prediction column appended to the dataset. A sample of ten records are shown in Fig. 11.15. The result tab also has the performance vector.

The performance vector shown as the result of the performance evaluation operator reports the RMSE and MAE of rating prediction. RMSE of the rating

Row No.	rating	userId	movieId	title	genres	prediction
1	2.500	1	2455	Fly, The (1986)	Drama|Horror|Sci...	2.367
2	3	2	339	While You Were Sleeping (1995)	Comedy|Romance	3.174
3	3	2	410	Addams Family Values (1993)	Children|Comedy...	3.003
4	3	2	539	Sleepless in Seattle (1993)	Comedy|Drama|R...	3.359
5	3	2	550	Threesome (1994)	Comedy|Romance	2.999
6	3	2	588	Aladdin (1992)	Adventure|Anima...	3.429
7	4	2	661	James and the Giant Peach (1996)	Adventure|Anima...	3.737
8	4	2	720	Wallace & Gromit: The Best of A...	Adventure|Anima...	4.053
9	3	4	431	Carlito's Way (1993)	Crime|Drama	4.746
10	5	4	1194	Cheech and Chong's Up in Smok...	Comedy	4.186

FIGURE 11.15
Predicted rating using content-based filtering.

Table 11.12 Item Profile With Class Label for One User

Movie	Tom Hanks	Helen Mirren	...	Joel Coen	Kathryn Bigelow	...	Romantic	Action	Class label for Olivia
Fargo				1					1
Forrest Gump	1								0
Queen		1							1
Sleepless in Seattle	1						1		0
Eye in the Sky		1						1	1

prediction is 0.915 stars for the neighborhood-based recommender using the MovieLens dataset. The MAE is 0.703 stars.

11.3.2 Supervised Learning Models

A supervised learning model-based recommender approaches the problem of user-item preference prediction at the individual user level. If a user has expressed interest in a few items and if those items have features, then the interest of the users to those features can be inferred. Consider the user-item ratings matrix shown in Table 11.8 and the item profile matrix shown in Table 11.10. The item profile matrix can be customized *just for one user*, say Olivia, by introducing a new column in the item profile to indicate whether Olivia likes the movie. This yields the item profile matrix for one user (Olivia) shown in Table 11.12. This matrix is strikingly similar to the training data used in the supervised models discussed in Chapter 4, Classification and Chapter 5, Regression Methods. With the exception of the first column (Movie title) which can be ignored as ID, all the attributes in the item profile table are features or independent variables in the training set. The last column, newly introduced indicator for one user, is the class label or the dependent variable. A classification model can be built to generalize the relationship between the attributes to the user preference and the resultant model can be used to predict the preference for any unseen new items for a specific user.

The classification model, say a decision tree, can be built by learning the attribute preferences for Olivia and the model can be applied to the catalog for all the movies not seen by Oliva. Classification models predict user preference of the item attributes. The supervised learning model-based approach treats recommendation tasks as a user-specific classification or regression problem and learns a classifier for the user's likes and dislikes based on the product features.

In the supervised learning model—based approach, each user has a personalized decision tree. Suppose one has a straightforward preference for movies: they only like it if the movie has Helen Mirren in the cast or is directed by the Coen brothers. Their personalized decision tree would be like the one in Fig. 11.16

The decision tree shown in Fig. 11.16 is a classification tree for the user Oliva using the item profile shown in Table 11.12. For another user, the tree would be different. For the ratings prediction problem, one could use regression models to predict the numerical ratings. Given that a user provides explicit ratings only for a few items, the challenge is inferring a pattern from a few positive ratings for items and from thousands of attributes of those items. Complementing the explicit ratings with the implicit outcomes (watching a movie, product views, items in the cart) will be helpful to boost the recommendations.

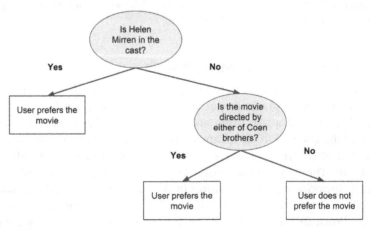

FIGURE 11.16
Personalized decision tree for one user in the system.

Supervised Learning Models – How to Implement

The supervised learning (classification) model approach for a content-based recommendation engine builds a classification model for each user. Hence, the model building is shown for one user and the process can be repeated in the loop for each user in the ratings matrix. The implementation step closely resembles the modeling process discussed in Chapter 4, Classification. The rule induction modeling technique is used in this recommender implementation. It can be replaced with various other classification or regression modeling techniques to suit the application and the data.

Dataset

The datasets used for the process is from MovieLens database with two datasets. The first dataset (ratings dataset) contains ratings, user ID and movie ID attributes. The second dataset (item dataset) contains limited metadata about each movie—movie ID, movie title, and concatenated genre attributes. To create the supervised learning model, these two datasets have to be merged to one dataset that has labels and attributes for one user.

Implementation steps

The outline of the complete RapidMiner process is shown in Fig. 11.17. The high-level process for a model-based approach to content-based recommendation engine contains: data preparation for classification modeling, model building, apply the model to test set and performance evaluation.

1. **Data Preparation:** The movie dataset structure is shown in Fig. 11.18A. Each movie has a title and the concatenated genres separated by | symbol. The first step is to convert this data structure to the structure

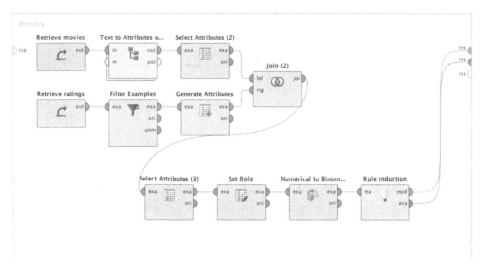

FIGURE 11.17

Classification process for one user in the system.

shown in Fig. 11.18B. The structure shown in Fig. 11.18B is conducive for classification modeling where each genre is shown as a separate attribute, with the value as 0 or 1 based on whether the movie is of that genre. For example, the movie *Toy story (movie id = 1)* is listed in

(A)

Row No.	movieId	title	genres
1	1	Toy Story (1995)	Adventure|Animation|Children|Comedy|Fantasy
2	2	Jumanji (1995)	Adventure|Children|Fantasy
3	3	Grumpier Old Men (1995)	Comedy|Romance
4	4	Waiting to Exhale (1995)	Comedy|Drama|Romance
5	5	Father of the Bride Part II (19...	Comedy
6	6	Heat (1995)	Action|Crime|Thriller
7	7	Sabrina (1995)	Comedy|Romance
8	8	Tom and Huck (1995)	Adventure|Children
9	9	Sudden Death (1995)	Action
10	10	GoldenEye (1995)	Action|Adventure|Thriller

(B)

movieId	(no genres ...	?	action	adventur	anim	children	comedi	crime	documentari
1	0	0	0	1	1	1	1	0	0
2	0	0	0	1	0	1	0	0	0
3	0	0	0	0	0	0	1	0	0
4	0	0	0	0	0	0	1	0	0
5	0	0	0	0	0	0	1	0	0
6	0	0	1	0	0	0	0	1	0
7	0	0	0	0	0	0	1	0	0
8	0	0	0	1	0	1	0	0	0
9	0	0	1	0	0	0	0	0	0
10	0	0	1	1	0	0	0	0	0

(C)

Row No.	userId	rating_b	(no genres ...	?	action	adventur	anim	children
1	549	false	0	0	0	0	0	0
2	549	true	0	0	0	0	0	0
3	549	false	0	0	0	0	0	0
4	549	true	0	0	0	0	0	0
5	549	true	0	0	0	0	0	0
6	549	false	0	0	0	0	0	0
7	549	true	0	0	0	0	0	0
8	549	true	0	0	0	0	0	0
9	549	true	0	0	0	0	0	0
10	549	true	0	0	0	0	0	0

FIGURE 11.18

(A) Item profile with concatenated genre. (B) Item profile with genre as attributes. (C) Item profile with class label for the user 549.

following categories: Adventure, Comedy, Animation, Children, and Fantasy.

Text mining data processing is used to convert the data structure from Fig. 11.18A to B. In the text mining subprocess, the genre attribute is converted to text. Each word is tokenized from the concatenated genre text using the delimiter |. Each token is then case converted and stemmed to provide word vector for each movie. The text mining subprocess is shown in Fig. 11.19.

The movie-genre vector shown in Fig. 11.18B, can now be merged with the preference information of a user. The ratings matrix is filtered for one user, user 549, using the *Filter example* operator. To simplify the rating scale, the 0−5 scale is converted to boolean true (3 or more) or false (below 3) using the formula in *Generate Attributes*. A numeric rating label is preferable in production models because it contains more information than the boolean true/false. The five-point rating is converted from numeric to categorical just to illustrate a simple classification model for this implementation. The rating information for the user can be merged to the movie profile using the inner *Join* operator. In this process, the result set will just contain the titles rated by the user. The resultant dataset is shown in Fig. 11.18C, where rating_b is the preference class label and the rest of the columns are predictors.

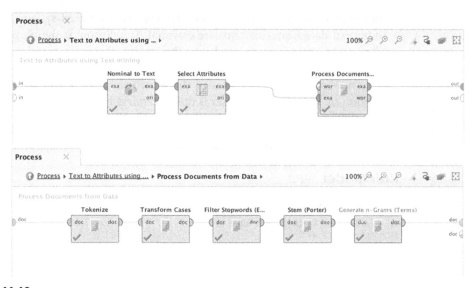

FIGURE 11.19

Subprocess to convert the item profile to classification training set.

2. **Modeling:** A rule induction is used for classification modeling. The rule induction model and parameters are discussed in Chapter 4, Classification. The parameters specified in this process are: criterion = information gain and sample ration = 0.9. A decision tree or logistic regression can be used as an alternative to the rule induction.

The whole process shown in Fig. 11.17 can be saved and executed. The result window shows the model from rule induction (Fig. 11.20). Ideally, this model should have been tested with a test dataset and performance evaluated. Based on the rule induction model, user 549 has a preference for the Crime genre. This model can be run against all other movies in the catalog which are not rated and the predicted rating can be used to recommend titles to the user 549.

The model built using the RapidMiner process is customized for one user, user 549. This entire process can be looped for each user and the model can be stored in a separate dataset. The looping process is discussed in Chapter 15 Getting started with RapidMiner. Each user in the system will have a personalized model. The effectiveness of the model depends on each user's past rating and is independent of ratings from other users.

Content-based recommendation engines are better at explaining why the system is making the recommendation because it has generalized the features the user is interested in. For example, the system might recommend *Apollo 13*, *Saving private Ryan*, and *Captain Phillips* because the user is interested in movies that have Tom Hanks in the cast. Unlike the collaborative filtering method, data from other users is not needed for the content-based systems, however, additional data from the items are essential. This feature is significant because when a new user is introduced into the system, the recommendation engine does not suffer from the cold start problem. When a new item is introduced, say a new movie, the attributes of the movie are already known. Hence, the addition of a new item or a user is quite seamless for the recommenders.

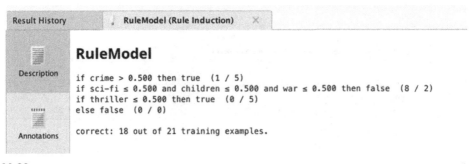

FIGURE 11.20

Rule induction model for one user in the system.

The key datasets involved in the recommendation, that is, the item profile, user profile or classification models, and the recommendation list, can be pre-computed. Since the main objective in many cases is finding the top recommended items instead of filling the complete ratings matrix, decision trees can focus only on the attributes relevant to the user.

Content-based recommenders tend to address unique preferences for the user. For example: users interested in Scandinavian crime thrillers. There may not be enough users who like this subgenre for collaborative filtering to be effective because a sizable cohort of users is needed to prefer these unique genres and other items in the catalog.

Even though rating information from other users are not necessary, an exhaustive item profile is essential for obtaining the relevant recommendations from content-based systems. The features of the item are hard to get to begin with and some attributes like genre taxonomy are difficult to master. Blockbuster items, are by definition, watched by a wider audience, beyond the fanatics of a particular genre. For example, one doesn't have to be a fan of science fiction to watch *Avatar*. Just because a user watched *Avatar* it doesn't mean that the recommender can be inundated with other science fiction movies. Special handling is required so the system doesn't conflate the success of blockbusters with the user preference for specific attributes in the blockbusters.

Content-based recommenders are content specific. For example, it makes logical sense to recommend Moroccan cooking utensils if the user has shown an interest in books focused on North African cuisine, if the ecommerce platform offers both the categories. Content-based systems will find this task to be difficult because the knowledge gained in a books category is hard to translate to a kitchen utensils category. Collaborative filtering is content agnostic.

11.4 HYBRID RECOMMENDERS

Each recommendation engine discussed in this chapter has a central idea and solves the problem of predicting the unseen user-item rating through a unique approach. Each recommendation model has its own strengths and limitations, that is, each works better in specific data setting than others. Some recommenders are robust at handling the cold start problem, have model biases, and tend to overfit the training dataset. As in the case of the ensemble classifiers, *hybrid recommenders* combine the model output of multiple base recommenders into one hybrid recommender. As long as the base models are independent, this approach limits the generalization error, improves the performance of the recommender, and overcomes the limitation of a single recommendation technique. The diversity of the base models can be imparted by selecting different

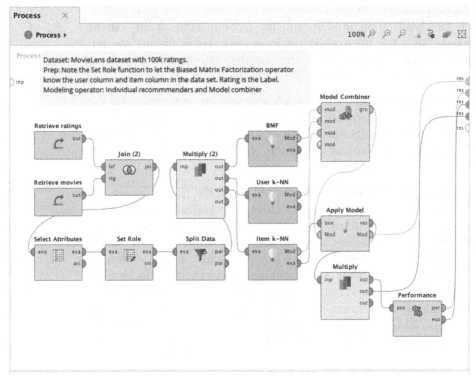

FIGURE 11.21

Hybrid recommenders using model combiner.

modeling techniques like neighborhood BMF, content-based and supervised model-based recommenders.

Fig. 11.21 shows the RapidMiner process of Hybrid recommender with base recommenders such as BMF, User K-NN and Item K-NN. The *Model Combiner* operator is the ensemble operator which combines all three models into one meta operator. It weighs the base models equally. All the base recommenders operate on the same training dataset. The performance of this hybrid recommender process for the MovieLens dataset is RMSE of 0.781 and MAE of 0.589. In this case, the performance of the Hybrid recommender is better than the results achieved with neighborhood or matrix factorization alone.

11.5 CONCLUSION

How does one know if the recommendations are relevant for the users? One would hope to see users taking up the offer of using the recommended items (watching, purchasing, reading,...) more than users acting on a random selection of items. An A/B experimental testing of "with" and "without" recommendation engines can help determine the overall impact of the recommendation engine in the system.

The data used by recommendation engines is considered sensitive under any standards because it is at the user level and indicates a user's preferences. A great deal of information about a person can be deduced when one knows the books they read, movies they watch, or the products they buy, let alone the combination of all three! (Siegel, 2016) Users implicitly entrust enterprises to safeguard their private information by implicitly or explicitly agreeing to the terms and conditions. Users prefer personalized experiences and they are willing to give some information about themselves by explicit rating information and implicit views or search information. How is the need for personalization balanced with the privacy of users? Transparency can be the enabler that strikes a balance between privacy and the benefits of personalization. Users have the right to know what inputs about them are used for recommenders: list of previously liked titles, searches, or any other clickstream data used as an input for recommenders. Users can inspect or remove their preference for the titles. The explainability of recommendations increases the trust that users have in the system. For example: one might like a list of titles because they have watched *Fargo*. In some jurisdictions for certain applications, users have the legal right to know why a recommendation or disposition is made about a user.

Personalization can lead to filter bubble, which is a state of intellectual isolation (Bozdag, 2013). Hyper personalized recommendation engines keep feeding items that a user is interested in and attenuate the usage of more diverse set of items. Personalization in news feeds causes reinforcement of one's political leaning and results in an echo chamber of viewpoints. Personalization, in a way, acts as a censor to filter out viewpoints that the user doesn't explicitly prefer. The algorithms that control personalization, especially in news sites and social media, play a significant role in shaping the political opinions of people. Enterprises have responded to the bias of filter bubbles by introducing the equivalent of best sellers: trending now, top news, etc.,—where a selection of un-personalized item selections are provided to the users, in addition to the personalized recommendations.

Summary of the Types of Recommendation Engines
See Table 11.13 for a summary of different types of recommendation engines.

Table 11.13 Comparison of Recommendation Engines

Type	Inputs	Assumption	Approach	Advantages	Limitations	Use Cases
Collaborative filtering	Ratings matrix with user-item preferences	Similar users or items have similar likes	Derives ratings from like-minded users (or items) and the corresponding known user-item interactions	The only input needed is the ratings matrix. Domain agnostic. More accurate than content-based filtering in most applications	Cold start problem for new users and items. Sparse entries in the rating matrix leads to poor coverage and recommendations. Computation grows linearly with the number of items and users.	eCommerce, music, new connection recommendations from Amazon, Last.fm, Spotify, LinkedIn, and Twitter
User-based CF (neighborhood)	Ratings matrix	Similar users rate items similarly	Finds a cohort of users who have provided similar ratings. Derives the outcome rating from the cohort users	User-to-user similarity can be pre-computed		
Item-based CF (neighborhood)	Ratings matrix	Users prefer items that are similar to previously preferred items	Finds a cohort of items which have been given similar ratings by the same users. Derives rating from cohort items	More accurate than user-based CF		
Latent matrix factorization	Ratings matrix	User's preference of an item can be better explained by their preference of an item's characteristics	Decomposes the User-Item matrix into two matrices (P and Q) with latent factors. Fills the blank values in the ratings matrix by dot product of P and Q	Works in sparse matrix. More accurate than neighborhood-based collaborative filtering.	Cannot explain why the prediction is made	

Content-based filtering	User-item rating matrix and item profile	Recommends items similar to those the user liked in the past	Abstracts the features of the item and builds an item profile. Uses the item profile to evaluate the user preference for the attributes in the item profile	Addresses cold start problem for new items and new users. Can provide explanations on why the recommendation is made. Provides descriptive recommendations.	Requires item profile dataset in addition to the ratings matrix. Recommenders are domain specific. Popular items skew the results	Music recommendation from Pandora and CiteSeer's citation indexing
User profile based	User-item rating matrix and item profile	User's preference for an item can be expressed by their preference for an item attribute	Builds a user profile with the same attributes as the item profile. Computes the rating based on similarity of the user profile and the item profile			
Supervised learning model based	User-item rating matrix and Item profile	Every time a user prefers an item, it is a vote of preference for the item's attributes	A personalized classification or regression model for every single user in the system. Learns a classifier based on user likes or dislikes of an item and its relationship with the item attributes	Every user has a separate model and could be independently customized.		

References

Bobadilla, J., Ortega, F., Hernando, A., & Gutiérrez, A. (2013). Recommender systems survey. *Knowledge-Based Systems*, *46*, 109−132. Available from https://doi.org/10.1016/J.KNOSYS.2013.03.012.

Bozdag, E. (2013). Bias in algorithmic filtering and personalization. *Ethics and Information Technology*, *15*(3), 209−227. Available from https://doi.org/10.1007/s10676-013-9321-6.

Cakir, O., & Aras, M. E. (2012). A Recommendation engine by using association rules. *Procedia−Social and Behavioral Sciences*, *62*, 452−456. Available from https://doi.org/10.1016/j.sbspro.2012.09.074.

Das, A.S., Datar, M., Garg, A., & Rajaram, S. (2007). Google news personalization. In: *Proceedings of the 16th international conference on World Wide Web−WWW '07* (p. 271). New York: ACM Press. <https://doi.org/10.1145/1242572.1242610>.

Gemulla, R., Nijkamp, E., Haas, P.J., & Sismanis, Y. (2011). Large-scale matrix factorization with distributed stochastic gradient descent. In: *Proceedings of the 17th ACM SIGKDD international conference on Knowledge discovery and data mining−KDD '11* (p. 69). New York: ACM Press. <https://doi.org/10.1145/2020408.2020426>.

Gupta, P., Goel, A., Lin, J., Sharma, A., Wang, D., & Zadeh, R. (2013). WTF: The who to follow service at twitter. In: *Proceedings of the 22nd international conference on World Wide Web - WWW '13* (pp. 505−514). New York: ACM Press. <https://doi.org/10.1145/2488388.2488433>.

Hu, Y., Koren, Y., & Volinsky, C. (2008). Collaborative filtering for implicit feedback datasets. In *2008 eighth IEEE international conference on data mining* (pp. 263−272). IEEE. <https://doi.org/10.1109/ICDM.2008.22>.

Isinkaye, F. O., Folajimi, Y. O., & Ojokoh, B. A. (2015). Recommendation systems: Principles, methods and evaluation. *Egyptian Informatics Journal*, *16*(3), 261−273. Available from https://doi.org/10.1016/J.EIJ.2015.06.005.

Koren, Y., Bell, R., & Volinsky, C. (2009). Matrix factorization techniques for recommender systems. *Computer*, *42*(8), 30−37. Available from https://doi.org/10.1109/MC.2009.263.

Lee, J., Sun, M., & Lebanon, G. (2012). *A comparative study of collaborative filtering algorithms*, pp. 1−27. Retrieved from <http://arxiv.org/abs/1205.3193>.

Mihelčić, M., Antulov-Fantulin, N., Bošnjak, M., & Šmuc, T. (2012). Extending RapidMiner with recommender systems algorithms. In: *RapidMiner community meeting and conference*.

Schafer, J. Ben, Konstan, J. A., & Riedl, J. (2001). E-commerce recommendation applications. *Data Mining and Knowledge Discovery*, *5*(1/2), 115−153. Available from https://doi.org/10.1023/A:1009804230409.

Siegel, Eric (2016). *Predictive analytics: The power to predict who will click, buy, lie, or die*. John Wiley & Sons Incorporated.

Thorson, E. (2008). Changing patterns of news consumption and participation. *Information, Communication & Society*, *11*(4), 473−489. Available from https://doi.org/10.1080/13691180801999027.

Underwood, C. (2017). *Use cases of recommendation systems in business−current applications and methods*. Retrieved on June 17, 2018, From <https://www.techemergence.com/use-cases-recommendation-systems/>.

Weise, E. (2017). That review you wrote on Amazon? Priceless. Retrieved on October 29, 2018, From <https://www.usatoday.com/story/tech/news/2017/03/20/review-you-wrote-amazon-priceless/99332602/>.

CHAPTER 12

Time Series Forecasting

Time series is a series of observations listed in the order of time. The data points in a time series are usually recorded at constant successive time intervals. Time series *analysis* is the process of extracting meaningful non-trivial information and patterns from time series. Time series *forecasting* is the process of predicting the future value of time series data based on past observations and other inputs. Time series forecasting is one of the oldest known predictive analytics techniques. It is widely used in every organizational setting and has deep statistical foundations. An example of a time series is shown in Fig. 12.1. It shows the time series value and period—monthly revenue of a product for a few years.

Up to this point in this book, supervised model building has been about collecting data from several different attributes of a *system* and using these attributes to fit a *function* to predict a desired quantity or target variable. For example, if the system was a housing market, the attributes may have been the price of a house, location, square footage, number of rooms, number of floors, age of the house, and so on. A multiple linear regression model or a neural network model could be built to predict the house price (target) variable given the independent (predictor) variables. Similarly, purchasing managers may use data from several different raw material commodity prices to model the cost of a product. The common thread among these predictive models is that predictors or independent variables that potentially influence a target (house price or product cost) are used to predict that target variable. The objective in time series forecasting is slightly different: to use historical information about a particular quantity to make forecasts about the value of the *same quantity* in the future.

In general, there are two important differences between time series analysis and other supervised predictive models. First, time is an important

Data Science. DOI: https://doi.org/10.1016/B978-0-12-814761-0.00012-5

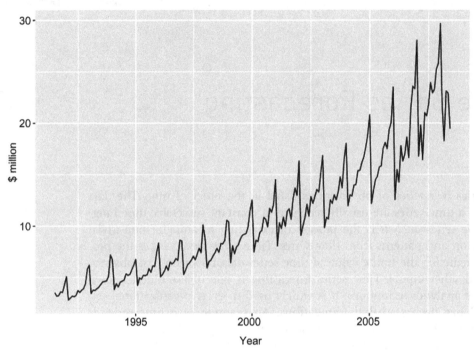

FIGURE 12.1
Time series of monthly antidiabetic drug sales.[1]

predictor in many applications. In time series analysis one is concerned with forecasting a specific variable, given that it is known how this variable has changed over time in the past. In all other predictive models discussed so far, the time component of the data was either ignored or was not available. Such data are known as *cross-sectional* data. Consider the problem of predicting the house price based on location, square footage, number of rooms, number of floors, and age of the house. The predictors are observed in a point in time (like a cross-section of a block of wood in Fig. 12.2) and the price is predicted in the same point in time. However, it is important to take the time variable (length of wood) to predict something like house prices. It fluctuates up and down based on economic conditions, supply and demand, etc., which are all influenced by time.

---

[1] Total monthly scripts for pharmaceutical products falling under ATC code A10, as recorded by the Australian Health Insurance Commission. July 1991–June 2008 (Hyndman & Athanasopoulos, 2018).

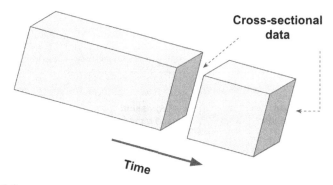

FIGURE 12.2
Cross-sectional data is a subset of time series data.

Second, one may not be interested in or might not even have data for other attributes that could potentially influence the target variable. In other words, independent or predictor variables are not strictly necessary for univariate time series forecasting but are strongly recommended for multivariate time series.

TAXONOMY OF TIME SERIES FORECASTING

The investigation of time series can also be broadly divided into *descriptive* modeling, called time series analysis, and *predictive* modeling, called time series forecasting. Time Series forecasting can be further classified into four broad categories of techniques: Forecasting based on time series decomposition, smoothing based techniques, regression based techniques, and machine learning-based techniques. Fig. 12.3 shows the classification of time series forecasting techniques.

Time series decomposition is the process of deconstructing a time series into the number of constituent components with each representing an underlying phenomenon. Decomposition splits the time series into a trend component, a seasonal component, and a noise component. The trend and seasonality components are predictable (and are called systematic components), whereas, the noise, by definition, is random (and is called the non-systematic component). Before forecasting the time series, it is important to understand and describe the components that make the time series. These individual components can be better forecasted using regression or similar techniques and combined together as an aggregated

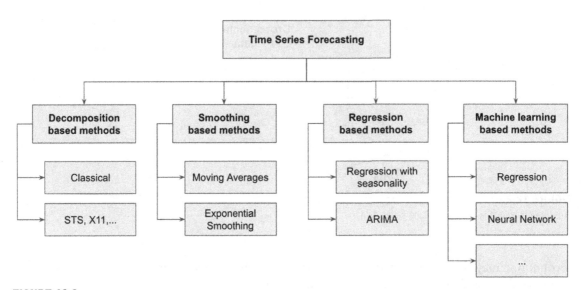

FIGURE 12.3

Taxonomy of time series forecasting techniques.

forecasted time series. This technique is called forecasting with decomposition.

Time series can be thought as past observations informing future predictions. To forecast future data, one can smooth past observations and project it to the future. Such time series forecasting methods are called smoothing based forecasting methods. In smoothing methods, the future value of the time series is the weighted average of past observations.

Regression based forecasting techniques are similar to conventional supervised predictive models, which have independent and dependent variables, but with a twist: the independent variable is now time. The simplest of such methods is of course a linear regression model of the form:

$$y_t = a \times t + b \tag{12.1}$$

where y_t is the value of the target variable at time t. Given a training set, the values of coefficients a and b can be estimated to forecast future y values. Regression based techniques can get pretty complicated with the type of function used to model the relationship between future value and time. Commonly used functions are exponential, polynomial, and power law functions.

Most people are familiar with the trend line function in spreadsheet programs, which offer several different function choices. The regression based time series forecast differs from a regular function-fitting predictive model in the choice of the independent variable. A more sophisticated technique is based on the concept of autocorrelation. Autocorrelation refers to the fact that data from adjacent time periods are correlated in a time series. The most well-known among these techniques is ARIMA, which stands for Auto Regressive Integrated Moving Average.

Any supervised classification or regression predictive models can be used to forecast the time series too, if the time series data are transformed to a particular format with a target label and input variables. This class of techniques are based on supervised machine learning models where the input variables are derived from the time series using a *windowing* technique. The windowing technique transforms a time series to a cross-sectional like dataset where the input variables are lagged data points for an observation. The artificial neural network-based time series forecasting has particular relevance because of its resemblance with the ARIMA technique.

FORECASTING DEMAND OF A PRODUCT

A common application of a time series is to forecast the demand for a product. A manufacturing company makes anti-corrosion wax tapes for use in gas and oil pipelines. The company makes more than a dozen varieties of wax tape products using a handful of assembly lines. The demand for these products varies depending on several factors. For example, routine pipeline maintenance is typically done during warm weather seasons. So, there could be a seasonal spike in the demand. Also, over the last several years, growth in emerging economies has meant that the demand for their products has been growing. Finally, any upcoming changes in pricing, which the company may announce ahead of time, may also trigger stockpiling by their customers, resulting in sudden jumps in demand. So, there can be both trend and seasonality factors, as shown in a sample series Fig. 12.4.

The product manager of the product needs to be able to predict the demand of their products on a monthly, quarterly, and annual basis so that they can plan the production using their limited resources and their department's budget. They make use of the time series forecasting models to predict the potential demand for each of their product lines. By studying the seasonal patterns and growth trends, they can better prepare their production lines. For example, studying seasonality in the sales for the #2 wax tape, which is heavily used in cold climates, reveals that March and April are the months with the highest number of orders placed as customers buy them ahead of the maintenance seasons starting in the summer months. So, the plant manager can dedicate most of their production lines to manufacturing the #2 tape during these months. This insight would not be known unless a time series analysis and forecasting was performed.

(Continued)

(Continued)

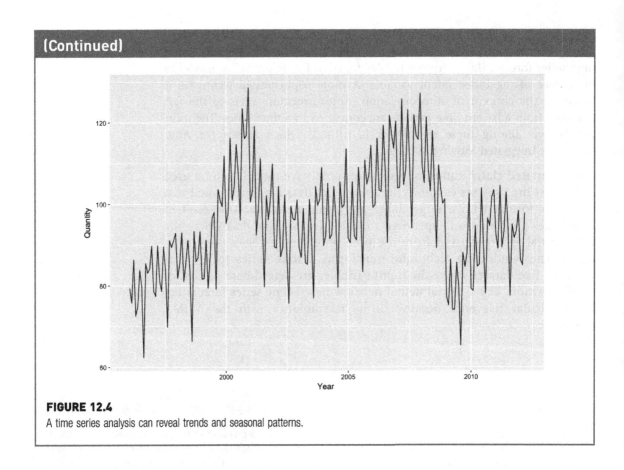

FIGURE 12.4

A time series analysis can reveal trends and seasonal patterns.

12.1 TIME SERIES DECOMPOSITION

Time series data, are univariate, an amalgamation of multiple underlying phenomenon. Consider the example shown in Fig. 12.1. It is a time series of monthly antidiabetic drug sales. A few observations can be made about this time series. Firstly, the overall drug sales is trending upward and the upward trend accelerates in the 2000s. Secondly, there is clear seasonality in the time series of drug sales. In particular, it is a yearly seasonality. There is a spike in drug sales at the start of the year and a dip in every February. This seasonal variation is consistent every year. However, even when accounting for the trend and the seasonal variations there is one more phenomenon that could not be explained. For example, the pattern in 2007 is odd when compared with prior years or 2008.

This unattributable phenomenon can be assumed as noise in the time series. Now that an intuitive understanding of the underlying phenomena of the time series has been developed, the formal definitions of different components that make up a time series can be discussed.

Trend: Trend is the long-term tendency of the data. It represents change from one period to next. If a trend line has been inserted in over a chart in a spreadsheet, it is the regression equation line that represents the trend component of a time series. The trends can be further split into a zero-basis trend and the level in the data. The level in the time series does not change with respect to time while the zero-basis trend does change with the time.

Seasonality: Seasonality is the repetitive behavior during a cycle of time. These are repeated patterns appearing over and over again in the time series. Seasonality can be further split into hourly, daily, weekly, monthly, quarterly, and yearly seasonality. Consider the revenue generated by an online finance portal, like Yahoo Finance or Morningstar. The visits would clearly indicate a daily seasonality with the difference in the number of people accessing the portal or the app during the day time, especially during the market open hours, and the nighttime. Weekdays will have higher traffic (and revenue) than during the weekends. Moreover, the online advertising spend shows quarterly seasonality as the advertisers adjust marketing spend during the end of the quarter. The revenue will also show yearly seasonality where end of the year, after Christmas, shows weakness in revenue because of holidays.

Cycle: Cyclic component represents longer-than-a-year patterns where there is no specific time frames between the cycles. An example here is the economic cycle of booms and crashes. While the booms and crashes exhibit a repeated pattern, the length of a boom period, the length of a recession, the time between subsequent booms and crashes (and even two consecutive crashes—double dip) is uncertain and random, unlike the seasonality components. Fig. 12.1, on the antidiabetic drug sales, shows an accelerated upward trend after the year 2000 which may represent a cyclic component or a non-linear trend. It is hard to conclude anything in this time series because of the limited time frame in the dataset.

Noise: In a time series, anything that is not represented by level, trend, seasonality, or cyclic component is the noise in the time series. The noise component is unpredictable but follows normal distribution in ideal cases. All the time series datasets will have noise. Fig. 12.5 shows the decomposition of quarterly production data, into trend, seasonality, and noise components.

The trend and seasonality are the systematic components of a time series. Systematic components can be forecasted. It is impossible to forecast

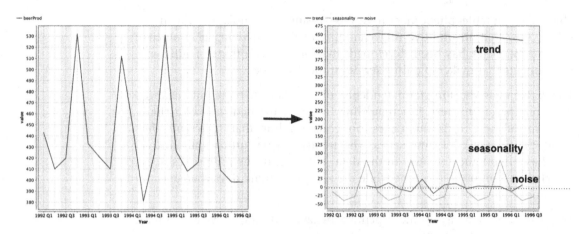

FIGURE 12.5
Decomposition of time series.

noise—the non-systematic component of a time series. In the time series decomposition can be classified into *additive decomposition* and *multiplicative decomposition*, based on the nature of the different components and how they are composed. In an additive decomposition, the components are decomposed in such a way that when they are added together, the original time series can be obtained.

Time series = Trend + Seasonality + Noise

In the case of multiplicative decomposition the components are decomposed in the such a way that when they are multiplied together, the original time series can be derived back.

Time series = Trend × Seasonality × Noise

Both additive and multiplicative time series decompostions can be represented by these equations:

$$y_t = T_t + S_t + E_t \tag{12.2}$$

$$y_t = T_t \times S_t \times E_t \tag{12.3}$$

where T_t, S_t, and E_t are trend, seasonal, and error components respectively. The original time series y_t is just an additive or multiplicative combination of components. If the magnitude of the seasonal fluctuation or the variation in trend changes with the level of the time series, then multiplicative time series decomposition is the better model. The antidiabetic drug sales time series from Fig. 12.1 shows increasing seasonal fluctuation and exponential rise in the long-term trend. Hence, a multiplicative model is more appropriate. Fig. 12.6 shows both the additive and multiplicative decomposition of the

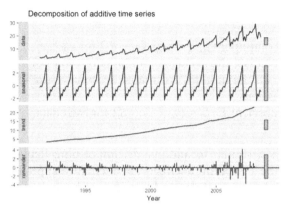 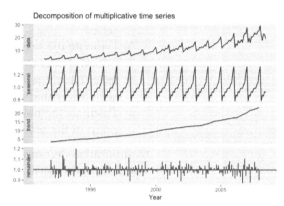

FIGURE 12.6
Additive and multiplicative decomposition of time series.

antidiabetic drug sales time series. Note the scale of the seasonal component is different for both decompositions. The noise in the additive decomposition is higher post 2005, as it ineffectively struggles to represent increases in the seasonal variation and trend changes. The noise is much smaller in the multiplicative decomposition.

To decompose the time series data to its individual components, there are a few different techniques available. In this section, some common approaches to describe time series data will be reviewed and how the knowledge can be used for forecasting time series to future time periods.

12.1.1   Classical Decomposition

The classical decomposition technique is simple, intuitive, and serves as a baseline of all other advanced decomposition methods. Suppose the time series has yearly seasonality with monthly data as shown in Fig. 12.1. m represents seasonal period, which is 12 for monthly data with yearly seasonality. The classical decomposition technique first estimates the trend component by calculating the long term (say 12 month) moving average. The trend component is removed from the time series to get remaining seasonal and noise components. The seasonal component can be estimated by average Jan, Feb, Mar, ..., variance in the remaining series. Once the trend and seasonal components are removed, what is left is noise. The algorithm for classic additive decomposition is:

1. Estimate the trend T_t: If m is even, calculate $2 \times m$ moving average (m-MA and then a 2-MA); if m is odd, calculate m-moving average. A moving average is the average of last m data points.

2. Calculate detrended series: Calculate $y_t - T_t$ for each data point in the series.
3. Estimate the seasonal component S_t: average $(y_t - T_t)$ for each m period. For example, calculate the average of all January values of $(y_t - T_t)$ and repeat for all the months. Normalize seasonal value in such a way that mean is zero.
4. Calculate the noise component E_t: $E_t = (y_t - T_t - S_t)$ for each data point in the series.

Multiplicative decomposition is similar to additive decomposition: Replace subtraction with division in the algorithm described. An alternative approach is to convert multiplicative decomposition into additive by applying the logarithmic function on both the sides of Eq. (12.3).

12.1.2 How to Implement

The decomposition algorithm is quite simple, and can be implemented in a spreadsheet. A practical example of a time series additive decomposition using RapidMiner will be briefly described. The process shown in Fig. 12.7 has simple data pre-processing operators to estimate the trend, seasonal, and error components. The data used in this process is the quarterly Australian beer production dataset[2] which can be found on the companion website www.IntroDataScience.com. Steps to convert the time series into the components are:

- *Trend*: Since the data show four quarter seasonality, a four period moving average operator and a two-period moving average operator is used to estimate the trend component.
- *Seasonality*: The *Generate attribute* operator is used to calculate the detrended series by finding the difference between the time series and the 2×4 month moving average values. The same operator also extracts quarter value (Q1, Q2, Q3, Q4) from the Year (e.g., 1996 Q1) attribute. The detrended series has seasonality and noise. To calculate the seasonality, the quarter values have to be averaged using the *Aggregate* operator. This gives seasonality values for one year. The *Join* operator is used to repeat the seasonal component for every Q1, Q2, Q3 and Q4 records.
- *Noise*: Noise is calculated by the difference of the time series with the combination of trend and seasonality.

The result of the process is shown in Fig. 12.8. The initial time series is decomposed into its components. Note that the noise is randomly

---

[2] Total quarterly beer production in Australia from 1956 to 2010. Australian Bureau of Statistics. Cat. 8301.0.55.001 (Hyndman & Athanasopoulos, 2018).

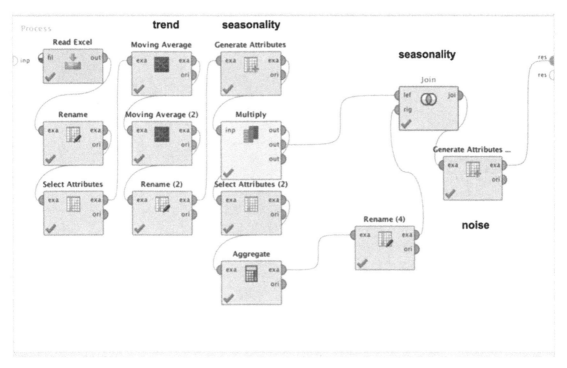

FIGURE 12.7
Process for time series decomposition.

distributed with the mean as zero. Even though the classical decomposition is straight forward, it has some serious limitations. Classical decomposition assumes the occurrence of the same seasonal pattern throughout the entire time series. That is too constrictive of an assumption for practical use cases. As the $2 \times m$ moving average is used, the first $m/2$ and the last $m/2$ data points are not used in the modeling. Moreover, classical decomposition is inept at handling anomalies in the data.

There are quite a range of advanced time series decomposition techniques. STL (Seasonal and Trend decomposition using Loess), SEATS (Seasonal Extraction in ARIMA Time Series), and X11 (from US Census Bureau) are some of the advanced decomposition techniques. All these methods have additional steps to deal with the limitations of the classical decomposition technique, particularly to deal with the change in the seasonality, decomposing quarterly, monthly, weekly, and daily seasonality, and handling changes in the trend.

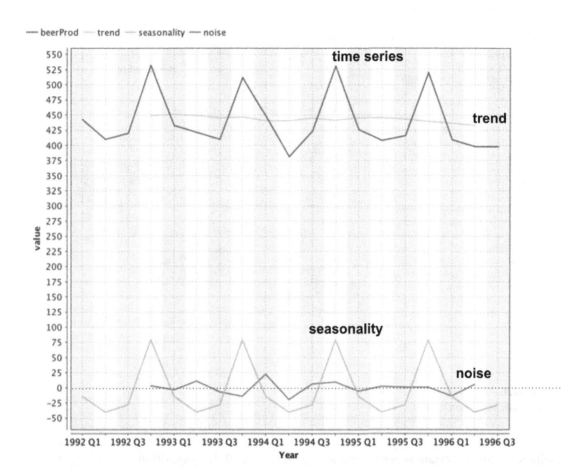

FIGURE 12.8
Time series and decomposed data.

Forecasting Using Decomposed Data

While decomposing the time series is used to describe and increase the understanding of time series data, it is useful for forecasting as well. The idea is to breakdown the time series into its parts, forecast the parts, and put it back together for forecasted future time series values. Why? Forecasting the time series through their components is a much easier task.

$$\hat{y}_t = \hat{S}_t + \hat{T}_t \tag{12.4}$$

It is assumed that the seasonal component of the time series does not change. Hence, the forecast of the seasonal component is the same as the values extracted from the time series. The time series data without the seasonal component is called *seasonally adjusted* time series. It contains just the trend component and noise in the data. The seasonally adjusted time series can be forecasted by relatively easier methods: linear or polynomial regression, Holt's method, or ARIMA. For example, the trend components in Figs. 12.6 and 12.8 can be extended using linear regression. Noise is normally distributed with the mean as zero. Hence, it is not forecasted. The time series forecast for the future value is the sum of the seasonal forecast and the seasonally adjusted forecast of the trend component.

12.2 SMOOTHING BASED METHODS

In the smoothing based approaches, an observation is a function of past few observations. It is helpful to start out with a basic notation system for time series in order to understand the different smoothing methodologies.

- *Time periods:* $t = 1, 2, 3, \ldots, n$. Time periods can be seconds, days, weeks, months, or years depending on the problem.
- *Data series:* Observation corresponding to each time period above: y_1, $y_2, y_3, \ldots y_n$.
- *Forecasts:* F_{n+h} is the forecast for the hth time period following n. Usually $h = 1$, the next time period following the last data point. However h can be greater than 1. h is called the *horizon*.
- *Forecast errors:* $e_t = y_t - F_t$ for any given time, t.

In order to explain the different methods, a simple time series data function will be used, $Y(t)$. Y is the *observed* value of the time series at any time t. Furthermore, the observations are made at a constant time interval. If in the case of intermittent data, one can assume that an interpolation scheme is applied to obtain equally spaced (in time) data points.

12.2.1 Simple Forecasting Methods

Naïve Method

Probably the simplest forecasting "model." Here one simply assumes that F_{n+1}, the forecast for the next period in the series, is given by the last data point of the series, y_n

$$F_{n+1} = y_n \tag{12.5}$$

Seasonal Naive Method

If the time series is seasonal, one can forecast better than the naive point estimate. The forecast can assume the value as the previous value of the same season. For example, the next January revenue can be assumed as the last known January revenue.

$$F_{n+1} = y_{n-s} \qquad (12.6)$$

where s is the seasonal period. In the case of monthly data with yearly seasonality, seasonal period is 12.

Average Method
Moving up a level, one could compute the next data point as an average of all the data points in the series. In other words, this model calculates the forecasted value, F_{n+1}, as:

$$F_{n+1} = \text{Average}(y_n, y_{n-1}, y_{n-2}, \ldots, y_1) \qquad (12.7)$$

Suppose one has monthly data from January 2010 to December 2010 and they want to predict the next January 2011 value, they would simply average the values from January 2010 to December 2010.

Moving Average Smoothing
The obvious problem with a simple average is figuring out how many points to use in the average calculation. As the observational data grows (as n increases), should one still use all the n time periods to compute the next forecast? To overcome this problem, one can select a window of the last "k" periods to calculate the average, and as the actual data grows over time, one can always take the last k samples to average, that is, $n, n-1, \ldots, n-k+1$. In other words, the window for averaging keeps moving forward and, thus, returns a moving average. Suppose in the simple example of the window $k = 3$; then to predict the January 2021 data, a three-month average would be taken using the last three months. When the actual data from January comes in, the February 2021 value is forecasted using January 2021 (n), December 2020 ($n-1$) and November 2020 ($n-3+1$ or $n-2$). This model will result in problems when there is seasonality in the data (e.g., in December for retail or in January for healthcare insurance), which can skew the average. Moving average smoothens the seasonal information in the time series.

$$F_{n+1} = \text{Average}(y_n, y_{n-1}, \ldots, y_{n-k}) \qquad (12.8)$$

Weighted Moving Average Smoothing
For some cases, the most recent value could have more influence than some of the earlier values. Most exponential growth occurs due to this simple effect. The forecast for the next period is given by the model:

$$F_{n+1} = (a \times y_n + b \times y_{n-1} + c \times y_{n-k})/(a+b+c) \qquad (12.9)$$

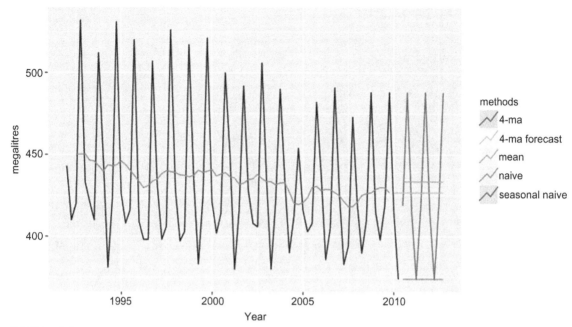

FIGURE 12.9
Comparing one-step-ahead forecasts for basic smoothing methods.

where typically $a > b > c$. Fig. 12.9 compares the forecast results for the simple time series introduced earlier. Note that all of the mentioned methods are able to make only one-step-ahead forecasts due to the nature of their formulation. The coefficients a, b, and c may be arbitrary, but are usually based on some previous knowledge of the time series.

12.2.2 Exponential Smoothing

Exponential smoothing is the weighted average of the past data, with the recent data points given more weight than earlier data points. The weights decay exponentially towards the earlier data points, hence, the name. The exponential smoothing is given by the equation 12.10.

$$F_{n+1} = \alpha y_n + \alpha(1 - \alpha)y_{n-1} + \alpha(1-\alpha)^2 y_{n-2} + \cdots. \tag{12.10}$$

α is generally between 0 and 1. Note that $\alpha = 1$ returns the naïve forecast of Eq. (12.5). As seen in the charts in Fig. 12.10, using a higher α results in putting more weight on actual values and the resulting curve is closer to the actual curve, but using a lower α results in putting more emphasis on

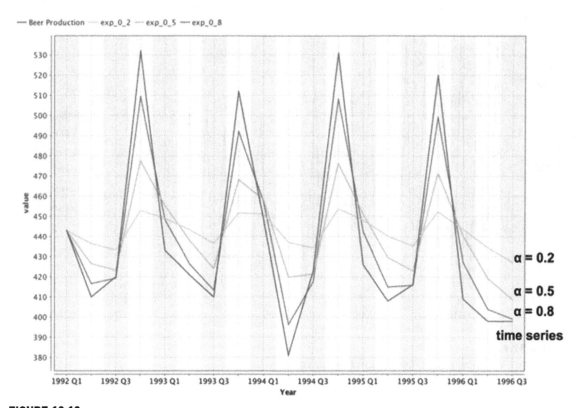

FIGURE 12.10

Fitted time series—exponential smoothing with different α levels.

previously forecasted values and results in a smoother but less accurate fit. Typical values for α range from 0.2 to 0.4 in practice.

To forecast the future values using exponential smoothing, Eq. (12.10) can be rewritten as:

$$F_{n+1} = \alpha \times y_n + (1 - \alpha) \times F_n \qquad (12.11)$$

Eq. (12.11) is more useful because it involves both actual value y_n and forecasted value F_n. A higher α value gives an exact fit and a lower value gives a smoother fit. Going back to the monthly example, if one wanted to make the February 2011 forecast using not only the actual January 2011 value but also the previously *forecasted* January 2011 value, the new forecast would have "learnt" the data better. This is the concept behind basic exponential smoothing (Brown, 1956).

This simple exponential smoothing is the basis for a number of common smoothing based forecasting methods. However, the model is suited only for time series *without clear trend or seasonality*. The smoothing model has only one parameter, α, and can help smooth the data in a time series so that it is easy to extrapolate and make forecasts. Like many methods discussed earlier, the forecast will be flat that is, there is no trend or seasonality factored in. Only the level is forecasted. Also, if Eq. (12.10) were examined, one would see that forecasts cannot be made more than one-step ahead, because to make a forecast for step $(n + 1)$, the data for the previous step, n, is needed. It is not possible to make forecasts several steps ahead, that is, $(n + h)$, using the methods described (where it was simply assumed that $F_{n+h} = F_{n+1}$), where h is the horizon. This obviously has limited utility. For making longer horizon forecasts, that is, where $h \gg 1$, the trend and seasonality information also needs to be considered. Once trend and seasonality are captured, one can forecast the value for any time in the future, not just the values for one step ahead.

Holt's Two-Parameter Exponential Smoothing

Anyone who has used a spreadsheet for creating trend lines on scatter plots intuitively knows what a trend means. A trend is an averaged long-term tendency of a time series. The simplified exponential smoothing model described earlier is not particularly effective at capturing trends. An extension of this technique, called Holt's two-parameter exponential smoothing, is needed to accomplish this.

Recall that exponential smoothing [Eq. (12.10)] simply calculates the average value of the time series at $n + 1$. If the series also has a trend, then an average slope of the series needs to be estimated as well. This is what Holt's two-parameter smoothing does by means of another parameter, β. A smoothing equation similar to Eq. (12.10) is constructed for the average trend at $n + 1$. With two parameters, α and β, any time series with a trend can be modeled and, therefore, forecasted. The forecast can be expressed as a sum of these two components, average value or "level" of the series, L_n, and trend, T_n, recursively as:

$$F_{n+1} = L_n + T_n \tag{12.12}$$

where,

$$L_n = \alpha \times y_n + (1 - \alpha) \times (L_{n-1} + T_{n-1}) \text{ and } T_n = \beta \times (L_n - L_{n-1}) + (1 - \beta) \times T_{n-1} \tag{12.13}$$

To make future a forecast over an horizon, one can modify Equation 12.12 to:

$$F_{n+h} = L_n + h \times T_n \tag{12.14}$$

The values of the parameter can be estimated based on the best fit with the training (past) data.

Holt-Winters' Three-Parameter Exponential Smoothing

When a time series contains seasonality in addition to a trend, yet another parameter, γ, will be needed to estimate the seasonal component of the time series (Winters, 1960). The estimates for value (or level) are now adjusted by a seasonal index, which is computed with a third equation that includes γ. (Shmueli, 2011; Hyndman, 2014; Box, 2008).

$$F_{t+h} = (L_t + {}_h T_t)\, S_{t+h-p} \tag{12.15}$$

$$L_t = \alpha y_t / S_{t-p} + (1-\alpha)(L_{t-1} + T_{t-1}) \tag{12.16}$$

$$T_t = \beta(L_t - L_{t-1}) + (1-\beta)T_{t-1} \tag{12.17}$$

$$S_t = \gamma(y_t / L_t) + (1-\gamma)\, S_{t-p} \tag{12.18}$$

where p is the seasonality period. One can estimate the value of the parameters α, β, and γ from the fitting of the smoothing equation with the training data.

12.2.3   How to Implement

Holt-Winters' three parameter smoothing provides a good framework to forecast time series data with level, trend, and seasonality, as long as the seasonal period is well defined. One can implement the time series forecasting model in RapidMiner using R extension. R[3] is a powerful, widely used statistical tool and this use case warrants the integration of RapidMiner with R functionality. The key operator in this process is *Execute R* which accepts the data as the input, processes the data, and outputs the data frame from R.

The data used in the process is the Australian Beer Production time series dataset used in prior time series process. After a bit of data pre-processing, like renaming the attributes and selecting the production data, R operator is invoked for Holt and Holt Winters' forecasting function (Fig. 12.11).

The *Execute R* operator executes the R script entered in the operator. The R script for the Holt-Winters' forecasting is shown below. It uses the forecast package library and invokes the forecasting function holt(inp, $h=10$) for Holts and hw(inp, $h=10$) for Holt-Winters' forecasting. The data frame (dataset in R) is returned to RapidMiner process.

---

[3] https://www.r-project.org/.

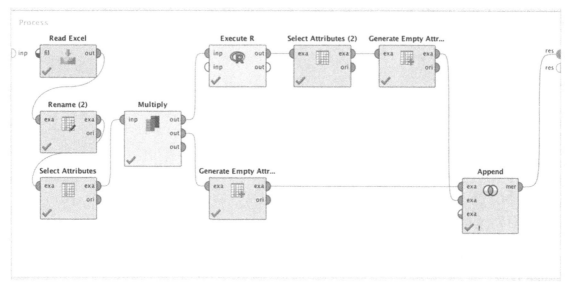

FIGURE 12.11
Holts and Holt-Winters' forecasting using R.

R Script for Holt-Winters' Forecasting

```
rm_main = function(data)
{
library(forecast)
  inp <- ts(data, freq = 4)
    y <- holt(inp, h = 10)    # or hw(inp, h = 10) for Holt Winters' smoothing
    df <- as.data.frame(y)
    return(list(df))
}
```

The output from the Execute R operator has point forecasts and the interval forecasts. For this implementation, the point forecast is selected using *Select Attributes* operator. The forecasted dataset is appended with the original dataset for better visualization using *Generate Attribute* and *Append* operators. Fig. 12.12 shows the forecasted result of both Holt's and Holt-Winters' exponential smoothing based forecast. Note that in Holt's forecast, only trend and level are forecasted and in Holt Winters' forecasting both trend and seasonality are forecasted.

12.3 REGRESSION BASED METHODS

In the regression based methods, the variable *time* is the predictor or independent variable and the time series value is the dependent

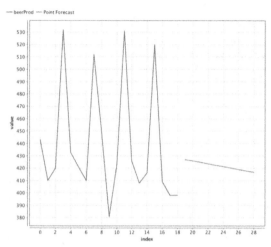

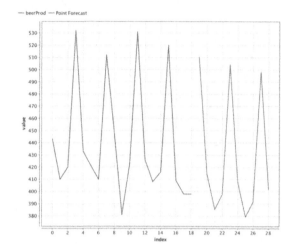

Holt's Two-Parameter Smoothing   Holt-Winters' Three-Parameter Smoothing

FIGURE 12.12

Holt's and Holt-Winters' smoothing.

variable. Regression based methods are generally preferable when the time series appears to have a global pattern. The idea is that the model parameters will be able to capture these patterns and, thus, enable one to make predictions for any step ahead in the future under the assumption that this pattern is going to be repeated. For a time series with local patterns instead of a global pattern, using a regression based approach requires one to specify how and when the patterns change, which is difficult. For such a series, smoothing approaches work best because these methods usually rely on extrapolating the most recent local pattern as seen earlier.

Fig. 12.13 shows two time series: Fig. 12.13A shows antidiabetic drug revenue and Fig. 12.13B shows the economy class passenger volume in Sydney-Melbourne[4] route. A regression based forecasting method would work well for the antidiabetic drug revenue series because it has a global pattern. However the passenger volume series shows no clear start or end for any patterns. It is preferable to use smoothing based methods to attempt to forecast this second series.

---

[4] Ansett Airlines (defunct). The dip shows the industrial dispute in 1989. FPP2 package in R.

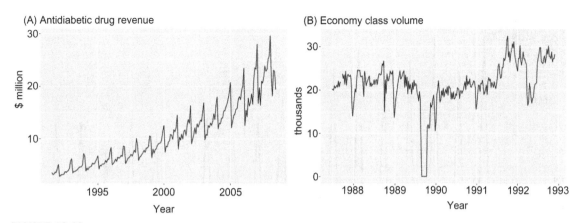

FIGURE 12.13

Global and local patterns. (A) Antidiabetic drug revenue - global pattern and (B) Airline economy class passenger volume between Sydney and Melbourne - local pattern.

12.3.1　Regression

The simplest of the regression based approaches for analyzing a time series is using linear regression. As mentioned in the introduction to the chapter, one assumes the time period is the independent variable and attempts to predict the time series value using this. For the Australian beer dataset used so far, the chart in Fig. 12.14 shows a linear regression fit. As can be seen, the linear regression model is able to capture the long-term tendency of the series, but it does a poor job of fitting the data.

Sophisticated polynomial functions can be used to improve the fit. Polynomial regression is similar to linear regression except that higher-degree functions of the independent variable are used (squares and cubes on the time variable). Since the global trend here is straight decline, it is difficult to argue that the cubic polynomial does a significantly better job. However in either of these cases, one is not limited to a one-step-ahead forecast of the simple smoothing methods.

12.3.2　Regression With Seasonality

The linear regression trend-fitting model can be significantly improved by simply accounting for seasonality. This is done by introducing *seasonal dummy variables* for each period (quarter), of the series, which triggers either 1 or 0 in the attribute values as seen in Fig. 12.15. In this example, four new attributes are added to the original dataset to indicate which quarter the record belongs to. The attribute value of (Quarter $=$ Q1) is turned 1 if the quarter is Q1 and so on.

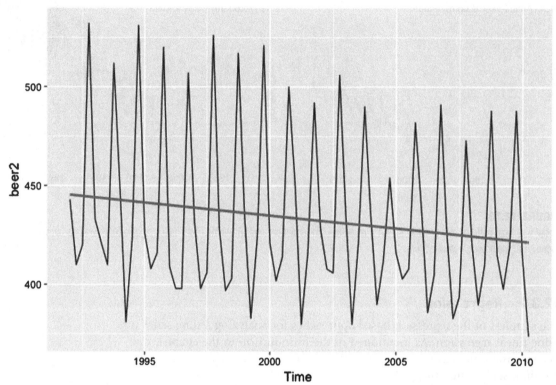

FIGURE 12.14
Linear regression model.

Just this trivial addition to the predictors of the linear regression model can yield a surprisingly good fit in most datasets with clear seasonality. Although the model equation may appear a bit complicated, in reality it is just a linear regression model with four variables: the time period and four dummy variables for each quarter of a year. The independent variable *time* captures the level and the long-term trend. The four dummy seasonal variables capture the seasonality. This regression equation can be used for predicting any future value beyond $n + 1$, and thus, has significantly more utility than the simpler counterparts in the smoothing side.

$$\text{Forecast} = 442.189 - 1.132 \times \text{time} - 27.268 \times (\text{Quarter} = Q2)$$
$$- 16.336 \times (\text{Quarter} = Q3) + 92.882 \times (\text{Quarter} = Q4)$$

There is of course no reason to use linear regression alone to capture both trend and seasonality. More sophisticated models can easily be built using polynomial equations along with the sine and cosine function to model seasonality.

Year	time	Quarter = Q1	Quarter = Q2	Quarter = Q3	Quarter = Q4	beerProd
1992 Q1	1	1	0	0	0	443
1992 Q2	2	0	1	0	0	410
1992 Q3	3	0	0	1	0	420
1992 Q4	4	0	0	0	1	532
1993 Q1	5	1	0	0	0	433
1993 Q2	6	0	1	0	0	421
1993 Q3	7	0	0	1	0	410
1993 Q4	8	0	0	0	1	512
1994 Q1	9	1	0	0	0	449
1994 Q2	10	0	1	0	0	381

FIGURE 12.15
Seasonal attributes.

How to implement

The implementation process for seasonal linear regression is similar to the linear regression model discussed in Chapter 5, Regression Methods. The additional step is to set up data pre-processing to add seasonal dummy variables. Fig. 12.16 shows the complete RapidMiner process for seasonal linear regression for the Australian beer production dataset. The steps in building the forecasting model are:

1. *Add time attribute*: After the dataset is read, a new attribute "time" is generated to indicate the consecutive time period of each example record. First record "1992 Q1" is tagged as 1 and the next as 2, and so on. This is essential in all regression based forecasting because *time* is the independent variable and will be part of the regression equation. It is important to sort the dataset before adding the sequential time attribute.
2. *Extract seasonal attribute*: The next step is to extract "Q1" from the "1992 Q1" attribute. It can be achieved with Generate attribute and cut () function to extract Q1 from the text. If the time series has weekly or monthly seasonality, corresponding identifiers like weekday or month id have to be extracted.
3. *Generation of independent seasonal attributes*: The quarter attribute has to be pivoted to "Is Q1", "Is Q2", ... attributes. The *Nominal to Numerical* conversion operator is used to generate these attributes. The value of the attribute is either 1 or 0, depending on the record's seasonal period.

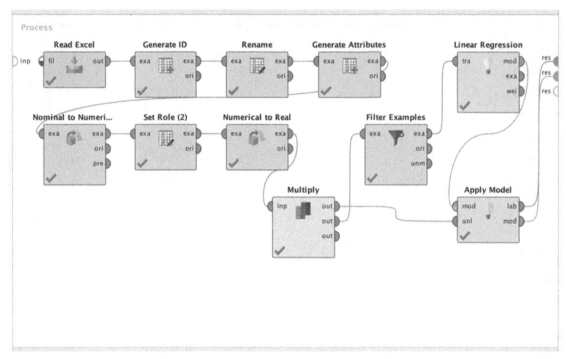

FIGURE 12.16
Process for seasonal linear regression.

4. *Modeling*: A linear regression model is used to fit the equation with the training data. A polynomial regression learner can be used for a better fit.
5. *Forecasting*: The dataset also contains the placeholders for future periods. The *Apply model* operator is used to visualize the fit of the model for the training period and to forecast the future horizon.

The process can be saved and executed. The result window shows the time series of both actual and forecasted data. As shown in Fig. 12.17, the seasonal linear regression forecasting has done a good job of fitting the model for the past data and projected the seasonality for the future horizon. Contrast this result with Fig. 12.14 where the linear regression model captures only the level and long-term trend.

12.3.3 Autoregressive Integrated Moving Average

ARIMA stands for Autoregressive Integrated Moving Average model and is one of the most popular models for time series forecasting. The ARIMA methodology originally developed by Box and Jenkins in the 1970s

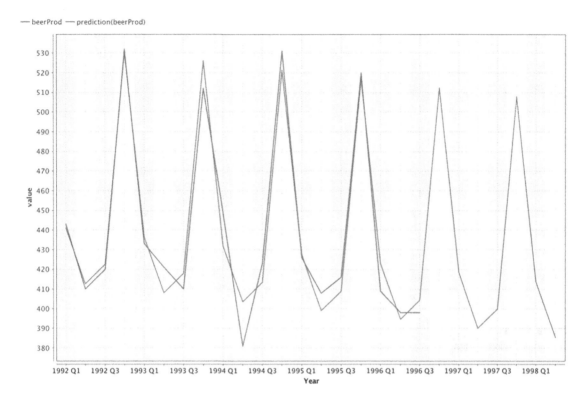

— beerProd — prediction(beerProd)

FIGURE 12.17
Forecasting using seasonal linear regression.

(Box, 1970). Even though the steps of training an ARIMA model are more involved, the implementation is relatively straightforward using statistical packages that support ARIMA functions. In this section, the concepts of auto-correlation, autoregression, stationary data, differentiation, and moving average of error are introduced, which are used to increase the understanding on time series and serve as the building blocks of ARIMA models.

Autocorrelation
Correlation measures how two variables are dependent on each other or if they have a linear relationship with each other. Consider the time series shown in Fig. 12.18. The second column "prod" shows the data for the simple time series. In the third column, data are lagged by one step. 1992 Q1 data is shown in 1992 Q2. This new series of values is termed a "1-lag" series. There are an additional 2-lag, 3-lag, ..., n-lag series in the dataset. Notice that there is a strong correlation between the original time series "prod" and 4-lag "prod-4." They tend to move together. This phenomenon is

Year	prod	prod-1	prod-2	prod-3	prod-4	prod-5	prod-6
1992 Q1	443	?	?	?	?	?	?
1992 Q2	410	443	?	?	?	?	?
1992 Q3	420	410	443	?	?	?	?
1992 Q4	532	420	410	443	?	?	?
1993 Q1	433	532	420	410	443	?	?
1993 Q2	421	433	532	420	410	443	?
1993 Q3	410	421	433	532	420	410	443
1993 Q4	512	410	421	433	532	420	410
1994 Q1	449	512	410	421	433	532	420
1994 Q2	381	449	512	410	421	433	532
1994 Q3	423	381	449	512	410	421	433
1994 Q4	531	423	381	449	512	410	421
1995 Q1	426	531	423	381	449	512	410

FIGURE 12.18

Lag series and autocorrelation.

called autocorrelation, where the time series is correlated with its own data points, with a lag.

As in a multivariate correlation matrix (Chapter 3: Data Exploration), one can measure the strength of correlation between the original time series and all the lag series. The plot of the resultant correlation matrix is called an *Autocorrelation Function* (ACF) chart. The ACF chart is used to study all the available seasonality in the time series. From Fig. 12.19 it can be concluded that the time series is correlated with the 4th, 8th, and 12th lagged quarter due to the yearly seasonality. It is also evident than Q1 is negatively correlated with Q2 and Q3.

Autoregressive Models

Autoregressive models are regression models applied on lag series generated using the original time series. Recall in multiple linear regression, the output is a linear combination of multiple input variables. In the case of autoregression models, the output is the future data point and it can be expressed as a linear combination for past p data points. p is the lag window. The autoregressive model can be denoted as the equation:

$$y_t = l + \alpha_1 y_{t-1} + \alpha_2 y_{t-2} + \cdots + \alpha_p y_{t-p} + e \tag{12.19}$$

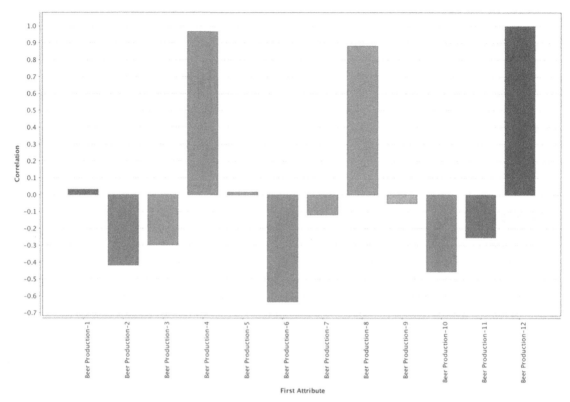

FIGURE 12.19

ACF chart. *ACF*, Autocorrelation Function.

where, l is the level in the dataset and e is the noise. α are the coefficients that need to be learned from the data. This can be referred to as an autoregressive model with p lags or an **AR(p)** model. In an AR(p) model, lag series is a new predictor used to fit the dependent variable, which is still the original series value, Y_t.

Stationary Data

In a time series with trends or seasonality, the value is affected by time (hence, one would be interested in this subject). A time series is called *stationary* when the value of time series is not dependent on time. For instance, random white noise is a stationary time series. Daily temperature at a location is not stationary as there will be a seasonal trend and it is affected by time. Meanwhile, the noise component of a time series is stationary. Stationary time series do not have any means of being forecasted as they are completely random. Fig. 12.20A is an example of nonstationary data because

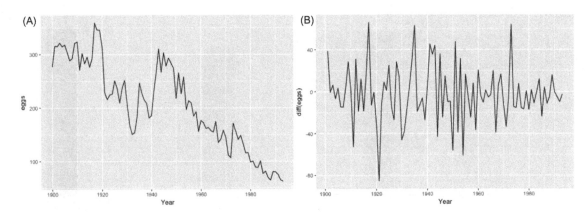

FIGURE 12.20

(A) Non-stationary Time series and (B) Stationary time series.

of the presence of both trend and seasonality and Fig. 12.20B is an example of stationary data because there is no clear trend or seasonality.

Differencing

A non-stationary time series can be converted to a stationary time series through a technique called differencing. Differencing series is the change between consecutive data points in the series.

$$y'_t = y_t - y_{t-1} \tag{12.20}$$

This is called first order differencing. Fig. 12.20 shows a time series and a first order differenced time series. In some cases, just differencing once will still yield a nonstationary time series. In that case a second order differencing is required. Second order differencing is the change between two consecutive data points in a first order differenced time series. To generalize, differencing of order **d** is used to convert nonstationary time series to stationary time series.

Seasonal differencing is the change between the same period in two different seasons. Assume a season has period, *m*.

$$y'_t = y_t - y_{t-m} \tag{12.21}$$

This is similar to the Year-over-Year metric used commonly in business financial reports. It is also called as m-lag first order differencing. Fig. 12.21 shows the seasonal differencing of the Australian Beer production dataset and the seasonal first order differencing of the same series with the seasonal lag as 4—to factor in the number of quarters in a year.

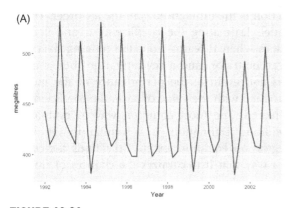 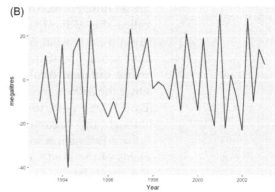

FIGURE 12.21

(A) Time series (B) Seasonal differencing of the time series.

Moving Average of Error

In addition to creating a regression of actual past "p" values as shown in Eq. (12.19), one can also create a regression equation involving forecast errors of past data and use it as a predictor. Consider this equation with:

$$y_t = I + e_t + \theta_1 e_{t-1} + \theta_2 e_{t-2} + \cdots + \theta_q e_{t-q} \tag{12.22}$$

where e_i is the forecast error of data point i. This makes sense for the past data points but not for data point t because it is still being forecasted. Hence, e_t is assumed as white noise. The regression equation for y_t can be understood as the weighted (θ) moving average of past q forecast errors. This is called Moving Average with q lags model or **MA(q)**.

Autoregressive Integrated Moving Average

The Autoregressive Integrated Moving Average (ARIMA) model is a combination of the differenced autoregressive model with the moving average model. It is expressed as:

$$y'_t = I + \alpha_1 y'_{t-1} + \alpha_2 y'_{t-2} + \cdots + \alpha_p y'_{t-p} + e_t + \theta_1 e_{t-1} + \theta_2 e_{t-2} + \cdots + \theta_q e_{t-q} \tag{12.23}$$

The AR part of ARIMA shows that the time series is regressed on its own past data. The MA part of ARIMA indicates that the forecast error is a linear combination of past respective errors. The I part of ARIMA shows that the data values have been replaced with differenced values of d order to obtain stationary data, which is the requirement of the ARIMA model approach. Why would one need to get to this level of complexity? The ARIMA model is effective in fitting past data with this combination approach and help forecast future points in a time series.

Eq. (12.23) shows the predictors are the lagged p data points for the autoregressive part and the lagged q errors are for the moving average part, which are all differenced. The prediction is the differenced y_t in the dth order. This is called the ARIMA(p,d,q) model. Estimating the coefficients α and θ for a given p,d,q is what ARIMA does when it learns from the training data in a time series. Specifying p,d,q can be tricky (and a key limitation) but one can tryout different combinations and evaluate the performance of the model. Once the ARIMA model is specified with the value of p,d,q, the coefficients of Eq. (12.23) need to be estimated. The most common way to estimate is through the Maximum Likelihood Estimation. It is similar to the Least Square Estimation for the regression equation, except MLE finds the coefficients of the model in such a way that it maximizes the chances of finding the actual data.

ARIMA is a generalized model. Some of the models discussed in this chapter are special cases of an ARIMA model. For example,

- ARIMA (0,1,0) is expressed as $y_{t}=y_{t-1} + e$. It is the naive model with error, which is called the Random walk model.
- ARIMA (0,1,0) is expressed as $y_{t}=y_{t-1} + e + c$. It is a random walk model with a constant trend. It is called random walk with drift.
- ARIMA (0,0,0) is $y_t = e$ or white noise
- ARIMA (p,0,0) is the autoregressive model

How to Implement
The dataset used to build an ARIMA trainer is the Australian beer production dataset. The task is to forecast the production for ten more quarters. RapidMiner provides an extension (Time Series Extension) for time series operators to describe and predict time series. ARIMA modeling and the forecasting are implemented by *ARIMA trainer* to build the model and *Apply forecast* to apply the model and forecast for ten more quarters. The process is shown in Fig. 12.22

Step 1: The Australian beer production dataset has two attributes: Year and beer production value in megaliters. The role of Year should be set as ID and the only attribute in the dataset should be the time series value. A sequential time period is generated and added to the dataset as an anchor for the charts.

Step 2: The *ARIMA trainer* operator can be found under Extension > Time Series > Forecast > ARIMA. The operator has these parameters:

- p: order of autoregression part. It is set as 1
- d: degree of differencing. Set as 0
- q: order of the moving average of the error part. Set as 1
- criterion: criterion to minimize for coefficient selection. Set as aic.

As a start, the model parameters are specified as ARIMA(1,0,1). One can further optimize the value of p,d,q using the *Optimize Parameters* operator where

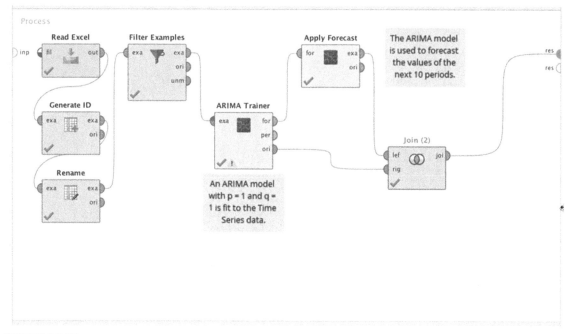

FIGURE 12.22

Process to implement ARIMA model. *ARIMA*, Autoregressive Integrated Moving Average.

all the combination of *p,d,q* are tried out to select the most optimal combination.

Step 3: The *Apply the forecast* operator takes the input of the forecasted model and applies the model for future horizon. Forecast horizon is set as 10 to predict 10 more data points at the end of the time series. The forecasted data is then joined with the original dataset using the *Join* operator so the forecasted data can be visualized along with the original dataset (Fig. 12.23).

The process shown in Fig. 12.22 can be saved and run. The result window has the output of the *Join* operator. The time series chart provides the plot of time series, both the original and forecasted value. The model has done a decent job of capturing the level and trend in the data, but the forecasted value does not have any seasonality, unlike the actual data. This is because seasonality was not expressed in the model. The ARIMA model discussed thus far does not take into account of the seasonality component. One would have a few additional steps to complete in order to incorporate the seasonality in the ARIMA modeling.

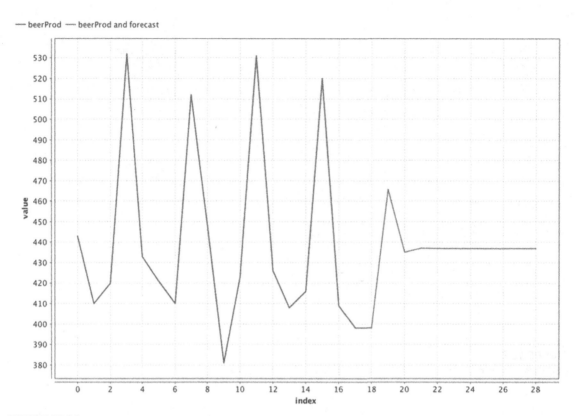

FIGURE 12.23
Forecast using ARIMA. *ARIMA*, Autoregressive Integrated Moving Average.

12.3.4 Seasonal ARIMA

The ARIMA model can be further enhanced to take into account of the seasonality in the time series. Seasonal ARIMA is expressed by the notion ARIMA$(p,d,q)(P,D,Q)_m$ where

> p is the order of nonseasonal autoregression
> d is the degree of differencing
> q is the order of nonseasonal moving average of the error
> P is the order of the seasonal autoregression
> D is the degree of seasonal differencing
> Q is the order of seasonal moving average of the error
> m is the number of observations in the year (for yearly seasonality)

In terms of the equation, the seasonal part of ARIMA is similar to the terms used in the nonseasonal part, except that it is *backshifted m times*, where m is the seasonal period. For example, the differencing is performed not with the consecutive data points but with the data points with m lags. If one has quarterly seasonality in monthly grain, each data point is differenced with the same month last quarter.

How to Implement

To implement seasonal ARIMA, *Execute R* operator from the *R* extension for RapidMiner is used. The RapidMiner process shown in Fig. 12.24 looks similar to the process built for the Holt-Winters' smoothing model. The difference is in the R code inside the *Execute R* operator. The process has a data preparation step before feeding data to *R* and a post process to combine the forecast and original data for visualization. The Australian beer production dataset is used for this process.

The R code inside the *Execute R* operator is shown here. It uses the Forecast package in R to activate the arima() function. In this processes the auto.arima() function was used, which automatically selects the best parameters for $(p,d,q)(P,D,Q)_m$. The optimal parameters for the Beer production dataset is ARIMA$(1,0,0)(1,1,0)_4$. The seasonal ARIMA model is used to forecast the future 12 data points using the forecast() function.

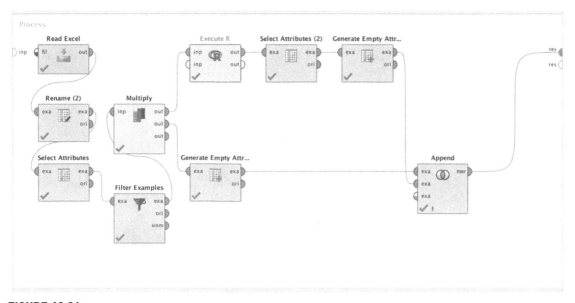

FIGURE 12.24

Seasonal ARIMA process using R. *ARIMA*, Autoregressive Integrated Moving Average.

```
rm_main = function(data)
{
library(forecast)
  inp <- ts(data, freq = 4)
  y <- auto.arima(inp)
    df <- as.data.frame(forecast(y, h = 12))
    return(list(df))
}
```

The process can be saved and executed. The forecast output is shown in Fig. 12.25. The model seems to have accounted for both the trend and seasonality in the time series. ARIMA is one of the most used forecasting techniques in businesses today. It has strong underpinning in statistics, has been field tested for decades, and is effective in modeling seasonal and

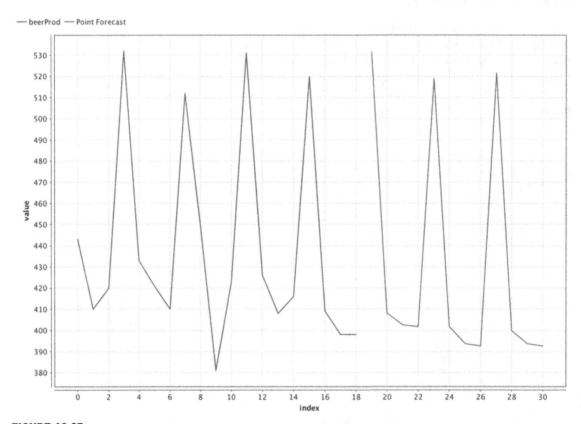

FIGURE 12.25

Forecast using seasonal ARIMA. *ARIMA*, Autoregressive Integrated Moving Average.

nonseasonal time series. Specifying the ARIMA modeling parameters before-hand might seem arbitrary. However, one can test the fit of the model for many combination or use meta functions like auto.arima() for the *Optimize parameters* operators. There is one more class of time series forecasting that has gained contemporary popularity—Machine learning–based time series forecasting.

12.4   MACHINE LEARNING METHODS

A time series is a unique dataset where the information used to predict future data points can be extracted from past data points. A subset of the past known data points can be used as inputs to an inferred *model* to compute the future data point as an output. Fig. 12.26 shows the general framework of the approach, which is similar to supervised learning techniques. Standard

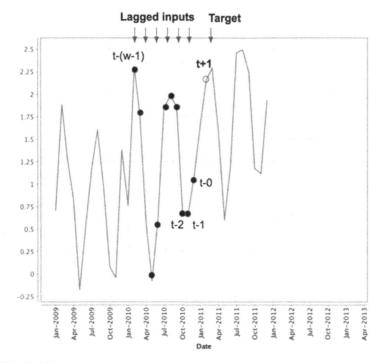

FIGURE 12.26
Lagged inputs and target.

machine learning techniques are used to build a model based on the inferred relationship between input (past data) and target (future data).

In order to use the supervised learners on time series data, the series is transformed into cross-sectional data using a technique called *windowing*. This technique defines a set of consecutive time series data as a window, where the latest record forms the target while other series data points, which are lagged compared to the target, form the input variables (Fig. 12.27). As consecutive windows are defined, the same data point in the series may function as the target for one cross-sectional window and the input variable for other cross-sectional windows. Once a sufficient number of windows are extracted from the dataset, a supervised model can be learned based on the inferred relationship between the lagged input variables and the target variable. This is similar to an autoregressive model where past p data points are used to predict the next data point. Any of the supervised learners discussed in the Classification or Regression chapter can be applied to learn and predict the target variable—the next time step in the series. The inferred model can be used to predict a future time series data point based on the last window of the time series. This gives visibility into one future data point. The new predicted data point can be used to define a new window and predict one more data point into the future. This subroutine can be repeated until all future predictions are made.

12.4.1 Windowing

The purpose of windowing is to transform the time series data into a generic machine learning input dataset. Fig. 12.28 shows a sample windowing and cross-sectional data extraction from the time series dataset.

The characteristics of the windows and the cross-sectional data extractions are specified by the parameters of the windowing process. The following parameters of windowing allow for changing the size of the windows, the

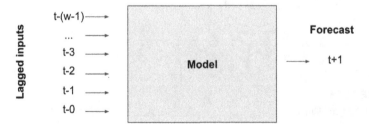

FIGURE 12.27
Machine learning model for time series.

Date	inputYt		Window id	inputYt + 1 (horizon)	inputYt - 5	inputYt - 4	inputYt - 3	inputYt - 2	inputYt - 1	inputYt - 0
Jan 1, 2009	0.709		0	1.169	0.709	1.886	1.293	0.822	-0.173	0.552
Feb 1, 2009	1.886		1	1.604	1.886	1.293	0.822	-0.173	0.552	1.169
Mar 1, 2009	1.293		2	0.949	1.293	0.822	-0.173	0.552	1.169	1.604
Apr 1, 2009	0.822		3	0.080	0.822	-0.173	0.552	1.169	1.604	0.949
May 1, 2009	-0.173		4	-0.040	-0.173	0.552	1.169	1.604	0.949	0.080
Jun 1, 2009	0.552		5	1.381	0.552	1.169	1.604	0.949	0.080	-0.040
Jul 1, 2009	1.169		6	0.761	1.169	1.604	0.949	0.080	-0.040	1.381
Aug 1, 2009	1.604		7	2.312	1.604	0.949	0.080	-0.040	1.381	0.761
Sep 1, 2009	0.949		8	1.795	0.949	0.080	-0.040	1.381	0.761	2.312
Oct 1, 2009	0.080		9	0.586	0.080	-0.040	1.381	0.761	2.312	1.795
Nov 1, 2009	-0.040		10	-0.077	-0.040	1.381	0.761	2.312	1.795	0.586
Dec 1, 2009	1.381		11	0.613	1.381	0.761	2.312	1.795	0.586	-0.077
Jan 1, 2010	0.761		12	1.845	0.761	2.312	1.795	0.586	-0.077	0.613
Feb 1, 2010	2.312		13	1.984	2.312	1.795	0.586	-0.077	0.613	1.845
Mar 1, 2010	1.795		14	1.861	1.795	0.586	-0.077	0.613	1.845	1.984
Apr 1, 2010	0.586		15	0.661	0.586	-0.077	0.613	1.845	1.984	1.861
May 1, 2010	-0.077									
Jun 1, 2010	0.613			**(B) Cross-sectional data set**						
Jul 1, 2010	1.845									

(A) Time series data set

FIGURE 12.28

Windowing process. (A) original time series and (B) cross-sectional data set with consecutive windows.

overlap between consecutive windows, and the prediction horizon which is used for forecasting.

1. *Window Size*: Number of lag points in one window excluding the target data point.
2. *Step*: Number of data points between the first value of the two consecutive windows. If the step is 1, maximum number of windows can be extracted from the time series dataset.
3. *Horizon width*: The prediction horizon controls how many records in the time series end up as the target variable. The common value for the horizon width is 1.
4. *Skip*: Offset between the window and horizon. If the skip is zero, the consecutive data point(s) from the window is used for horizon.

In Fig. 12.28, the window size is 6, step is 1, horizon width is 1, and skip is 0.

Thus, the series data are now converted into a generic cross-sectional dataset that can be predicted with learning algorithms like regression, neural networks, or support vector machines. Once the windowing process is done, then the real power of machine learning algorithms can be brought to bear on a time series dataset.

Model Training

Consider the time series dataset shown in Fig. 12.28A. The dataset refers to historical monthly profits from a product, from January 2009 to June 2012. Suppose the objective in this exercise is to develop profitability forecasts for the next 12 months. A linear regression model can be used to fit the cross-sectional dataset shown in Fig. 12.28B using the technique described in Chapter 5, Regression Methods. The model will be:

$$\text{input } Y_{t+1}(\text{label}) = 0.493 \times \text{input } Y_{t-5} + 0.258 \times \text{input } Y_{t-4} + 0.107 \times \text{input } Y_{t-3}$$
$$- 0.098 \times \text{input } Y_{t-2} - 0.073 \times \text{input } Y_{t-1} + 0.329 \times \text{input } Y_{t-0} + 0.135$$

Training the model is quite straightforward. The inferred relationship between a data point in the time series with the previous six data points is established. In other words, if one knows six consecutive data points in a time series, they can use the model to predict the seventh unseen data point. Since a new data point has been forecasted, it can be used along with the five preceding data points to predict one more data point and so on. That's time series forecasting one data point at a time!

How to Implement

Implementing a time series forecasting process using supervised learning is similar to a classification or regression process. The distinguishing step in time series forecasting is the conversion of a time series dataset to a cross-sectional dataset and stacking the forecast one data point at a time. The RapidMiner process is shown in Fig. 12.29. It uses operators from the Time Series extension. Although the process looks complicated, it consists of three functional blocks: (1) conversion to cross-sectional data, (2) training an machine learning model, and (3) forecasting one data point at a time in a loop. The dataset used in the process is the Product profit[5] dataset (the dataset can be downloaded from www.IntroDataScience.com) shown in Fig. 12.28. The time series has two attributes: Date and Input Y_t.

Step 1: Set Up Windowing

The process window in Fig. 12.29 shows the necessary operators for windowing. The time series dataset has a date column, and this must be treated with special care. The operator must be informed that one of the columns in the dataset is a date and should be considered as an "id." This is accomplished with the *Set Role* operator. If the input data has multiple time series, *Select Attributes* operator can be used to select the one to be forecasted. In this case, only a one value series is used and strictly speaking this operator is not needed. However, to make the process generic it has been included and the

---

[5] Available for download from www.IntroDataScience.com.

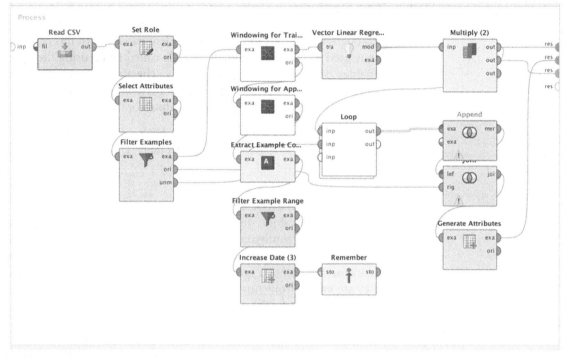

FIGURE 12.29
Process for time series forecasting using machine learning.

column labeled "inputYt" has been selected. Optionally, one may want to use the *Filter Examples* operator to remove any data points that may have missing values. The central operator for this step is the *Windowing* operator in the Time series extension. The main parameters for the *Windowing* operator are:

1. *Window size:* Determines how many "attributes" are created for the cross-sectional data. Each row of the original time series within the window size will become a new attribute. In this example, $w = 6$ was chosen.
2. *Step size:* Determines how to advance the window. $s = 1$ was used.
3. *Horizon width:* Determines how far out to make the forecast. If the window size is 6 and the horizon is 1, then the seventh row of the original time series becomes the first sample for the "label" variable. $h = 1$ was used.

Fig. 12.28 shows the original data and the transformed output from the windowing process. The window operator adds six new attributes named input Y_{t-5} through input Y_{t-0}.

Step 2: Train the Model

When training any supervised model using this data, the attributes labeled input Y_{t-5} through input Y_{t-0} form the independent variables. In this case, *linear regression* is used to fit the dependent variable called label, using the independent variables input Y_{t-5} through input Y_{t-0}. The *Vector Linear Regression* operator is being used to infer the relationship between six dependent variables and the dependent variable. The model output for the dataset is:

$$label = 0.493 \times input\ Y_{t-5} + 0.258 \times input\ Y_{t-4} + 0.107 \times input\ Y_{t-3} - 0.098$$
$$\times input\ Y_{t-2} - 0.073 \times input\ Y_{t-1} + 0.329 \times input\ Y_{t-0} + 0.135$$

Step 3: Generate the Forecast in a Loop

Once the model fitting is done, the next step is to start the forecasting process. Note that given this configuration of the window size and horizon, one can now only make the forecast for the next step. In the example, the last row of the transformed dataset corresponds to December 2011. The independent variables are values from June–November 2011 and the target or label variable is December 2011. The regression equation is be used to predict December 2011 value. The same regression equation is also used for predicting January 2012 value. All one needs to do is insert the values from July–December into the regression equation to generate the January 2012 forecast. Next, a new row of data needs to be generated that would run from August–*January* to predict February 2012 using the regression equation. All the (actual) data from August–December is available as well as the predicted value for January. Once the predicted February value is obtained, there is nothing preventing the actual data from September–December plus the predicted January and February values from being used to forecast March 2012.

To implement this in RapidMiner process, one would need to break this up into two separate parts. First, take the last forecasted row (in this case, December 2011), drop the current value of input Y_{t-5} (current value is 1.201), rename input Y_{t-4} to input Y_{t-5}, rename input Y_{t-3} to input Y_{t-4}, rename input Y_{t-2} to input Y_{t-3}, rename input Y_{t-1} to input Y_{t-2}, rename input Y_{t-0} to input Y_{t-1}, and finally rename predicted *label* (current value is 1.934) to input Y_{t-0}. With this new row of data, the regression model can be applied to predict the next date in the series: January 2012. Fig. 12.30 shows the sample steps. Next, this entire process need to be put inside a *Loop* operator that will allow these steps to be repeatedly run for as many future periods as needed.

The *Loop* operator will contain all the mechanisms for accomplishing the renaming and, of course, to perform the forecasting (Fig. 12.31). Set the *iterations* in the *Loop* operator to the number of future months to forecast

Date	prediction(I...	inputYt−5	inputYt−4	inputYt−3	inputYt−2	inputYt−1	inputYt−0
Dec 1, 2011...	1.694	1.201	2.466	2.497	2.245	1.179	1.119
Jan 1, 2012 ...	2.597	2.466	2.497	2.245	1.179	1.119	1.694
Feb 1, 2012...	2.693	2.497	2.245	1.179	1.119	1.694	2.597
Mar 1, 2012...	2.196	2.245	1.179	1.119	1.694	2.597	2.693
Apr 1, 2012...	1.457	1.179	1.119	1.694	2.597	2.693	2.196
May 1, 201...	1.457	1.119	1.694	2.597	2.693	2.196	1.457
Jun 1, 2012 ...	2.087	1.694	2.597	2.693	2.196	1.457	1.457
Jul 1, 2012 ...	2.784	2.597	2.693	2.196	1.457	1.457	2.087
Aug 1, 2012...	2.807	2.693	2.196	1.457	1.457	2.087	2.784
Sep 1, 2012...	2.265	2.196	1.457	1.457	2.087	2.784	2.807
Oct 1, 2012...	1.720	1.457	1.457	2.087	2.784	2.807	2.265
Nov 1, 2012...	1.816	1.457	2.087	2.784	2.807	2.265	1.720
Dec 1, 2012...	2.433	2.087	2.784	2.807	2.265	1.720	1.816
Jan 1, 2013 ...	2.974	2.784	2.807	2.265	1.720	1.816	2.433
Feb 1, 2013...	2.911	2.807	2.265	1.720	1.816	2.433	2.974

FIGURE 12.30
Forecasting one step ahead.

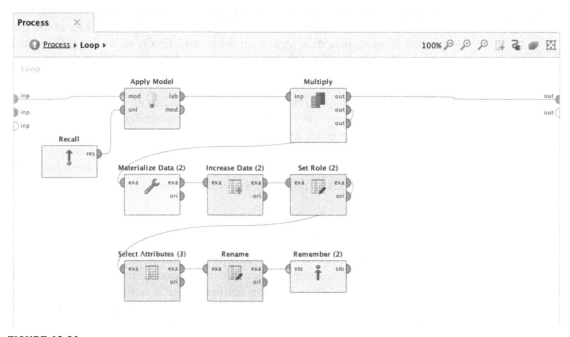

FIGURE 12.31
Looping subroutine to forecast one data point at a time.

(horizon). In this case, this is defined by a process variable called *futureMonths* whose value can be changed by the user before process execution. It is also possible to capture the Loop counts in a macro if the *set iteration macro* box is checked. A *macro* in RapidMiner is nothing but a process variable that can be called by other operators in the process. When *set iteration macro* is checked and a name is provided in the *macro name* box, a variable will be created with that name whose value will be updated each time, one loop is completed. An initial value for this macro is set by the *macro start value* option. Loops may be terminated by specifying a *timeout*, which is enabled by checking the *limit time* box. A macro variable can be used by any other operator by using the format %{macro name} in place of a numeric value.

Before the looping is started, the last forecasted row needs to be stored in a separate data structure. This is accomplished by a new *Windowing* operator and the macro titled *Extract Example Set*. The *Filter Example* operator simply deletes all rows of the transformed dataset except the last forecasted row. Finally the *Remember* operator stores this in memory and allows one to "recall" the stored value once inside the loop.

The loop parameter *iterations* will determine the number of times the inner process is repeated. Fig. 12.31 shows that during each iteration, the model is applied on the last forecasted row, and bookkeeping operations are performed to prepare application of the model to forecast the next month. This includes incrementing the month (date) by one, changing the role of the predicted label to that of a regular attribute, and finally renaming all the attributes. The newly renamed data are stored and then recalled before the next iteration begins.

The output of this process is shown in Fig. 12.32 as an overlay on top of the actual data. As seen, the simple linear regression model seems to adequately capture both the trend and seasonality of the underlying data. The *Linear Regression* operator of *Step 2: Train the model* can be quickly swapped to a *Support Vector Machine* operator and its performance tested without having to do any other programming or process modifications.

12.4.2 Neural Network Autoregressive

The windowing process allows time series dataset to be transformed to a cross-sectional horizontal dataset that is conducive to learners to create a forecasting model. That includes artificial neural networks to forecast the time series. Consider a simple ANN architecture with six inputs, one hidden layer with five nodes and an output, as shown in Fig. 12.33. It is multi-layer feed forward network that maps nonlinear functions.

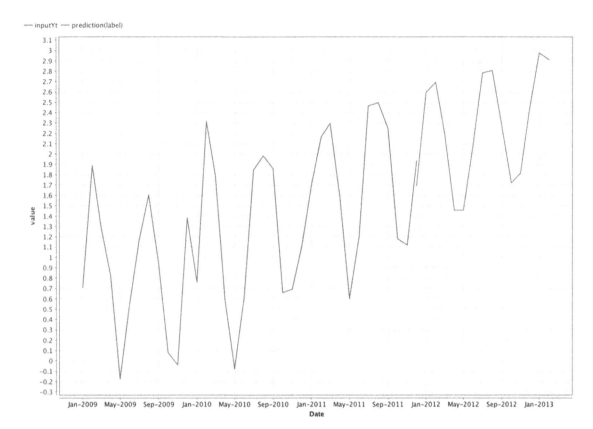

FIGURE 12.32
Forecasted time series.

Time series data, which is transformed into a cross-sectional dataset, can be fed into a neural network as inputs to predict the output. The weights for the links can be estimated with the training dataset, with lagged inputs and label, to build the neural network model. A feed forward neural network with one hidden layer, in the context of Time series is denoted as Neural Network Autoregressive—NNAR$(p,P,k)_m$ where p is the number of lagged inputs (order of the autoregressive model), k is the number of nodes in the hidden layer, P is the auto regressive part of the seasonal component and m is the seasonal period. The neural network NNAR$(p,P,k)_m$ has a particular relevance when it comes to time series forecasting. A NNAR$(p,P,k)_m$ functions *similarly* to a seasonal ARIMA $(p,0,0)$ $(P,0,0)_m$ model (Hyndman & Athanasopoulos, 2018).

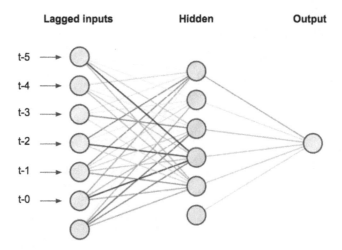

Lagged inputs   **Hidden**   **Output**

t-5
t-4
t-3
t-2
t-1
t-0

FIGURE 12.33
Neural network autoregressive model.

How to Implement

The implementation of NNAR is the same as the previous Windowing process shown in Fig. 12.29 with the *Neural Net* operator replacing the *Vector Linear Regression* modeling operator. The neural network operator has a parameter called *Hidden layer* where one can specify the number of hidden layers and nodes within each layer. For the NNAR model, the number of hidden layers is 1 and the number of nodes is one less than the number of the input nodes (Hyndman & Athanasopoulos, 2018). Fig. 12.34 shows the Rapidminer process for NNAR. This process has six lagged inputs and the number of nodes in the hidden layer is 5.

The forecasting is done one step ahead. The *Loop* operator takes the latest output and applies it to the input for the next iteration. The process can be saved and executed. The time series forecast is shown in Fig. 12.35. It can be observed that the NNAR forecast is different from the forecast achieved with the linear regression model.

An important point about any time series forecasting is that one should not place too much emphasis on the point forecasts. A complex quantity like sales demand for a product is influenced by too many factors and to claim that any forecasting will predict the exact value of demand three months in advance is unrealistic. However, what is far more valuable is the fact that recent undulations in the demand can be effectively captured and predicted.

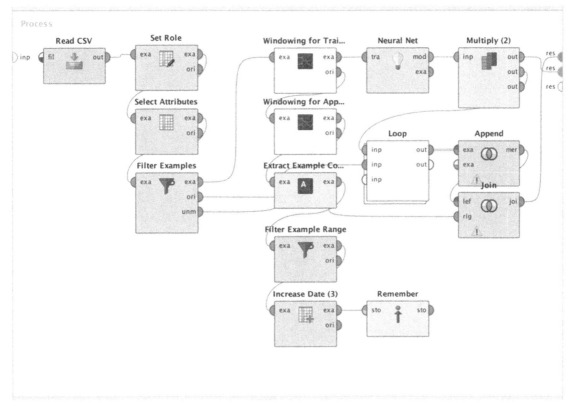

FIGURE 12.34
Process for neural network autoregressive model.

12.5 PERFORMANCE EVALUATION

How does one know if the time series forecasting model provides accurate forecasts? forecast accuracy metrics have to be created to compare the performance of one model with another and to compare the models across different use cases. For example, the performance of a revenue forecasting model can be contrasted with other models built by different techniques or different parameters; and even to compare with models to forecast the customer complaints for a product.

12.5.1 Validation Dataset

One way to measure accuracy is to measure the actual value post-fact and compare against the forecast and calculate the error. However, one would

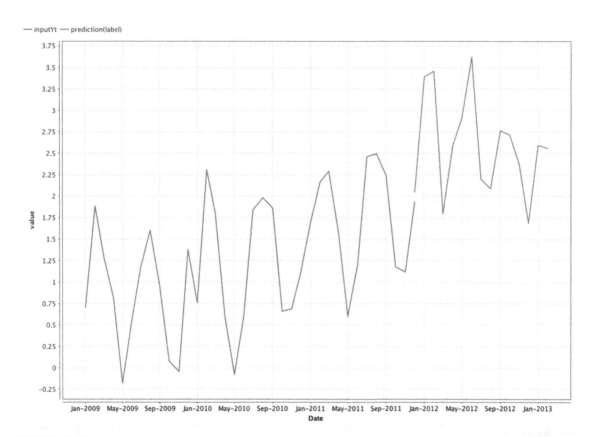

FIGURE 12.35
Forecast using neural network autoregression.

have to wait for the time to pass and the actual data to be measured. Residues are calculated when a forecast model is fitted on training data. By all means, the model might have overfitted the training data and perform poorly with unseen future forecasts. For this reason, training residuals are not a good way to measure how the forecast models are going to perform in the real world. Recall that in the case of the supervised learners, a set of known data is reserved for model validation. Similarly, some data points can be reserved in the time series as a *validation dataset* just to test the accuracy of the model. The training process uses data by restricting it to a point and the rest of the later time series is used for validation as shown in Fig. 12.36. As the model has not seen the validation dataset, deviation of actuals from the forecast is the forecast error of the model. The forecast error is the difference

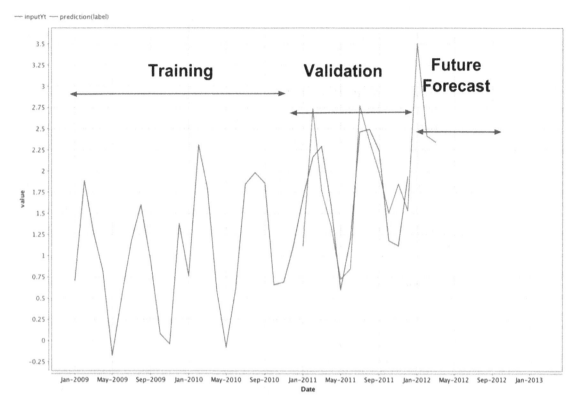

FIGURE 12.36
Validation dataset.

between the actual value y_i and the forecasted value $\hat{y}_i$. The error or the residue for the ith data point is given by Eq. (12.24)

$$e_i = y_i - \hat{y}_i \tag{12.24}$$

The forecast error shown in Eq. (12.24) is scale dependent. The error measured for each of the data points and can be aggregated to one metric to indicate the error of the forecasting model. Some of the commonly used forecast accuracy aggregate metrics are:

Mean Absolute Error

The error of the individual data point may be positive or negative and may cancel each other out. To derive the overall forecast for the model, calculate the absolute error to aggregate all the residuals and average it.

Mean absolute error = $\text{mean}(|e_i|)$ $\qquad$ (12.25)

MAE is a simple metric and it is scale dependent. It is convenient to communicate the error of the revenue forecasting model as, for example, $\pm$ \$900,000 per day.

Root Mean Squared Error

In some cases it is advantageous to penalize the individual point error with higher residues. Even though two models have the same MAE, one might have consistent error and the other might have low errors for some points and high error for other points. RMSE penalizes the latter.

$$\text{Root mean squared error} = \sqrt{\text{mean}\,(e^2)} \qquad (12.26)$$

RMSE is scale dependent and is used in situations where penalizing high relative residue is necessary. On the other hand, it is slightly difficult to understand the RMSE for a stand-alone model.

Mean Absolute Percentage Error

Percentage error of a data point is $p_i = 100\,\frac{e_i}{y_i}$. It is a scale independent error that can be aggregated to form mean absolute percentage error.

$$\text{Mean absolute percentage error} = \text{mean}\big(|p_i|\big) \qquad (12.27)$$

MAPE is useful to compare against multiple models across the different forecasting applications. For example, the quarterly revenue forecast, measured in USD, for a car brand might be $\pm 5\%$ and the forecast for world-wide car demand, measured in quantity, might be $\pm 3\%$. The firm's ability to forecast the car demand is higher than the revenue forecast for one brand. Even though MAPE is easy to understand and scale independent, MAPE has a significant limitation when it applies to intermittent data where zero values are possible in actual time series. For example, profit or defects in a product. Zero value in the time series yields an infinite error rate (if the forecast is non-zero) and skews the result. MAPE is also meaningless when the zero point is not defined or arbitrarily defined, as in non-kelvin temperature scales.

Mean Absolute Scaled Error

MASE is scale independent and overcomes the key limitations of MAPE by comparing the forecast values against a naive forecast. Naive forecast is a simple forecast where the next data point has the same value as the previous data point (Hyndman & Koehler, 2006). Scaled error is defined as:

$$\text{MASE} = \frac{\sum_{i=1}^{T} |e|}{\frac{T}{T-1}\sum_{i=2}^{T} |\bar{y}_i - \bar{y}_{i-1}|} \qquad (12.28)$$

T is the total number of data points. Scaled error is less than one if the forecast is better than naive forecast and greater than one if it is worse than naive forecast. One would want a scaled error much less than one for a good fore-casting model.

12.5.2 Sliding Window Validation

Sliding window validation is a process of backtesting time series models built through machine learning based methods. The whole cross-sectional dataset is divided into different training *windows* by specifying the window width. A model is trained using a training window and applied on the testing window to compute the performance for the first run. For the next run, the training window is slid to new set of training records and the process is repeated until all the training windows are used. By this technique, an average performance metric can be calculated across the entire dataset. The performance metric derived through sliding window validation is generally more robust than split validation technique.

12.6 CONCLUSION

Time series forecasting remains one of the cornerstones of data science tech-niques. It is one of the most widely used analytical applications in business and organizations. All organizations are forward looking and want to plan for the future. Time series forecasting, thus, forms a lynchpin to look into the *most probable* future and plan accordingly. Time series forecasting, like any other data science technique, has a diverse set of techniques and methods. This chapter covered the most important techniques that have practical rele-vance in a business setting.

Univariate time series forecasting treats prediction, essentially, as a single-variable problem, whereas, multivariate time series may use many time-concurred value series for prediction. If one has a series of points spaced over time, conventional forecasting uses smoothing and averaging to *predict* where the next few points will likely be. However, for complex systems such as the economy or demand of a product, point forecasts are unreliable because these systems are functions of hundreds if not thousands of variables. What is more valuable or useful is the ability to predict trends, rather than point forecasts. Trends can be predicted with greater confidence and reliability (i.e., Are the quantities going to trend up or down?), rather than the values or levels of these quantities. For this reason, using an ensemble of different modeling schemes such as artificial neural networks or support vector machines or polynomial regression can sometimes give highly accurate trend forecasts. If the time series is not highly volatile (and, therefore, more pre-dictable), time series forecasting can help understand the underlying struc-ture of the variability better. In such cases, trends or seasonal components have a stronger signature than random components do.

12.6.1   Forecasting Best Practices

While the science part of time series forecasting is covered in this chapter, there is a bit of *art* in getting robust forecasts from the time series models. Here is a list of suggested practices to build a robust forecasting model.

1. *Understand the metric*: Investigate how the time series metric is derived. Is the metric influenced by other metrics or phenomenon that can be better candidates for the forecasting? For example, instead of forecasting profit, both revenue and cost can be forecasted, and profit can be calculated. This is particularly suitable when profit margins are low and can go back and forth between positive and negative values (loss).
2. *Plot the time series*: A simple time series line chart reveals a wealth of information about the metric being investigated. Does the time series have a seasonal pattern? Long-term trends? Are the seasonality and trend linear or exponential? Is the series stationary? If the trend is exponential, can one derive log() series? Aggregate daily data to weeks and months to see the normalized trends.
3. *Is it forecastable*: Check if the time series is forecastable using stationary checks.
4. *Decompose*: Identify trends and seasonality using decomposition methods. These techniques show how the time series can be split into multiple meaningful components.
5. *Try them all*: Try several different methods mentioned in the forecasting taxonomy in Fig. 12.3, after splitting, training, and validation samples. For each method:
   a. Perform residual checks using MAE or MAPE metric.
   b. Evaluate forecasts using the validation period.
   c. Select the best performing method and parameters using optimization functions.
   d. Update the model using the full dataset (training + validation) for future forecasts.
6. *Maintain the models*: Review models on a regular basis. Time series forecast models have a limited shelf life. Apart from feeding the latest data to the model, the model should be refreshed to make it relevant for the latest data. Building a model daily is not uncommon.

References

Box, G. A. (1970). *Time series analysis: Forecasting and control*. San Francisco, CA: Holding Day.

Box, G. J. (2008). *Time series analysis: Forecasting and control*. Wiley Series in Probability and Statistics.

Brown, R. G. (1956). *Exponential smoothing for predicting demand*. Cambridge, MA: Arthur D. Little.

Hyndman R.A. (2014). *Forecasting: Principles and practice.* <Otexts.org>.

Hyndman, R. J., & Athanasopoulos, G. (2018). *Forecasting: Principles and practice.* 2nd edition. <Otexts.org>.

Hyndman, Rob J., & Koehler, Anne B. (2006). Another look at measures of forecast accuracy. *International Journal of Forecasting, 22*, 679−688.

Shmueli G. (2011). *Practical time series forecasting: A hands on guide.* <statistics.com>.

Winters, P. (1960). Forecasting sales by exponentially weighted moving averages. *Management Science, 6*(3), 324−342.

CHAPTER 13

Anomaly Detection

Anomaly detection is the process of finding outliers in a given dataset. Outliers are the data objects that stand out amongst other data objects and do not conform to the expected behavior in a dataset. Anomaly detection algorithms have broad applications in business, scientific, and security domains where isolating and acting on the results of outlier detection is critical. For identification of anomalies, algorithms discussed in previous chapters such as classification, regression, and clustering can be used. If the training dataset has objects with known anomalous outcomes, then any of the supervised data science algorithms can be used for anomaly detection. In addition to supervised algorithms, there are specialized (unsupervised) algorithms whose whole purpose is to detect outliers without the use of a labeled training dataset. In the context of unsupervised anomaly detection, algorithms can either measure distance from other data points or density around the neighborhood of the data point. Even clustering techniques can be leveraged for anomaly detection. The outlier usually forms a separate cluster from other clusters because they are far away from other data points. Some of the techniques discussed in previous chapters will be revisited in the context of outlier detection. Before discussing the algorithms, the term outlier or anomaly has to be defined and the reason such data points occur in a dataset will need to be understood.

13.1 CONCEPTS

An outlier is a data object that is markedly different from the other objects in a dataset. Hence, an outlier is always defined in the context of other objects in the dataset. A high-income individual may be an outlier in a middle-class neighborhood dataset, but not in the membership of a luxury vehicle ownership dataset. By nature of the occurrence, outliers are also rare and, hence, they stand out amongst other data points. For example, the majority of computer network traffic is legitimate, and the one malicious network attack would be the outlier.

Data Science. DOI: https://doi.org/10.1016/B978-0-12-814761-0.00013-7

13.1.1   Causes of Outliers

Outliers in the dataset can originate from either error in the data or from valid inherent variability in the data. It is important to understand the provenance of the outliers because it will guide what action, if any, should be performed on the identified outliers. However, pinpointing exactly what caused an outlier is a tedious task and it may be impossible to find the causes of outliers in the dataset. Here are some of the most common reasons why an outlier occurs in the dataset:

Data errors: Outliers may be part of the dataset because of measurement errors, human errors, or data collection errors. For example, in a dataset of human heights, a reading such as 1.70 cm is obviously an error and most likely was wrongly entered into the system. These data points are often ignored because they affect the conclusion of the data science task. Outlier detection here is used as a preprocessing step in algorithms such as regression and neural networks. Data errors due to human mistake could be either intentional introduction of error or unintentional error due to data entry error or significant bias.

Normal variance in the data: In a normal distribution, 99.7% of data points lie within three standard deviations from the mean. In other words, 0.26% or 1 in 370 data points lie outside of three standard deviations from the mean. By definition, they don't occur frequently and yet are a part of legitimate data. An individual earning a billion dollars in a year or someone who is more than 7 ft tall falls under the category of outlier in an income dataset or a human height dataset respectively. These outliers skew some of the descriptive statistics like the mean of the dataset. Regardless, they are legitimate data points in the dataset.

Data from other distribution classes: The number of daily page views for a customer-facing website from a user IP address usually range from one to several dozen. However, it is not unusual to find a few IP addresses reaching hundreds of thousands of page views in a day. This outlier could be an automated program from a computer (also called a bot) making the calls to scrape the content of the site or access one of the utilities of the site, either legitimately or maliciously. Even though they are an outlier, it is quite "normal" for bots to register thousands of page views to a website. All bot traffic falls under the distribution of a different class "traffic from programs" other than traffic from regular browsers that fall under the human user class.

Distributional assumptions: Outlier data points can originate from incorrect assumptions made on the data or distribution. For example, if the data measured is usage of a library in a school, then during term exams there will be an outlier because of a surge in the usage of the library. Similarly, there will be a surge in retail sales during the day after

Thanksgiving in the United States. An outlier in this case is expected and does not represent the data point of a typical measure.

Understanding why outliers occur will help determine what action to perform after outlier detection. In a few applications, the objective is to isolate and act on the outlier as can be seen in credit card transaction fraud monitoring. In this case, credit card transactions exhibiting different behavior from most normal transactions (such as high frequency, high amounts, or very large geographic separation between points of consecutive transactions) has to be isolated, alerted, and the owner of the credit card has to be contacted immediately to verify the authenticity of the transaction. In other cases, the outliers have to be filtered out because they may skew the final outcome. Here outlier detection is used as a preprocessing technique for other data science or analytical tasks. For example, ultra-high-income earners might need to be eliminated in order to generalize a country's income patterns. Here outliers are legitimate data points but are intentionally disregarded in order to generalize conclusions.

DETECTING CLICK FRAUD IN ONLINE ADVERTISING

The rise in online advertising has underwritten successful Internet business models and enterprises. Online advertisements make free Internet services, like web searches, news content, social networks, mobile application, and other services, viable. One of the key challenges in online advertisement is mitigating *click frauds*. Click fraud is a process where an automated program or a person imitates the action of a normal user clicking on an online advertisement, with the malicious intent of defrauding the advertiser, publisher, or advertisement network. Click fraud could be performed by contracting parties or third parties, like competitors trying to deplete advertisement budgets or to tarnish the reputation of the sites. Click fraud distorts the economics of advertising and poses a major challenge for all parties involved in online advertising (Haddadi, 2010). Detecting, eliminating, or discounting click fraud makes the entire marketplace trustworthy and even provides competitive advantage for all the parties.

Detecting click fraud takes advantage of the fact that fraudulent traffic exhibits an atypical web browsing pattern when compared with typical clickstream data.

Fraudulent traffic often does not follow a logical sequence of actions and contains repetitive actions that would differentiate from other regular traffic (Sadagopan & Li, 2008). For example, most of the fraudulent traffic exhibits either one or many of these characteristics: they have very high click depth (number of web pages accessed deep in the website); the time between each click would be extremely short; a single session would have a high number of clicks on advertisements as compared with normal users; the originating IP address would be different from the target market of the advertisement; there would be very little time spent on the advertiser's target website; etc. It is not one trait that differentiates fraudulent traffic from regular traffic, but a *combination* of the traits. Detecting click fraud is an ongoing and evolving process. Increasingly, the click fraud perpetrators are getting more sophisticated in imitating the characteristics of a normal web browsing user. Hence, click fraud cannot be fully eliminated, however, it can be contained by constantly developing new algorithms to identify fraudulent traffic.

To detect click fraud outliers, first clickstream data would need to be prepared in such a way that detection using

(Continued)

(Continued)

data science is easier. A relational column-row dataset can be prepared with each visit occupying each row and the columns being traits like click depth, time between each click, advertisement clicks, total time spent in target website, etc. This multidimensional dataset can be used for outlier detection using data science. Clickstream traits or attributes have to be carefully considered, evaluated, transformed, and added into the dataset. In multidimensional data space, the fraudulent traffic (data point) is distant from other visit records because of their attributes, such as the number of ad clicks in a session. A regular visit usually has one or two ad clicks in a session, while a fraudulent visit would have dozens of ad clicks. Similarly, other attributes can help identify the outlier more precisely. Outlier-detection algorithms reviewed in this chapter assign an outlier score (fraud score) for all the clickstream data points and the records with a higher score are predicted to be outliers.

13.1.2   Anomaly Detection Techniques

Humans are innately equipped to focus on outliers. The news cycle experienced every day is mainly hinged on outlier events. The interest around knowing who is the fastest, who earns the most, and who wins the most medals or scores the most goals is in part due to increased attention to outliers. If the data is in one dimension like taxable income for individuals, outliers can be identified with a simple sorting function. Visualizing data by scatter, histogram, and box-whisker charts can help to identify outliers in the case of single attribute datasets as well. More advanced techniques would fit the data to a distribution model and use data science techniques to detect outliers.

Outlier Detection Using Statistical Methods

Outliers in the data can be identified by creating a statistical distribution model of the data and identifying the data points that do not fit into the model or data points that occupy the ends of the distribution tails. The underlying distribution of many practical datasets fall into the Gaussian (normal) distribution. The parameters for building a normal distribution (i.e., mean and standard deviation) can be estimated from the dataset and a normal distribution curve can be created like the one shown in Fig. 13.1.

Outliers can be detected based on where the data points fall in the standard normal distribution curve. A threshold for classifying an outlier can be specified, say, three standard deviations from the mean. Any data point that is more than three standard deviations is identified as an outlier. Identifying outliers using this method considers only one attribute or dimension at a time. More advanced statistical techniques take multiple dimensions into account and calculate the *Mahalanobis distance* instead of the standard

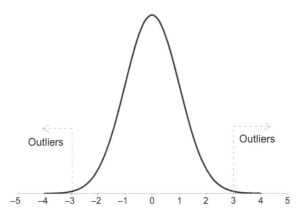

FIGURE 13.1
Standard normal distribution and outliers.

deviations from the mean in a univariate distribution. Mahalanobis distance is the multivariate generalization of finding how many standard deviations away a point is from the mean of the multivariate distribution. Outlier detection using statistics provides a simple framework for building a distribution model and for detection based on the variance of the data point from the mean. One limitation of using the distribution model to find outliers is that the distribution of the dataset is not previously known. Even if the distribution is known, the actual data don't always fit the model.

Outlier Detection Using Data Science

Outliers exhibit a certain set of characteristics that can be exploited to find them. Following are classes of techniques that were developed to identify outliers by using their unique characteristics (Tan, Steinbach, & Kumar, 2005). Each of these techniques has multiple parameters and, hence, a data point labeled as an outlier in one algorithm may not be an outlier to another. Hence, it is prudent to rely on multiple algorithms before labeling the outliers.

> *Distance-based:* By nature, outliers are different from other data objects in the dataset. In multidimensional Cartesian space they are distant from other data points, as shown in Fig. 13.2. If the average distance of the nearest N neighbors is measured, the outliers will have a higher value than other normal data points. Distance-based algorithms utilize this property to identify outliers in the data.

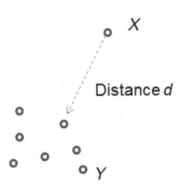

FIGURE 13.2
Distance-based outlier.

Density-based: The density of a data point in a neighborhood is inversely related to the distance to its neighbors. Outliers occupy low-density areas while the regular data points congregate in high-density areas. This is derived from the fact that the relative occurrence of an outlier is low compared with the frequency of normal data points.

Distribution-based: Outliers are the data points that have a low probability of occurrence and they occupy the tail ends of the distribution curve. So, if one tries to fit the dataset in a statistical distribution, these anomalous data points will stand out and, hence, can be identified. A simple normal distribution can be used to model the dataset by calculating the mean and standard deviation.

Clustering: Outliers by definition are not similar to normal data points in a dataset. They are rare data points far away from regular data points and generally do not form a tight cluster. Since most of the clustering algorithms have a minimum threshold of data points to form a cluster, the outliers are the lone data points that are not clustered. Even if the outliers form a cluster, they are far away from other clusters.

Classification techniques: Nearly all classification techniques can be used to identify outliers, if previously known classified data are available. In classification techniques for detecting outliers, a known test dataset is needed where one of the class labels should be called "Outlier." The outlier-detection classification model that is built based on the test dataset can predict whether the unknown data is an outlier or not. The challenge in using a classification model is the availability of previously labeled data. Outlier data may be difficult to source because they are rare. This can be partially solved by stratified sampling where the outlier records are oversampled against normal records.

Supervised classification methods have been discussed in past chapters and unsupervised outlier-detection methods will be discussed in the coming sections. The focus will mainly be placed on distance and density-based detection techniques in the coming sections.

13.2 DISTANCE-BASED OUTLIER DETECTION

Distance or proximity-based outlier detection is one of the most fundamental algorithms for anomaly detection and it relies on the fact that outliers are distant from other data points. The proximity measures can be simple Euclidean distance for real values and cosine or Jaccard similarity measures for binary and categorical values. For the purpose of this discussion, consider a dataset with numeric attributes and Euclidean distance as the proximity measure. Fig. 13.3 shows a two-dimensional scatterplot of a sample dataset.

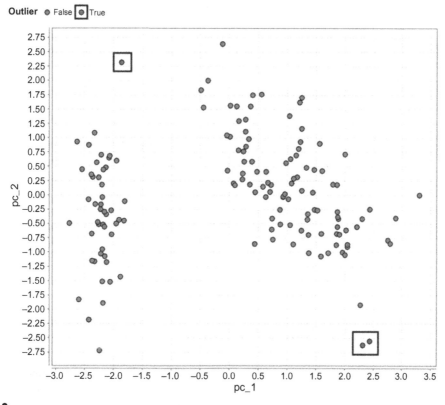

FIGURE 13.3

Dataset with outliers.

Outliers are the data points marked as gray and can be visually identified away from the groups of data. However, when working with multidimensional data with more attributes, visual techniques show limitations quickly.

13.2.1 How It Works

The fundamental concept of distance-based outlier detection is assigning a *distance score* for all the data points in the dataset. The distance score should reflect how far a data point is separated from other data points. A similar concept was reviewed in the k-nearest neighbor (k-NN) classification technique in Chapter 4, Classification. A distance score can be assigned for each data object that is the distance to the kth-nearest data object. For example, a distance score can be assigned for every data object that is the distance to the third-nearest data object. If the data object is an outlier, then it is far away from other data objects; hence, the distance score for the outlier will be higher than for a normal data object. If the data objects are sorted by distance score, then the objects with the highest scores are potentially outlier(s). As with k-NN classification or any algorithm that uses distance measures, it is important to normalize the numeric attributes, so an attribute with a higher absolute scale, such as income, does not dominate attributes with a lower scale, such as credit score.

In distance-based outlier detection, there is a significant effect based on the value of k, as in the k-NN classification technique. If the value of $k = 1$, then two outliers next to each other but far away from other data points are not identified as outliers. On the other hand, if the value of k is large, then a group of normal data points which form a cohesive cluster will be mislabeled as outliers, if the number of data points is less than k and the cluster is far away from other data points. With a defined value of k, once the distance scores have been calculated, a distance threshold can be specified to identify outliers or pick the top n objects with maximum distances, depending on the application and the nature of the dataset. Fig. 13.4 shows the results of two different outlier-detection algorithms based on distance for the Iris dataset. Fig. 13.4A shows the outlier detection with $k = 1$ and Fig. 13.4B shows the detection of the same dataset with $k = 5$.

13.2.2 How to Implement

Commercial data science tools offer specific outlier-detection algorithms and solutions as part of the package either in the modeling or data cleansing sections. In RapidMiner, unsupervised outlier-detection operator can be found in Data Transformation > Data Cleansing > Outlier Detection > Detect Outlier Distance. The example set used in this process is the Iris dataset with four numerical attributes and 150 examples.

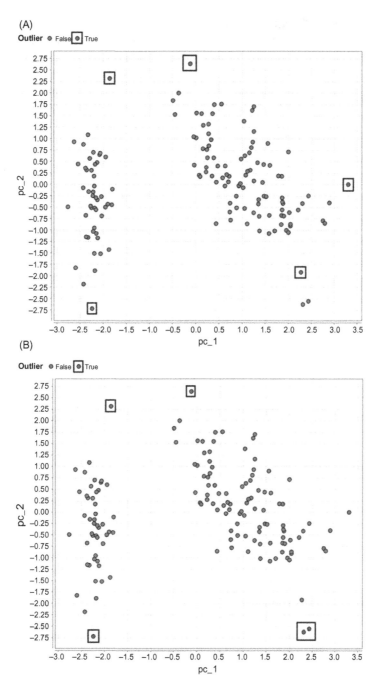

FIGURE 13.4
Top five outliers of Iris dataset when (A) $k = 1$ and (B) $k = 5$.

Step 1: Data Preparation

Even though all four attributes of the Iris dataset measure the same quantity (length) and are measured on the same scale (centimeters), a normalization step is included as a matter of best practice for techniques that involve distance calculation. The *Normalize* operator can be found in Data Transformation > Value modification > Numerical. The attributes are converted to a uniform scale of mean 0 and standard deviation 1 using Z-transformation.

For the purposes of this demonstration, a two-dimensional scatterplot with two attributes will be helpful to visualize outliers. However, the Iris dataset has four attributes. To aid in this visualization objective, the four numerical attributes will be reduced to two attributes (principal components) using the *principal component analysis (PCA)* operator. Please note that the use of the *PCA* operator is optional and not required for outlier detection. The results of the outlier detection with or without *PCA* in most cases will be unchanged. But visualization of the results will be easy with two-dimensional scatterplots. *PCA* will be discussed in detail in Chapter 14, Feature Selection. In this process a variance threshold has been specified for the *PCA* operator of 0.95. Any principal component that has a variance threshold more than 0.95 is removed from the result set. The outcome of the *PCA* operator has two principal components.

Step 2: Detect Outlier Operator

The *Detect Outlier (Distances)* operator has a data input port and outputs data with an appended attribute called *outlier*. The value of the output outlier attribute is either true or false. The *Detect Outlier (Distances)* operator has three parameters that can be configured by the user.

Number of neighbors: This is the value of k in the algorithm. The default value is 10. If the value is made lower, the process finds smaller outlier clusters with less data points.

Number of outliers: The individual outlier score is not visible to the users. Instead the algorithm finds the data points with the highest outlier scores. The number of data points to be found can be configured using this parameter.

Distance function: As in the k-NN algorithm, the distance measurement function needs to be specified. Commonly used functions are Euclidean and cosine (for document vectors).

In this example, $k = 1$, number of outliers $= 10$, and the distance function is set to Euclidian. The output of this operator is the example set with an appended outlier attribute. Fig. 13.5 provides the RapidMiner process with

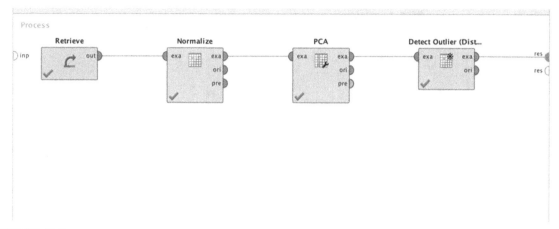

FIGURE 13.5
Process to detect outliers based on distance.

data extraction, PCA dimensional reduction, and outlier-detection operators. The process can now be saved and executed.

Step 3: Execution and Interpretation

The result dataset can be sorted by outlier attribute, which has either a true or false value. Since 10 outliers have been specified in the parameter of the *Detect outlier* operator, that number of outliers can be found in the result set. An efficient way of exploring the outliers is to look at the scatterplot in the Chart view of results set. The X- and Y-axes can be specified as the principal components and the color as the outlier attribute. The output scatterplot shows the outlier data points along with all the normal data points as shown in Fig. 13.6.

Distance-based outlier detection is a simple algorithm that is easy to implement and widely used when the problem involves many numeric variables. The execution becomes expensive when the dataset involves a high number of attributes and records, because the algorithm has to calculate distances with other data points in high-dimensional space.

13.3 DENSITY-BASED OUTLIER DETECTION

Outliers, by definition, occur less frequently compared to normal data points. This means that in the data space outliers occupy low-density areas and normal data points occupy high-density areas. Density is a count of data points in a normalized unit of space and is inversely proportional to the

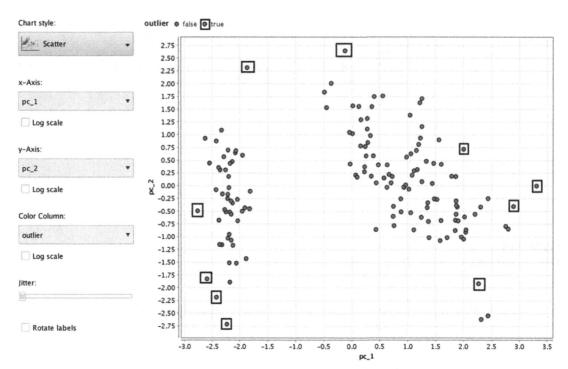

FIGURE 13.6
Outlier detection output.

distances between data points. The objective of a density-based outlier algorithm is to identify those data points from low-density areas. There are a few different implementations to assign an outlier score for the data points. The inverse of the average distance of all k neighbors can be found. The distance between data points and density are inversely proportional. Neighborhood density can also be calculated by calculating the number of data points from a normalized unit distance. The approach for density-based outliers is similar to the approach discussed for density-based clustering and for the k-NN classification algorithm.

13.3.1 How It Works

Since distance is the inverse of density, the approach of a density-based outlier can be explained with two parameters, distance (d) and proportion of data points (p). A point X is considered an outlier if at least p fraction of points lie more than d distance from the point (Knorr & Ng, 1998). Fig. 13.7 provides a visual illustration of outlier detection. By the given definition, the point X occupies a low-density area. The parameter p is specified

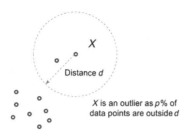

FIGURE 13.7
Outlier detection based on distance and propensity.

as a high value, above 95%. One of the key issues in this implementation is specifying distance. It is important to normalize the attributes so that the distance makes sense, particularly when attributes involve different measures and units. If the distance is specified too low, then more outliers will be detected, which means normal points have the risk of being labeled as outliers and vice versa.

13.3.2   How to Implement

The RapidMiner process for outlier detection based on density is similar to outlier detection by distance, which was reviewed in the previous section. The process developed for previous distance-based outliers can be used, but the *Detect Outlier (Distances)* operator would be replaced with the *Detect Outlier (Densities)* operator.

Step 1: Data Preparation
Data preparation will condition the data so the *Detect Outlier (Densities)* operator returns meaningful results. As with the outlier detection by distance technique, the Iris dataset will be used with normalization and the *PCA* operator so that the number of attributes is reduced to two for easy visualization.

Step 2: Detect Outlier Operator
The *Detect Outlier (Densities)* operator can be found in Data Transformation > Data Cleansing > Outlier Detection, and has three parameters:

   Distance (d): Threshold distance used to find outliers. For this example, the distance is specified as 1.
   Proportion (p): Proportion of data points outside of radius *d* of a point, beyond which the point is considered an outlier. For this example, the value specified is 95%.
   Distance measurement: A measurement parameter like Euclidean, cosine, or squared distance. The default value is Euclidean.

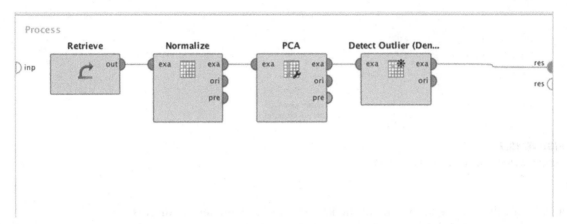

FIGURE 13.8

Process to detect outliers based on density.

Any data point that has more than 95% of other data points beyond distance *d* is considered an outlier. Fig. 13.8 shows the RapidMiner process with the *Normalization, PCA,* and *Detect Outlier* operators. The process can be saved and executed.

Step 3: Execution and Interpretation

The process adds an outlier attribute to the example set, which can be used for visualization using a scatterplot as shown in Fig. 13.9. The outlier attribute is Boolean and indicates whether the data point is predicted to be an outlier or not. In the scatterplot, a few data points marked as outliers can be found. The parameters *d* and *p* of the *Detect Outlier* operator can be tuned to find the desired level of outlier detection.

Density-based outlier detection is closely related to distance-based outlier approaches and, hence, the same pros and cons apply. As with distance-based outlier detection, the main drawback is that this approach does not work with varying densities. The next approach, local outlier factor (LOF) is designed for such datasets. Specifying the parameter distance (*d*) and proportion (*p*) is going to be challenging, particularly when the characteristics of the data are not previously known.

13.4 LOCAL OUTLIER FACTOR

The LOF technique is a variation of density-based outlier detection, and addresses one of its key limitations, detecting the outliers in varying density. Varying density is a problem in simple density-based methods, including

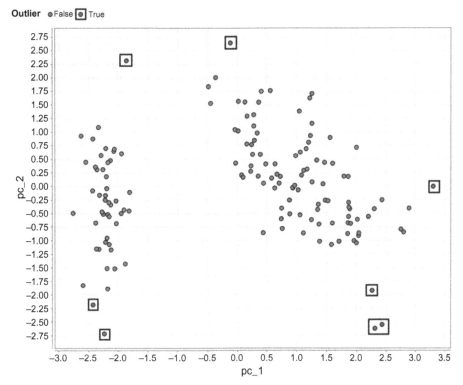

FIGURE 13.9
Output of density-based outlier detection.

DBSCAN clustering (see Chapter 7: Clustering). The LOF technique was proposed in the paper *LOF: Identifying Density-Based Local Outliers* (Breunig,
Kriegel, Ng, & Sander, 2000).

13.4.1 How it Works

LOF takes into account the density of the data point and the *density of the
neighborhood* of the data point as well. A key feature of the LOF technique is
that the outlier score takes into account the relative density of the data point.
Once the outlier scores for data points are calculated, the data points can be
sorted to find the outliers in the dataset. The core of the LOF lies in the calculation of the relative density. The relative density of a data point X with k
neighbors is given by the following equation:

$$\text{Relative density of } X = \frac{\text{Density of } X}{\text{Average density of all data points in the neighborhood}} \quad (13.1)$$

where the density of X is the inverse of the average distance for the nearest k data points. The same parameter k also forms the locality of the neighborhood. By comparing the density of the data point and density of all the data points in the neighborhood, whether the density of the data point is lower than the density of the neighborhood can be determined. This scenario indicates the presence of an outlier.

13.4.2   How to Implement

A LOF-based data science process is similar to the other outlier processes explained in RapidMiner. The *Detect Outlier (LOF)* operator is available in Data Transformation > Data Cleansing > Outlier Detection. The output of the *LOF* operator contains the example set along with a numeric outlier score. The LOF algorithm does not explicitly label a data point as an outlier; instead the score is exposed to the user. This score can be used to visualize a comparison to a threshold, above which the data point is considered an outlier. Having the raw score means that the data science practitioner can "tune" the detection criteria, without having to rerun the scoring process, by changing the threshold for comparison.

Step 1: Data Preparation
Similar to the distance- and density-based outlier-detection processes, the dataset has to be normalized using *Normalize* operator. The *PCA* operator is

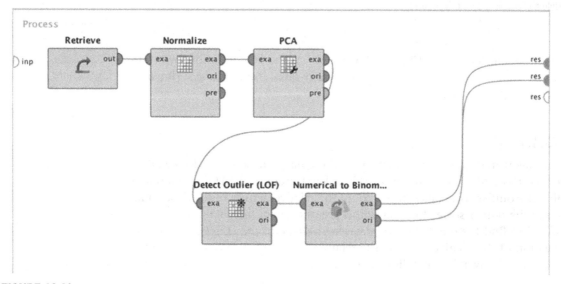

FIGURE 13.10
RapidMiner process for LOF outlier detection. *LOF*, Local outlier factor.

used to reduce the four-dimensional Iris dataset to two dimensions, so that the output can be visualized easily.

Step 2: Detect Outlier Operator
The *LOF* operator has minimal points (*MinPts*) lower bound and upper bound as parameters. The *MinPts* lower bound is the value of k, the neighborhood number. The LOF algorithm also takes into account a *MinPts* upper bound to provide more stable results (Breunig et al., 2000). Fig. 13.10 shows the RapidMiner process.

Step 3: Results Interpretation
After using the *Detect Outlier* operator, the outlier score is appended to the result dataset. Fig. 13.11 shows the result set with outlier score represented as the color of the data point. In the results window, the outlier score can be used to color the data points. The scatterplot indicates that points closer to the blue spectrum (left side of the outlier scale in the chart legend) are predicted to be regular data points and points closer to the red spectrum

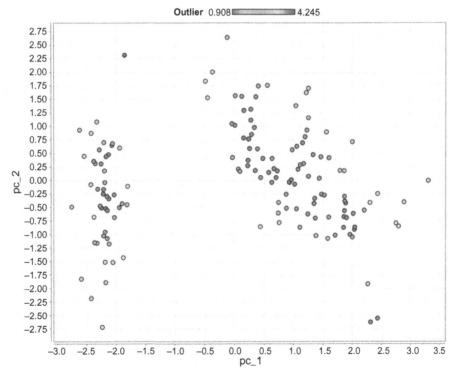

FIGURE 13.11
Output of LOF outlier detection. *LOF*, Local outlier factor.

(right side of the outlier scale in the chart legend) are predicted to be out-liers. If an additional Boolean flag indicating whether a data point is an out-lier or not is needed, a *Numeric to Binominal* operator can be added to the result dataset. The *Numeric to Binominal* operator converts the numeric outlier score to a binominal true or false based on the threshold specification in the parameter of the operator and to the score output from the *LOF* operator.

In addition to the three data science techniques discussed for outlier detec-tion, the RapidMiner Anomaly *Detection extension* (RapidMiner Extension: Anomaly Detection, 2014) offers more algorithms to identify outliers. RapidMiner extensions can be installed by accessing Help > Updates and Extensions.

13.5 CONCLUSION

In theory, any classification algorithm can be used for outlier detection, if a previously classified dataset is available. A generalized classification model tries to predict outliers the same way it predicts the class label of the data point. However, there is one key issue in using classification models. Since the proba-bility of occurrence of an outlier is really low, say, less than 0.1%, the model can just "predict" the class as "regular" for all the data points and still be 99.9% accurate! This method clearly does not work for outlier detection, since the *recall measure* (see Chapter 8: Model Evaluation for details about recall) is 0%. In practical applications, like detecting network intrusion or fraud preven-tion in high-volume transaction networks, the cost of not detecting an outlier is very high. The model can even have an acceptable level of false alarms, that is, labeling a regular data point as an outlier. Therefore, special care and prepa-ration is required to improve the detection of the outliers.

Stratified sampling methods can be used to increase the frequency of occur-rence of outlier records in the training set and reduce the relative occurrence of regular data points. In a similar approach, the occurrence of outliers and regular records can be sampled with replacements so that there are an equal number of records in both classes. Stratified sampling boosts the number of outlier records in the test dataset with respect to regular records in an attempt to increase both the accuracy and recall of outlier detection. In any case, it is important to know the biases in any algorithm that might be used to detect outliers and to specially prepare the training dataset in order to make the resulting model effective. In practical applications, outlier-detection models have to be updated frequently as the characteristics of an outlier changes over time, and hence, the relationship between outliers and normal records changes as well. In constant real time data streams, outlier detection creates additional challenges because of the dynamic distribution of the data and dynamic relationships within the data (Sadik & Gruenwald, 2013). Outlier detection remains one of the most profound applications of data science as it impacts the majority of the population through financial transaction monitoring, fraud prevention, and early identification of anomalous activity in the context of security.

References

Breunig, M. M., Kriegel, H., Ng, R. T., & Sander, J. (2000). LOF: Identifying density-based local outliers. In *Proceedings of the ACM SIGMOD 2000 international conference on management of data* (pp. 1−12).

Haddadi, H. (2010). Fighting online click-fraud using bluff ads. *ACM SIGCOMM Computer Communication Review, 40*(2), 21−25.

Knorr, E. M., & Ng, R. T. (1998) Algorithms for mining distance-based outliers in large datasets. In *Proceedings of the 24th VLDB conference* (pp. 392−403). New York, USA.

RapidMiner Extension: Anomaly Detection. (2014). *German research center for artificial intelligence.* DFKI GmbH. Retrieved from <http://madm.dfki.de/rapidminer/anomalydetection>.

Sadagopan, N., & Li, J. (2008) Characterizing typical and atypical user sessions in clickstreams. In *Proceeding of the 17th international conference on World Wide Web—WWW '08 885.* <https://doi.org/10.1145/1367497.1367617>.

Sadik, S., & Gruenwald, L. (2013). Research issues in outlier detection for data streams. *ACM SIGKDD Explorations Newsletter, 15*(1), 33−40.

Tan, P.-N., Steinbach, M., & Kumar, V. (2005). *Anomaly detection. Introduction to data mining* (pp. 651−676). Boston, MA: Addison Wesley.

CHAPTER 14

Feature Selection

In this chapter the focus will be on an important component of dataset preparation for data science: feature selection. An overused rubric in data science circles is that 80% of the analysis effort is spent on data cleaning and preparation and only 20% is typically spent on modeling. In light of this it may seem strange that this book has devoted more than a dozen chapters to modeling techniques and only a couple to data preparation! However, data cleansing and preparation are things that are better learned through experience and not so much from a book. That said, it is essential to be conversant with the many techniques that are available for these important early process steps. In this chapter the focus will not be on data cleaning, as it was partially covered in Chapter 2, Data Science Process, but rather on reducing a dataset to its essential characteristics or features. This process is known by various terms: feature selection, dimension reduction, variable screening, key parameter identification, attribute weighting or regularization. Regularization was briefly covered in Chapter 5 as applied to multiple linear regression. There it was introduced as a process that helps to reduce overfitting, which is essentially what feature selection techniques implicitly achieve. [Technically, there is a subtle difference between dimension reduction and feature selection. Dimension reduction methods—such as principal component analysis (PCA), discussed in Section 14.2—combine or merge actual attributes in order to reduce the number of attributes of a raw dataset. Feature selection methods work more like filters that eliminate some attributes.]

First a brief introduction to feature selection along with the need for this preprocessing step is given. There are fundamentally two types of feature selection processes: *filter type* and *wrapper type*. Filter approaches work by selecting only those attributes that rank among the top in meeting certain stated criteria (Blum & Langley, 1997; Yu & Liu, 2003). Wrapper approaches work by iteratively selecting, via a feedback loop, only those attributes that improve the performance of an algorithm (Kohavi & John, 1997). Among the filter-type methods, one can further classify based on the data types: numeric versus nominal. The most common wrapper-type methods are the ones

Data Science. DOI: https://doi.org/10.1016/B978-0-12-814761-0.00014-9

associated with multiple regression: stepwise regression, forward selection, and backward elimination. A few numeric filter-type methods will be explored: PCA, which is strictly speaking a dimension reduction method; information gain—based filtering; and one categorical filter-type method: chi-square-based filtering.

14.1 CLASSIFYING FEATURE SELECTION METHODS

IDENTIFYING WHAT MATTERS

Feature selection in data science refers to the process of identifying the few most important variables or attributes that are essential to a model for an accurate prediction. In today's world of big data and high-speed computing, one might be forgiven for asking, why bother? What is the reason to filter any attributes when the computing horse-power exists? For example, some argue that it is redundant trying to fit a model to data; rather one should simply use a fast brute-force approach to sift through data to identify meaningful *correlations* and make decisions based on this (Bollier, 2010).

However, models are still useful for many reasons. Models can improve decision making and help advance knowledge. Blindly relying on correlations to predict future states also has flaws. The now popular "My TiVo thinks I'm gay" example (Zaslow, 2002), illustrated how the TiVo recommendation engine, which works on *large data* and correlations, resulted in a humorous mismatch for a customer. As long as the use of models is needed, feature selection will be an important step in the process. Feature selection serves a couple of purposes: it optimizes the performance of the data science algorithm and it makes it easier for the analyst to interpret the outcome of the modeling. It does this by reducing the number of attributes or features that one must contend with.

There are two powerful technical motivations for incorporating feature selection in the data science process. First, a dataset may contain highly correlated attributes, such as the number of items sold, and the revenue earned by the sales of the item. Typically, there is no new information gained by including both of these attributes. Additionally, in the case of multiple regression—type models, if two or more of the independent variables (or predictors) are correlated, then the estimates of coefficients in a regression model tend to be unstable or counter intuitive. This is the *multicollinearity* discussed in Section 5.1. In the case of algorithms like naïve Bayesian classifiers, the attributes need to be independent of each other. Further, the speed of algorithms is typically a function of the number of attributes. So, by using only one among the correlated attributes the performance is improved.

Second, a dataset may also contain redundant information that does not directly impact the predictions: as an extreme example, a customer ID number has no bearing on the amount of revenue earned from the customer. Such attributes may be filtered out by the analyst before the modeling process begins. However, not all attribute relationships are that clearly known in advance. In such cases, one must resort to computational methods to detect and eliminate attributes that add no new information. The key here is to include attributes that have a strong correlation with the predicted or dependent variable.

So, to summarize, feature selection is needed to *remove* independent variables that may be strongly correlated to one another, and to *keep* independent variables that may be strongly correlated to the predicted or dependent variable.

Feature selection methods can be applied before the modeling process starts and, thus, unimportant attributes will get filtered out, or feature selection methods can be applied iteratively within the flow of the data science process. Depending on the logic, there are two feature selection schemes: filter schemes or wrapper schemes. The filter scheme does not require any learning algorithm, whereas the wrapper type is optimized for a particular learning algorithm. In other words, the filter scheme can be considered unsupervised and the wrapper scheme can be considered a supervised feature selection method. The filter model is commonly used:

1. When the number of features or attributes is really large
2. When computational expense is a criterion

The chart in Fig. 14.1 summarizes a high-level taxonomy of feature selection methods, some of which will be explored in the following sections, as indicated. This is not meant to be a comprehensive taxonomy, but simply a

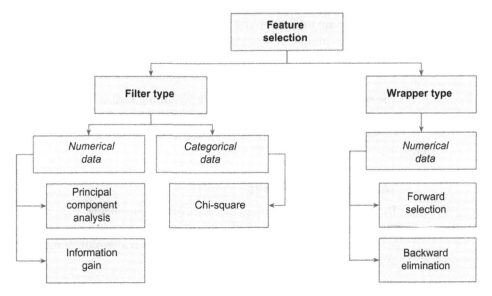

FIGURE 14.1

Taxonomy of common feature selection methods and the sections in this chapter that discuss them.

useful depiction of the techniques commonly employed in data science and described in this chapter.

14.2   PRINCIPAL COMPONENT ANALYSIS

To start with a conceptual introduction to PCA will be provided before the mathematical basis behind the computation is shown. Then a demonstration of how to apply PCA to a sample dataset using RapidMiner will be given.

Assume that there is a dataset with m attributes. These could be for example, commodity prices, weekly sales figures, number of hours spent by assembly line workers, etc.; in short, any business parameter that can have an impact on a performance that is captured by a label or target variable. The question that PCA helps to answer is fundamentally this: Which of these m attributes explain a significant amount of variation contained within the dataset? PCA essentially helps to apply an 80/20 rule: Can a small subset of attributes explain 80% or more of the variation in the data? This sort of variable screening or *feature selection* will make it easy to apply other data science techniques and also make the job of interpreting the results easier.

PCA captures the attributes that contain the greatest amount of variability in the dataset. It does this by transforming the existing variables into a set of principal components or *new variables* that have the following properties (van der Maaten, Postma, & van den Herik, 2009):

1. They are uncorrelated with each other.
2. They cumulatively contain/explain a large amount of variance within the data.
3. They can be related back to the original variables via weighting factors.

The original variables with very low weighting factors in their principal components are effectively removed from the dataset. The conceptual schematic in Fig. 14.2 illustrates how PCA can help in reducing data dimensions with a hypothetical dataset of m variables.

14.2.1   How It Works

The key task is computing the principal components, z_m, which have the properties that were described. Consider the case of just two variables: v_1 and v_2. When the variables are visualized using a scatterplot, something like the one shown in Fig. 14.3 would be observed.

As can be seen, v_1 and v_2 are correlated. But v_1 and v_2 could be transformed into two new variables z_1 and z_2, which meet the guidelines for principal components, by a simple linear transformation. As seen in the chart, this

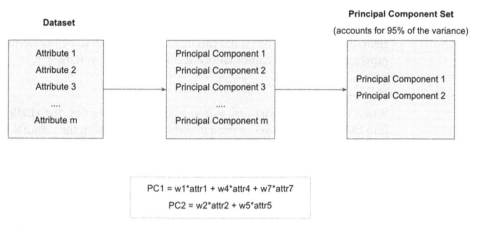

FIGURE 14.2
A conceptual framework illustrating the effectiveness of using PCA for feature selection. The final dataset includes only PC 1 and PC 2.
PCA, Principal Component Analysis.

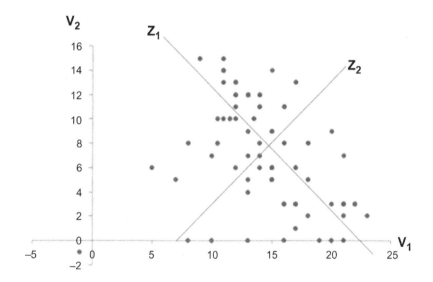

FIGURE 14.3
Transforming variables to a new basis is at the core of PCA. *PCA*, Principal Component Analysis.

amounts to plotting the points along two new axes: z_1 and z_2. Axis z_1 contains the maximum variability, and one can rightly conclude that z_1 explains a significant majority of the variation present in the data and is the first principal component. z_2, by virtue of being orthogonal to z_1, contains the next highest amount of variability. Between z_1 and z_2, 100% of the total variability in the data can be accounted for (in this case of two variables).

Furthermore, z_1 and z_2 are uncorrelated. As the number of variables, v_m, increases it's possible that only the first few principal components are sufficient to express all the data variances. The principal components, z_m, are expressed as a linear combination of the underlying variables, v_m:

$$z_m = \sum w_i \times x_i \qquad (14.1)$$

When this logic is extended to more than two variables, the challenge is to find the transformed set of principal components using the original variables. This is easily accomplished by performing an *eigenvalue analysis* of the *covariance matrix* of the original attributes.[1] The eigenvector associated with the largest eigenvalue is the first principal component; the eigenvector associated with the second largest eigenvalue is the second principal component and so on. The covariance explains how two variables vary with respect to their corresponding mean values—if both variables tend to stay on the same side of their respective means, the covariance would be positive, if not it would be negative. (In statistics, covariance is also used in the calculation of correlation coefficient.)

$$\mathrm{Cov}_{ij} = E\left[V_i V_j\right] - E[V_i]E\left[V_j\right] \qquad (14.2)$$

where expected value $E[v] = v_k\, P(v = v_k)$. For the eigenvalue analysis, a matrix of such covariances between all pairs of variables v_m is created. For more details behind the eigenvalue analysis refer to standard textbooks on matrix methods or linear algebra (Yu & Liu, 2003).

14.2.2   How to Implement

In this section, with the use of a publicly available dataset,[2] RapidMiner will be used to perform the PCA. Furthermore, for illustrative reasons, non-standardized or non-normalized data will be used. In the next part the data will be standardized and why it may be important to sometimes do so will be explained.

The dataset includes information on ratings and nutritional information on 77 breakfast cereals. There are a total of 16 variables, including 13 numerical parameters (Table 14.1). The objective is to reduce this set of 13 numerical predictors to a much smaller list using PCA.

---

[1] Let A be an $n \times n$ matrix and x be an $n \times 1$ vector. Then the solution to the vector equation $[A][x] = \lambda[x]$, where λ is a scalar number, involves finding those values of λ for which this equation is satisfied. The values of λ are called eigenvalues and the corresponding solutions for x ($x \neq 0$) are called eigenvectors.

[2] https://www.kaggle.com/jeandsantos/breakfast-cereals-data-analysis-and-clustering/data.

Table 14.1 Breakfast Cereals Dataset for Dimension Reduction Using PCA

Name	mfr	Type	Calories	Protein	Fat	Sodium	Fiber	Carbo	Sugars	Potass	Vitamins	Shelf	Weight	Cups	Rating
100%_Bran	N	C	70	4	1	130	10	5	6	280	25	3	1	0.33	68.402973
100%_Natural_Bran	Q	C	120	3	5	15	2	8	8	135	0	3	1	1	33.983679
All-Bran	K	C	70	4	1	260	9	7	5	320	25	3	1	0.33	59.425505
All-Bran_with_Extra_Fiber	K	C	50	4	0	140	14	8	0	330	25	3	1	0.5	93.704912
Almond_Delight	R	C	110	2	2	200	1	14	8	-1	25	3	1	0.75	34.384843
Apple_Cinnamon_Cheerios	G	C	110	2	2	180	1.5	10.5	10	70	25	1	1	0.75	29.509541
Apple_Jacks	K	C	110	2	0	125	1	11	14	30	25	2	1	1	33.174094
Basic_4	G	C	130	3	2	210	2	18	8	100	25	3	1.33	0.75	37.038562

Step 1: Data Preparation

Remove the non-numeric parameters such as Cereal name, Manufacturer, and Type (hot or cold), as PCA can only work with numeric attributes. These are the first three columns in Table 14.1. (In RapidMiner, these can be converted into ID attributes if needed for reference later. This can be done during the import of the dataset into RapidMiner during the next step if needed; in this case these variables will simply be removed. The *Select Attributes* operator may also be used following the *Read Excel* operator to remove these variables.) Read the Excel file into RapidMiner: this can be done using the standard *Read Excel* operator as described in earlier sections.

Step 2: PCA Operator

Type in the keyword PCA in the operator search field and drag and drop the *PCA* operator into the main process window. Connect the output of Read Excel into the ports of the *PCA* operator.

The three available parameter settings for dimensionality reduction are *none*, *keep variance*, and *fixed number*. Here use *keep variance* and leave the *variance threshold* at the default value of 0.95% or 95% (see Fig. 14.4). The variance threshold selects only those attributes that collectively account for or explain 95% (or any other value set by user) of the total variance in the data. Connect all output ports from the *PCA* operator to the results ports.

Step 3: Execution and Interpretation

By running the analysis as configured above, RapidMiner will output several tabs in the results panel (Fig. 14.5). By clicking on the PCA tab, three PCA related tabs will be seen—Eigenvalues, Eigenvectors, and Cumulative Variance Plot.

Using Eigenvalues, information can be obtained about the contribution to the data variance coming from each principal component individually and cumulatively.

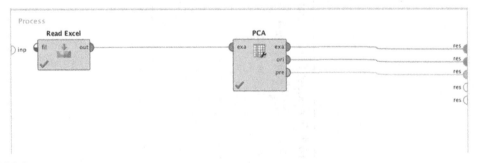

FIGURE 14.4
Configuring the PCA operator. *PCA*, Principal Component Analysis.

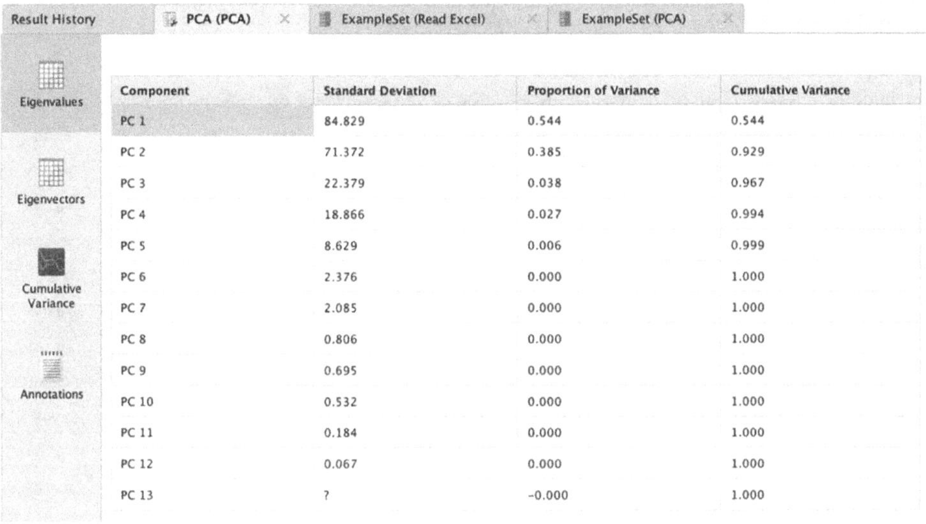

Component	Standard Deviation	Proportion of Variance	Cumulative Variance
PC 1	84.829	0.544	0.544
PC 2	71.372	0.385	0.929
PC 3	22.379	0.038	0.967
PC 4	18.866	0.027	0.994
PC 5	8.629	0.006	0.999
PC 6	2.376	0.000	1.000
PC 7	2.085	0.000	1.000
PC 8	0.806	0.000	1.000
PC 9	0.695	0.000	1.000
PC 10	0.532	0.000	1.000
PC 11	0.184	0.000	1.000
PC 12	0.067	0.000	1.000
PC 13	?	−0.000	1.000

Tabs: Result History | PCA (PCA) | ExampleSet (Read Excel) | ExampleSet (PCA)
Sidebar: Eigenvalues, Eigenvectors, Cumulative Variance, Annotations

FIGURE 14.5
Output from PCA. *PCA*, Principal Component Analysis.

If, for example, our variance threshold is 95%, then PC 1, PC 2, and PC 3 are the only principal components that need to be considered because they are sufficient to explain nearly 97% of the variance. PC 1 contributes to a majority of this variance, about 54%.

One can then deep dive into these three components and identify how they are linearly related to the actual or real parameters from the dataset. At this point only those real parameters can be considered that have significant weight contribution to the each of the first three PCs. These will ultimately form the subset of reduced parameters for further predictive modeling.

The key question is how does one select the real variables based on this information? RapidMiner allows the eigenvectors (weighting factors) to be sorted for each PC and one can decide to choose the two to three highest (absolute) valued weighting factors for PCs 1–3. As seen from Fig. 14.6, the highlighted real attributes have been chosen—calories, sodium, potassium, vitamins, and rating—to form the reduced dataset. This selection was done by simply identifying the top three attributes from each principal component.[3]

For this example, PCA reduces the number of attributes from 13 to 5, a more than 50% reduction in the number of attributes that any model would need

[3] More commonly, only the top three principal components are directly selected for building subsequent models. This route was taken here to explain how PCA, which is a dimension reduction method, can be applied for feature selection.

| Result History | | PCA (PCA)   × | | ExampleSet (Read Excel)   × | | ExampleSet (PCA)   × | | |

Attribu...	PC 1	PC 2	PC 3	PC 4	PC 5	PC 6	PC 7	PC 8	PC 9
calories	−0.076	0.010	0.612	0.613	0.464	0.131	0.082	−0.011	0.030
protein	0.001	−0.008	−0.000	−0.002	0.056	0.229	0.042	0.468	−0.533
fat	0.000	−0.003	0.016	0.026	−0.017	0.174	−0.181	−0.309	−0.198
sodium	−0.983	−0.112	−0.142	0.004	0.015	0.014	0.020	−0.000	−0.004
fiber	0.005	−0.030	−0.019	−0.020	0.017	0.091	0.259	−0.577	0.377
carbo	−0.020	0.018	0.015	−0.031	0.348	−0.835	−0.324	−0.022	−0.051
sugars	−0.006	−0.002	0.100	0.112	−0.287	−0.420	0.796	0.052	−0.181
potass	0.107	−0.991	0.028	0.044	−0.041	−0.029	−0.042	0.016	−0.001
vitamins	−0.101	−0.022	0.703	−0.703	−0.024	0.024	0.012	0.006	0.008
shelf	0.001	−0.004	0.012	−0.006	−0.005	−0.008	−0.042	−0.586	−0.704
weight	−0.001	−0.001	0.004	0.003	0.004	−0.007	0.013	0.006	0.020
cups	−0.000	0.002	0.001	−0.001	0.002	−0.015	−0.008	0.072	0.021
rating	0.075	−0.066	−0.316	−0.337	0.758	0.128	0.385	0.006	−0.042

Left sidebar labels: Eigenvalues, Eigenvectors, Cumulative Variance, Annotations

FIGURE 14.6

Selecting the reduced set of attributes using the Eigenvectors tab from the PCA operator. *PCA*, Principal Component Analysis.

to realistically consider. One can imagine the improvement in performance as one deals with the larger datasets that PCA enables. In practice, PCA is an effective and widely used tool for dimension reduction, particularly when all the attributes are numeric. It works for a variety of real-world applications, but it should not be blindly applied for variable screening. For most practical situations, domain knowledge should be used in addition to PCA analysis before eliminating any of the variables. Here are some observations that explain some of the risks to consider while using PCA.

1. *The results of a PCA must be evaluated in the context of the data.* If the data is extremely noisy, then PCA may end up suggesting that the noisiest variables are the most significant because they account for most of the variation! An analogy would be the total sound energy in a rock concert. If the crowd noise drowns out some of the high-frequency vocals or notes, PCA might suggest that the most significant contribution to the total energy comes from the crowd—and it will be right! But this does not add any clear value if one is attempting to distinguish which musical instruments are influencing the harmonics, for example.

2. *Adding uncorrelated data does not always help. Neither does adding data that may be correlated, but irrelevant.* When more parameters are added to the

dataset, and if these parameters happen to be random noise, effectively the same situation as the first point applies. On the other hand, caution also has to be exercised and spurious correlations have to looked out for. As an extreme example, it may so happen that there is a correlation between the number of hours worked in a garment factory and pork prices (an unrelated commodity) within a certain period of time. Clearly this correlation is probably pure coincidence. Such correlations again can muddy the results of a PCA. Care must be taken to winnow the dataset to include variables that make business sense and are not subjected to many random fluctuations before applying a technique like PCA.

3. *PCA is very sensitive to scaling effects in the data.* If the data in the example is closely examined, it will be observed that the top attributes that PCA helped identify as the most important ones also have the widest range (and standard deviation) in their values. For example, potassium ranges from -1 to 330 and sodium ranges from 1 to 320. Comparatively, most of the other factors range in the single or low double digits. As expected, these factors dominate PCA results because they contribute to the maximum variance in the data. What if there was another factor such as sales volume, which would potentially range in the millions (of dollars or boxes), that were to be considered for a modeling exercise? Clearly it would mask the effects of any other attribute.

To minimize scaling effects, one can range normalize the data (using for example, the *Normalize* operator). When this data transformation is applied, all the attributes are reduced to a range between 0 and 1 and scale effects will not matter anymore. But what happens to the PCA results?

As Fig. 14.7 shows, eight PCs are now needed to account for the same 95% total variance. As an exercise, use the eigenvectors to filter out the attributes that are included in these eight PCs and it would be observed that (applying the top three rule for each PC as before), none of the attributes would be eliminated!

This leads to the next section on feature selection methods that are not scale sensitive and also work with non-numerical datasets, which were two of the limitations with PCA.

14.3 INFORMATION THEORY-BASED FILTERING

In Chapter 4, Classification, the concepts of information gain and gain ratio were encountered. Recall that both of these methods involve comparing the *information exchanged* between a given attribute and the target or label

Component	Standard Deviation	Proportion of Variance	Cumulative Variance
PC 1	0.459	0.306	0.306
PC 2	0.392	0.224	0.530
PC 3	0.302	0.132	0.663
PC 4	0.287	0.120	0.782
PC 5	0.212	0.065	0.848
PC 6	0.187	0.051	0.898
PC 7	0.162	0.038	0.937
PC 8	0.140	0.029	0.965
PC 9	0.122	0.022	0.987
PC 10	0.067	0.006	0.993
PC 11	0.053	0.004	0.997
PC 12	0.043	0.003	1.000
PC 13	?	-0.000	1.000

FIGURE 14.7
Interpreting RapidMiner output for principal component analysis.

attribute (Peng, Long, & Ding, 2005). As discussed in Section 14.1, the key to feature selection is to include attributes that have a strong correlation with the predicted or dependent variable. With these techniques, one can rank attributes based on the amount of information gain and then select only those that meet or exceed some (arbitrarily) chosen threshold or simply select the top k (again, arbitrarily chosen) features.

Recall the golf example discussed first in Chapter 4, Classification. The data is presented here again for convenience in Fig. 14.8A. When the information gain calculation methodology that was discussed in Chapter 4, Classification, is applied to compute information gain for all attributes (see Table 4.2), the feature ranking in Fig. 14.8B will be reached, in terms of their respective influence on the target variable Play. This can be easily done using the *Weight by Information Gain* operator in RapidMiner. The output looks almost identical to the one shown in Table 4.2, except for the slight differences in the information gain values for Temperature and Humidity. The reason is that for that dataset, the temperature and humidity had to be converted into nominal values before computing the gains. In this case, the numeric attributes are used as they are. So, it is important to pay attention to the discretization of the attributes before filtering. Use of information gain feature selection is also restricted to cases where the label is nominal. For fully numeric datasets, where the label variable is also numeric, PCA or correlation-based filtering methods are commonly used.

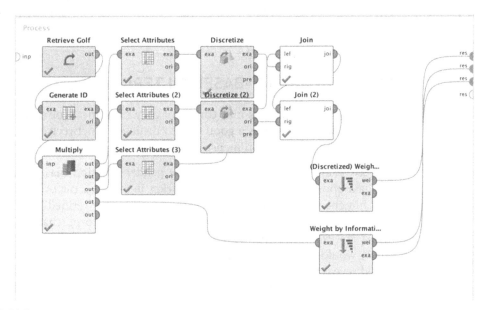

Row No.	id	Play	Outlook	Temperature	Humidity	Wind
1	1	no	sunny	85	85	false
2	2	no	sunny	80	90	true
3	3	yes	overcast	83	78	false
4	4	yes	rain	70	96	false
5	5	yes	rain	68	80	false
6	6	no	rain	65	70	true
7	7	yes	overcast	64	65	true
8	8	no	sunny	72	95	false
9	9	yes	sunny	69	70	false
10	10	yes	rain	75	80	false
11	11	yes	sunny	75	70	true
12	12	yes	overcast	72	90	true
13	13	yes	overcast	81	75	false
14	14	no	rain	71	80	true

(A)

(B)

attribute	weight ↓
Outlook	0.247
Temperature	0.113
Humidity	0.102
Wind	0.048

FIGURE 14.8
(A) Revisiting the golf example for feature selection. (B) Results of information gain—based feature selection.

FIGURE 14.9
Process to discretize the numeric Golf dataset before running information gain—based feature selection.

Fig. 14.9 describes a process that uses the sample Golf dataset available in RapidMiner. The various steps in the process convert numeric attributes, Temperature and Humidity, into nominal ones. In the final step, the *Weight by Information Gain* operator is applied to both the original data and the converted dataset in order to show the difference between the gain computed using different data types. The main point to observe is that the gain computation depends not only on the data types, but also on how the nominal

Table 14.2 Results of Information Gain Feature Selection

Attribute	Info Gain Weight (Not Discretized)	Info Gain Weight (Discretized)
Outlook	0.247	0.247
Temperature	0.113	0.029
Humidity	0.102	0.104
Wind	0.048	0.048

data is discretized. For example, one gets slightly different gain values (see Table 14.2) if Humidity is divided into three bands (high, medium, and low) as opposed to only two bands (high and low). These variants can be tested easily using the process described. In conclusion, the top-ranked attributes are selected. In this case, they would be Outlook and Temperature if one chose the non-discretized version, and Outlook and Humidity in the discretized version.

14.4   CHI-SQUARE-BASED FILTERING

In many cases the datasets may consist of only categorical (or nominal) attributes. In this case, what is a good way to distinguish between high influence attributes and low or no influence attributes?

A classic example of this scenario is the gender selection bias. Suppose one has data about the purchase of a big-ticket item like a car or a house. Can the influence of gender on purchase decisions be verified? Are men or women the primary decision makers when it comes to purchasing big-ticket items? For example, is gender a factor in color preference of a car? Here attribute 1 would be gender and attribute 2 would be the color. A chi-square test would reveal if there is indeed a relationship between these two attributes. If there are several attributes and one wishes to rank the relative influence of each of these on the target attribute, the chi-square statistic can still be used.

Back to the golf example in Fig. 14.10—this time all numeric attributes have been converted into nominal ones. Chi-square analysis involves *counting* occurrences (number of sunny days or windy days) and *comparing* these variables to the target variable based on the frequencies of occurrences. The chi-square test checks if the frequencies of occurrences across any pair of attributes, such as Outlook = overcast and Play = yes, are correlated. In other words, for the given Outlook type, overcast, what is the probability that Play = yes (existence of a strong correlation)? The multiplication law of probabilities states that if event A happening is independent of event B, then the probabilities of A and B happening together is simply $p_A \times p_B$. The next step

Row No.	id	Play	Humidity	Temperature	Outlook	Wind
1	1	no	High	hot	sunny	false
2	2	no	High	hot	sunny	true
3	3	yes	Normal	hot	overcast	false
4	4	yes	High	mild	rain	false
5	5	yes	Normal	cool	rain	false
6	6	no	Normal	cool	rain	true
7	7	yes	Normal	cool	overcast	true
8	8	no	High	mild	sunny	false
9	9	yes	Normal	cool	sunny	false
10	10	yes	Normal	mild	rain	false
11	11	yes	Normal	mild	sunny	true
12	12	yes	High	mild	overcast	true
13	13	yes	Normal	hot	overcast	false
14	14	no	Normal	mild	rain	true

FIGURE 14.10
Converting the golf example set into nominal values for chi-square feature selection.

Table 14.3 Contingency Table of Observed Frequencies for Outlook and the Label Attribute, Play

Outlook	Sunny	Overcast	Rain	Total
Play = no	3	0	2	5
Play = yes	2	4	3	9
Total	5	4	5	14

is to convert this joint probability into an expected frequency, which is given by $p_A \times p_B \times N$, where N is the sum of all occurrences in the dataset.

For *each* attribute, a table of observed frequencies, such as the one shown in Table 14.3, is built. This is called a *contingency table*. The last column and row (the margins) with heading 'Totals' are simply the sums in the corresponding rows or columns as can be verified. Using the contingency table, a corresponding *expected frequency table* can be built using the expected frequency definition ($p_A \times p_B \times N$) from which the chi-square statistic is then computed by comparing the difference between the observed frequency and expected frequency for *each* attribute. The expected frequency table for *Outlook* is shown in Table 14.4.

Table 14.4 Expected Frequency Table

Outlook	Sunny	Overcast	Rain	Total
Play = no	1.785714	1.428571	1.785714	5
Play = yes	3.214286	2.571429	3.214286	9
Total	5	4	5	14

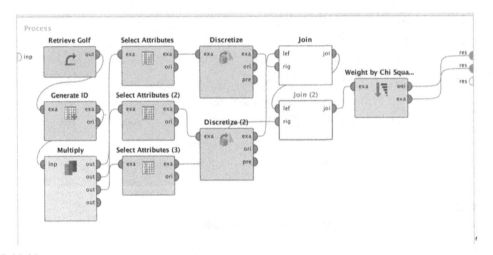

FIGURE 14.11

Process to rank attributes of the Golf dataset by the chi-square statistic.

The expected frequency for the event [Play = no and Outlook = sunny] is calculated using the expected frequency formula: $(5/14 \times 5/14 \times 14) = 1.785$ and is entered in the first cell as shown. Similarly, the other expected frequencies are calculated. The formula for the chi-square statistic is the summation of the square of the differences between observed and expected frequencies, as given in Eq. (14.3):

$$\chi^2 = \sum\sum \frac{(f_o - f_e)^2}{f_e} \tag{14.3}$$

where f_o is the observed frequency and f_e is the expected frequency. The test of independence between any two parameters is done by checking if the observed chi-square is less than a critical value which depends on the confidence level chosen by the user (Black, 2007). In this case of feature weighting, all the observed chi-square values are simply gathered and used to rank the attributes. The ranking of attributes for the golf example is generated using the process described in Fig. 14.11 and is shown in the table of observed chi-square values in Fig. 14.14. Just like in information gain feature selection, most of the operators shown in the process are simply transforming the data into nominal values to generate it in the form shown in Fig. 14.10.

Compare the output of the chi-square ranking to the information gain−based ranking (for the nominalized or discretized attributes) and it will be evident that the ranking is identical (see Fig. 14.12).

Note that the Normalize weights option is sometimes also used, which is a range normalization onto the interval 0 to 1.

attribute	weight ↓
Outlook	3.547
Humidity	1.998
Wind	0.933
Temperature	0.570

FIGURE 14.12
Results of the attribute weighting by the chi-square method.

14.5 WRAPPER-TYPE FEATURE SELECTION

In this section of the chapter, wrapper scheme feature reduction methods will briefly be introduced using a linear regression example. As explained earlier, the wrapper approach iteratively chooses features to add or to remove from the current attribute pool based on whether the newly added or removed attribute improves the accuracy.

Wrapper-type methods originated from the need to reduce the number of attributes that are needed to build a high-quality regression model. A thorough way to build regression models is something called the "all possible regressions" search procedure. For example, with three attributes, $v1$, $v2$, and $v3$, one could build the different regression models in Table 14.5.

In general, if a dataset contains k different attributes, then conducting all possible regression searches implies that one builds $2^k - 1$ separate regression

Table 14.5 All Possible Regression Models With Three Attributes

Model	Independent Variables Used
1	$v1$ alone
2	$v2$ alone
3	$v3$ alone
4	$v1$ and $v2$ only
5	$v1$ and $v3$ only
6	$v2$ and $v3$ only
7	$v1$, $v2$, and $v3$ all together

models and picks the one that has the best performance. Clearly this is impractical.

A better way, from a computational resource consumption point of view, to do this search would be to start with one variable, say $v1$, and build a baseline model. Then add a second variable, say $v2$, and build a new model to compare with the baseline. If the performance of the new model, for example, the R^2 (see Chapter 5: Regression Methods), is better than that of the baseline, this model can be made to be the new baseline, add a third variable, $v3$, and proceed in a similar fashion. If, however, the addition of the second attribute, $v2$, did not improve the model significantly (over some arbitrarily prescribed level of improvement in performance), then a new attribute $v3$ can be chosen, and a new model built that includes $v1$ and $v3$. If this model is better than the model that included $v1$ and $v2$, proceed to the next step, where the next attribute $v4$ can be considered, and a model built that includes $v1$, $v3$, and $v4$. In this way, one steps forward selecting attributes one by one until the desired level of model performance is achieved. This process is called *forward selection*.[4]

A reverse of this process is where the baseline model with all the attributes is started, $v1$, $v2$, ..., vk and for the first iteration, one of the variables, vj, is removed and a new model is constructed. However, how does one select which vj to remove? Here, it is typical to start with a variable that has the lowest t-stat value, seen in the case study described below.[5] If the new model is better than the baseline, it becomes the new baseline and the search continues to remove variables with the lowest t-stat values until some stopping

---

[4] Forward selection is considered a "greedy" approach, and does not necessarily yield the globally optimum solution.

[5] RapidMiner typically tries removing attributes one after the other. Vice versa for forward selection: first it tries out all models having just one attribute. It selects the best, then adds another variable, again trying out every option.

criterion is met (usually if the model performance is not significantly improved over the previous iteration). This process is called *backward elimination*.

As observed, the variable selection process wraps around the modeling procedure, hence, the name for these classes of feature selection. A case study will now be examined, using data from the Boston Housing dataset first introduced in Chapter 5, Regression Methods, to demonstrate how to implement the backward elimination method using RapidMiner. Recall that the data consists of 13 predictors and 1 response variable. The predictors include physical characteristics of the house (such as the number of rooms, age, tax, and location) and neighborhood features (schools, industries, zoning), among others. The response variable is the median value (MEDV) of the house in thousands of dollars. These 13 independent attributes are considered to be predictors for the target or label attribute. The snapshot of the data table is shown again in Table 14.6 for continuity.

14.5.1 Backward Elimination

The goal here is to build a high-quality multiple regression model that includes as few attributes as possible, without compromising the predictive ability of the model.

The logic used by RapidMiner for applying these techniques is not linear, but a nested logic. The graphic in Fig. 14.13 explains how this nesting was used in setting up the training and testing of the *Linear Regression* operator for the analysis done in Chapter 5, Regression Methods, on the Boston Housing data. The arrow indicates that the training and testing process was nested within the *Split Validation* operator.

In order to apply a wrapper-style feature selection method such as backward elimination, the training and testing process will need to be tucked inside another subprocess, a learning process. The learning process is now nested inside the *Backward Elimination* operator. Therefore, a double nesting as schematically shown in Fig. 14.13 is now obtained. Next, the Backward Elimination operator can be configured in RapidMiner. Double clicking on the *Backward Elimination* operator opens up the learning process, which can now accept the *Split Validation* operator that has been used many times.

The *Backward Elimination* operator can now be filled in with the *Split Validation* operator and all the other operators and connections required to build a regression model. The process of setting these up is exactly the same as discussed in Chapter 5, Regression Methods, and, hence, is not repeated here. Now the configuration of the *Backward Elimination* operator will be examined. Here one can specify several parameters to enable feature

Table 14.6 Sample View of the Boston Housing Dataset

CRIM	ZN	INDUS	CHAS	NOX	RM	AGE	DIS	RAD	TAX	PTRATIO	B	LSTAT	MEDV
0.00632	18	2.31	0	0.538	6.575	65.2	4.09	1	296	15.3	396.9	4.98	24
0.02731	0	7.07	0	0.469	6.421	78.9	4.9671	2	242	17.8	396.9	9.14	21.6
0.02729	0	7.07	0	0.469	7.185	61.1	4.9671	2	242	17.8	392.83	4.03	34.7
0.03237	0	2.18	0	0.458	6.998	45.8	6.0622	3	222	18.7	394.63	2.94	33.4
0.06905	0	2.18	0	0.458	7.147	54.2	6.0622	3	222	18.7	396.9	5.33	36.2
0.02985	0	2.18	0	0.458	6.43	58.7	6.0622	3	222	18.7	394.12	5.21	28.7
0.08829	14.5	7.87	0	0.524	6.012	66.6	5.5605	5	311	15.2	395.6	14.43	22.9
0.14455	14.5	7.87	0	0.524	6.172	96.1	5.9505	5	311	15.2	396.9	19.15	27.1

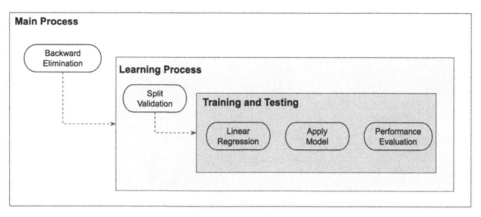

FIGURE 14.13
Wrapper function logic used by RapidMiner.

selection. The most important one is the *stopping behavior*. The choices are "with decrease," "with decrease of more than," and "with significant decrease." The first choice is highly parsimonious—a decrease from one iteration to the next will stop the process. But if the second choice is chosen, one now has to now indicate a "maximal relative decrease." In this example, a 10% decrease has been indicated. Finally, the third choice is very stringent and requires achieving some desired statistical significance by allowing one to specify an alpha level. But it has not been said by how much the performance parameter should decrease yet! This is specified deep inside the nesting: all the way at the *Performance* operator that was selected in the Testing window of the *Split Validation* operator. In this example, the performance criterion was squared correlation. For a complete description of all the other *Backward Elimination* parameters, the RapidMiner help can be consulted.

There is one more step that may be helpful to complete before running this model. Simply connecting the *Backward Elimination* operator ports to the output will not show the final regression model equation. To be able to see that, one needs to connect the example port of the *Backward Elimination* operator to another *Linear Regression* operator in the main process. The output of this operator will contain the model, which can be examined in the Results perspective. The top level of the final process is shown in Fig. 14.14.

Comparing the two regression equations (Fig. 14.15 and in Chapter 5: Regression Methods, see Fig. 5.6A) it is evident that nine attributes have been eliminated. Perhaps the 10% decrease was too aggressive. As it happens, the R^2 for the final model with only three attributes was only 0.678. If the stopping criterion was changed to a 5% decrease, one would end up with an

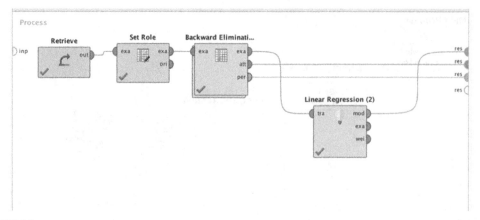

FIGURE 14.14
Final setup of the backward elimination wrapper process.

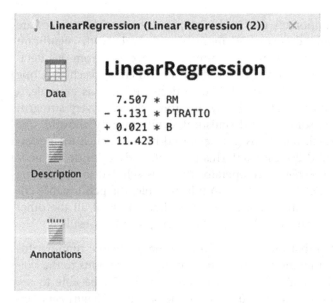

FIGURE 14.15
Aggressive feature selection. Maximal relative decrease = 10%.

R^2 of 0.812 and now have 8 of the 13 original attributes (Fig. 14.16). It is also evident that the regression coefficients for the two models are different as well. The final judgment on what is the right criterion and its level can only be made with experience with the dataset and of course, good domain knowledge.

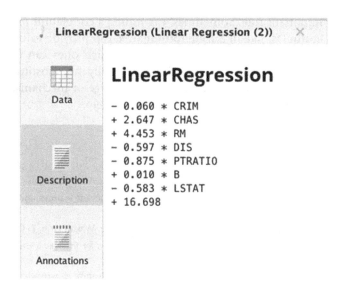

FIGURE 14.16
A more permissive feature selection with backward elimination. Maximal relative decrease = 5%.

Each iteration using a regression model either removes or introduces a variable, which improves model performance. The iterations stop when a preset stopping criterion or no change in performance criterion (such as adjusted r^2 or RMS error) is reached. The inherent advantage of wrapper-type methods are that multicollinearity issues are automatically handled. However, no prior knowledge about the actual relationship between the variables will be gained. Applying forward selection is similar and is recommended as an exercise.

14.6 CONCLUSION

This chapter covered the basics of an important part of the overall data science paradigm: feature selection or dimension reduction. A central hypothesis among all the feature selection methods is that good feature selection results in attributes or features that are highly correlated with the class, yet uncorrelated with each other (Hall, 1999). A high-level classification of feature selection techniques were presented and each of them were explored in some detail. As stated at the beginning of this chapter, dimension reduction is best understood with real practice. To this end, it is recommended that one applies all the techniques described in this chapter on all the datasets provided. The same technique can yield quite different results based on the selection of analysis parameters. This is where data visualization can play an important role. Sometimes, examining a correlation plot between the various attributes, like in a scatterplot matrix, can provide valuable clues about which attributes are likely redundant and which ones can be strong predictors of the label variable. While there is usually no substitute for domain knowledge, sometimes data are simply too large or mechanisms are unknown. This is where feature selection can actually help.

References

Black, K. (2007). *Business statistics*. New York: John Wiley and Sons.

Blum, A. L., & Langley, P. (1997). Selection of relevant features and examples in machine learning. *Artificial Intelligence*, 97(1–2), 245–271.

Bollier, D. (2010). *The promise and perils of big data*. Washington, D.C.: The Aspen Institute.

Hall, M.A. (1999). *Correlation based feature selection for machine learning* (Ph.D. thesis). University of Waikato: New Zealand.

Kohavi, R., & John, G. H. (1997). Wrappers for feature subset selection. *Artificial Intelligence*, 97 (1–2), 273–324.

Peng, H., Long, F., & Ding, C. (2005). Feature selection based on mutual information: Criteria of max-dependency, max-relevance and min-redundancy. *IEEE Transactions on Pattern Analysis and Machine Intelligence*, 27(8), 1226–1238.

van der Maaten, L. J. P., Postma, E. O., & van den Herik, H. J. (2009). Dimensionality reduction: A comparative review. In: *Tilburg University technical report. TiCC-TR*.

Yu, L., Liu, H. (2003). Feature selection for high dimensional data: A fast correlation based filter solution. In: *Proceedings of the twentieth international conference on machine learning (ICML-2003)*. Washington, DC.

Zaslow, J. (December 4, 2002). Oh No! My TiVo thinks I'm gay. *Wall Street Journal*.

CHAPTER 15

Getting Started with RapidMiner

For someone who has never attempted any analysis using RapidMiner, this chapter would be the best place to start. In this chapter the attention will be turned away from the data science concepts and processes toward an actual tool set needed for data science. The goal for this chapter is to get rid of any trepidation that one may have about using the tool if this entire field of analytics is totally new. If perhaps someone has done some data science with RapidMiner but gotten frustrated or stuck somewhere during the process of self-learning using this powerful set of tools, then this chapter should hopefully help.

RapidMiner is an open source data science platform developed and maintained by RapidMiner Inc. The software was previously known as YALE (Yet Another Learning Environment) and was developed at the University of Dortmund in Germany (Mierswa, 2006).

RapidMiner Studio is a graphical user interface or GUI-based software where data science *workflows* can be built and deployed. Some of the advanced features are offered at a premium. In this chapter, some of the common functionalities and terminologies of the RapidMiner Studio platform will be reviewed. Even though one specific data science tool is being emphasized, the approach, process, and terms are all similar to other commercial and open source data science tools.

Firstly a brief introduction to the RapidMiner Studio GUI will be given to set the stage. The first step in any data analytics exercise is of course to bring the data to the tool, and this is what will be covered next. Once the data is imported, one may want to actually visualize the data and if necessary select subsets or transform the data. Basic visualization is covered, followed by selecting data by subsets. An overview of the fundamental data scaling and transformation tools will be provided and data sampling and missing value handling tools will be explained. Then some advanced capabilities of RapidMiner will be presented such as process design and optimization.

Data Science. DOI: https://doi.org/10.1016/B978-0-12-814761-0.00015-0

15.1 USER INTERFACE AND TERMINOLOGY

It is assumed at this point that the software is already downloaded and installed on a computer.[1] Once RapidMiner is launched, the screen in Fig. 15.1 will be seen.

We start by assuming that a new process needs to be created. With that in mind, a brand new process is started with by clicking on the "Blank" option seen at the top of Fig. 15.1. Once this is done, the view changes to that shown in Fig. 15.2. Only two of the main sections: Design and Results panels will be introduced, as the others (Turbo Prep and Auto Model) are not available in the free edition.

Views: The RapidMiner GUI offers two main *views*. The Design view is where one can create and design all the data science processes and can be thought of as the canvas where all the data science programs and logic will be created. This can also be thought of as a workbench. The Results view is where all the recently executed analysis results are available. Switching back and forth between the Design and Results views several times during a session is very

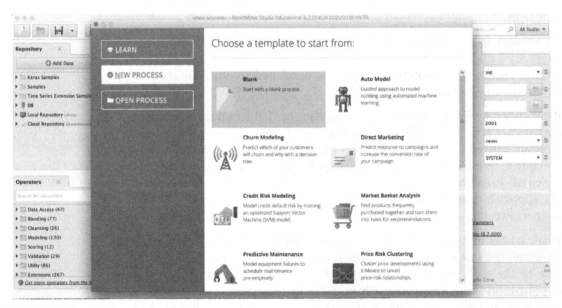

FIGURE 15.1

Launch view of RapidMiner.

---

[1] Download the appropriate version from http://rapidminer.com.

FIGURE 15.2

Activating different views inside RapidMiner.

much an expected behavior for all users. When a new process is created one starts with a blank canvas or uses a wizard-style functionality that allows starting from predefined processes for applications such as direct marketing, predictive maintenance, customer churn modeling, and sentiment analysis.

Panel: When a given view is entered, there will be several display elements available. For example, in the Design view, there is a panel for all the available operators, stored processes, help for the operators, and so on. These panels can be rearranged, resized, removed, or added to a given view. The controls for doing any of these are shown right on the top of each panel tab.

First-time users sometimes accidentally delete some of the panels. The easiest way to bring back a panel is to use the main menu item View → Show View and then select the view that was lost or reset using View → Restore Default View, see Fig. 15.2.

Terminology

There are a handful of terms that one must be comfortable with in order to develop proficiency in using RapidMiner.

Repository: A *repository* is a folder-like structure inside RapidMiner where users can organize their data, processes, and models. The repository is, thus, a central place for all the data and analysis processes. When RapidMiner is launched for the first time, an option to set up the New Local Repository will be given (Fig. 15.3). If for some reason this was not done correctly, it can always be fixed by clicking on the New Repository icon (the one with a " + Add Data" button) in the Repositories panel. When that icon is clicked on, a dialog box like the one shown in Fig. 15.3 will be given where one can specify the name of a repository under *Alias* and its location under *Root Directory*. By default, a standard location automatically selected by the software is checked, which can be unchecked to specify a different location.

Within this repository, folders and subfolders can be organized to store data, processes, results, and models. The advantage of storing datasets to be analyzed in the repository is that metadata describing those datasets are stored alongside. This metadata is propagated through the process as it is built. Metadata is basically data about the data and contains information such as the number of rows and columns, types of data within each column, missing values if any, and statistical information (mean, standard deviation, and so on).

FIGURE 15.3
Setting up a repository on one's local machine.

Attribute

Row No.	Play	Outlook	Temperature	Humidity	Wind
1	no	sunny	85	85	false
2	no	sunny	80	90	true
3	yes	overcast	83	78	false
4	yes	rain	70	96	false
5	yes	rain	68	80	false
6	no	rain	65	70	true
7	yes	overcast	64	65	true
8	no	sunny	72	95	false
9	yes	sunny	69	70	false
10	yes	rain	75	80	false
11	yes	sunny	75	70	true
12	yes	overcast	72	90	true
13	yes	overcast	81	75	false
14	no	rain	71	80	true

Example — row 5

FIGURE 15.4

RapidMiner terminology: attributes and examples.

Attributes and examples: A *data set* or data table is a collection of columns and rows of data. Each column represents a type of measurement. For example, in the classic Golf data set (Fig. 15.4) that is used to explain many of the algorithms within this book, there are columns of data containing Temperature levels and Humidity levels. These are numeric data types. There is also a column that identifies if a day was windy or not or if a day was sunny, overcast, or rainy. These columns are categorical or nominal data types. In all cases, these columns represent attributes of a given day that would influence whether golf is played or not. In RapidMiner terminology, columns of data such as these are called *attributes*. Other commonly used names for attributes are variables, factors, or features. One set of values for such attributes that form a row is called an *example* in RapidMiner terminology. Other commonly used names for examples are records, samples, or instances. An entire dataset (rows of examples) is called an *example set* in RapidMiner.

Operator: An *operator* is an atomic piece of functionality (which in fact is a chunk of encapsulated code) performing a certain task. This data science task can be: importing a data set into the RapidMiner repository, cleaning it by getting rid of spurious examples, reducing the number of attributes by using feature selection techniques, building predictive models, or scoring new datasets using models built earlier. Each task is handled by a chunk of code, which is packaged into an operator (see Fig. 15.5).

Thus, there is an operator for importing an Excel spreadsheet, an operator for replacing missing values, an operator for calculating information gain—based feature weighting, an operator for building a decision tree, and an operator for applying a model to new unseen data. Most of the time an operator requires some sort of input and delivers some sort of output (although there are some operators that do not require an input). Adding an operator to a process adds a piece of functionality to the workflow. Essentially, this amounts to inserting a chunk of code into a data science program and, thus, operators are nothing but convenient visual mechanisms that will allow RapidMiner to be a GUI-driven application rather than an application which uses programming language like R or Python.

Process: A single operator by itself cannot perform data science. All data science problem solving requires a series of calculations and logical operations. There is typically a certain flow to these problems: import data, clean and prepare data, train a model to learn the data, validate the model and rank its performance, then finally apply the model to score new and unseen data. All of these steps can be accomplished by connecting a number of different operators, each uniquely customized for a specific task as seen earlier. When such a series of operators are connected together to accomplish the desired data science, a *process* has been built which can be applied in other contexts. A process that is created visually in RapidMiner is stored by RapidMiner as a platform-independent XML code that can be exchanged between RapidMiner users (Fig. 15.6). This allows different users in different locations and on different platforms to run *your* RapidMiner process on *their* data with minimal

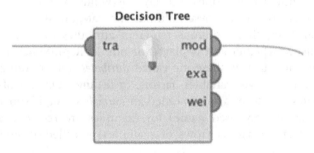

FIGURE 15.5

An operator for building a decision tree.

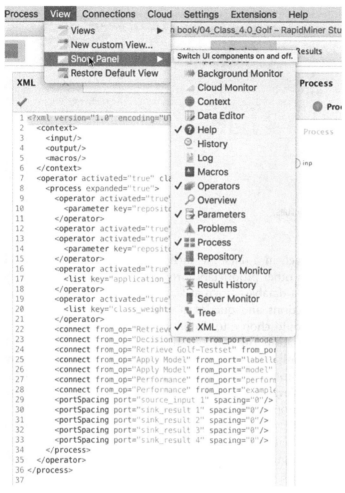

FIGURE 15.6
Every process is automatically translated to an XML document.

reconfiguration. All that needs to be done is to send the XML code of the process to a colleague across the aisle (or across the globe). They can simply copy and paste the XML code in the XML tab in the Design view and switch back to the Process tab (or view) to see the process in its visual representation and then run it to execute the defined functionality.

15.2 DATA IMPORTING AND EXPORTING TOOLS

RapidMiner offers dozens of different operators or ways to connect to data. The data can be stored in a flat file such as a comma-separated values (CSV)

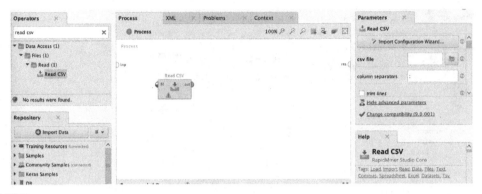

FIGURE 15.7

Steps to read in a CSV file. *CSV*, Comma-Separated Values.

file or spreadsheet, in a database such as a Microsoft SQLServer table, or it can be stored in other proprietary formats such as SAS or Stata or SPSS, etc. If the data is in a database, then at least a basic understanding of databases, database connections and queries is essential in order to use the operator properly. One could choose to simply connect to their data (which is stored in a specific location on disk) or to import the data set into the local RapidMiner repository itself so that it becomes available for any process within the repository and every time RapidMiner is opened, this data set is available for retrieval. Either way, RapidMiner offers easy-to-follow wizards that will guide through the steps. As shown in Fig. 15.7, to simply connect to data in a CSV file on disk using a *Read CSV* operator, drag and drop the operator to the main process window. Then the *Read CSV* operator would need to be configured by clicking on the Import Configuration Wizard, which will provide a sequence of steps to follow to read the data in[2]. The search box at the top of the operator window is also useful—if one knows even part of the operator name then it's easy to find out if RapidMiner provides such an operator. For example, to see if there is an operator to handle CSV files, type "CSV" in the search field and both Read and Write will show up. Clear the search by hitting the red X. Using search is a quick way to navigate to the operators if part of their name is known. Similarly try "principal" and the operator for principal component analysis can be seen, if there is uncertainty about the correct and complete operator name or where to look initially. Also, this search shows the hierarchy of where the operators exist, which helps one learn where they are.

---

[2] Data example shown here is available from IMF, (2012, October). World economic outlook database. International Monetary Fund. Retrieved from < http://www.imf.org/external/pubs/ft/weo/2012/02/weodata/index.aspx > Accessed 15.03.13.

On the other hand, if the data is to be imported into a local RapidMiner repository, click on the down arrow "Import Data" button in the Repositories tab (as shown in Fig. 15.7) and select Import CSV File. The same five-step data import wizard will immediately be presented. In either case, the data import wizard consists of the following steps:

1. Select the file on the disk that should be read or imported.
2. Specify how the file should be parsed and how the columns are delimited. If the data have a comma "," as the column separator in the configuration parameters, be sure to select it.
3. Annotate the attributes by indicating if the first row of the dataset contains attribute names (which is usually the case). If the dataset has first row names, then RapidMiner will automatically indicate this as Name. If the first few rows of the dataset has text or information, that would have to be indicated for each of the example rows. The available annotation choices are "Name," "Comment," and "Unit." See the example in Fig. 15.8.
4. In this step the data type of any of the imported attributes can be changed and whether each column or attribute is a regular attribute or a special

Annota...	att1	att2	att3	att4	att5	att6
Name ▼	Current ...	General...	Gross d...	Gross n...	Total in...	Country
–	3.877	21.977	0.037	30.398	26.521	Afghani...
Name						
Comment	−11.372	25.835	0.032	14.509	25.886	Albania
Unit	7.489	36.458	0.337	48.947	41.428	Algeria
–	9.024	43.479	0.147	21.692	12.668	Angola
–	−13.109	22.43	0.002	16.194	29.303	Antigua ...
–	0.658	37.199	0.863	22.595	24.451	Argentina
–	−14.653	20.97	0.023	16.66	31.313	Armenia
–	−2.87	31.846	1.175	23.925	26.794	Australia
–	3.009	48.105	0.447	24.611	21.602	Austria
–	28.423	45.652	0.122	46.955	18.532	Azerbai...
–	3.578	27.174	0.04	34.544	30.965	Bahrain
–	1.646	11.514	0.349	29.356	24.808	Banglad...

FIGURE 15.8
Properly annotating the data.

type of attribute can be identified. By default, RapidMiner autodetects the data types in each column. However, sometimes one may need to override this and indicate if a particular column is of a different data type. The special attributes are columns that are used for identification (e.g., patient ID, employee ID, or transaction ID) only or attributes that are to be predicted. These are called "label" attributes in RapidMiner terminology.

5. In this last step, if connecting to the data on disk using Read CSV, simply hit Finish (Fig. 15.9). If the data are being imported into a RapidMiner repository (using Import CSV File), then the location in the repository for this will need to be specified.

☑ Preview uses only first 100 rows.

Current acc	General gov	Gross dome	Gross natio	Total invest	Country
real ▼	real ▼	real ▼	real ▼	real ▼	polyn... ▼
attribute ▼	attribute ▼	attribute ▼	attribute ▼	attribute ▼	label ▼
3.877	21.977	0.037	30.398	26.521	Afghani...
−11.372	25.835	0.032	14.509	25.886	Albania
7.489	36.458	0.337	48.947	41.428	Algeria
9.024	43.479	0.147	21.692	12.668	Angola
−13.109	22.430	0.002	16.194	29.303	Antigua ...
0.658	37.199	0.863	22.595	24.451	Argentina
−14.653	20.970	0.023	16.660	31.313	Armenia
−2.870	31.846	1.175	23.925	26.794	Australia
3.009	48.105	0.447	24.611	21.602	Austria
28.423	45.652	0.122	46.955	18.532	Azerbai...
3.578	27.174	0.040	34.544	30.965	Bahrain

FIGURE 15.9
Finishing the data import.

When this process is finished, there should be either a properly connected data source on disk (for Read CSV) or a properly imported example set in their repository that can be used for any data science process. Exporting data from RapidMiner is possible in a similar way using the *Write CSV* operator.

15.3 DATA VISUALIZATION TOOLS

Once a dataset is read into RapidMiner, the next step is to explore the dataset visually using a variety of tools. Before visualization is discussed, however, it is a good idea to check the metadata of the imported data to verify if all the correct information is there. When the simple process described in Section 15.2 is run (be sure to connect the output of the read operator to the "result" connector of the process), an output is posted to the Results view of RapidMiner. The data table can be used to verify that indeed the data has been correctly imported under the *Data* tab on the left (see Fig. 15.10).

By clicking on the Statistics tab (see Fig. 15.11), one can examine the type, missing values, and basic statistics for all the imported dataset attributes. The data type of each attribute (integer, real, or binomial), and some basic statistics can also be identified. This high-level overview is a good way to ensure that a dataset has been loaded correctly and exploring the data in more detail using the visualization tools described later is possible.

Row No.	Country	Current account balance	General government revenue	Gross domestic pr...	Gross nati...	Total inves...
1	Afghanistan	3.877	21.977	0.037	30.398	26.521
2	Albania	−11.372	25.835	0.032	14.509	25.886
3	Algeria	7.489	36.458	0.337	48.947	41.428
4	Angola	9.024	43.479	0.147	21.692	12.668
5	Antigua and...	−13.109	22.430	0.002	16.194	29.303
6	Argentina	0.658	37.199	0.863	22.595	24.451
7	Armenia	−14.653	20.970	0.023	16.660	31.313
8	Australia	−2.870	31.846	1.175	23.925	26.794
9	Austria	3.009	48.105	0.447	24.611	21.602
10	Azerbaijan	28.423	45.652	0.122	46.955	18.532
11	Bahrain	3.578	27.174	0.040	34.544	30.965
12	Bangladesh	1.646	11.514	0.349	29.356	24.808

FIGURE 15.10
Results view that is shown when the data import process is successful.

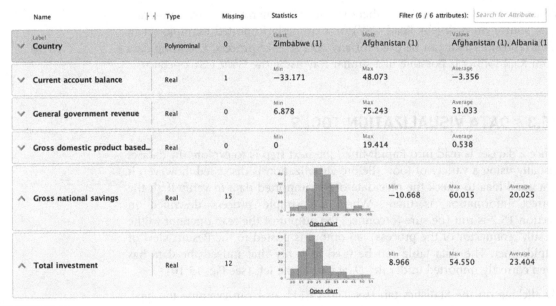

Name		Type	Missing	Statistics			Filter (6 / 6 attributes):	Search for Attribute
Label **Country**	✓	Polynominal	0	Least Zimbabwe (1)	Most Afghanistan (1)		Values Afghanistan (1), Albania (1	
Current account balance	✓	Real	1	Min −33.171	Max 48.073	Average −3.356		
General government revenue	✓	Real	0	Min 6.878	Max 75.243	Average 31.033		
Gross domestic product based...	✓	Real	0	Min 0	Max 19.414	Average 0.538		
Gross national savings	∧	Real	15		Min −10.668	Max 60.015	Average 20.025	
Total investment	∧	Real	12		Min 8.966	Max 54.550	Average 23.404	

FIGURE 15.11

Metadata is visible under the Statistics tab.

There are a variety of visualization tools available for univariate (one attribute), bivariate (two attributes), and multivariate analysis. Select the Charts tab in the Results view to access any of the visualization tools or plotter. General details about visualization are available in Chapter 3, Data Exploration.

Univariate Plots

1. *Histogram:* A density estimation for numeric plots and a counter for categorical ones.
2. *Quartile (Box and Whisker):* Shows the mean value, median, standard deviation, some percentiles, and any outliers for each attribute.
3. *Series (or Line):* Usually best used for time series data.

Bivariate Plots

All 2D and 3D charts show dependencies between tuples (pairs or triads) of variables.[3]

---

[3] A 2D plot can also depict three dimensions, for example using color. Bubble plots can even depict four dimensions! This categorization is done somewhat loosely.

1. *Scatter:* The simplest of all 2D charts, which shows how one variable changes with respect to another. RapidMiner allows the use of color; the points can be colored to add a third dimension to the visualization.
2. *Scatter Multiple:* Allows one axis to be fixed to one variable while cycling through the other attributes.
3. *Scatter Matrix:* Allows all possible pairings between attributes to be examined. Color as usual adds a third dimension. Be careful with this plotter because as the number of attributes increases, rendering all the charts can slow down processing.
4. *Density:* Similar to a 2D scatter chart, except the background may be filled in with a color gradient corresponding to one of the attributes.
5. *SOM:* Stands for a self-organizing map. It reduces the number of dimensions to two by applying transformations. Points that are similar along many attributes will be placed close together. It is basically a clustering visualization method. There are more details in Chapter 8, Model Evaluation, on clustering. Note that SOM (and many of the parameterized reports) do not run automatically, so switch to that report, there will be a blank screen until the inputs are set and then in the case of SOM the calculate button is pushed.

Multivariate Plots

1. *Parallel:* Uses one vertical axis for each attribute, thus, there are as many vertical axes as there are attributes. Each row is displayed as a line in the chart. Local normalization is useful to understand the variance in each variable. However, a deviation plot works better for this.
2. *Deviation:* Same as parallel, but displays mean values and standard deviations.
3. *Scatter 3D:* Quite similar to the 2D scatter chart but allows a three-dimensional visualization of three attributes (four, the color of the points is included)
4. *Surface:* A surface plot is a 3D version of an area plot where the background is filled in.

These are not the only available plotters. Some additional ones are not described here such as pie, bar, ring, block charts, etc. Generating any of the plots using the GUI is pretty much self-explanatory. The only words of caution are that when a large dataset is encountered, generating some of the graphics intensive multivariate plots can be quite time consuming depending on the available RAM and processor speed.

15.4 DATA TRANSFORMATION TOOLS

Many times the raw data is in a form that is not ideal for applying standard machine learning algorithms. For example, suppose there are categorical attributes such as gender, and the requirement is to predict purchase amounts based on (among several other attributes) the gender. In this case, the categorical (or nominal) attributes need to be converted into numeric ones by a process called *dichotomization*. In this example, two new variables are introduced called Gender = Male and Gender = Female, which can take (numeric) values of 0 or 1.

In other cases, numeric data may be given but the algorithm can only handle categorical or nominal attributes. A good example, is where the label variable being numeric (such as the market price of a home in the Boston Housing example set discussed in Chapter 5 on regression) and one wants to use logistic regression to predict if the price will be higher or lower than a certain threshold. Here the need is to convert a numeric attribute into a binomial one.

In either of these cases, the underlying data types may need to be transformed into some other types. This activity is a common data preparation step. The four most common data type conversion operators are:

1. *Numerical to Binominal:* The *Numerical to Binominal* operator changes the type of numeric attributes to a binary type. Binominal attributes can have only two possible values: true or false. If the value of an attribute is between a specified minimal and maximal value, it becomes false; otherwise it is true. In the case of the market price example, the threshold market price is $30,000. Then all prices from $0 to $30,000 will be mapped to false and any price above $30,000 is mapped to true.

2. *Nominal to Binominal:* Here if a nominal attribute with the name "Outlook" and possible nominal values "sunny," "overcast," and "rain" is transformed, the result is a set of three binominal attributes, "Outlook = sunny," "Outlook = overcast," and "Outlook = rain" whose possible values can be true or false. Examples (or rows) of the original dataset where the Outlook attribute had values equal to sunny, will, in the transformed example set, have the value of the attribute Outlook = sunny set to true, while the value of the Outlook = overcast and Outlook = rain attributes will be false.

3. *Nominal to Numerical:* This works exactly like the *Nominal to Binominal* operator if one uses the Dummy coding option, except that instead of true/false values, one would see 0/1 (binary values). If unique integers option was used, each of the nominal values will get assigned a unique integer from 0 upwards. For example, if Outlook was sunny, then "sunny" gets replaced by the value 1, "rain" may get replaced by 2, and "overcast" may get replaced by 0.

4. *Numerical to Polynominal:* Finally, this operator simply changes the type (and internal representation) of selected attributes, that is, every new numeric value is considered to be another possible value for the polynominal attribute. In the golf example, the Temperature attribute has 12 unique values ranging from 64 to 85. Each value is considered a unique nominal value. As numeric attributes can have a huge number of different values even in a small range, converting such a numeric attribute to polynominal form will generate a huge number of possible values for the new attribute. A more sophisticated transformation method uses the discretization operator, which is discussed next.

5. *Discretization:* When converting numeric attributes to polynominal, it is best to specify how to set up the discretization to avoid the previously mentioned problem of generating a huge number of possible values—each numeric value should not appear as a unique nominal one but would rather be binned into some intervals. The Temperature in the golf example can be discretized by several methods: one can discretize using equal-sized bins with the *Discretize by Binning* operator. If two bins (default) are selected there will be two equal ranges: [below 74.5] and [above 74.5], where 74.5 is the average value of 64 and 85. Based on the actual Temperature value, the example will be assigned into one of the two bins. The number of rows falling into each bin (*Discretize by Size* operator) can instead be specified rather than equal bin ranges. One could also discretize by bins of equal number of occurrences by choosing to *Discretize by Frequency*, for example. Probably the most useful option is to *Discretize by User Specification*. Here explicit ranges can be provided for breaking down a continuous numeric attribute into several distinct categories or nominal values using the table shown in Fig. 15.12A. The output of the operator performing that discretization is shown in Fig. 15.12B.

Sometimes the structure of an example set may need to be transformed or rotated about one of the attributes, a process commonly known as pivoting or creating pivot tables. Here is a simple example of why this operation would be needed. The table consists of three attributes: a customer ID, a product ID, and a numeric measure called Consumer Price Index (CPI) (see Fig. 15.13A). It can be seen that this simple example has 10 unique customers and 2 unique product IDs. What should preferably be done is to rearrange the data set so that one gets two columns corresponding to the two product IDs and aggregate[4] or group the CPI data by customer IDs. This is

---

[4] CAUTION: The Pivot operator does not aggregate! If the source dataset contains combinations of product ID and customer ID occurring multiple times, one would have to aggregate before applying the Pivot operator in order to produce a dataset containing only unique combinations first.

(A)

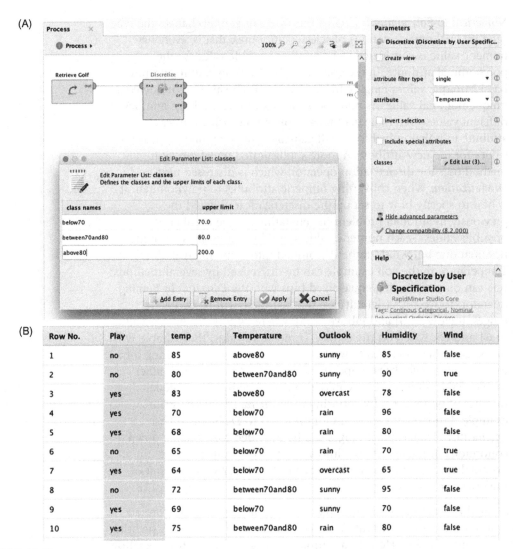

(B)

Row No.	Play	temp	Temperature	Outlook	Humidity	Wind
1	no	85	above80	sunny	85	false
2	no	80	between70and80	sunny	90	true
3	yes	83	above80	overcast	78	false
4	yes	70	below70	rain	96	false
5	yes	68	below70	rain	80	false
6	no	65	below70	rain	70	true
7	yes	64	below70	overcast	65	true
8	no	72	between70and80	sunny	95	false
9	yes	69	below70	sunny	70	false
10	yes	75	between70and80	rain	80	false

FIGURE 15.12

(A) Discretize operator. (B) The output of the operation.

because the data needs to be analyzed on the customer level, which means that each row has to represent one customer and all customer features have to be encoded as attribute values. Note that there are two missing values (Fig. 15.13A, in the 'customer id' column indicated by the thin rectangles. These are missing entries for customer ids 6 and 8. However the result of the pivot operation will have 10 x 2 = 20 entries because there are 10 customers (c1:c10) and 2 products (v1:v2).

(A)

Row No.	customer id	product id	CPI
1	c1	v1	0.970
2	c2	v1	0.860
3	c3	v1	?
4	c4	v1	0.530
5	c5	v1	0.330
6	c7	v1	0.190
7	c9	v1	0.650
8	c10	v1	0.440
9	c1	v2	0.790
10	c2	v2	0.600
11	c3	v2	0.730

(B)

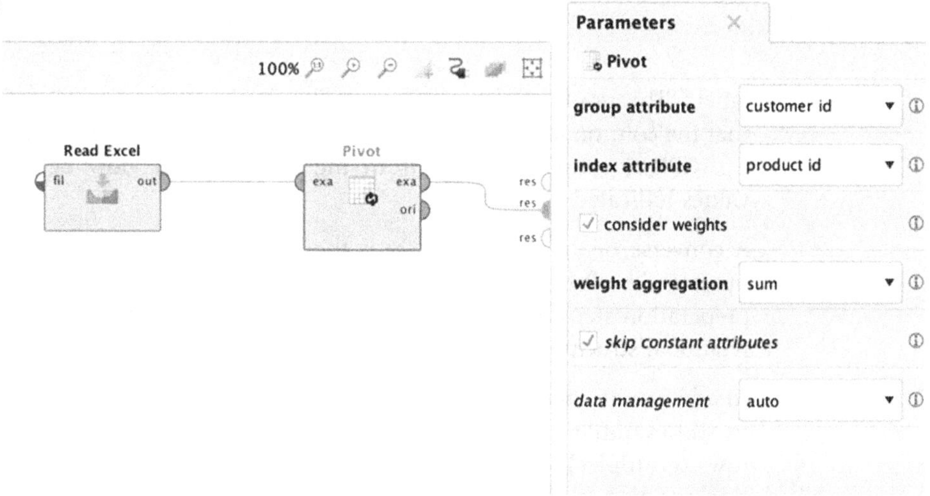

FIGURE 15.13

(A) A simple dataset to explain the pivot operation using RapidMiner. (B) Configuring the Pivot operator. (C) Results of the pivot operation.

This is accomplished simply with the *Pivot* operator. Select "customer id" as the group attribute and "product id" as the index attribute as shown in Fig. 15.13B. If familiar with Microsoft Excel's pivot tables, the group attribute parameter is similar to "row label" and the index attribute is akin to "column

(C)

Row No.	customer id	CPI_v1	CPI_v2
1	c1	0.970	0.790
2	c10	0.440	0.420
3	c2	0.860	0.600
4	c3	?	0.730
5	c4	0.530	0.660
6	c5	0.330	0.780
7	c6	?	?
8	c7	0.190	?
9	c8	?	0.040
10	c9	0.650	0.910

FIGURE 15.13
(Continued).

label." The result of the pivot operation is shown in Fig. 15.13C. Observe that the column labels are prefixed by the name of the column label attribute e.g. CPI_v1. Missing entries from the original table now become missing values indicated by "?".

A converse of the *Pivot* operator is the *De-pivot* operator, which reverses the process described and may sometimes also be required during the data preparation steps. In general a *De-pivot* operator converts a pivot table into a relational structure.

In addition to these operators, one may also need to use the *Append* operator to add examples to an existing dataset. Appending an example set with new rows (examples) works just as the name sounds— the new rows end up getting attached to the end of the example set. One has to make sure that the examples match the attributes exactly with the main dataset. Also useful is the classic *Join* operator, which combines two example sets with the same observations units but different attributes. The *Join* operator offers the traditional inner, outer, and left and right join options. An explanation for joins is available in any of the books that deal with SQL programming as well as the RapidMiner help, which also provides example processes. They will not be repeated here.

Some of other common operators used in the various chapters of the book (and are explained there in context) are: Rename attributes, Select attributes, Filter examples, Add attributes, Attribute weighting, etc.

15.5 SAMPLING AND MISSING VALUE TOOLS

Data sampling might seem out of place in today's big data—charged environments. Why bother to sample when one can collect and analyze all the data they can? Sampling is a perhaps a vestige of the statistical era when data was costly to acquire and computational effort was costlier still. However, there are many situations today where "targeted" sampling is of use. A typical scenario is when building models on data where some class representations are extremely low. Consider the case of fraud prediction. Depending on the industry, fraudulent examples range from less than 1% of all the data collected to about 2%–3%. When classification models are built using such data, the models tend to be biased and would not be able to detect fraud in the majority of the cases with new unseen data, literally because they have not been trained on enough fraudulent samples!

Such situations call for balancing datasets where the training data needs to be sampled and the proportion of the minority class needs to be increased so that the models can be trained better. The plot in Fig. 15.14 shows an example of imbalanced data: the negative class indicated by a circle is disproportionately higher than the positive class indicated by a cross.

This can be explored using a simple example. The dataset shown in the process in Fig. 15.15 is available in RapidMiner's Samples repository and is called "Weighting." This is a balanced dataset consisting of about 500 examples with the label variable consisting of roughly 50% positive and 50% negative classes. Thus, it is a balanced dataset. When one trains a decision tree to classify this data, they would get an overall accuracy of 84%. The main thing to note here is that the decision tree recall on both the classes is roughly the same: ∼86% as seen in Fig. 15.15.

A sub-process called *Unbalance* is now introduced, which will resample the original data to introduce a skew: the resulting dataset has more positive class examples than negative class examples. Specifically, the dataset is now with 92% belonging to the positive class (as a result the model inflates the predicted class recall to 99.2%) and 8% belonging to negative class (as a result the model underestimates the predicted class recall to 21.7%). The process and the results are shown in Fig. 15.16. So how do we address this data imbalance?

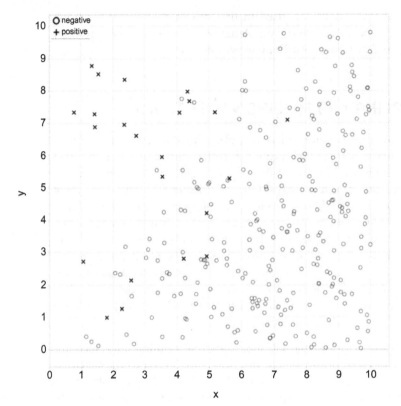

FIGURE 15.14
Snapshot of an imbalanced dataset.

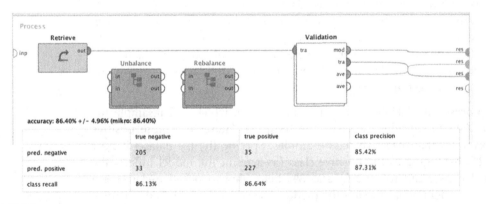

accuracy: 86.40% +/- 4.96% (mikro: 86.40%)

	true negative	true positive	class precision
pred. negative	205	35	85.42%
pred. positive	33	227	87.31%
class recall	86.13%	86.64%	

FIGURE 15.15
Performance of decision trees on well-balanced data.

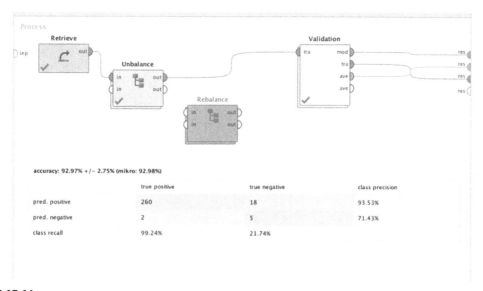

accuracy: 92.97% +/- 2.75% (mikro: 92.98%)

	true positive	true negative	class precision
pred. positive	260	18	93.53%
pred. negative	2	5	71.43%
class recall	99.24%	21.74%	

FIGURE 15.16
Unbalanced data and the resulting accuracy.

There are several ways to fix this situation. The most commonly used method is to resample the data to restore the balance. This involves undersampling the more frequent class—in this case, the positive class—and oversampling the less frequent negative class. The *rebalance* sub-process achieves this in the final RapidMiner process. As seen in Fig. 15.17, the overall accuracy is now back to the level of the original balanced data. The decision tree also looks a little bit similar to the original (not visible in the figures shown, but the reader can verify with the completed processes loaded into RapidMiner), whereas, for the unbalanced dataset it was reduced to a stub. An additional check to ensure that accuracy is not compromised by unbalanced data is to replace the accuracy by what is called *balanced accuracy*. It is defined as the arithmetic mean of the class recall accuracies, which represent the accuracy obtained on positive and negative examples, respectively. If the decision tree performs equally well on either class, this term reduces to the standard accuracy (i.e., the number of correct predictions divided by the total number of predictions).

There are several built-in RapidMiner processes to perform sampling: sample, sample (bootstrapping), sample (stratified), sample (model-based), and sample (Kennard-stone). Specific details about these techniques are well described in the software help. Only the bootstrapping method will be remarked on here because it is a common sampling technique. Bootstrapping works by sampling repeatedly within a base dataset with replacement. So, when this operator is used to generate new samples, one

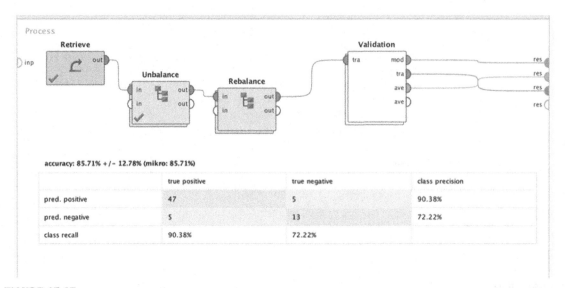

accuracy: 85.71% +/- 12.78% (mikro: 85.71%)

	true positive	true negative	class precision
pred. positive	47	5	90.38%
pred. negative	5	13	72.22%
class recall	90.38%	72.22%	

FIGURE 15.17
Rebalanced data and resulting improvement in class recall.

may see repeated or nonunique examples. There is the option of specifying an absolute sample size or a relative sample size and RapidMiner will randomly pick examples from the base data set with replacement to build a new bootstrapped example set.

This section will be closed with a brief description of missing value handling options available in RapidMiner. The basic operator is called *Replace Missing Values*. This operator provides several alternative ways to replace missing values: minimum, maximum, average, zero, none, and a user-specified value. There is no median value option. Basically, all missing values in a given column (attribute) are replaced by whatever option is chosen. A better way to treat missing values is to use the *Impute Missing Values* operator. This operator changes the attribute with missing values to a label or target variable, and trains models to determine the relationship between this label variable and other attributes so that it may then be predicted.

15.6   OPTIMIZATION TOOLS[5]

Recall that in Chapter 4: Classification, on decision trees, there was an opportunity to specify parameters to build a decision tree for the credit risk

---

[5] Readers may skip this section if completely new to RapidMiner and return to it after developing some familiarity with the tool and data science in general.

example (Section 4.1.2, step 3) but default values were simply used. Similar situations arose when building a support vector machine model (Section 4.6.3) or logistic regression model (Section 5.2.3), where the default model parameter values were simply chosen. When a model evaluation was run, the performance of the model is usually an indicator as to whether the right parameter combinations were chosen for the model.[6] But what if one is not happy with the model accuracy (or its r-squared value)? Can it be improved? How?

RapidMiner provides several unique operators that will allow one to discover and choose the best combination of parameters for pretty much all of the available operators that need parameter specifications. The fundamental principle on which this works is the concept of a nested operator. A nested operator was first encountered in Section 4.1.2, step 2—the *Split Validation* operator. Another nested operator was also described in Section 14.5 in the discussion on wrapper-style feature selection methods. The basic idea is to iteratively change the parameters for a learner until some stated performance criteria are met. The *Optimize* operator performs two tasks: it determines what values to set for the selected parameters for each iteration, and when to stop the iterations. RapidMiner provides three basic methods to set parameter values: grid search, greedy search, and an evolutionary search (also known as genetic) method. Each method will not be described in detail, but a high-level comparison between them will be done and when each approach would be applicable will be mentioned.

To demonstrate the working of an optimization process, consider a simple model: a polynomial function (Fig. 15.18). Specifically, for a function $y = f(x) = x^6 + x^3 - 7x^2 - 3x + 1$ one wishes to find the minimum value of y within a given domain of x. This is of course the simplest form of optimization—to select an interval of values for x where y is minimum. As seen in the functional plot, for x in $[-1.5, 2]$, there are two minima: a local minimum of $y = -4.33$, $x = -1.3$ and a global minimum of $y = -7.96$, $x = 1.18$. It will be demonstrated how to use RapidMiner to search for these minima using the *Optimize* operators. As mentioned before, the optimization happens in a nested operator, what is placed inside the optimizer will be discussed first before discussing the optimizer itself.

The nested process itself, also called the inner process, is quite simple as seen in Fig. 15.19A: *Generate Data* randomly generates values for x between an upper bound and a lower bound (see Fig. 15.19B).

---

[6] Normally one can't judge from just one performance estimate whether the right parameters were chosen. Multiple performance values and their dependency on the parameter values would need to be examined to infer that the right/optimal parameter values were chosen.

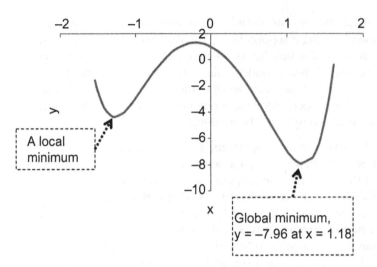

FIGURE 15.18
A simple polynomial function to demonstrate optimization.

Generate Attributes will calculate y for each value of x in this interval. *Performance (Extract Performance)* will store the minimum value of y within each interval. This operator has to be configured as shown on the right of Fig. 15.19A in order to ensure that the correct performance is optimized. In this case, y is selected as the attribute that has to be minimized. The *Rename, Select Attributes,* and *Log* operators are plugged in to keep the process focused on only two variables and to track the progress of optimization.

This nested process can be inserted into any of the available *Optimize Parameters* operators. It will be described how one can do this with the *Optimize Parameters (Grid)* operator first. In this exercise, the interval [*lower bound, upper bound*] is basically being optimized so that the objective of minimizing the function y = f(x) can be achieved. As seen in the function plot, the entire domain of x has to be traversed in small enough interval sizes so that the exact point at which y hits a global minimum can be found.

The grid search optimizer simply moves this interval window across the entire domain and stops the iterations after all the intervals are explored (Fig. 15.20). Clearly it is an exhaustive but inefficient search method. To set this process up, simply insert the inner process inside the outer *Optimize Parameters (Grid)* operator and select the *attributes upper bound* and *attributes lower bound* parameters from the *Generate Data* operator. To do this, click on the *Edit Parameter Settings* option for the optimizer, select *Generate Data* under the *Operators* tab of the dialog box, and further select *attributes_upper_bound* and *attributes_lower_bound* under the *Parameters* tab (Fig. 15.21).

(A)

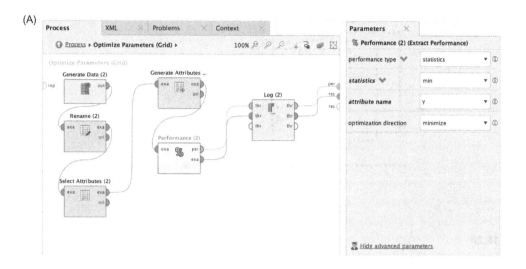

(B)

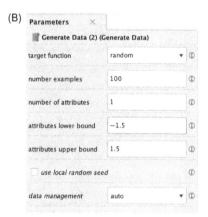

FIGURE 15.19

(A) The inner process that is nested inside an optimization loop. (B) Configuration of the generated data.

One would need to provide ranges for the grid search for each of these parameters. In this case, the lower bound is set to go from −1.5 to −1 and the upper bound to go from 0 to 1.5 in steps of 10. So the first interval (or window) will be $x = [−1.5, 0]$, the second one will be $[−1.45, 0]$ and so on until the last window, which will be $[−1, 1.5]$ for a total of 121 iterations. The *Optimize Performance (Grid)* search will evaluate y for each of these windows and store the minimum y in each iteration. The iterations will only stop after all 121 intervals are evaluated, but the final output will indicate the window that resulted in the smallest minimum y. The plot in Fig. 15.22 shows the progress of the iterations. Each point in the chart

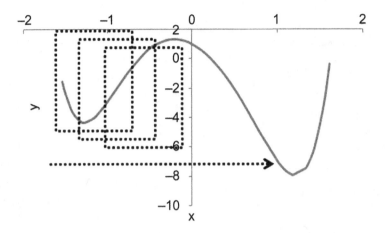

FIGURE 15.20
Searching for an optimum within a fixed window that slides across.

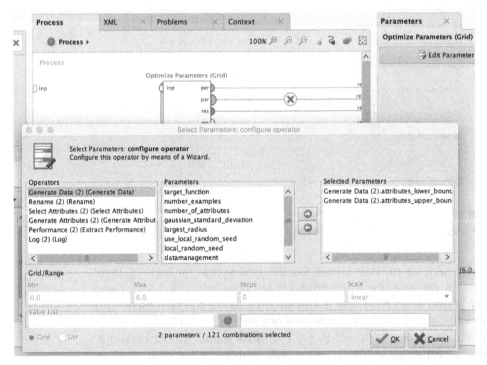

FIGURE 15.21
Configuring the grid search optimizer.

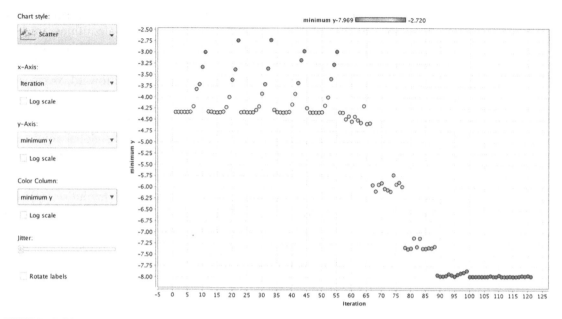

Chart style:

Scatter

x–Axis:

Iteration

Log scale

y–Axis:

minimum y

Log scale

Color Column:

minimum y

Log scale

Jitter:

Rotate labels

FIGURE 15.22
Progression of the grid search optimization.

corresponds to the lowest value of y evaluated by the expression within a given interval. The local minimum of $y = -4.33$ @ $x = -1.3$ is found at the very first iteration. This corresponds to the window $[-1.5, 0]$. If the grid had not spanned the entire domain $[-1.5, 1.5]$, the optimizer would have reported the local minimum as the best performance. This is one of the main disadvantages of a grid search method.

The other disadvantage is the number of redundant iterations. Looking at the plot above, one can see that the global minimum was reached by about the 90th iteration. In fact, for iteration 90, $y_{minimum} = -7.962$, whereas, the final reported lowest $y_{minimum}$ was -7.969 (iteration 113), which is only about 0.09% better. Depending on the tolerances, the computations could have been terminated earlier. But a grid search does not allow early terminations and there end up running nearly 30 extra iterations. Clearly as the number of optimization parameters increase, this would become a significant cost.

The *Optimize Parameters (Quadratic)* operator is next applied to the inner process. Quadratic search is based on a *greedy* search methodology. A greedy methodology is an optimization algorithm that makes a locally optimal decision at each step (Ahuja, 2000; Bahmani, 2013). While the decision may be locally optimal at the current step, it may not necessarily be the best for all future steps. k-Nearest neighbor is one good example of a greedy algorithm.

In theory, greedy algorithms will only yield local optima, but in special cases, they can also find globally optimal solutions. Greedy algorithms are best suited to find approximate solutions to difficult problems. This is because they are less computationally intense and tend to operate over a large dataset quickly. Greedy algorithms are by nature typically biased toward coverage of a large number of cases or a quick payback in the objective function.

In this case, the performance of the quadratic optimizer is marginally worse than a grid search requiring about 100 shots to hit the global minimum (compared to 90 for a grid), as seen in Fig. 15.23. It also seems to suffer from some of the same problems encountered in the grid search.

Finally the last available option: Optimize Parameters (Evolutionary) will be employed. Evolutionary (or genetic) algorithms are often more appropriate than a grid search or a greedy search and lead to better results, This, is because they cover a wider variety of the search space through mutation and can iterate onto good minima through cross-over of successful models based on the success criteria. As seen in the progress of iterations in Fig. 15.24, the global optimum was hit without getting stuck initially at a

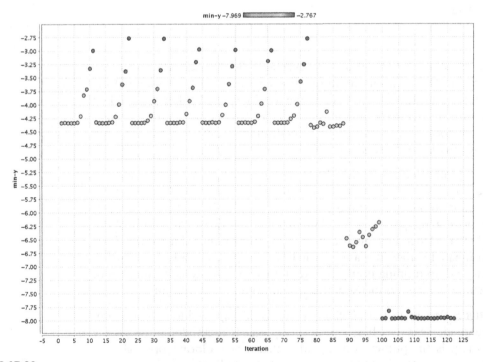

FIGURE 15.23

Progression of the quadratic greedy search optimization.

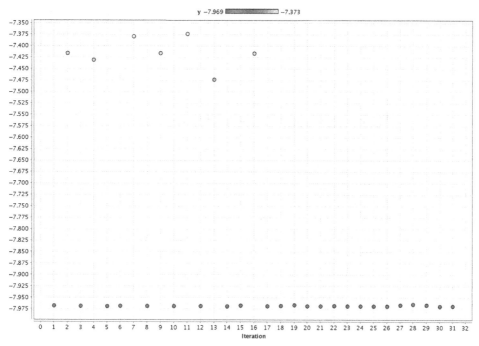

FIGURE 15.24
Progression of the genetic search optimization.

local minimum—right from the first few iterations it can be seen that the neighborhood of the lowest point has been approached. The evolutionary method is particularly useful if one does not initially know the domain of the functions, unlike in this case where they are known. It is evident that it takes far fewer steps to get to the global minimum with a high degree of confidence—about 18 iterations as opposed to 90 or 100. Key concepts to understanding this algorithm are *mutation* and *cross-over*, both of which are possible to control using the RapidMiner GUI. More technical details of how the algorithm works are beyond the scope of this book and some excellent resources are listed at the end of this chapter (Weise, 2009).

To summarize, there are three optimization algorithms available in RapidMiner all of which are nested operators. The best application of optimization is for the selection of modeling parameters, for example, split size, leaf size, or splitting criteria in a decision tree model. One builds their machine learning process as usual and inserts this process or nests it inside of the optimizer. By using the Edit Parameter Settings . . . control button, one can select the parameters of any of the inner process operators (for example a *Decision Tree*, *W-Logistic*, or *SVM*) and define ranges to sweep. Grid search is an exhaustive search process for finding the right settings, but is expensive and cannot guarantee a global optimum. Evolutionary algorithms are extremely flexible and fast and are usually the best choice for optimizing machine learning models in RapidMiner.

15.7 INTEGRATION WITH R

R is a popular programmable open source statistical package that can execute scripts. The RapidMiner process can invoke R, send data, process it in R and receive back the data for further processing, modeling, and visualization in RapidMiner. RapidMiner offers an operator *Execute R* to invoke R and run the script that is contained in the operator. The script can be edited under the *Edit Text* parameter. Fig. 15.25 shows a process with the R operator and a sample script.

The script contains a function rm_main that can accept the datasets connected to the input port of the Execute R operator. Similarly, the return part

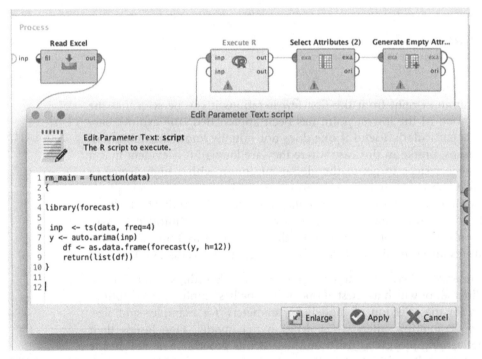

FIGURE 15.25

Integration with R.

of the function sends the dataframe (dataset in R) back to the output port of the operator.

15.8   CONCLUSION

As with other chapters in this book, the RapidMiner process explained and developed in this discussion can be accessed from the companion site of the book at www.IntroDataScience.com. The RapidMiner process (*.rmp files) can be downloaded to the computer and can be imported to RapidMiner from File > Import Process. The data files can be imported from File > Import Data.

This chapter provided a high-level view of the main tools that one would need to become familiar with in building data science models using RapidMiner. Firstly the basic graphical user interface for the program was introduced. Then options by which data can be brought into and exported out of RapidMiner were discussed. An overview of the data visualization methods that are available within the tool were provided, because quite naturally, the next step of any data science process after ingesting the data is to understand in a descriptive sense the nature of the data. Tools were then introduced that allow one to transform and reshape the data by changing the type of incoming data and restructuring them in different tabular forms to make subsequent analysis easier. Tools that would allow us to resample available data and account for any missing values were also introduced. Once familiar with these essential data preparation options, it is possible to apply any of the appropriate algorithms described in the earlier chapters for analysis. Optimization operators were also introduced that allow one to fine-tune their machine learning algorithms so that an optimized and good quality model can be developed to extract any insights.

With this overview, one can go back to any of the earlier chapters to learn about a specific technique and understand how to use RapidMiner to build models using that machine learning algorithm.

References

Ahuja, R. O. (2000). A greedy genetic algorithm for quadratic assignment problem. *Computers and Operations Research, 27*(10), 917−934.

Bahmani, S.R. (2013). Greedy sparsity-constrained optimization. *Statistical Machine Learning, 14*, 807−841.

Mierswa, I.W. (2006). YALE: Rapid prototyping for complex data mining tasks. *Association for computing machinery − Knowledge discovery in databases* (pp. 935−940).

Weise, T. (2009). *Global optimization algorithms − Theory and application.* <http://www.it-weise.de/>.

Comparison of Data Science Algorithms

Classification: Predicting a categorical target variable

Algorithm	Description	Model	Input	Output	Pros	Cons	Use Cases
Decision trees	Partitions the data into smaller subsets where each subset contains (mostly) responses of one class (either "yes" or "no")	A set of rules to partition a data set based on the values of the different predictors	No restrictions on variable type for predictors	The label cannot be numeric. It must be categorical	Intuitive to explain to nontechnical business users. Normalizing predictors is not necessary	Tends to overfit the data. Small changes in input data can yield substantially different trees. Selecting the right parameters can be challenging	Marketing segmentation, fraud detection
Rule induction	Models the relationship between input and output by deducing simple "IF/THEN" rules from a data set	A set of organized rules that contain an antecedent (inputs) and consequent (output class)	No restrictions. Accepts categorical, numeric, and binary inputs	Prediction of target variable, which is categorical	Model can be easily explained to business users. Easy to deploy in almost any tools and applications	Divides the data set in rectilinear fashion	Manufacturing, applications where description of model is necessary
k-Nearest neighbors	A lazy learner where no model is generalized. Any new unknown data point is compared against similar known data points in the training set	Entire training data set is the model	No restrictions. However, the distance calculations work better with numeric data. Data needs to be normalized	Prediction of target variable, which is categorical	Requires very little time to build the model. Handles missing attributes in the unknown record gracefully. Works with nonlinear relationships	The deployment runtime and storage requirements will be expensive. Arbitrary selection of value of *k*. No description of the model	Image processing, applications where slower response time is acceptable
Naïve Bayesian	Predicts the output class based on the Bayes' theorem by calculating class conditional probability and prior probability	A lookup table of probabilities and conditional probabilities for each attribute with an output class	No restrictions. However, the probability calculation works better with categorical attributes	Prediction of probability for all class values, along with the winning class	Time required to model and deploy is minimum. Great algorithm for benchmarking. Strong statistical foundation	Training data set needs to be representative sample of population and needs to have complete combinations of input and output. Attributes need to be independent	Spam detections, text mining

Continued

Continued

Algorithm	Description	Model	Input	Output	Pros	Cons	Use Cases
Artificial neural networks	A computational and mathematical model inspired by the biological nervous system. The weights in the network learn to reduce the error between actual and prediction	A network topology of layers and weights to process input data	All attributes should be numeric	Prediction of target (label) variable, which is categorical	Good at modeling nonlinear relationships. Fast response time in deployment	No easy way to explain the inner working of the model Requires preprocessing data. Cannot handle missing attributes	Image recognition, fraud detection, quick response time applications
Support vector machines	Boundary detection algorithm that identifies/ defines multi-dimensional boundaries separating data points belonging to different classes	The model is a vector equation that allows one to classify new data points into different regions (classes)	All attributes should be numeric	Prediction of target (label) variable, which can be categorical or numeric	Extremely robust against overfitting. Small changes to input data do not affect boundary and, thus, do not yield different results. Good at handling nonlinear relationships	Computational performance during training phase can be slow. This may be compounded by the effort needed to optimize parameter combinations	Optical character recognition, fraud detection, modeling "black-swan" events
Ensemble models	Leverages wisdom of the crowd. Employs a number of independent models to make a prediction and aggregates the final prediction	A meta-model with individual base models and an aggregator	Superset of restrictions from the base model used	Prediction for all class values with a winning class	Reduces the generalization error. Takes different search space into consideration	Achieving model independence is tricky Difficult to explain the inner working of the model	Most of the practical classifiers are ensemble

Regression: Predicting a numeric target variable

Algorithm	Description	Model	Input	Output	Pros	Cons	Use Case
Linear regression	The classical predictive model that expresses the relationship between inputs and an output parameter in the form of an equation	The model consists of coefficients for each input predictor and their statistical significance. A bias (intercept) may be optional	All attributes should be numeric	The label may be numeric or binominal	The workhorse of most predictive modeling techniques. Easy to use and explain to nontechnical business users	Cannot handle missing data. Categorical data are not directly usable, but require transformation into numeric	Pretty much any scenario that requires predicting a continuous numeric value
Logistic regression	Technically, this is a classification method. But structurally it is similar to linear regression	The model consists of coefficients for each input predictor that relate to the "logit." Transforming the logit into probabilities of occurrence (of each class) completes the model	All attributes should be numeric	The label may only be binominal	One of the most common classification methods. Computationally efficient	Cannot handle missing data. Not intuitive when dealing with a large number of predictors	Marketing scenarios (e.g., will click or not click), any general two-class problem

Association analysis: Unsupervised process for finding relationships between items

Algorithm	Description	Model	Input	Output	Pros	Cons	Use Case
FP-Growth and Apriori	Measures the strength of co-occurrence between one item with another	Finds simple, easy to understand rules like {Milk, Diaper} → {Beer}	Transactions format with items in the columns and transactions in the rows	List of relevant rules developed from the data set	Unsupervised approach with minimal user inputs. Easy to understand rules	Requires preprocessing if input is of different format	Recommendation engines, cross-selling, and content suggestions

Clustering: An unsupervised process for finding meaningful groups in data

Algorithm	Description	Model	Input	Output	Pros	Cons	Use case
k-Means	Data set is divided into k clusters by finding k centroids	Algorithm finds k centroids and all the data points are assigned to the nearest centroid, which forms a cluster	No restrictions. However, the distance calculations work better with numeric data. Data should be normalized	Data set is appended by one of the k cluster labels	Simple to implement. Can be used for dimension reduction	Specification of k is arbitrary and may not find natural clusters. Sensitive to outliers	Customer segmentation, anomaly detection, applications where globular clustering is natural
DBSCAN	Identifies clusters as a high-density area surrounded by low-density areas	List of clusters and assigned data points. Default cluster 0 contains noise points	No restrictions. However, the distance calculations work better with numeric data. Data should be normalized	Cluster labels based on identified clusters	Finds the natural clusters of any shape. No need to mention number of clusters	Specification of density parameters. A bridge between two clusters can merge the cluster. Cannot cluster varying density data set	Applications where clusters are nonglobular shapes and when the prior number of natural groupings is not known
Self-organizing maps	A visual clustering technique with roots from neural networks and prototype clustering	A two-dimensional lattice where similar data points are arranged next to each other	No restrictions. However, the distance calculations work better with numeric data. Data should be normalized	No explicit clusters identified. Similar data points occupy either the same cell or are placed next to each other in the neighborhood	A visual way to explain the clusters. Reduces multi-dimensional data to two dimensions	Number of centroids (topology) is specified by the user. Does not find natural clusters in the data	Diverse applications including visual data exploration, content suggestions, and dimension reduction

Anomaly detection: Supervised and unsupervised techniques to find outliers in data

Algorithm	Description	Model	Input	Output	Pros	Cons	Use Case
Distance–based	Outlier identified based on distance to kth nearest neighbor	All data points are assigned a distance score based on nearest neighbor	Accepts both numeric and categorical attributes. Normalization is required since distance is calculated	Every data point has a distance score. The higher the distance, the more likely the data point is an outlier	Easy to implement. Works well with numeric attributes	Specification of k is arbitrary	Fraud detection, preprocessing technique
Density-based	Outlier is identified based on data points in low-density regions	All data points are assigned a density score based on the neighborhood	Accepts both numeric and categorical attributes. Normalization is required since density is calculated	Every data point has a density score. The lower the density, the more likely the data point is an outlier	Easy to implement. Works well with numeric attributes	Specification of distance parameter by the user. Inability to identify varying density regions	Fraud detection, preprocessing technique
Local outlier factor	Outlier is identified based on calculation of relative density in the neighborhood	All data points as assigned a relative density score based on the neighborhood	Accepts both numeric and categorical attributes. Normalization is required since density is calculated	Every data point has a density score. The lower the relative density, the more likely the data point is an outlier	Can handle the varying density scenario	Specification of distance parameter by the user	Fraud detection, preprocessing technique

Deep learning: Training using multiple layers of representation of data

Layer Type	Description	Input	Output	Pros	Cons	Use Cases
Convolutional	Based on the concept of applying filters to incoming two-dimensional representation of data, such as images. Machine learning is used to automatically determine the correct weights for the filters.	A tensor of typically three or more dimensions. Two of the dimensions correspond to the image while a third is sometimes used for color/channel encoding.	Typically the output of convolutional layer is flattened and passed through a dense or fully connected layer which usually terminates in a softmax output layer.	Very powerful and general purpose network. The number of weights to be learned in the conv layer is not very high.	For most practical classification problems, conv layers have to be coupled with dense layers which result in a large number of weights to be trained and thus lose any speed advantages of a pure conv layer.	Classify almost any data where spatial information is highly correlated such as images. Even audio data can be converted into images (using fourier transforms) and classified via conv nets.
Recurrent	Just as conv nets are specialized for analyzing spatially correlated data, recurrent nets are specialized for temporally correlated data: sequences. The data can be sequences of numbers, audio signals, or even images	A sequence of any type (time series, text, speech, etc).	RNNs can process sequences and output other sequences (many to many), or output a fixed tensor (many to one).	Unlike other types of neural networks, RNNs have no restriction that the input shape of the data be of fixed dimension.	RNNs suffer from vanishing (or exploding) gradients when the sequences are very long. RNNs are also not amenable to many stacked layers due to the same reasons.	Forecasting time series, natural language processing situations such as machine translation, image captioning.

Recommenders: Finding the user's preference of an item

Algorithm	Description	Assumption	Input	Output	Pros	Cons	Use Case
Collaborative Filtering - neighborhood based	Find a cohort of users who provided similar ratings. Derive the outcome rating from the cohort users	Similar users or items have similar likes	Ratings matrix with user-item preferences.	Completed ratings matrix	The only input needed is the ratings matrix Domain agnostic	Cold start problem for new users and items Computation grows linearly with the number of items and users	eCommerce, music, new connection recommendations
Collaborative Filtering - Latent matrix factorization	Decompose the user-item matrix into two matrices (P and Q) with latent factors. Fill the blank values in the ratings matrix by dot product of P and Q	User's preference of an item can be better explained by their preference of an item's character (inferred)	Ratings matrix with user-item preferences.	Completed ratings matrix	Works in sparse matrix More accurate than neighborhood based collaborative filtering	Cannot explain why the prediction is made	Content recommendations
Content-based filtering	Abstract the features of the item and build item profile. Use the item profile to evaluate the user preference for the attributes in the item profile	Recommend items similar to those the user liked in the past	User-item rating matrix and Item profile	Completed ratings matrix	Addresses cold start problem for new items Can provide explanations on why the recommendation is made	Requires item profile data set Recommenders are domain specific	Music recommendation from Pandora and CiteSeer's citation indexing
Content-based - Supervised learning models	A personalized classification or regression model for every single user in the system. Learn a classifier based on user likes or dislikes of an item and its relationship with item attributes	Every time a user prefers an item, it is a vote of preference for item attributes	User-item rating matrix and Item profile	Completed ratings matrix	Every user has a separate model and could be independently customized. Hyper personalization	Storage and computational time	eCommerce, content, and connection recommendations

Time series forecasting: Predicting future value of a variable

Algorithm	Description	Model	Input	Output	Pros	Cons	Use Case
Decomposition	Decompose the time series into trend, seasonality, and noise. Forecast the components	Models for the individual components	Historical value	Forecasted value	Increased understanding of the time series by visualizing the components	Accuracy depends on the models used for components	Application where the explanation of components is important

Continued

Continued

Algorithm	Description	Model	Input	Output	Pros	Cons	Use Case
Exponential smoothing	The future value is the function of past observations	Learn the parameters of the smoothing equation from the historical data	Historical value	Forecasted value	Applies to wide range of time series with or without trend or seasonality	Multiple seasonality in the data make the models cumbersome	Cases where trend or seasonality is not evident
ARIMA (autoregressive integrated moving average)	The future value is the function of auto correlated past data points and the moving average of the predictions	Parameter values for (p,d, q), AR, and MA coefficients	Historical value	Forecasted value	Forms a statistical baseline for model accuracy	The optimal p,d,q value is unknown to begin with	Applies on almost all types of time series data
Windowing-based machine learning	Create cross-sectional data set with time lagged inputs	Machine learning models like regression, neural networks, etc.	Historical value	Forecasted value	Uses any machine learning approaches on the cross-sectional data	The windowing size, horizon, and skip values are arbitrary	Applies to user cases where the time series has trend and/or seasonality

Feature selection: Selection of most important attributes

Algorithm	Description	Model	Input	Output	Pros	Cons	Use Case
PCA (principal component analysis) filter-based	combines the most important attributes into a fewer number of transformed attributes	Each principal component is a function of attributes in the dataset	Numerical attributes	Numerical attributes (reduced set). Does not really require a label	Efficient way to extract predictors that are uncorrelated to each other. Helps to apply Pareto principle in identifying attributes with highest variance	Sensitive to scaling effects, i.e., requires normalization of attribute values before application. Focus on variance sometimes results in selecting noisy attributes	Most numeric-valued data sets require dimension reduction
Info gain (filter-based)	Selecting attributes based on relevance to the target or label	Similar to decision tree model	No restrictions on variable type for predictors	Data sets require a label. Can only be applied on data sets with nominal label	Same as decision trees	Same as decision trees	Applications for feature selection where target variable is categorical or numeric
Chi-square (filter-based)	Selecting attributes based on relevance to the target or label	Uses the chi-square test of independence to relate predictors to label	Categorical (polynominal) attributes	Data sets require a label. Can only be applied on data sets with a nominal label	Extremely robust. A fast and efficient scheme to identify which categorical variables to select for a predictive model	Sometimes difficult to interpret	Applications for feature selection where all variables are categorical

Continued

Continued

Algorithm	Description	Model	Input	Output	Pros	Cons	Use Case
Forward Selection (wrapper-based)	Selecting attributes based on relevance to the target or label	Works in conjunction with modeling methods such as regression	All attributes should be numeric	The label may be numeric or binominal	Multicollinearity problems can be avoided. Speeds up the training phase of the modeling process	Once a variable is added to the set, it is never removed in subsequent iterations even if its influence on the target diminishes	Data sets with a large number of input variables where feature selection is required
Backward elimination (wrapper-based)	Selecting attributes based on relevance to the target or label	Works in conjunction with modeling methods such as regression	All attributes should be numeric	The label may be numeric or binominal	Multicollinearity problems can be avoided. Speeds up the training phase of the modeling process	Need to begin with a full model, which can sometimes be computationally intensive	Data sets with few input variables where feature selection is required

About the Authors

VIJAY KOTU

Vijay Kotu is Vice President of Analytics at ServiceNow. He leads the implementation of large-scale data platforms and services to support the company's enterprise business. He has led analytics organizations for over a decade with focus on data strategy, business intelligence, machine learning, experimentation, engineering, enterprise adoption, and building analytics talent. Prior to joining ServiceNow, he was Vice President of Analytics at Yahoo. He worked at Life Technologies and Adteractive where he led marketing analytics, created algorithms to optimize online purchasing behavior, and developed data platforms to manage marketing campaigns. He is a member of the Association of Computing Machinery and a member of the Advisory Board at RapidMiner.

BALA DESHPANDE, PHD

Dr. Deshpande has extensive experience in working with companies ranging from startups to Fortune 5 in fields ranging from automotive, aerospace, retail, food, and manufacturing verticals delivering business analysis; designing and developing custom data products for implementing business intelligence, data science, and predictive analytics solutions. He was the Founder of SimaFore, a predictive analytics consulting company which was acquired by Soliton Inc., a provider of testing solutions for the semiconductor industry. He was also the Founding Co-chair of the annual Predictive Analytics World-Manufacturing conference. In his professional career he has worked with Ford Motor Company on their product development, with IBM at their IBM Watson Center of Competence, and with Domino's Pizza at their data science and artificial intelligence groups. He has a Ph.D. from Carnegie Mellon and an MBA from Ross School of Business, Michigan.

Index

Praise

"A wonderful book to take on the broad topic of Data Science. It covers all the relevant algorithms from the classical to the newly reborn to the latest innovations. The content is presented in a way that is both accessible and tangible by describing practical applications in recommendation engines, time series forecasting, and the like. The book provides the vocabulary and taxonomy to discern the right approach for each application."

Eric Colson
Chief Algorithms Officer, Stitch Fix.

"If you are business leader, a data practitioner or just someone who is curious about how Data Science and AI work in practice, then this book is a must read. I received tremendous value when I read through the book the first time to get a discipline overview, and I also find myself referring back to specific chapters time and time again as a reference guide. The content is well presented and the book provides practical examples to illustrate important concepts."

David Dowhan
CEO, TruSignal.

"This book is an important work to help analytics teams rapidly bridge the data science skills gap. The hands-on application of advanced analytics and machine learning will enable readers to competently solve high value use cases."

Peter Lee
CEO, RapidMiner.

"Kotu and Deshpande have delivered a comprehensive and accessible a-to-z on data science. The book enables leadership teams from organizations of all sizes to grasp and implement data science principles and approaches to unlock the value of their data."

Jonathan Murray
CEO, myVR.

"This book is a must have for you and your organization to align and learn the best methods to exploit the best competitive advantages you have: your own data. Data science provides a method to understand, activate, and make prescriptive decisions and recommendations about your data. This book provides a level of baseline for the organization; to understand and drive a pathway on techniques used to do just that."

Sy Fahimi
Operating Partner, Symphony Technology Group.

"AI and Data Science is at a critical inflection point for businesses; the transformation potential not seen since the infancy of the Internet. Those who fail to embrace this transformation will be disrupted. Kotu and Deshpande have created a comprehensive and powerful manifest for both the practitioner and the business leader seeking to understand the potential. This is your basis to Play to win with Data Science & AI"

Andrew J. Walter
VP, IT and Commercial Services (ret), P&G.

"Only marketers living under a rock would deny the paramount importance of data science now and in the future. Authors of this book do a fantastic job of both explaining the fundamentals of data science and also providing practical tips on how to make your data work for your business."

David Rodnitzky
CEO, 3Q Digital.

"A great resource for anyone interested in learning more about data analysis and associated data science techniques. A deeper dive on machine learning, association analysis and other emerging analytical tools is available for the serious practitioners. All in all, a great tool and a handy reference for those interested in data science in general."

Badal Choudari
SVP, Products, Symantec.

"Data science is challenging, transforming and re-inventing every business sector. This comprehensive and hands-on guide delivers the conceptual framework and the concrete examples that make data science accessible and realizable in any organization"

Meri Gruber
Co-founder, Decision Management Solutions.

"This book provides the quick start into practical data analysis. Without overburdening the reader with theory, the book covers all standard data mining topics, ranging from data preparation over classification and regression to deep learning and time series forecasting. Showing ready-to-use configurations in RapidMiner, readers can directly apply the methods to their problems at hand, allowing for a quick transition from theory to practice."

Prof. Heiko Paulheim
Professor, Data and Web Science Group, University of Mannheim.

"There is a lot being written about how data science will transform our world, but for most of us, it can be hard to get beneath the superficial excitement or fear that these claims elicit and what they will mean to our everyday lives. This book accomplishes the rare task of investigating these mechanics, not just for experts, but for non-technicians whose lives and livelihoods will be impacted by data science. Whether you're a CEO or a salesman or a stock clerk, reading this book will allow you to understand where we're headed, and thrive in the data science revolution."

Charlie Stack
Head of Data & Analytics Practice, Spencer Stuart.

"This book does an amazing job of clearly organizing, explaining and then presenting a practical implementation for various data science techniques. As a business executive, this book has enabled me to better understand, what previously seemed like a foreign language. In today's highly competitive digital environment I highly recommend adding this to your must-read list."

Cindy Brown
Chief Revenue Officer, ViralGains.

"From our operating rooms, to our schools, financial markets, concert halls and art galleries; data science and machine learning have disrupted traditional processes and expanded the borders that previously served as our limitations. This book democratizes the concepts of Data Science for readers across all job types and skill sets and arms them with the necessary concepts and tools to begin applying them to their daily lives."

Eoin Ryan
Head of Investor Relations, Naspers.

"From business leaders and emerging executives seeking to better understand the concepts of data science, and how to use this field to better understand their business and make better decisions; to emerging data scientists seeking a stronger foundation in this field and a better sense of how to apply its concepts and techniques in the real world, this text is a touchstone resource."

Jeff Russakaw
CEO, Boosted.

"Whether you are a company driving disruption or undergoing disruption in your industry, deriving data-driven business insights via application of Data Science, AI/ ML technologies for making the right strategic decisions is very foundational. This book breaks down the concepts of Data Science fluidly and couples them with very practical implementation tips. A must read for the novice as well as experts in this field."

Milind Wagle
Chief Information Officer, Equinix.

Printed in the United States
By Bookmasters